Crisis
Intervention
Strategies

Crisis Intervention Strategies

Burl E. Gilliland
Richard K. James

Memphis State University

Brooks/Cole Publishing Company
Pacific Grove, California

Brooks/Cole Publishing Company
A Division of Wadsworth, Inc.

Printed in the United States of America
10 9 8 7 6 5 4 3 2 1

Library of Congress Cataloging in Publication Data

Gilliland, Burl E.
   Crisis intervention strategies / Burl E. Gilliland, Richard K. James.
     p.   cm.
   Includes bibliographies and index.
   ISBN 0-534-09054-0
   1. Crisis intervention (Psychiatry)   I. James, Richard K., [date]
   II. Title.
RC480.6.G55   1988
616.89025—dc 19

Sponsoring Editor: *Claire Verduin*
Editorial Associate: *Linda Ruth Wright*
Production Editor: *Linda Loba*
Manuscript Editor: *Meredy Amyx*
Permissions Editor: *Carline Haga*
Interior and Cover Design: *Sharon L. Kinghan*
Typesetting: *Interactive Composition Corp.*
Printing and Binding: *The Maple-Vale Book Manufacturing Group*

The authors wish to recognize and honor the numerous individuals, groups, and agency workers who so willingly shared their knowledge, skill, love, and encouragement.

We especially dedicate this book to our students, clients, and colleagues in crisis agencies, and our respective families.

Preface

PURPOSE OF THE BOOK

The primary purpose of this book is to organize and present *applied* thera-peutic counseling in general, and crisis intervention in particular, in such a way that it effectively *deals with* and *describes* actual strategies. It has been our experience that most of the clients who enter counseling or psychother-apy do so because of some sort of crisis in their lives. Although "preventive" counseling is an idealistic concept, personal crisis generally provides the im-petus that impels the clients of the real world into personal contact with a helping person. We have endeavored to provide a perspective that *puts you into the crisis situation as it is occurring,* enabling you to experience what the crisis worker is experiencing.

RATIONALE

Primacy of Crisis Intervention

We believe that practically all counseling is initiated as crisis intervention. As much as we would prefer otherwise, people tend either to avoid presenting their problems to a helper until those problems have grown to crisis propor-tions, or to allow themselves to become ensconced in situational dilemmas which wind up in unforseen crises. In any event, one of the goals of the hu-man service professions has been to follow the example of medicine and dentistry and work with people in preventive modes from developmental perspectives. Our ideal objective, as human service workers, is to establish primary prevention programs so effectively that crisis intervention or crisis counseling will seldom be needed. However, it appears that people will not be as quick to adapt preventive measures to their psychological health as they are to their physical health. Therefore, we believe that the application of crisis intervention strategies is appropriate to practically all counseling, not just to crisis situations. It is from that perspective that we consider this book to be applicable to the total scope of counseling.

The Case for an Applied Viewpoint

The material and techniques we promote in this book come from two sources: first, our own experiences in teaching and counseling in crisis situations; second, interviews with people who are currently engaged in and successfully performing the trench warfare of counseling and crisis intervention. We have obtained opinions from many different individuals in the helping professions, whose daily and nightly work is dealing directly with human dilemmas, and related their views to the best of current theory and practice from the professional literature. Through many hours of dialogue, these experts have provided the most contemporary strategies and techniques in use in their particular fields. They have also reviewed our rendition of each crisis category and have provided much helpful commentary and critique on the ecology and etiology, tactics and procedures, terminology, and developmental stages of the specific crises with which they work. Therefore, what you read in the case-handling strategies comes from the horse's mouth.

Where controversies exist in regard to treatment modalities, we have attempted to present as many perspectives as possible. If you encounter problems with the tactics and techniques presented, the fault is undoubtedly in our rendition and not in the modalities themselves, which work well for the people who described them to us.

We have endeavored to incorporate, synthesize, and integrate the case-handling strategies of these resource people in a comprehensive, fluid, and dynamic way that will provide crisis workers with a basic set of tenets about effective crisis intervention. The book is not about long-term therapy or theory. Neither is it a volume dealing with crisis from one theoretical perspective, such as a psychoanalytic approach or a behavioral system only. The book incorporates a wide diversity of therapeutic modalities and reflects our eclectic approach.

Specific crises demand specific interventions that span the whole continuum of therapeutic strategies. The strategies presented in this book should not be construed as the only ones available for a particular crisis. They are presented as "best bets" based on what current research and practice indicate to be appropriate and applicable. Yet these strategies may not be appropriate for all practitioners with all clients in all situations. Good crisis intervention, as well as good therapy of any other kind, is a serious professional activity that calls for creativity and the ability to adapt to changing conditions of the therapeutic moment. To that extent, crisis intervention at times is more art than science and is not always prescriptive. Therefore, we would caution you that there are no clear-cut prescriptions or simple cause-and-effect answers in this book.

The Case for an Experiential Viewpoint

The fact that no single theory or strategy applies to every crisis situation is particularly problematic to those who are looking for simple, concrete answers to resolve the client problems they will face. If you are just beginning your career in the human service business, we hope that while reading and trying out activities in this book you will suspend your judgment for a while and be open to the experience.

Basic relationship skills. This admonition is particularly appropriate for Chapter 2, which deals with basic listening and responding skills. The listening and responding skills are critical to everything else the worker does in crisis intervention. Yet on cursory inspection these techniques and concepts would seem at best simplistic and at worst inane. They do not appear to fix anything because they are not "fixing" skills. What they do is give the crisis worker a firm basis of operation to explore clearly the dilemmas the client is facing. Basic listening and responding skills are the prerequisites for opening gateways into all other therapeutic modalities. Our experience has shown us over and over that students and trainees who scoff at and dismiss these basic relationship skills are the ones who will invariably have the most trouble meeting the experiential requirements of our courses and workshop training sessions. We feel very strongly about this particular point and thus ask you to read Chapter 2 with an open mind.

If this volume is used as a structured learning experience, the case studies and the exercises at the end of each chapter will be a valuable resource for experiential learning. It is essential that you observe effective crisis intervention models at work, and then follow up by actually practicing and enacting the procedures you have observed. Intensive and extensive role play is an excellent skill builder.

Role play. A critical component of training is not just talking about problems but practicing the skills of handling them as well. Talking about a problem is fine, but attempting to handle a live situation allows the trainee to get involved in the business of calming, managing, controlling, and motivating clients. Role play is one of the best ways of practicing what is preached, and it prepares human service workers for developing creative ways to deal with the variety of contingencies they may face. Role play allows human service workers the chance to find out what works and does not work for them in the safety of a training situation and affords their fellow students and trainees an opportunity to give them valuable feedback. We have included exercises at the end of each chapter that provide readers numerous opportunities to try out their skills in role-playing situations.

A major problem in role playing is the embarrassment of standing up in a class or workshop and risking making a fool of oneself. We want to assure you that in our classes and training sessions we do not expect perfection. If our students and trainees were perfect at crisis intervention, they would not be taking instruction in the first place! Therefore, put your inhibitions on the shelf for a while and become engaged in the role plays as if the situations were real, live, and happening right now. Further, be willing and able to accept critical comments from your peers, supervisors, or instructors. Your ego may be bruised a bit in the process, but that is far better than waiting until you are confronted with an out-of-control client before you think about what you are going to do.

Give the exercises provided in each chapter your best effort, process them with fellow students or trainees, and see what fits best with your own feelings, thoughts, and behaviors. Many times our students and trainees attempt to imitate us. Although it is gratifying to see students or trainees attempting to be "Burl" or "Dick," it is generally an exercise in futility for them. What they need to do is view us critically as we model the procedures and then incorporate their own style and personhood into the procedures. We would urge you to do the same whether you are reading this book in the context of a class or as a part of a training exercise in a crisis agency.

ORGANIZATION OF THE BOOK

Part One: Crisis Intervention Theory and Application

Part One of the book introduces the basic concepts of crisis intervention. It is comprised of Chapters 1 and 2.

Chapter 1, Introduction. Chapter 1 contains the basic rationale and the theoretical and conceptual information needed for understanding and enhancing the study of applied crisis intervention.

Chapter 2, Six Steps in Crisis Intervention. Chapter 2 is a conceptual as well as skill-building model of crisis intervention that applies to all crisis categories. It contains background information, relationship skills, strategies, and practical guidelines for initial intervention in all crises.

Part Two: Crisis Categories: Going into the Trenches

Part Two (Chapters 3 through 11) addresses a variety of important categories or types of crisis. For each chapter in Part Two the background and dynamics of the particular crisis type are detailed to provide a basic grasp of the driving forces behind the dilemma. While some theory is presented to highlight the therapeutic modalities used, comprehensive theoretical systems are beyond the scope of this book. For that information, turn to the reference section at the end of each chapter.

In Part Two we have provided scripts from live interventions, highlighted by explanations of why the crisis workers did what they did. Throughout this section the emphasis is on live tryout, experiencing, and processing of the cases and issues.

Chapter 3, Suicide: Strategies for Assessment and Intervention. Chapter 3 focuses on strategies that crisis workers need in working with suicidal people. Suicidal ideation permeates many other problems that assail people the human service worker is likely to confront and has general applicability to all providers of crisis intervention service.

Chapter 4, Women in Crisis: Battering. Chapter 4 deals with the crisis which many women face: being treated violently by their spouses. Battering also refers to being psychologically abused. This chapter provides strategies needed to help women who are attempting to work their way out of such pernicious relationships.

Chapter 5, Institutional Crises: Controlling Violent Behavior. Chapter 5 tackles the little-publicized, and badly neglected, category which crisis workers in many institutions face daily: violent behavior within the walls of the institution. Regardless of the organizational settings where they are employed, workers will find in this chapter useful concepts and practical strategies which they can put to immediate use with agitated and potentially assaultive clients.

Chapter 6, Crisis of Severe Physical Limitation. Chapter 6 examines individuals with severe physical limitations and the special crises they encounter. The major focus is on wheelchair-bound survivors of spinal cord injury.

Chapter 7, Post Traumatic Stress Disorder. Chapter 7 treats a fairly new crisis problem, posttraumatic stress disorder (PTSD). Although it concentrates heavily on PTSD among war veterans, the background, principles, and strategies explained here are relevant to dealing with PTSD clients whose traumas were derived from any human-generated source.

Chapter 8, Substance Abuse. Chapter 8 deals with one of the most timely and pressing issues of our day, addiction to substances. Since addiction is such a pervasive scourge on society, no human service worker in the public arena can escape the effects, the need to know about, and the urgency of possessing competence in dealing with people who present problems of addiction.

Chapter 9, Sexual Assault. Chapter 9 addresses another societal crisis which practically every human service worker will eventually encounter—clients who have either experienced or been affected by sexual abuse. Sexually abused clientele are a special population because of the negative moral and social connotations associated with the dehumanizing acts perpetrated on them.

Chapter 10, Hostage Crisis: Negotiation Strategies. Chapter 10 represents another hot topic in our modern world. The taking of hostages has become well publicized through terrorism and other acts of violence. However, many hostage takings occur within the confines of human service work settings. This chapter provides basic negotiation strategies that may allow a human service worker to contain and survive a hostage situation.

Chapter 11, Personal Loss: Bereavement, Grief, and Separation. Chapter 11 presents a crisis category which every crisis worker as well as every other person will sooner or later face: personal loss. Even though the phenomenon of loss has been with us as long as the human species has existed, many people in our culture are poorly prepared and ill equipped to deal with it. This chapter provides models and strategies for coping with unresolved grief. It uses ultimate loss, death, to examine a variety of problems associated with termination of relationships, both for the client and the crisis worker.

Part Three: Focus on Improving the Crisis Worker or Counselor

Part Three (Chapter 12) focuses directly on the problems of crisis workers and their employing institutions.

Chapter 12, Human service workers in crisis: burnout. Chapter 12 is about us: all human service workers who are in the helping professions. No worker is immune to stress, burnout, and the crises which go with human service work. Chapter 12 should prove to be invaluable for any worker anywhere whose work environment is frenetic or whose personality tends to generate compulsive behavior, perfectionism, or other stressors which may lead to burnout.

In summary we have not been so concerned about intellectualizing, philosophizing, or using theoretical interpretations as much as simply focusing on the practical matters of how, when, and what to do in crisis situations.

ACKNOWLEDGMENTS

In writing a book that covers so many diverse areas of the human condition, it would be extremely presumptuous of us to rely solely on our own expertise to propose crisis intervention techniques based on what we theoretically thought was truth, beauty, and goodness. While we tend at times to think a good bit of ourselves as therapists, we are not so vain or foolish as to believe we have all the answers to all the problems one may encounter in this book. We decided the only realistic and honest way to present the most current, reliable, and practical techniques available would be to go straight to the human service workers who deal with the problems you will encounter in this book. The people are not "big names" in the therapy business. In fact, they consider themselves to be normal human service workers who meet their clientele day in and day out. What makes them "world class" in the human service business is that on a day in and day out basis, they do their job very, very well. They are an encyclopedia of practical knowledge in dealing with the gut-wrenching problems addressed in this text.

All of these people graciously agreed to be interviewed at length by us. Taped transcriptions were made of each interview session. Techniques and cases presented by the human services workers were then incorporated and blended into each chapter. Upon completion of each chapter's rough draft, the manuscripts were sent to the respective workers for their critical review. We hope the final product reflects clearly what these people so skillfully do in crisis intervention.

In alphabetical order we would like to thank the following human service professionals: Steve Allen, Counseling Department, Newman School District, Newman, Illinois; Bill Brewi, Vietnam Veterans Center, Memphis, Tennessee; Sharon Butts, Marriage and Family Practice, Urbana, Illinois; Rich Cevasco, Psychology Department, Trenton State Maximum Security Penitentiary; Deborah Cunningham, Center for Independent Living, Memphis, Tennessee; Angie Dagastino, YWCA Wife Abuse Service and YWCA Wife Abuse Shelter, Memphis, Tennessee; Dotsie Graham, Alcohol and Drug Unit, Charter Lakeside Hospital, Memphis, Tennessee; John Hathcock, undergraduate student, Memphis State University; Ann Kirkpatrick, Memphis Police Department; Ann Lewellyn, TLC Center, Eastern Illinois Special Education District, Mattoon, Illinois.

Carol McCown, Southeast Mental Health Center, Memphis, Tennessee; Joyce McCrory, ACE Care Unit, St. Francis Hospital, Memphis, Tennessee; Ollie Mannino, Methodist Outreach, Methodist Hospital, Memphis, Tennessee; Marilyn Miller, graduate student, Memphis State University, Memphis, Tennessee; Barbara Moore, graduate student, Memphis State University; Connie Nelson, Rape Crisis Center, Memphis, Tennessee; Carolyn Parker, Rediscovery Unit, Jackson Regional Hospital, Jackson, Tennessee; Bruce Reed, Northeast Mental Health Center, Memphis, Tennessee; Ray Richardson, ACE Care Unit, St. Francis Hospital, Memphis, Tennessee; Mike Rohr, Family Link/Runaway House, Memphis, Tennessee; Mary Sewell, Crisis Center, Memphis, Tennessee; B. J. Stone, Vietnam Veterans Center, Memphis, Tennessee; Milt Trapold, Department of Psychology, Memphis State University; Barry Vinick, Adolescent Unit, Memphis Mental Health Institute; Ed Wallin, Vietnam Veterans Center, Memphis, Tennessee.

We would like to thank the students in our Crisis Intervention and Theories of Counseling courses at Memphis State University who served as willing "guinea pigs" as we field tested the exercises in this book.

A special note of thanks goes to the men in the Wednesday night "rap" group at the Memphis Vietnam Veterans Center for their willingness to include us in their group and willingness to share openly some of the trauma they are still experiencing.

We thank also the reviewers of our manuscript for their helpful comments: Dr. Gary Belkin, Long Island University; Dr. Lawrence Brammer, University of Washington; Dr. L. Sherilyn Cormier, West Virginia University; Professor Don M. Hartsough, Purdue University; Professor Iris Heckman, Washburn University, Topeka, Kansas; and Mary Sewell, former Executive Director, Suicide and Crisis Intervention Service, Memphis, Tennessee.

We wish to express the utmost of appreciation and gratitude for the editorial expertise, assistance, support, and encouragement provided by Brooks/Cole during the entire writing and production process. Our admiration and thanks are particularly accorded to Claire Verduin, Managing Editor, Linda Loba, Production Editor, and Meredy Amyx, Manuscript Editor. We believe that they are the best of the best in the book publishing business.

Finally, we would like to thank our spouses, Martha and Susan, for again refraining from taking us to divorce court while we were having this love affair for the past three years.

Burl Gilliland and Dick James

Contents

PART TWO

PART THREE

Focus on Improving the Crisis Worker or Counselor

439

CHAPTER 12 *Human Service Workers in Crisis: Burnout*

441

Index

Crisis Intervention Strategies

CRISIS INTERVENTION THEORY AND ITS APPLICATION

Part One introduces you to the fundamental concepts and theoretical and applied techniques, strategies, methodologies, procedures, and relationship skills needed to understand and conduct effective crisis counseling and intervention in a general sense. Chapter 1 is mainly introductory and conceptual. Chapter 2 serves as a key to the application of relationship skills and counseling strategies to the whole scope of crisis intervention. Crisis workers and counselors will find that the skills and strategies represented here also apply broadly to *all* human problems, crisis or otherwise.

Introduction

DEFINITIONS OF CRISIS

There are many definitions of *crisis.* Five are presented here for your thought and study. We believe that they collectively represent and define crisis, as well as preparing you to consider the theoretical constructs that follow in this chapter. These definitions should also set the stage for the remainder of the book.

1. We may say that people are in a state of crisis when they face an obstacle to important life goals—an obstacle that is, for a time, insurmountable by the use of customary methods of problem solving. A period of disorganization ensues, a period of upset, during which many abortive attempts at solution are made (Caplan, 1961, p. 18).

2. Crisis results from impediments to life goals that people believe they cannot attain through customary choices and behaviors (Caplan, 1964).

3. Crises are crises because the individual has no response to deal with a situation (Carkhuff & Berenson, 1977, p. 165).

4. Crises are personal difficulties or situations that immobilize people and prevent them from consciously controlling their lives (Belkin, 1984, p. 424).

5. Crisis is a state of disorganization in which helpees face frustration of important life goals or profound disruption of their life cycles and methods of coping with stressors. The term *crisis* refers usually to the helpee's feelings of fear, shock, and distress *about* the disruption, not the disruption itself (Brammer, 1985, p. 94).

To summarize these definitions, *crisis is a perception of an event or situation as an intolerable difficulty that exceeds the resources and coping mechanisms of the person.* Unless the person obtains relief, the crisis has the potential to cause severe affective, cognitive, and behavioral malfunctioning.

PRINCIPLES AND CHARACTERISTICS OF CRISIS

The following general principles and characteristics of crisis represent an expanded definition and clarification of what crisis means.

Both Danger and Opportunity

Crisis is a danger because it can overwhelm the individual to the extent that it may result in serious pathology, including homicide and suicide. It is also an opportunity because the nature of the pain it induces impels the person to seek help (Aguilera & Messick, 1982, p. 1). If the individual takes advantage of the opportunity, the intervention can help plant the seeds of self-growth and self-realization (Brammer, 1985, p. 95).

Individuals who do not seek therapeutic assistance may experience any one of three outcomes. Under ideal circumstances, many individuals can cope effectively with crisis and develop strength from the experience. They change and grow in a positive manner and come out of the crisis both stronger and more compassionate. Other people appear to survive the crisis, but effectively block out the hurtful affect from awareness, only to have it haunt them in innumerable ways throughout the rest of their lives. There are also those who break down psychologically at the onset of the crisis and clearly demonstrate that they are incapable of going any further with their lives unless provided with immediate and intensive assistance.

Transcrisis States

Crises are time limited, usually persisting to a maximum of six to eight weeks, at the end of which the subjective discomfort diminishes (Janosik, 1984, p. 9). However, what occurs during the immediate aftermath of the crisis event determines whether or not the crisis will become a disease reservoir that will be transformed into a chronic and long-term state. Although the original crisis event may be submerged from awareness and the individual may believe the problem has been resolved, appearance of new stressors may bring the individual to the crisis state again. This emotional roller coaster occurs frequently and for extended periods of time, ranging from months to years. An adult who was sexually abused as a child is an excellent example of a person who is in a *transcrisis state.* The adult may have attained what appears to be good mental health. However, this appearance is gained at the cost of warding off and repressing the original trauma from conscious memory. Later, during the stress of a divorce, the repressed material from the original event may resurface in symptomatic ways that seem to have nothing in common with the original traumatic event or the current stressful problem. Another example would be the client entering treatment for an acute substance abuse problem. While the substance abuse problem becomes a high priority for treatment, it is also a symptom of the psychological roller coaster ride that started with the childhood sexual abuse. The divorce may be reconciled or the substance abuse treated, but the original crisis has not been expunged. It has merely subsided and a temporary state of equilibrium is achieved, but the original trauma will usually reemerge and instigate a new crisis the moment new stressors are introduced. Dynamically, this pattern is defensive repression. Therapeutically, this transcrisis state calls for crisis intervention techniques.

Transcrisis points. A frequent part of transcrisis states are *transcrisis points* occurring within the therapeutic intervention. These points are generally marked by the client coming to grips with new developmental stages or other dimensions of the problem.

Transcrisis points do not occur in regular, predictable, linear progression. For example an abused spouse may go through crisis point after crisis point talking to a helper over the telephone before making a decision to leave the battering relationship, often calling helping persons a dozen times in the course of a few days. The abused spouse may then make a decision to leave the battering relationship and go to a spouse abuse shelter only to find that the necessity of making a geographical move or finding a job may instigate a crisis that is almost as potent as the battering. Many times, human service workers who practice long term therapy are shocked, confused, and overwhelmed by the sudden disequilibrium their clients experience. Handling these transcrisis points may be the psychological equivalent of trying to gather quicksilver from the floor. Behaviorally, such clients may vacillate from a placid to an agitated state so fast that the worker puts out one brushfire only to be confronted by yet another. It is at these transcrisis points that standard therapeutic strategies and techniques are suspended and the human service worker must operate from a crisis intervention mode.

Once the individual has made a clear-cut choice to seek help, transcrisis points continue to occur in therapy and may be seen as benchmarks that are critical to progressive stages of positive therapeutic growth. These points are characterized by approach-avoidance behavior in seeking help, taking risks, and initiating action steps toward forward movement. Encountering these transcrisis points, a person will experience the same kind of disorganization, disequilibrium, and fragmentation that surrounded the original crisis event. Leaping one hurdle does not necessarily mean that the entire crisis is successfully overcome. Quite the contrary is true. Spouse-abuse victims may extricate themselves from a battering relationship, only to become so terrified at having to make their own way in the world that they return to the batterer. Substance abusers may become detoxified in a difficult battle with their drug of choice, only to be undone by an inability to come to terms with another member of the family. Survivors of a catastrophe may expunge the event from memory and then be faced with repairing gaping wounds in personal relationships which have been torn apart by their long term pathological behavior. Persons having spinal cord injuries may be successfully rehabilitated physically but retreat into substance addiction or become depressed and/or suicidal as they attempt to begin a new lifestyle from a wheelchair. Crisis workers may be faced with a series of these transcrisis points as they help clients work through their problems.

Therefore, it is not only the initial crisis with which the worker must contend but also each transcrisis point, as it occurs, if clients are not to slip back into the pathology that assailed them in the first place. Transcrisis points should not be confused with the jumps and starts that go with the working through of typical adjustment problems. Although these points may be forecast with some degree of reliability by workers who are expert in the particular field, their onset is sudden, dramatic, and extremely potent. In that regard, these psychological aftershocks can be just as damaging as the initial tremor and may require extraordinary effort on the part of the human service worker to assist the client in regaining control. It is with these transcrisis states and points that this book is also concerned and cases have been portrayed that consider both of these components.

Complicated Symptomology

Crisis is *not* simple; it is complex and difficult to understand, and it defies cause-and-effect description (Brammer, 1985, p. 91; Kliman, 1978, p. xxi). The symptoms that overlay precipitating crisis events become tangled webs that crisscross all environments of an individual. When an event reaches a fulminating point, there may be so many compounding problems that the worker has to intervene directly in a variety of areas. Further, the environment of individuals in crisis figures prominently in the ease or difficulty with which the crisis can be handled. Families, employing organizations, and the state of the economy are among many salient factors that may have direct effects on problem resolution and a return to stability.

Value of Life Experiences

The worker handles the crisis or not as he or she is a whole person or not (Carkhuff & Berenson, 1977, pp. 162–163). A whole person has a rich and varied background of life experiences. These life experiences serve as a resource for emotional maturity that, combined with training, allow workers to be stable, consistent, and well integrated not only within the crisis situation but also in a broad span of other environments in their daily lives.

However, life experiences alone are not sufficient to qualify one to be a crisis worker and may be debilitating if they continue to influence the worker in negative ways. This issue is central to crisis intervention because many of the people who work as volunteers, support personnel, and professionals are products of their own crisis environments. They have chosen to work with people experiencing the same kind of crisis they themselves have suffered, and they use their experiential background as a resource in working with others. For example, there are recovering addicts who work in alcohol and drug units, battered women who work in spouse-abuse centers, and PTSD victims who counsel in Vietnam veterans' centers. These professionals have had first-hand experience with the trauma that their clients have experienced. Does this background give them an edge over other workers who have not suffered the malady?

The answer is a qualified yes: qualified in that a person who carries emotional baggage into the helping relationship may be even less effective than the person who has had few if any life experiences. We see examples of emotional carryover into the intervention process in the proselytizing alcoholic who vilifies others in order to assuage his own insecurities and fears about "falling off the wagon" and in the child-abuse worker, herself a former victim of sexual abuse, who castigates mothers for their failure to confront abusing fathers. Such human service workers may have tremendous difficulties because they commingle many of their own problems with those of their clients. These workers alternate among feeling states characterized by sympathy, anger, disappointment, and cynicism, which are detrimental both to themselves and to their clients.

We do not believe that crisis workers must have "lived in the crisis" to be able to understand and deal with it effectively. We do believe that interventionists who have successfully overcome some of life's problems and have put those problems into perspective will have assets of maturity, optimism, tenacity, and tough-mindedness that will help them marshal their psychological resources to aid their clients.

We are not proposing that people lacking a variety of life experiences should actively pursue trauma as a means of becoming seasoned enough to be effective interventionists. We would also caution that on-the-job training in this business is a very arduous way to win one's spurs, particularly if the worker who has spent a sheltered, constricted life decides through misguided idealism to become a Florence Nightingale and fix the problems of the world. This rose colored view does little for clients in general and may do much harm to workers as their good intentions pave the road to burnout. We hasten to add that chronological age has very little to do with having or not having self-enhancing life experiences and a broader, more resilient viewpoint. We know people ranging in age from 21 to 65 who are emotional adolescents. They are threatened by face-to-face encounters with the real world and may be characterized by rigidity, insularity, and insecurity.

The ideal crisis worker we envision is one who has experienced life, has learned and grown from those experiences, and supports those experiences in his or her work by thorough training, knowledge, and supervision. This individual constantly seeks to integrate all these aspects into his or her therapeutic intervention in particular and into living in general.

Seeds of Growth and Change

In the disequilibrium that accompanies crisis, anxiety is always present, and the discomfort of anxiety provides an impetus for change (Janosik, 1984, p. 39). Many times the dilemma is that anxiety must reach the boiling point before an individual is ready to admit that the problem has gone beyond control. One need look no further than the substance abuser for affirmation of this point. By waiting so long, the substance abuser may be so entrenched that a therapeutic jackhammer has to be applied to break the addiction down into manageable pieces. Even so, a threshold point for change is reached, albeit in last-ditch desperation, where the abuser finally surrenders to the fact that something must be done.

No Panaceas or Quick Fixes

People in crisis are generally amenable to help through a variety of forms of intervention, some of which can be described as *brief therapy* (Cormier & Hackney, 1987, p. 240). For problems of long duration, quick fixes are rarely available. Many of the problems of clients who are suffering from severe crises stem from the fact that they sought quick fixes in the first place, usually through a pill. Whereas the "fix" may dampen the dreadful responses, it does nothing for the instigating stimulus, and therefore the crisis deepens.

The Meaning of Choices

Life is a process of interrelated crises and challenges that we confront or not, to live or not (Carkhuff & Berenson, 1977, p. 173). When we *choose to act* we are making a choice that is clearly pro-life! When we *choose not to act*, we are signing a death warrant for living. In the realm of crisis, *not to choose is a choice*, and this choice usually turns out to be negative and destructive. *Choosing to do something* at least contains the seeds of growth and allows a person the chance to set goals and formulate a plan to begin to overcome the dilemma.

Universality and Idiosyncrasy

Disequilibrium or disorganization accompanies every crisis, whether universal or idiosyncratic (Janosik, 1984, p. 13). Crisis is universal because no one is immune to breakdown, given the right constellation of circumstances. It is idiosyncratic because what one person may successfully overcome, another may not, even though the circumstances are virtually the same. Maintaining a belief that one is immune to psychic assaults, that one can handle any crisis in a stable, poised, and in-command fashion is foolhardy. Thousands of "tough" Vietnam veterans, suffering from PTSD, who have turnstiled through VA hospitals and veterans' centers are convincing proof that when the crisis boils over, disorganization, disequilibrium, disorientation, and fragmentation of the individual's coping mechanisms will occur no matter how conditioned against psychological trauma a person may be.

Interrelatedness of Crises and the Personhood of Crisis Workers

The pattern of helping, as of life, consists of a series of interrelated crises. We benefit or not as we act constructively or not. Each crisis encapsulates a process leading to the potential for constructive change, not only for the client but also for the helper (Carkhuff & Berenson, 1977, pp. 162–163).

The crisis helping relationship is reciprocal and is greater than the sum of its parts. The helper changes as a result of every contact with a client. Successful resolution of the crisis results in two products: (1) helping the client overcome the crisis and (2) effecting positive change in the helper as a result of the encounter.

Positive change is not merely summed up in so many cases successfully handled or so many techniques effectively employed. Successful intervention is enhancing, not only professionally but also personally, to the extent that what has impact upon us in the therapeutic moment transfers to the rest of our environments. Successfully helping a client negotiate a crisis allows us to incorporate the experience into our own life and become more holistic, enabling, and competent in all our endeavors. The power and benefit are not merely arithmetically additive but geometrical in their potential impact. Seen from this standpoint, successful intervention with another human being is one of the most intrinsically rewarding endeavors a professional helper may undertake.

CHARACTERISTICS OF EFFECTIVE CRISIS WORKERS

Effective crisis workers need to have not only comprehensive life experiences, but also professional and personal skills commensurate with the intensity of crisis intervention. Many crisis workers begin in the field as volunteers or support persons. They may or may not have been victims of crisis in the particular category with which they work. If these people remain in the field for any length of time they usually find that their initial zeal and commitment need to be enhanced by professional training. Many volunteers professionalize themselves by returning to school just to take a course "because they don't know enough" and end up seeking a degree in the human service field.

Our own classes and workshop sessions comprise people as diverse as homemakers, business executives, and retirees enrolled in counseling courses and specialized training because of a desire to learn in a systematic manner the therapeutic skills necessary to do their volunteer work. It is not uncommon for us also to find people who are successful in a vocation completely unrelated to human service work and who, by virtue of the intrinsic rewards they receive from their volunteer or support work, decide to make a career shift into the helping professions. A classic example is recovering alcoholics who turn the twelfth step of Alcoholics Anonymous, "helping others," into a profession, seeking a graduate degree to go with their personal experience of substance abuse.

Professional Skills

Professionally, we seek to inculcate in our students the following helping strategies:

attentiveness
accurate listening and responding
congruence between thinking, feeling, and acting therapeutically
reassuring and supporting skills

rudimentary ability to analyze, synthesize, and diagnose
basic assessment and referral skills
ability to explore alternatives and solve problems
specific techniques such as behavioral contracting, relaxation training, and
   assertion skills.

This is not an all-inclusive list, but it should provide a flavor of the outcome goals we expect of people who go through our crisis intervention course at Memphis State University.

Although these skills would be the hallmark of those who perform any human service work, the difference in crisis intervention is that these skills must be used when problem onset is sudden and dramatic, emotions are highly volatile, and background information may be sketchy at best. Although we can model and process the therapeutic skills necessary to intervene in these circumstances, inculcating the personal skills necessary to do effective crisis intervention work is another matter.

Poise

The nature of crisis intervention is that the worker is often confronted with shocking and threatening material from clients who are completely out of control. Probably the most significant help the interventionist can provide at this juncture is to remain calm, poised, and in control (Belkin, 1984, p. 427). Creating a stable and rational atmosphere provides a model for the client that is conducive to restoring equilibrium to the situation. Practicing relaxation techniques is one way of keeping calm in such highly charged situations, but more important is the worker's faith that the client can be pulled through the crisis. In our teaching we can model patience and understanding with troubled clients. What we cannot model is faith and belief in the client's ability to overcome the situation. This trait is one that must abide deep within the interventionist; we know of no easy way to teach it.

Creativity and Flexibility

Creativity and flexibility are major assets to those confronted with perplexing and seemingly unsolvable problems (Aguilera & Messick, 1982, p. 24). It is one thing to teach a person a repertoire of skills. It is quite another thing to teach the use of those skills in ways that are adaptable to clients' needs. Clearly, most traditional schooling has to do with learning material in rote ways. Most training programs known to us pay scant attention to creative therapeutic functioning. In our own courses and training workshops, students and trainees have difficulty when confronted with conducting role plays with peers because they have no formula for getting the "right" answer. Imagine their trepidation when we invite into our classes drama students who can really act out the problems our students are likely to face! Although practice in tough role-play situations builds confidence, how creative individuals are in difficult situations depends to a large measure on how well they have nur- tured their own creativity over the course of their lives by taking risks and practicing divergent thinking.

Energy

Functioning in the unknown areas that are characteristic of crisis interven- tion requires energy, organization, direction, and systematic action (Carkhuff & Berenson, 1977, p. 194). Professional training can provide organizational guidelines and principles for systematic acting. What it cannot do is provide the energy requisite to perform this work. The chapter on burnout in this book (Chapter 12) speaks to many of the maladies that workers suffer and suggests ways to bolster morale, but being energized is still largely incum- bent on the worker. Feeling good enough about oneself to tackle perplexing problems day after day calls for not only an initial desire to do the work but also the ability to take care of one's physical and psychological needs so that energy levels remain high.

Time

Crisis work is different from typical therapeutic intervention in that time is a critical factor. Crisis intervention requires more activity and directiveness than ordinary therapeutic endeavors usually do. Time to reflect and mull over problems is a rare commodity in crisis intervention. The worker must have fast mental reflexes to deal with the constantly emerging and changing issues that occur in the crisis. We know of no video tape or spa that provides fitness activities in these areas. The worker who cannot think fast and accu- rately is going to find the business very frustrating indeed.

Other Characteristics

The following chapters will reveal that tenacity, the ability to delay gratifi- cation, courage, optimism, a reality orientation, calmness under duress, ob- jectivity, a strong self-concept, and abiding faith that human beings are strong, resilient, and capable of overcoming seemingly insurmountable odds are all attributes of world-class crisis interventionists. Poll yourself on these traits. All of them are of utmost importance to you and your clients.

We also want you to understand that admission into the inner circle of the profession is not solely reserved for a few supermen and superwomen. Most interventionists we know, including ourselves, are at times perplexed, frus- trated, angry, afraid, threatened, incompetent, foolish, vain, troubled, and otherwise unequal to the task. We allow ourselves and our students and trainees at least one mistake a day and go on from there. We would like you to remember that cognitive billboard and place it squarely in the forefront of your mind.

If you are now feeling pessimistic about going into the field of crisis intervention or even reading this book, do not give up yet. Standing up to the intense heat of the crisis situation to help people through seemingly unsolvable problems is some of the most gratifying and positively reinforcing work we know. The intense personal rewards that accrue to crisis workers lead us to believe that this work would be high on Glasser's (1976) list of positively addicting behaviors.

If you are not starting out in the field, but are a seasoned veteran of the human service wars, the utility of this book should become readily apparent. We know of no human service workers who have not encountered or will not encounter crisis situations at some time in their career. This book has a variety of resources that should be helpful in those situations and add to the effectiveness of your short-term work.

For those who may decide that human service work (and particularly crisis intervention) is not their calling, this book also has applicability. Consider, for a moment, yourself as a client. Everyone is at times subject to the whims of a randomly cruel universe, and the kinds of crises that are dealt with in this book are apt to be visited upon all of us. Understanding how to navigate through these constellations of problems is a valuable resource. How well we live depends on our ability to handle the problems that confront us when we least expect them. As you read through the material you may find yourself "living into" some of these problems and asking yourself, "I wonder how I'd fare if I were a client?" We believe that this too is a worthwhile perspective if one can also look beyond the dilemmas to the coping techniques and bank them for future reference and use.

THEORIES OF CRISIS AND CRISIS INTERVENTION

There is no single theory or school of thought that encompasses every view of human crisis or all the models or systems of crisis intervention. We will give a brief overview of theories relevant both to crisis (as a phenomenon) and to crisis intervention (as an intentional helping response). Janosik (1984) conceptualized crisis theory on three different levels: basic crisis theory, expanded crisis theory, and applied crisis theory.

Basic Crisis Theory

The research, writings, and teachings of Lindemann (1944, 1956) gave professionals and paraprofessionals a new understanding of crisis. Lindemann helped caregivers to promote crisis intervention for many sufferers of loss who had no specific pathological diagnoses but who were exhibiting symptoms that appeared to be pathological. Lindemann's basic crisis theory and work made a substantive contribution to our understanding of behavior in clients whose grief crises were precipitated by loss. He helped professionals and paraprofessionals to recognize that behavioral responses to crises associated with grief are normal, temporary, and amenable to alleviation through short-term intervention techniques. These "normal" grief behaviors include (1) preoccupation with the lost one, (2) identification with the lost one, (3) expressions of guilt and hostility, (4) some disorganization in daily routine, and (5) some evidence of somatic complaints (Janosik, 1984, p. 11). Lindemann negated the prevailing perception that clients manifesting crisis responses should necessarily be treated as abnormal or pathological.

Whereas Lindemann focused mainly on immediate resolution of grief after loss, Caplan (1964) expanded Lindemann's constructs to the total field of traumatic events. Caplan views crisis as a state resulting from impediments to life goals that are unattainable through customary behaviors. These impediments can arise from both developmental and situational events. Both Lindemann and Caplan deal with crisis intervention following psychological trauma on an equilibrium/disequilibrium paradigm. The stages in Lindemann's paradigm are (1) disturbed equilibrium, (2) brief therapy or grief work, (3) client's working through the problem or grief, and (4) restoration of equilibrium (Janosik, 1984, pp. 10–12). Caplan linked Lindemann's concepts and stages to all developmental and situational events and extended crisis intervention to eliminating the cognitive, emotional, and behavioral distortions that precipitated the psychological trauma in the first place.

The work of both Lindemann and Caplan gave impetus to the use of crisis intervention strategies in counseling and brief therapy with people manifesting universal human reactions to traumatic events. Basic crisis theory, following their lead, focuses on helping people in crisis recognize and correct temporary cognitive, emotional, and behavioral distortions brought on by traumatic events.

All people experience psychological trauma at some time during their lives. Neither stress nor emergency conditions of the trauma in itself constitute crisis. It is only when the traumatic event is subjectively perceived as a threat to needs, safety, or meaningful existence that an individual enters a state of crisis (Caplan, 1964). A crisis is accompanied by temporary disequilibrium and contains potential for human growth. The resolution of crisis may lead to positive and constructive outcomes such as self-enhancing coping ability and a decrease in negative, self-defeating, dysfunctional behavior (Janosik, 1984, pp. 3–21).

Expanded Crisis Theory

Expanded crisis theory was developed because basic theory, which depended on a psychoanalytic approach alone, did not adequately satisfy all the social, environmental, and situational factors that make an event a crisis. As crisis theory and crisis intervention have expanded, it has become clear that an approach that identifies predisposing factors as the main or only causal agent falls short of the mark. A prime example of this restrictive view was the erroneous diagnosis by practitioners who first encountered PTSD victims that pathology preceding the crisis event was the real cause of the trauma. As crisis theory and intervention have grown, it has become apparent that, given the right combination of developmental, sociological, psychological, environmental, and situational determinants, anyone could fall victim to transient pathological symptoms. Therefore, expanded crisis theory draws not only from psychoanalytic but also from general systems, adaptational, and interpersonal theory (Janosik, 1984). The following are synopses of the major theoretical components of an expanded view.

Psychoanalytic theory. Psychoanalytic theory (Fine, 1973), applied to expanded crisis theory, is based on the view that the disequilibrium that accompanies a person's crisis can be understood through gaining access to the individual's unconscious thoughts and past emotional experiences. Psychoanalytic theory presupposes that some early childhood fixation is the primary explanation of why an event becomes a crisis. This theory may be used to help clients develop insight into the dynamics and causes of their behavior as the crisis situation acts upon them.

Systems theory. Systems theory (Haley, 1973, 1976) is based not so much on what happens within an individual in crisis as on the interrelationships and interdependence among people and between people and events. The fundamental concept of systems theory is analogous "to ecological systems in which all elements are interrelated, and in which change at any level of those interrelated parts will lead to alteration of the total system" (Cormier & Hackney, 1987, p. 217). Belkin (1984) added that this theory "refers to an emotional system, a system of communications, and a system of need fulfillment and request" in which all members within an intergenerational relationship bring something to bear on the others and each of whom derives something from the others (pp. 350–351).

Systems theory represents a turning away from traditional approaches, which focus only on what is going on within the person of the client, and adopts an interpersonal-systems way of thinking. There is great value in looking at crises in their total social and environmental perspectives—not simply as one individual being affected in a linear progression of cause-and-effect events.

Adaptational theory. Adaptational theory, in our use of the term, depicts a person's crisis as being sustained through maladaptive behaviors, negative thoughts, and destructive defense mechanisms. Adaptational crisis theory is based on the premise that the person's crisis will recede when these maladaptive coping behaviors are changed to adaptive behaviors.

Breaking the chain of maladjusted functioning means changing to adaptive behavior, promoting positive thoughts and constructing defense mechanisms that will help the person overcome the immobility created by the crisis and move to a positive mode of functioning. As maladaptive behaviors are learned, so may adaptive behaviors be learned. Aided by the interventionist, the client may be taught to replace old, debilitating behaviors with new, self-enhancing ones. Such new behaviors may be applied directly to the context of the crisis and ultimately result in either success or reinforcement for the client in overcoming it (Cormier & Cormier, 1985, p. 148).

Interpersonal theory.   Interpersonal theory (Rogers, 1977) is built on many of the dimensions that Cormier and Hackney (1987) describe as enhancing personal self-esteem (openness, trust, sharing, safety, unconditional positive regard, accurate empathy, and genuineness) (pp. 35–64). The essence of interpersonal theory is that people cannot sustain a personal state of crisis for very long if they believe in themselves and others and have confidence that they can become self-actualized and overcome the crisis.

When people confer their locus of self-evaluation on others, they become dependent on others for validation of their being. Therefore, as long as a person maintains an external locus of control the crisis will persist. The outcome goal, in interpersonal theory, is returning the power of self-evaluation to the person. Doing so enables the person once again to control his or her own destiny and regain the ability to take whatever action is needed to cope with the crisis situation.

Applied Crisis Theory

The application of crisis theory requires a nontraditional approach. Each person and each crisis situation are different. Thus, crisis workers must view each person and the setting events precipitating the crisis as unique. Brammer (1985, pp. 94–95) characterizes applied crisis theory as encompassing three domains: (1) normal *developmental* crises, (2) *situational* crises, and (3) *existential* crises.

Developmental crises.   Developmental crises are events in the normal flow of human growth and evolvement whereby a dramatic change or shift occurs that produces abnormal responses. For example, developmental crises may occur in response to the birth of a child, graduation from college, midlife career change, or retirement. Developmental crises are considered normal; however, all persons and all developmental crises are unique and must be assessed and handled in unique ways.

Situational crises.   A situational crisis emerges with the occurrence of uncommon and extraordinary events that an individual has no way of forecasting or controlling. Situational crises may follow such events as automobile accidents, kidnappings, rapes, corporate buyouts and loss of jobs, and sudden illness and death. The key to differentiating a situational crisis from other crises is that a situational crisis is random, sudden, shocking, intense, and catastrophic.

Existential crises. "Existential crisis" refers to the inner conflicts and anxieties that accompany important human issues of purpose, responsibility, independence, freedom, and commitment. An existential crisis might accompany the realization, at age 40, that one will never make a significant and distinct impact upon a particular profession or organization; remorse, at age 50, that one chose never to marry or leave one's parents' home, never really made a separate life, and now has lost forever the possibility of being a fully happy and worthwhile person; or a pervasive and persistent feeling, at age 60, that one's life is meaningless—that there is a void that can never be fulfilled in a meaningful way.

CRISIS INTERVENTION MODELS

Three basic crisis intervention models discussed by both Leitner (1974) and Belkin (1984) are the *equilibrium* model, the *cognitive* model, and the *psychosocial transition* model. These three models provide the groundwork for many different crisis intervention strategies and methodologies. All crisis intervention models are based on theory. Nowhere is this fact better exemplified than in the work of Strickler and Bonnefil (1974, p. 38), who linked crisis theory with a psychosocial approach to psychotherapy through the following points:

1. Treatment goals are structured to enhance the client's competency in coping with difficulties by using problem-solving skills.
2. The treatment targets specific and pertinent problem areas that involve the client's interpersonal conflicts and role dysfunctioning.
3. The client's attention is kept on the specific problem area through active focusing techniques.
4. The treatment is geared primarily to the level of the client's conscious and near-conscious emotional conflicts. These conflicts are handled by searching out their situational references and by keeping a focus within them.
5. Precipitating events are recognized as very important to the dynamics of the problem situation.
6. The modification of the client's character traits or personality patterns is not a fundamental objective of the treatment.
7. The phenomenon of client transference to the interventionist is normally *not* considered important to the therapeutic process unless such transference presents an impediment to treatment.
8. Treatment is based on background information derived from a knowledge of personality, ego functioning, and sociocultural functioning.

These important principles provide the bridge between crisis theory and applied crisis intervention. They clearly demonstrate that the principles of crisis psychology provide the foundation for clinical practice (Belkin, 1984, p. 427). They also set the stage for a brief examination of the equilibrium, cognitive, and psychosocial transition models of crisis intervention.

The Equilibrium Model

The equilibrium model is really an equilibrium/disequilibrium model. People in crisis are in a state of psychological or emotional disequilibrium, in which their usual coping mechanisms and problem-solving methods fail to meet their needs. The goal of the equilibrium model is to help people attain a state of precrisis equilibrium (Caplan, 1961).

The equilibrium model would seem most appropriate for early intervention, when the person is out of control, disoriented, and unable to make appropriate choices. Until the person has regained some coping abilities, the main focus is on stabilizing the individual. Up to the time the person has reacquired some definite measure of stability, little else can or should be done. For example, it does little good to dig into the underlying factors that cause suicidal ideation until the person can be stabilized to the point of agreeing that life is worth living for at least another week. This is probably the purest model of crisis intervention and is most likely to be used at the onset of the crisis (Caplan, 1961; Leitner, 1974; Lindemann, 1944).

The Cognitive Model

The cognitive model of crisis intervention is based on the premise that crises are rooted in *faulty thinking* about the events or situations that surround the crisis—not in the events themselves or the facts about the events or situations (Ellis, 1962). The goal of this model is to help people become aware of and to change their views and beliefs about the crisis events or situations. The basic tenet of the cognitive model is that people can gain control of crises in their lives by changing their thinking, especially through recognizing and disputing the irrational and self-defeating parts of their cognitions, and by retaining and focusing on the rational and self-enhancing elements of their thinking.

The messages that people in crisis send themselves become very negative and twisted in context of the reality of the situation. Dilemmas that are constant and grinding wear people out, pushing their internal state of perception more and more toward negative self-talk about the situation until their cognitive sets are such that no amount of preachment can convince them that anything positive will ever come from the situation. Their behavior soon follows this negative self-talk and begets a self-fulfilling prophecy that the situation is hopeless. At this juncture, crisis intervention becomes a job of rewiring the individual's thoughts to more positive feedback loops by practicing and rehearsing new self-statements about the situation until the old, negative, debilitating ones are expunged. The cognitive model seems most appropriate after the client has been stabilized and returned to an approximate state of precrisis equilibrium. Basic components of this approach are found in the rational-emotive work of Ellis (1982), the cognitive-behavioral approach of Meichenbaum (1977), and the cognitive system of Beck (1976) and Beck, Rush, Shaw, and Emery (1987).

The Psychosocial Transition Model

The psychosocial transition model assumes that people are products of their hereditary endowments plus the learning they have absorbed from their particular social environments. Since people are continually changing, developing, and growing and their social environments and social influence (Dorn, 1986) are continuously evolving, crises may be related to internal or external (psychological, social, or environmental) difficulties. The goal of crisis intervention is to collaborate with clients in their assessment of both internal and external difficulties contributing to the crises and to help them choose workable alternatives to their current behaviors, attitudes, and use of environmental resources. The incorporation of adequate internal coping mechanisms, social supports, and environmental resources may be needed to assist the clients in attainment of autonomous (noncrisis) control over their lives.

The psychosocial model does not perceive crisis as simply an internal state of affairs that resides totally within the individual. It reaches outside the individual and asks what systems need to be changed. Peers, family, occupation, religion, and community are but a few of the external dimensions that promote or hinder psychological adaptiveness. With certain kinds of crisis problems, few lasting gains will be made unless the social systems that affect the individual are also changed or the individual comes to terms with and understands the dynamics of those systems and how they affect adaptation to the crisis. Like the cognitive model, the psychosocial transition model seems to be most appropriate after the client has been stabilized. Theorists who have contributed to the psychosocial transition model include Adler (Ansbacher & Ansbacher, 1956), Erikson (1963), and Minuchin (1974).

ECLECTIC CRISIS INTERVENTION THEORY

Eclectic crisis intervention involves the intentional and systematic selection and integration of valid concepts and strategies from all available approaches to helping clients. As such, eclecticism has few major concepts, but is a hybrid of all other available approaches. As opposed to concepts, it operates from a task orientation. Its major tasks (Gilliland, James, Roberts, & Bowman, 1984, p. 273; Thorne, 1973, p. 451) are

1. to identify valid elements in all systems and to integrate them into a internally consistent whole that does justice to the behavioral data to be explained
2. to consider all pertinent theories, methods, and standards for evaluating and manipulating clinical data according to the most advanced knowledge of time and place
3. to identify with no specific theory, keep an open mind, and continuously experiment with those formulations and strategies that produce successful results.

Throughout this volume, the reader will find an eclectic theory integrated into interventions presented. Distinctive threads of the equilibrium/disequilibrium model, the cognitive model, and the psychosocial transition model will be woven into the fabric of crisis intervention strategies for each crisis category explored. The eclectic theory fuses two pervasive themes: (1) all people and all crises are unique and distinctive, and (2) all people and all crises are similar. We do not see these themes as mutually exclusive.

All people and all crises are similar in that there are global perspectives to specific crisis types. The dynamics of bereavement are generic and provide us with general guidelines for intervention. However, treating individual cases of bereavement is anything but generic. How a family perceives the impact of the death of a member depends on a number of factors: the deceased member's place in the family, what each member of the family does in response to the death, and how the changed family system now operates. Treatment of surviving family members who have lost a child after rearing five others, as opposed to those who have lost their only child, born late in the parents' life, who had become the focus of existence for the couple, may call for far different interventional strategies even if bereavement is the generic issue.

An eclectic approach does not mean taking a therapeutic shotgun and aimlessly blasting away at the crisis. Using an eclectic approach means not being bound by and locked into any one theoretical approach in a dogmatic fashion. Rather, it means being well versed in a number of approaches and theories and being able to assess the client's needs so that appropriate techniques can be planned and fitted to them. Many human service workers avow an eclectic approach but in actuality use the word as a rationalization for not being able to do anything very well. Being a true eclectic means lots of hard work by reading, studying, experiencing, and being supervised and critiqued by other professionals. It also means taking risks and having a willingness to abandon an approach that on first inspection might seem reasonable and proper but, once entered, is fruitless for the particular situation.

Eclecticism performed well is equal parts of skill and intuition. Paying attention to one's affect as much as to one's cognition about the situation is critical. Many times changing to more affective interventions is no more scientific than "feeling" that something is amiss. Although having a feeling is little justification in the remotest scientific sense for doing something, it can nevertheless be a sound basis for action. We know of no formula for deciding when to move from a nondirective to a highly directive stance with a client in crisis, nor is there an equation that tells us that mental imagery may be more effective than confrontation as an interventional technique. Unabashedly, we believe that in an eclectic approach the performing art of crisis intervention clearly reaches its zenith.

SUMMARY

In this chapter we discussed five definitions of crisis. We consider all of these definitions of crisis to be valid and useful and we have incorporated elements of all of them into the book. Our composite definition of crisis, derived from all five sources, is: *a crisis is a perception of an event or situation as an intolerable difficulty that exceeds the resources and coping mechanisms of the person.* This general definition is useful throughout the book, but the worth of the definition is enhanced by considering several important principles and characteristics of crisis:

1. crisis embodies both danger and opportunity for the person experiencing the crisis;
2. crisis is usually time limited but may develop into a series of recurring transcrisis points;
3. crisis is oftentimes complex and difficult to resolve;
4. the life experiences of workers may greatly enhance their effectiveness in crisis intervention;
5. crisis contains the seeds of growth and impetus for change;
6. panaceas or quick fixes are not applicable to crisis situations;
7. crisis confronts people with choices;
8. emotional disequilibrium and disorganization accompany crisis; and,
9. the resolution of crisis and the personhood of crisis workers interrelate.

Workers will find these principles and characteristics of crisis to be of enormous value in their role as helpers.

We have identified and discussed a number of characteristics of effective crisis workers. They demonstrate competency in their professional skills. They maintain poise while confronting the difficult issues of their clients. Effective workers are both creative and flexible in their dealing with client problems. They possess a great deal of energy and know how to organize and direct their energy toward systematic action. They manage time efficiently and wisely. Finally, effective crisis workers are positive in their outlook, work, philosophy, and approach to helping clients.

Three theoretical thrusts were discussed in the chapter: basic, expanded, and applied. *Basic crisis theory*, founded in the works of Lindemann (1944; 1956) and Caplan (1964), helps us to view crisis as situational or developmental rather than pathological in nature. *Expanded crisis theory* added to and enhanced basic theory by incorporating and adapting components from general systems, psychoanalytic, adaptational, and interpersonal theory. *Applied crisis theory* integrates the concepts of developmental, situational, and existential crises into a holistic theoretical structure containing both basic and expanded crisis theory concepts. Applied crisis theory provides the conceptual framework for us to put both basic and expanded theory into practice.

Three fundamental crisis intervention models were identified and discussed: equilibrium, cognitive, and psychosocial transition. The *equilibrium model*, probably the most widely known model of the three, defines equilibrium as an emotional state in which the person is stable, in control, or psychologically mobile. It also defines disequilibrium as an emotional state which accompanies instability, loss of control, and psychological immobility. The *cognitive model* views the crisis state as resulting from faulty thinking and belief about life's dilemmas and traumas. The *psychosocial transition model* assumes that people are products of both hereditary endowment and environmental learning and that crisis may be caused by psychological, social, or environmental factors. The psychosocial transition model therefore instructs us to look for intervention strategies in all three realms: psychological, social, and environmental.

An eclectic theoretical position, which we believe incorporates and integrates all valid concepts of crisis intervention, was presented and discussed. The strength of eclectic crisis intervention theory is that it encourages workers to select, integrate, and apply useful concepts and strategies from all available approaches to helping clients.

REFERENCES

Aguilera, D. C., & Messick, J. M. (1982). *Crisis intervention: Theory and methodology* (4th ed.). St. Louis: C.V. Mosby Co.

Ansbacher, H. L., & Ansbacher, R. R. (1956). *The individual psychology of Alfred Adler.* New York: Greenberg.

Beck, A. T. (1976). *Cognitive therapy and the emotional disorders.* New York: International Universities Press.

Beck, A. T., Rush, A. J., Shaw, B. F., & Emery, G. (1987). *Cognitive therapy of depression.* New York: Guilford Press.

Belkin, G. S. (1984). *Introduction to counseling* (2nd ed.). Dubuque, IA: William C. Brown.

Brammer, L. M. (1985). *The helping relationship: Process and skills* (3rd ed.). Englewood Cliffs, NJ: Prentice-Hall.

Caplan, G. (1961). *An approach to community mental health.* New York: Grune & Stratton.

Caplan, G. (1964). *Principles of preventive psychiatry.* New York: Basic Books.

Carkhuff, R. R., & Berenson, B. G. (1977). *Beyond counseling and therapy* (2nd ed.). New York: Holt, Rinehart & Winston.

Cormier, L. S., & Hackney, H. (1987). *The professional counselor: A process guide to helping.* Englewood Cliffs, NJ: Prentice-Hall.

Cormier, W. H., & Cormier, L. S. (1985). *Interviewing strategies for helpers: Fundamental skills and cognitive behavioral interventions* (2nd ed.). Pacific Grove, CA: Brooks/Cole.

Dorn, F. J. (Ed.). (1986). *The social influence process in counseling and psychotherapy.* Springfield, IL: Charles C Thomas.

Ellis, A. E. (1962). *Reason and emotion in psychotherapy.* New York: Lyle Stuart.

Ellis, A. E. (1982). Major systems. *The Personnel and Guidance Journal, 61,* 6–7.

Erikson, E. (1963). *Childhood and society* (2nd ed.). New York: Norton.

Fine, R. (1973). Psychoanalysis. In R. J. Corsini (Ed.), *Current psychotherapies* (pp. 1–33). Itasca, IL: F.E. Peacock.

Gilliland, B. E., James, R. K., Roberts, G. T., & Bowman, J. T. (1984). *Theories and strategies in counseling and psychotherapy.* Englewood Cliffs, NJ: Prentice-Hall.

Glasser, W. (1976). *Positive addiction.* New York: Harper & Row.

Haley, J. (1973). *Uncommon therapy.* New York: Norton.

Haley, J. (1976). *Problem-solving therapy.* New York: McGraw-Hill.

Janosik, E. H. (1984). *Crisis counseling: A contemporary approach.* Monterey, CA: Wadsworth Health Sciences Division.

Kliman, A. S. (1978). *Crisis: Psychological first aid for recovery and growth.* New York: Holt, Rinehart & Winston.

Leitner, L. A. (1974). Crisis counseling may save a life. *Journal of Rehabilitation, 40,* 19–20.

Lindemann, E. (1944). Symptomatology and management of acute grief. *American Journal of Psychiatry, 101,* 141–148.

Lindemann, E. (1956). The meaning of crisis in individual and family. *Teachers College Record, 57,* 310.

Meichenbaum, D. H. (1977). *Cognitive-behavior modification: An integrative approach.* New York: Plenum.

Minuchin, S. (1974). *Families and family therapy.* Cambridge, MA: Harvard University Press.

Rogers, C. R. (1977). *Carl Rogers on personal power: Inner strength and its revolutionary impact.* New York: Delacorte.

Strickler, M., & Bonnefil, M. (1974). Crisis intervention and social casework: Similarities and differences in problem solving. *Clinical Social Work Journal, 2,* 36–44.

Thorne, F. C. (1973). Eclectic psychotherapy. In R. Corsini (Ed.), *Current psychotherapies* (pp. 445–486). Itasca, IL: F.E. Peacock.

CHAPTER 2

Six Steps in Crisis Intervention

INTRODUCTION

The purpose of this chapter is to provide a general overview of crisis intervention from a practitioner's standpoint. To that end we will present and fully describe an applied crisis intervention model. Throughout the chapter we will augment the model by including fundamental skills and intervention concepts. We will provide dialogues between client and worker to illustrate many of the skills and concepts. Finally, we will share some thoughts on using referrals, give some suggestions regarding counseling with difficult clients, and provide a laboratory exercise.

This chapter is a prerequisite for succeeding chapters, and we would urge you to consider carefully this foundation material for successful interventional work. By "considering" we do not mean a cursory reading. Read, think, and react. Examine the examples of the techniques carefully. Discuss our responses and formulate your own. Practice the laboratory exercises. To obtain the necessary skills to become a successful crisis worker, you will need to learn some new practices in the ways you deal with people in volatile situations. What we propose in this chapter will not make you perfect, but it will give you, with practice, some proven methods and start-up abilities. We have never, repeat never, seen a consistently successful crisis interventionist who did not practice what we are about to preach to you. If you can learn the techniques in this chapter, you should find them adaptable to any crisis situation.

We do not purport to repeat the fundamental skills and steps of crisis intervention in every chapter or to apply them in a step by step explicit manner to every crisis category in the book. These basic principles contained in Chapter 2 should be used as an essential guideline for applying the art and skill of intervention to the process of helping any client in any category of crisis.

Even though human crises are never simple, we have found that it is desirable for the crisis worker to have a relatively straightforward and efficient model of intervention. The six steps presented in this chapter (Gilliland, 1982) may be used as such a model. Volunteers and professional human services

workers such as nurses, ministers, police officers, psychologists, social workers, and counselors may be called upon at any time to deal with a unique crisis surprising in content and heavy in emotional tone. We have found that
many crisis workers, especially telephone counselors and other workers in
centers dealing with acute crises, appreciate a set of guidelines that are un-
complicated and practical. The six steps illustrated in Figure 2-1 have been
used by both professional counselors and lay workers in helping clients with
many different kinds of crises.

The action-oriented, situationally based method of crisis intervention,
which we have outlined in Figure 2-1, is our preferred method for systematically applying several worker-initiated skills. The process of applying these
skills is fluid rather than mechanistic. The entire six-step process is carried
out under an umbrella of *assessment* by the crisis worker. The first three
steps of (1) defining the problem, (2) ensuring client safety, and (3) providing
support are more *listening* activities than they are acting. The latter three
steps of (4) examining alternatives, (5) planning, and (6) obtaining commitment to positive action are largely *action* behaviors on the part of the worker,
even though listening is always present along with assessment.

STEPS IN CRISIS COUNSELING

The six-step model shown in Figure 2-1 is the hub around which the crisis
intervention strategies in this book revolve. We have constructed the model to
clarify for students and human service workers the intervention techniques
we advocate. Again, we remind the users of the model that, although the
steps may appear to be locked into a mechanical or compartmentalized format, it is important to use them in a fluid manner. The effective crisis worker
is flexible and resilient in the use of the six steps. In the actual intervention
process, steps 4, 5, and 6, for instance, appear to flow together in a natural,
smooth, and systematic whole. The steps are designed to operate as an integrated problem-solving process.

Defining the Problem

The first step in crisis intervention is to define and understand the problem
from the client's point of view. Unless the worker perceives the crisis situation as the client perceives it, all the intervention strategies and procedures
the helper might use may miss the mark and be of no value to the client. An
accurate definition of the problem facilitates the entire counseling process.
All of the dimensions of assessing the client's situation depend upon the ac-
curacy of the definition; throughout the crisis intervention process workers
direct their listening and acting skills according to the dictates of the
definition. To assist workers in defining crisis problems, we recommend that
intervention sessions begin with crisis workers practicing what we call the
core listening skills: empathy, genuineness, and acceptance. These skills and
the exercises described later in this chapter should greatly enhance the
reader's competency in this first step of crisis intervention.

Figure 2-1 Steps in Crisis Counseling

ASSESSING: Overarching, continuous, and dynamically on-going throughout the crisis; evaluating the client's present and past situational crises in terms of the client's ability to cope, personal threat, mobility or immobility, and making a judgment regarding type of action needed by the crisis worker. (See crisis worker's action continuum below.)

Listening →

LISTENING: Attending, observing, understanding, and responding with empathy, genuineness, respect, acceptance, nonjudgment, and caring.

1. *DEFINE THE PROBLEM.* Explore and define the problem from the client's point of view. USE ACTIVE LISTENING such as is practiced by Rogerian counselors (Rogers, 1977). May include open-ended questions. Attend to both verbal and nonverbal messages of the client.

2. *ENSURE CLIENT SAFETY.* Assessment of lethality, criticality, immobility, or seriousness of threat to the client's physical, emotional, and psychological safety. Assess both the client's internal events and the environmental situation surrounding the client, and, if necessary, ensure that client is made aware of alternatives to impulsive, self-destructive actions.

3. *PROVIDE SUPPORT.* Communicate to the client that the crisis worker is a valid support person. Demonstrate (by words, voice, and body language) a caring, positive, non-possessive, nonjudgmental, acceptant, personal involvement with the client.

Acting  →

ACTING. Crisis worker involvement in the intervention is non-directive, collaborative, or directive, according to the assessed needs of the client and the availability of environmental supports.

4. *EXAMINE ALTERNATIVES.* Assist client in exploring the choices he/she has available to him/her now. Facilitate a search for immediate situational supports, coping mechanisms, and positive thinking.

5. *PLAN.* Assist client in developing a short-term plan that:
   a. identifies additional persons and groups that may be contacted for immediate support.
   b. provides coping mechanisms (something concrete and positive for the client to do now)—definite action steps that the client can own and comprehend; a variety of constructive psychomotor activities may be considered, such as running, playing a musical instrument, reading, etc., whenever appropriate.
   c. is realistic in terms of the client's coping ability.
   d. may utilize appropriate and available referral resources.

e. may include many forms of client/crisis worker collaboration; for example, facilitation of relaxation techniques, emotive imagery, etc.

f. Focuses on systematic problem-solving for the client.

6. *COMMITMENT:* Help client commit himself/herself to definite positive action steps that the client can own and can realistically accomplish or accept.

a. Ask client to *verbally summarize* the plan/commitment.

b. Crisis worker demonstrates (models) responsibility in carrying out his/her part of the commitment if the worker is in a collaborative role.

c. Crisis worker follows up on client's performance or obtaining assistance.

Crisis Worker's Action Continuum

Crisis Worker is Non-directive	**Crisis Worker is Collaborative**	**Crisis Worker is Directive**
Threshold *Varies* From Client to Client		Threshold *Varies* From Client to Client
Client is Mobile	**Client is Partially Mobile**	**Client is Immobile**

The crisis worker's level of action/involvement may be anywhere on the continuum according to a valid and realistic assessment of the client's level of mobility/immobility.

Ensuring Client Safety

It is imperative that crisis workers continually keep client safety at the forefront of all crisis intervention procedures. We define client safety simply as minimizing the physical, emotional, and psychological danger to self and others. Although we position client safety in the second step, we apply this step in a fluid way, meaning that safety is a primary consideration throughout crisis intervention. The dimension of safety receives equal consideration in the worker's assessing, listening, and acting strategies. In this book and pervading our teaching and practice of crisis intervention, client safety is present, whether we overtly state it or not. We encourage students and crisis workers to make the safety step a natural part of their thinking and behaving.

Providing Support

The third step in crisis intervention emphasizes communicating to the client that the worker is a person who cares about the client. Workers cannot assume that a client experiences feeling valued, prized, or cared for. The support step provides an opportunity for the worker to assure the client that "here is one person who really cares about you." Throughout this book, the exercises, dialogues, and cases are presented in a way that shows workers feeling and showing support for clients in appropriate ways. It is important to note that the word "support" in crisis intervention usually refers to people and their personal attitudes and behaviors.

In step 3, the person providing the support is the worker. This means that workers must be able to accept, in an unconditional and positive way, all their clients, whether the clients can reciprocate or not. The worker who can truly provide support for clients in crisis is able to accept and value the person no one else is willing to accept and to prize the client no one else prizes.

Examining Alternatives

Step 4 in crisis intervention addresses an area which both clients and workers often neglect—exploring a wide array of appropriate choices available to the client. Many times clients, in their immobile state, do not adequately examine their best options. Some clients in crisis actually believe there are no options.

In the fourth step, effective workers help clients to recognize that many alternatives are available and that some choices are better than others. It may help for workers to realize that there are different ways to think about alternatives: (1) *situational supports*, which may represent excellent sources of help, are people, known to the client in the present or past, who might care about what happens to the client; (2) *coping mechanisms* are those actions, behaviors, or environmental resources which the client might use to help get through the present crisis; and, (3) *positive and constructive thinking patterns*, on the part of the client, which might substantially alter the client's view of the problem and lessen the client's level of stress and anxiety. Crisis workers who can objectively examine a great number of alternatives from these three perspectives can be of great assistance to clients who are feeling hopelessly stuck and lacking in choices.

The effective crisis worker may think about an infinite number of alternatives pertaining to the client's crisis but discuss only a few of them with the client. Clients experiencing crisis do not need excessive choices; they need appropriate choices which are realistic to their situation. The exercises, dialogues, and cases in this book reflect crisis workers who have competency in assisting clients to explore and discover alternatives that uniquely apply to alleviating the particular crisis state being experienced.

Making Plans

The fifth step in crisis intervention, making plans, flows logically and directly from step 4. Much of the material throughout this book focuses either directly or indirectly on the crisis worker's involvement with clients in planning action steps which have a good chance of restoring the emotional equilibrium of the clients. Figure 2-1 lists several important considerations for workers. It is important that planning be done in collaboration with clients so that clients know that they helped to develop, and therefore, feel a sense of ownership of the plan. We have seen too many instances where helpers in many fields decided for clients what they should do. The critical element in developing a plan is that clients do not feel robbed of their power, independence, and self-respect.

We believe that clients prefer to commit themselves to and carry out actions which they know they had a part in developing. Some clients may not object when a helper decides for them what they should do. At the moment, such clients may be so engrossed in their crisis that it really does not matter to them. They may even believe that a plan imposed on them is what they should have. It is often easy to manipulate emotionally distraught clients to accept a plan which is benevolently imposed upon them.

The central issues in planning are *control* and *autonomy* of clients. The reasons for clients to carry out plans are to restore their sense of control and to ensure that they do not become dependent on support persons such as the worker. These central issues in the planning process are emphasized in helping clients in every crisis category in this book.

Obtaining Commitment

The sixth step, commitment, flows directly from step 5, and the issues of control and autonomy, discussed under "Making Plans," apply equally to the process of obtaining an appropriate commitment. If the planning step is effectively done, the commitment step is apt to be easy. Many times the commitment step is brief and simple: "Now that we have gone over what you plan to do next time you start to get angry with her, summarize for me what actions you will take to ensure that you do not lose your temper and what you will do to make sure you keep it from escalating into another crisis."

During the sixth step the crisis worker does not forget about all the other helping steps and skills such as assessment, safety, and supports. The worker is careful to obtain an honest, direct, and appropriate commitment from the client before terminating the crisis intervention session. Later, when the worker checks up on the client's progress, the checking is done in an empathic and supportive stance. The core listening skills are as important to the commitment step as they are to the problem definition or any other step.

Clarifying Terms

The model of crisis intervention presented in Figure 2-1 emphasizes actively, assertively, intentionally, and continuously assessing, listening, and acting in a six-step approach to systematically helping the client regain as much of the precrisis equilibrium, mobility, and autonomy as possible. Two of those terms, *equilibrium* and *mobility*, and their antonyms, *disequilibrium* and *immobility*, are commonly used by crisis workers to identify client states of being and coping. Since we will be using these terms as common parlance, we would like to define them first by their dictionary meaning and then give a common analogy so their meaning becomes thoroughly understood.

Equilibrium. A state of mental or emotional stability, balance, or poise in the organism.

Disequilibrium. Lack or destruction of emotional stability, balance, or poise in the organism.

Mobility. A state of physical being whereby the person can autonomously change or cope in response to different moods, feelings, emotions, needs, conditions, influences; being flexible or adaptable to the physical and social world.

Immobility. Not immediately capable of autonomously changing or coping in response to different moods, feelings, emotions, needs, conditions, influences; unable to adapt to the immediate physical and social world.

A typical, normal, healthy person will be in a state of approximate equilibrium. That is to say, the typical, normal person will be like a motorist driving with some starts and stops, down the road of life—in both the short and the long haul. The person may hit some potholes but does not break any psychological axles. Aside from needing an occasional tune-up, the person remains more or less equal to the task of making the drive. In contrast, the person in crisis, whether it be acute or chronic, is experiencing serious difficulty in steering and successfully navigating life's highway. The individual is at least temporarily out of control, unable to command personal resources or those of others in order to stay on safe psychological pavement.

A normal, healthy person is capable of negotiating hills, curves, ice, fog, stray animals, and most other obstacles that impede progress. No matter what roadblocks may appear, such a person adapts to changing conditions, applying brakes, putting on fog lights, and estimating passing time. This person may have fender-benders from time to time but avoids head-on collisions. The person in a dysfunctional state of equilibrium and mobility has failed to pass inspection. Careening down hills and around dangerous curves, knowing the brakes have failed, the person is frozen with panic and despair and has little hope of handling the perilous situation. The result is that the person has become a victim of the situation, has forgotten all about emergency brakes, downshifting, or even easing the car into guard railings. He or she flies headlong into catastrophe and watches transfixed as it happens.

Our analogy of equilibrium and mobility applies to most crisis situations. Thus, it becomes every crisis worker's job to figuratively get the client back into the driver's seat of the psychological vehicle. As we shall demonstrate, sometimes this means leaving the driving to us, sometimes sitting alongside and pointing out the rules of the road, and sometimes just pretty much going along for the ride!

ASSESSING IN CRISIS INTERVENTION

Overarching the six-step model is assessment. As Figure 2-1 shows, assessment is a pervasive, intentional, and continuous activity of the crisis worker. Assessment is critically important because it enables the worker to (1) determine the severity of the crisis, (2) determine the client's current emotional status—the client's level of emotional mobility or immobility, (3) determine the alternatives, coping mechanisms, support systems, and other resources available to the client, and (4) determine the client's level of lethality (danger to self and others).

Assessing Severity of Crisis

It is important for the crisis worker to evaluate the crisis severity as quickly as possible during the initial contact with the client. The degree of severity of the crisis may affect the client's mobility, which, in turn, gives the worker a basis for judging how directive to be. The length of time the client has been in the present crisis will determine how much time the worker has to safely defuse the crisis. Crisis is time limited; that is, most acute crises persist only a matter of days before some change—for better or worse—occurs. The severity of the crisis is assessed from the client's subjective viewpoint and from the worker's objective viewpoint. Objective assessment is based on an appraisal of the client's functioning in three areas: cognitive (thinking patterns), affective (feeling or emotional tone), and psychomotor (behavioral) functioning.

Cognitive state.   The worker's assessment of the client's thinking patterns may provide answers to several important questions: How realistic and consistent is the client's thinking about the crisis? To what extent, if any, does the client appear to be rationalizing, exaggerating, or believing part-truths, to exacerbate the crisis? How long has the client been engaged in crisis thinking? How open does the client appear to be to changing beliefs about the crisis situation? The answers to these and other open-ended questions about the client's thought patterns may provide some directions for crisis intervention. The worker may use such cognitive assessment to determine how to help the client refute irrational or confused thinking and develop more positive and productive thought patterns about the crisis and about workable alternatives.

Affective state.   The crisis worker who is sensitive to the client's emotional tone can mentally record affective reactions to assess the seriousness of the crisis as well as discern ways to help the client. Abnormal or impaired affect is often the first sign that the client is in a state of disequilibrium. The client may be overemotional and out of control, underemotional and lethargic, or severely withdrawn and detached. Often the worker can assist the client to regain control and mobility by helping that person express feelings in appropriate and realistic ways. Some questions the worker may address are: Do the client's affective responses indicate that the client is denying the situation or attempting to avoid involvement in it? Is the emotional response normal or congruent with the situational crisis? Do people typically show this kind of affect in situations such as this? Certainly, to ignore an unusual or unhealthy display of affect would be a mistake on the part of the worker.

Psychomotor activity.   The crisis worker focuses much attention upon *doing, acting out, taking active steps, behaving,* or any number of other psychomotor activities. In crisis intervention we believe that the quickest (and often the best) way to get the client to become mobile is to facilitate positive actions that the client can take at once. Persons who successfully cope with crisis and later evaluate their experiences report that the most helpful alternative during a crisis is to engage in some concrete and immediate activity. However, it is important for the worker to remember that it may be very difficult for immobilized people to take independent and autonomous action even though that is what they need to do most. These are appropriate questions that the worker might ask himself or herself before assisting the client to do something constructive: In cases like this in the past, what actions did you take that helped you get back in control? What would you have to do now to get back on top of the situation? Name one or two persons who, if you contacted them right now, would be supportive to you in this crisis. The fundamental problem in immobility is loss of control. Once the client becomes involved in doing something concrete, which is a step in a positive direction, an element of control is restored, a degree of mobility is provided, and the climate for forward movement is established. The crisis worker uses these small steps in helping a crisis client move toward equilibrium. The foregoing is the crux of assessing the client's psychomotor functioning.

Assessing Client's Current Emotional Status

Two major factors in assessing the client's emotional stability are the *duration* of the crisis and the *degree* of emotional stamina or coping at the disposal of the client at the moment. The duration factor has to do with the time frame of the crisis. Is it a one-time crisis? Is it recurring? Has it been plaguing the client for a long period of time? A one-time, relatively short-duration crisis is what we call *acute* or *situational*. We would label a long-term pattern of recurring crisis as *chronic, long-term,* or *transcrisis*. (The latter recurring crisis is described in detail in Chapter 1.) The degree factor refers to the client's current reservoir of emotional coping stamina. Whereas during normal periods of the client's life the reservoir is relatively full, during crisis periods the client's reservoir is relatively empty. Assessment of the degree factor, then, involves the crisis worker's determination of how much emotional coping strength is left in the client's reservoir. Has the client run out of gas or can the client make it over a small hill?

Client's current acute or chronic state.   In assessing the crisis client's emotional functioning, it is important that the crisis worker determine whether the client is a normal individual who is in a *one-time* situational crisis or a person with a *chronic,* crisis-oriented life history. The one-time crisis is assessed and treated quite differently from the chronic crisis. The one-time crisis client usually requires direct intervention to facilitate getting over the one event or situation that precipitated the crisis. Having reached a state of precrisis equilibrium, the client can usually draw on normal coping mechanisms and support persons and manage independently. The chronic crisis client usually requires a greater length of time in counseling. That individual typically needs the help of a crisis worker in examining adequate coping mechanisms, finding support persons, rediscovering strategies that worked during previous crisis periods, generating new coping strategies, and gaining affirmation and encouragement from the worker and others as sources of strength by which to move beyond the present crisis. The chronic case frequently requires referral for long-term professional help.

Client's reservoir of emotional strength.   The client who is totally devoid of emotional strength needs more direct response from the crisis worker than the client who obviously retains a good deal of emotional strength. The worker must be very sensitive to the client's emotional functioning in order to formulate an objective judgment. A feeling of hopelessness or helplessness is a clue to a low reservoir of emotional strength. In some cases, the assessment can be enhanced by asking open-ended questions for the specific purpose of measuring that reservoir. Typically, if the reservoir is low the client will have a distorted view of the past and present and cannot envision a future. Questions like these can reveal the *degree* of emotional stamina remaining: "Picture yourself after the current crisis has been solved. Tell me what you're seeing yourself doing and how you're feeling. How would you wish to be feeling? How were you feeling about this before the crisis got so bad? Where do you see yourself headed with this problem?" The answers may be of great value to the worker in establishing the degree of emotional control retained by the client. In general, the lower the reservoir of emotional strength, the less the client can get hold of the future. The client with an empty reservoir might respond by a blank stare or by saying something like "There are no choices" or "No, I can't see anything. The future is blank. I can see no future." The worker's assessment of the client's current degree of emotional strength will have definite implications for the strategies and level of action to be employed by the worker during the remainder of the counseling.

Strategies for assessing emotional status. The crisis worker who assesses the client's total emotional status may look at a wide array of factors that affect both the duration (chronic versus acute) and the degree (reservoir of strength) of emotional stability. Some of the factors to be considered are the client's age, educational level, family situation, marital status, vocational maturity and job stability, financial stability and obligations, drug and/or alcohol use, legal history (arrests, convictions, probations), social background, level of intelligence, lifestyle, religious orientation, ability to sustain close personal relationships, tolerance for ambiguity, physical health, medical history, and past history of dealing with crises. A candid look at factors like these helps the crisis worker decide whether the client will require quick referral (for medical treatment or examination), brief counseling, long-term therapy, or referral to a specific agency.

No two client situations are ever alike. Every client's profile of emotional stability can be expected to be different. No one factor alone can ordinarily be used to conclude that the client's reservoir of emotional coping ability is empty. However, some patterns often can be pieced together to form a general picture. A person in middle age who has experienced many disappointments related to undereducation would be viewed differently from a young person who has experienced a first career disappointment. A person who has been through several bitter divorces would be expected to respond differently from a person who has recently begun to sense the first strains of marital discord. The person who is addicted to a chemical substance would be expected to emote differently from a person who is experiencing a rare hangover. A person who was raised as an only child in a protected environment would be expected to respond differently from one who grew up in the milieu of a large family with lots of freedom. A person who has experienced many serious medical problems and hospital stays would feel differently from a person who is having a first encounter with a medical problem.

Carefully phrased open-ended questions are a valuable assessment tool for enabling the worker to judge the client's emotional background and status and for involving the client in the ongoing assessment in a way that is facilitative for the client. For example, the worker might ask: "How is your current treatment different from the treatments you've received in the past? How has your increased level of drinking affected your feelings toward your wife and children? What could you do to make yourself feel better? What do you want to see happen to your self-esteem now? How can you make sure you never feel this way again?" The number and wording of open-ended questions are virtually infinite.

What we have been talking about is the facilitative assessment of the individual. By "facilitative assessment" we mean that data gleaned about the client are used as a part of the ongoing helping process, not simply filed away or kept in the worker's head. The key to facilitative assessment is to focus on the client's inner emotional world—not the worker's analysis of that world. Only the client can tell us what his or her real, inner emotional state is like.

Assessing Alternatives, Coping Mechanisms, Support Systems, and Other Resources

Throughout the helping process the crisis worker keeps in mind and builds a repertory of options, evaluating their appropriateness for the client. In assessing alternatives available to the client, the worker must first consider the client's viewpoint, mobility, and capability of taking advantage of the alternatives. The worker's own objective view of available alternatives is an additional dimension. Alternatives include a repository of appropriate referral resources available to the client. Even though the client may be looking for only one or two concrete action steps or options, the worker brainstorms, in collaboration with the client, to develop a list of possibilities that can be evaluated. Most of them will be discarded before the client can own and commit to a definite course of action. The word "own" has a special connotation in planning and committing to a course of action. "Owning" means that options are not imposed on the client by the worker. The important thing for clients is that they feel a deep and genuine commitment to their choices and that they do not depend upon or merely agree to choices they believe workers have discovered for them. We believe this ownership of options is a key factor in motivating clients to explore their choices and to predispose them to expect their planned action steps to succeed.

The worker ponders questions such as "What actions or choices does the client have now that would restore the person to a precrisis state of autonomy? What realistic actions can the client take? What institutional, social, vocational, or personal strengths or supports are available? Who would care about and be open to assisting the client? What are the financial, social, vocational, and personal impediments to client progress?"

Assessing for Suicide Potential

Not every crisis involves the client's contemplating suicide. However, in dealing with crisis clients, workers must always explore the possibility of suicide because suicidal behavior takes many forms and wears many masks. What may appear to the crisis worker as the main problem may camouflage the real issue. That issue is the intent of the client to take his or her life. Contrary to popular belief, most suicidal clients give off definite clues and believe that they are calling out for help. However, even the client's closest friends may ignore those clues and do nothing about them. For that reason, we believe that *every* crisis problem should be assessed as to its potential for suicide. The most important aspect of suicidal evaluation is the crisis worker/evaluator's realization that suicide is an ever-present possibility in all types of clients. It occurs in every age and socioeconomic group. There are a number of factors that may assist the crisis worker to judge the lethality potential in a specific client. Three of them—the client's personal/family history, physical/emotional history, and suicide plan—are of utmost importance because the best predictors of suicide are prior attempts and current spoken or written intent.

Personal/family history.   The level of lethality increases with the number and degree of seriousness of personal and family problems. The worker's assessment might take note of personal/family problems such as marital status (separated, divorced, widowed, living alone, family difficulty, destabilized family), recent death or serious illness in the family, financial stability and condition, employment and vocational stability, legal history (court action, jail terms, probation, arrest record), level of drug or alcohol use, social lifestyle and level of satisfaction, interpersonal relationships and peer group relationships, level of satisfaction with life and achievement at current age level, coping level at developmental stages (midlife, attainment of age 30, age 40, and so on), relationships with siblings and in-laws, and other personal or family matters that might have recently contributed to the client's stress or anxiety level. The worker will be interested in taking into account and probing into each area affecting the client to determine its possible impact on the current crisis.

Physical/emotional history.   The client's level of lethality may be increased as a result of one or more physical or emotional problems. The lethality assessment must not overlook substantive areas affecting the client, such as poor health, recent hospitalization, having a diagnosis of a serious medical problem, chronic physical impairment or problem, serious or chronic emotional problem, history of emotional problems (nervous breakdowns, loss of appetite, loss of energy, insomnia, withdrawal, depression, loneliness, helplessness, hopelessness, guilt, fear, apathy, extreme suspiciousness or fearfulness, poor recovery from surgery or emotional illness, inability to communicate, fear of leaving one's home or bed, and so forth), and hypochondria. The presence of one or more of these physical or emotional aspects may have a bearing on the client's current coping level, depending on an assessment of that individual's total functioning. The crisis worker would certainly want to weigh and consider such factors and definitely not overlook them in the assessment process.

Suicide plan.   Another important factor for the crisis worker to consider in assessing suicide lethality is to closely examine whether the client's statements and actions represent a suicidal intent or plan. Incisive questioning may be necessary to determine the facts: How serious is the intent or plan? How available is the means of suicide? How serious is the client about carrying out the plan? Does the plan represent crying out for help rather than a serious intent to commit suicide? Does the plan place the client in a situation in which rescue is probable? Will the client be totally isolated and beyond rescue? Does the client have a prior record of attempts? The answers to questions such as these can give the worker some good clues about the client's level of lethality. In general, the worker can assume that lethality increases with specificity of the plan and immediate access to the means. If the client has a plan definitely mapped out and settled and possesses the means to do it, the danger is substantially increased. If the client has a loaded gun or a bottle of pills in hand, the danger is increased. If the client has attempted suicide in the past, the danger is increased. If the client has it planned in a way that makes rescue impossible or highly improbable, the danger is increased. A highly specific and lethal plan would be cause for the worker to assess a high lethality risk even if the client's personal/family history and physical/emotional history yielded no strong indication of danger.

Summary of Assessment

One of the major differences between crisis intervention and other human service endeavors such as counseling, social work, and psychotherapy is that the crisis worker generally does not have time to either gather or analyze all the background and other assessment data that might normally be available under less stressful conditions. A key component of a highly functioning crisis worker is the ability to take the data available and make some meaningful sense out of it. Cases and exercises throughout this book provide an approximation of the amount and type of data that a crisis worker might normally expect to obtain. This may be somewhat unsettling to those students who are accustomed to having complete social and psychological work-ups available to them before they proceed with intervention. However, the ability to make a quick evaluation of the degree of client disequilibrium and immobility—and to be flexible enough to change one's evaluation as changing conditions warrant—is a priority skill that students should seek to cultivate as the various chapter exercises are attempted.

From onset to resolution of crisis, assessment is a central, continuous process. It is essential that the crisis worker not assume that, because the crisis appears on the surface to have been resolved, assessment is no longer needed. The balance sheet of assessing the client's crisis in terms of severity, current emotional status, alternatives, situational supports, coping mechanisms, resources, and level of lethality is never complete until the client has achieved his or her precrisis level of mobility, equilibrium, and autonomy. Only then are the psychological debts of the client reconciled.

The resumption of precrisis equilibrium does not imply that the client needs no developmental or long-term therapy or medical treatment. It does mean that the worker's job is done, and the acute phase of the crisis is over.

LISTENING IN CRISIS INTERVENTION

Crisis intervention is a pragmatic system of counseling, helping, and assisting individuals that abbreviates the therapeutic schedule and condenses strategies. Crisis intervention is not a long, drawn-out procedure that deals with either restorative or developmental issues. This compression of time and strategies often requires the crisis worker to be more proactive and assertive than the long-term counselor or therapist. It is a procedure that may be used by both professionals and laypersons with some training. We believe that accurate and well-honed listening skills are a necessary and, indeed, sometimes sufficient skill that all helping persons must have, whether lay or professional, performing short- or long-term counseling, and this is absolutely true for crisis workers.

For that reason, listening skills are a major component of our intervention model outlined in Figure 2-1 and described in this chapter. Our preferred conceptual model for effective listening comes from person-centered counseling (Rogers, 1977; Egan, 1982). We will present brief descriptions of selected Rogerian techniques, which are applicable to any kind of helping relationship, crisis or otherwise.

Climate of Human Growth

According to Rogers (1977), the most effective helper is one who can provide three necessary and sufficient conditions for client growth. These conditions he named *empathy, genuineness,* and *acceptance* (pp. 9–12). To create a climate of empathy means that the crisis worker accurately senses the inner feelings and meanings the client is experiencing and directly communicates to the client that the worker understands how it feels to be the client. The condition of genuineness (also called *realness* or *congruence*) means that the worker is being completely open in the relationship; that nothing is being hidden; that there are no façades; that there are no professional fronts. The term *transparent* is sometimes used to describe the crisis worker's attitude of genuineness. If the worker is clearly open and willing to be fully himself or herself in the relationship, the client is encouraged to reciprocate. The term *acceptance* (also referred to as *caring* or *prizing*) means that the crisis worker feels an unconditional positive regard for the client. It is an attitude of accepting and caring for the client without the client's necessarily reciprocating. The condition of acceptance is provided for no other reason than that the client is a human being in need.

If these conditions of empathy, genuineness, and acceptance can be provided for the client, then the probability that the client will experience positive emotional movement is increased.

Communicating Empathy

In describing the use of empathy by crisis workers who are effective listeners, we will focus on four important techniques for using empathy to help clients: (1) attending, (2) verbally communicating empathic understanding, (3) nonverbally communicating empathic understanding, and (4) silence as a way of communicating empathic understanding (Cormier & Cormier, 1985; Gilliland, James, Roberts, & Bowman, 1984).

Attending. The first step in listening has little to do with words and a lot to do with looking, acting, and being attentive. In most initial counseling and therapy sessions the client enters with some anxiety related to the therapy itself in addition to the stress brought on by the crisis. In crisis such anxiety is increased exponentially. Whatever crisis has traumatized the client, it will have the effect of putting the client in a state of extreme disequilibrium. Shame, guilt, rage, and sorrow are but a few of the feelings that may be manifested. Such feelings may be blatant and rampant or they may be subtle and disguised. Whatever shape or form such feelings take, the inattentive crisis worker can miss the message the client is attempting to convey if the worker is not tuned in to the client's world. Worse, an inattentive attitude implies lack of interest on the part of the worker and does little to establish a trusting relationship.

The effective crisis worker focuses fully on the client both in facial expression and in body posture. By nodding, keeping eye contact, smiling, showing appropriate seriousness of expression, leaning forward, keeping an open stance, and sitting or standing close to the client without invading the client's space, the crisis worker conveys a sense of involvement, concern, commitment, and trust.

Vocal tone, diction, pitch, modulation, and smoothness of delivery also tell clients a great deal about the attentiveness of crisis workers. Crisis workers, by attending closely to clients' verbal and nonverbal responses, can quickly tell whether they are establishing an empathic relationship or exacerbating the clients' feelings of distrust, fear, and uncertainty about becoming involved in the relationship.

Attentiveness, then, is both an attitude and a skill. It is an attitude in that the worker focuses fully on the client right here and now. In such moments the crisis worker's own concerns are put on hold. It is a skill in that conveying attending takes practice. It is just as inappropriate for the crisis worker to look too concerned and be too close in proximity as it is to lean back with arms folded and legs crossed, giving a cold stare. A happy medium between appearing overly concerned and entirely unconcerned comes by practicing with and getting feedback from clients and by being critiqued by professionals through video and audio taping, role play, and live crisis counseling sessions. An example of an appropriate blend of both verbal and nonverbal skill in attending to a client may help to clarify what we mean. Rita is a client who is having serious marital problems. (Rita's case history is recounted in Exercise I at the end of this chapter; we suggest that you read it for background.)

Rita: [*Enters room, sits down in far corner, warily looks about the room, crosses her legs and fidgets with her purse, and avoids direct eye contact, manifesting the appearance of a distraught woman who is barely holding together.*]

CW: [*Rises behind desk. Observing the behavior and physical appearance of the client, moves to a chair a comfortable distance and a slight angle from Rita's, sits down, leans forward in an open stance, and with an appearance of concern and inquisitiveness looks directly at Rita.*] I'd like to be of help. Where would you like to start?

The crisis worker sees the apprehension in the client and immediately becomes proactive. The crisis worker moves close to the client but does not sit directly in front of her in what could be construed as a confronting stance. The worker inclines forward to focus attention—eyes, ears, brain, and whole body—into the client's world. The whole posture of the crisis worker is congruent with the verbal message of offering immediate acceptance and willingness to help. In summary, effective attending is unobtrusive, natural, and without pretense. It is a necessary condition for effective listening.

Verbally communicating empathic understanding. When we can accurately hear and understand the core emotional feelings that are inside the client and accurately and caringly communicate that understanding to the client, we are demonstrating effective listening. The deeper our level of listening (understanding), the more helpful we will be to our clients. For instance, reflecting a client's message at the interchangeable level is helpful.

Rita: I'm thinking about just walking in and telling Jake I want a divorce—regardless of what Sam is ready to do. I don't think I can go on much longer. My ulcer is beginning to act up, I'm an emotional wreck, and everyone is expecting more of me than I can give.

CW: You're feeling a sense of urgency because it's adversely affecting your physical and emotional being.

A deeper level of listening and communicating empathic understanding to Rita might be expressed thus:

CW: Rita, your sense of urgency is getting to the point where you're about ready to take a big risk with both Jake and Sam. I sense that your physical and emotional stresses have about reached their limits and you're realizing that no one else is going to act to give you relief—that you are the one who is going to have to decide and act.

The second response is more helpful because it confirms to Rita a deeper understanding than the first response. Both responses are helpful because they are accurate and neither add to nor detract from the client's verbal, nonverbal, or emotional messages. Whereas the first response is considered minimally helpful, the second response is more facilitative because it lets the client know the worker heard a deeper personal meaning (risk) and a personal ownership of possible action. A word of caution to the worker, however: beware of reading into the client's statements more than the client is saying, and take care to keep your response as brief as possible.

Effective communication of empathic understanding to the client means focusing on the client's expressed affective and cognitive messages. The worker deals *directly with* the client's concerns and does not veer off into talking *about* the client's concerns or some tangential person or event. That distinction is important.

Rita: I'm afraid Jake might attack me even worse if I tell him I want a divorce.

CW: He did beat you pretty badly. Sam would probably go bananas at that. Jake, your husband, has such a violent temper. [*Talking about the situation and tangentially focusing on Jake.*]

CW: You're feeling some reservations about telling Jake because you really don't want to be beaten up again. [*Dealing with Rita's current feelings and concerns.*]

The latter response is preferred because it stays on target with Rita's feelings and concerns in the here-and-now and because it avoids getting off onto Jake, Sam, or any other third party or issue. The central issue in empathic understanding is to home in on the client's current core of feelings and concerns and communicate to the client (in the worker's own words) the gist of what the client is experiencing.

Nonverbal communication.   Empathic understanding means accurately picking up and reflecting more than verbal messages. It involves accurately sensing and reflecting all the unspoken cues, messages, and behaviors that the client emits. Nonverbal messages may be transmitted in many ways. Body posture, body movement, gestures, grimaces, vocal pitch, movement of eyes, movement of arms and legs, and other body indicators should be carefully observed by the worker. Clients may transmit emotions such as anger, fear, puzzlement, doubt, rejection, emotional stress, and hopelessness by different body messages. Crisis workers should be keenly aware of whether nonverbal messages are consistent with the client's verbal messages. A part of empathic understanding is the communication of such inconsistency to the client who may not be consciously aware of the difference. For example:

CW: [*Observing the way Rita's face lights up whenever she speaks or thinks about Sam.*] Rita, I notice you are talking about all the trouble it is for you to keep seeing Sam on the sly. But your body tells me that those are the moments you live for— that, right now, your only ecstasy is when you're with Sam.

It is important that the crisis worker avoid reading more into body language than it warrants. Communicating empathy in the nonverbal realm is no place for fishing expeditions or long-shot hunches.

The crisis worker's main concern with nonverbal communication, however, involves the worker's own messages. All the dynamics of the client's body language apply to the worker as well. Remember that your own body, voice, facial expression, posture, muscle activity, and so on serve as a constant vehicle of communication to the client. You are a living model. Your nonverbal messages must be consistent with your verbal messages. It would not be empathic or helpful if your words were saying to the client, "I understand precisely what you're feeling and desiring," but your body were saying, "I don't care," or, "I'm bored," or, "My mind isn't fully focused on what you're saying." Your voice, facial expression, posture—even the office arrangement and environment—must say to the client: "I'm fully tuned in to your world while you're with me. I want to give my total mental and emotional energy to understanding your concerns, feelings, alternatives, and choices while you're here. I will not be distracted." If your body can communicate such messages so that they are unmistakenly understood by the client, then you will have effectively communicated empathy to the client nonverbally, and you will stand a better chance of being helpful.

Silence.   Silence is golden. Beginning crisis workers often feel compelled to initiate talk to fill any void or lapse in the dialogue because they believe they "would not be doing their job otherwise." Nothing could be further from the truth. Clients need time to think. To throw up a barrage of questions or engage in a monologue says more about the crisis worker's insecurity in the situation than it does about resolving the crisis. Silence gives the client thinking time—and the crisis worker too.

Indeed, at such times, verbiage from the crisis worker may be intrusive and even unwelcome. Remaining silent, but attending closely to the client, can convey deep, empathic understanding. Nonverbally, the message comes across: "I understand your struggle trying to put those feelings into words and it's OK. I know it's tough, but I believe you can handle it. However, I'm right here if you need me."

Rita: The last beating . . . I was so ashamed, yet I couldn't seem to do anything except go back to him.

CW: It hurts you not only to get beaten but also that others might find out—which seems even worse. As a result, you don't see any alternatives.

Rita: [*Thinks hard, eyes focused into the distance for more than a minute.*] Yes and no! I see alternatives, but I guess until now I haven't had the guts to do anything. I rationalized that something must be wrong with me, or that the situation would get better, but it hasn't for five years. It has gotten worse.

CW: [*Silence. Looks at Rita for some 30 seconds while collecting thoughts*).] A couple of things strike me about what you said. First, you've decided to quit blaming yourself. Second, by the fact that you're here now, you've chosen at least one alternative to that five-year merry-go-round of abuse.

In this sense, silence is allowed to work for both the client and the worker. The client needs time to work through her response to the worker and she is unconditionally allowed to do this. The same is true of the crisis worker. The client's comment is synthesized and processed for its full meaning. By reacting immediately, the crisis worker might make less than a potent response. Taking time to digest both the content and the affect of the client enables the worker to formulate a response that is more likely to be on target and helpful.

Communicating Genuineness

Contrary to the thinking of most beginning human service workers, as evidenced by their behavior, being fully oneself and not some pseudotherapist or mimic of a particular therapist one has heard or seen is an absolutely necessary condition, particularly in crisis intervention. Rogers (1969, p. 228) says it in clear, simple, and succinct terms:

When I can accept the fact that I have many deficiencies, many faults, make a lot of mistakes, am often ignorant where I should be knowledgeable, often prejudiced when I should be open-minded, often have feelings which are not justified by the circumstances, then I can be much more real.

Applied to the behavior of crisis workers, Rogers' statement means putting on no false fronts, but rather, being oneself in the relationship and communicating what "oneself" is to the client. In short, it is being honest both with the client and with oneself. The advice to be honest is not simply a platitude. To be honest is to be congruent; it means that the crisis worker's awareness of self, feelings, and experience is freely and unconditionally available and communicable, when appropriate, during intervention in a crisis.

Egan (1975, 1982, 1986) has listed five components of genuineness that would serve the beginning crisis worker well. These components are generally good rules for any therapist to live by.

1. *Being role free.* The crisis worker is genuine in life as well as in the therapeutic relationship and is congruent both in experiencing and communicating feelings (Egan, 1975, p. 91).
2. *Being spontaneous.* The crisis worker communicates freely, with tact and without constantly gauging what to say, because such helpers behave freely without being impulsive or inhibited and are not rule bound or technique bound. Worker behavior is based on a feeling of self-confidence (p. 92).
3. *Being nondefensive.* Crisis workers who behave nondefensively have an excellent understanding of their strengths and weaknesses. Thus, they can be open to negative, even hostile, client expressions without feeling attacked or defensive. The crisis worker who is genuine understands such negative expressions as saying more about the client than the worker and tries to facilitate exploration of such comments rather than defending against them (pp. 92–93).
4. *Being consistent.* People who are genuine have few discrepancies between what they think, feel, and say and their actual behavior. Crisis workers who are consistent do not think one thing and tell a client another or engage in behavior that is contrary to their values (pp. 93–94).
5. *Being a sharer of self.* When it is appropriate to the situation, people who are genuine engage in self-disclosure, allowing others to know them through open verbal and nonverbal expression of their feelings (p. 94).

The following dialogue between the crisis worker and Rita demonstrates comprehensively the points both Rogers and Egan make.

Rita: Just what the hell gives? Here I am going crazy and you put it back on my shoulders. You're supposed to help get me out of this mess!

CW: I can see that you're really mad at me because I don't behave the way you think I ought to.

Rita: Well, how can you be such a caring person if you let me hang out there, pushing me to take such risky chances? I could lose everything.

CW: You see me as being a real hypocrite because I'm pushing you to take some action rather than sympathizing with you.

Rita: God knows I could use some . . . and when you act so callously [*Cries.*] . . . you're like every other damn man!

CW: What would I be doing if I were acting in the most helpful way I possibly could, in your opinion, right now?

Rita: Well, I know you can't solve this for me, but I'd sure as hell like for you to point the way or help me solve this.

CW: So, what you're really wanting is to be able to solve this dilemma on your own, and what you're wanting from me is to help you find your own inner choices that are best for you. What I want to do is to help you find those choices. Let's look at your current options right now.

The dialogue aptly depicts the crisis worker owning feelings, using "I" statements, and focusing on the client's emergent concerns rather than allowing the focus to shift to tangential matters or defensive responses of the worker. The listening exercises and owning feelings activities at the end of this chapter expand upon the worker's use of owning feelings and using "I" statements. Such statements allow the crisis worker to retain integrity, squarely face client hostility without becoming hostile in turn, and model a safe and trusting atmosphere in which clients see that it is all right for them to demonstrate angry feelings and still be accepted by the crisis worker. At the same time, the crisis worker stands by and is consistent with a therapeutic approach without being intimidated by or defensive with the client. The crisis worker above all has the self-confidence and congruence to make such statements in a way that is facilitative for the client.

Communicating Acceptance

The crisis worker who interacts with complete acceptance of clients exudes an unconditional positive regard for clients that transcends clients' personal qualities, beliefs, problems, situations, or crises. The worker is able to prize, care for, and fully accept clients even if they are doing things, saying things, and experiencing situations that are contrary to the worker's personal beliefs and values. The worker is able to put aside personal needs, values, and desires and does not require clients to make specific responses as conditions of full acceptance as they are at that moment.

Rita: I hate to bother you with all my problems. I know you're married and have never been divorced. You must think I'm a terribly screwed up mess.

CW: I hear your concern and I want you to know that what has happened to you and what you choose to do have nothing to do with my regard for you. What I'm really hoping we can do is to help you arrive at those choices that will best help you get through this crisis and successfully get back in total control of your life.

Rita: I appreciate that very much. But sometimes I wonder whether my running around with Sam doesn't strike you as unwise and immature.

CW: I hope I'm not giving off negative vibes to give you that impression, because your personal preferences have nothing to do with my caring for you. It seems like you really have a concern about my feelings about how you should act.

Rita: Not really. It's just something inside me—that if I were you, I'd be wondering.

CW: So, a source of concern inside you is whether I may evaluate you negatively. What I want you to know is that my esteem for you is not based on what you do.

Even when clients persist in projecting onto the crisis worker negative evaluations or notions such as those expressed by Rita, the worker doesn't have to buy into such notions. If the worker can truly feel an unconditional positive regard for the client, there will be no need for denial, defensiveness, or diversion from the reality of the worker's true feelings. If the worker demonstrates caring and prizing of the client, regardless of the client's situation or status, the client will be more likely to accept and prize himself or herself. That is the essence of acceptance in crisis intervention.

Facilitative Listening

Listening is the first imperative in crisis intervention. When we use the word *listening,* we are applying the term broadly to several important behavioral and communications skills discussed in this chapter. To function in a facilitative way, workers must *give full attention* to the client by

1. focusing their total mental power into the client's world
2. attending to the client's verbal and nonverbal messages (what the client does not say is sometimes more important than what is actually spoken)
3. picking up on the client's current readiness to enter into emotional and/ or physical contact with others, especially with the worker
4. emitting attending behavior by both verbal and nonverbal actions, thereby strengthening the relationship and predisposing the client to trust the crisis intervention process.

One important aspect of listening is for the worker to make initial, owning statements that express exactly what he or she is going to do.

CW: Rita, I can see you're really hurting. So that I can fully understand what's going on and what needs to be done, I'm going to focus as hard as I can on what you're saying and how you're saying it. As well as listening to what you do say, I'm going to be listening for those things that aren't said because they may have some bearing on your problems too. So if I seem to be really concentrating on you, it's because I want to fully comprehend in as helpful and objective a way as possible what the situation is and your readiness to do something about it.

The *second* important aspect of listening is to *respond* in ways that let the client know that the crisis worker is *accurately hearing* both the facts and the emotional state from which the client's message comes. Here we are searching for both the affective and content dimensions of the problem. The crisis worker combines the dilemma and feelings by using restatement and reflection.

CW: As you lay the problem out—the abuse by your husband, the job pressures, the wonderful yet guilt-ridden times with Sam—I get the feeling of an emotional switchboard with all the lines plugged in and even crossed over, and you're a beginning operator who might be able to handle one or two incoming calls, but now you're just sitting paralyzed wishing you'd never taken the job, wondering how you can get out, wanting answers, but having so many problems that you don't even know the right questions to ask.

The *third* facet in effective listening is facilitative responding. It provides positive impetus for clients to gain a clearer understanding of their feelings, inner motives, and choices. Facilitative responses allow clients to feel hopeful and to sense an inclination to begin to move forward, toward resolution and away from the central core of the crisis. Clients begin to be able to view the crisis from a standpoint of more reality or rationality, which immediately gives them a sense of control. Here the crisis worker targets an action.

CW: So, given all the wires running into the switchboard, which ones do you want to pull and which ones do you want to keep plugged in? You've given me all kinds of information about how well you've handled the business up to this crisis point. Look back on how you handled that particular phone line. What worked then that might work now? Using that as an example, can we sort each one of these out and get the circuits plugged in or just say that particular call isn't important right now and unplug the line?

The *fourth* dimension of effective listening is evidenced by the worker's helping clients to understand the *full impact* of the crisis situation. Such an understanding allows clients to become more like objective, external observers of the crisis and to *refocus* it in rational ways rather than remaining stuck in their own internal frame of reference and emotional bias.

Rita: I feel like the whole world is caving in on me. I wonder if I'll ever be able to get out from under all the mess I'm in now.

CW: You're sounding emotionally frozen by what is happening. I'm wondering what would happen if we could step back for a moment and look at it as if we were third-party observers to your situation—as if you were someone else in a soap opera. What would you say to that person?

Rita: Well . . . [*Moment of thought.*] I'd say she's not the first or only one to experience lots of trouble—that things may look horrible now, but that eventually things get worked out—especially if she's lucky and can bear up long enough.

CW: Then looking at it from outside yourself does give you an additional view.

Helping clients refocus on the full impact is not a solution in itself. It is an extension of the art of listening that may facilitate forward movement when clients are emotionally stuck in their emotional view.

These four aspects of listening are not operative in a fragmented or mechanical way. Such listening requires skill, practice, an emotionally secure listener, and both physical and emotional stamina on the part of the listener. The following dialogue gives a brief but comprehensive demonstration of how effective listening is combined in its many dimensions. The client now is Jean, the daughter of Rita. Don't be perplexed at our shift in clients. One person in crisis may well put a significant other into a crisis situation also. In this instance, Rita's problems have boiled over into her 13-year-old daughter's life.

Jean: I feel put down and ignored by my mother. Every time anything is mentioned about Sam, that's her secret boyfriend, she gets mad and leaves the room. Everything has changed. It's like I'm no longer important to her. I don't know what's happening or what to do.

CW: You're feeling hurt and disappointed, and you're also bewildered by her responses to you.

Jean: [*Crying and very emotionally upset.*] I . . . I feel like I no longer count. I'm feeling like I'm in the way. Like I'm suddenly no good . . . I feel like now I'm the problem.

CW: You're blaming yourself, even though you're trying to understand what has happened and what you should do.

Jean: [*Crying is slowing down.*] By Sunday night I felt like killing myself. I planned to do it that night. I was feeling abandoned, alone, and hopeless. I just wanted to find some way to end the hurting. I didn't think I could go on another day. I felt like I was no longer her daughter—like she had either disowned me or had been living a lie. I don't know if I can go on.

CW: Even though you were feeling you were at the brink of death, you somehow managed to pull out of it. What did you do and what are you doing now to keep from killing yourself?

Jean: [*Not crying—pondering the crisis worker's last response.*] Well, Marlene and her parents came by. I spent the night with them. That really helped. It was lucky for me that they came by and invited me. They were so kind and understanding. I had a bad night. Worrying about all that stuff. But they, especially Marlene, helped me so much.

CW: Let's see if you can tell me what you have learned from that experience that can help you the next time you feel like killing yourself.

Jean: [*Pause, as if studying the crisis worker's response.*] To get away . . . with someone who cares and understands.

CW: Tell me someone you can contact whenever you feel hopeless and lonely and suicidal so that next time you won't have to depend on "luck."

Jean: Well, I'd call Marlene again . . . or my uncle and aunt. They'd be quick to invite me over . . . and there are several friends at school I could call.

[*Dialogue continues.*]

This segment of dialogue contains several of the elements of listening that we have described. It contains accurate reflective listening, open-ended questions, and attention to the client's safety (without asking closed questions, giving advice, or encroaching on the client's prerogatives and autonomy).

Also, the crisis worker keeps the focus right on the central core of the client's current concerns, paving the way to facilitating the client's forward movement from the immediate crisis toward safer and more adjustive actions. The worker's selective responses are geared toward enabling the client to become aware of and pursue immediate short-term goals. The worker does not digress onto external events, past events, the mother, the secret boyfriend, gathering background information, or conducting long-term therapy.

It is also important to make a distinction between what the worker is doing and what we might call *rescuing* the client. Crisis intervention is a lot more than rescuing. Alleviating the current crisis and helping the client progress to a state of precrisis equilibrium are the main objectives of crisis intervention. Another objective of crisis intervention is to make appropriate referrals so that the client can preserve equilibrium, safety, and autonomy while working toward maintaining a state of noncrisis and progressing toward positive growth and prevention of future crises.

Given the situation as it stands now, with Rita's crisis having boiled over and involved other members of the family in crises beyond Rita's knowledge, one of the crisis worker's major referral thrusts is to ensure that Rita and members of her family become involved in family therapy, once her precrisis equilibrium has been restored. The family therapy we would strongly recommend would go beyond crisis intervention, involving Rita's family in regular meetings with one or more therapists who would facilitate communication, trust, cooperation, and basic problem-solving skills within the family.

ACTING IN CRISIS INTERVENTION

As shown in Figure 2-1, the crisis worker's level of action/involvement in the client's world, based on a valid and realistic assessment, may be anywhere on a continuum ranging from nondirective through collaborative to directive. Finding and implementing alternative coping mechanisms hinge on the client's mobility. Thus, assessment of client mobility is a key concept governing the degree of the crisis worker's involvement.

A major goal of crisis intervention is to assist the client in finding and implementing alternatives for coping with the events that precipitated the crisis, thereby progressing to a manageable precrisis level of control. We do not view crisis intervention as a part of a client's long-term or developmental therapy. Rather, we see crisis intervention as a form of brief therapy designed to get clients back on their feet and in control of their lives. One of the first things the worker must determine is what event precipitated the crisis. What brought on the disequilibrium? The answer may not be very clear in the client's complex and rambling story. So the worker may have to ask, early in the interview, "What *one event* brought you to seek counseling today?" When you discover the major precipitating event that took away the client's autonomous coping ability, it will likely signal your primary focus with the client.

The worker should have a current file of local medical, mental health, social, financial, and other pertinent resources for referral to assist clients in choosing appropriate postcrisis actions. During the worker's *acting* mode (helping clients examine alternatives, plan action steps, and make a commitment), the worker may function mainly in one of three ways: nondirective, collaborative, or directive.

Nondirective Counseling

The nondirective approach is desirable whenever clients are able to initiate and carry out their own action steps. As a general rule, the less severe the crisis, the less directive the crisis worker will have to be. The worker uses a great amount of active listening and open-ended questions to help clients clarify what they really want to do and examine what outcomes various choices might produce. These are some possible questions: "What do you wish to have happen?" "How can you make it happen?" "What will occur if you choose to do that?" "What could you do to begin that process?" "What persons are available now who could and would assist you in this?" "Picture yourself doing that—vividly see yourself choosing that route. Now, how does that image fit with what you're really trying to accomplish?" "How is that choice going to change things for the better for you?" "What activities did you do in the past that helped you in situations similar to this?" These are only a few of the possible open-ended questions the crisis worker may pose. Nondirective questions and reflections are geared to a sensitive and accurate identification of the client's current inner feelings, needs, and goals. Accurate empathy, genuineness, and unconditional acceptance are the main skills employed in the nondirective approach.

In nondirective counseling the worker focuses on the client's inner world, determines that the client has the capability, energy, mobility, and autonomy to make reasonable choices, and facilitates realistic forward movement of the client. The worker does not manage, manipulate, prescribe, dominate, or control. It is the client who owns the problem, the coping mechanisms, the plan, the action, the commitment, and the outcomes. The worker is a support person who may listen, encourage, reflect, reinforce, self-disclose, and suggest. Nondirective counseling assists clients in mobilizing what already is inside them—the capacity, ability, and coping strength to solve their own problems in ways that are pretty well known to them already but that are temporarily out of reach. Here is an example of a nondirective response:

Rita: This is it. I've had the last beating I'm going to take from that jerk! I'm simply going to get myself out of this hell!

CW: You've made a decision to choose a different life for yourself, and you've decided that *you* are the one who is going to start it.

Collaborative Counseling

The collaborative approach enables the crisis worker to forge a real partnership with the client in evaluating the problem, generating acceptable alternatives, and implementing realistic action steps. When the assessment indicates that the client cannot function successfully in a nondirective mode but has enough mobility to be a partner in the crisis intervention process, the worker is collaborative to that degree. Collaborative counseling is a "we" approach, whereas nondirective counseling is a "you" approach. Consider some typical worker statements in the collaborative mode: "You have asked me where you might find a safe place to spend the night. Let's consider the places we know of around here." "You've come up with a lot of good ideas, but you sound a little confused about which one to act on. Could we put our heads together and make a priority list of alternatives?" Usually the collaborative client's crisis is more severe that that of the nondirective client. But the collaborative client is a full partner in identifying the precipitating problem, examining realistic alternatives, planning action steps, and making a commitment to carrying out a realistic plan. The collaborative client is not as self-reliant and autonomous as the nondirective client but does possess sufficient ego strength and mobility to participate in resolving the problem. The worker is needed to serve as a temporary catalyst, consultant, facilitator, and support person. The concept of collaborative counseling is based on the precept that the worker serves as a catalyst to help the client map out immediate action steps in order to get started. The client can then take over, having once achieved a state of precrisis equilibrium. Here is an example of a collaborative response to a client:

Rita: I've thought about going to my mother's or going to the Wife Abuse Shelter, or even calling my school-counselor friend for a place to stay tonight.

CW: Let's examine these three choices and maybe some others available to you that I know of to see which one will best meet your requirements for tonight.

Directive Counseling

The directive approach is necessary when the client is assessed as being too immobile to cope with the current crisis. The crisis worker is the principal definer of the problem, searcher for alternatives, and developer of an adequate plan, and instructs, leads, or guides the client in the action. Directive counseling is an "I" approach. This is an example of a worker-directed statement: "I want you to try something right now. I want you to draw a deep breath, and while you are doing it, I want you to just focus on your breathing. Don't let any other thoughts enter your mind. Just relax and notice how your tensions begin to subside." By using a very directive stance, the worker takes temporary control, authority, and responsibility for the situation.

Rita: I don't know which way to turn. My whole world has caved in. I don't know what I'll do tonight. It's all so hopeless. I'm scared to even think about tonight. [*Rita appears stunned and in a state of panic.*] I don't know what to do.

CW: I don't want you to go home in the state you're in now. I'm going to call the Wife Abuse Service, and, if they have room for you at their shelter, I want you to consider spending at least one night there. The Wife Abuse Service has offices and a counseling service at one location and a shelter at a different address, which is unlisted. I don't want you to worry. We have a van that can take you to the shelter. In the morning you may leave the shelter and go talk with the Wife Abuse Service counselors or you can come back and talk with me; but right now my main concern is that you are safe for today and tonight.

There are many kinds of immobile clients: (1) clients who need immediate hospitalization due to chemical use or organic dysfunction, (2) clients who are suffering from such severe depression that they cannot function, (3) clients who are experiencing a severe psychotic episode, (4) clients who are suffering from severe shock, bereavement, or loss, (5) clients whose anxiety level is temporarily so high that they cannot function until the anxiety subsides, (6) clients who, for any reason, are out of touch with reality, and (7) clients who are currently a danger to themselves or others. The directive client is more apt to be suicidal than the nondirective or the collaborative client, so the directive client's level of lethality must be assessed early. How does the worker accomplish the degree of directedness necessary to manage the cases of these immobile clients? No one strategy is appropriate for all immobile clients. The worker needs a great deal of supervised experience, training, and self-confidence in order to deal effectively with a wide array of problems.

Most lay workers or paraprofessionals make it a practice to deal with the nondirective and collaborative clients and to refer many of the directive clients to professionally trained persons, hospitals, or clinics. In the *real* world of crisis intervention, every crisis worker must deal with a great many directive clients. The worker must be able to make a fairly accurate and objective assessment of the client's level of *mobility*. However, if the worker makes an error of judgment (believing a client to be immobile who in fact is not), no harm is usually done because the client may simply respond by refusing to accept the worker's direction. In most cases of this sort, the worker can then shift into a collaborative mode and continue the helping session. Many times a worker will begin in a directive mode and then shift into a collaborative mode during the session. For example, with a highly anxious client the worker may begin by directing the client in relaxation exercises, which may lower the client's anxiety level to the point where the worker can make a natural shift into a collaborative mode to continue the counseling.

Action Strategies for Crisis Workers

Crisis workers who use the six-step model we have described may begin each session using a nondirective approach and shift to a more directive approach as the ongoing assessment indicates. A number of action strategies and considerations may enhance the worker's effectiveness in dealing with clients in crisis.

Recognition of individual differences.   View and respond to each client and each crisis situation as unique. Even for experienced workers, staying attuned to the uniqueness of each person is difficult. Under the pressures of time and exhaustion, and misled by overconfidence in their own expertise, workers find it all too easy to lump problems and clients together and provide pat answers and solutions. Treating clients generically is likely to cost the worker and the client a great deal more in the long run than they save in time and effort in the short run. Stereotyping, labeling, and taking for granted any aspect of crisis intervention are definite pitfalls.

Self-analysis. Ongoing self-analysis on the part of the worker is mandatory. At all times, workers must be fully and realistically aware of their own values, limitations, physical and emotional status, and personal readiness to deal objectively with the client and the crisis at hand. Crisis workers need to run continuous perceptual checks to ascertain if they have has gotten in over their heads. (See the chapter on the crisis worker in crisis, Chapter 12, for a complete description of this phenomenon.) If for any reason the worker is not ready for or capable of dealing with the crisis or the client, the worker must immediately make appropriate referral.

Regard for client's safety. The worker's style, choices, and strategies must reflect a continuous consideration of the client's physical and psychological safety as well as the safety of others involved. The safety consideration includes the safety of the worker as well as the ethical, legal, and professional requirements mandated in counseling practice. The greatest intervention strategies and tactics are absolutely useless if clients leave the crisis worker and go out and harm themselves or others. The golden rule is, "When in doubt about client safety, get help." The safety requirement may mean appropriate referral interventions that include immediate hospitalization.

Client support. The crisis worker should be available as a support person during the crisis period. You help the client to develop a list of possible support persons, but if no appropriate support person emerges in the examination of alternatives, you can serve as a primary support person right now. Making sure the client knows how to reach you, you can assure the client that you can be—and wish to be identified as—a crisis support, at least until the crisis is over. You may need to employ a warm, empathic, and assertive counseling strategy with clients who are extremely lonely and devoid of supports. For example, "I want you to know that I am very concerned about your safety during this stressful time, and that I'm available to help. I want you to keep this card with you until you're through this crisis, and call me if you feel yourself sliding back into that hopeless feeling again. If you call either of these numbers and don't get an answer or get a busy signal, keep trying until you get me. You *must* make contact with *me*. I will be very disturbed if you are in a seriously threatening situation again without letting me become involved with you. I really want to impress upon you my genuine concern for you and the importance of making an agreement or contract to call me whenever your safety is threatened. Will you give me that assurance?"

Clear definition of the problem. Many clients have complicated and multiple problems. Make sure that each problem is clearly and accurately defined from the client's viewpoint and from a practical, problem-solving viewpoint. Many clients define the crisis as someone else's problem or as some external event or situation that has happened. Attempting to solve the crisis of some third party (who isn't present) is counterproductive. Pinpoint the client's own problem with the event or situation and keep the focus on the client's central core of concern. Also, attempt to distill multiple problems down into an immediate, workable problem. It is generally better to isolate the one precipitating problem or aspect of the situation that caused the client to seek help today and to concentrate on that problem first. We cannot overemphasize the tenacity with which the worker must avoid being drawn off on tangents by some highly emotional or defensive clients with difficult problems. Consider these exchanges with Rita's husband Jake:

Jake: You don't seem to like me much.

CW: Right now, that's not the issue of importance. What I'm trying to do is help you identify the main source of your problem.

Another example:

Jake: Haven't you ever hit your wife too?

CW: No, but that's not what we're working on now. I'm trying to help us figure out a way for you to avoid fighting with her whenever you first get home each evening.

In both instances the worker stays focused on the client and does not get caught up on side issues such as worker competency, beliefs, and attitudes.

Examine and analyze alternatives. In most problem situations, the alternatives are infinite. But crisis clients (and sometimes workers) have a limited view of the many options available. It is a good strategy for the worker to think of as many options as possible. Through the use of open-ended questions, elicit the maximum number of choices from the client. Then add your own list of possible alternatives to the client's list. For example: "I get the feeling that it might help if you could get in contact with a counselor at the Credit Counseling Bureau. How would you feel about our adding that to our list?" Examining, analyzing, and listing alternatives to consider should be as collaborative as possible. The best alternatives are ones that client truly *owns*. Take care to avoid imposing your alternatives on the client. The alternatives on the list should be workable and realistic. They should represent the right amount of action for the client to undertake now—not too much, not too little. The client will generally express ownership of an option by words such as, "I would really like to call him today." Worker-imposed options are usually signaled by the worker's words, such as *"You need to* go to his office and do that right away." *Beware* of the latter! An important part of the quest for appropriate alternatives is to explore with the client what options worked before in situations like the present one. Many times, the client can come up with the best choices, derived from coping mechanisms that have worked well in the past. But the stresses created by the immediate crisis may keep clients from identifying the most obvious and appropriate alternatives for them. Here the crisis worker facilitates the client's examination of alternatives:

CW: Rita, you say you're feeling frightened and trapped right now and you don't know where to turn. But it sounds like you'd take a step in a positive direction if you could get some of your old zip back. What are some actions you took or some persons you sought out in previous situations when you felt frightened or stuck?

Rita: Oh, I don't know that I've been in a mess quite this bad before.

CW: Well, that may be true. But what steps have you taken or what persons have you contacted before in a mess like this, even if it wasn't this bad?

Rita: Hmm . . . Well, a time or two I did go talk to Mr. Jackson, one of my auto mechanics instructors when I was at the Area Vo-Tech School. He's very understanding and helpful. He always seemed to understand me and believe in me.

CW: How would you feel about reestablishing contact with him whenever you're down again?

Plan action steps. In crisis intervention the worker endeavors to assist the client to develop a short-term plan that will help the client get through the immediate crisis, as well as making the transition to long-term coping. The plan should include the client's internal coping mechanisms, as well as sources of help in the environment. The coping mechanisms are usually brought to bear on some concrete, positive, constructive action that clients can take to regain better control of their lives. Actions that initially involve some physical movement are preferred. The plan should be realistic in terms of the client's current emotional readiness and environmental supports. It may involve collaboration with the worker until the client can function independently. The effective crisis worker is sensitive to the need of the client to function autonomously as soon as feasible.

Rita: Right now I'd like to just be free of the whole mess for a few days . . . just get off this dizzy merry-go-round long enough to collect my thoughts.

CW: It sounds to me like you really mean that. Let's see if together we can examine some options that might really get you the freedom and breathing space you need to pull the pieces back together.

Rita: I can't really let go. Too many people depending on me. That's just wishful thinking. But it would be wonderful to get some relief.

CW: Even though you don't see any way to get it, what you're wanting is some space for yourself right now—away from work, kids, Jake, Sam, and the whole dilemma.

Rita: The only way that would happen is for my doctor to order it—to prescribe it, medically.

CW: How realistic is that? How would that help you?

Rita: It would call a halt to some of the pressures. The treadmill would have to stop, at least temporarily. Yes, I guess that kind of medical reason wouldn't be so bad.

CW: Sounds like consulting your physician, and laying at least part of your cards on the table, might be one step toward getting medical help in carving out some breathing space for yourself.

Rita: I think so. Yeah, that's it! That's one thing I could do.

CW: Let's together map out a possible action plan—for contacting your physician and requesting assistance in temporarily letting go. Let's look at *when* you want to contact your physician, *what* you're going to say, and *how* you're going to say it—to make sure you get the results you must have right now.

The crisis worker is attempting to work collaboratively with Rita and to facilitate Rita's real ownership of her plan. The worker also implies a view of Rita as competent and responsible.

Use the client's coping strengths.   In crisis intervention it is important not to overlook the client's own strengths and coping mechanisms. Often the crisis events temporarily immobilize the individual's usual strengths and coping strategies. If they can be identified, explored, and reinstated they may make an enormous contribution toward restoring the client's equilibrium and reassuring the client. For example, one woman had previously relieved stress by playing her piano. She told the worker that she was no longer able to play the piano because her piano had been repossessed. The crisis worker was able to explore with her several possible places where she could avail herself of a piano in times of stress.

Attend to client's immediate needs.   It is important for crisis clients to know that their immediate needs are understood and attended to by the crisis worker. If a client is extremely lonely, attempt to arrange for the client to be with someone. The client may need to make contact with relatives, friends, former associates, or former friends. The client may need follow-up appointments with the crisis worker or referral to another worker, counselor, or agency. The client may simply need to be heard—to ventilate about a loss, a disappointment, or a specific hurtful event.

Use referral resources.   An integral aspect of crisis intervention is the accessibility and use of referral resources. A ready list of names, phone numbers, and contact persons is a necessity. It is also important for the crisis worker to develop skill in making referrals as well as in working with a wide variety of referral agencies. Many clients need to be referred early to make contact with sources of help regarding financial matters, assistance from social agencies, legal assistance, long-term individual therapy, family therapy, substance abuse, severe depression, or other personal matters. A worker might use referral resources for purposes like these: to obtain emergency eyeglasses for a junior high school student whose family cannot buy them; to get dental care for a child who is suffering excruciating pain and whose family cannot pay; to prevail upon a parole officer to mandate that a specific parolee cease abusing his wife and children; to ensure that a client disabled by an automobile accident receives help for his vocational rehabilitation as well as for his depressed mental state. We have compiled a list of suggestions and cautions that we have found to be useful in working with a variety of agencies. Most of these fall into the realm of what is known as common sense, but it is often easy to forget them. Generally, we find that a breakdown in our communication with agencies follows our having overlooked a few obvious and simple cautions.

1. Keep a handy, up-to-date list of frequently used agencies. Keep up with personnel changes.
2. In communities that publish a directory of human services, have available the most recent edition.
3. Cultivate a working relationship with key persons in agencies you frequently use.
4. Identify yourself, your agency, and your purpose when telephoning.
5. Know secretaries and receptionists by name; use their names when you call. Treat them with dignity, respect, and equality.
6. Follow up on referrals you make.
7. Don't assume that all clients have the skill to get the services they need. Be prepared to assist, to avoid runarounds and bureaucratic red tape.
8. Whenever necessary, go with clients to the referral agencies to assist and to ensure that effective communication takes place.
9. Be sensitive to the client's needs for transportation and child care.
10. Write thank-you messages (with copies to their bosses) to persons who are particularly helpful to you and your clients.
11. Don't criticize fellow professionals or the agencies they represent, and don't carry tales about either workers or agencies.
12. Keep accurate records of referral activities.
13. Remember that police and fire departments are referral resources also.
14. Know frequently used agencies' hours, basic services, mode of operation, limitations, and, if possible, policies such as insurance, sliding scale fees, and so forth.
15. Be aware of any agency services the client is already using.
16. Use courtesy and good human relations skills when dealing with agency personnel. Put yourself in their shoes and treat them as you would like to be treated.
17. Give agencies feedback on how they did; obtain feedback from them, too.
18. Avoid perfectionism.
19. If possible, talk with an agency when the client is *present*.
20. Think of how it affects the pride of the client—especially the older client—to accept help.
21. Be aware of sensory impairment in clients, especially in older adults.

22. If the client needs personal counseling, it is a good idea to ask the client to make the call.
23. Persevere until the client receives services.
24. If the agency has an orientation session, seek to participate in it, or at least attend.
25. Practice honesty! Avoid hidden agendas, part-truths, and other dishonest or misleading practices.
26. Rules of confidentiality and rights of privacy apply to all clients and fellow workers.

Develop and use networking.   Closely allied with referral is a function we call *networking*. Networking, for us, is having and using personal contacts within a variety of agencies that directly affect our ability to serve clients effectively and efficiently. Although each person in our network is a referral resource, it is the relationship we have with that individual that defines it as a network. Effective crisis workers can't sit behind a desk and wait for assistance to come to them. They must get out into the community and get to know personally the key individuals who can provide the kinds of services their clients require. A personal relationship based on understanding and trust between the worker and vital network persons is invaluable in helping the worker cut through bureaucratic red tape, expedite emergency assistance, and personalize many services that might otherwise not be available to clients.

As crisis workers, we do not operate alone in the world. We are interdependent on one another. Networking permits us to spread the responsibilities among other helping professionals. It is, indeed, an admission ticket into the community of helpers. We mean "helping professionals" in the broadest possible context: lawyers, judges, parole officers, ministers, school counselors, federal, state, and local human service workers, directors and key persons in crisis agencies, business and civic leaders, medical doctors, dentists, police, and political leaders may play important roles in the networking process. The development and use of effective networking is an indispensable function of the successful worker.

Commitment.   One of the vital aspects of crisis intervention is getting a commitment from the client to follow through on the action or actions planned. The crisis worker should ask the client to summarize verbally the steps to be taken. This verbal summary helps the worker understand the client's perception of both the plan and the commitment, and it gives the worker an opportunity to clear up any distortions. It also provides the worker an opportunity to establish a follow-up checkpoint with the client. The commitment step can serve both as a motivational reminder to the client and a verbal set which is a comment by the worker to encourage and predispose the client to believe that the action steps will succeed. Without a definite and positive commitment on the part of the client, the best of plans may fall short of the objectives that have been worked out by the worker and the client.

Step 6, the commitment step, does not stand alone. It would be worth little without the foundation of the five preceding steps. The actions that a client in crisis owns and to which the client commits are derived from the solid planning (Step 5) which is, in turn, based on systematic examination of alternatives (Step 4). The three acting steps (Step 4, 5, and 6) are based on effective listening or relational skills found in Steps 1, 2, and 3. All six of these steps are carried out under the umbrella of *assessing*.

Commitment is individually tailored to the specific client crisis situation. Volumes could be written without adequately describing the ideal strategy for generating the process and content for every possible crisis client's commitment. The art and skill of facilitating the commitment step depends on the sensitivity, training, experience, motivation, and natural talent of each crisis worker. The following segment is one example of a crisis worker functioning during the commitment step.

CW: So, Rita, it seems to me that what you've decided to do is to reinitiate some kind of meaningful contact with Mr. Jackson. That seems to be one thing you've decided that might really help right now. So that we're both very clear on what you've committed yourself to doing, would you please summarize how and when you're going to proceed?

Rita: I'm going straight to my office today and phone him at school. I'll either talk to him or leave a message for him to call me. As soon as I talk to him, I'll set up a definite day and time to meet with him.

CW: And when you've set up. . . .

Rita: Oh, yes! And when I've set up my appointment with him I'm going to phone you and let you know how it went.

CW: Good. And in the meantime, you have my number on the card if you need me—especially if it looks like the safety of either you or your children becomes jeopardized.

Rita: That's right, and I'll call if I lose my nerve with Sam. I've got to get some space for myself there—at least some temporary space.

Not all commitments are handled as smoothly and definitely as Rita's. Hard work, good training, and experience will greatly enhance the crisis worker's proficiency at getting effective commitments from clients. Experienced crisis workers are generally able to sense how far and how fast the client is able to act. Usually the client is encouraged to commit to as much action as feasible. If we cannot get them to make a giant leap forward, we'll accept one small step in a positive direction. The main idea is to facilitate some commitment that will result in movement of the client in a constructive direction.

COUNSELING WITH DIFFICULT CLIENTS

We are frequently asked by crisis workers, counselors-in-training, counselors in community agencies, and volunteer workers for suggestions for dealing with "difficult" clients. Individuals in agencies that do a lot of crisis intervention as well as general counseling sometimes have to deal with clients who are angry, uncooperative, or less articulate than we would choose them to be. Generally, we are requested to provide specific strategies that a crisis worker may use to help difficult clients effectively, both individually and in small groups (such as mediating with couples or a family in crisis). This brief discussion is intended to speak to this recurring need.

The worker usually has several options available for helping and dealing with difficult clients, whether they are being seen individually, by couples, or in small groups. Prior to the start of the counseling session, one can obtain an understanding and a commitment from clients who are known to be difficult. At the time the appointment is made, the worker can set a tone of positive expectancy.

Ground Rules

A set of ground rules can be agreed upon at the outset. The ground rules can be structured to help avoid defensive, uncommunicative, defiant, and other problem behaviors before such behaviors actually have a chance to occur in the session. The ground rules may vary according to the particular situation. We offer a typical set of ground rules for dealing with difficult clients. Workers who must deal with difficult clients regularly may wish to print a set of ground rules to place in the hands of selected client groups at the initial session or prior to the first meeting.

1. We start on time and quit on time; if couples are involved, both parties must be present; we will not meet unless both parties are present.
2. There will be no physical violence or threats of violence.
3. Everyone speaks for himself or herself.
4. Everyone has a chance to be fully heard.
5. We deal mainly with the here and now; we try to steer clear of getting bogged down in the past and in blaming others.
6. Everyone faces all the issues brought up—nobody gets up and leaves just because the topic is uncomfortable, and everyone stays for the entire session.
7. Everyone gets an opportunity to define the current problems, suggest realistic solutions, and make at least one commitment to do something positive; at least *one positive action step* is desired from each person present.
8. Everyone belongs, because he or she is a human being and because he or she is here.
9. The crisis worker will not take sides.
10. There will be no retribution, retaliation, or grudges over what is said in the session; whatever is said in the session belongs and stays in the session.
11. The time we spend together is for working on the concerns of persons in the group—not for playing games, making personal points, diversion, ulterior purposes, or carrying tales or gossip outside the session.

12. When we know things are a certain way, we will not pretend they are another way—we will confront and deal with each other as honestly and objectively as we possibly can.
13. We will not ignore the nonverbal or body messages that are emitted—we will deal with them openly if they occur.
14. If words or messages need to be expressed to clear the air, we will say them either directly or with role playing; we will not put them off until later.
15. We will not expect each other to be perfect.
16. In the event the ground rules are broken, the consequences will be discussed in the group. People who comply with the rules will not be denied services because one person disobeys the rules.

The crisis worker may go over the ground rules, in person or over the phone, prior to the first session. If this is not possible, a brief orientation, which includes the ground rules, is advisable at the start of the first meeting.

Confronting Difficult Clients

In dealing with difficult clients (such as highly emotional or defensive persons, those who deny any involvement in either the problem or the solution, and belligerent individuals) the worker may have to *confront* such behavior directly. We can confront clients with what they are doing by paying particular attention to the *nonverbal behavior* and giving immediate feedback: "You're saying one thing, but seem to be doing another; look how you're turning away and frowning whenever she says she wants the marriage to last." It is also essential to use good, focused *open-ended questions* with difficult clients. If the worker is helping a couple, one of whom is uncooperative or blocking, the worker must remain neutral. Regardless of how difficult a client is, the worker must not take sides, exhibit frustration, or show preference for one or the other.

There is a possibility that a client may be so difficult that the session may have to be terminated. (This should happen very, very infrequently.) In such a rare case, the worker would openly admit, "We're getting nowhere, so let's adjourn and see if we can figure out a way to try again." The worker might then reword the ground rules. The individuals may have to be seen separately for a while before they are ready to meet as a couple or in the group again. Consultation with a professional colleague for suggestions would be one of the first steps the group leader would take following such an adjournment. Also, we must recognize that we cannot succeed with every client. Sometimes, all we can do is let some of the clients ventilate, admit that we cannot help the situation, and perhaps refer the clients to a different worker, counselor, or agency.

The worker must be prepared to deal with various kinds of difficult clients: the nonverbal (nontalking) person, clients sent by a court order, clients from a particular ethnic or social group who are uncomfortable when talking with or facing a crisis worker, and clients who are "forced" or coerced into coming. The worker uses the utmost empathy when needed. We must also be sensitive to the need for confrontation, assertion, and directive tactics and ready to use them ("I will not permit you to violate our ground rules by attacking her that way."). Role playing may be needed to model appropriate assertion among group members.

The worker has the option of "staffing," or seeking the expert professional assistance of other highly trained, experienced, and skilled professionals. Often, getting consultatory assistance from a competent professional colleague provides a key to dealing with a specific difficult case. Knowing when to seek professional assistance and supervision ourselves is an important strategy in the referral, networking, and counseling process. Learning to leave difficult problems behind is an essential worker skill. We cannot afford to burn ourselves out by taking our clients' problems home with us.

SUMMARY

This chapter presents an overview of crisis intervention from a practitioner's standpoint by incorporating fundamental counseling skills into a six-step model of systematic helping. Figure 2-1 provides the central organizing focus: facilitative *listening* and *acting* within an overarching *assessing* paradigm. The six-step model follows an organized and fluid process of applying crisis intervention skills to the emerging feelings, concerns, and crisis situations that clients having any type of trauma might present.

The six steps in crisis intervention serve to organize and simplify the work of the crisis worker. Step 1 helps to explore and define the problem from the client's point of view. Step 2 ensures the client's physical and psychological safety. Step 3 provides personal supports for the person in crisis. Step 4 examines alternatives available to the client. Step 5 assists the client in developing a plan of action. Finally, Step 6 helps the client to make a commitment to carry out a definite action plan.

Assessment of the person and the crisis situation is the keystone for initiating intervention. Assessment techniques such as evaluating the severity of the crisis, appraising clients' thinking, feeling, emoting, and behaving patterns, assessing the chronicity and lethality of the crisis, looking into the client's background for contributing factors, and evaluating the client's resources, coping mechanisms, and support systems are presented and explored.

Listening is a fundamental imperative for *all* successful counseling, including crisis intervention. The chapter describes essential components of effective listening and communication, such as the application of effective attending, empathy, genuineness, and acceptance.

Action skills such as nondirective, collaborative, and directive worker strategies, showing consideration for individual differences and client safety, examining alternatives with clients experiencing crises, helping clients plan for and commit themselves to facilitative choices, wise use of referral resources, and techniques for dealing with difficult clients are explored.

The fundamental relationship skills such as attending, listening, communicating, showing empathy and acceptance, exhibiting genuine responses, and ensuring client safety are demonstrated or modeled through excerpts of worker/client dialogue with a client named Rita. The appropriate utilization of the six steps in the dialogue with Rita provides a thumbnail view of therapeutic counseling in action.

REFERENCES

Blocher, D. H. (1987). *The professional counselor.* New York: Macmillan.

Carkhuff, R. (1983). *The art of helping* (5th ed.). Amherst, MA: Human Resources Development Press.

Cormier, L. S., & Hackney, H. (1987). *The professional counselor: A process guide to helping.* Englewood Cliffs, NJ: Prentice-Hall.

Cormier, W. H., & Cormier, L. S. (1985). *Interviewing strategies for helpers: Fundamental skills and cognitive behavioral interventions* (2nd ed.). Pacific Grove, CA: Brooks/Cole.

Egan, G. (1975). *The skilled helper: A model for systematic helping and interpersonal relating.* Pacific Grove, CA: Brooks/Cole.

Egan, G. (1982). *The skilled helper: Model, skills, and methods for effective helping* (2nd ed.). Pacific Grove, CA: Brooks/Cole.

Egan, G. (1986). *The skilled helper: A systematic approach to effective helping* (3rd ed.). Pacific Grove, CA: Brooks/Cole.

Fujimura, L. E., Weis, D. M., & Cochran, J. R. (1985, June). Suicide: Dynamics and implications. *Journal for Counseling and Development. 63(10),* 612–615.

Gilliland, B. E. (1982). *Steps in crisis counseling.* Memphis, TN: Memphis State University, Department of Counseling and Personnel Services. Unpublished curricular handout distributed to crisis counseling classes.

Gilliland, B. E., James, R. K., Roberts, G. T., & Bowman, J. T. (1984). *Theories and strategies in counseling and psychotherapy.* Englewood Cliffs, NJ: Prentice-Hall.

Lillibridge, M., & Klukken, G. (no date). *Crisis intervention training* [six audio casette tapes]. Tulsa, OK: Affective House.

Rogers, C. R. (1969). *Freedom to learn: A view of what education might become.* Columbus, OH: Chas. E. Merrill.

Rogers, C. R. (1977). *Carl Rogers on personal power: Inner strength and its revolutionary impact.* New York: Delacorte.

Shneidman, E. S., Farberow, N. L., & Litman, R. E. (1976). *The psychology of suicide.* New York: Aronson.

■ Classroom Exercises: Case Example

The case of Rita, based on a real situation in our counseling practice, is presented here for you to consider because it clearly demonstrates and emphasizes the six steps in crisis intervention. We suggest that you make notes as you read and reread it. Suppose that you were the crisis worker to whom Rita had come for help (in person, not on the telephone). As an exercise to discover how well you have learned the six-step crisis counseling model, write a personal narrative description of how you might use the six-step model to help Rita during the initial session you have scheduled with her. (We have also written our description. Please write your description before reading ours, found at the end of this case example; then compare your crisis intervention strategies with the narrative we have prepared. Remember, in crisis intervention, there is no one best way. Yours may be as effective as ours, or more so. We hope the exercise will prove instructive for you.)

The Case of Rita

Rita is a 35-year-old businesswoman. She is a graduate of high school and a post–high school vocational-technical institute. She holds a certificate in auto mechanics. She has never been to a counselor before. She has come to the crisis worker at the suggestion of a close friend who is a school counselor. Rita owns and operates an automobile tune-up and service shop. She employs and supervises a crew of mechanics, tune-up specialists, and helpers. She works very hard and keeps long hours, but maintains some flexibility by employing a manager. Rita's husband Jake is a college-educated accountant. They have two children: a daughter, 13, and a son, 8. The family rarely attends church, and they don't consider themselves to be religious. But they are church members. Their close friends are neither from their church nor from their work.

Rita's presenting problem is complex. She constantly feels depressed and unfulfilled. She craves attention but has difficulty getting it in appropriate ways. For diversion, she participates in a dance group that practices three nights a week and performs on many Friday and Saturday evenings. Rita, Jake, and their children spend most of their Sundays at their lake cottage, which is an hour's drive from their home. Their circle of friends is mainly their neighbors at the lake.

Rita's marriage has been going downhill for several years. She has become sexually involved with Sam, a wealthy wholesaler of used automobiles. She met him through a business deal whereby she contracted to do the tune-up and service work on a large number of cars for Sam's company. Sam's contracts enable Rita's business to be very successful. Rita states that the "chemistry" between her and Sam is unique and electrifying. She says she and Sam are "head over heels in love with each other." She lives with Jake but no longer feels any love for him.

According to Rita, Sam is unhappily married too, and Sam and his current wife have two small children. Rita states that she and Sam want to get married, but she doesn't want to subject her two children to a divorce right now and she's very fearful of her own mother's wrath if she files for a divorce. Sam fears his wife will "take him to the cleaners" if he leaves her for Rita right now. Lately, Sam has been providing Rita with expensive automobiles, clothing, jewelry, and trips out of town. Also, Sam has been greatly overpaying Rita's service contracts, making her business flourish. Jake doesn't know the details of Rita's business dealings with Sam, but he is puzzled, jealous, frustrated, impulsive, and violent. Jake used to slap Rita only occasionally. Recently, however, he has become more frustrated, impulsive, and violent. Jake has beaten Rita several times in recent months. Last night he beat her worse than ever. Rita has no broken bones, but she has several bruises on her body, legs, and arms. The bruises do not show as long as she wears pantsuits.

Rita has told her problems only to her school-counselor friend. She fears that her boyfriend would kill her husband if he found out about the beatings. Rita is frustrated because she cannot participate with the dance group until her bruises go away. Rita is feeling very guilty and depressed. She is not especially suicidal, however. She is feeling a great deal of anger and hatred toward Jake, and she suffers from very low self-esteem. She is feeling stress and pressure from her children, from her mother, from Jake, and even from Sam, who wants to spend more and more time with Rita. Recently, Rita and Sam have been taking more and more risks in their meetings. Rita's depression is getting to the point where she doesn't care. She has come to the crisis worker in a state of lethargy—almost in a state of emotional immobility. But Rita has decided to share her entire story with the worker because she feels she is at her "wit's end," and she wouldn't dare talk with her minister, her physician, or other acquaintances. Rita has never met the crisis worker, and she feels this is the best approach, even though she is uncomfortable in sharing all this with a stranger.

STOP. Don't continue until you have written your own description of your use of the six steps in crisis intervention with Rita. Furthermore, if you are participating in a class, workshop, or other study group, make sure you get together with others (preferably in small groups of five to seven persons) to share descriptions of your particular method of crisis intervention. Immediately following this case example is our own description, which you should read only after participating in small group discussions.

A CRISIS WORKER'S NARRATIVE

Description of the Six-Step Crisis Counseling Process for the Case of Rita

(Read this narrative (1) following the writing of your own narrative description of your suggested case handling, and (2) after completion of small group discussions of group members' individually written summaries of their case handling in which they demonstrated competency using the Six-Step Crisis Counseling Process for the case of Rita.)

First, I would explore and *define Rita's problem* from her point of view. I would use active listening techniques. I would avoid closed questions. Apparently Rita is feeling trapped because of several situational conditions: her marriage; her relationship with Sam; her own web of unfulfilling activity; and the beatings by her husband, Jake. I would try to identify the one area which precipitated the crisis and immediately focus on that. After Rita's whole story had been fully examined, I might say, "Rita, what one thing caused you to come to see me today?" I would start with that one event or stressor. *Active Listening* would bring us to that point.

Second, I would take whatever steps I deemed necessary to *ensure Rita's safety.* From the case data, I assume that Jake does not physically abuse the children, but he might do so. If my assessment indicated that Rita was in imminent danger, I would refer her to the Wife Abuse Services and inform her of their shelter options. Other safe places could be explored with Rita to ensure the safety of both herself and her children.

Third, I would offer myself as an immediate *support person.* I would also attempt, during the session, to develop other viable support persons to whom Rita could turn, especially in an emergency. I would assume that Rita's school counselor friend is a positive support person, and I would encourage Rita to maintain that relationship as well as explore others.

Fourth, I would encourage Rita to *examine the various alternatives available to her.* I would give special attention to the options that Rita could own and do for herself which would contribute directly toward restoring her pre-crisis level of equilibrium.

Fifth, I would attempt to help Rita *develop a plan* of action which she could own, and which would represent a *positive action step* toward her pre-crisis level of equilibrium. The plan would have to be concrete, positive, realistic, and clearly oriented toward alleviating her crisis. If her stress level were high, I might immediately use relaxation techniques to assist her through the current stressful and anxious state. This could be one method by which Rita might begin to learn to deal with future stresses as they are encountered in her life.

Sixth, before the termination of the session with Rita, I would try to get a *commitment* from her to carry out some action which would be positive and would help her restore her equilibrium or make a step toward it. I would ask her to summarize the commitment as a means of helping to solidify it in her mind as an immediate objective and to motivate her toward attainment of the stated goal. I would assure Rita of my support and encouragement and make arrangements for the two of us to check back with each other to follow-up on her progress.

In terms of problem-solving, I would covertly brainstorm two important components while I listened and responded to Rita: (1) I would make a mental list of *adequate situational supports*; and, (2) I would make a mental list of *adequate coping mechanisms.* I would not disclose all of these to Rita. The mental options would be available to me to effect referrals or to ask appropriate open-ended questions in helping her to discover the alternatives available to her. I would take care not to impose my own solutions, alternatives, or plans on Rita.

Throughout the crisis intervention session, I would be engaged in assessing Rita's situation. During the listening, safety, and support phases of the session, I would be *active* with Rita. My degree of action would depend on my *assessment* of Rita's mobility or criticalness. If Rita were assessed as immobile, I would be quite *directive*; if she were partially mobile, I would be *collaborative*. If she were totally mobile, I would be *nondirective*. From the case data, I assume that Rita is fairly mobile, so initially, I would function in a *collaborative* mode. Depending on my own ongoing assessment, I would move toward either directive or nondirective, but I believe I would function largely in the collaborative mode most of the time.

I would certainly avoid asking closed questions. By continuing to focus on Rita's situation with open-ended questions, I would try to get her to concentrate on what she wants to do; that is, I would focus on alternatives. I would hope to get her to consider as many realistic alternatives as possible. I would assist her in brainstorming to identify these alternatives. From a repertory of choices, I would hope that her plan, mentioned in Step 5, would be a sound one which would move her toward attainment and success. The optimum plan would be simple and realistic. I would not be attempting to get her to solve all her situational problems. My first goal would be to help her get the present crisis under control, and then work toward having the mobility to independently take charge of her life.

In *Problem-solving* Rita's case with her, I would start with a list of support persons gleaned from the case data. In crisis intervention, a support person is someone whom the client trusts and who is always available. That person or persons could be an acquaintance, a friend, relative, coworker—anyone who could be called upon to provide temporary comfort, encouragement, or support. In Rita's case, the most obvious support persons would be the crisis worker (myself), her school counselor friend, her own children, other dancers in her dance group, her "lake" friends, her shop manager and shop employees, and her former vocational-technical instructors. Other possible supports might include her mother, her physician, other members of her family, and even former classmates from school. These are the kinds of persons who would be identified and saved in the crisis worker's mind as possible appropriate supports for Rita to consider. Normally, we recommend using only one or two support persons at a time, not a whole host of people. I would encourage Rita to choose and contact one or two appropriate support persons.

Adequate *coping mechanisms* stored in the crisis worker's mental repertory for possible assistance to Rita could be: leaving Jake the next time he beats her; breaking off the relationship with Sam; setting priorities on the amount of time she is spending on various activities; devising better or different ways to obtain positive attention when she needs it; calling a support person on the phone; calling the Crisis Center or the Wife Abuse Service; calling me (the crisis worker); consulting an attorney for legal advice; consulting her physician for a complete physical examination, diagnosis, and advice; initiating marriage counseling with Jake, if he agrees; initiating couples' counseling with Sam, if he agrees; planning ways to spend time with and engage in activities with her school counselor friend; entering individual counseling on a continuing basis; doing something that is recreational or relaxing for herself, such as working on cars or developing a new dance routine; enrolling in an assertiveness training course to enhance her self-esteem and improve her coping behaviors; wearing tights or colored hose to her dance rehearsals until her bruises heal; and thinking of something innovative or creative that she would enjoy to get away from the turmoil.

In helping Rita (using the Six-Step Crisis Counseling Model), I would seek to involve Rita in *prioritizing* any of the alternatives, plans, support persons, or coping mechanisms she might wish to pursue. If chosen *action steps* can truly represent Rita's own priorities, the chances of success will be greatly increased. Finally, and most importantly, I would reemphasize getting Rita to commit herself to one or more of the actions which we collaboratively developed as her plan. I would ask her to summarize her plan so that both she and I could agree on what she was committing herself to. I would try to respond to her during the committment phase in a way in which she would feel supported by me, but *not dependent* on me. I would certainly want her to be motivated and predisposed toward success.

Crisis Intervention Laboratory Exercise

A. Group members form pairs.
B. You will practice two roles: (1) being a crisis worker and (2) reliving a real crisis from your past experience. All sessions must be tape-recorded; to begin each tape, the person serving as crisis worker obtains the client's spoken permission to record the session.
C. The crisis worker practices accurate listening skills: attending, observing, understanding, and responding with empathy, genuineness, respect, acceptance, nonjudgment, and caring.
D. The client relates the past crisis to his or her partner as if the crisis event were being reexperienced in the present moment.
E. Whenever each partner has had an opportunity to play the roles of both crisis worker and client in the laboratory experience, the class will be regrouped for discussion. Here are some possible discussion questions:
   1. To you as a client, what aspects of the process were most helpful? What aspects would you like to see improved?
   2. To you as a client, what was the most threatening part of the exercise?
   3. For you as a worker, what did you perceive to be your strongest and most positive intervention technique?
   4. For you as a worker, what did the exercise bring out that you wish to improve upon?
   5. What additional skills or learnings do you need to make your next session more successful?
F. Homework assignment: Take the taped session home, listen to it, and, in your role as the crisis worker, write a six-step plan for intervention. At the next class meeting, share that plan with the client, and obtain verbal feedback from that person.

Listening Exercises

Most of us would like to improve the odds that we really do accurately interpret clients' messages when they talk to us. There are many hints to aid us in listening to clients. We will deal with two methods in these exercises.

A. *Restatement of ideas.* Make a simple statement in your own words telling the client what you heard him or her say. This helps to be sure that you and the client are talking about the same thing. Example:

Client: I don't think I can go back home tonight—just too many heavy problems for me to handle.

Worker: You don't think you can face what's at home.

B. *Reflection of feelings.* Reflecting feelings means sending the client a message that confirms your understanding of what the client must be feeling. In that way you let the client know you heard him or her, giving the client a chance to correct or clarify (you may have received half the message, but not all of it). Reflective listening also helps the client see the basis for his or her behavior. Example:

Client: My boss really chewed me out in front of my friends last night.

Worker: Sounds like it really embarrassed you.

To help you learn to make appropriate responses that contain both restatement and reflection, we have prepared a listening practice sheet (Table 2-1). Do the practice exercises on the sheet without consulting anyone else. Then obtain feedback from others as the directions indicate. The individual effort followed by feedback in small groups sharpen your restatement and reflective skills.

Open-ended Statements

Often workers are frustrated by a client's lack of response and enthusiasm. Workers may make statements such as, "All my clients ever do is grunt or shake their heads indicating yes or no." We can do something about getting fuller, more meaningful responses if we ask questions that are not dead ends.

There are two types of statement: *open* and *closed.* Closed statements usually begin with verbs like *do, did, does, can, will,* and *doesn't.* ("Do you like this story?" "Yup." "Did you have fun on vacation?" "Nope.") Closed statements elicit one-word, abrupt responses. Examples: "How old is your mother?" and "Do you like your job?"

Open statements encourage clients to respond with full statements and at deeper levels of meaning. Remember that open-ended comments are used to elicit from clients something about their feelings, thoughts, and behaviors. Here are some guidelines for forming open verbalizations.

1. Request description: "Please tell . . . ," "Tell me about . . . ," "Show me . . . ," "In what way does . . . ?"

Table 2-1 Listening Practice

DIRECTIONS: In your own words write a restatement of the client's statement. The yes/no column is a feedback device for you. Then write a reflective statement. In small groups, give one another feedback, making check marks under "yes" or "no" to indicate whether or not others find your responses appropriate.

Client's statement	Worker's restatement	Worker's reflection	Yes	No
1. When he says those hateful things to me I wish I could die.				
2. I don't need her and I frankly don't think I need counseling. She's the one with problems.				
3. You're so wonderful. Nobody else understands me, but you do. I think I love you.				
4. Life is like a roller coaster—up and down. Isn't that kind of the way it is with you?				

2. Focus on plans: "What will you do . . . ?" "How will you make it happen?" "How will that help you to . . . ?"

3. Own your own desires: "I'd like you to add more to what you've said . . . ," "I want you to describe what that means to you," "What would you like to have happen in the relationship?"

Asking open-ended questions does not guarantee that every client will respond with full statements. The purpose of this exercise is to help you become aware of how you state your questions so that you can get fuller, deeper levels of response.

Recognizing Open-Ended Verbalizations

	Open	Closed	Counselor Statement
Example A		X	Do you have a girlfriend?
Example B	X		Tell me about your family.
1.			How old are you?
2.			How did that happen?
3.			When will you go?
4.			Tell me about school.
5.			What happened next?
6.			Isn't that a silly choice?

Change the following closed leads to open leads.

1. How long have you been out of work?
2. Can I help?
3. Did you like that story?
4. Are you angry with me?
5. Do you have to hit Sally every time you get drunk?

Owning Feelings

Owning means communicating possession: "That's mine." Often in conversation we avoid specific issues by "disowning" statements with phrases like these: "They say . . . ," "I heard the other day that you . . . ," "It's not right for you to . . . ," and "Don't you think you ought to . . . ?" Whether it is intentional or not, such verbal manipulation functions to escape ownership of responsibility for what's being said or to avoid awareness of one's own position on thoughts and feelings concerning an issue.

When working with a client it is very important to *own* your feelings and behaviors because many clients are using you as a model. So if you imply "We think this way" (meaning I and the world, the universe, all other people) or "God thinks this way," then the client doesn't have much chance to question such an awesome cast of thinkers.

Also, many of us chronically disown many human qualities. As workers, we are never confused, jealous, shallow, bored, or proud! Small wonder that some clients learn to distrust such all-knowing, well-integrated individuals. Let's just take, for example, my feeling of confusion. If I am pretending to understand when I'm really confused, I have split my energy right down the middle, and the client who is listening to me is doubly confused.

A deeper aspect of checking my own behavior and eliciting responses from clients is to own confusions. This means that I am aware of being confused by a client's response or behavior and that I do not pretend that I understand. Being willing to own my confusion or frustration and to attempt to eliminate it is a trust-reinforcing event for the client for two reasons: (1) both client and worker can reduce the need to pretend or fake understanding one another and begin to see more clearly where communication wires are getting crossed, and (2) the client can begin to become actively involved with the worker in an attempt to work together.

Further, to be genuine is to say what *I* feel at times. When a client has done well and I'm happy and feel good about it, I say it! Likewise, when clients start trying to control, browbeat, or otherwise put me on the hot seat, it does little good to try to hide my anger, disappointment, or hurt feelings. If I am congruent, I need to let the client know how I feel.

Table 2-2 is a practice exercise designed to let you try out owning your own feelings and expressing them in responses that indicate that you are owning them. We call such messages *"I" messages*. When we disown a feeling, we usually give someone else the responsibility for it and begin statements with words that refer outside ourselves, such as *"they," you, people,* and *all people.*

Worker/Client Communications

Communication is often not a simple matter. Words come so fast and easily at times that we have our responses formulated in our heads before we hear the full message of the client who is speaking.

The exercises in Table 2-3 are designed to emphasize (1) attentive listening and (2) formulating responses that communicate acceptance of the feeling behind the message as well as awareness of the message's content. An accepting response combines (1) restatement, (2) reflection, (3) owning one's feelings, and (4) an open lead designed to get to the fuller meaning. Thus, the instrument contained in Table 2-3 is to be seen as a culminating activity for better communications skills.

Look at the grid in Table 2-3. Break into dyads (pairs) and write the answers to at least two of the examples. (Allow about 15 minutes.) You need not

Table 2-2 Owned Message Practice

DIRECTIONS: Read the situation in the first column. Examine the "you" or the disowned message in the second column. Then write in the third column an "I" message that indicates you take responsibility for your feelings. The purpose is *not* to resolve the problem, but rather to communicate that you are aware of your feelings and are being honest about them at this moment. After you have completed the exercise individually, form groups of three or four persons. Give each other feedback on whether or not the message indicates owning one's own feelings. The yes/no column is a feedback device for you. If, after you have shared your responses, others feel that most of your responses are not "I" messages, please elicit help in restating your message.

Situation	Disowned Messages	Owned Messages	Yes	No
1. Client has been sulking and acting sad all session.	Come on, now. Stop moping around. Life isn't that bad.	I'm really puzzled. You say things are OK! Yet your behavior doesn't fit with OK.		
2. Macho man brags about beating wife. Has just responded, "Women need to be kept in control."	Well, I wonder if you'd do that to the Raider line backers.			
3. People complain about client's body odor. (It's bothering you, too.)	James, you really should bathe more frequently.			
4. Cynthia has a reputation for being promiscuous and has talked at some length about it.	We workers feel that talk only leads to acting out behavior.			
5. John is extremely over-weight. Wants to lose weight but doesn't seem to be able to stick to a plan.	Face it, John. You're fat. I'm sorry, but that's it. No wonder you can't get dates. Why not try jogging?			

Table 2-3 Total Listening Practice

Client's Message	Restatement	Reflection	Owning "I" statement	Open-ended statement
I used to like him as a boss. But he chewed me out today. I hate his guts.				
He beat the daylights out of me last night.				
Well, I really wonder what life's all about; love, too, for that matter.				
You're just like all the rest. You don't really care about me. I think I'll kill myself.				

write out anticipated client responses. However, there must be agreement between the two members on appropriate client responses.

Each pair should be prepared to role-play the client and the worker in dialogue beyond initial responses in one of the exercises. To improve worker/client communication and to provide practice in total listening, partners should treat the exercise in Table 2-3 as if they represented real clients in a crisis intervention situation.

PEOPLE IN CRISIS:
GOING INTO THE TRENCHES

Part Two represents a multifaceted application of intervention strategies to several of the most prevalent and timely crisis categories in the human experience. The purpose of Part Two is to provide crisis workers, counselors, caregivers, and various other professionals with the background, dynamics, and intervention methodologies needed to effectively help individuals or groups in crisis. We believe you will appreciate the strong emphasis on the *applied* art and science of crisis intervention.

We have several objectives in mind for organizing and presenting discussion of crises in these categories: (1) to provide valid, useful, and interesting material, (2) to deal with areas of current importance in our culturally pluralistic world, (3) to promote sound practice, based on the best available research and theoretical foundations, and (4) to demonstrate a wide number of alternatives available to workers who are in the business of crisis counseling or crisis intervention.

Part Two contains a wide array of crisis case illustrations, the usual and accepted practices, and many innovative strategies for intervention. It examines crises in these categories: suicide, battering of women, institutional violence, severe physical handicaps, posttraumatic stress disorder, substance addiction, sexual assault, hostage crisis negotiation, and coping with loss and grief. Several central themes pervade these chapters (which often deal with devastating human dilemmas):

1. Some crises are *time limited* and some are *transcrisis* in that the person in crisis may progressively experience severe problems, either deal with or suppress them, and then experience and exhibit repeated responses and symptoms of the same crisis over a period of many years.
2. Crises are characterized by both danger and opportunity.
3. No one set of theories, assumptions, strategies, or procedures is appropriate for intervening in *all* crisis situations; rather, a systematic and eclectic approach is recommended and demonstrated as the preferred mode of helping in a broad assortment of crisis problems and settings.

CHAPTER 3

Suicide: Strategies for Assessment and Intervention

In crisis work the possibility of dealing with suicidal clients is ever present. That is why we addressed the issue of assessing the lethality level of suicidal clients in Chapter 2. Here, our concentration on counseling and prevention is predicated on the crisis worker's continuous awareness and assessment of the level of suicidal risk of all clients in crisis. In this chapter we will present strategies to help crisis workers strengthen their skills by means of assessing, counseling, intervention, and prevention. The strategies addressed in this chapter are solidly based upon the concepts, including the six steps in crisis intervention, found in Chapter 2. All of the examples, cases, and exercises are presented with the assumption that workers understand and use these fundamental crisis intervention concepts in dealing with suicidal clients as well as with clients in any other category of crisis. We do not wish to continually call attention to the six steps, but we want to make it clear that the fundamental concepts are presumed to apply in every instance.

BACKGROUND

Although crisis workers may not be able to identify every client having high suicidal risk and may not succeed in preventing suicide in 100% of high-risk clients encountered, it is possible to provide the kinds of support and intervention that have proved to be helpful to self-destructive persons (Fujimura, Weis, & Cochran, 1985). A wealth of literature on counseling with suicidal clients is available (Allen, 1977; Fujimura, Weis, & Cochran, 1985; Getz, Allen, Myers, & Linder, 1983; Hatton, Valente, & Rink, 1977; Hersh, 1985; Hipple & Cimbolic, 1979; Morgan, 1981; Motto, 1978; Ray & Johnson, 1983; Shneidman, Farberow, & Litman, 1976; Wekstein, 1979). Crisis workers who deal with suicidal clients and their families and associates have found that keeping up to date through regular reading is an excellent way of enhancing their knowledge and skill as helpers.

Suicide can strike any family. It is among the top five to ten causes of death in the Western world (Toughy, 1974); it is occurring among all segments of the population ("Tidewater Psychiatric," 1985). It is prevalent in all age and racial/ethnic groups. Women attempt suicide more than men; men succeed in killing themselves more often than women. The highest-risk group for many years has been Caucasian men over 35, but the suicide rate among teenagers and young Black males has been dramatically increasing over the past 30 to 35 years (Fujimura, Weis, & Cochran, 1985; Shneidman, Farberow, & Litman, 1976). Even though the elderly make up roughly 10% of the total population, 25% of all suicides occur in the over-65 population. Women over 65 kill themselves twice as frequently as the total population and men over 65 kill themselves at a rate four times the national norm (Janosik, 1984, p. 153).

The suicide rate among children and adolescents tripled between 1950 and 1985 (American Association for Counseling and Development, 1985). It is the second leading cause of death among children and teens. Nearly 2 million high school seniors in the United States report having attempted suicide, and nearly 2000 youngsters under age 19 took their own lives in 1980. By 1985, youth suicide had become epidemic. The search for solutions reached the U.S. Congress, where two youth suicide prevention bills were introduced (H.R. 1099 and H.R. 1894) (AACD, 1985, p. 1).

Despite the vast amount of attention being focused on suicide, especially teenage suicide, professionals have a difficult time identifying a common denominator for the cause of so many adolescent suicides ("Teenage suicide," 1985). Dr. Donald Reay, a Seattle medical examiner, conducted a two-year study on teenage suicides. On the basis of his data, he stated, "We didn't find any outstanding characteristic. . . . In other words, take 100 teenagers and, on the basis of what we looked at, we wouldn't be able to identify a potential suicide victim" (p. 3). Dr. Reay's conclusions substantiate the premise that the mythical "suicidal type" does not exist and underscore the complexity and the difficulty encountered when we attempt to predict, identify, type, assess, and prevent potential suicides among any segment of the population. Perhaps the best assumption to begin with is that no two potential suicidal situations are ever alike, but that there are common threads and clues that are useful in treatment and prevention work with suicidal clients and their loved ones.

DYNAMICS OF SUICIDE

According to Fujimura, Weis, and Cochran (1985), two different approaches have been advanced to explain suicidal behaviors: Freud's psychodynamic approach (Allen, 1977) and Durkheim's (1951) sociological approach. In the psychodynamic view suicide is held to be an intrapsychic conflict that emerges when a person experiences great psychological stress. Sometimes such stress causes regression to a more primitive ego state in which one's aggression is directed toward the self.

In Durkheim's approach, societal pressures and influences are major determinants of suicidal behavior. Durkheim (1951) identified three types of suicide: egoistic, anomic, and altruistic (pp. 152–276). *Egoistic* suicide is related to one's lack of integration or identification with a group. *Anomic* suicide arises from a perceived or real breakdown in the norms of society. *Altruistic* suicide is related to perceived or real social solidarity, such as the traditional Japanese hara-kiri or, to put it in a current context, the episodes of suicidal attacks by Middle East extremist groups. A fourth type of suicide, identified by Fujimura, Weis, and Cochran (1985), is *dying with dignity*. This type of suicide is typified by a person's choosing death in the face of an incurable illness.

Characteristics of Suicide

When we try to understand the inner dynamics of the committed suicide, at the moment of its occurrence, we are often moved to ask, "What are the common characteristics of the self-destructive act?" We have often heard statements such as, "The suicide makes perfect sense at that particular moment to the person who accomplishes it." Assuming that this is true, however, the statement somehow begs the question. Shneidman (1985) made a substantial contribution toward clarifying what suicide is like when he formulated ten common characteristics occurring within an individual when the act is accomplished.

Shneidman's (1985, 1987) ten common characteristics are grouped under six aspects of suicide, which he calls *situational, conative, affective, cognitive, relational,* and *serial* (1985, pp. 121–149).

Situational characteristics: (1) "The common *stimulus* in suicide is unendurable psychological pain" (p. 124), and (2) "The common *stressor* in suicide is frustrated psychological needs" (p. 126).

Conative characteristics: (1) "The common *purpose* of suicide is to seek solution" (p. 129), and (2) "The common *goal* of suicide is cessation of consciousness" (pg. 129).

Affective characteristics: (1) "The common *emotion* in suicide is hopelessness–helplessness" (p. 131), and (2) "The common *internal attitude* toward suicide is ambivalence" (p. 135).

Cognitive characteristic: "The common *cognitive state* in suicide is constriction" (p. 138).

Relational characteristics: (1) "The common *interpersonal act* in suicide is communication of intention" (p. 143), and (2) "The common *action* in suicide is egression" (p. 144).

Serial characteristic: "The common *consistency* in suicide is with life-long coping patterns" (p. 147).

The characteristics of suicide are not meant to portray all suicides as being alike. In using the word *common*, Shneidman is careful to note that suicides, taken together, do reflect similarities. However, he also reminds us that each suicide is idiosyncratic; that there are no absolutes or universals (1985, pp. 121–122).

These characteristics are important dynamics in that they point us toward what makes sense to the individual about to embark on suicide. Commonalities contribute to our understanding even though suicidology is not a precise science.

Myths about Suicide

There are a number of commonly held myths about suicide that the crisis worker should know and take into account while assessing potentially suicidal clients (Shneidman, Farberow, & Litman, 1976, p. 130; Fujimura, Weis, & Cochran, 1985). These are some of the myths.

1. *Discussing suicide will cause the client to move toward doing it.* The opposite is generally true. Discussing it with an empathic person will more likely provide the client with a sense of relief and a desire to buy time to regain control.

2. *Clients who threaten suicide don't do it.* This is untrue. A large percentage of people who kill themselves have previously threatened it or disclosed their intent to others.

3. *Suicide is an irrational act.* Maybe so, but nearly all suicides and suicide attempts make *perfect sense* when viewed from the perspective of the persons doing them.

4. *Persons who commit suicide are insane.* Again, not so. Only a small percentage of persons attempting or committing suicide are psychotic or crazy. Most of them appear to be normal people who are severely depressed, lonely, hopeless, helpless, newly aggrieved, shocked, deeply disappointed, jilted, or otherwise overcome by some emotionally charged situation.

5. *Suicide runs in families—it is an inherited tendency.* This may appear, at times, to be true, but suicidal tendency is not inherited. It is either learned or situational.

6. *Once suicidal, always suicidal.* Again, this is untrue. A large proportion of people contemplate suicide at some time during their existence. Most of these individuals recover from the immediate threat, learn appropriate responses and controls, and live long, productive lives, free of the threat of self-inflicted harm.

7. *When a person has attempted suicide and pulls out of it, the danger is over.* This is not true. Probably the greatest period of danger is during the upswing period, when the suicidal person becomes energized following a period of severe depression. One danger signal is a period of euphoria following a depressed or suicidal episode. The appearance of being over the suicidal tendency and into a period of renewed vigor and high spirits may simply mean that the person has finally made a definite plan and has settled on a specific time. So, to the client, the euphoria is a sign that it is all settled and there is no need to worry about it any more. Such vigor and apparent well-being, coming immediately after a suicidal episode, is a signal to the crisis worker to be taken seriously and monitored closely, and it should be cause to question the client directly with the intention to uncover and deal with any new or revised plan the client has made, before it is too late.

8. *A suicidal person who begins to show generosity and share personal possessions is showing signs of renewal and recovery.* Not necessarily so. Many suicidal persons begin to dispose of their most prized possessions once they

experience enough upswing in energy to make a definite plan. Such disposal of personal effects is sometimes tantamount to acting out the last will and testament. Beware of recently suicidal clients who go around distributing their most valued and cherished belongings to friends. Their behavior may be indicative of another form of presuicidal euphoria.

9. *Suicide is always an impulsive act.* Not always. There are several types of suicide. Some involve impulsive actions. Some are very deliberately planned and carried out.

These are only a few of the myths about suicide. All of them are relevant to the crisis worker's assessment of a client's lethality. There are many factors to be considered in the complex arena of assessing suicide lethality level, which is not an exact area of assessment. The worker must be quite objective, sensitive, alert, and honest. The worker must also be ready to question, confront, and challenge the client in a caring, nonthreatening, empathic, but assertive way.

Dynamics of Suicide Assessment

Three categories of assessment dynamics that are of concern to workers who deal with suicidal clients are risk factors, suicidal clues, and cries for help. The reason we urge crisis workers to focus so much attention on these assessment dynamics is that most suicidal clients will manifest a number of them. A necessary part of the crisis worker's assessment function is to be able to pick up on the client's risk factors, clues, and cries for help.

Risk factors. Bernard and Bernard (1985), Gilliland (1985), and Hersh (1985) have identified a number of risk factors that may help the crisis worker in assessing suicidal potential. We recommend that the following list be used as a risk-assessment checklist. Whenever a person manifests four or five of these risks, that should be an immediate signal for the crisis worker to treat the person as a high risk in terms of suicide potential.

1. Client has a family history of suicide.
2. Client has a history of previous attempts.
3. Client has formulated a specific plan.
4. Client has experienced loss of a parent through death, divorce, or separation.
5. Client's family is destabilized as a result of loss.
6. Client is preoccupied with the anniversary of a particularly traumatic loss.
7. Client is psychotic.
8. Client has a history of drug and/or alcohol use.
9. Client is seriously depressed.
10. Client has a history of unsuccessful medical treatment or recent physical trauma.

11. Client is living alone and cut off from contact with others.
12. Client is coming out of depression or has recently been hospitalized for depression.
13. Client is giving away prized possessions or putting personal affairs in order.
14. Client displays *radical shifts* in characteristic behaviors or moods, such as apathy, withdrawal, isolation, irritability, panic, anxiety, or changed social habits, eating habits, or school or work habits.
15. Client is delusional, schizophrenic, or manic.
16. Client is experiencing a pervasive feeling of hopelessness/helplessness.
17. Client is preoccupied, troubled, or trapped by earlier episodes of experienced physical, emotional, or sexual abuse.
18. Client exhibits *profound degree of one or more emotions* such as anger, aggression, loneliness, guilt, hostility, grief, or disappointment, which are uncharacteristic of the individual's normal emotional behavior.

This risk-assessment checklist is supplementary to our previous discussion, despite a seeming overlap with the section on lethality in Chapter 2 or contradiction of what we said about suicide myths. The crisis worker must realize, however, that assessing suicide risk is no simple matter. There are no direct "if–then" connections. Some risk factors are more lethal than others and must be given more weight or attention. Assessment is a complex, ongoing art, science, and skill that requires workers to be alert, attentive, sensitive, caring, and practiced in attending and responding to verbal, behavioral, situational, and "syndromatic" clues. (The latter is Shneidman's term for constellations of syndromes. Shneidman, Farberow, & Litman, 1976, p. 433.)

Strother (1986) states that suicide is the third most common cause of death among persons between the ages of 15 and 24—accounting for more than 5000 deaths per year. She lists (p. 756) the following risk factors for young people in that age bracket:

1. a family history of alcohol and drug abuse
2. family breakdown (destabilized family situation)
3. symptoms of delinquency, aggression, or depression
4. nonspecific crises such as conflict with parents, peers, or school officials
5. impulsive responses to crisis or loss.

Some crisis centers and practitioners have developed weighted scales for crisis workers to use in assessing clients' suicide lethality. One such instrument, the *Scale for Assessment of Suicidal Potentiality* (Battle, 1985), is a checklist containing 121 weighted items in the 9 risk categories of (1) demographics, (2) symptoms of behavior, (3) stress, (4) resources outside of self, (5) personal and social history, (6) suicidal plan, (7) prior suicidal behavior, (8) suicidal communication, and (9) personality features and other clinical signs. Instruments such as the Battle scale are not meant to be highly precise, but they are quite helpful to crisis workers in evaluating and considering all the factors relevant to a client's total risk level.

Counseling in the realm of suicide intervention is no easy or simple matter. The dynamics and causes are so complex that no one has yet been able to develop completely successful and specific ways of assessing suicide risks or to devise strategies for counseling and prevention that will work in every case. From the enormous body of writing and research on the subject, we know enough about suicide to help people who are at risk if we can be aware of their crisis and can be in contact with them at the time of their greatest need. According to Fujimura, Weis, and Cochran (1985), people in the emotional vicinity of suicidal persons are in key positions for preventing suicides. The important thing is that those support persons (family members, crisis workers, counselors, teachers, and friends) learn to recognize, evaluate, and intervene whenever suicidal persons give off clues and cries for help (p. 613). It is also vital that support persons know enough to refer suicidal persons close to them to appropriate agencies or persons who can help them regain their precrisis state of equilibrium.

Suicidal clues. Most suicidal clients, feeling high levels of ambivalence or inner conflict, either emit some clues or hints about their serious troubles or call for help in some way (Shneidman, Farberow, & Litman, 1976, pp. 429–440). The clues may be verbal, behavioral, situational, or syndromatic. *Verbal clues* are spoken or written statements, which may be either direct ("I'm going to do it this time—kill myself") or indirect ("I'm of no use to anyone any more"). *Behavioral clues* may range from purchasing a grave marker for oneself to slashing one's wrist as a "practice run" or suicidal gesture. Even so, such behavioral clues are more often interpreted as "cries for help" than as genuine wishes to die (Shneidman, Farberow, & Litman, 1976, pp. 129, 432). *Situational clues* might include concerns over a wide array of conditions such as the death of a spouse, divorce, a painful physical injury or terminal illness, sudden bankruptcy, preoccupation with the anniversary of a loved one's death, or other drastic changes in one's life situation. *Syndromatic clues* include such constellations of suicidal symptoms as severe depression, loneliness, hopelessness, dependence, and dissatisfaction (Shneidman, Farberow, & Litman, 1976, pp. 431–434).

Cries for help. Fortunately for the crisis worker, nearly all suicidal persons reveal some kind of clues or cries for help. Some of the clues or cries for help are easy to recognize and some are very hard to identify. According to Shneidman, Farberow, and Litman (1976), no person is 100% suicidal. People with the strongest death wishes are invariably ambivalent, confused, and gasping for life (p. 128). Their emotions and their perspectives are paralyzed. Their patterns are illogical and their sense of available options is frozen in an all-or-nothing, black-or-white mode. They may be able to see only two alternatives—misery and death. They are typically unable to project themselves ahead to happier, more successful times. Each suicidal person is unique. Whether the crisis worker encounters a clue indicative of an outright strong desire to die or senses a subtle hopeless threat attendant to a suicidal gesture, it is still an essential component of assessment to identify the level of intent and lethality and intervene in an appropriate manner. People of all ages and circumstances cry out for help in definite but unique ways.

The assessment dynamics we have described can be translated into life-saving actions by crisis workers or anyone else in the physical or emotional proximity of suicidal persons. However, if the risk factors, clues, or cries for help go unnoticed or unrecognized, the chances for effective intervention are greatly reduced. The client problems in the selected cases in the next section contain many of the dynamics we have described. Recognition of and attention to suicidal risk factors, clues, and cries for help are the keys to the doors of intervention and counseling.

COUNSELING SUICIDAL CLIENTS

This section contains examples of general counseling strategies for suicidal children, adolescents, adults, and older adults. These strategies include attending to risk factors and clues in initial assessment and counseling. Case examples, emphasizing appropriate responses to cries for help, are used to illustrate counseling with clients of different ages.

Billy, age 11. In a group counseling session, children ages 9 to 12 (including Billy) were engaged in relaxation training, emotive imagery, and self-esteem building. The children were taking turns disclosing "a positive image" each was experiencing.

Billy had been rather quiet and complacent in previous counseling sessions.

Billy: I see myself beside the highway. There's a big 18-wheeler—going fast. I'm feeling like I'm gonna die. I want to die. I see myself jumping in front of it.

CW: Billy, it frightens me terribly to hear you say that! Could you and I talk about that after the others leave? And, Billy, I want you to know that I'm glad you didn't keep that image a secret from us. I'm sure we all want to help you to stay alive and to learn how to be safe.

The crisis worker was shaken and surprised at Billy's sudden, unexpected description of his images. The suicidal risk was assessed to be high because of the content and the context of the disclosure (the group activity had been clearly structured to facilitate sharing only positive, growth-promoting images, which other members of the group had done). Billy's nonverbal body posture and profoundly serious facial expression communicated that he was not fooling. The clues were sudden and definite. The crisis worker did not deny, refute, or admonish Billy. Recognizing that Billy was taking a great risk by disclosing his death wish, the worker responded by assuring Billy that he had received the message as sent and conveying to members of the group the worker's willingness to attend to and answer Billy's cry for help.

In Billy's case, the worker's attending to the cry for help precipitated several intervention strategies: (1) contact and counseling with Billy's parents, (2) evaluation of Billy's school situation and development of appropriate actions for the principal, counselor, and teachers to use in helping Billy, (3) immediate referral of Billy for medical evaluation, and (4) intensive individual therapy for Billy and family therapy for Billy and his parents.

Lester, age 14. Lester was an intelligent youngster who made good grades in school and had a reputation for being quiet, cooperative, and well behaved. Following his parents' bitter divorce, while living with his mother and a younger sister and brother, Lester began to get into trouble in school because of his overt acting out and belligerent behavior. He lost interest in his studies and school activities and his grades began to tumble. He became rebellious with his mother, and his appetite decreased to the degree that he just picked at his food. He became very withdrawn—seldom leaving his room—in contrast to his previous behavior of being actively engaged in outside activities whenever possible.

Lester's mother and the school counselor decided to place him in a student support group consisting of male and female middle school students, all of whom were experiencing severe difficulty following the separation and/ or divorce of their parents. At the conclusion of one of the group sessions, Lester asked to speak with the crisis worker.

CW: Lester, sounds like something happened in the group today that got pretty close to you.

Lester: (Hesitant; looking down; nervous.) I . . . I've been feeling weird lately. Strange. Like I'm somewhere else.

CW: You mean like you're outside your own body observing yourself?

Lester: Yeah. Even at night. I don't understand it. I've even thought I might be going crazy.

CW: (Closely observing Lester's body language.) Lester, it sounds like this is so serious you may have even been wishing you were dead.

Lester: Yeah. I've been scared. I've just thought about how it would be to just go to sleep and not wake up.

CW: Have you thought about making that happen? Killing yourself, so that you'd never wake up?

Lester: Thought about it, yeah. Thought about it more lately.

The crisis worker had sensed prior to the interview that Lester might be suicidal. The clues were there before he cried out for help. Lester's changing family life, his changing behavior and attitudes, his body language, his eating habits, his social habits, his grades—any one of these alone would have been an important signal. At least five indicators on the risk-assessment checklist pointed to the conclusion that Lester was suicidal. The worker continued the session, attending to Lester's safety needs. Once Lester's immediate safety was ensured, a crisis intervention team developed the long-term referrals that Lester needed. The crisis intervention team consisted of Lester's counselor, guidance supervisor, homeroom teacher, principal, school psychologist (the crisis worker), and mother. It addressed the areas of family, medical assessment, school, and personal needs.

Jennifer, age 17. Jennifer was terrified. Although she had suffered from depression, loneliness, and low self-esteem for several years, she had managed to have a satisfactory social life, maintain average grades in school, and regain her equilibrium following each depressive episode. Several stressors during the past year combined to complicate and disrupt her life. Her parents' separation and divorce were unexpected and bitter. Her maternal grandmother, to whom she had been very close, died from rapidly moving intestinal cancer. Jennifer was living with her mother and two younger sisters. The mother began dating a single man and permitted him to move in with them. Jennifer changed schools during the middle of the year when her parents' original home was sold. Due to her lack of social adjustment and academic achievement in the new school, Jennifer was placed in a support group at the school and was also seen regularly by an individual counselor.

Following a weekend episode of severe depression, Jennifer was terrified, physically and emotionally exhausted, pale, and withdrawn.

CW: Jennifer, it frightens me to see you this way. What's happening to cause you so much pain right now?

The crisis worker could see the physical and emotional devastation Jennifer was feeling. It was important to communicate to Jennifer the worker's affective concern and to provide a direct and open opportunity for Jennifer to feel safe and to respond. The crisis worker's voice and body language provided Jennifer with reassuring clues: the worker was calm, sensitive, caring, genuine, and accurate in gauging Jennifer's situation; there were no barriers, facades, pity, or other negative clues. Immediately, Jennifer felt accepted and valued.

Jennifer: (After a long pause, in a very low, subdued voice.) I . . . I've never been this scared before in my life. (Pause.) All weekend I've been at the end of my rope. I've just thought, "There's no use going on anymore."

CW: Well, Jennifer, I'm glad you're here now. And that we have this time together right now. Tell me what's happening to cause you to feel like not going on anymore.

The crisis worker wanted to get at the events or sources of Jennifer's present crisis.

Jennifer: It all started Saturday when my daddy came by the apartment. He was really mad when he saw Ronnie with my mom. He was going to kill them both, he said. Mom called the police. Four squad cars came. It was an awful mess. I was very embarrassed for all the neighbors to see my family like this. I feel like we kids are just in the way. It would be better if we'd never been born. I just don't think I can stand any more of this.

CW: So the weekend confrontation was so bad you wished you were not even here to see it. Jennifer, I want you to know that I'm glad you're here now and that we're talking. The very first thing I want us to do is talk about any suicidal feelings you're having now so that I can rest easy knowing you're safe. We can then talk and plan together about what we can do right now and in the future to ensure your safety.

We can also make plans to help you cope with your fears and loneliness. Now that you and I are safely talking about it, tell me what you think about when you wish you had never been born.

The crisis worker was struggling to listen accurately to Jennifer and assess her level of lethality. The worker also wanted to know the extent of Jennifer's mobility in order to make a judgment about whether to provide supports in a directive, collaborative, or nondirective way. Finally, the worker attempted to lead Jennifer to view her suicidal plans as being in the past, so that they could go forward together, perceiving the weekend episode and the current suicidal crisis as a receding rather than a looming condition. The worker's interaction with Jennifer over the course of several days resulted in Jennifer's restored emotional and social mobility. The worker was successful in getting Jennifer referred for psychiatric evaluation and care.

Ruby, age 21. Ruby was a senior in a large university. She achieved average grades through college except for her freshman year. During her freshman year at a small liberal arts college she had experienced an emotional and suicidal breakdown as the anniversary date of her older sister's suicide approached. She left the small college, returned home, and underwent psychiatric treatment. Ruby later enrolled in the university in her home town, where she lived in a residence hall. She went home frequently but managed to succeed fairly well in her studies and social life. Ruby was referred to the crisis worker by her mother following a weekend mother–daughter discussion during which Ruby disclosed some recurring suicidal ideations to her mother. The mother expressed concern that the fifth anniversary of the sister's suicide seemed to be looming in Ruby's mind and asked the crisis worker to call Ruby in for a conference. During the first interview with Ruby, the worker established that Ruby did not have a specific, highly lethal plan, but that she did have a lot of suicidal ruminations.

Ruby: I think Mother thinks I'm crazy. Sometimes I wonder if she's right. (Long pause.) It's weird, you calling me in this way. Do you think I may be going crazy?

CW: No, I certainly don't. What I'm hearing is a lot of confusion and unsettled emotion. I'm glad you feel comfortable enough to ask me. I'm wondering what's happening in you to bring up the question.

Ruby: Well, as I told you before, I've just been sitting in the room by myself, staring at the wall. Not sleeping, not eating, not going out. And I've had this strange sensation—of both wanting to run and scream, and just giving up. And I've thought about my sister's death constantly. More than at any time since I was a freshman. It's like I'm destined to go the way she went. Sometimes I think I can't stand it any longer. Then I catch myself and wonder if I *am* crazy.

Ruby's mother cried out for help. As a result, Ruby received the treatment she needed. She got over the fifth anniversary of her sister's suicide, thanks to an alert and sensitive mother and a team of competent professional workers in her university and community. The sessions between Ruby and the crisis worker led to the establishment of a network of supports for her. Eventually Ruby recovered from her depression and provided valuable assistance to the counseling center in setting up suicide support groups and in helping with several programs to educate students, faculty, and staff regarding suicide awareness and counseling. Ruby graduated from college and became successful in her career. She admitted that she probably would never have reentered counseling if her mother had not intervened during the critical time of her senior year.

Deborah, age 27. Deborah had been in therapy, off and on, for eleven years—since she was 16. She had been hospitalized as an inpatient in psychiatric wards several times as a result of suicide attempts and/or suicidal threats. Because her regular therapist was out of town, Deborah was referred to the crisis worker on an emergency basis because of a suicide threat. During the early part of the interview, Deborah told the worker that she (1) had a history of suicide attempts, some of them serious, some of them gestures; (2) had used a wide variety of drugs in her college years—in fact, she had dropped out of college after two years because of drug use and resulting poor academic performance; (3) had a history of episodes of severe depression, loneliness, hopelessness, and helplessness followed by mood swings to euphoric and deep religious activity and commitment; (4) had been hospitalized numerous times for psychiatric care; (5) had experienced a sense of great loss and grief at the divorce of her parents when she was 22 years old; (6) had recently gone into self-imposed isolation and remorse—cutting herself off from friends, family, and co-workers; (7) was feeling a new sense of meaninglessness related to her career—she had been seeking something that she really chose to do (as opposed to working for her father). In relation to point 7, the crisis worker learned that Deborah had, all her life, sought to both appease and oppose her father; that Deborah now worked as a real estate salesperson in her father's firm; that Deborah had obtained her realtor license to please her father, yet constantly blamed him for keeping her bonded to him; that Deborah had both resented and appreciated the fact that her father planned for her to inherit and manage the lucrative real estate brokerage firm at the time of his retirement; that Deborah had vacillated between gratitude for inheriting a lot of money and security and resentment of her father's dominating her and deciding her career for her. Deborah, in tears, was trembling and in a state of acute anxiety.

CW: So, Deborah, I'm picking up that you're right back again at the very brink of death. How specific is your suicide plan this time, and how close are you today—to doing it?

Deborah: Well, I can see you've zeroed right in. I was halfway hoping you wouldn't ask that. Well, I might as well tell you, I've got it mapped out to a T . . . have had for some time now. I'm just going to end the hurting . . . just end it all. . . .

CW: Deborah, when? And how?

Deborah: Simple . . . easy . . . and smooth! I'm gonna do it with exhaust fumes. And I don't know just when. Soon, though . . . very soon.

The crisis worker was having a difficult time remaining calm. Deborah's risk factors and nonverbal clues were too numerous and too lethal to take a chance on making a contract with her and letting her leave. Over Deborah's verbal protests, the crisis worker took the necessary steps of contacting Deborah's regular therapist's consulting psychiatrist, who was on call for emergencies. The psychiatrist knew Deborah, had treated her on previous occasions, and agreed to meet Deborah and the worker at the hospital. The worker drove with Deborah to the hospital, where the doctor had already arranged by phone for her admission.

The crisis worker had correctly assessed Deborah's lethality and appropriately used directive methods to get her to safety and help. That's about all the crisis worker could do when presented with Deborah's lethal situation. Even though the hospital and psychiatric staff did everything they knew to do to help Deborah, she carried out her plan a few weeks later, following her release from the hospital. She killed herself with exhaust fumes just as she had said she would. She left several suicide notes in her bedroom. All the professionals and crisis workers who had known and cared for Deborah were saddened and felt a deep sense of grief and loss. But they did not blame themselves. Few felt guilt. They tried to listen, learn, and appreciate Deborah's life and her messages. They vowed to go on working with their living clients and learning to be better helpers. They also participated in the post-suicide mental health team staffings both for their own mental health and for documentation and research, so they would know how to deal more effectively with future "Deborahs."

Gertrude, age 61. Gertrude was an eminent and successful primary school principal who had devoted her life to children and the teaching profession. She was exceptionally capable, hard working, conscientious, and efficient. She was also compulsive and perfectionistic in her work and personal habits. At age 61, Gertrude faced some life and career decisions that she regarded as catastrophic: (1) she had been "cured" of TB only to discover she had cancer of the colon, and she could not bear to think about her physician's recommendation to accept early retirement, for which she had been qualified since age 55; (2) she felt trapped between the two unacceptable choices of continuing to hold the principalship in her debilitating physical condition and becoming the ex-principal who had been forced into early retirement; and (3) she was totally unprepared to alter her whole identity, which had included serving the students, faculty, parents, community, school, and the teaching profession. Gertrude had no family. She had never married because she had devoted all her energies and talents to education. She came to the crisis worker in desperation. The dialogue took place some ten minutes into the initial interview.

Gertrude: (In tears.) It is so hopeless. Why me? Why has God forsaken me? What have I done to cause me to come to this? I don't think I can bear it. (Sobs. Pause.) It's so unfair. I have no choice. (Sobs.)

CW: You're feeling hurt, hopeless, and vulnerable—and you're looking for better answers and choices than you've been able to find so far.

Gertrude: (Still in tears.) I guess I'm just getting too old and cranky to do this job.

CW: Well, Gertrude, I want you to know that I'm glad you have the courage to discuss it. And I don't view you as being old and cranky. What scares me is the desperation and danger you're feeling. You're feeling that, right now, there are no acceptable choices, but what you'd like to find are some choices other than pain and oblivion in your future.

Gertrude: (Still in tears; nonverbal clues show that she is experiencing acute fear, anxiety, and hopelessness, and has almost given up.) There is no future. There are no choices. None. None at all.

CW: Gertrude, it sounds to me like you've considered suicide. I feel a need to know your thinking on this subject.

Gertrude: (Still in tears.) Oh God! I've thought about that a lot. Toyed with it a lot. And I'll have to admit that it becomes more appealing all the time.

The crisis worker did not suddenly jump to the conclusion that Gertrude was suicidal. As the crisis interview progressed, more and more of the background clues, verbal clues, and nonverbal clues pointed toward suicide. When Gertrude said, "There is no future," the worker immediately judged that her words and her nonverbal signs of desperation must not be ignored or pushed aside. The alertness and forthright response of the crisis worker provided the pivotal point from which to help start Gertrude on her way out of her desperate course toward oblivion. Crisis counseling was followed by medical and psychiatric referrals. Long-term therapy was required to bring Gertrude from the brink of self-destruction to the point where she could come to accept the unacceptable—medical retirement, life away from the school, and steadily deteriorating physical health. The choices in cases like Gertrude's are never simple or easy. Crisis workers, therapists, and medical professionals cannot completely solve problems in such difficult situations. The best they can do is to listen, assess, care, understand, and intervene in ways as objective and appropriate as humanly possible.

Roy, age 75. Roy had been a farmer all his life. At age 73 he went into semiretirement, turning his land, equipment, buildings, and livestock over to his two sons, who also were career farmers. One year after he began his semiretirement, his wife died. About a year later, he was despondent and could find no purpose in life even though he was in excellent health and had the good fortune of financial independence. The dialogue occurred after several minutes in the initial interview.

Roy: Well, I never did think I'd be in here talking to you.

CW: Roy, I can understand that. You're obviously very self-sufficient. I'd be curious to know—just what brought you in to talk today?

Roy: That's just it. Nothing. That is, no one thing. But it's everything too. My world has changed. There's nothing left for me. I'm really not needed any more.

CW: So it's your whole life situation that brings you here. Any one thing? Any one happening or situation in particular that stands out today to make life so meaningless?

Roy: Well, nothing but just pure loneliness—and the fact that my usefulness is over. All my life is in the past.

CW: It's true that you've accomplished a great deal during your life. Right now it sounds like you're feeling that *all* your life is over. And the fact that you've taken the time to come in to talk about it tells me that you've very serious about it. What's different for you now from, say, six months or a year ago?

Roy: Well, now there's really nothing else to live for. A man's got to have some purpose. I've got nothing to go to—nothing to get up for in the morning.

CW: Then the situation sounds so bad and so hopeless for you that it sounds to me like you're considering ending it all. Are you thinking about killing yourself?

Roy: You bet I am! It's a wonder I'm even here now. I've been close to it many times lately.

The crisis worker followed the usual procedure of attempting to discover the specificity of Roy's plan, the time, place, and so on, as a means of assessing Roy's imminent risk. Roy proved to have a definite plan.

Roy: When I do it, I won't be fooling around. I've got a good, stout rope down there in the barn. It will do the job. No doubt about it. That barn loft is high and those beams are sound. There'll be no way to miss. That'll do the job all right. And it will be early in the morning. If I do it, it'll be soon. It'll be at the end of another one of my long, sleepless nights. I'll be the only one around.

In assessing Roy's responses the worker quickly concluded that he definitely exhibited six of the lethality characteristics that Fujimura, Weis, and Cochran (1985) defined as high-risk factors: (1) the plan was definite and readily accessible, (2) the method was irreversible, (3) there was indication of sleep disruption, (4) support persons would not be around, (5) rescue would not be probable, and (6) the most valued possessions had been disposed of. Also, the crisis worker knew that among men Roy's age there are very few suicidal gestures or attempts. They are more likely to accomplish the act than to merely attempt it (Shneidman, Farberow, & Litman, 1976). The worker knew that this was a life-or-death situation and that there was little time to act. A person as fiercely independent as Roy would not easily go to see a crisis worker or therapist; that person would more than likely go to the barn and hang himself and be done with it! The worker, who managed to get Roy referred for medical evaluation and long-term psychiatric care, felt that it was fortunate that Roy had come in for help in the first place.

Dennis, age 88. Dennis had a long, productive, and successful career as a carpenter. He and his wife had reared seven children. Dennis worked until he was 70 and remained physically alert and healthy until he was 84, at which time he had a stroke that paralyzed the right half of his body from head to toe. Following his partial recovery and release from the hospital, he gradually regained a small percentage of the psychomotor control of the impaired right half of his body. His hearing loss, which had been getting progressively worse over a number of years, declined to the point where he had a serious hearing deficit. It became increasingly difficult for him to communicate. He became feeble and slow at walking, but he refused to use a cane or a walker. Since his seven children were involved in plying their own careers and rearing their own families, Dennis became totally dependent on his wife,

Millie, age 81. Although his wife was in relatively good health and of sound mental status, the situation became quite serious. Maintaining the household and providing total care for her husband quickly became a greater responsibility than she was able to assume.

Dennis became more and more withdrawn; he refused to exercise, he refused to go out of the house except to go to the doctor; he became self-conscious about his unsteady pattern of walking; and he soon began to make statements such as, "I'm no good to anyone now," "I should have just passed on instead of being left like I am," "People would be better off without me around," and "Some day I may just take that rifle and end it all." At first his wife, children, and grandchildren attempted to refute him and discount such statements. Finally, Dennis was taken to the family physician, who prescribed medication to deal with his suicidal symptoms. Nothing was done to provide psychiatric, psychotherapeutic, or physical therapy treatment. Dennis became even more withdrawn, he slept most of the time, and he lost interest in much of the family activity.

Following one of his verbally expressed wishes to die, the crisis worker was summoned for a home visit. The worker began by obtaining permission for a private interview with Dennis. The worker was sensitive to Dennis's hearing loss and also judged by Dennis's body language that Dennis would respond to the crisis worker's sitting close and physically touching him. The worker sat very close to Dennis, took him by the hand, and gently stroked the back side of the impaired but sensitive right hand and arm as they talked. The worker used a very loud, clear, calm, and even voice to talk with Dennis. The worker sought to provide clear, nonthreatening, caring messages combined with the gentle physical stroking. Dennis responded positively. The worker provided long periods of time for Dennis to formulate ideas and speak them. (Family members had rarely waited for Dennis to respond. They would ask him a question, and, before he was able to respond, would go on to something else. Dennis felt that they ignored him and that he was being treated like a retarded child.) The worker was able to establish good rapport with Dennis.

CW: (Loudly, while gently stroking Dennis.) So, you are feeling like you aren't being listened to lately, and you really do miss talking to people.

Dennis: (Long pause; eyes and facial expression show him formulating a response.) Yeah. They . . . won't . . . wait . . . for . . . me to finish. Some . . . won't wait . . . for me to start.

CW: What you'd like is for someone to let you talk at your own speed. It bothers you for them to "run off and leave you."

Dennis: (Long pause; tears in his eyes.) I . . . guess it's hard . . . for them to . . . to talk to me. I . . . have to have time . . . to get it . . . out.

CW: (Still gently stroking, looking him in the eyes, and waiting for his responses.) It makes you feel sad, not to be understood. You really want people to take time to hear what you have to say.

Dennis: (Tears in his eyes; long pause.) I guess they . . . don't think . . . I . . . have . . .

anything . . . worth saying. I'm . . . so . . . old and stove up . . . guess I'm no account now.

CW: Being, as you say, "stove up" doesn't mean you're worth any less. They tell me you've built lots of this town with your own hands. You've accomplished lots of things in your life, which you must be proud of. Tell me something you've done, which really makes you proud you did it.

Dennis: (Long pause; thoughtful; no tears; smiles.) I've . . . raised . . . helped raise . . . a bunch of fine children. . . . I've been a good dad . . . a good provider.

CW: (Still gently stroking.) That's true, I'm sure. I want you to think back to raising those kids. Think back to the happiest times you had with your growing kids, and just imagine you're back there now. Just take your mind back. Tell me exactly what you're doing with them that makes you feel good—a good daddy.

Dennis: (Long pause; smile; look of intensity and reminiscence.) We'd all go down to the . . . swimming hole . . . on Sunday afternoon. . . . We took a basket of . . . of sandwiches . . . and melons . . . and a great big ball. We . . . we played games . . . their mother . . . Millie and I . . . we'd play all kinds of games . . . big ones . . . little ones. . . . All the children . . . running, playing, squealing. . . . Yeah, . . . (Laughs.) . . . all sorts of games. . . . We had a time! . . . Millie and I . . . we had some good times with those children . . . had a real good time . . . a good life.

The worker continued using what are called *reminiscence techniques* (Ebersole, 1976a, 1976b). Many interesting facets of Dennis's past were highlighted, remembered, and relished: family, carpentry, social life, travel, hardships. His whole life was reviewed and appreciated. These reminiscence techniques (American Association of Retired People, 1986) have been used quite effectively in working with many elderly people—to strengthen their sense of value of how their life has been lived. The worker went back to see Dennis several times and used the reminiscence technique during a part of each visit. The worker was able to facilitate several productive strategies to help Dennis: part-time help was hired to assist with the daily care of Dennis; physical therapy was prescribed by the family physician to enhance Dennis's muscular functioning; a counselor provided communications skills that the family members could learn, including verbal and nonverbal skills, delayed responding, and touching; and the crisis worker called in a gerontologist, who taught family members how to use the reminiscence technique with their father. The crisis worker did not ignore the suicide threats that Dennis voiced. Along with reminiscence, Dennis was encouraged to talk about his self-destructive feelings. Finally, the family counselor held a group session concerning the suicide issue, after which Dennis never mentioned it again.

Assessing and responding to cries for help from the elderly are difficult and delicate tasks. They normally involve friends, relatives, and support persons from several age groups and disciplines. Workers aren't always successful. Work with the elderly must invariably take into account their age, physical impairments, experiences, and needs. Even though they are unique, they are reachable, responsive, and appreciative. The crisis worker who visited Dennis made a statement that is typical of those who develop a closeness and rapport with the elderly: "I can truly say that I received much more from

Dennis than I gave. I was blessed and enriched by the experience. I think I learned more than he did."

INTERVENTION STRATEGIES

Suicide intervention involves the set of strategies that "consists of interrupting a suicide attempt that is imminent or in the process of occurring" (Fujimura, Weis, & Cochran, 1985, p. 612). Since every person and every problem situation are unique, every suicidal situation is also unique. There are no clear, simple strategies that are recommended for every case. In this chapter's section on assessment, we purposely showed the crisis worker moving from assessing to acting. That is the way crisis intervention works—in a fluid, ongoing, emerging process. We now present an encapsulation of some additional strategies that crisis workers might use in continuing to intervene with the eight representative clients we have described.

Children and Adolescents

The actions of the crisis workers in the cases of Billy, age 11, Lester, age 14, and Jennifer, age 17, are good examples to keep in mind. Suicides of children and adolescents have received increasing attention from the public. Here are some of the strategies most commonly suggested by psychologists in the media ("Teenage Suicide," 1985) for anyone (crisis worker or layperson) who comes in contact with a child or adolescent suspected of being suicidal:

1. Trust your suspicions that the young person may be self-destructive.
2. Tell the person you're worried about them, then listen to the person.
3. Ask direct questions, including whether the youngster is thinking about suicide and, if so, has a plan. *GET SPECIFIC !!!*
4. Don't act shocked at what the youngster tells you. Don't debate whether suicide is right or wrong, or counsel the person yourself if you're not qualified. Don't promise to keep the youngster's intentions a secret.
5. Don't leave the youngster alone if you think the risk of suicide is immediate.
6. If necessary, get help from a competent counselor, therapist, or other responsible adult ("Teenage Suicide," 1985, p. E3).
7. Ensure that the youngster is safe and that the appropriate adults responsible for the youngster are notified and become actively involved with the youngster.
8. Assure the youngster that something is being done, that the youngster's suicidal urges are real, and that, in time, the emergency will pass. Advise the youngster not to expect the urges to disappear right away. Rather, apprise him or her that survival is a step-by-step, day-to-day process; that help is at hand; and that calling for help in a direct manner is necessary whenever the impulsive suicidal urge gets strong.

9. Assume as active and authoritarian a role as needed to protect the person at risk. The youngster may need such directive action to enable him or her to become sufficiently involved with support persons to resume self-responsibility.

10. After the youngster has apparently resolved the high-risk crisis, monitor the progress very closely. Many persons have been known to suddenly commit suicide after they seemed to be renewed and strong. Remember that previously depressed suicidal clients may decide to kill themselves once they gain enough energy to do it. Helping persons must continue to be proactive and involved with suicidal youngsters until the apparent danger has definitely subsided (Fujimura, Weis, & Cochran, 1985, pp. 612–613).

Crisis workers, counselors, and other adults who work with youngsters must pay attention to the real clues rather than trusting their own desires and hopes.

CW: Lester, I asked for this conference because I'm worried about you again. I thought you were doing great! And I hoped you could keep it up, but now, frankly, I'm scared to death for you.

Lester: Oh, I'm OK. Things are going great.

CW: (In a calm, soft, caring, empathic voice—not a lecturing or agitated tone.) They may seem OK to you, but what concerns me right now is the amount and direction of energy you're spending lately. Your mother is very upset and puzzled because you've given your stereo to a friend and the principal is livid because you've picked two fights on the way home from school this week. I've noticed that the last two days in the hallways and cafeteria you've been like an entirely different person. I don't know what's behind these observations, but if these things say what they appear to say, I don't think I can leave here today until I can be sure you're safe. I don't want to wake up in the morning and hear that you're dead!

Lester: It's really not anything you should be worried about. I'm OK, really I am.

CW: (Soft, empathic vocal tone continued.) Fine, then you can help me feel OK by discussing with me what's going on because, if these observations are even partially true, your actions have really taken an unusual turn. I just want you to know that the clues I'm picking up spell danger, and that I'm as concerned for you as I've ever been. And I need to know that you're safe, even though you say you're OK. I really care about you.

The crisis worker was confrontive and persistent even though it would have been desirable and comforting to believe that Lester was "OK." As it turned out, Lester was indeed on the threshold of suicide again. Fortunately, the worker reinstituted the necessary medical and therapeutic referrals needed to help Lester. The important thing was that the worker interpreted Lester's unusual and energetic actions as clues that called for help—whether the client overtly called for help or not. It was also fortunate for Lester that the worker acted directively and decisively to intervene in his life again. The clues and calls for help may take many forms in children and adolescents.

Workers must be alert and proactive in checking out the clues and intervening whenever and however it is needed to stem the suicidal plans of youngsters. Suicidal youngsters need to know that adults are available who will respond in mature, sensitive, responsible, and caring ways.

Adults

When we speak of intervention we are referring to those procedures and actions that the crisis worker employs to interrupt a suicide attempt that is imminent or in the process of occurring. Nearly all the intervention strategies applicable to children and adolescents may also be appropriate for adults, so there's no need to repeat them. It should be mentioned that intervention in suicidal behavior sometimes raises complex philosophical questions about the individual's right to commit suicide (Zinner, 1985, p. 75). For example, does a terminally ill cancer patient have a right to die with dignity, through an act of suicide, to avoid prolonged pain and suffering? Also, in institutional settings, the worker should be sensitive to the legal and ethical issues that may arise when one adult intervenes in the suicidal behavior of another (Bernard & Bernard, 1980, 1982).

The intervention strategies employed in the cases of Ruby, age 21, and Deborah, age 27, provide some representative examples of crisis work with adults. Even though Ruby was a young adult, in college, her responses, emotions, and needs were those of an adult. Most of the counseling and treatment strategies used by Ruby's crisis worker have wide applicability to adult clients in general. There are no panaceas in crisis intervention, counseling, and methodology, but there are things that can help.

The following considerations provide both attitudinal and behavioral guidelines for crisis workers who are involved in suicide work with adult clients. Most of them may also apply to younger or older populations, but they are particularly appropriate for intervening with adults. We have incorporated a number of considerations from our own repertory of guidance tips along with those of other contributors (Bernard & Bernard, 1985; Gilliland, 1985; Hersh, 1985; Hipple, 1985; Hipple & Cimbolic, 1979; Hipple & Hipple, 1983). These suggestions have implications for crisis workers, community and media, educational, training, and mental health institutions, and family, friends, and associates.

Considerations for crisis workers. At the beginning of the interview, the crisis worker must establish a sense of rapport and trust right away in order to create a working relationship and provide clients with an anchor to life. It is also important to begin to reestablish in clients a sense of hope and to diminish their sense of helplessness—to take immediate steps to speak and act on the clients' current pain. The worker will want to look for the hidden messages behind the suicidal behavior, trying to discover what the behavior in its simplest form is saying and to whom. In many instances it is necessary to establish stay-alive contracts that provide clients with some concrete and immediate structure.

Another area of importance is to help clients discover their ambivalence and ambiguity: part of them may be oriented toward self-destruction and part toward living. The worker can help clients clarify and understand the real but opposing poles of existence.

Always, client safety is primary. Even though confidentiality of the suicidal person's communication is important, confidentiality must be reconsidered if life is at risk. The crisis worker must consider whether important others need to be contacted to gather information, rally community support, or establish a network of support persons interested in and committed to keeping the client alive.

The crisis worker can use history taking to evaluate the client's developmental background and show how the current suicidal crisis evolved. The worker can also determine whether the crisis is situational or systemic; that is, do the roots go deep into the client's personal history? The worker can be as directive, active, or collaborative as the crisis situation dictates. One point to remember is to follow up on missed appointments. The suicidal person must not be ignored. During the crisis interview itself, the crisis worker must attend to the client's verbal or behavioral cries for help. Ignoring these cries may be interpreted by the client as confirmation of a feeling of worthlessness.

The crisis worker should realize that suicidal behavior is a symptom of complex interactions of biological, psychological, and sociological factors. Different clients may require different strategies. Many clients will respond to cognitive strategies. The worker may assist those suicidal persons to (1) separate thought from action, (2) reinforce expression of affect, (3) anticipate consequences of action, and (4) focus on precipitating events and constructive alternatives.

Crisis workers must be prepared to provide simple, clear-cut, and appropriate referral sources. Clients may need access to a central telephone number for crisis referral. Clients may need a safe place to stay where overnight observation is available. A repertory of referral resources is a necessity if the crisis worker is to be effective with suicidal clients.

Considerations for community and media.   The community and the local media can be instrumental in helping to stem the tide of loss of life by suicide. The channels of public information (newspapers, radio, television, newsletters, and other networks) can be used to educate the total population, communicating the essential information, attitudes, and behaviors needed to deal with suicide. Of particular importance is to get the message across to the community that all suicidal behavior (ideation, gestures, threats, or attempts) can result in completed suicides, and thus must be taken seriously.

The community and media can establish and support crisis hot lines and advertise suicide and crisis intervention services as a first line of help for troubled persons. They can also ensure that emergency shelters for safe overnight observation and support are available for persons who find themselves in temporary suicidal or severe crisis situations. Another source of help in almost every community is its religious organizations.

The media can serve as advocates to counter the fears, myths, prejudices, and punitive attitudes that may exist toward suicidal persons and their families. The media can have a positive influence by showing the realities of suicide and appropriate ways of preventing and responding to it.

Considerations for institutions. Educational, training, and mental health institutions in the community can do much to prevent and respond to the phenomenon of suicide. A starting point is assessing the existing knowledge and attitudes about suicide in the community. Institutions need (1) to become familiar with research, legal, and ethical issues involved in suicides and to disseminate relevant information to the community and its leaders and (2) to engage in the research and exchange of data on suicide prevention and intervention. They can sponsor educational programs and transmit information on suicide awareness, risks, prevention, and intervention to the public, to work places, and to community agencies.

Institutions can provide educational leadership to help reduce suicides. Such leadership might result in providing lectures on potential suicides, risks, indicators, gauging lethality, causes, and so forth, in adult education courses and in instructional areas such as counseling, psychology, social work, sociology, home economics, marriage and family therapy, and others. The institutions can also establish peer support groups of persons who have survived suicidal urges and attempts and who are willing to share their knowledge and experience to help others. To a large degree, institutions can also teach and encourage empathic responses to suicidal persons by family, friends, co-workers, and peers.

One of the most important roles that institutions can play is helping to train volunteers, paraprofessionals, and community support persons to deal with suicidal persons. Suicidal persons may be encountered anywhere at any time. A trained citizenry is a great asset. Institutions can also provide a ready mechanism for the hospitalization of the acutely suicidal person. Institutions responsible for suicidal clients should provide for close follow-up of acute cases after discharge from the hospital—for at least 90 days following the high-risk period. And finally, they should provide appropriate procedures for notifying and dealing with family, associates, and friends who were close to the person who completed the suicide act.

Considerations for family, friends, and associates. The family, friends, and associates of the suicidal person can do many things to contribute to prevention as well as coping with acts of suicide. They can focus on prevention by correcting the alienated lifestyle that cuts off the suicidal person's connectedness with others. They can learn and become attuned to the risk factors, cues, and cries for help that suicidal persons generally display in some way.

Family, friends, and associates can provide the suicidal person with permission to live and accept himself or herself: the suicidal person may need to hear directly that he or she is a person of value and worth and therefore deserves to live. They can also help the suicidal person to gain permission to be human—to accept his or her own fallibility and to give up perfectionism. This may mean that people around the suicidal person learn to deal with the suicidal person's perception of loss and despair without encouraging helplessness or dependency.

Family, friends, and associates who attend to the many cues we have described can help the suicidal person by genuinely and assertively confronting suicidal issues. For instance, they can watch for the suicidal person's preoccupation with an anniversary date of a significant loss, such as the death of a loved one, and intervene in a directive manner if needed. Finally, significant others can help the survivors cope with suicide after it happens. When bereaved groups cannot get past the shock of the suicide and/or exhibit excessive blame or guilt, someone should meet with them and talk about their grief over the loss.

Some don'ts. Hipple (1985) has identified some don'ts of suicide management that also serve to supplement the intervention considerations we have listed:

1. Don't lecture, blame, or preach to clients.
2. Don't criticize clients or their choices or behaviors.
3. Don't debate the pros and cons.
4. Don't be misled by the client's telling you the crisis is past.
5. Don't deny the client's suicidal ideas.
6. Don't try to challenge for shock effects.
7. Don't leave the client isolated, unobserved, and disconnected.
8. Don't diagnose and analyze behavior or confront the client with interpretations during the acute phase.
9. Don't be passive.
10. Don't overreact. Keep calm.
11. Don't keep the client's suicidal risk a secret (be trapped in the confidentiality issue).
12. Don't get sidetracked on extraneous or external issues or persons.
13. Don't glamorize, martyrize, glorify, or deify suicidal behavior in others, past or present.
14. Don't forget to follow up.

Older Adults

All the strategies for helping suicidal clients, from children through adults, are valuable assets in helping older adults, such as Gertrude, age 61, Roy, age 75, and Dennis, age 88. The crisis worker must keep in mind what research into the age factor among suicidal clients has shown: "In general, for both sexes, the intensity of the wish to kill and the wish to be killed decreases with advancing age, while the intensity of the wish to die increases with age" (Shneidman, Farberow, & Litman, 1976, p. 165). The research indicates that the percentage of "failed" attempted suicides decreases with age and the percentage of "successes" increases with age. It would seem that workers may have fewer second chances at helping persons above 60 than they would normally expect among youths and younger adults.

In intervening with older adults, workers should pay particular attention to all forms of verbal and behavioral gestures that might be clues to suicidal risk. The worker's own silent assessment during the interview helps bring to the forefront a special consideration for dealing with older persons. An excerpt from an interview with Roy, age 75 (showing parenthetical worker self-talk), is one example.

Roy: Well, now there's really nothing else to live for. A man's got to have some purpose. I've got nothing to go to—nothing to get up for in the morning.

CW: ("Wow, he's not fooling! I'm remembering his age, his male image, his having disposed of all his property, his wife's death—it's a wonder he's even in here talking about it. I sense how lethal he may be. I'm thankful he's here. I'd better not take any chances now.") Then the situation sounds so bad and so hopeless for you that it sounds to me like you're considering ending it all. Are you thinking about killing yourself?

Roy: You bet I am! It's a wonder I'm even here now. I've been close to it a good many times lately.

CW: ("I've lucked in again! It's a good thing I know that many of these older folks don't play around too long with gestures.") Roy, that really scares me. How about telling me just how you've been thinking of doing it—the method, I mean.

Once Roy had described a specific and lethal plan, the worker's silent self-talk immediately leaped forward.

CW: ("OK, this is it! Look at all these risk factors! I don't need much more clarity than this. I'm lucky he came in. My immediate goal is to make sure we don't find him swinging by a rope in the barn!") Roy, there are several things that I think you and I can do. Let me assure you that I'm thankful you're here talking to me this way. And I want you to know that I'm ready to start right now, working on some definite things with you to reduce the loneliness, the sleepless nights, and the risks to your life. I want you to know that, now that you've reached out to me, I'm returning that reaching hand, and together we will work toward making things safer for you.

[Dialogue continues.]

Roy's situation was unique. But it contained similarities to problems experienced by many other older persons. The worker's knowledge of risks associated with Roy's age group and sensitivity to Roy's present emotional functioning were key assessment factors in the helping process. The worker's clear and accurate inner self-talk enhanced and facilitated the intervention and referral.

PREVENTION

Crisis workers helping suicidal clients are also primary prevention workers. But prevention is the work of everyone. Effective suicide prevention involves comprehensive educational and communications programs designed to touch, influence, sensitize, and educate every segment of society. Since every segment of society is affected by suicides, effective and pervasive prevention must also involve every segment of society. This means taking suicide out of the closet and publicly dealing with all its dimensions in an honest, realistic, and responsible manner. It also means learning from our mistakes and being willing to accept our joys, failures, fallibilities, responsibilities, and interdependence on one another as mutual life-support persons.

An important point for crisis workers to remember is that we cannot prevent all suicides. What do we do when one of our clients takes his or her own life despite our best efforts? The case of Deborah in this chapter provides at least a partial answer. In her case, even though a number of professionals, laypersons, and support persons had worked and hoped for Deborah's survival, they knew that they could not save all clients. Deborah died, but these professionals had done their best. Knowing that, they vowed to learn, by carefully reviewing the case, how to be successful with future Deborahs who would come into their lives. They did not place blame or wallow in their own guilt.

When crisis workers fail to save a suicidal person, they must go home, renew themselves, be kind to themselves and their associates, get some rest and sleep, and awaken with vigor, sensitivity, and resolve. Never forgetting the Deborahs of the world, they must go forward, ready to meet, understand, and help future clients. Even though crisis workers try as much as they can, they cannot be successful 100% of the time. They are not perfect. They are 100% human.

All of our institutions, as well as individuals, can contribute to suicide prevention (Morgan, 1981; Pretzel, 1972; Shneidman, Farberow, & Litman, 1976; Wekstein, 1979). The techniques, strategies, and attitudes reflected throughout this chapter can be used in educational institutions, business and industry, the printed media, television, radio, churches and religious organizations, governmental and community agencies, and professional offices to help alleviate the pain and loss of life accompanying the phenomenon of suicide ("Horror of suicide," 1985). As it is in all other plagues to human existence, prevention is the preferred mode of treatment (Morgan, 1981). In suicide, it is even more so: an ounce of prevention may be worth more than ten thousand pounds of cure.

Shneidman (1987) developed the technique that is commonly called *psychological autopsy* for the purpose of compiling detailed post mortem mental histories following suicides. Psychological autopsies provide some of the most valuable data we have for suicide prevention. On the basis of nearly 40 years of study, treatment, and prevention work with people who manifest suicidal tendencies, Shneidman states (p. 56) that suicide

> is not a bizarre and incomprehensible act of self-destruction. Rather, suicidal people use a particular logic, a style of thinking that brings them to the conclusion that death is the only solution to their problems. This style can be readily seen, and there are steps we can take to stop suicide, if we know where to look.

The most effective means of suicide prevention appears to be educating the general public, mental health professionals, and agency personnel regarding the characteristic thinking and behavior of suicidal persons.

From a societal standpoint, there are compelling reasons why we must prevent suicides: grief suffered by friends and family, financial loss to family and community, societal stigma on the family, financial burden to community, loss of human talent, and many others. In our early history the laws and social attitudes about suicide were so punitive and restricted by taboo that little help was available to the potential suicide victim. Even though many of our earlier fears and attitudes persist today, we are beginning to realize that suicide prevention is everybody's business.

It is not really possible or desirable to separate and compartmentalize intervention and prevention. For example, most of the treatment considerations listed in the sections entitled "Counseling Suicidal Clients" and "Intervention Strategies" in this chapter are indeed preventive in thrust. The intent of this section is to augment what we have already emphasized in the name of counseling and intervention.

According to Shneidman, Farberow, and Litman (1976), effective prevention begins with the realization that suicide affects everyone: clients, medical staff, family, friends, rich, poor, educated, uneducated, professional, laypersons, persons of status, and persons who are unknown. The optimal starting point in prevention is that people in all levels of society become sensitive to the possibility of suicidal potential in everybody (p. 439). Since suicide is "democratic" (p. 438) in its occurrence, we must be democratic in our prevention efforts. Co-workers, family, friends, and colleagues can contribute to prevention by not running scared whenever they encounter symptoms of suicide.

We may be prone to overlook suicidal clues in high-status persons such as ministers, physicians, politicans, business executives, and the like. But these individuals need and deserve our help just as much as the poor vagrant. Therefore, we must not hold back from becoming a support person or notifying appropriate others when we encounter individuals of any status who are at risk. For example, we might ordinarily tend to overlook the presuicidal message of a well-known surgeon who may need to be hospitalized for treatment. Our fear of becoming involved or of embarrassing that person should not impede our willingness to hear and respond to a legitimate and real cry for help and to become assertive in assisting that person to examine options and counter constricted thinking (Goleman, 1985).

Shneidman, Farberow, and Litman (1976) have identified four routes, avenues, or thrusts to effect a reduction in the suicide rate in this country (pp. 145–146).

1. Increase the acumen for recognition of potential suicide among all potential rescuers.
2. Facilitate the ease with which each citizen can utter a cry for help.
3. Provide resources for responding to the suicidal crisis.
4. Disseminate the facts about suicide.

Hipple (1985) advocates a comprehensive educational and communications program that includes the schools, PTAs, family, and the medical community. Hipple, Shneidman, and others recommend postintervention programs to assist the survivors to cope, grieve, understand, and become instruments for prevention in the future. Postintervention programs are important to family, friends, and crisis workers.

SUMMARY

The phenomenon of suicide is democratic in that it affects every segment of society. It is a serious problem which is on the rise among all groups, especially youth, but the highest risk group is, and has remained for many years, Caucasian males over 65. Researchers find few common denominators in their quest to study ways to identify suicide risk types and to predict and prevent suicide.

In this chapter we have attempted to strengthen crisis workers' knowledge and competency in dealing with suicidal clients by acquainting them with the dynamics of suicide, counseling techniques, intervention strategies, and prevention considerations. Background information, concepts, and applications are provided. It is assumed that the fundamental concepts of crisis intervention found in Chapter 2, including the six steps emphasized there, are an integral part of working with suicidal clients.

Dynamics of suicide are important because crisis workers who deal with suicidal clients need to know that there are several different types and characteristics of suicide. There are many reasons why people kill or attempt to kill themselves and there are differing points of view about suicide among various social, ethnic, and age groups. A thorough knowledge of the dynamics of suicide should sensitize workers to the causes and signs of suicide. A good many myths about suicide complicate the assessment, counseling, intervention, and prevention which workers attempt to do.

Despite the difficulties, however, we now know enough about suicide to be of great help to suicidal people. A great number of risk factors have been identified that serve as danger signals and help to determine levels of lethality. We have provided two lists which give a total of 23 risk factors. This is a formidable collection of important criteria for both assessing and acting in the realm of suicide work. Workers who are perceptive of the dynamics find that suicidal persons often send out subtle but definite clues and/or cries for help. We have provided suggestions for deciphering and assessing the behavioral cues of potential suicide victims.

Examples of counseling with eight different suicidal clients were included to illustrate several techniques which workers might use. Samples of counseling included a wide variety of problems presented by clients whose ages were 11, 14, 17, 21, 27, 61, 75, and 88. The counseling vignettes clearly demonstrated that crisis workers do not have to be expert suicidologists to help clients who are at risk. Rather, the examples showed crisis workers being reasonably knowledgeable and sensitive to the cues and needs of suicidal people.

The intervention strategies we portrayed showed crisis workers being appropriately assertive, directive, and forceful. In work with suicidal clients, workers cannot be passive. We gathered a list of "do's" and "don'ts" which pertain exclusively to intervention with suicidal clients. We discussed a number of special considerations for coping with the act of suicide and with suicidal people. In suicide intervention, workers have to consider many environmental and social factors in addition to attending to client safety.

Several ideas were given on the topic of suicide prevention. There is wide agreement that the most effective means of keeping people from killing themselves is through education. This is an enormous task because it involves all of society. Preventive suicide education is a continuous process which involves every institution and every mode of communication. Making the general public aware of the dynamics, dangers, cues, myths, and rudimentary techniques for counseling and intervention is the primary goal of prevention.

REFERENCES

Aguilera, D. C., & Messick, J. M. (1982). *Crisis intervention: Theory and methodology* (4th ed.). St. Louis: C.V. Mosby.

Allen, N. (1977). History and background of suicidology. In C. L. Hatton, S. M. Valente, & A. Rink (Eds.), *Suicide assessment and intervention* (pp. 1–19). New York: Appleton-Century-Crofts.

American Association for Counseling and Development (AACD). (1985, September 5). Congress eyes youth suicide; AACD to testify. *Guidepost, 28*(3), pp. 1, 5.

American Association of Retired People (AARP). (1986). Reminiscence: Thanks for the memory. *News Bulletin, 27*(8), p. 2.

Battle, A. O. (1985, November). Outpatient management of the suicidal adolescent (paper, presentation, and assessment instrument). Symposium on Suicide in Teenagers and Young Adults, University of Tennessee, College of Medicine, Department of Psychiatry, Memphis.

Bernard, J. L., & Bernard, M. L. (1980). Institutional responses to the suicidal student: Ethical and legal considerations. *Journal of College Student Personnel, 21*(2), 109–113.

Bernard, J. L., & Bernard, M. L. (1982). Factors related to suicidal behavior among college students and the impact of institutional response. *Journal of College Student Personnel, 23*(5), 409-413.

Bernard, J. L., & Bernard, M. L. (1985). Suicide on campus: Response to the problem. In E. S. Zinner (Ed.), *Coping with death on campus* (pp. 69–83). San Francisco: Jossey-Bass.

Durkheim, E. (1951). *Suicide*. New York: Free Press.

Ebersole, P. (1976a, August). Reminiscing. *American Journal of Nursing, 76*, 1304–1305.

Ebersole, P. (1976b, November–December). Problems of group reminiscing with institutional aged. *Journal of Gerontological Nursing, 2*, 23–27.

Fujimura, L. E., Weis, D. M., & Cochran, J. R. (1985). Suicide: Dynamics and implications for counseling. *Journal of Counseling and Development, 63*, 612–615.

Getz, W. L., Allen, D. B., Myers, R. K., & Linder, K. C. (1983). *Brief counseling with suicidal persons*. Lexington, MA: D. C. Heath.

Gilliland, B. E. (1985, November). Surviving college: Teaching college students to cope (paper and presentation). Symposium on Suicide in Teenagers and Young Adults, University of Tennessee, College of Medicine, Department of Psychiatry, Memphis.

Goleman, D. (1985, October 8). Painful path to suicide studied: Biological factors play role in pushing people to brink. *The Commercial Appeal*, Memphis, Section A, p. 2.

Hatton, C. L, Valente, S. M., & Rink, A. (1977). *Suicide: Assessment and intervention*. New York: Appleton-Century-Crofts.

Hersh, J. B. (1985, January). Interviewing college students in crisis. *Journal of Counseling and Development, 63*, 286–289.

Hipple, J. (1985). Suicide: The preventable tragedy (mimeographed monograph, 25 pp.). Denton, TX: North Texas State University.

Hipple, J., & Cimbolic, P. (1979). *The counselor and suicidal crisis.* Springfield, IL: Charles C Thomas.

Hipple, J., & Hipple, L. (1983). *Diagnosis and management of psychological emergencies: A manual for hospitalization.* Springfield, IL: Charles C Thomas.

Horror of suicide: Young people have a right to know. (1985, September 24). *The Commercial Appeal,* Memphis, Section A, p. 4 (editorial).

Janosik, E. H. (1984). *Crisis counseling: A contemporary approach.* Belmont, CA: Wadsworth.

Morgan, L. B. (1981). The counselor's role in suicide prevention. *Personnel and Guidance Journal, 59,* 284–286.

Motto, J. A. (1978). Recognition, evaluation, and management of persons at risk for suicide. *Personnel and Guidance Journal, 56,* 537–543.

Pretzel, P. (1972). *Understanding and counseling the suicidal person.* Nashville: Abingdon Press.

Ray, L. Y., & Johnson, N. (1983). Adolescent suicide. *Personnel and Guidance Journal, 62,* 131–134.

Shneidman, E. S. (1985). *Definition of suicide.* New York: Wiley.

Shneidman, E. S. (1987, March). At the point of no return: Suicidal thinking follows a predictable path. *Psychology Today, 21,* pp. 54–58.

Shneidman, E. S., Farberow, N. L., & Litman, R. E. (1976). *The psychology of suicide.* New York: Aronson.

Strother, D. B. (1986, June). Suicide among the young. *Phi Delta Kappan, 67:* 756–759.

Teenage suicide (1985, September 22). *The Commercial Appeal,* Memphis, Section E, pp. 1, 3.

Tidewater Psychiatric Institute's SOS sessions help "victims" left behind after a loved-one's suicide (1985, July). *Network* (employee publication of National Medical Enterprise), *15,* p. 3.

Toughy, W. (1974, October 25). World health agency zeros in on suicide. *Los Angeles Times,* pp. 1–3.

Wekstein, L. (1979). *Handbook of suicidology.* New York: Brunner/Mazel.

Zinner, E. S. (Ed.). (1985). *Coping with death on campus.* San Francisco: Jossey-Bass.

■ Classroom Exercises: Case of Tom

Tom, his wife Sheila, and daughter Renee (age 7) live in a small town surrounded by a large agricultural area. Tom is employed as a heavy equipment operator. He likes the outdoors, particularly hunting, and he prides himself on being macho. He was an excellent high school athlete and could have gone to a small college on a football scholarship. But he took a job working for his father and an uncle, married Sheila (who had been his classmate and the high school homecoming queen), and obligated himself with a large mortgage on a home next door to his parents. Tom began to drink heavily, drive fast cars, frequently take risks on the highways, get into fights at taverns, come home late at night, neglect his physical health, and felt remorseful, guilty, depressed, and suicidal following each fling at a tavern. Sheila and her supervisor repeatedly attempted to persuade Tom to see a therapist. Sheila finally prevailed upon Tom to call the tricounty crisis line after she walked into their bedroom at 7:30 P.M. Saturday and discovered him preparing to shoot himself in the head with his deer rifle. The volunteer crisis worker received the call from Tom later that evening.

Tom: (In a fearful, tense, and anxious voice.) I wouldn't have called, but my wife insisted. She caught me trying to shoot myself tonight. Now I'm scared as hell. She sort of demanded that I get help.

CW: Tom, I'm glad you called. You did the right thing when you called, because you can be helped, and I want us to start right now. I can hear the tenseness in your voice. What I want to do first is for you to stay on the line, sit down, and tell me what's happening in your life right now—in the past day or so—that's brought you so close to killing yourself. That's what I want to know first.

Tom: Well, everything. All these pressures. Everybody expecting big things from me, and I'm not really worth a shit! My wife and kid would be better off if I was out of the way, and I would be too. I ain't the happy-go-lucky guy I look like on the surface.

CW: So, Tom, you're really down; you've had a very close call, and you're frightened. What happened to cause the stress at this time?

Tom: Well, it's a buildup of lots of things. I'm getting nowhere on a treadmill. And yesterday—it just hit me—I realized I'm a nothing. A dependent kid in a man's clothing. One of my friends I went to high school with has his M.B.A. Another one owns a car dealership. I'm still working for my daddy—can't get away from Mamma. I'm a dud—a nobody. And I'm stuck. A nobody, going nowhere.

CW: So, you're trying yourself, sentencing yourself, and you've nearly executed yourself because you're stuck—and you're realizing that what you're really wanting is to be in a successful career, independent from your folks. And it really hurts when you face it head on. You're feeling powerless right now.

Tom: That's it. And Sheila deserves a better man than that! I'm stuck, so she's stuck with me, and I ain't much to look at.

Simulated Telephone Interview

Generate a telephone crisis counseling modeling session to carry the interview forward, with a volunteer taking the role of Tom and another volunteer taking the role of the crisis worker. Place two chairs back to back in the middle of the room in a "fishbowl" configuration, to simulate the telephone interview. A sound tape recording of the interview should be made. To make it realistic, Tom and the crisis worker must not be able to see each other. Continue the simulated telephone call with the objective of taking Tom through the six-step crisis counseling model described in Chapter 2. If possible, obtain a realistic commitment from Tom to take some constructive action step, such as making a commitment not to kill himself without first meeting with the crisis worker, going to a hospital, or going directly to a therapist. If the person taking the role of the crisis worker gets stuck, have someone else take over and continue the telephone counseling. When the simulated telephone session is completed, convene the whole group for discussion and suggestions. Upon completion of the exercise, time should be taken to disassociate themselves from the characters they have portrayed during the role play. Here are some questions to facilitate discussion:

1. What were the advantages and drawbacks of the lack of visual contact between the crisis worker and Tom?
2. If this client/worker simulation were repeated, what could you do to improve upon the first session?

3. What other strategies could the worker use?
4. What other alternatives might the worker help Tom to explore?
5. What feelings (frustration, stress, and so on) were experienced by members of the group who were observers?
6. What are the implications and suggestions from the group with respect to helping suicidal clients who call on crisis hot lines? (See Aguilera & Messick, 1982, pp. 8–12).

Interview, Take Two

Listen to the tape recording of the session in Exercise I. Two new volunteers will now repeat Exercise I, including all six questions. Compare the tape recordings of the two sessions.

Postintervention Meeting

Suppose that the entire group were the tricounty crisis center staff and volunteer workers in a called meeting a week following Exercise I. The purpose of the meeting is to deal with the death of Tom, who shot himself the following Friday, despite the best efforts of the center, support persons, and other intervention and referral resources. Make a list of the points that need to be addressed and discuss the issues that need to be brought before the combined group. All participants should have opportunities to express their feelings and concerns. Make a list of actions the center might want to take as a result of the experience with Tom.

CHAPTER 4

Women in Crisis:
Battering

BACKGROUND

In current usage, "rule of thumb" means a measure or guideline based on an educated guess, particularly in the carpentry or masonry trade. However, the origins of this expression are not so innocuous. For "rule of thumb" in the original sense refers to a passage of British Common Law that allowed a husband to beat his wife with a rod no thicker than his thumb so as to spare her permanent physical injury (Davidson, 1977, p. 18). The history of wife beating in Western society goes as far back as the patriarchal system. Whereas an assault or rape of another man's wife caused and still causes immediate and severe legal punishment and moral outrage, abuse by a man of his own wife is quite another story. Throughout this chapter we refer to terms such as "wife," "spouse," and "husband." It should be clearly understood that the concepts involved in the crisis of battering apply to partners or people in any established relationship.

Common law in the United States early acknowledged the right of a man to chastise his wife for misbehavior without being prosecuted for doing so (*Bradley* v. *State of Mississippi*, 1824). Indeed, the law's attitude toward wife beating to the current day is aptly summarized in the case of the *State of North Carolina* v. *Oliver* in 1874. The court ruled that ". . . if no permanent injury has been inflicted, it is better to draw the curtains, shut out the public eye, and leave the parties to forgive and forget. . . ." Although laws have changed, there is little doubt that for much of the legal justice system the North Carolina comments still prevail in the contemporary scene. The implications of such blind justice are ominous.

First, there is no more anxiety-provoking call for a police officer than a domestic disturbance call. More police die as a result of intervening in domestic violence calls than in any other type of crime (Resnik, 1976, p. 9). Further, domestic disturbance calls far outnumber other types of police calls in which the possibility of violence exists (Benjamin & Walz, 1983, p. 63). And violence does exist, in a big way. Approximately one-fourth of all murders in the United States occur within the family and one-half of those are spouse killings (Margolin, 1979, p. 13). Although overall statistics remain cloudy because of victims' reluctance to report battering incidents, conservative estimates indicate that abuse has occurred with 1.8 million victims. It has been reported that one-quarter of all American couples experience at least one violent incident during their married lives; one-sixth of the couples experience at least one incident per year; and one-tenth of the couples experience extreme physical abuse on a regular and continuing basis (Barnett, Pittman, Ragan, & Salus, 1980; Margolin, 1979).

A common myth is that such violence occurs only among lower socioeconomic and ethnically distinct families. Nothing could be further from the truth. Wife abuse, at least in the contemporary United States, cuts across class, ethnic, religious, and age groups (Fields, 1976; Flynn, 1977; Pagelow, 1977). Gelles (1972, 1977) found in his controlled studies that wives in high socioeconomic groups were as prone as those in low socioeconomic groups to experience abuse, if not more so. The reason for the myth is simply that women in lower socioeconomic classes come to the attention of social service agencies and the legal justice system because they do not have the financial means to do otherwise (Benjamin & Walz, 1983, p. 64).

Yet, despite the long history of wife abuse, it has been only since 1974 that a consistent and planned systematic approach to the problem has evolved. Erin Pizzey's book *Scream Quietly or the Neighbors Will Hear* (1974) was responsible for the start of the first women's shelter in England. Subsequently, in the United States, the National Organization of Women, along with grassroots organizations such as the Massachusetts Coalition of Battered Women Service Groups, has taken to the forefront in developing funding sources, shelters, support groups, organizing and training manuals, and legislation for battered women. At the present time, these efforts do not begin to address the severity and range of the problem, even though from 1975 to 1978 the number of shelters grew from zero to more than 400. Organized in 1978, the National Coalition Against Domestic Violence was formed to promote a national power base for battered women. By 1982, there were 46 state coalitions (Capps, 1982).

One of the major debates that has come out of the movement is who shall control services to battered women. Grassroots groups, for the most part made up of battered women, have allied themselves with feminists and identified wife battering as a feminist issue. They see the government's slow entrance into the problem not as one of choice but as a way of co-opting their power and destroying the nontraditional nature of the grassroots shelters. Ardent supporters of the grassroots and feminist movements feel that the government's intervention has much more to do with political and economic considerations than with a "social" problem (Capps, 1982).

On the other side, the very complex nature of the problems that battered women bring to abuse centers has called for more professional expertise and increased financial support than grassroots organizations can supply. Such expertise ranges from gaining funds to providing expert crisis intervention. Because of the size and scope of the problem, it does not seem realistic to expect that wife abuse programs can run without outside help and trained personnel (Dagastino, 1984).

We have attempted to walk a tightwire in regard to this issue. Undoubtedly, grassroots feminists within the battered women's program will not be extraordinarily pleased with our push for professional training. However, we would quickly respond that we are not advocating educational degrees in place of skills. We believe that volunteers, battered women, and professionals alike can do worthwhile work in this area. Experience and compassion are necessary, but we do not consider them sufficient. Conversations we have had with people directly involved in shelter programs indicate that learning thoroughly the kind of crisis intervention and supervision skills advocated by Woods (1981) is necessary for those who would engage in this demanding work (Dagastino, 1984). It is from that standpoint that we present this chapter.

DYNAMICS

Psychosocial and Cultural Dynamics

The overarching dynamic of wife battering is male supremacy. It is the natural result of a long-term sexist, paternalistic social order that rewards aggressive behavior in men but expects women to be passive and submissive (Benjamin & Walz, 1983, p. 65). Combined with the emergent status of women outside the home, this tradition has produced a volatile mix of personality dynamics. The flash point of such a mix occurs when the man who lives the traditional male image of chief breadwinner and director of the family perceives himself as losing power in the conjugal relationship.

The question of power is the fuse that ignites this explosive mixture. The woman's position is to obey, conciliate, perform traditional domestic duties, and, in general, be subservient. Any attempt to establish herself in her own right is likely to be met with punishment for overstepping her bounds (Benjamin & Walz, 1983, pp. 74–77). Violence, though, is not something that develops only in families. It involves a complex interplay of social, cultural, and psychological factors.

Social factors. Societal attitudes about the legitimate use of violence to achieve personal ends have their roots in a tradition of perceived "national interest." There is a long and true history of civilization that shows one group violently retaliating against other groups aspiring for power. As a nation, we promote and glorify the controlled use of aggression for protection, law and order, self-defense, and national interest (Benjamin & Walz, 1983, pp. 65–66). There is little question that we still accept as a standard Teddy Roosevelt's dictum, "Speak softly and carry a big stick."

Given the violent world we live in, there is some truth in what Roosevelt said. However, this notion has been extended to the family by at least implicit permission of the state. For the state, the family is the basic disciplinary agent—family over individual, male over female, adult over child. Control is direct, continuous, personalized, and an efficient way of keeping intact the past social order of the state (Capps, 1982).

Cultural factors. Our cultural heritage goes far back in aiding and abetting the family as a cradle of violence and learned aggression for the male. Supported by the Judeo-Christian ethic, "Spare the rod and spoil the child" can easily be translated into the same homily for "the wife." Given the excellent role models of learned aggression that such long-standing messages and behaviors imply, it is not too difficult to see that families in which this principle is carried out become excellent training grounds for violent behavior (Gelles, 1972, p. 10). Evidence substantiates the hypothesis that the cycle of violence continues: males from such families mature and practice similar behavior on their spouses (Steinmetz & Strauss, 1973). Between what is modeled in families and the extremely violent role models presented in the media, it is little wonder that violence occurs in the home.

Psychological factors. Psychologically, both parties of a battering situation have some or all of the following characteristics. Men in a battering relationship

1. demonstrate excessive dependency and possessiveness toward their women—although they deny it
2. are unable to express any emotion except anger and generally have poor communications skills where emotional issues are concerned
3. have unrealistic expectations of their spouses and idealize marriage or the relationship far beyond what realistically may be expected
4. have a lack of self-control and, paradoxically, set up rigid family boundaries for everyone else
5. are alcohol or drug abusers
6. were abused as children or saw their mothers abused
7. deny and minimize problems, particularly battering, that they generate in families
8. emotionally cycle from hostility, aggressiveness, and cruelty when they don't get their way to charm, manipulation, and seductiveness when they do
9. may be characterized as jealous, denying, impulsive, self-deprecating, depressive, demanding, aggressive, and violent

(Barnett et al., 1980; Ganley & Harris, 1978; Mott-MacDonald, 1979; Symonds, 1978; Walker, 1984, p. 11).

Encompassing the foregoing personal factors of abusing men are four general personality patterns: the controller, the defender, the approval seeker, and the incorporator (Elbow, 1977).

1. *The controller.* This individual uses threats and force to get his way. Women are regarded as objects. There is little or no emotional reciprocity. Violence occurs when he feels unable to control his wife. Halleck (1976) has

cast this personality pattern as an extremely dangerous, criminally violent individual who may be described as narcissistic, immature, and sociopathic. Total dominance is the end product; therefore the killing of the wife is a distinct possibility, since death of the spouse represents complete control over her.

2. *The defender.* This individual is insecure and afraid of being hurt. Such a man is able to feel strong only if his mate continuously clings to and depends on him. His spouse may punish him for being aggressive toward her—particularly by withholding sex. To render her nonpunitive and powerless so that he will not be vulnerable to attack, he may resort to violence.

3. *The approval seeker.* This individual has high expectations of himself but low self-esteem. His self-esteem is contingent on acceptance and approval by others. The prospect of losing a mate for any reason is highly threatening because such a loss would confirm his low regard for himself. As a result, he will do anything, including becoming violent, to keep his self-esteem intact.

4. *The incorporator.* This individual cannot see himself as a whole person without incorporating his mate into his persona. By doing so he gains from his mate a degree of self-validation. Fear of losing her results in ego deterioration, which must be avoided at all costs. The ultimate cost may be violence.

Women in a battering relationship

1. have a lack of self-esteem as a result of being told over and over that they are stupid, incompetent, and otherwise inadequate
2. experience a lack of control and little confidence in their ability to take any meaningful steps to improve their marriage
3. have experienced a history of abuse that leads them to accept their role as victim or saw their mothers abused and accept it as their lot
4. are so ashamed that they hide their physical and emotional wounds and become socially and emotionally isolated
5. lack personal, physical, educational, and financial resources that would allow them to get out of the battering situation
6. are extremely dependent and are willing to suffer grievous insult and injury to have their needs met
7. have an idealized view of what a relationship should be and somehow feel they can "fix or change" the man
8. do not have good communications skills, particularly in regard to asserting their rights and feelings
9. learn stereotyped sex roles and thus feel guilty if they do not adhere to a rigid patriarchial system
10. are unable to differentiate between sex and love and believe that love is manifested through intense sexual relationships

(Barnett et al., 1980; Benjamin & Walz, 1983, p. 72; Ibrahim & Herr, 1987; Walker, 1984, pp. 8–11, 51).

In one way or another, all the concepts we've just enumerated have to do with power. Whether its presence or absence is perceived or real makes little difference because the outcome—abuse and battering—is the same. To chalk wife battering up to something other than this basic enculturated dynamic is not valid. If men acted on impulse or some other drive, they would beat up their bosses, secretaries, friends, or neighbors as often as their mates and children. Only in a conjugal relationship do many men generally believe in and exercise their ability to coerce and abuse their spouses and children (Hart, 1980).

Stressors

If power is the fuse, then stress is the match that lights the fuse. As the idealized image of the relationship breaks down and environmental stresses build up, couples become engaged in an ever-upward spiral of violent interaction (Barnett et al., 1980). When the social system does not provide a family member with sufficient resources to maintain his or her position, tension rises, and physical force is often used as a means of trying to stabilize the situation (Steinmetz & Strauss, 1974, p. 9).

Common stress factors. Although not generic to all battering, a variety of stress factors that seem to appear over and over have been compiled by Barnett et al. (1980, pp. 7–9), Gelles (1972, pp. 116–117), and Walker (1984, p. 51).

1. *Geographic isolation.* Because of geographic location, the victim has no friends or family near that can provide a support system. A farm woman who cannot drive is an example of the worst case: literally being marooned and held captive by an abusive husband.

2. *Social isolation.* Because of extreme emotional dependence, the woman expects all needs to be met by her partner and has no significant others to turn to when she is assaulted.

3. *Economic stress.* When a woman is unemployed or underemployed, has inadequate housing, is pressured by creditors, and cannot feed and clothe her children by herself, she becomes human chattel to her abusive partner. In the case of the man, unemployment means idle time to sit and brood on his inability to perform his head-of-household role, and he feels further demeaned when his spouse is working.

4. *Medical problems.* Long-term, chronic medical problems for either spouse or children exact tremendous financial and emotional cost.

5. *Inadequate parenting skills.* A lack of knowledge of parenting skills and conflict over parental roles can lead to situations that start as minor disciplinary problems and escalate into violence in the family.

6. *Pregnancy.* Ranging from heralding an unwanted child through creating anxiety over providing for the new baby to arousing jealousy over a wife's attention to a newborn, pregnancy is an especially acute crisis point for potential abuse.

7. *Family structure and homeostasis.* A veritable kaleidoscope of problems causes dysfunction in the family. Some of these problems are related to age

and number of children, presence of stepchildren, loyalty conflicts, death, desertion, and career change.

8. *Alcohol and drug abuse.* Chemical dependence serious enough to cause economic chaos and severe emotional disturbance characterizes addictive families and has spinoffs that commonly include spouse abuse. The insidious problem with alcohol and drugs is that they are often used as an excuse for behavior (battering) that is normally prohibited by societal norms and standards.

Precipitating factors.   Barnett et al. (1980) have schematically represented the phases leading to the explosion of these volatile dynamics into violence. Walker's (1984) cycle theory of violence closely parallels these phases and her research supports the theory (p. 95).

Phase I. Tranquillity prevails. The relationship may have been characterized as calm to this point, with no previous violent incidents, or a period of calm may follow an earlier violent episode.

Phase II. Tension starts to build. A variety of stresses impinge on the relationship. They may come in combination or singularly from the common group we have already mentioned. However, there is no reduction of tension and the situation grows more severe.

Phase III. A violent episode occurs. The episode may range from harsh words to a severe beating. At this phase, communication has broken down and the situation is out of control.

Phase IV. The relationship takes on crisis proportions. A variety of options becomes available.

    A. The abuser becomes remorseful and asks forgiveness. Sooner or later the victim forgives the abuser and calmness is restored.

    B. The abuser is not remorseful and feels his control over the situation has been established. The victim gives in and relinquishes control, and calmness is restored.

    C. The victim takes new action. Within this option are two possibilities: the abuser negotiates the situation, and, given that the negotiation is agreeable to the victim, calmness is restored; or the abuser rejects the new action and a crisis state continues.

It is at this last point, in which no possibility of resolution exists, that the victim is most likely to seek help by referring herself to a wife abuse center. If effective assessment and intervention do not occur when the violence emerges (Phase II), the likelihood that the violence will recur and will be of greater intensity is dramatically increased (Barnett et al., 1980, p. 34).

Myths of Wife Abuse

To summarize this section on dynamics and to illuminate the problem further, we would like to explore and explode a number of existing myths. The following myths have been encapsulated from a number of sources (Heppner, 1978; Massachusetts Coalition of Battered Women Service Groups, 1981; Pagelow, 1977; Schultz, 1960).

1. *Battered women overstate the case.* Any person who has contusions, lacerations, and broken bones is not overstating anything. In any other instance such outcomes are referred to as assault and battery.

2. *Battered women provoke the beating.* While some women may be classified as the stereotypical "nag," there can certainly be many significant others in a man's life who fit into the "nag" category. Yet such people do not get assaulted with the regularity that wives do.

3. *Battered women are masochists.* If such women did have masochistic tendencies they would find a variety of ways to suffer pain that would not be exclusive to an abusive mate.

4. *Battering is a private, family matter.* When beaten women are disenfranchised from their homes, and the children of battering relationships learn the pathological roles a battering father models, battering transcends the home and becomes society's problem.

5. *Alcohol abuse is the prime reason for wife abuse.* Although alcohol plays a part in many cases of abuse, it may be only an excuse for, and not the cause of, violent behavior.

6. *Battering occurs only in problem families.* The dynamic representation of stress factors that assail families shows that any family at any given point may be classified as "problem."

7. *Only low-income and working-class families experience violence.* Members of those socioeconomic classes do come to the attention of the police and welfare agencies to a much greater degree than middle- or upper-class members, but statistics from wife abuse shelters indicate that battering has no class boundaries.

8. *The battering cannot be that bad or she would not stay.* The host of personal factors that tie the woman to the relationship militate heavily against simply picking up and leaving.

9. *A husband has patriarchal rights.* What a man does in his own family is not his own business when the emotional overflow of what he does spills over into the community. No amount or kind of justification from the Bible or any other authority—be it person, institution, or book—can excuse spouse abuse.

10. *The beaten spouse exaggerates the problem to exact revenge.* Reporting a beating—whether committed by a total stranger or one's spouse—is no exaggeration. If revenge were the motive, there would be a host of ways of going about it that would be far less traumatic than calling or showing up at a wife abuse shelter.

11. *Women are too sensitive, especially when they are pregnant.* If a person is too sensitive who objects to being kicked in the stomach or vagina, thrown down a flight of stairs, or hit in the face with a lamp, then we would suppose that everyone is overly sensitive.

Realities of Wife Abuse

Why, then, do women stay in an abusing relationship? Benjamin and Walz (1983) and Conroy (1982) have developed a list stating the real reasons for remaining in the battering situation, and these realities have little to do with the myths we've just examined.

1. The woman has a fear of reprisal or of aggravating the attacks even more.
2. Even though the situation may be intolerable for the woman, her children do have food, clothing, and shelter.
3. The woman would suffer shame, embarrassment, humiliation, and even ridicule if her secret got out.
4. Her self-concept is so strongly dependent on the relationship and perceived social approval that leaving would be very destructive to her.
5. Early affection and prior love in the relationship persist and, by staying, the woman hopes to salvage them.
6. If financially well off, the woman is unable to forego a reduction in her financial freedom.
7. In the cyclic nature of abuse, her mate may not be terrible twenty-four hours a day, seven days a week. There may be good times when a lot of caring and tenderness are professed and shown. The victim may tend to forget the batterings and remember only the good times.
8. Early role models of an abusive parent may lead her to believe that relationships exist in no other way.
9. The woman may hold religious values that strongly militate against separation, divorce, or anything less than filial subjugation to the man's wishes.

We believe that there are strong social and psychological forces that serve to rationalize and deny some very complex dynamics with which few people or social institutions are willing to grapple. As a result, any woman who attempts to break free of a battering relationship will most likely meet active discouragement from the church, police, courts, welfare agencies, legal services, family, and friends (Schuyler, 1976, p. 489). It is little wonder that a woman making her first call to an abuse center may be taking only an initial step in a series that sometimes goes on for years before she can make a complete break from the battering relationship.

INTERVENTION STRATEGIES

Throughout our discussion of the intervention process, we will be speaking of the crisis worker in the feminine gender. After careful consideration, both from a review of the literature and from dialogues with wife abuse workers, we believe that men are likely to be unsuccessful as wife abuse workers. This is true for two reasons. First, the trauma that battered women undergo at the hands of their mates tends to generalize to all men. Dealing with battered women is a difficult enough task without having to wade through issues involving fear of the crisis worker. Second, the crisis worker must be an advocate, but at the same time not allow the client to manipulate the situation. Many battered women have learned to relate to men in a charming and seductive way. Thus, a great deal of extra time may be needlessly spent in teaching battered women how to relate to a male worker in positive and nonseductive ways (Walker, 1979, p. 76). Whereas one long-term goal of therapy may be teaching such women more equitable relationships with men, it is not the goal of crisis intervention.

Assessment

Analysis. Assessment of battered women by personality measures is somewhat confounding and contradictory to what one might logically believe. Using the Minnesota Multiphasic Personality Inventory (MMPI), Rosewater (1982) found that the profiles of battered women appear to be similar to those of other emotionally disturbed individuals. However, investigation of subscale inconsistencies indicated battered women to be different from others who have serious mental illness. This is an important distinction that debunks the notion that most battered women are unstable. As an example, battered women may have real reasons to be fearful about their safety, and such fears are not indicative of paranoid ideation (Walker, 1984, p. 75).

Walker's (1984) in depth study of the personality constructs of battered women sheds some interesting light on how they perceive themselves. Contrary to popular notions that such women would assume a subservient, conservative sex role, she found battered women to be highly liberal in their sex-role views and saw themselves as much more liberated than controlled. Further, such women did not see their male counterparts as more powerful than they were, but rather saw themselves as equals in the battering relationship. It might also be expected that these women would have extremely low self-esteem. To the contrary, battered women were found to have very high positive views of themselves. However, these women were subject to depression and became more depressed after they left the battering relationship than while they were in it (pp. 77–83). This last point has important transcrisis ramifications for the crisis worker and indicates that resolving initiating events is only one component of the intervention process.

Diagnosis. Overall, battered women present many of the symptoms of posttrauma stress disorder (for a complete description of this disorder, see Chapter 7) and can be placed for diagnostic purposes within the PTSD category of the *Diagnostic and Statistical Manual of Mental Disorders III* (American Psychiatric Association, 1980, p. 238).

Whereas it is interesting and helpful to know these personality patterns in assessing battered women, crisis workers who provide help to victims most often do not have time to obtain an in-depth personality assessment. Walker

(1984, p. 122) has one major rule of assessment that supersedes all others and to which we strongly subscribe: when a woman calls or comes in to report a battering, believe her and start intervention immediately. It is a safe bet that whenever a battered woman seeks help, she is not carrying out the act as some impetuous, hysterical, spur-of-the-moment way to get back at her mate. Battered women refer themselves only after their problems have become exceedingly serious. Walker (1984, p. 26) found that only 14% of battered women surveyed would seek help after a first incident, 22% would seek help after a second incident, and finally, 49% would seek help only after a series of incidents had taken place.

Components of Intervention

As a call comes into the wife abuse center and the crisis worker picks up the phone, the assessment process begins with active listening. The crisis worker immediately has to be concerned with a variety of roles. She not only must be a good listener but also must be supportive, facilitative, and concerned with the caller's safety and must act as an advocate (Barnett et al., 1980, p. 44).

Listening. Facilitative listening and responding are crucial. The victim must know that the crisis worker understands and accepts her present situation in a nonjudgmental, non-value-laden way. Only then will the battered woman be able to open up and share her feelings about her predicament (Heppner, 1978). The crisis worker also immediately reflects that she understands the difficulty and urgency of the situation by positively reinforcing the battered woman for calling and taking a first step toward resolving her problem.

CW: You did the right thing by calling. No matter how bad it seems and what terrible things have happened, you've made a big step on the road to straightening it out. We're here to help and we'll stick with it as long as it takes.

Victim: I . . . I . . . don't know. It's gone on so long. I feel so ashamed. I don't know what to do! It's so confusing.

CW: I understand how you feel and how difficult it was to make this call. The hurt, the fear, the uncertainty of it all. So start anywhere you want. We won't do anything unless *you* decide it's best for you. Right now, though, so I can get a good idea of what your situation is, I want to listen to what you have to say. I'll listen for as long as it takes, so take your time and tell me what's happened.

Supporting. The caller is given both explicit and implicit permission to ventilate. The free flow of the victim's anger, hurt, fear, guilt, and other debilitating feelings may take from a few minutes to two hours to an extended period of months. Supportiveness means empathizing but not sympathizing with the victim. Many victims are only partially mobile and any action steps they take may be months away from happening. Thus, support of a victim does not mean intervention on a one-shot basis. The crisis worker may have to exert an excruciating amount of patience over a long period of time as the victim slowly moves toward making a decision to take action. No matter how

bad the victim's situation looks to the worker, only the victim herself can decide when she is ready to take action to alleviate her traumatic situation (Dagastino, 1984).

CW: OK! I understand it's a hard decision to make—getting out. Your marriage has
had some good times and you'd really like to hang onto that part of it, even though
the beatings are happening more often. You say you want some time to think about
it. That's OK! It's your decision and we'll help whenever you need us.

Breaking away from a battering relationship is a slow, developmental process. The crisis worker cannot move the victim any faster than she is willing
to go. The crisis worker must be acutely aware of being manipulated into becoming sympathetic to the victim's needs and attempting to "fix" things for
her. Many times the victim will project anger onto the police, a minister, or
other significant persons. The victim at some point needs to see that displacement and shifting of responsibility to others is not going to solve the
problem. The crisis worker must be aware of this possibility and not get
trapped into proposing external remedies. For example, the crisis worker
would be in error by communicating to a battered woman a message such as,
"Why don't you come out, bring him along, and let us talk with both of you. I
know we can straighten it out."

The victim is actually demonstrating what Heppner (1978) calls the
"wishing and hoping syndrome." The victim wishes the situation would
change, that her spouse would treat her the way he used to, and hopes the
crisis worker can effect a change in her husband. However, cessation of battering by the abuser rarely happens without legal or therapeutic intervention
(Dagastino, 1984). Under no circumstances should the crisis worker attempt
to rescue the victim in this manner. It is dangerous and takes responsibility
and autonomy away from the victim. Instead, the conversation should be
redirected away from what can be done to "fix" the husband and toward
what the victim is now able to do.

CW: While I hear you wanting me to come and straighten your husband out and
make things the way they were, I can't do that. I wish I could, but I'm not a marriage counselor. If you think marriage counseling would work, I can give you some
names of people who do that. What I can do is help you make some decisions
about what you want to do right now.

A typical response to the crisis worker's refusal to fix the problem is anger.

Victim: You're no damn help at all. You're just as bad as the rest. You're a horrible
counselor. I'm gonna have to go back to him and he'll kill me just because you
wouldn't do anything.

Because abuse workers do not want to lose clients, such ploys often rub a
raw nerve in the worker and propel her to do something she may later regret.
The worker should understand that she is working not merely with a battered woman but with the whole woman. If she responds to only the battered part, it will be very difficult for her not to become overly sympathetic
with the victim. This approach may salve the wounded pride of the worker

but will do little to help the victim in the long run. The crisis worker should realize that when a victim doubts the worker's ability, she is also doubting her own ability. She is probably looking for a way to resume the relationship and may be displacing her own incompetence to make changes by blaming the worker (Dagastino, 1984).

The best response the crisis worker can make is not to be confrontive but to be empathic, realizing that right now the woman is looking for a way to go back to her mate.

CW: I'm sorry you're angry with me because I won't talk to your husband. I realize the frustration you feel. Yet I'm also not like the others who'll tell you how to act and what to do. What I'd most like to do is to help you move off dead center because I feel you're really wanting to take some kind of action. If you don't believe you're quite ready to do that, OK. You have our phone number and I want you to know I'd be happy to sit down with you at any time and together we can work on a plan of action you want to take.

The excerpt typifies the response of a crisis worker who is being supportive yet not taking over for the victim. The crisis worker must do her best to give power and control to the battered woman, from the initiating interview to entering a shelter and finally being on her own. Usually abuse victims have not been independent to any degree and quickly fall back into a dependent state. If the crisis worker keeps foremost in her mind that the woman she is now talking to is ultimately going to have to be her own defender and protector, then the crisis worker is not likely to fall into a sympathy trap. The crisis worker who becomes angry or engages in denouncing or criticizing the husband is making a fundamental mistake. She may provoke the victim to defend the violent husband and to attack the crisis worker (Dagastino, 1984).

Facilitating. To facilitate the movement of a victim to action takes a great deal of tenacity and patience. Typically the crisis worker will have to deal with feelings of dependency, ambivalence, and depression, which are all clear-cut signs of the client's immobility. Overarching these immobilizing feelings is the concept of *learned helplessness*. Learned helplessness may be defined as noncontingent negative reinforcement, which leads people to believe that they cannot control the outcome by any voluntary actions they perform. The motivation of battered women to act independently is extinguished by repeated beatings and is generalized to the belief that no response will help. The result is a woman who becomes helpless and passive in the battering relationship (Davies & Janosik, 1984, pp. 208–209; Walker, 1984, pp. 33, 89).

Steinmetz (1978) has suggested that the phenomenon of the passive victim of abuse is much like that of brainwashing. She is isolated from support systems, her only validation of self-worth comes from her captor, and the inconsistent, contradictory, and threatening treatment interspersed with kindness leaves her alone with her feelings of anxiety, fear, guilt, and shame. To generate movement of the victim, the crisis worker strongly reinforces the victim's attempts at rational decision making, self-control, and statements of personal power (Heppner, 1978).

CW: You said that you couldn't do anything, but that's not true. You called here, didn't you? When you first started talking you were crying uncontrollably and now you're speaking in a rather level, controlled voice. I also notice a lot of "I" statements, which say to me you're starting to take responsibility. Maybe you don't know it, but those are all signs that you're starting to feel some personal power for the first time in a long while, and I think that's great!

Ambivalence about the situation is predominant in most women who seek help from wife abuse centers. Ambivalence is particularly strong with regard to the husband, who, after he beats his wife, apologizes and showers her with gifts. He tells her what she wants to hear and what society leads her to believe. The message is that if women remain married and stay in the home and mind their husbands, everything will be fine (Conroy, 1982). Consequently, even though the victim knows something is terribly wrong, there is still an extremely powerful pull to try to hold the relationship together. To deal with this ambivalent state the crisis worker cycles between asking open-ended questions and reflecting and clarifying the victim's feelings. The questions that follow, and their variations, represent effective means of helping the victim to begin to examine previously denied feelings and thoughts.

CW: What were you thinking and feeling while he was beating you?

Victim: It was like I was standing off to the side watching a movie of this. It was like this can't really be happening, especially to me.

CW: So that's how you cope with it. Kind of separating yourself from the beating, as if it's happening to someone else.

Victim: Yes, I guess I've done it that way for a long time. I'd go crazy otherwise.

CW: What is your understanding of why you're being battered?

Victim: I don't know. I guess I'm just not a good wife.

CW: You're not living up to his expectations, then. How about your own?

Victim: I'm not sure. I mean, I've never thought of that. It's always been what he wants.

CW: How do you cope with the beating other than just kind of separating yourself from the situation when it happens?

Victim: I try to do what he wants, but when it starts to build—the tension—I just try to stay out of his way and be nice, although I know sooner or later I'm gonna get it. I dread the waiting. Actually sometimes I push the issue just to get it over with. I know he'll always apologize afterwards and treat me nice.

CW: So you do what he wishes even though you know the bottom line is a beating. Yet because of the anxiety you may even push things to get it over with. Seems like you're willing to pay a steep price to get his love back.

Victim: When you say that, I can't believe I'm letting this happen to me. What a fool . . . a stupid fool!

CW: Then you feel foolish about paying that price. What's keeping you in the relationship?

Victim: God! I don't know. Love! Honor! Obey! The kids. The good times. Martyrdom. I don't have a job and I'm pregnant again. Even then, it's no good, but I stay. I've got to get out. This is nuts. He'll wind up killing me.

Using open-ended questions, restatement, and reflection, the crisis worker relentlessly hammers at the victim's faulty and illogical perception of the abusive situation. In assessing the situation, the worker tries to gain an understanding of the victim's interpretation of what being battered means to her. Only by looking and listening through the victim's eyes and ears can the crisis worker form an accurate perception of what steps to take and how she will operate on the nondirective-to-directive continuum of intervention.

Women who have been abused also have in common the feeling of depression. Invariably, once a victim has related the details of the assault, her affect becomes flat. Depression has taken over. The victim is like a rat that gets shocked at both ends of a Skinner box. She is wrong whatever she does and becomes frozen and immobilized. Beneath the depression is a volcano of residual anger that is trying to find an outlet. The crisis worker's job is to help move the victim out of her depressed state and let the angry feelings out (Dagastino, 1984). This is the first step toward taking action.

CW: As you relate the details it sounds like you're reporting it but not living it. I wonder if that's a typical way you hold it in . . . control it.

Victim: I guess . . . if I really thought about it, I'd kill the S.O.B. How could the bastard do this to me?

CW: How does it feel to let some of those angry feelings out?

Victim: Scary! I'm really scared I would kill him if I got the chance.

CW: That is a legitimate feeling after what you've been through, but that won't get you where you want to go. Let's take a look at some of the alternatives between killing and being killed.

In summarizing the facilitation of the victim's movement from an immobile to a mobile state, the Massachusetts Coalition of Battered Women Service Groups (1981, pp. 25, 67) has made these points. We agree with them in totality.

1. *Be real.* Don't hide behind a role. You are what you are. To pretend to be something else makes the crisis worker false and uncreditable in the eyes of the victim.

2. *Set limits.* The crisis worker is not Superwoman. Owning feelings of puzzlement, anger, stupidity, tiredness, and so forth allows the crisis worker to stay on top of the game. Nowhere is it written that a crisis worker has to become a victim. If the worker is tired, is taking on a lot of anger, and cannot work it through with the victim, she should own the feelings, ask for time out, and get out of the situation until the problem can be gone over with a fellow professional and a fresh start can be taken.

3. *Give the victim space and time to "freak out."* Remember that the victim is experiencing a flood of emotions that have been building over a long period of time. Knowing that anger is one step on the way to becoming her own person can be reassuring and empowering to the victim. Give her time to ventilate before settling down to a plan of action.

4. *Allow the victim to go through the pain, but stay with her.* A crisis worker's first response may be to become a psychological crutch because the victim is so fragile that she cannot hold together. If the crisis worker remembers that the victim has been down a long road of pain and is just now beginning to experience that pain, she will realize that the victim possesses a lot of staying power. Belief in the victim's ability to get out of the mess she is in is of overriding importance.

5. *Maintain eye and ear contact.* Both nonverbal and verbal responses of the victim are important; they tell the crisis worker whether what the victim is saying is congruent with what she is doing. Reading nonverbal responses may be difficult over the phone, but the worker needs to be aware of intonations, pauses, and sighs. How something is said may be as important as what is said. Also, what is not said may be as important as what is said.

6. *Being respectful and nonjudgmental of the victim is a must.* The victim's actions must be carefully separated from the victim herself. What the victim does may be asinine. That does not mean the victim is an ass.

7. *Restate and reflect the victim's thoughts and feelings.* Simple as this sounds, it is often extremely difficult. There is no greater therapeutic help than manifesting these skills.

8. *Set priorities together.* Two heads are better than one. This is why the crisis worker is there. If the victim could handle the problem alone, she would. Likewise, the wife abuse worker is not in business to run the victim's life for her.

9. *Look at options.* Brainstorming can uncover a variety of previously hidden ideas and actions.

10. *Stay away from whys.* Asking *why* a person does something, like staying in a battering relationship, is an open invitation to philosophizing, rationalizing, and intellectualizing. These are all detours away from dealing with the real issue, the person's situation at that particular time. Further, a "why" question often leads the victim, rightly or wrongly, to assume she is being judged. When a victim feels she is being judged, she is apt to respond in defensive ways that do little to help her or her situation.

11. *Give the victim time to experience catharsis, but do not let her get stuck in self-pity.* The client needs to accomplish movement, and the crisis worker needs to move gently from nurturing emotional release to helping the client start to make plans, however small, concerning her own predicament.

12. *Touch the victim.* Both verbally and nonverbally, the worker must show she remembers that most victims are isolated psychologically. To touch deeply a feeling the victim is struggling with and, indeed, to lean over and touch the victim's hand in a appropriate and empathic way may be worth much.

13. *Get back to the victim.* No matter how the battered woman says, "I guess I can make it now," get her phone number and call a few days later to make sure she is getting along all right. Many abused women are so embarrassed by their plight and their own self-assessed stupidity that they cannot bring themselves to make another call and admit they have failed again.

14. *Peer supervision and feedback are essential for wife abuse workers.* The intensity of wife abuse is such that few, if any, crisis workers can remain totally objective all the time. Cross-supervision by trusted coprofessionals keeps the worker on track, reduces personal stress, and helps avoid burnout.

Ensuring safety. The crisis worker's first job is to determine how critical the situation is (Walker, 1984, p. 122). All the listening and responding skills known to humanity are of little use if the victim has multiple fractures or if her spouse has threatened to come back and kill her. The crisis worker calmly and cautiously makes an assessment of how bad the situation is. Does the victim need and want medical attention, shelter, a place to send her children, a way out of the house if her husband returns? All these questions are posed in a measured, deliberate way to avoid adding to the panic the victim already feels. Although the situation may be critical, and the best alternative might be for the victim to come directly to the shelter, the crisis worker has to remember that the woman cannot be forced into making that choice. This does not mean, however, that the worker cannot make such a recommendation.

CW: From what you've said, it sounds like the situation is pretty bad. Bad enough that you might consider leaving and coming to the shelter.

Because of a fear of the unknown, the victim may balk at this alternative (Dagastino, 1984). Patiently, the crisis worker explains the role and function of the shelter, answers any questions the victim has, and tries to allay her fears. If, after all this, the victim is still unwilling to make a decision, the worker does not push the issue. The worker shifts attention to other critical needs of the victim. How physically abused is the client? Is this the first time she has been abused or is this the latest in a continuing series of abusive events? In either case, how severe has the abuse been? Are her feelings hurt, or is her body injured?

Even though most women insist the beatings are random, there may be a subtle correlation between environmental events and occurrence of abuse (Heppner, 1978). All the foregoing questions are important in determining a baseline of what is going on with the victim. It is this kind of information the worker must have to be of the most assistance, both in getting the victim the help she needs immediately and in assessing what long-term help may be needed.

In initially reporting the battering, victims often appear to feel that it is an isolated incident and not abuse. They refuse to see it on an ever-escalating continuum. They delude themselves with the belief, "He really does love me, and if I'm a better person, it'll never happen again."

As the crisis worker intervenes, she should be aware that such incidents are not isolated. Indeed, there is a consistent pattern leading up to the climax of battering (Walker, 1984, p. 24). The crisis worker endeavors to lay that pattern out so that the victim sees it not as isolated but as continuous and predictable. Seeing the pattern is particularly important when the victim is not sure whether to leave or stay.

CW: As you tell me about it, I hear a sort of pattern. For about a week he gets surly, starts criticizing the way the house looks, the way you look, the food you cook, and your control over the kids. Those criticisms start out mild, but become more severe until you finally have had enough and say something to the effect that he ought to take more responsibility if he doesn't like things. That winds up with your getting beat up. As you report that, I wonder if you can look back and see how the situation has repeated itself.

Victim: Well, I don't know. I really think it was different this time. I mean this was the first time I needed emergency treatment. He was really sorry afterward. I don't know.

CW: OK. Granted the beating was more severe, but I believe from what you're saying that there's a very definite pattern to it. What's different is that the pattern seems to be repeating itself more frequently and it's getting more intense.

Many times the client may be in a high degree of immobility and may not even hear the question, so the worker may need to refer to it again (Dagastino, 1984).

CW: When did he say he'd be back and what'd he say he'd do?

Victim: I just don't know whether to take it any more. I love him, but I'm really scared.

CW: Ok, I understand you are afraid, but I need to know how much time we've got and what threats he made.

By gently guiding the victim back to immediate and pressing issues, the crisis worker keeps the session on track but does not deny the emotional hurt and confusion the victim is experiencing.

By the time the battered woman becomes desperate enough to make the call for help, she does not have time to be analyzed, nor does she have time to go into all kinds of self-analysis. What she does need is some behavioral action-oriented techniques she can use on a short-term basis (Walker, 1979, pp. 75–77). The crisis worker's major task is to get the victim back to a semblance of equilibrium and control. This is accomplished by attempting to get the abused woman to commit to some plan, however small. By just knowing and having a plan, the victim is able to regain some composure and feel that she has obtained some control over the situation. The whole focus of the conversation is to prepare her to get through that one day. At this time, the worker does not worry about tomorrow or any other time. Tomorrow, the worker may call the victim and talk about the next day. If the worker attempts to deal with future events that extend beyond a week, the victim gets lost (Dagastino, 1984).

Because of the flood of critical needs the victim faces, the worker must realistically judge which needs may require immediate action and which ones can be deferred. To help make sense of the heavy flow of information, the crisis worker writes down what the victim tells her so that she can quickly identify and prioritize the very practical concerns that are pressing in on the victim. Issues such as getting enough money for the children's lunch the next day may be just as important as taking care of a broken nose, and the worker will need to remember this. By calmly, clearly, and concisely feeding back to the victim her written summary, the crisis worker takes the victim step by step through a review of her most critical needs. In doing so, the worker shows the victim that although she has many problems, they are not insurmountable. By dissecting the crisis in this manner, the worker assures the victim that her problems can be broken down and managed (Dagastino, 1984).

CW: Here are all the things I hear happening to you right now. No wonder you're feeling paralyzed; anyone in that situation would feel the same. You've said you have no job, the children don't want to leave, and that he might kill you. Let's take them one at a time and sort through each problem and put them back together.

A careful examination of the woman's fears about these problems, how they need to be prioritized, and the options she has in dealing with them is extremely important. Until the abused woman can confront such fears openly, she cannot begin developing strategies to deal with her problems (Heppner, 1978).

CW: You're afraid to leave because you feel sure he will come after you when he comes back, and you're not sure what he might do, so that causes tension to build. Yet I really believe if we make a plan right now you'll feel better, even if you don't have to use it.

If the victim states that she does not know what to do, the crisis worker immediately looks at the two basic alternatives—staying and leaving. A considerable amount of exploration time is given over to the possible options in each of the two alternatives. A key ingredient is determining the level of danger at home. Is the husband really going to act out, or is the fear of his acting out propelling the woman into making the call? To learn what has happened before, the crisis worker asks questions such as, "When he's gone out and got drunk before, what has he done? Has he torn up the house, beat you or the kids? What has he done?" From the answers, the crisis worker gains a realistic assessment of the danger level of the situation. If the victim is unwilling to leave the house, then the crisis worker role-plays the scene of the drunken spouse returning home. Assuming the role of the abuser, the worker goes through, in a systematic way, each situation of potential confrontation and then discusses the potential positive and negative outcomes of the victim's attempt to handle the confrontation (Dagastino, 1984).

CW: (In role.) Hey, honey! Come on into the bedroom. I need you real bad.

Victim: (Typical response.) I can't stand having sex with you when you are drunk.

CW: (As self.) Now, look at how you responded to that. When you shut him off like that he gets angry, right? What could you do or say differently? How could you change things? How about turning the tables so he had no desire for you at all? What'd happen if you had a facial on and your hair up in curlers, and had on a frowzy housecoat? While that might not make you very alluring, would that turn him off?

By looking at options and posing alternative ways of behaving, the worker attempts to provide coping techniques that may defuse the crisis. By the time the worker is done, the victim is feeding back a plan, point by point, either for staying in the house or for moving out. Having an escape plan is critical (Walker, 1984, p. 122).

CW: All right! You've figured out how to get out of the house. You'll keep the back door open. You've given the kids a note to go over to the neighbors. You've got our number and you know you can get to your car, parked out back, and get to a phone booth and call us.

In summary, both short- and long-term safety depends on helping abused women take action steps rather than remaining immobilized. Wife abuse crises are different from other types of crises in this respect. For many victims, it may not be a question of returning to a precrisis equilibrium. The equilibrium was never there in the first place. Therefore, for many women, taking first, tentative steps toward action is likely to be extremely frightening, confusing, and full of trepidation.

The following points seem worthwhile for crisis workers to know and understand in helping abused women make such decisions and take action (Massachusetts Coalition of Battered Women Service Groups, 1981, pp. 25, 67).

1. Help women think and act on their situation by providing legitimate reinforcement for their efforts.
2. Help women figure out what they want by providing a sounding board for examining ideas and alternatives.
3. Help women to identify feelings that prevent them from making decisions.
4. Be honest. The worker cannot tell a person what to do, but can clearly state from her own life how the situation would affect her.
5. Help women to do things for themselves, but do not let them become dependent on the worker.
6. Know and offer resources from which battered women can get specific kinds of assistance: spell out who, what, where, when, and how.
7. Help women gain a sense of self-confidence and ability to take care of themselves.
8. Be challenging. Support women, but do not be afraid to push them toward a decision-making point.
9. Be open to choices. Each woman has control over her life; the crisis worker must not attempt to assume control for clients.
10. Hear and understand what women have to say, particularly if it does not run parallel to the worker's own beliefs, attitudes, and outlooks.

11. Build on the commonalities that women, particularly battered women, share, but recognize the worth of the individual differences of each person.

12. Assess lethality. "I'm fed up and whipped" may really mean "I'm ready to commit suicide."

The following wife abuse worker's response to a battered woman, who after two hours of talking on the telephone still could not make up her mind about what to do, aptly illustrates application of the 12 points just made.

CW: I understand your mixed feelings of wanting to stay and wanting to leave, also the constant fear you live with while waiting for the next time, maybe even wishing it would happen quickly so the tension will ease off. But my guess is that tension reduction only occurs for a short period and then starts to build all over again. I also understand that you feel like you're locked into this, but there are some alternatives, which we have gone over. I want you to pick at least one of those, whichever seems best for you, and do it. I won't take no for an answer. Do something that will make you feel better right now. Go take a hot bath if that'll help and don't spare the bath oil. I think it would be safer for you to come to the shelter right now, but if you don't really feel you can do that, I understand. However, if you feel the tension start to rise and feel like you just can't take it any more, I want you to promise to call back here. I won't take no for an answer. Whatever, I'll call you tomorrow afternoon to see how things are going. What would be a good time?

Advocacy. Because battered women have been isolated for much of their lives, they generally have little knowledge of alternatives open to them. This is especially true with respect to their rights and options with both legal and welfare systems. Therefore, a major responsibility of the crisis worker is to know not only the formal but also the informal workings of these monolithic systems. Understanding the laws and how to make them work for abused women in crisis is a must. Knowing how to weave through bureaucratic obstacles and how to cut through the red tape that is often put in the way of someone seeking help from the system is of paramount importance. The wife abuse worker who excels has an excellent networking system that she can tap into and get immediate help for a variety of problems. Further, the competent crisis worker will know how the game in each system is played and will know how to bend the rules to get help for the victim. (For an excellent summary of advocacy, see Chapter 4, "Advocacy—Welfare and Legal," *For Shelter and Beyond: An Educational Manual for Working with Women Who Are Battered* [Massachusetts Coalition of Battered Women Service Groups, 1981], and *Battered Women* [Moore, 1979]).

Transcrisis perspective. All of the foregoing intervention procedures cannot be accomplished in a 20-minute phone call. Even minor crises may require two or three calls to get the client stabilized, in touch with her feelings, and into some semblance of preabuse equilibrium. The crisis worker is not providing a short-term elixir that merely calms the victim and then blithely sending her on her way. What is being provided is a blend that not only deals with the immediate crisis but also has a long-term application. Many battered women need to go through a complete reeducation process about who they are and what they can do. This process should not be hurried even if it takes a year to accomplish the goal. One of the most difficult problems in dealing with battered women is that they have lived at such peak energy levels for such long periods of time. Battered women seem never to come down from their state of anxiety and frenetic tension.

In response to this continuing high-pitched state of emotional existence, a crisis worker must be prepared to deal with emotional brushfires that occur frequently and last for extended periods of time. Indeed, the transcrisis of the battered woman does not end when she gets off the phone and decides to come into the center or go to the shelter. The initiating interview or hot line call is only the first part of the crisis resolution. Other and probably more severe crises will continue to plague the victim. The guidelines we have described in this first stage still apply, but other problems lie ahead.

Ibrahim and Herr's (1987) work with battered women who were involved in a group counseling format that concentrated on vocational exploration and economic independence is an excellent example of a transcrisis point. When these women reached the stage of vocational implementation, ready actually to go out into the world of work and test their skills, they experienced all kinds of threatening and anxious feelings and became immobile and paralyzed. Fifteen two-hour sessions of intensive support by the group leaders were needed to help the women work through this stage!

CENTER AND SHELTER

A center and a shelter are generally two different entities within a wife abuse program. The center deals with telephone and on-site, short-term crisis intervention and counseling. The shelter is a longer-term facility where women and their families can stay for short or extended periods of time. A comprehensive program will have both a center and a shelter and will be staffed around the clock with a 24-hour hot line and an open-door policy for walk-ins (Barnett et al., 1980). There will be tie-ins to other social service agencies: law enforcement personnel, free or sliding-scale legal services, hospitals, medical staff and mental health facilities, mobile crisis teams that provide transportation for abuse victims, and direct links to emergency housing facilities with follow-up services (Benjamin & Walz, 1983, p. 83). Such a comprehensive program is the ideal. In reality, shortages of funds and personnel make the ideal a rarity.

The typical shelter is linked to the wife abuse center and is well publicized, but for security reasons its location may not be made public. For the same reason, it will be well patrolled by the police and will be secure. Staffed by both professionals and volunteers, it will have adequate cooking, sleeping, bath, child- and infant-care facilities for a number of families, and funds for clothing, food, and transportation (Langley & Levy, 1977). It should also provide a variety of counseling services to assist women to ventilate feelings, explore alternatives, and make immediate plans for what they will do next (Benjamin & Walz, 1983, p. 84). This ideal, again, is a rarity.

Counseling Women at Shelters

Women who enter the shelter fit into two categories: those who are unsure about leaving the battering relationship and those who have made a definite commitment to leave it (Dagastino, 1984). Women who fall into the first category need to be monitored on an hour-by-hour basis and are the more critical of the two categories. The crisis worker maintains constant contact with these women and reinforces them for having had the courage to come to the shelter.

CW: I'm glad you made it. I know it took a lot of courage.

CW: (10 minutes later.) Getting settled in? Come on with me, there's some other women I would like you to meet.

CW: (2 hours later.) How are things going? Got the kids settled in? They're great-looking children. Want to have a cup of coffee and talk?

Vacillation between going back and staying is characteristic of these women. The worker does not try to force women to stay at the shelter, but does try to get them to take some psychological "time out" to review their situation in a more objective way (Dagastino, 1984).

CW: Let's assume you're taking a one-day vacation so you can get some rest before you go back and deal with it. It's fine if you want to go back home, but do this much for me—just take it easy for a while. I can see that you're physically all right and not hurt, and I'm relieved. This is a great time to talk about what you can do when you go back and it is a good time to make some concrete plans.

The shelter worker checks repeatedly with the new arrival and reinforces her decision to come. She conveys her concern for the victim and with the help of other women in the shelter, sees that the victim and her family are settled. The focus is on the here and now. During the first few hours of the victim's separation from her abuser, the worker will probably have to be very directive. Few women, at this time, have the ego strength to stand on their own and need an abundance of support and help. The objective is to keep the victim moving, thinking, and acting so that she is preoccupied and does not have time to let fear, guilt, or any other debilitating and anxiety-ridden emotions overcome her. Domestic chores such as cleaning and cooking seem to be particularly helpful in this regard. In all instances, the worker should be carefully attuned to the victim's needs. Some may find help sitting, talking, or crying with a worker or a group of other women. Others may be so exhausted that they need to go to bed and sleep. Whatever the victim needs, the worker should be adaptable to those needs and flexible enough to change as circumstances demand (Dagastino, 1984).

A variety of positive dynamics occurs at shelters. There is substantial support from other women who have experienced the same kind of trauma. This enables victims to begin gaining the courage to face people, recovering their lost self-esteem, and learning that the beatings were not their fault (Schecter, 1982, pp. 55–60).

Wife abuse shelters are not vacation spas where one's every whim is catered to. Although an abundance of caring and sharing occurs, women who live in shelters are encouraged to start trusting themselves to make decisions. Part of the decision-making process includes determining what is best for the shelter. This is not an easy task. Limits have to be set with respect to pets, children, cooking, and so on (Schecter, 1982, pp. 63–64). Women get bored, boss each other around, miss their men, miss sex (pp. 55–60), and have problems relating to people from different ethnic and racial backgrounds and sociocultural milieus (Massachusetts Coalition of Battered Women Service Groups, 1981, p. 28).

Victim: Getting used to a shelter is overwhelming. You like it, but you don't want to be there 'cause it isn't home. You've got to put together all your psychological know-how in getting along with different types of people. Wondering if you're going to make it, especially when you see all the pain and confusion and don't know whether it's yours or theirs or what, and hoping nobody finds out you're here. Trying to be understood and feeling like you are a blabbermouth here when you couldn't talk at home. Trying to look forward and all the time wanting to forget . . . wanting to forget . . . wanting to forget (Schecter, 1982, pp. 59–60).

At a shelter everything is not always as it seems. Many women who come to the shelter are extremely dependent and exceptionally adept at manipulating the workers there (Walker, 1984, p. 126). A statement like "You really understand—you've made my whole life better" is reinforcing to the worker, but she is actually being manipulated. The woman is using the house and the worker as a security blanket and is not making any progress toward getting out on her own (Dagastino, 1984). The wise shelter worker comes to see the manipulation for what it is, a refusal to take responsibility for oneself and a shift from dependency on an abusive husband to dependency on a caring shelter worker (Weincourt, 1985). Gently but firmly, the worker extinguishes such behavior.

CW: I appreciate what you said, and I appreciate your wanting to cook my dinner and all the other things you want to do for me. Yet I believe your time and mine could be better spent working on getting you set up in an apartment and looking for a job.

Besides being dependent, many women go through a grieving process. They talk about their furniture, homes, vacations, and so forth, as they relive their past. There are a lot of "yes, buts" as workers start to confront them with making a new future. As victims shift from a depersonalized view of their situation to depression over it, the process can be extremely frightening to a shelter worker unless she knows that this, too, is another step in the transcrisis battered women go through (Dagastino, 1984). When grieving occurs, the crisis worker is empathic and lets the victim work through it, then slowly pulls her back to the present and the rest of her life by reflecting and connecting past to present.

CW: It's really hard to say good-bye to all those things that were and that might have been. In some ways it's like a close friend or relative died. Yet there's also something new, too. As you work through those farewells I kind of see a new, different, better, stronger person coming out of it, tough as it is.

Depression comes in many guises. Many women who come into the shelter sleep much of the time. On first appearance, they may seem to be lazy. Actually, they may be going through a stage of trying to regroup their psychic energy. The worker's task becomes one of trying to help them move past their inactivity, but not by pressuring them or taking them on a guilt trip (Massachusetts Coalition of Battered Women Service Groups, 1981, p. 27).

CW: I've noticed you pretty much sticking to your room and sleeping a lot. I was a little concerned and was wondering how you were feeling. I wonder if you've had a chance to talk to anyone about how you feel since you got here.

For many women, a stress-related syndrome similar to agoraphobia arises after they have been in the shelter for a while (Massachusetts Coalition of Battered Women Service Groups, 1981, p. 27). They may have extreme and unexplainable attacks of terror that are touched off by seemingly innocuous incidents. These incidents greatly restrict their activities and new freedom. The fear of their mates, the fear of their predicament, the fear of their separation from a definable past, and the fear of an undefinable future can all cause the onset of terror. Under no circumstances should the shelter worker allow it to continue. Victims must be encouraged and helped step by step to pull themselves away from the security blanket of the shelter and out into the real world. Such progress may take place in very small, slow steps, but the steps must be taken. As women take these steps, they receive very specific, positive reinforcement for what they have accomplished, enabling them not to fall back into learned helplessness but instead to take responsibility for their behavior (Weincourt, 1985). Invariably, victims will not be able to see that they have done much of anything, or they tend to diminish their successes.

CW: I know you're still scared to death to go down and talk to them at Federal Express about that job. It's a big step, but a week ago you couldn't walk down to the grocery store and now you're doing that fine. So let's take it a step at a time. Look at what you overcame. We can go through the job interview, play it a step at a time, talk about those steps right here where it's safe, and give you a chance to really become confident about going down there.

The second category of women who come to the shelter are in for a long haul and are not going back to the battering situation. For women who are in for the duration, the crisis worker deals with immediate specifics such as finding a place to live, financial aid, and child care. Emotional support has a low priority because these women are so busy that all they want and need is very practical advice and help. These women are very different from those experiencing acute crisis because they are highly motivated to change their lives. They are much easier to work with because they have made a decision to get out of their domestic pressure cooker (Dagastino, 1984).

For all women who come to wife abuse centers and shelters, a continuing and pervasive problem is their inability not only to say they will not be beaten but also to own that statement behaviorally (Dagastino, 1984). The whole thrust of this type of transcrisis work is to teach victims to view themselves as survivors dependent only on themselves, and to realize that the traumas they have been forced to deal with are not unique to them, but rather are political issues with deep sociocultural roots that all women have to deal with either directly or indirectly (Schecter, 1982, p. 66).

The crisis worker may then, while the victim is in transition, broach larger societal issues that keep her in the battering situation, if, and this is a big if, she is ready to handle such issues. Many women who initiate contact with an abuse center are isolated to the extent that they feel as if no one else were in their situation, and they are so wrapped up in themselves that they cannot see the ways that societal norms conspire to keep them in the battering situation. If victims can begin to understand that the system does impinge on them, the crisis worker can then start to do something to help them take responsibility for meeting the world and finding a place in it without getting battered in the process.

Follow-Up

Once women leave the shelter, they should be provided with follow-up. As immediate demands are relieved, the emotional impact of their decision should be dealt with over the long term. These women are urged to go for counseling with the idea that no one can be beaten even once without suffering some psychological damage. It is not uncommon for a woman to be so busy getting her act together that her emotional reactions are delayed. The victim may be out on her own, well established, and watching television at the time that she experiences a sudden emotional breakdown. The crisis worker apprises the victim of what to expect in the way of emotional aftershocks. Such residual psychological trauma seems to be particularly characteristic of women who initially appear to be very much in control (Dagastino, 1984).

CW: Even though you feel like you've made the break from your husband, don't be surprised if later on you get depressed and really feel like you need and miss your husband. That's to be expected. We know that and we're here to help then too!

Indeed, in the worst of scenarios, the victim may become lonely, forget about the terrible abuse she suffered in the past, invite her ex-mate over for dinner, and get beaten up again. Therefore, in following up with the victim, the crisis worker should understand that there may be relapses and that the victim may fall into old ways of behaving. Thus, crisis workers not only may have to check up on their clients but also may have to be indirect about it so the women do not become dependent on them (Dagastino, 1984).

CW: Hello, Jane. Just called to see if you've been able to make that appointment for counseling at the Human Services Clinic. I know it's hard to get in there at times and thought if you hadn't, I could call the clinic and we'd have one of the people here drive you down and help you get started.

If the victim volunteers to enter therapy, the worker continues to check on her until she has really settled into her therapy and is mobile. The crisis worker continues to be a support system until the victim is well connected to a long-term support source, and only then will the crisis worker fade from the victim's life.

SUMMARY

Wife abuse has deep roots in the psychological, sociological, and cultural makeup of this country that go back to the beginning of the patriarchal system. Battering is pervasive through all socioeconomic levels of society and knows no ethnic, racial, or religious boundaries.

Dynamically, wife abuse may be seen as having much to do with the concept of power. A variety of stressors that insinuate themselves into a relationship can escalate relational problems to violence and wife battering.

To be an effective worker in wife abuse normally means being a woman. Otherwise the victim's fear of men interferes too much with the ongoing process. In the complex arena of wife abuse, there are no simple answers. Each case and each situation must be handled as unique. Different victims will feel, think, and behave differently at different times. It is clear that no one can or should tell a victim that she must leave a battering situation. Only the victim is qualified to decide when she is ready to take action steps. The worker's job is to provide options and, working with the victim, to help her explore and choose among them.

Wife abuse work is sequential, developmental, and dynamic. The situation of the abused woman is unlike many other crises in that it has the nature of a transcrisis; that is, it is cyclic, reaching many peak levels over extended periods of time.

Wife abuse crisis intervention is less than twenty years old. In a field so young, much research still needs to be done to determine the most effective ways to handle wife abuse. We have tapped the experiences of both workers and victims in this fluid and changing field and attempted to present them as the current state of the art in a practical and helpful fashion. This does not mean that we have the final word on the subject.

We do not believe that being a battered wife is a sufficient reason for becoming an interventionist in a spouse abuse center. We believe that professional crisis worker training and emotional maturity are required ingredients for functioning without becoming overly involved to the detriment of both the worker and the client. What we have written in this chapter is a start toward that training. Experience gained through well-supervised volunteer work or practicums is a necessary adjunct.

Because of the intense emotional pressure of the job, there is a pronounced tendency for workers to become over involved and demonstrate feelings of depression, anger, and frustration. Such problems go with the territory. To help workers avoid the emotional drainage that goes with the job, weekly case conferences should reserve some time for crisis workers to vent some of their own feelings about the trials, tribulations, and emotional effects of their jobs. (For a complete analysis of the crisis worker in crisis, see Chapter 12.)

In our home state of Tennessee a law has recently raised the marriage license fee to $25. The additional money has been earmarked to fund wife abuse centers and shelters throughout the state. If state bureaucracy does not interfere with the excellent job that wife abuse centers like the one we have in Memphis are doing, then the additional money will make possible a gigantic step forward in helping battered women in Tennessee reclaim their lives.

REFERENCES

American Psychiatric Association. (1980). *Diagnostic and statistical manual of mental disorders* (3rd ed.). Washington, DC: Author.

Barnett, E. R., Pittman, C. R., Ragan, C., & Salus, M. K. (1980). *Family violence: Intervention strategies* (DHHS Publication No. OHD 580-30258). Washington, DC: U.S. Government Printing Office.

Benjamin, L., & Walz, G. R. (1983). *Violence in the family: Child and spouse abuse* (Report No. EDN00001). Washington, DC: National Institute of Education. (ERIC Document Reproduction Service No. ED 226–309).

Bradley v. State, 1 Miss. 156 (1824).

Capps, M. (1982, April). *The co-optive and repressive state versus the battered women's movement.* Paper presented at annual meeting of Southern Sociological Society, Memphis.

Conroy, K. (1982). Long term treatment issues with battered women. In J. P. Flanger (Ed.), *The many faces of family violence.* Springfield, IL: Charles C Thomas.

Dagastino, A. (Speaker). (1984). *Crisis intervention series: Helping abused women in wife abuse centers and shelters* (Cassette Recording No. 4-1). Memphis: Memphis State University Department of Counseling and Personnel Services.

Davidson, T. (1977). Wife beating: A recurring phenomenon throughout history. In M. Roy (Ed.), *Battered women: A psychosocial study of domestic violence.* New York: Van Nostrand Reinhold.

Davies, J. L., & Janosik, E. H. (1984). Disorganized families in crisis: Spouse abuse. In E. H. Janosik (Ed.), *Crisis counseling: A contemporary approach* (pp. 202–220). Monterey, CA: Wadsworth Health Sciences Division.

Elbow, M. (1977). Theoretical considerations of violent marriages. *Social Casework, 31,* 515–523.

Fields, M. D. (1976). Wife beating: The hidden offense. *New York Law Journal, 175,* 1–7.

Flynn, J. P. (1977). Recent findings relative to wife abuse. *Social Casework, 58*(1), 13–20.

Ganley, A. L., & Harris, L. (1978, August). *Domestic violence: Issues in designing and implementing programs for male batterers.* Paper presented at the annual meeting of the American Psychological Association, Toronto. (ERIC Document Reproduction Service No. ED 167871).

Gelles, R. J. (1972). *The violent home: A study of physical aggression between husbands and wives.* Beverly Hills, CA: Sage Publications.

Gelles, R. J. (1977). No place to go: The social dynamics of marital violence. In M. Roy (Ed.), *Battered women: A psychosocial study of domestic violence.* New York: Van Nostrand Reinhold.

Halleck, S. L. (1976). Psychodynamic aspects of violence. *Bulletin of American Academy of Psychiatry and Law, 4,* 328–335.

Hart, B. (1980, June). Testimony at a hearing before the U.S. Commission on Civil Rights, Harrisburg, PA.

Heppner, M. J. (1978). Counseling the battered wife: Myths, facts, and decisions. *Personnel and Guidance Journal, 56,* 522–525.

Ibrahim, F. A., & Herr, E. L. (1987). Battered women: A developmental life–career counseling perspective. *Journal of Counseling and Development, 65,* 244–248.

Langley, R., & Levy, R. C. (1977). *Wife beating: The silent crisis.* New York: Dutton.

Margolin, G. (1979). *Conjoint marital therapy to enhance anger management and reduce spouse abuse.* Los Angeles: University of Southern California Psychological Research and Service Center.

Massachusetts Coalition of Battered Women Service Groups (1981). *For shelter and beyond: An educational manual for working with women who are battered.* Boston, MA: Red Sun Press.

Moore, D. M. (Ed.). (1979). *Battered women.* Beverly Hills, CA: Sage Publications.

Mott-MacDonald, L. (1979). Report on the Belmont Conference on Spouse Abuse. Washington, DC: Center for Women Policy Studies.

Pagelow, M. D. (1977). *Battered women: A new perspective.* Berkeley, CA: University of California.

Pizzey, E. (1974). *Scream quietly or the neighbors will hear.* London: Penguin Books.

Resnik, M. (1976). *Wife beating: Counselor training manual.* Ann Arbor, MI: NOW Domestic Violence Project.

Rosewater, L. B. (1982). *An MMPI profile for battered women.* Unpublished doctoral dissertation, Union Graduate School. Ann Arbor, MI: *Dissertation Abstracts,* 1982.

Schecter, S. (1982). *Women and male violence.* Boston: South End Press.

Schultz, L. G. (1960). The wife assaulter. *Corrective Psychiatry and Journal of Social Therapy, 6,* 103–111.

Schuyler, M. (1976). Battered wives, an emerging social problem. *Social Work, 21,* 488–491.

State v. Oliver, 70 N. C. 60, 61–62 (1874).

Steinmetz, S. K. (1978). Wife beating: A critique and reformulation of existing theory. *Bulletin of American Academy of Psychiatry and the Law, 6,* 322–334.

Steinmetz, S. K., & Strauss, M. A. (1973). Family as a cradle of violence. *Society, 10,* 50–56.

Steinmetz, S. K., & Strauss, M. A. (Eds.). (1974). *Violence in the family.* New York: Harper & Row.

Symonds, M. (1978). The psychodynamics of violence prone marriages. *American Journal of Psychoanalysis, 38,* 213–222.

Walker, L. (1979). How battering happens and how to stop it. In D. Moore (Ed.), *Battered women* (pp. 59–78). Beverly Hills, CA: Sage Publications.

Walker, L. (1984). *The battered woman syndrome.* New York: Springer Publishing Co.

Weincourt, R. (1985, March). Never to be alone: Existential therapy for battered women. *Journal of Psychosocial Nursing, 23,* 24–29.

Woods, F. B. (1981). *Living without violence: A community approach to working with battered women and their children.* Fayetteville, AR: Project for Victims of Domestic Violence, Inc.

■ Classroom Exercises: Case of Joyce

The following is a typical case of an abused wife. Joyce is a 34-year-old woman who has been married ten years. She has three children, all under 10 years old: Sheena, age 9; Jack, age 6; and Beth, age 2. Her husband is a prominent attorney. The family presents an ideal picture of an upper-middle-class family. They live in a fashionable suburb. The husband has been successful to the extent that he has been made a full partner in a large law firm. The family is very active in church, the country club, and various other social organizations. Joyce is an active member of several charitable, civic, and social groups. Joyce's initial call to the wife abuse center was vague and guarded. She expressed an interest for "another woman" in regard to the purpose of the center. After she had received information and an invitation to call back, a number of weeks elapsed. Joyce's second call occurred after receiving a severe beating from her husband. This is a segment of that conversation.

CW: (Answering phone.) Wife abuse center. May I help you?

Joyce: I feel terrible calling you so many times, but I've gotta have help right away. (Sobbing.)

CW: OK! Tell me what's happened that you need help now.

Joyce: Well, last night he beat me worse than ever. I thought he was really going to kill me this time. It had been building up for the past few weeks. His fuse was getting shorter and shorter, both with me and the kids. It's his work, I guess. Finally he came home late last night. Dinner was cold. We were supposed to go out and I guess it was my fault . . . I complained about his being late and he blew up. Started yelling that he was gonna teach me a lesson. He started hitting me with his fists . . . knocked me down . . . and then started kicking me. I got up and ran into the bathroom. The kids were yelling for him to stop and he cuffed Sheena . . . God, it was horrible! (Wracked with sobs for more than a minute. CW waits.) I'm sorry, I just can't seem to keep control.

CW: After all that I think anyone would be insane if they weren't feeling out of control. Right now, I'm concerned about your and your children's safety. Do you need medical attention? A safe place to come and stay, like right now?

Joyce: No . . . I guess I'm OK . . . I guess . . . I don't know. Then, he broke down the door and started in again and the next thing I knew Sheena was wiping blood off my face with a washcloth and he'd left.

CW: What do you want to do now?

Joyce: Well, I was going to get a divorce but when I went to see a lawyer a couple of years ago I thought I'd lose the children if I went through with it. So I just figured I'd put up with it. (Voice trembles.) I'd rather die than lose the children. I was afraid he might kill me, too.

CW: Did he ever threaten you?

Joyce: No, but somehow I just thought he would. Besides, when I went to our minister he told me to pray about being a better wife and I just felt like maybe he was right. So there wasn't any help from him or anyone else. I just felt so bad and guilty, too. I mean, he provides a good home and all. Kids go to the best schools. Even my best girlfriend says, "It's no big deal—he could be a womanizer or a drug addict." Besides, it'd really be a scandal if everybody found out. I just didn't have any place to turn. What can I do? (Begins sobbing again.)

Simulated Telephone Interview

In small groups of five or six, one person takes the role of Joyce and one person takes the role of the crisis worker. The remaining group members are observers. The crisis worker picks up where the telephone dialogue left off, following the six-step model discussed in Chapter 2. Pursue the crisis intervention session through to gaining a commitment, if possible, from Joyce. At the conclusion of the intervention, the observers will provide feedback to both crisis worker and client. These are typical discussion questions:

1. Did the crisis worker *really* hear what the victim was saying, both verbally and nonverbally?
2. What did the crisis worker do to attend to the client's safety and security needs?
3. What evidence was shown to indicate that the client understood and owned realistic options?
4. What typical dynamics did you see occurring—denial, guilt, fear, rationalization, withdrawal, and so on—in the victim? How did the crisis worker handle them?
5. Did the crisis worker attempt to impose solutions or alternatives on Joyce?

After these questions have been discussed, all those who played the role of Joyce should have the opportunity to disassociate themselves from the simulated role. They each make a statement to members of the group, explaining why they are *not* Joyce and noting ways in which they are personally different from that person. Typically we say, "Word your statement in such a way that all of us who observed will never again associate you with that role." Then we call for a round of applause from the group for the persons doing the role play.

Simulated Support Group

Five or six female volunteers from the group take the roles of abused wives who are now in residence at the wife abuse shelter. Either the instructor or a volunteer crisis worker from the group conducts a short session of a support group for abused wives. Use a "fishbowl" arrangement—that is, the support-group players are seated in the center of the room. Role players should draw upon their own experience and reading of this chapter to make the exercise as realistic as possible. During the process the crisis worker will want to focus on these issues:

1. the effects of being transplanted from one's own home to crowded conditions of living in a socioeconomically and ethnically diverse group of women
2. the desire to reestablish contact with the husband even though the consequences may be extremely negative (particularly note any dependency needs)
3. bringing to the surface and dealing with the dynamic responses of victims, including disbelief, denial, fear, anger, negotiation, pride, striving for independence, and resolution

4. typical problems such as employment, finances, child care, transportation, legal aid, food, clothing, permanent shelter, schooling for children, and vocational skills

5. what each abuse victim wants to do over the long term.

Following the role-playing session, discuss questions like these: How does the crisis worker act as facilitator of solutions to these problems? Does she let group members take responsibility or is she responsible for them? How does she resolve conflict? How does she respond to group members who exhibit overt helplessness and dependency? Again, after the discussion the role players should disassociate themselves from their roles, as they did in Exercise I, and receive a round of applause.

CHAPTER 5

Institutional Crises: Controlling Violent Behavior

BACKGROUND

This chapter deals with a problem that many institutions and human service workers do not care to acknowledge: violent clients. A variety of hazards now put human service professionals more at risk to violent behavior than they have been in the past. Probably the most noteworthy event has been the increase in number of substance-abuse clients. Given the variety of drugs and the erratic behavior that accompanies them, the human service worker is confronted with a complex and sometimes dangerous job of assessment and treatment (Piercy, 1984).

Second has been the release of many mental patients back into the community. Since the least-restrictive-environment movement and subsequent deinstitutionalization of patients in the 1970s, day care, halfway houses, and shelters have been plugged into the gap left when the warehousing facilities of state mental institutions were emptied. Although deinstitutionalization is a commendable idea, lack of facilities for transients, shortage of staff, and inability to monitor medication closely have created a fertile breeding ground for clients to regress to their previous pathological states (Reid, 1986).

Third has been the growth of crime. With increased societal and judicial awareness of the part that mental illness plays in crime, a number of individuals who would formerly have been incarcerated are now remanded to mental health facilities. Also, because of prison overcrowding, potentially violent people are released on early parole. Farmed out to halfway houses that are also understaffed, and assigned to parole officers who have tremendous caseloads, parolees do not always get the follow-up and supervision they need. Thus, human service workers are now being asked to deal with a wider variety of ex-felons than before (Appelbaum, 1984).

Finally, the increase in the number of the elderly now institutionalized in nursing homes and hospitals has created a whole new population of potentially violent individuals. Casually dismissed as infirm and incapable of rendering harm to anyone, geriatric patients represent a disproportionate percentage of violent behavior committed against human service workers (Petrie, 1984, p. 107).

Institutional Culpability

While human service organizations have been inundated with heavier and heavier caseloads and more and more problematic kinds of clients, many care providers have not taken commensurate measures to upgrade security for their staff or train workers in how to handle violent clients. By their very nature, most care providers are readily accessible to clientele and have minimal security checks. Therefore they are also easy prey to anyone who walks in off the street with intentions other than seeking services (Turner, 1984, pp. v–vi). Further, training for security and implementation of security devices cost time and money. Administrators trained in handling the financial, logistical, and personnel functions of institutions plus the responsibility of maintaining adequate patient care are unaware of what it takes to provide an adequately secure environment for their staff (Dyer, Murrell, & Wright, 1984).

Because of the negative publicity that accrues from violent incidents, institutions are loath to admit that they occur (Lanza, 1985). Such denials do not help the morale of workers and lead the staff to feel powerless and frustrated (Lenehan & Turner, 1984, p. 253). The significant role that contextual variables play in triggering violent behavior suggests the need to examine the environmental demands the institution places on its staff (Katz, Cohen, & Stokman, 1985). High staff turnover, absenteeism, on-the-job accidents, poor or incomplete communication between administration and staff, and lack of unifying treatment philosophy allow frustration to build within the staff and disrupt the treatment routine. As the staff transfer their frustration to the clients, the clients in turn become more threatened and start testing the limits of what will be tolerated. When staff attempt to impose behavioral limits under these erratic conditions, the outcome is often manifested in violent behavior by clients (Piercy, 1984, pp. 141–142).

Staff Culpability

Staff members are also culpable. There is a prevailing philosophy that because human service workers are caring, well-intentioned people, recipients of their services will act in reciprocal ways toward them (Turner, 1984, p. vii). The ostrichlike assumption that "It can't happen to me, and besides, there are so few violent incidents that I really don't need to be concerned" is fallacious (Dyer, Murrell, & Wright, 1984, p. 1). Even after violence has occurred, many take the position, "That goes with the territory!" Other staff members, in an effort to deny their own vulnerability, may shun the victim by either labeling the victim as inadequate to the task or blaming the victim for provoking the incident (Lenehan & Turner, 1984, pp. 251–253).

Incidence

Mainly because of fear of bad publicity and inadequate reporting, statistics on violent behavior of clients toward workers in human service agencies are either poor or unavailable in most settings (Turner, 1984, p. v). The few studies conducted present a profile of violence that should serve as an eye opener for human service workers in general and crisis workers in particular. Lanza (1983) found that psychiatric nurses reported having been assaulted an average of seven times during an average of six years' service. Ruben, Wolkon, and Yamamoto (1980) found that 48% of psychiatric interns reported being assaulted during training. Other studies have shown that 24% of human service workers experienced violent acts committed against them during their first year of service, and the rate escalated to 74% at some time during their tenure (Whitman, Armao, & Dent, 1976). Information garnered from congressional hearings on violence in federal hospitals during the years 1977 to 1980 showed increases of 16% in robbery, 33% in rape, 27% in assault, and 16% in physical arrests (House of Representatives Committee on Veterans Affairs, 1981). Even with these increases, Lion, Snyder, and Merrill (1981) believe that the incidence of assaults on patients and staff is underreported at a rate of about 5 to 1.

Although these various statistics may mean little to human service workers who rarely encounter violent incidents (Dyer, Murrell, & Wright, 1984, p. 1) (or suppose that they won't), it appears that an attack upon such individuals is almost inevitable (Whitman, Armao, & Dent, 1976), particularly if they are front-line workers in the business of crisis intervention (Marohn, 1982). The point of citing these statistics is that the subject concerns you—not just somebody who works down the hall from you. For anyone who has ever seen a client wildly out of control and who has been injured or scared senseless in trying to contain that violence, one time is once too many (Lanza, 1985).

Legal Liability

Another more odious problem for health care providers and institutions is legal liability. Although health care providers may be the victims of assaults, they may also become legally liable for their actions, no matter how well intended those actions may be (Monahan, 1984). Such liability extends to the institutions and directors of those institutions, who may fall under a heading of "vicarious" liability. As a consequence, employers and institutions may be subject to both civil and criminal liability (Dyer, Murrell, & Wright, 1984, p. 23).

DYNAMICS

Assessment

In 1974, the American Psychiatric Association did a study on the ability of the psychiatric profession to predict violence. Its conclusion was that such predictions were unreliable and lacked validity (American Psychiatric Association, 1974) and was confirmed in other studies (Mulvey & Lidz, 1984; Valliant, Aser, Cooper, & Mammola, 1984). Recently, however, research studies on violence have at least started to move in the direction of better prediction. Tanke and Yesavage (1985) have used the Brief Psychiatric Rating Scale successfully to differentiate high- and low-profile violence-prone clients from nonviolent controls. Also, Ostrow, Marohn, Offer, Crutiss, & Feczko (1980) have developed the Adolescent Anti-Social Behavior Checklist using Wechsler Intelligence Scale subtests and Rorschach personality profiles to predict violent behavior in adolescents.

However, the current status of prediction and the "real world" of mental health care provision lead us to believe that the ability to predict clearly who will and who will not become violent at what times and under what conditions has not been clearly established (Vinick, 1986). Predictions are especially likely to be erroneous when crisis workers have little background information on clients and may not have time to make more than an "eyeball" assessment of the situation before they have to act. Yet data do exist to present general profiles of clients who are more likely than others to become violent, given the right constellation of conditions.

Bases

There are biological, psychological, and social bases for violence. Biologically, low intelligence, hormonal imbalances, organic brain disorders, neurological and systemic changes of a psychiatric nature, disease, chemicals, or traumatic injury may lead to more violence-prone behavior. Psychologically, specific situational problems, certain functional psychoses, and character disorders are predisposing to violence. Socially, modeling the behavioral norms of family, peers, and the milieu within which one lives can exacerbate violent tendencies (Tardiff, 1984a, p. 45; Wood & Khuri, 1984, p. 60). Finally, specific on-site physical environmental stressors such as heat, crowding, noise, conflict, and poor communication are triggers that can cause violence. When all these ingredients are mixed together, the results start to resemble the kinds of people and environments with which the crisis worker is likely to come in contact. Therefore, the environment within which the factors combine is of critical significance in whether the outcome will be violent or not (Tardiff, 1984a, p. 45). Understanding that we cannot extract absolute, "true" types from the conditions described, we nevertheless believe that the following are representative observations of clients that crisis workers need to be aware of as they ply their human service trade.

Age. Males between the age of 15 and 30 who come from the inner city and are members of a minority tend to be the most violent subgroup (Fareta, 1981; Kroll & Mackenzie, 1983). Next come elderly clients, who are disproportionately represented in the population that may be violent (Petrie, 1984, p. 107). Crisis workers tend to dismiss this group as being harmless. Nothing could be further from the truth. In a study of 200 cases of assault at the Cincinnati Veteran's Administration Medical Center, Jones (1985) discovered that 58.5% of the assaults took place in the geriatric facility. This statistic is noteworthy because the institution also had a large psychotic and substance-abuse population.

Substance abuse.   Simonds and Kashani (1980) found high positive relationships between crimes committed against people and the use of amphetamines, phencyclidine (PCP), barbiturates, cocaine, and Valium®. Rada
(1981) found that toxic reactions to illicit drugs such as PCP, LSD, barbiturates, amphetamines, and cocaine are common causes of violence in the
emergency room. It is not within the purview of this book to deal with the
medical aspects of crisis; however, those who abuse drugs are endemic to the
human services setting, and at times they are so highly volatile that a working
knowledge of the behavioral and psychological ramifications of drugs is of
critical importance in handling crisis situations. Therefore, for any human
service worker, resources should include a *Physician's Desk Reference* (PDR)
and the availability of a consulting physician for a fast diagnosis of the possible substance involved. Any initial assessment should be concerned not only
with drug type but also with whether the drug is a prescription drug or of
"street" manufacture so its potency may be determined (Piercy, 1984, p. 129).

A common myth is that only a person who has been on stimulants or hal-
lucinogens or has active alcohol psychoses will be violence prone. Whereas
barbiturates are commonly understood to depress the central nervous system, on occasion barbiturates may have an excitatory effect. Anyone coming
off sedatives or depressants may be as likely or even more disposed to violent
acting out as those who take stimulants. One of the most popular prescribed
and abused drugs, Valium, is a classic example. Many people suffering from
alcohol addiction will stop drinking and substitute large doses of Valium for
alcohol. Effects of withdrawal from Valium may be even more prolonged than
those of the original drug of choice, alcohol, and may result in irritability and
opposition to the health care setting and workers within that setting (Piercy,
1984, pp. 131–132).

Although many other exotic drugs have replaced heroin as an abused
agent, the popularized versions of withdrawal from heroin as depicted by the
media and press are close to reality. Particularly when addicts are suffering
withdrawal, attempts to obtain money to purchase more heroin make them
high-potential perpetrators of violence if they cannot secure the drug or the
means to obtain it (Piercy, 1984, p. 135).

Amphetamines, particularly when used by the violence-prone individual,
can cause feelings of power, euphoria, and extreme excitability. Other effects
can include suspiciousness, wide fluctuations in mood, feelings of grandiosity, and extreme physical activity. Amphetamine abusers may overreact to
mild and minor stimulations in their environment and at their worst become
indistinguishable from paranoid or acute paranoid schizophrenics (Piercy,
1984, p. 132). Although downplayed in the media in comparison with users of
other drugs, amphetamine abusers make up a large portion of the clientele
that find their way into groups we run in the penal setting, and they have almost always been incarcerated because of violent crimes.

Although alcohol is undoubtedly the most abused drug in existence and its
evils have been "cussed" and discussed for centuries, it has played a secondary role to more glamorous forms of intoxication. Yet alcohol has been associ-

ated with more than one-half of reported cases of violence in emergency rooms and one-fourth of reported cases in psychiatric institutions (Bach y Rita, Lion, & Climent, 1971). Alcohol releases the individual from fear of retribution and reduces cortical control to the point that inhibitions of morally and socially acceptable conduct are lost (Piercy, 1984, p. 130). In the withdrawal stage, the individual may behave violently either because of being denied alcohol or, less commonly, because of hallucinosis, which causes the individual to fear imagined harm. A compounding problem of alcohol abuse may be that in an initial assessment, alcohol is diagnosed as the major contributing factor, but in actuality it camouflages other drug abuse (Piercy, 1984, pp. 135–136).

Predisposing history of violence. A history of serious violence, including homicide, sexual attacks, assault, or threat of assault with a deadly weapon, is one of the best predictors of future violence (Fareta, 1981; Monahan, 1981). Any background material that indicates a history of violence should automatically put the human service worker on notice to be extremely cautious with the client.

Psychological disturbance. A variety of mental disorders fall within the category of psychological disturbance: the antisocial personality type who has a history of violent behavior, emotional callousness, impulsivity, and manipulative behavior; the borderline personality who floats in and out of reality, lacks adequate ego strength to control intense emotional drives, and repeatedly exhibits emotional outbursts; the paranoid who is on guard against and constantly anticipating external threat and is willing and able to take action against that threat; the manic who has elevated moods, hyperactivity, and excessive involvement in activities that may have painful consequences; and the explosive personality who has sudden escalating periods of anger followed by periods of tranquility (Wood & Khuri, 1984, p. 63).

Family history. A recent or past history of violence within the family is often carried into other environments. An early childhood characterized by an unstable and violent home is an excellent model for future violence (Wood & Khuri, 1984, pp. 65–66).

Time. Time in relation to the person's admission and tenure in the facility is critical. Admission on Friday or Saturday night during "party hours" significantly increases the potential for violence. The evening hours in geriatric and mental hospitals, with the onset of darkness, change of shift, and decrease in staff, often lead to client disorientation and states of confusion. The effects of this time period have become so notorious that they have been labeled the *sundown syndrome* (Piercy, 1984, p. 139). Mealtime, toileting, and bathing are also prime times for violent outbursts (Jones, 1985; Stokeman, 1982).

Patients in both general and forensic psychiatric hospitals are more likely to be violent immediately after admission to the hospital (Star, 1984). For most patients committed involuntarily, the possibility of assault is significantly increased during the first 10 to 20 days after admission, and for paranoids it remains high during their first 45 days (Rofman, Askinazi, & Fant, 1980).

Interactive participants. Violent behavior may be contingent on those who bring the person to the institution. Family members or friends who bring patients in for treatment often interact in a volatile manner with admitting staff, particularly if the staff are seen as abrasive and callous (Ruben, Wolkon, & Yamamoto, 1980) and treat either the patient or support persons in a curt or uncaring manner (Wood & Khuri, 1984, p. 58). Arguments that may be occurring between the client and support persons are easily transferred to staff. Further, when admonitions by distraught or intoxicated supporters to "fix" the client are not given immediate attention, they or the client may express grievances against the institution and staff by acting out. Any client who is accompanied to the institution by a police officer should be viewed as potentially violent (Piercy, 1984, pp. 140–141).

Motoric cues. Close observation by the human service worker of physical cues will often give clues to emergent states predisposing to physical violence (Petrie, 1984, p. 115). Early warning signs include tense muscles; bulging, darting eye movements; staring or completely avoiding eye contact; closed, defensive body posture; twitching muscles, fingers, and eyelids (Wood & Khuri, 1984, p. 77). If the client is pacing back and forth, alternately approaching and then retreating from the worker, this may be a sign that the individual is gathering courage for an assault. The agitated client may have an expanded sense of personal space of up to eight feet in circumference, instead of three to four feet, and may be extremely sensitive to any intrusion into that space (Moran, 1984, pp. 244–246).

A number of verbal cues are precursors to violent action by the client. Heightened voice pitch, volume, and rapidity of speech may occur, particularly if the client has been using amphetamines. Alternately, if speech and movement are slowed dramatically, the client may be using depressants. Confused speech content is reflective of confused thought. Finally, there is a high correlation between threats of violence and acting on those threats. All these aberrant speech patterns may be assessed as possible antecedents to the onset of a violent episode (Atkinson, 1982; Marohn, 1982; Piercy, 1984, pp. 140–141).

INTERVENTION STRATEGIES

Physical Setting

Handling potentially violent clients is a bit different from dealing with other crises discussed in this book. Most crisis situations involve a one-to-one relationship between client and human service worker. Yet because the institution itself plays such a large part in the whos, whats, whys, hows, and whens of treatment, it may be viewed as an equal and contributing partner in resolving problems with clients who are disposed to becoming physically and verbally assaultive.

No two institutions are alike with respect to a number of variables that affect what the institution can do about the problem of violence. Purposes, methods, philosophies, finances, staffing, and clientele differ dramatically from setting to setting. The differences among a private, long-term mental health hospital for substance abusers, a state-supported halfway home for parolees, and a runaway shelter for teenagers supported by charity are great. Yet when confronted with clienteles that may be distraught, angry, fearful, and experiencing disequilibrium, they all have a common core of problems. Given the financial, legal, treatment, organizational, and philosophical limits that are idiosyncratic to each setting, the following intervention strategies should be viewed as a best "general" approach. Therefore, dealing effectively with potentially violent clients means knowing clearly and in depth what the institution is about and what its resources and commitments are.

Safety of Staff and Clients

Security analysis. One of the first steps in preventing violence is understanding what precautions the institution has taken to ensure safety of clients and staff. Although a health care facility should not strive for prison-like security, certain precautions may be taken to ensure that workers are not put at extreme risk by their clientele. First and foremost, a security management analysis should be conducted by management with experts in the security field (Ishimoto, 1984, p. 211). The following questions are representative of what Ishimoto believes a security management analysis should entail in the areas of prevention, detection, response, and security education (pp. 211–216):

1. What are the institution's goals, functions, operations, organizational structure, and responsibilities?
2. Who is in charge of what security provisions?
3. What image considerations limit the amount of security?
4. What balance needs to be maintained between security of staff and provision of human services?
5. What is the geographical, environmental, and socioeconomic setting in which services are rendered?
6. What kinds of clientele make use of the facilities and what are their risk factors to others?
7. What kinds of provisions have already been made for staff, clients, visitors, and neighborhood security?
8. What kinds of training have staff received for emergencies?
9. What screening devices are available to monitor clientele, and are they reliable and valid?

10. What screening devices are used for personnel selection, and are they reliable and valid?
11. What physical security is available in the form of barriers, lighting, locks, and dispensing of keys?
12. What security personnel will be needed? Where, and when?
13. Are there emergency contingency plans for a variety of problems and do staff know what is expected of them under varying circumstances?
14. How do these outcome goals fit with Occupational Health and Safety Act requirements?

Security plan. The foregoing are a few of the many security questions that need to be raised by management so that a total risk assessment of the institution may be made. All staff should have input into these questions and a comprehensive security plan should be worked out antecedent to the occurrence of any crisis. Such a plan should be comprehensive and simple, detailing who is responsible for what under which conditions. The plan should cover the entire domain of the institution starting with the parking lot, moving through the front door to admissions, and proceeding through the building to encompass day-treatment facilities, staff offices, food services, pharmaceutical dispensaries, and client rooms (Ishimoto, 1984, p. 209–223). Although initial costs in time and money for this service may be seen as burdensome by the administration, its net cost will be minimal if it avoids just one law suit by a client or staff member (Moran, 1984, p. 249). If such a survey is not taken, not only does the facility risk outbreaks of violence but also the staff will perceive it as not being greatly concerned about what happens to them (Lewellyn, 1985).

Training. Planning is of little consequence if no training follows. Rice, Helzel, Varney, and Quinsey (1985) evaluated comprehensive crisis intervention and prevention training for staff in minimum, medium, and maximum security areas of a psychiatric hospital. The training for staff consisted of five days of verbal and physical techniques of preventing violence and injury. Staff who had training improved significantly in skill and knowledge of intervention techniques over a control group who had not received training. Outcomes on the wards indicated better relations with the patients and a significant reduction in violent episodes.

Training should include both knowledge and skill building and be ongoing (Dyer, Murrell, & Wright, 1984, pp. 12–15). It should begin with the fundamental crisis intervention skills, including the six steps, which were emphasized in Chapter 2. In addition, it should cover such topics as security procedures, volatile situations, client assessment, behavioral and verbal cues, techniques for verbal defusing, self-defense, and follow-up staffing procedures (Rice et al., 1985). A critical component of training is not just talking about problems but gaining practice in solving them. Any new member of the treatment team should immediately be introduced to a well-defined set of training procedures designed to familiarize the worker with staff procedures and techniques (Lewellyn, 1985). As we indicated in the Preface, there is no better way of doing this than role-playing situations.

Assumptions and precautions. Adequate training should endow the crisis worker with the ability to make certain assumptions and take certain precautions when dealing with potentially violent clients (Zold & Schilt, 1984, pp. 98–99):

1. Assume the need to set limits and provide routine and negative sanctions against behavior that is predisposing to violence.
2. Assume that the client manifests a number of debilitating emotions, such as anxiety, depression, fear, anger, and feelings of rejection, and provide love, care, warmth, and unconditional positive regard in a general sense while specifically reinforcing and modeling prosocial behavior such as appropriate communication of feelings.
3. Assume frustration of normal activity and boredom when the client is in residence and provide activities to keep the client fruitfully busy.
4. Assume a threat to the client's self-esteem, independence, and self-control and provide choices and opportunities to help in carrying out medical and psychological activities.
5. Assume tension and arousal and provide a calm and relaxing atmosphere, particularly during high-tension periods.
6. Assume confusion and provide a careful explanation of all procedures to be employed, being particularly sure that all staff are operating from the same frame of reference.
7. Assume responsibility and provide for one primary staff member to act as chief caretaker and advocate of each client.
8. Assume disconnectedness and rootlessness if the client is to be institutionalized for any length of time and provide familiarity and psychologically calming anchors associated with pleasant memories.

While providing support through the foregoing proactive behaviors, the wise human service worker should observe a number of precautionary measures (Moran, 1984, p. 244; Piercy, 1984, p. 143; Wood and Khuri, 1984, p. 69):

1. Don't deny the possibility of violence when early signs of agitation are first noticed in the client.
2. Don't underestimate information given by others regarding behavioral clues that are antecedent to violence.
3. Don't become isolated with potentially violent clients unless you have made sure that enough security precautions have been taken to prevent or limit a violent outburst. Although perhaps the ideal condition for therapy, being alone allows too much of the client's attention to be focused on one person.
4. Don't engage in certain behaviors that may be interpreted as aggressive, such as moving too close, staring directly into the client's eyes for extended periods of time, pointing fingers, or displaying facial expressions and body movements that would appear threatening.

5. Don't allow a number of the institution's workers to interact simultaneously with the client in confusing multiple dialogues.
6. Don't make promises that cannot be kept.
7. Don't allow feelings of fear, anger, or hostility to interfere with self-control and professional understanding of the client's circumstances.
8. Don't argue, give orders, or disagree when not absolutely necessary.
9. Don't be placating by giving in and agreeing to all the real and imagined ills the client is suffering at the hands of the institution.
10. Don't become condescending by using childish responses that are cynical, satirical, or otherwise designed to denigrate the client.
11. Don't let self-talk about your own importance be acted out in an officious and "know-it-all" manner.
12. Don't raise your voice, put a sharp edge on responses, or use threats to gain compliance.
13. Conversely, don't mumble, speak hesitantly, or use a tone of voice so low that the client has trouble understanding what you are saying.
14. Don't argue over small points, given strong opposition from the client.
15. Don't attempt to reason with any client who is under the influence of a mind-altering substance.
16. Don't attempt to gain compliance based on the assumption that the client is as reasonable about things as you are.
17. Don't keep the client waiting or leave a potentially violent client alone with freedom to move about.
18. Don't allow a crowd to congregate as spectators to an altercation.

These injunctions are not a recipe for avoiding violent confrontations, but they are general working procedures that will help the human service worker move adroitly with the client through the intervention stages.

Critical areas: Admissions and offices. The following are a few minimal safety precautions that deal with the physical settings of the institution in which staff members are most likely to become involved in potentially violent situations with clients. Two critical areas important to all crisis workers are the admissions area and the worker's office.

The reception or waiting-room area should offer a television set, reading material, and accessibility to snack areas. Availability of entertainment and food and drink gives clients and visitors an opportunity to become engaged in a pleasurable activity to offset the hostile feelings that may be engendered by the problems they are facing and defuse the stressful situation of admission (Wood & Khuri, 1984, pp. 79–80). One admonition is necessary with regard to food and drink. Clients who are extremely rebellious about entering the institution may attempt to choke themselves on foodstuffs or even swallow pull tabs from metal cans. The admissions staff should be sure that potential problems like this do not occur by having a snack area available, but not immediately accessible, and should carefully monitor clients if they are allowed to eat or drink (McCown, 1986).

The admissions area should be clean and well kept, with furniture, carpet, and wall coverings well maintained. First impressions do make lasting impressions. If the client's first impression of a facility is that staff have little regard or respect for the facility, the client will have little reason to respect what goes on there either (Marohn, 1982). No sharp, movable objects, including furniture, should be available as potential weapons (McCown, 1986).

The area should be set up so that it is a choke point. Only one way into the rest of the facility should be available from the admissions area (Annis, McClaren, & Baker, 1984, p. 30). Depending on how much security is needed, the reception area may have electronically locked doors that separate it from the rest of the facility, sign-in sheets, identity check procedures, and metal detectors (Jones, 1984).

The admissions worker will make the first contact with the client and will be engaging the person in one of the most potentially violent moments the institution is likely to encounter. The admissions worker should be highly skilled in crisis intervention techniques and should have one primary job—*staying with and attending to the client being admitted!* Under no circumstances should a secretary, receptionist, or any other support person who is not professionally well versed in crisis intervention or who has other tasks to perform, such as typing letters or answering the telephone, be delegated to handle this important assignment. The admissions worker does not leave the client until all admitting procedures have been accomplished and the client is safely settled (McCown, 1986).

The admissions worker should never be left in a position of isolation from the rest of the staff. Security support equipment such as a body alarm (a button-activated device that when triggered will automatically send an alarm and position fix to security), an automatic dialer preset to in-house security and 911, convex mirrors to monitor the whole waiting area, panic buttons, closed-circuit-television monitoring equipment, button locks on elevators, and a metal detector at the entrance should be available (Doms, 1984, pp. 225–229; Jones, 1984; Wood & Khuri, 1984, pp. 79–80; McCown, 1986).

Personal work environments should also be safe. Desks should be set so that they allow for separation of client and worker, even though communicating across a desk is not the most desirable counseling setup. Space should be arranged to permit both the worker and the client clear access to the door. Any interview setting should provide an easy exit for the human service worker and should be so situated that the worker can leave the room without having to confront or cross within the personal space of the client. No potential weapons such as paperweights, letter openers, and sharpened pencils should be openly displayed or within easy reach of the client. The same personal warning devices and procedures recommended for the reception area should also be in place in workers' offices. This precaution is particularly critical because of the isolated nature of the therapy setting (Tardiff, 1984a, p. 50).

Although the institution and its precautions may cause human service workers some embarrassment and chagrin, workers should not disregard them. Our own work in penal institutions is a good example of what we are talking about. There have been very few times when we personally have felt threatened or even remotely believed that we would suffer harm at the hands of the men we were counseling. Yet it must be remembered that these men did not become incarcerated for receiving a traffic summons. The corrections facility we work in mandates that a body alarm be worn at all times by the counselor, that a cocounselor be present in all groups, and that a guard be posted at all times within easy access of the group room. Occasionally group members may make snide remarks about these precautions. The worker may easily respond by stating, "I don't much like it either, but you guys know the rules," and injecting a little humor: "It's probably because they're afraid we might beat up on group members and want to protect you guys."

Stages of Intervention

Management techniques for potentially violent situations should be built in the following sequential manner, based in part on a nine-stage model developed by Piercy (1984, pp. 147–148). For each of these stages, we wish to stress that personal responsibility is paramount. Passing the buck is too easy and is likely to cause the very problems we are trying to avoid. Further, whether by circumstance or by design, the first person who comes in contact with the problem is the most likely to be the agitated client's focus of attention. As a result, that human service worker is the person who will most likely have to confront the problem, no matter what other resources are available (Moran, 1984, pp. 233–234).

Stages one through five all rely heavily on talking instead of acting, in accordance with one of the primary goals of crisis intervention with violence-prone individuals: getting them to talk out rather than act out. This approach may seem obvious, but it is difficult to achieve. The agitated client clearly indicates a limited ability to talk and think through problems, as opposed to acting on them and giving little thought to the consequences (Tardiff, 1984a, p. 52).

CASE OF JASON

As we move through the nine stages, we will follow Jason, a 15-year-old white male client, and Carol, a therapist, who by most standards is an old pro. She has been at Seashore Village, an adolescent treatment facility, for four years. Many people have burned out of Carol's job in less than two years. Carol survives and prospers in the setting not only because she cares very much for children but because she is extremely street smart in the ways of disturbed and disruptive children that come through these doors.

Jason is new to the business of institutions. He is not new to being angry, which he is right now as he sits with a deputy sheriff in the reception area waiting for Carol to come through the door. Jason's teenage years have been filled with petty larceny, truancy, alcohol and drug use, and parents who have gotten him out of one scrape after another. His latest escapade of stealing a car landed him in front of a juvenile court and adjudication to Seashore as an alternative to the state juvenile correction system. His father, fed up with Jason's behavior and over the objections of his wife, has pushed for this placement. Jason feels betrayed and is extremely angry at his father for doing so.

Seashore itself is representative of a broad sample of institutions. It is neither the best nor the worst in terms of clients, staff, resources, and security measures. If you are familiar with more rigorous procedures, rules, and operations of institutions such as psychiatric hospitals and correctional facilities, you may find reason to criticize the following intervention procedures for failure to meet institutional or legal mandates. We are endeavoring to paint as representative a picture as possible, asking you to withhold judgments about the efficacy and appropriateness of these strategies in every institution. It is absolutely impossible to speak to all circumstances. Our hope is that the procedures used in the case of Jason will cause you to think carefully about your own present or future role in an institution, compare the ideas proposed here with the requirements imposed upon you, analyze the procedures used, and make thoughtful comparisons between these techniques and the real world within which you operate. Given that rather large disclaimer, let us now turn to Jason, Carol, and Seashore Residential Facility.

Jason: (Thinking to himself, hands sweating, slight tremors racing through his body.) Man, this place is scaring the hell out of me. How'd I ever get in this fix? What are they gonna do to me? I'll just bet a wrap-around suit with no arms in it. I'll be at the mercy of the rest of the crazies in here. I'll really go nuts if I stay here. I gotta get out of this place if it's the last thing I ever do.

Jason is extremely angry and anxious about what will happen to him, frustrated that he has lost control of his life and that what he has considered to be normal activity is going to be severely curtailed. He also feels extremely vulnerable, confused, bewildered, and alone. Jason's feelings are typical of those of a client who is being introduced to a long-term treatment facility for the first time (Zold & Schilt, 1984, p. 96).

As soon as Jason enters Seashore, admissions immediately calls the adolescent unit. At that time Carol, the worker in the unit whose name is up for the next admission, comes quickly to the reception area and meets Jason. The human service worker (HSW) immediately makes a fast visual assessment of Jason's verbal and nonverbal behavior as she enters the room and monitors Jason closely to see what his reaction to her initial query will be (McCown, 1986).

HSW: (Thinking to herself.) What's going on with this kid? Any signs he is agitated? Yes! He's pacing around, eyes darting to and fro, keeps cracking his knuckles, looking at the door and the cop. He'll run if he gets the chance! Muttering to himself. Who brought him in? Nobody else here but that cop over there. He keeps watching him. Must be an adjudication. If a cop brought him here, be careful until you know what's happening.

Carol goes over to the reception desk and picks up the file the deputy has brought, quickly looks it over, and finds the boy's name and rap sheet. A fast review tells her that Jason has been in a series of escalating scrapes with the law, that his parents are fed up with his behavior and feel he's out of control, and that he has been involved in fights when his explosive personality got out of control. Carol then stops briefly with the deputy and finds out what kind of a trip Jason had from the juvenile detention center.

HSW: (Thinking to herself.) OK! Check him out and see how stabilized he is and let him find out what's going to happen to him.

Stage 1: Education.   Clients need to be educated about what is happening to them and why and how it is happening. Reasoning and reassurance are given. One way of doing this is to assume the role of the client's advocate (Pisarick, 1981). Owning statements that indicate concern over the client's welfare are a good opening gambit. It must be assumed that in this new, strange, and alien environment the primary feeling of the client will be fear and anger (Rada, 1981). Open-ended questions and reflection of the client's feelings are crucial to conveying that the client's feelings count for something and are being taken into consideration.

HSW: Hi! My name's Carol, and you must be Jason. I'm the person who'll be working with you.

Jason: (Gives a menacing look.) Yeah! So what? (Points to officer.) The cop got me in here but I ain't gonna go any farther.

HSW: I understand how you feel. Most people who come here feel about the same way. Seems like everybody's against you, telling you what to do. I'd be angry too! I want you to know, though, that here at Seashore you're going to have some options about what happens.

Jason: Screw your options. I ain't stayin' here. (Makes a menacing move toward the HSW.)

HSW: (Senses move and moves back and a little to Jason's left, giving him some increased space.) One of your immediate options is that I'd like you to come with me and meet some of the other kids here and have them tell you what's going on and see if what they have to say fits with what you're about. On the other hand, the court sent you here, and if you don't like the first option and want to fight it out, you could be carried back to the unit and we can wait until you've got yourself together. I understand you're angry, and I'd be angry too, but I'd like to know if you feel that fighting or running is gonna make it better for you and improve your situation rather than checking things out. So you've got a choice. I think you might be interested in meeting some of the other kids, but it'll have to be under peaceful conditions and you'll have to show me you can handle that starting right now.

In this initial meeting, the worker uses the technique of providing options. She is letting the client have some semblance of control of the situation, but is also clearly outlining what the consequences of his choices are. The human service worker takes a well-gauged risk. She is satisfied that Jason is not on any addictive substance or flirting with a psychotic break. Although she is sure he has a lot of volatile emotions seething just below the surface, she also assumes he is open to logic. As soon as possible she is going to model option therapy (McCown, 1986). Option therapy, in simple terms, says, "You always have a choice. You need to start deciding as soon as possible who's going to have control over those choices, you or us." Indeed, this will be the first of a long series of choices Jason will have to make as he goes through his extended-care program. Poor choices about appropriate behavior undoubtedly got Jason here in the first place. The worker immediately starts the educative process by proposing optional behaviors for Jason that will allow him opportunities to see clearly what his choices are and what the consequences of those choices will be (McCown, 1986).

Jason: Well . . . all right . . . lady, I'll give it a look-see, but I ain't promisin' nothin' after that.

HSW: I don't expect any more than that at the moment. What I want most for you is to see what's going on here and what some of the other kids think about what we do before you make any kind of promises. We don't lie and we don't make promises we can't keep, so let's go back and see the unit and meet some of the kids.

The worker has to make a quick judgment about how directive or nondirective to be. She is directive only to the extent of setting boundaries equivalent to how out of control the client is. Her other mission is to establish rapport and credibility with the client. She does this by accepting and acknowledging the client where he is and in turn stating the same from the institution's perspective. She offers no platitudes or false promises (Vinick, 1986). Her technique of letting the client talk to other people on the unit is designed to let the client hear and see with his own ears and eyes what is going on without feeling he is getting a lot of propaganda. However, she will not provide a format for him to act out, and if in her judgment Jason is not controlled enough to make a tour with her, she will summon assistance and Jason will be escorted to an observation room (McCown, 1986).

HSW: (Walking down the hall, with Jason two steps in front of her and a bit to the side.) At each stop along our tour, I'll tell you what goes on. We have a lot of activities, so if you don't clearly understand what's happening or you want to know some more about it, just ask. For example, here's the community meeting room. You can have free time to play ping pong, cards, games, or just talk with the other kids here during your free time from 8:00 to 9:00 in the evening. The whole community meets here twice a day. Once right after breakfast for about 15 minutes to find out what's going on for the day and once in the evening from 7:00 to 8:00 to plan community activities. You'll also be in here for a problem-solving meeting each afternoon from 2:00 to 3:00.

Jason's Schedule

7:00–8:00.	Stretch period, clean up room, lavatory, breakfast.
8:00–8:15.	Community meeting, announcements.
8:15–12:00.	School.
12:00–12:45.	Lunch.
12:45–2:00.	School.
2:00–3:00.	Group problem solving.

3:00–4:00.	Individual counseling.
4:00–5:00.	Quiet time in room.
5:00–5:45.	Dinner.
5:45–7:00.	Special groups: assertiveness training, social skills, group counseling, family therapy, Alcoholics Anonymous, art therapy, etc.
7:00–8:00.	Group recreation in gym.
8:00–9:00.	Free time. Recreation, phone calls, etc. (privileges depend on level achieved).
9:00–9:30.	Shower, clean-up, bedtime. Bedtime extended to 10:00 or 10:30 depending on level achieved.

Carol first explains each of these activities in general terms. If Jason has questions about any activity, she adds more details. Very little free time is available. For most individuals who enter a facility such as Seashore, a major problem has been too much free time and the inability to handle it well. Structuring the environment brings some badly needed discipline back into their lives. Particularly for adolescents, burning up energy in constructive ways is paramount. Further, too much free time is a fertile breeding ground for acting out behavior. The maxim "Idle hands are the devil's playground" holds true at Seashore (Vinick, 1986).

Seashore is also on a behavior management program that makes use of levels. Jason starts at entry level. Depending on how Jason operates in his environment, he will go up or down on the level system and will concomitantly receive more or fewer privileges. At an entry level, he will have few privileges—early bedtime, no passes—and will be under fairly close supervision. By conducting himself in a responsible manner, he may increase his level designation and gain access to a broader array of recreational activities, later bedtime, ground privileges, and weekend passes. The system is explained to Jason in a careful and clear manner, with emphasis on the fact that whether or not he moves to higher levels is his responsibility.

Once the client has had an opportunity to check the institution out and see for himself that he is not being imprisoned in a "snake pit," an interview is conducted. It would certainly be helpful if the worker had a psychosocial history of the client, but in emergency situations this may not always be possible. The worker may well have to make a rapid assessment from his or her initial observation of the client and plan strategy accordingly, particularly in a large institution, which is likely to have persons with a variety of disorders cross its threshold under crisis conditions (Rohr, 1986).

Educating a client about what is to happen medically and psychologically needs to be done slowly, methodically, and in nontechnical terms with numerous perceptual checks. Keeping explanations simple and helping the client to gain understanding ameliorates the situation, whereas complexity only increases the chance for violent behavior to occur (Moran, 1984, p. 234). This approach in no way means that the treatment procedure is minimized. Not only does deliberate pacing diminish fear in the client but it also slows the volatile emotion down and models a calm, rational atmosphere (Wood & Khuri, 1984, p. 76).

Jason: (Somewhat belligerently.) Like, what's this group meeting?

HSW: The group meets every day. We do two things there. First, putting this many kids together means that problems are going to arise. Within the limits of the institution we decide on a group basis how these problems will be handled. It's a one-person–one-vote program, and that includes the staff. The group decides how to tackle a community problem and then collectively makes a commitment to do something about it. Second, when problems between people arise, we all put our heads together and see how those problems can be solved. You don't necessarily have to accept an idea, but you must listen to what's being said.

Jason: I don't think I got anything to say to these nerds.

HSW: Maybe you don't. However, a lot of kids here do. You're not going to be here forever. Therefore, we look pretty hard at what's going on with you right now as you deal with other people here, how that behavior may or may not cause you problems, and what's down the road for you if you do decide to change some things in your life and what's likely if you don't. We don't ask you to love everybody here, but we do ask you to respect what they're trying to do, just as we ask them to respect you. Most of the kids really like the problem-solving meetings, but that's for you to decide.

The human service worker's responses are straight out of Glasser's reality therapy (1965, 1969) and focus on the issues of becoming involved, looking at alternatives, making value judgments, accepting no excuses, and assuming responsibility and consequences for one's actions. In this manner Carol goes over the entire schedule with Jason, who is given a copy of his schedule and the rules and regulations of Seashore. She slowly and clearly explains each component of the schedule, the level system, his treatment program, and the various other rules and regulations of the institution. While she explains the content of the program, she also makes sure to assess and reflect the emotional content of Jason's responses, again and again reinforcing the idea of options, responsibilities, and commitments. From the time Jason gets up at 7:00 A.M. to the time he goes to bed at 9:30 P.M., he is going to be very busy.

Stage 2: Avoidance. Avoidance of conflict and confrontation is attempted whenever possible. Matching threat for threat is likely to obtain for the human service worker exactly the opposite of control and containment of the situation (Dubin, 1981). If individuals can cool down on their own, with minimal monitoring, they should be given the option of doing so. A major error that human service workers sometimes make is letting their egos get in the way of good rational thinking. Workers who delight in continuously pushing and escalating issues are not practicing good therapeutic intervention techniques and are clearly asking for trouble.

One week has elapsed since Jason's admission.

Jason: (Standing in the hallway, shouting, shaking, and trembling, face flushed.) If you think you or anybody else can make me stay in my room or in this place, you're crazier than I am. I just wanted a drink of water and Mr. Richardson started yelling at me that it was past quiet time. Just try stopping me and see what happens.

HSW: (Quietly and calmly.) Jason, if you'll calm down, I'll bring you a cup of water. Please go in your room. You can have your drink and we can talk about it.

If the client is fast approaching a point of no return, let ventilation of feelings occur. Although shouting, cursing, and yelling are not pleasant, they are better than hand-to-hand combat (McCown, 1986; Vinick, 1986). The worker should attempt to remove the agitated client from the vicinity of other residents who may aggravate the situation. This is best done by immediately asking the client to go to an area that is away from the other residents (McCown, 1986). If the client retains some semblance of control, the client's own room may be an appropriate place. If the client is fast losing control and cannot calm down, a better choice is a room that is devoid of stimuli. Such a place should be specifically prepared and reserved for this sort of occurrence. Once the client has relaxed to some degree, then the human service worker may establish the cause and degree of agitation by determining what occurred and then pointing out consequences (Vinick, 1986).

HSW: What are you angry about?

Jason: (Still standing in the hallway, quite agitated.) He was treating me just like my old man, just making me feel like a baby.

HSW: And what were you doing?

Jason: Hey, I was just going to get a drink of water. I still had two minutes until quiet time. He made me so mad I wanted to pick up a chair and bust him. I still feel like going after that jerk.

HSW: What will that accomplish?

Jason: It'll show him he can't push me around like my old man does.

HSW: If you do that, it'll just confirm that you need to be here. That you can't control yourself. Is that what you want?

Jason: Maybe I just don't care.

For those clients who do not respond to verbal attempts to defuse the situation, the next step for the human service worker is to give assurance that violent behavior by anybody, including both staff and clients, is unacceptable and then indicate what the person's choices and consequences will become if the behavior persists (Wood & Khuri, 1984, pp. 67–68).

HSW: You can choose to pick up a chair, Jason, but that'll mean a number of things will happen. First, nobody is allowed to hit anybody else here, and that goes for both staff and kids. We won't permit anybody to do that because we don't want to see anybody hurt here. If it comes to that, we won't hurt you, but we will restrain you, something I'd not like to see happen. Second, if you choose to do that, no one else will get to hear your side of it and we won't have a chance to work your problem out with Mr. Richardson. Another choice would be to go back to your room, and then ask for a drink. If you do that, I will get Mr. Richardson and we'll all sit down and work this through. Would you be willing to do that?

Clients should be confronted with their inappropriate behavior, but in a caring, supportive, and problem-solving way that is not tinged with sarcasm or challenge. If the situation is deteriorating so rapidly that the worker no longer feels that communication can be maintained, it may be fruitful to have someone else enter the scene who will be perceived as a neutral party by the client. This tactic is risky and involves a judgment call on the worker's part. Allowing clients to be rewarded for acting out by getting other people to come to the scene may reinforce inappropriate behavior and lead clients to believe that they and not the institution control the situation.

Jason: It ain't just Richardson, this whole place sucks. They won't let me do nothin'. And you don't understand either. Chaplain Gentry's the only guy who I can really talk to.

HSW: I understand that you're really disappointed and mad that you couldn't get a drink. I also know you're pretty angry at me and everybody else right now and about the last thing you want to do is go peacefully back to your room. I know that you and Chaplain Gentry are pretty close. Would you be willing to go to your room and wait quietly while I get him?

At this juncture the client is being given the option of going to voluntary time out until the arrival of a third party who may be able to de-escalate the situation. If the client does not choose this option then the worker will have to move the client to a safe place, which will be a time-out room. A show of force may be necessary to send a clear message: "If you can't handle yourself, we will."

HSW: Jason, I want you to go down to observation for fifteen minutes and think this out. (Speaking to technicians.) Bob and Jerry, will you see that Jason gets to observation. In fifteen minutes I'll be down to see if you're ready to talk this through.

Stage 3: Appeasement. Stages 3 and 4 are probably most appropriate in emergency situations in which the worker has little basis to judge the client's aggressiveness and violence and is unable to obtain immediate assistance. Appeasement is not applicable in a number of settings under ordinary circumstances, and if Jason had reached the point of being removed to involuntary time out, appeasement or deflection of feelings (Stage 4) would be highly inappropriate and run counter to good therapeutic practice.

However, in all situations we believe it is better to err on the side of humility than to project a "tough guy" image, regardless of the client's verbal barbs, threats, and exhortations. This recommendation does not mean that the human service worker should become a doormat to be walked all over by the client. It does mean that by operating in an empathic mode we should see just how frightening and alarming the situation is to the client. Alternately, any attempts by the worker to counter threat with threat in an emergency situation are likely to confirm the client's suspicions that bad things are going to happen.

Appeasement can be attempted if the client's demands are simple and reasonable, even if those demands are made in a bellicose manner. Early on it is better to grant demands and let worry about what "lessons" need to be taught wait until later (Piercy, 1984, p. 148). This approach may be difficult for some human service workers to accept because it is based on the idea that there is no winner or loser in a potentially violent confrontation between an agitated client and the institution (Moran, 1984, p. 234).

Jason: (Enters the human service worker's office without an appointment, fists clenched, and starts shouting in an agitated, high-pitched voice.) Listen, big shot! I wanted to mail this letter to my girl, she doesn't know what's happened to me, and that jerk Richardson won't give me a stamp. I could bust all yer heads!

HSW: (In a calm, collected voice.) He's going by the rules, but I understand your concern. Please sit down at the table there and I'll see what can be done about getting a stamp.

The human service worker meets this demand because it is easily done and does not seriously conflict with institutional rules. She is also alone with an extremely agitated client who may or may not act out. There may be a discussion afterwards with the other worker who gave the original order, but there needs to be a clear understanding among all workers that in emergencies judgment calls may bend the rules a bit or countermand orders of others.

Stage 4: Deflection.   Deflection of angry feelings is attempted by shifting to other, less threatening topics. This may be done in a variety of ways. Asking the client to take a physically less threatening position focuses away from agitated motoric activity to problem solving (Wood & Khuri, 1984, p. 68).

HSW: (Repeating her statement patiently, firmly, and respectfully.) Jason, I understand how important it is for you to be able to write to your girlfriend. Please sit down, then I'll get you a stamp and see if we can iron out this problem.

The human service worker literally and figuratively gets the client off his feet and in a less threatening operating mode. The worker is also quietly but firmly setting limits by asking the client to sit. Since agitated individuals seldom listen closely to requests for compliance, Carol acknowledges Jason's feeling state and then uses the broken-record routine (Canter & Canter, 1982) of repeating her request. She is also employing another behavior management technique. By making a reward contingent upon a compliant behavior, Carol is using "Grandma's Law" (Becker, 1971). "Grandma's Law" basically states: "First you eat your spinach and then you get your ice cream."

By using problem-solving techniques, no matter how small the real or imagined injustice is, the human service worker conveys to the client an interest in the client as an individual and not just as another name in the institutional computer (Wood & Khuri, 1984, p. 71). Parceling out the problems into workable pieces, the worker removes them from the realm of the enormous and makes them solvable. A week later, in another confrontation over a variety of issues, the worker seeks to make the problem manageable.

Jason: I can't get nothin' done here. Everything's screwed up. School, home, people, the food, my freedom. It's a concentration camp.

HSW: OK. There seem to be at least three things that are really bugging you right now. Not being able to get a pass yet, the way your dad got angry in family therapy, and your problem with the math assignment yesterday. Together, I can see how it'd become overwhelming. Let's take them one at a time and see what can be done about each.

Until absolutely sure what the problem is, the human service worker should never make promises about what can or cannot be done when attempting to calm an agitated client (Wood & Khuri, 1984, p. 71).

HSW: I know that weekend pass is really important. You'd get to see your girlfriend, and you feel like you really deserve it. I'd like to see what could be done, but I can't give you a guarantee. A pass is based on good behavior and your level status. If you feel like you've gotten jerked around, griping about it won't help much. Very specifically, write down why you think you deserve the pass. I'll take it to the staffing this afternoon. Understand, though, I'll not use this as bait to get you to calm down.

Having the client write down problems also defuses angry feelings and acting out. In many instances, the client may just be testing limits. To write down clearly and logically what the problem is calls for time and effort, which very few clients will invest if the problem is not important. Writing down the particulars of the problem is also cathartic for clients, allowing them to gain some emotional distance from it and view the situation in a more objective light.

When other more overt ploys are ineffective, the client may use manipulation and threat to obtain demands.

Jason: If you don't get that pass for me, you ain't much of a counselor and they'll be real sorry they didn't give it to me.

HSW: When you try and lay that guilt trip on me and make threats about what you'll do if you don't get your way, that's a pretty good indication that the staff's judgment was right and makes it even more difficult to act as your advocate. It's not so much any of the demands that you want met, but more like pushing the limits to see how far you can get by manipulating and threatening me.

The response the human service worker makes is one from Adlerian psychotherapy called "Avoiding the Tar Baby" (Dinkmeyer, Pew, & Dinkmeyer, 1979, p. 118). By responding directly to the client, the human service worker does not allow herself to be caught up in the manipulative trap the client lays for her. Although the response is confrontive, it is exceedingly effective with manipulative individuals because it deflects them from their game plan and causes them to consider the consequences of their actions (Wood & Khuri, 1984, p. 71).

When clients become agitated, despite the normal busy day and physical activity that help to burn up energy, deflection of anger through the use of physical activity can be helpful. Clients can take out their frustrations through activities that range from pounding on a heavy bag (Vinick, 1986) to tearing up telephone directories (McCown, 1986). At the same time the human service worker can reinforce the client for acting in more appropriate ways.

Jason: (Tearing up the Yellow Pages.) Umphf! I . . . get so mad . . . I . . . Arggh! I . . . wish this phone book was that no-good S.O.B.'s face.

HSW: But in fact you haven't torn anybody's face off. You've made a good choice. Much better than when you were going around clobbering people. You don't have to pay any consequences at all for tearing up the phone book. You get it out of your system and get back in control.

Jason: (Continues ventilating, until finally he runs out of energy and lets arms hang limply at side.)

HSW: (Continues to reinforce Jason for acting appropriately and within limits.) Look at what you could have done. You could have swung a chair at Mr. Richardson, you could have punched me out, or trashed your room, all of which would have got you in hot water. The very kinds of things that got you here in the first place. But you didn't do that. What you did was perfectly acceptable and within the limits here. And we have plenty of used telephone books.

Stage 5: Time out. When clients cannot contend with the emotion of the moment, they are asked to go to a place that has a reduced-stimulus environment, to be alone and think things out. A clear assessment of how agitated the client is needs to be made at this point. In an initial meeting, the worker can estimate the client's remaining degree of control by the client's response to certain questions (Wood & Khuri, 1984, p. 68): How dangerous does the client feel in regard to self and others? Is the client able and willing to leave a high-stimulus situation for a few minutes to rest and think things over? If the worker has no prior knowledge of the client or feels the client may be in danger of hurting self or others, close observation is called for. The client should not be left alone without someone to keep an eye on the time-out area. If the client is not overly reactive, then the worker may ask the client to take a minimal time out in living quarters.

Jason: I don't want to sit, talk, or be reasonable. I want this scumbag place to do something!

HSW: Right now I can see there's no way this is going to get solved. You can go to your room and think things over. Go for fifteen minutes. If you can come back and show me you're in control, that's it, no reduction in level, no write-ups, and it's forgotten.

If the client is noncompliant, the worker escalates time out.

Jason: So shove it! I'll take anybody on here and that's no bull! I am not going back to my room, period, paragraph!

If a threat is made directly to the human service worker, other staff, or clients, the policy should be mandatory time out with a clear and strong statement of reason (Vinick, 1986).

HSW: I've tried to work this through with you and you clearly don't want to hear it.

When you continue to make threats, you're saying to me you're not willing to abide by the rules and are choosing to have rules enforced. I want you to go to the observation room for thirty minutes right now. At the end of that time I'll be around to see you. If you don't feel like talking you don't have to, but you can go back in the room for another thirty minutes. You can continue to do that until you're willing to talk to me about how you think you've been treated unfairly.

The human service worker states these conditions in a matter-of-fact manner and does not press the issue (Vinick, 1986). If Jason is not in control of himself after thirty minutes, the sequence will continue until he is able to behave in a rational manner. Carol suggests that Jason go to the time-out room for two reasons. First, it is safer there for both the worker and the client. There are fewer things to throw than there are in an office or Jason's room (McCown, 1986). Second, Jason is unlikely to draw a crowd, which might well agitate him to act out even more (Vinick, 1986). If the client is so agitated as to be beyond the grasp of reality and is unwilling to be compliant to the human service worker's request, then the worker needs help to contain the situation.

Stage 6: Show of force.   If the client is unable to proceed to time out or is otherwise noncompliant or acting out, then a show of force is needed (Piercy, 1984, p. 148). If the client is already agitated enough to warn the human service worker that help may be warranted, the interview should be carried out in an open hallway or large meeting room where the participants are in plain view of other staff members and the client can be restrained easily (Viner, 1982). The show of force indicates that any display of violence or threat of violence will not be tolerated and often helps disorganized clients to regain control of themselves (Wood & Khuri, 1984, p. 68). By this time, someone has decided that talking the problem through is probably going to be ineffective and stronger measures will have to be taken (Vinick, 1986). If this stage is reached, the potential for violence is high and the worker should not attempt to deal with the client alone. Either by paging help through an emergency code or by having assistance readily available, the worker needs to be able to summon enough help to demonstrate that compliance is now required.

The problem is that not all individuals give indications that they are about to become violent. Therefore, there are times when, through no fault of the worker, potentially violent situations occur when the worker is alone and not immediately able to call for assistance. Some simple procedures may then keep the worker out of harm's way (Moran, 1984).

First and foremost, the institution should have provided training, written guidelines, and rehearsed procedures for handling such an agitated client. If so, as Moran (1984, pp. 238–248) indicates, the human service worker is going to know the following:

1. *Stay calm and relaxed.* Tensing of muscles and agitated movement only fuel the situation and cause the client to expect that something bad (for the client) is about to happen. Knowing relaxation techniques such as simple

deep breathing is extremely helpful because one is able to stay loose, antici-pate client responses, and move quickly.

2. *Practice positive self-talk.* Even in the worst situations, running positive "billboards" through the mind's eye will help keep control of the situation.

3. *Do not stare at the client.* Whereas eye contact is fine in most counseling situations, it may be construed as a challenge in this situation. Focus on an imaginary spot on the client's upper chest about where the first button on a shirt would be, occasionally glancing at the eyes and other parts of the indi-vidual's body. Keeping focus on the centerline of the client's body will also let the human service worker avoid being faked out by extremity or eye move-ments.

4. *Arm's length.* Make a judgment about how long the client's arms are and stay an arm's length and a bit more away. Estimating this distance on a con-tinuous basis with other staff will keep the human service worker's distance perception well honed.

5. *Dominance.* Know which of the client's hands is dominant and stay to the client's weak side. Chances are nine out of ten the client will be right-handed. In an aggressive stance, a person invariably places the foot of the weak side forward, and wristwatches are usually worn on the weak arm. If the worker keeps to the weak side of the assailant, any blow aimed by the client is likely to have less power and be a glancing one.

6. *Keep arms at side.* Folded arms are bad for two reasons. They imply hos-tility or authority and they put the worker at a distinct disadvantage because of the time it takes to unfold them and defend oneself.

7. *Assume a defensive posture.* Stand with feet slightly spread, face to face with the client but tending a bit to the client's weak side. Move the dominant leg slightly to the rear with the knee locked. Move the other leg slightly for-ward of the body and bent slightly at the knee. This position will allow the worker the best chance to stay upright, and staying upright is the best safe-guard against being hurt.

8. *Avoid cornering.* Cornering occurs in three ways. When the client is placed in an angle formed by two walls or other objects, with the human ser-vice worker directly in front of the client, the only way out is through the worker. Exit cornering occurs when the individual cannot get out of a room without first crossing the personal space of the worker. Contact cornering oc-curs when the worker attempts to subdue a client by physical means. The client has two choices, either to submit or to resist.

The premise in avoiding cornering is that even an agitated individual will seek to disengage if given the opportunity to do so without losing face. The human service worker should be careful to give the client space to exit the situation safely. A problem occurs in a private office where the worker does not have an easy escape exit. The easiest solution is to be so situated in an office that both the worker and the client can exit the room without having to cross the personal space of one another.

Although we would advise the worker to have a basic understanding of self-defense, under none but the most extreme circumstances do we believe that a worker should ever attempt bodily restraint of a client. The risk of physical injury is far too great and the client's trust in the worker will be destroyed.

9. *Avoid ordering.* When a client is threatening violence, attempting to order or command a client to do something is likely to aggravate the situation further. Staying with the basic empathic listening and responding skills used throughout this book is far more likely to lead to satisfactory results.

Although it is not within the purview of this book to provide instruction on self-defense, we do believe that all human service providers and especially crisis workers should undergo training in simple self-defense and take-down procedures. This precaution seems especially important in small outpatient facilities where specially trained help may not be readily available. Neglecting to learn how to deal with a noncompliant teenager who one of our co-workers thought could be manhandled cost the worker a broken rib. Following the incident, all human service personnel in the facility underwent training in physical self-defense and containment procedures. Numerous subsequent incidents were handled effectively without injury either to the clients or to the staff.

There are numerous facilities that provide such training for little or no charge. Local YMCAs or YWCAs and college continuing-education courses may offer such instruction, or the local high school wrestling coach may even be prevailed upon. Instruction should be a priority of the institution, and *all* personnel should receive training.

Stage 7: Seclusion.   Seclusion may be generally differentiated from time out by its length, its setting, and its involuntary nature. If clients are unable to extricate themselves from the volatile situation then they may have to be involuntarily secluded. Seclusion is a more severe type of limit setting that provides temporary ego boundaries for the client in a safe and secure environment where the client can reorganize thinking, feeling, and behavior (Holmes & Werner, 1966; Mattson & Sacks, 1978). There are three reasons for seclusion: (1) the client is agitated, hyperactive, verbally threatening, or damaging property; (2) the client is impulsive or intrusive and does not respond to limit setting; (3) the client is making suicidal gestures and is unable or unwilling to make a verbal contract about controlling behavior (Baradell, 1985).

Secluding clients who will not voluntarily seclude themselves calls for application of force. First, a response team that is trained to apply restraints to a client should be formed and be on call at all times (Wood & Khuri, 1984, p. 81). If the person is to be restrained, then adequate staff should be available and should consist of at least one person for each limb and another person who serves as leader, for a total of five members. Written guidelines and constant rehearsal of procedures with observation and critique should be made to keep the team's skills well honed (Tardiff, 1984b).

If at all possible, the crisis worker should not be involved in the episode, since involvement may erect barriers to future therapeutic endeavors. Once the decision to restrain the client has been made, then the team should move fast and no further attempts at communication should be made. In an emergency, if not enough staff are present to contain the client adequately, tossing a sheet over the client's head will provide enough distraction and be confining enough to enable staff to control the client (Vinick, 1986). At a predetermined signal, each staff member seizes and controls one extremity. With a backward motion the client is brought gently to the ground. The leader controls the client's head to prevent biting, and without choking, hitting, or verbal abuse the client is carried face down with four-point restraints to a room where five-point restraints may be applied and the client's condition monitored (Tardiff, 1984a, p. 47).

In the confrontation with Jason, a response team has been called and is ready to take Jason to seclusion. Carol has slowly and carefully removed her jewelry to avoid cutting anyone in case she becomes involved.

HSW: I'd really like you to go on your own down to time out. It's up to you. You can go on your own right now or the technicians will take you to seclusion.

Even at this late hour, the worker is still attempting to allow Jason to exercise options and make choices (Baradell, 1985).

Jason: I ain't gonna go nowhere 'ceptin' outta here.

Carol backs away and the response team moves in. On a predetermined signal by the leader, they quickly take Jason down. One member holds his head, and the other four carry him to seclusion.

Once placed in seclusion, the client is oriented to what is going to occur, and a staff member will be assigned to monitor the client. Checks will be made at 15-, 30-, or 60-minute intervals, depending on the mental status of the client. Copies of nursing and general-care orders will be given to both staff and the client. Seclusion will have a low level of sensory input—no radio or television, no visitors—and emphasis will be on biological needs. "Low level" does not mean that the client is sensorily deprived. It is important to prevent feelings of abandonment. The client is shown acceptance by the human service worker and reassured that seclusion is necessary and temporary and that the client can return to normal routine when behavior calms down (Baradell, 1985).

HSW: I'm sorry you chose to go to seclusion, Jason. You decided to exercise that option, but when you can agree to not make threats, control your behavior to the point you can talk this through, and make a written contract as to what you will do, you can come back out.

In an acute stage of agitation such as Jason has just experienced, it is no longer appropriate to explore conflicts or feelings (Ruesch, 1973). Carol's communication with the client is brief, direct, concrete, but kind. Given the sensory overload of the client, sleep is an excellent therapeutic modality, and the client should be allowed to use it (Baradell, 1985).

Seclusion or extended time out also has an effect upon other members of the community (Jones, 1976). Other residents will demonstrate a variety of feelings ranging from concern to fear. It is important that questions of the residents be answered as fully as possible and plans made that incorporate their help in expediting the client's return to the community. Having a community meeting specifically for dealing with the concerns of the other residents is worthwhile. Typical questions include whether to speak to the client, how to act around the client, and whether the time away from the group should be mentioned (Baradell, 1985). Many times the group can act as a therapeutic agent; encourage members to discuss how they can help the client by reinforcing or ignoring particular behaviors that caused the problem in the first place.

Indeed, in school settings where a student has been placed on seclusion or extended periods of time out, we have negotiated contracts between the class and the student detailing very specifically what behaviors were to be performed by both parties for the student to gain reentry to the classroom. Classroom meetings based on the Glasser model (1969) provide an excellent format for problem solving and exploring the feelings of the group when a radical procedure such as seclusion is used. We see no reason why this cannot and should not be used in other institutional settings.

As the client is able to regain control, successive approximation is used to reintegrate the client back into the community. The goal of successive approximation is to break the total task into attainable small steps. A major fault of attempts to manage behavior is requiring total and immediate compliance to task. In Jason's case, if he were allowed access to the community on the basis of his agreement to be "good" it is doubtful, no matter how good his intentions were, that he could handle the immediate increase in the environmental stimuli that got him in trouble in the first place. Periods away from the seclusion room become longer and longer as the client demonstrates increased ability to handle the environment. Verbal and written contracts ensure understanding of limits. The client discusses feelings about the experience with the human service worker and fully explores feelings of trepidation and stigma about returning to the community (Baradell, 1985). One negative footnote is appropriate here. A few clients may use seclusion as a way of achieving notoriety and a macho image (Gutheil, 1978). Under no circumstances should a client be allowed to gain image enhancement through seclusion. If such a hidden agenda is suspected, the human service worker should thoroughly discuss this problem with the other residents and obtain their help in being nonresponsive to the client's "tough" behavior.

Stage 8: Restraints.   If the client is acting out and will not go to seclusion, the client may have to be restrained. Restraints should be employed if the etiology of the violence is unknown. Specific examples include organic mental disorders, fear that the client might be harmful to self or others, and worsening of the client's condition while in seclusion (Tardiff, 1984a, p. 48). Restraints are most often employed in psychiatric facilities and are used in conjunction with a request from the nursing staff and backed by a doctor's order. Care needs to be taken in the use of restraints, and specific procedures as outlined in the American Nurses Association's (1974) *A Plan for the Implementation of the Standards of Nursing Practice* should be followed. When a client is placed in restraints, whether two, four, or five point, close observation is absolutely necessary. Under no circumstances should clients be restrained without such guidelines and available professional medical staff.

Stage 9: Sedation.   If all else fails, then the client needs to be sedated. The problem now becomes clearly medical, and until the medical staff feels that medication is no longer necessary, there is little the human service worker can do.

Whether Jason learns anything from his experiences is difficult to say. If he continues to act out in increasingly violent ways, he will have to be sedated. However, if sedation is needed, it does not mean the end of Jason's story. Stage 9 is essentially a complete time out for both Jason and the staff. For Jason, it will allow the sensory overload he is experiencing to diminish and return to normal limits. For the staff, it will give them time to reorganize their thoughts on how best to deal with this highly agitated adolescent. The overriding philosophy is that while plans may fail, people do not. This philosophy especially holds true for clients such as Jason who are resistant, aggressive, and noncompliant to treatment. When Jason comes out of sedation, the staff will start down the treatment road with him again and, hopefully, will have developed a new plan to deal effectively with this angry young man.

THE VIOLENT GERIATRIC CLIENT

The geriatric client belongs to a growing population that human service workers are likely to encounter. While medical science has been able to prolong the lives of Americans, the neuropsychiatric disorders concomitant with increased longevity remain beyond the reach of medical science at present. Alzheimer's disease is but one of many of the organic brain problems that the geriatric population currently faces. Accompanying the neuropsychiatric problems of the geriatric client are reduced judgment and increased impulsivity, which are precursors of violent behavior (Petrie, 1984, p. 107).

The assumption that the elderly are passive recipients of care is misguided. Study after study indicates this clientele to be at risk with regard to violent behavior (Climent & Ervin, 1972; Johnson, Frankel, & Ferrence, 1975; Ochitill & Krieger, 1982; Petrie, Lawson, & Hollender, 1982; Tardiff & Sweillam, 1980, 1982). With the intact extended nuclear family generally becoming a curiosity of history, the elderly who are no longer able to care for themselves are placed in nursing care facilities by their families. Dealing with the agitated geriatric client is one of the most frustrating tasks with which the staff of such facilities contend (Miller, 1986).

The case of Cliff demonstrates how the agitated and mildly disoriented elderly client may be stabilized without the use of medication. Reality orientation (Taulbee & Folsom, 1966), reminiscence (Butler, 1963), and remotivation (Garber, 1965) techniques are presented as workable options for the mildly disoriented elderly. The case of Grace shows how validation therapy (Feil, 1982) may be used with the severely disoriented elderly. The cases, presented in condensed form, illustrate that the psychologically infirm elderly do not always have to spend this final stage of their lives in a chemically induced compliant state.

CASE OF CLIFF

Cliff Hastings had lived a full and eventful life, but now, at the age of 74, he is a resident of a skilled nursing care facility. He was a strapping man who had worked all over the world on big construction projects until he was 72 years of age. He had invented many engineering techniques in steamfitting and chilled water cooling systems. He was well respected by his men as a fair boss and had earned a worldwide reputation as a man whom one could call when there was an impossible job to be done. He lost his wife to cancer ten years ago, but submerged himself in his work and lived a highly productive life as a widower. He has had excellent relationships with his two children, Jane and Robert. Although they and their families are geographically distant from Cliff, they love their father very much and are very concerned about him.

At age 73, Cliff got up one morning, prepared to go to work, and fell flat on his face with a stroke. Although he recovered to the extent that he was able to shuffle around the house, lung complications set in. He was diagnosed as having emphysema and went on oxygen. Six months later, he was no longer able to take care of himself physically, was starting to have memory lapses, and was moved to Hursthaven Nursing Home by his children, who made the agonizing decision to place him there because of his physical and psychological infirmities.

At Hursthaven, he has become progressively more confused about people, places, and times and when asked to do something has been either rebellious or passively resistant. A crisis was precipitated when he knocked an oxygen bottle over in the middle of the night because the "Arabs were after him" and broke the nose of a male attendant who tried to calm him down as he was attempting to struggle out of his bed. Cliff is about to meet a new type of human service worker. Her name is Marilyn and she is a gerontological counselor. She has just been retained by Hursthaven to deal with crisis situations like Cliff's.

Assessment

Marilyn has thoroughly reviewed Cliff's chart and has discussed his case with the medical and primary care staff. Many of the primary care staff maintain that Cliff is noncompliant, badly disoriented, and dangerous, and they would like to keep him heavily sedated. Cliff's stroke, his unplanned aggressive outburst, hostile and uncooperative behavior, fear of the medical equipment, and depression, plus the fact that his outburst was at night, all point toward vascular impairment (Petrie, 1984, pp. 110–111) and support the staff's contention that little but chemical restraints is left for Cliff. Marilyn takes these facts and the staff's comments under advisement, but she decides to conduct her own assessment by interviewing Cliff. As the worker heads toward the interview, she has three purposes in mind: first, to determine the client's degree of disorientation and agitation; second, to use her therapeutic skills to reduce his disruptive behavior and help him return to a state of equilibrium with as little reliance on medication as possible; and third, to help Cliff use whatever resources he has to live this final stage of his life as fully as he is able.

The medical staff has decided that Cliff not be given any more sedatives so that Marilyn may identify a behavioral baseline to determine just how much in touch with reality the client is. As the worker enters the room, Cliff is sitting in a specially equipped chair with a cloth belt strapped around his midsection. He has just finished swearing vigorously at an attendant who refused to take the belt off.

Intervention

CW: Hello, I'm Marilyn. I don't believe I've met you. You seem pretty angry about something.

Cliff: (Suspiciously.) Who the hell are you?

CW: I'm new here, part of the staff, and I'm getting around meeting all the residents. Sorry you're so angry. What can I do to help?

Cliff: I'm Cliff Hastings, and I'm mad as hell. Look at what those S.O.B.s have done to me. I pay $1500 a month for this place to strap me down. I'll kill the bastards if I get a chance. Can you get me out of here?

CW: (Speaking in a strong but soft and empathic voice, while pulling up a chair and sitting down directly in his line of sight.) No! I can't right now. I guess I'd be mad too if I were strapped in like that. Do you know where you are?

Cliff: I'm in Hell and these people are all devils.

CW: It may feel like that right now, but this is Hursthaven Nursing Home. Do you know that?

Cliff: Too damn well.

CW: Do you know what day it is?

Cliff: Who cares? They're all the same in here.

Testing reality. The worker assesses Cliff's degree of contact with reality by determining how well oriented he is to person, place, and time. Although the client does not give specific, concrete responses, his retorts indicate that he is fairly well in touch with reality, given his present agitated state.

CW: I'm sorry you're feeling so angry. Can I get you a drink of water?

Eliciting trust.   Offering food or drink to agitated clients tends to defuse the situation and make them more accepting of initiating overtures the worker may tender (Wood & Khuri, 1984, p. 67). The worker also sits down by Cliff and meets him at eye level. She places herself on his physical level and in his direct line of sight. Standing over a client who is confused tends to distort the caregiver's image in grotesque ways and may be very threatening (Wolanin & Phillips, 1981, p. 106).

Cliff: (Takes a sip of water from cup Marilyn offers.) Yeah, that's the least somebody around this place could do for the money I pay to be doped up and trussed up like a pig.

CW: How do you feel?

Cliff: How the hell do you think I feel, young lady?

CW: I guess I'd not only feel like a pig all trussed up, but mad as a wildcat in a gunnysack. How did this happen?

The crisis worker matches the vernacular of the client and interjects a bit of humor (Tomine, 1986). The worker is interested in knowing what happened, but her major concern is to continue posing open-ended questions to assess how much in touch with reality Cliff is and also to let him know she is interested and concerned about him. Cliff continues to vilify the attendants, the nursing home, and everybody else in a long, profane, and rambling discourse. Part of his diatribe is couched in realistic terms and part appears not to be. Overall, though, the client does understand where he is, who he is, and what time frame he is in. The worker manages to gain a working rapport with the client and explores the incident.

CW: So what happened last night that got you in that fix?

Cliff: The Arab, he was after me. He was gonna strangle me, but nobody believes me. (Points to attendant.) That guy said it was one of the guys that work here at night. Said I busted his nose. Well, it was the Arabs. Sneaky devils.

CW: Why do you think it was the Arabs?

Reality orientation.   The worker is taking a first step in attempting to relieve Cliff's confusion by using reality orientation (Taulbee & Folsom, 1966). Reality orientation focuses on anchoring clients to who they are, where they are, and why they are there. When a client's response or behavior is out of touch with reality, the worker asks the client a "why" question, in an approach contrary to that of most therapeutic interventions (Taulbee, 1978, p. 207). Marilyn does this because she is trying to find out the reason for the behavior. Once the worker knows that, then she may start to reorient the client.

Cliff: I spent a lot of time in Arabia, you know. Worked in construction. Put up a lot of refrigeration plants and steam systems. Hard to believe you'd need steam in that hothouse. Sometimes I wish I was back in Arabia. But that doesn't mean any damn camel choker can come in here in the middle of the night and kill me. I had plenty of close scrapes back there, and they didn't get me and they won't get me here.

CW: (Genuinely interested.) Hey! That sounds pretty exciting. I've hardly been out of the Midwest. I'll bet you've seen some pretty hair-raising things and I can guess how you might think somebody was an Arab, being in a strange place like this.

Cliff rambles on for quite a while about his experiences there, with Marilyn listening and responding using person-centered techniques of attending, affirming, restating for clarification, reflecting feelings, and asking open-ended questions.

Pacing.   Cliff's response about working in Arabia gives the worker a clue about the image he saw attacking him in the night. However, she does not try to change his mind about what happened. The worker keeps pace with Cliff. She lets him tell his story without hurrying or trying to persuade him that he was mistaken last night. Patience is of maximum benefit in gaining the trust she will need if she is to accomplish anything with the client (Taulbee, 1978, p. 210). This approach is in direct contrast to that of most of the staff in the facility, who are pressed to get tasks accomplished in a specified time. Indeed, trying to gain compliance by coercing the client to meet institutional needs is likely to engender more agitated behavior.

Reminiscence therapy.   The worker's approach in urging Cliff to talk about his past is again contradictory to most standard operating procedures and generally accepted counseling technique. Most therapeutic systems try very hard to keep clients in present time and view trips to the past as counterproductive to changing real-time problems. However, allowing geriatric clients to ruminate about past experiences can be therapeutically effective (Ebersole, 1978a, p. 145). Sparking recollection of past experiences in which the client was proactive, vibrant, and alive says in effect, "You have lived a good, positive, and fulfilling life and have every right to recall those really positive times." Reminiscence therapy (Butler, 1963) is designed both to calm and to enhance credibility (Miller, 1986). Reminiscence can be therapeutic and healing for the client, while at a more basic level it is a simple, enjoyable sharing of anecdotes that allows the worker to form a closer affiliation with the client (Ebersole, 1978a, p. 145). Over the long term, using reminiscence may allow these positive outcomes to occur (McMahon & Rhudick, 1964, pp. 292–298):

1. maintaining self-esteem in the face of declining physical capacities
2. coping with grief and depression resulting from personal losses
3. contributing significantly to a society of which the elderly client is still a member
4. retaining a sense of identity in an increasingly estranged environment.

Cliff: Yeah . . . (Voice trails off.) . . . I used to be hot stuff . . . but I'm not so hot now. Hell, half the time I don't even know who, what, or where I am.

CW: (Touches client's arm lightly with her hand.) It sounds like that's pretty scary, having run things most of your life and now things are out of control.

Cliff: I hate to admit it, but that's right. All my life doing a job. Now I got to have help getting to the john! If that isn't something. How'd you like that? It embarrasses the hell out of me. They treat me like a 2-year-old.

CW: So being embarrassed and not being treated like a man is one of the worst parts of being here. I wonder what we might do to change that?

Control.   The worker uses a reflective statement of feeling to integrate the client's past with his present. By bringing up past incidents and hooking them to the present, the worker attempts to reinforce and help the client reassert his competence. She also uses touch to anchor Cliff psychologically to someone in the institution (Wolanin & Phillips, 1981, pp. 105–106). Prior to the assault, a kind but sterile atmosphere had existed for Cliff at Hursthaven. Like most human beings, he has not responded well to living in an emotional vacuum. Since the attack, the atmosphere between Cliff and the staff has become adversarial in nature. Marilyn needs to change Cliff's view of the staff as being against him and likewise the staff's view that Cliff is to be avoided. The worker will instruct primary care staff to start Cliff on a twenty-four hour orientation program once the present crisis is over. All staff members who come in contact with Cliff during the course of the day will introduce themselves, call Cliff by name, state the date, give a short preview of the next few hours' activities, and also explain any procedures, medical or otherwise, that they are carrying out. By consistently orienting the client, the staff takes a first step in treating confusion (Taulbee, 1978, p. 209).

The worker also picks up on Cliff's fear of losing control. Having violent urges and not remembering what happened is frightening for clients when they regain lucidity. Being wildly out of control is competely out of character for clients like Cliff, who are frightened at the prospect of losing their minds. Even more fears are generated when elderly clients sense someone is afraid of them or avoiding them because of fear of violence (Lion & Pasternak, 1973).

The crisis worker engages in a number of activities in this dialogue. The most important is that she has made a small but significant change in the interactional system that currently exists between Cliff and the staff by representing herself as an empathic, caring spokesperson for the institution and as an advocate for the client (Fisch, Weakland, & Segal, 1983). Second, she reflects his anger, fear, and loss of control. She acknowledges and validates his experiences. She is not just being platitudinous. She knows that the more he lacks current orientation, the more the staff will tend to avoid him. The more he is avoided and the less contact he has with people, the more out of touch and disoriented he is likely to become (Petrie, 1984, pp. 114–115). The cycle can become deeper and deeper if uninterrupted and may cause even more disorientation and aggressive acts in the future (Miller, 1986).

Illusions versus hallucinations.   While Cliff is engaged in reminiscence, Marilyn is busily attempting to figure out what may have prompted Cliff to believe that an Arab was indeed invading his room. Marilyn further understands that what agitated Cliff was probably not a hallucination, as the staff thinks, but more than likely an illusion. While piecing together the tale of the night before, she determines that one of the Sisters of Charity who works at the nursing home made rounds about the time Cliff became agitated. The sister's veil may have made her look like an Arab in the dim light. Thus, what Cliff saw was probably an illusion based in fact, not fiction. By proposing an explanation of the event, she allows Cliff to understand that he was not delusional but was misperceiving reality. The two problems are very different, and the difference is of great significance in calming the client. Although this may sound like a very pat conclusion, such happenings are all too common among mildly confused and disoriented clients. Many times, very definite, concrete stimuli create illusions that disrupt peace of mind for geriatric clients, leaving them to doubt their own perceptions. By being a bit of a detective, the worker may often be able to ascertain what is responsible for the illusion. It is extremely important for the worker to relate such a hypothesis to mildly confused clients like Cliff who are very much concerned about keeping in touch with reality (Wolanin & Phillips, 1981, p. 107).

CW: (Relates her hypothesis to the client.) So I believe that you weren't really crazy last night, but actually saw Sister Lucy making rounds. If you think about it, it makes sense.

Cliff: I don't know. I still really believe there was an Arab in here.

CW: From all you've told me about your experiences there, I can understand that. But I also know that when you're zonked out in a strange place with the medical equipment around and strangers passing to and fro, suddenly waking up and seeing things differently is not uncommon and doesn't mean you're nuts. I'll bet if you think about it, it has happened before. I know it has happened to me. There's a big difference between misunderstanding what you see and seeing something that isn't there. I'm not trying to change your mind, but maybe it's possible. I'd like you to think about it.

Sundown syndrome. Because the event happened in the early evening, the sundown syndrome must be considered. Events that accompany the end of the day in an institution are strange and unsettling to residents who have been used to a regimen of activities based on their own time and the security of their own home. Unmet toilet needs, absence of a snack, different noises, decreased light, effects of sedatives, and presence of fewer personnel all add up to fear and strangeness without the support of another human being. These conditions can lead the client to act out (Wolanin & Phillips, 1981, p. 107). The worker will need to study the events surrounding the assault to determine if other factors in the institution caused Cliff to act out. Given the need to further assure Cliff about the reality of the situation, Marilyn relates the problems that occur with the approach of evening in the institution and makes some suggestions about how things might be changed to make this time less threatening.

CW: So a lot of times when evening comes at Hursthaven things can get exciting for the reasons I mentioned. If you could make things here a bit more like home, what would they be?

Cliff: Well, I used to put my earphones on and listen to some country music and have a beer before I hit the hay. I don't know much else, just watch TV and stuff. No special furniture or anything. I lived in apartments most of my life.

CW: I notice that there's not much of you in this room. It looks like a hospital room instead of Cliff's room. You mentioned a lot of items you collected over the years and picture albums of all your travels. Where are they?

Cliff: Oh, my kids just stored them away.

CW: I'd like to see if we couldn't get some of those in here, dress the place up a bit so when people come by they'd know this was Cliff Hastings, world class engineer, who lives here.

Security blankets. The worker is proposing that articles familiar to Cliff be brought into the room for two reasons. First, creating a familiar environment may go a long way toward creating a basis in reality for the fact that this is now Cliff's home and reconciling him to this stage in his life (Petrie, 1984, p. 116). Second, suddenly awakening in a medical environment with a variety of strange machines and tubes running in and out of one's body is extremely threatening because such foreign objects alter a person's body images and surroundings in a very negative way (Wolanin & Phillips, 1981, p. 106). Having familiar objects immediately visible can help the client reorient without becoming agitated in the process. Marilyn will check with administrative staff to see if Cliff's stereo equipment can be brought into his room. The worker will also check with medical staff to see if a bottle of beer in the evening will confound his medication. If possible, providing these amenities will further approximate the client's routine at home and provide orientation and security (Miller, 1986).

Remotivation. Finally, the worker will attempt to involve Cliff in the activities of the institution. It is important to involve clients interpersonally and have them become physically and psychologically active in their environment. For people like Cliff who have been highly active throughout their lives, it is critical to fill idle time in meaningful ways to keep such clients from drifting into depression (Donahue, 1965). This does not mean forcing and cajoling clients into doing something contrary to what interests them. Playing bingo might be fun for many people, but forcing a person to engage in such an activity is inappropriate (Miller, 1986). After listening to Cliff, the worker makes a proposal designed to reinvolve him with the human race.

CW: I don't know if this would be your cup of tea or not, but I'd like you to consider a proposition I have to make. Hursthaven has an alliance with St. Peter's Orphanage. None of those kids have anybody to care about them. I have a couple of boys in mind that I think you could do some good with. You've got some great stories that they'd love and probably some wisdom that could be helpful to those guys. They just mainly need a man to talk to and I wonder if you'd be willing to help out?

The worker's agenda is twofold. She is truthful in what she tells Cliff. She also knows that the two boys will have a positive effect on Cliff in turn. Aged people seem particularly interested in sharing their experiences with the young (Ebersole, 1978b, p. 241). Cliff's candidness, wisdom, and trove of stories are likely to have a positive effect on two boys who are as anchorless as Cliff. He will have to get involved in the planning that the residents of Hursthaven carry out in coordinating activities with St. Peter's. Involvement with other members of the community, heretofore nil, will gently push him back into the mainstream, reinforce his dignity, and provide him with interaction that he will find meaningful and enjoyable. Engaging in this activity will give the client a stake in the community and will, Marilyn hopes, focus his psychic energy on something besides his own outcast state (Miller, 1986).

The worker is engaging in a variation of remotivation therapy at this point. Remotivation therapy is a group technique that is used to stimulate and revitalize individuals who are no longer interested in the present or the future (Dennis, 1978, p. 219). It is based on a combination of reminiscence and reality orientation. Remotivation attempts to persuade the client that he is accepted by others as an individual who has unique and important traits that make him distinguishable from everyone else (Garber, 1965). Remotivation therapy creates a bridge between the individual's self-perception and the perception of others. Reminiscing about one's experiences with the concrete world and identifying and asserting one's experiences through interactions with others often lead to strengthening the concept of reality. Being encouraged to describe oneself concretely as a person with roles and specific social functions and speaking accurately about past and present experiences gives a person strength (Dennis, 1978, p. 220).

Validation therapy. Whereas Cliff is only mildly confused and fairly coherent as he ruminates about his past, many geriatric clients the worker will encounter have lost touch with reality. Verbalization of past events becomes commingled with fantasy. The standard regimen for working with geriatric clients has been to attempt to reality-orient them to the present. Such an approach becomes problematic for moderately confused clients and profoundly so for those who have almost entirely retreated from the reality of the present. Attempts to orient moderately-to-severely confused old, old clients to person, place, and time are generally futile. For many of these clients nothing could be less worthwhile, for there is clearly not much in the present worth remembering (Miller, 1986).

Naomi Feil has seized upon this notion and has developed validation therapy (Feil, 1982). Her thesis is to acknowledge the feelings of the person no matter how irrational they may seem to be. By dignifying feelings the worker validates the person. To deny the feelings of the client is to deny past existence and thus deny the personhood of the individual.

Feil also believes that validating early memories allows clients to resolve the past and justify their role in old age. Positive outcomes for using the approach are restoration of self-worth, reduction of stress, justification of living, resolution of unfinished conflicts, and a better and more secure feeling for the client (Feil, 1982, p. 1). The worker continuously validates the client as a first step in restoring self-worth and affirming that at least one person is interested and concerned enough to listen to what the client's life has been. Anyone overhearing a dialogue between a worker and a client who has severely regressed into an irrational past would probably wonder at first whether the worker had also become senile. The worker must have some creative insight into the verbal meanderings and repetitive behaviors of the client in order for validation therapy to be effective (Miller, 1986). Listen to Marilyn as she attempts to convince an 83-year-old woman to go to dinner.

────────────────── **CASE OF GRACE** ──────────────────

The woman, Grace, is standing in the hallway refusing to be moved. She is engaging in a rocking motion with her arms and softly humming to herself. Staff's efforts to get her to go to dinner have been fruitless and she is becoming increasingly agitated as a number of staff members are attempting to orient her and get her to comply with their requests. Marilyn enters this scene and asks the rest of the staff to leave them.

Grace: There, there! Don't you cry.

CW: I see you're really concerned about your baby.

Grace: Yes, I've been up all night with Ellen. She must have colic, but I can't seem to get her to settle down. I need to get Dr. Heinz, he's our family doctor, a very good one, but I don't have anyone to hitch the team to go to town and get him.

CW: It really worries you that Ellen doesn't seem to be getting any better. You must be awfully tired and hungry!

Grace: Even though Ellen's cranky, she's no bother, she's really a beautiful baby. It's just that her father isn't around much, he works on the railroad and I could use some help sometimes.

CW: You must love her very much. Maybe we could go down to dinner together and you could tell me some more about her.

Grace: She's got to have quiet to get to sleep. It's too noisy there.

CW: It's important to you that she gets to sleep. Perhaps we could have dinner served in your room. It'd be quiet there.

Grace: Well, I suppose, if you'd really like to.

In this short exchange the worker demonstrates two critical components of validation therapy. The client may well have lost the ability to comprehend and reason with any degree of complexity. By keeping communication short and simple, the worker avoids losing the client in a variety of ideas that may rapidly become overwhelming. The worker also responds directly and continuously to Grace's feelings, validating to her that the symbolic act she is engaging in is highly important (Miller, 1986).

Although the purpose of validation therapy is not to manipulate the client, the worker's approach is far better than forcibly taking the client to the dining room, where she will probably be so distraught over having to neglect her baby that she will not eat anyway. Whether Grace has ever had a baby named Ellen, or whether she is trying to resolve some shortcomings she has long felt in regard to mothering, is of little concern in the present moment. What is of concern is that the worker treat the situation as if it were real and of importance to the client and acknowledge the client's scattered thoughts and feelings in a congruent, empathic manner. Validation therapy is not intended to return the client to reality. However, for the human service worker who has to intervene in a crisis situation with the severely disoriented elderly, it does have the potential to calm them down, avoid situations conducive to acting out, and provide an effective therapeutic technique in an area where few have been found (Miller, 1986).

FOLLOW-UP WITH STAFF VICTIMS

Staff who are victims of violent attacks by clients may have emotional responses that include hypervigilance, startle responses, intrusive thoughts, and unresolved anger (Lenehan & Turner, 1984, p. 256), much like the victims of PTSD. Lanza (1984) found that nurses who had experienced such attacks had negative emotional, cognitive, and behavioral reactions up to a year afterward. It is extremely important to work through the aftermath of violent behavior suffered by staff, first, so that the victim does not become debilitated personally and professionally by the incident, and second, because other members of the staff will perceive that the institution takes such events very seriously and is concerned for their safety as well.

After an attack, staff members initially ascribe blame to the victim to ease their own fear and trepidation about the possibility that it could happen to them. Under no circumstances should this be allowed to happen. While empathy and support for the victim are vital, pity, condescension, or subtle implications about provoking the assault are not. Instead staff should give immediate help with problem solving and decision making, such as determining injuries, providing medical transportation, staying with the victim, providing moral support, and helping with medical, legal, and police reports (Lenehan & Turner, 1984, 255–256).

As soon as the victim is able, a psychological autopsy should be performed on the incident. A psychological autopsy examines in detail the situation that led to the violent episode. All staff members who are involved with the client attend the autopsy. It dissects what the staff and the client did behaviorally before, during, and after the incident. Further attention is given to the environmental setting to determine if it played a role in instigating the aggressive behavior. Hopefully, the autopsy will provide clues as to the "whys," "hows," and "whats" of the incident so it does not reoccur. The victim's opinions should be solicited and should be used as expert testimony. Staff gathers to discuss what happened, work through feelings about the event, and generate options for preventing a recurrence (Lenehan & Turner, 1984, p. 259). By reviewing the traumatic experience, the victim is also able to deal with feelings of loss of security and control. As with any other type of violence, the victim needs to be able to review the assault for clues and causes as a way of resolving the traumatic experience (Lenehan & Turner, 1984, pp. 254–255). If the victim continues to have problems, then therapeutic help is called for and should be provided by the institution.

SUMMARY

Violence in the human service setting has increased exponentially in the past two decades. Increased abuse of drugs, closing down of the large state mental hospitals, increased adjudication of felons to mental health facilities, and increases in the geriatric population have been major contributors to this phenomenon. The problem pervades all parts of human services. Both service providers and their staff have largely looked the other way, and when violence against staff has occurred it has been seen as going with the territory, or the victim has been blamed for being stupid and careless.

Since the range and type of institutions that provide extended care for clients with every conceivable type of problem is so broad, this chapter has endeavored to present interventional approaches that represent generically what all crisis workers need to know to stay out of harm's way and still provide effective service to their clientele. We examined two representative types of client: the male adolescent who is adjudicated as delinquent and the geriatric client who is suffering disorientation.

The techniques presented in this chapter range from option therapy to validation therapy. Designed to help clients, these techniques and others we have discussed are also intended to prevent the human service worker from being the object of an assault. Although neophytes to the human service business may dismiss the idea of being hurt by one of their clients, statistics indicate a strong likelihood that sometime during their career they will become victims of violence. The objective of this chapter has been to provide techniques that will minimize that chance.

REFERENCES

American Nurses Association. (1974). *A plan for the implementation of the standards of nursing practice.* Kansas City, MO: Author.

American Psychiatric Association. (1974). *Clinical aspects of the violent individual.* Washington, DC: American Psychiatric Association Press.

Annis, L. V., McClaren, H. A., Baker, C. A. (1984). Who kills us? In J. T. Turner (Ed.), *Violence in the medical care setting: A survival guide* (pp. 19–31). Rockville, MD: Aspen Systems Corp.

Appelbaum, P. S. (1984). Hospitalization of the dangerous patient: Legal pressures and clinical responses. *Bulletin of the American Academy of Psychiatry and the Law, 12,* 323–329.

Atkinson, J. H. (1982). Managing the violent behavior in the general hospital. *Postgraduate Medicine, 71,* 193–201.

Bach y Rita, G., Lion, J. R., & Climent, C. E. (1971). Episodic dyscontrol: A study of 630 violent patients. *American Journal of Psychiatry, 128,* 1473–1478.

Baradell, J. G. (1985, February). Humanistic care of the patient in seclusion. *Journal of Psychosocial Nursing and Mental Health Services, 23,* 9–14.

Becker, W. C. (1971). *Parents are teachers.* Champaign, IL: Research Press.

Butler, R. (1963). The life review: An interpretation of reminiscence in the aged. *Psychiatry, 26,* 65–76.

Canter, L., & Canter, E. (1982). *Assertive discipline for parents.* Santa Monica, CA: Canter Associates.

Climent, C. E., & Ervin, F. R. (1972). Historical data in the evaluation of violent subjects. *Archives of General Psychiatry, 27,* 621–624.

Dennis, H. (1978). Remotivation therapy groups. In I. M. Burnside (Ed.), *Working with the elderly: Group processes and techniques* (pp. 219–235). North Scituate, MA: Duxbury Press.

Dinkmeyer, D. C., Pew, W. L., & Dinkmeyer, D. C., Jr. (1979). *Adlerian counseling and psychotherapy,* Pacific Grove, CA: Brooks/Cole.

Doms, R. W. (1984). Personal distress devices for health care personnel. In J. T. Turner (Ed.), *Violence in the medical care setting: A survival guide* (pp. 225–229). Rockville, MD: Aspen Systems Corp.

Donahue, H. H. (1965). Expanding the program. *Hospital and Community Psychiatry, 17,* 117–118.

Dubin, W. R. (1981). Evaluating and managing the violent patient. *Annals of Emergency Medicine, 10,* 481–484.

Dyer, W. O., Murrell, D. S., & Wright, D. (1984). Training for hospital security: An alternative to training negligence suits. In J. T. Turner (Ed.), *Violence in the medical care setting: A survival guide* (pp. 1–18). Rockville, MD: Aspen Systems Corp.

Ebersole, P. P. (1978a). A theoretical approach to the use of reminiscence. In I. M. Burnside (Ed.), *Working with the elderly: Group processes and techniques* (pp. 139–154). North Scituate, MA: Duxbury Press.

Ebersole, P. P. (1978b). Establishing reminiscence groups. In I. M. Burnside (Ed.), *Working with the elderly: Group processes and techniques* (pp. 236–254). North Scituate, MA: Duxbury Press.

Fareta, G. (1981). A profile of aggression from adolescence to adulthood: An 18 year follow-up of psychiatrically disturbed and violent adolescents. *American Journal of Orthopsychiatry, 51,* 439–453.

Feil, N. (1982). *Validation: The Feil method.* Cleveland, OH: Edward Feil Productions.

Fisch, R., Weakland, J. H., & Segal, L. (1983). *The tactics of change.* San Francisco: Jossey-Bass.

Garber, R. S. (1965). A psychiatrist's view of remotivation. *Mental Hospitals, 16,* 219–221.

Glasser, W. (1965). *Reality therapy.* New York: Harper & Row.

Glasser, W. (1969). *Schools without failure.* New York: Harper & Row.

Gutheil, T. G. (1978). Observation on the theoretical basis for seclusion of the psychiatric inpatient. *American Journal of Psychiatry, 135,* 325–328.

Holmes, M. J., & Werner, J. A. (1966). *Psychiatric nursing in a therapeutic community.* New York: Macmillan.

House of Representatives Committee on Veterans Affairs. (1981, July 15). *Subcommittee on Hospital Health Care and Security Forces at VA Medical Center.* Washington, DC: U.S. Government Printing Office.

Ishimoto, W. (1984). Security management for health care administrators. In J. T. Turner (Ed.), *Violence in the medical care setting: A survival guide* (pp. 209–223). Rockville, MD: Aspen Systems Corp.

Johnson, F. G., Frankel, B. G., & Ferrence, R. G. (1975). Self-injury in London, Canada: A prospective study. *Canadian Journal of Public Health, 66,* 307–316.

Jones, J. (Speaker). (1984). *Counseling in correctional settings* (Cassette Recording No. 25-6611). Memphis: Memphis State University, Department of Counseling and Personnel Services.

Jones, M. (1976). *Maturation of the therapeutic community.* New York: Human Services Press.

Jones, M. K. (1985, June). Patient violence: Report of 200 incidents. *Journal of Psychosocial Nursing and Mental Health, 23,* 12–17.

Katz, S. E., Cohen, R., & Stokman, C. L. (1985). Violence in psychiatric institutions. *New York State Journal of Medicine, 85,* 64–66.

Kroll, J., & Mackenzie, T. B. (1983). When psychiatrists are liable: Risk management and violent patients. *Hospital and Community Psychiatry, 34,* 29–37.

Lanza, M. L. (1983). The reactions of nursing staff to physical assault by a patient. *Hospital and Community Psychiatry, 34,* 422–425.

Lanza, M. L. (1984). A follow-up study of nurses' reaction to physical assault. *Hospital & Community Psychiatry, 35,* 492–494.

Lanza, M. L. (1985, June). How nurses react to patient assault. *Journal of Psychosocial Nursing and Mental Health, 23,* 6–11.

Lenehan, G. P., & Turner, J. T. (1984). Treatment of staff victims of violence. In J. T. Turner (Ed.), *Violence in the medical care setting: A survival guide* (pp. 251–260). Rockville, MD: Aspen Systems Corp.

Lewellyn, A. (Speaker). (1985). Counseling emotionally disturbed high school students: The Mattoon, Illinois, TLC program (Cassette Recording No. 12-6611). Memphis: Memphis State University, Department of Counseling and Personnel Services.

Lion, J. R., & Pasternak, S. A. (1973). Countertransference reactions to violent patients. *American Journal of Psychiatry, 130,* 207–210.

Lion, J. R., Snyder, W., & Merrill, G. L. (1981). Underreporting of assaults on staff in state hospitals. *Hospital and Community Psychiatry, 32,* 497–498.

Marohn, R. C. (1982). Adolescent violence: Causes and treatment. *Journal of the American Academy of Child Psychiatry, 21,* 354–360.

Mattson, M. R., & Sacks, M. H. (1978). Seclusion: Uses and implications. *American Journal of Psychiatry, 135,* 1210–1212.

McCown, C. (Speaker). (1986). Counseling in an adolescent psychiatric treatment facility (Cassette Recording No. 7). Memphis: Memphis State University, Department of Counseling and Personnel Services.

McMahon, A., & Rhudick, P. (1964). Reminiscing: Adaptional significance in the aged. *Archives of General Psychiatry, 10,* 292–298.

Miller, M. (Speaker). (1986). Counseling geriatric clients (Cassette Recording No. 14). Memphis: Memphis State University, Department of Counseling and Personnel Services.

Monahan, J. (1981). *The clinical prediction of violent behavior.* Rockville, MD: National Institute of Mental Health.

Monahan, J. (1984). The prediction of violent behavior: Toward a second generation of theory and policy. *American Journal of Psychiatry, 141,* 10–15.

Moran, J. F. (1984). Teaching the management of violent behavior to nursing staff: A health care model. In J. T. Turner (Ed.), *Violence in the medical care setting: A survival guide* (pp. 231–250). Rockville, MD: Aspen Systems Corp.

Mulvey, E. P., & Lidz, C. W. (1984). Clinical considerations on the prediction of dangerous mental patients. *Clinical Psychology Review, 4,* 379–401.

Ochitill, H. N., & Kreiger, M. (1982). Violent behavior among hospitalized medical and surgical patients. *Southern Medical Journal, 75,* 151–155.

Ostrow, E., Marohn, R. C., Offer, D., Crutiss, G., & Feczko, M. (1980). The adolescent antisocial behavior checklist. *Journal of Clinical Psychology, 36,* 594–601.

Petrie, W. M. (1984). Violence: The geriatric patient. In J. T. Turner (Ed.), *Violence in the medical care setting: A survival guide* (pp. 107–122). Rockville, MD: Aspen Systems Corp.

Petrie, W. M., Lawson, E. C., & Hollender, M. H. (1982). Violence in geriatric patients. *Journal of the American Medical Association, 248,* 443–444.

Piercy, D. (1984). Violence: The drug and alcohol patient. In J. T. Turner (Ed.), *Violence in the medical care setting: A survival guide* (pp. 123–152). Rockville, MD: Aspen Systems Corp.

Pisarick, G. (1981, September). The violent patient. *Nursing,* pp. 63–65.

Rada, R. T. (1981). The violent patient: Rapid assessment and management. *Psychosomatics, 22,* 101–109.

Reid, B. (Speaker). (1986). Counseling in half-way houses (Cassette Recording No. 9). Memphis: Memphis State University, Department of Counseling and Personnel Services.

Rice, M. E., Helzel, M. F., Varney, G. W., & Quinsey, V. L. (1985). Crisis prevention and intervention training for psychiatric hospital staff. *American Journal of Community Psychiatry, 13,* 289–304.

Rohr, M. (Speaker). (1986). Counseling in a runaway house for adolescents (Cassette Recording No. 10). Memphis: Memphis State University, Department of Counseling and Personnel Services.

Rofman, E. S., Askinazi, C., & Fant, E. (1980). The prediction of dangerous behavior in emergency civil commitment. *American Journal of Psychiatry, 137,* 1061–1064.

Ruben, I., Wolkon, G., & Yamamoto, J. (1980). Physical attacks on psychiatric residents by patients. *Journal of Nervous and Mental Disease, 168,* 243–245.

Ruesch, J. (1973). *Therapeutic communication.* New York: Norton.

Simonds, J. F., & Kashani, J. (1980). Specific drug use and violence in delinquent boys. *American Journal of Drug and Alcohol Abuse, 7,* 305–322.

Star, B. (1984). Patient violence/therapist safety. *Social Work, 29,* 225–230.

Stokeman, C. L. (1982). Questions and answers: Violence among hospitalized mental patients. *Hospital and Community Psychiatry, 33,* 986.

Tanke, E. D., & Yesavage, J. A. (1985). Characteristics of assaultive patients who do and do not provide visible cues of potential violence. *American Journal of Psychiatry, 142,* 1409–1413.

Tardiff, K. (1984a). Violence: The psychiatric patient. In J. T. Turner (Ed.), *Violence in the medical care setting: A survival guide* (pp. 33–55). Rockville, MD: Aspen Systems Corp.

Tardiff, K. (1984b). *The psychiatric uses of seclusion and restraint.* Washington, DC: American Psychiatric Association Press.

Tardiff, K., & Sweillam, A. (1980). Assault, suicide, and mental illness. *Archives of General Psychiatry, 37,* 164–169.

Tardiff, K., & Sweillam, A. (1982). The occurrence of assaultive behavior among chronic psychiatric inpatients. *American Journal of Psychiatry, 139,* 212–215.

Taulbee, L. R. (1978). Reality orientation: A therapeutic group activity for elderly persons. In I. M. Burnside (Ed.), *Working with the elderly: Group processes and techniques* (pp. 206–218). North Scituate, MA: Duxbury Press.

Taulbee, L. R., & Folsom, J. C. (1966). Reality orientation for geriatric patients. *Hospital and Community Psychiatry, 17,* 133–135.

Tomine, S. (1986). Private practice in gerontological counseling. *Journal of Counseling and Development, 68,* 406–409.

Turner, J. (Ed.). (1984). *Violence in the medical care setting: A survival guide.* Rockville, MD: Aspen Systems Corp.

Valliant, P. M., Aser, M. E., Cooper, D., & Mammola, D. (1984). Profile of dangerous and non-dangerous offenders referred for pre-trial psychiatric assessment. *Psychological Reports, 54,* 411–418.

Viner, J. (1982). Toward more skillful handling of acutely psychotic patients, Part I: Evaluation. *Emergency Room Report, 3,* 125–130.

Vinick, B. (Speaker). (1986). Counseling in a state mental hospital (Cassette Recording No. 13). Memphis: Memphis State University, Department of Counseling and Personnel Services.

Whitman, R. M., Armao, B. B., & Dent, O. B. (1976). Assault on the therapist. *American Journal of Psychiatry, 133,* 426–431.

Wolanin, M. O., & Phillips, L. R. (1981). *Confusion: Prevention and care.* St. Louis, MO: C.V. Mosby.

Wood, K. A., & Khuri, R. (1984). Violence: The emergency room patient. In J. T. Turner (Ed.), *Violence in the medical care setting: A survival guide* (pp. 57–84). Rockville, MD: Aspen Systems Corp.

Zold, A. C., & Schilt, S. C. (1984). Violence: The child and the adolescent patient. In J. T. Turner (Ed.), *Violence in the medical care setting: A survival guide* (pp. 85–106). Rockville, MD: Aspen Systems Corp.

■ Classroom Exercises: Dealing with Verbal Abuse

The group is divided into dyads. One person in each pair assumes the role of the human service worker and the other person assumes the role of an agitated, verbally abusive client. The human service worker's job is to get the client under control. Since the dialogue will probably become rather loud, it is suggested that dyads be housed in separate offices or rooms if at all possible, or the exercise done outside of class. The exercise may be difficult for people who are not used to being bellicose. Think back for a moment and conjure the memory of a really angry, obnoxious person you have either met or seen.

The client will take a standing position and the human service worker will remain seated (all the better to intimidate the worker!). Another chair should be available for the client, but in the beginning the client must not sit down. The client may threaten, be noncompliant, yell, berate, gripe, say terrible things about the worker or the worker's parents, or otherwise try to cow and manipulate the worker into submission. However, when asked a question, the client must respond to the content being asked. Also, when a reflective statement is made by the worker, the client must respond by indicating the feeling state felt.

The worker may use any of the techniques discussed in this chapter or, for that matter, anything else that comes to mind. The mission for this exercise is to get the client to sit down. Continue the exercise for five to ten minutes with tape recorder on. At the end of the time switch roles. Whenever dyad partners have concluded their experiences of enactment of both worker and client roles, make sure that both persons verbally disassociate themselves from the roles to one another. At the end of both sessions, come back together as a group. Discuss the following questions:

1. How did you feel as the worker?
2. Were you able to stay relaxed and keep your wits about you?
3. How did you do that without becoming agitated yourself?
4. How did you attempt to gain compliance from the client?
5. What techniques worked and what didn't?

Staffing and Plotting a Strategy

Select some of the tapes made in Exercise I. In groups of four or five, listen to the tapes and brainstorm what might be a more effective approach. Solicit the client for feedback on what seem to be the most effective ideas and why. See if the group agrees on what techniques for handling the client would be best. Is the group willing to commit as a team to employing the techniques? Process how the group feels about its decision after it has finished, particularly taking note of and discussing any ideas that may seem repugnant to some of the members.

Using Validation Therapy with a Disoriented Client

Working in dyads, one member assumes the role of a disoriented client who would like to talk about a past event that is of great importance. To make this event realistic, clients should think back to an important moment in their childhood and attempt to report that moment as if it were present time.

While they are doing this, the human service workers should be doing their utmost to disregard this senseless patter and should be attempting to orient their clients to person, place, and time. The workers should also try to get their clients to complete some task. When approximately five minutes have elasped, stop the dialogue and switch roles. At the end of another five minutes, again stop the dialogue and rejoin the group. Discuss these questions:

1. As the counselor, how did you feel in trying to orient the client?
2. How frustrated, if at all, did you become?
3. What did you try to do to get the client to be compliant?
4. How would you feel and what would you do if you had a busy schedule and had to gain compliance from the client?
5. As the client, what was your feeling about the worker's attempt to get you off your childhood memory and back to reality?
6. How did you respond when the worker kept trying to get you on task?

In the same dyads, the clients go back again to the early childhood memories. The workers will use validation therapy and pace with their clients as if the memories were real, alive, important, and very much here and now. Again the workers should attempt to have their clients comply with a task, but this purpose is secondary to responding empathically to the feelings and content of the memory. After the dialogue has continued for approximately five minutes, stop and switch roles. After another five minutes, again stop and rejoin the group. Discuss the following questions:

1. As the worker, how did you feel as you paced with the client?
2. How frustrated, if at all, did you become?
3. What did you do to stay at an empathic level with the client?
4. How compliant was the client to any requests you made?
5. As the client, how did you feel about the worker's attempts to listen and understand what you were saying?
6. How did you feel and what did you do when the worker attempted to gain compliance with the requested task?

CHAPTER 6

Crisis of Severe Physical Limitation

BACKGROUND

In this chapter we will examine a kind of crisis that millions of people have faced—severe physical trauma that begins with acute crisis and develops into chronic and often irreversible physical limitation. The basic philosophy in our approach to dealing with severe physical limitation is to focus away from specific impairments or restricted activities. The physically handicapped are insistently reminded of what their bodies can and cannot do. We prefer to focus on what they can do and what the able-bodied ought to do in response to them.

The fundamental approach to helping people in crises of severe physical limitation is that of the six steps in crisis intervention which we discussed in Chapter 2. You will notice that the application of the basic skills and concepts of the six steps has been woven into the intervention strategies while concomitantly considering the unique aspects of physical limitation. Undergirding our work with handicapped clients is an emphasis on the worker's total acceptance of clients' abilities, resources, and aspirations as well as recognizing their limitations. We prefer to perceive them more accurately as *survivors* than as victims or impaired individuals.

Kleinfield (1979) pointed the way when he reported on how most physically impaired persons continuously engage in unheralded struggles to lead independent lives. The pictures he gave were not of heroic or inspirational accomplishments against extraordinary obstacles, but rather of human beings engaged in uncompromising, sometimes astonishingly hopeful, quests to lead their lives from day to day. Zola (1982) put it another way. Instead of looking at the disabled through tales of superhuman heroism and courage (which may be true), he encouraged the public to learn that just because people become severely disabled, it does not follow that they may not still be "a mother, father, lover, doctor, writer, and accomplish great deeds" in those mundane occupational and parental roles (p. 11).

The onset of severe physical impairment generally represents the crisis phase. Whenever people recognize that they or their loved ones (such as their children) are seriously and permanently limited—following an accident or disease, for example—their worlds may seem to be shattered. Crisis intervention is concerned with getting such persons (both the physically limited and their loved ones) past the period of devastation and on to a phase of emotional and physical mobility, problem solving, networking, and acquiring supports needed to progress toward relatively independent coping and equilibrium. This chapter deals mainly with the *crisis phase* of intervention. The long-term treatment of the handicapped is extensively covered in the literature of rehabilitation and rehabilitation counseling (DeLoach & Greer, 1981).

Physically Limiting Conditions

A physically debilitating condition may occur rapidly, following an accident (such as an automobile collision or a diving mishap); the condition may occur progressively (as do cancer and multiple sclerosis); or the condition may be related to some congenital or internal cause such as cerebral palsy. A wide variety of severely limiting conditions may leave a person without sight or hearing or otherwise physically disabled. Accidents, physical assault, and disease are examples of causative factors (Holzhauser, 1986). A few representative categories of handicapping conditions are amputation, polio, neuromuscular disease, congenital disabilities, Alzheimer's disease, object loss, and spinal cord injury.

Amputation. According to Hathcock (1986), crises experienced by amputees may vary from person to person. The extent and circumstances of the loss, the age and physical and psychological functioning of the individual, and other factors govern the way amputees respond to the loss (Whipple, 1980). Amputations and other serious physical disabilities may produce object losses, causing people to experience unique but traumatic emotions (Parkes, 1972). Workers should be aware that, in referring to amputees, "object loss" means the physical loss of the limb or body part plus the psychological void the person feels as a result of the event. Examples of such psychological voids might include (1) a feeling of the loss of identity as a whole person without one's arm or leg; (2) a feeling of loss of one's femininity or womanhood resulting from the surgical removal of a breast; and (3) a feeling of loss of one's virility or manhood as a result of the removal of a testicle. Whipple (1980) reported that individual amputees experience different degrees of feelings of loss and varying stages of crisis, from the initial phases of shock and grief through denial, depression, anger, reality, and readjustment.

Polio. Poliomyelitis (polio) vaccines have greatly reduced the number of cases of the crippling disease during recent years. There are, however, still some new cases. There are also large numbers of people in society who continue to be directly impaired by the effects of polio. In addition to the crises experienced by persons who have polio, there are many obstacles that they and their families face: problems with medical care and facilities; difficulties with prosthetics; public prejudice and ignorance; acquisition of appropriate training and career opportunities; male–female relationships; and the inner personal struggles to live normal lives (Cunningham, 1986; Marx, 1974; Warren & Kirkendall, 1973). Some individuals who have been recovering from polio for years encounter a resumption of crisis, later in life, caused by additional neuromuscular impairment. According to Cunningham (1986), the additional impairment is believed to center in the complex anterior horn cells that were originally damaged by the polio virus. Later in life, survivors may believe that their condition is stable when, in fact, the impairment is progressing and their functioning is gradually deteriorating. Survivors who are used to leading active business, social, and recreational lives may find it increasingly difficult to keep up the pace they have set for themselves. They may revert to previous crisis states such as anger, denial, bargaining, and depression whenever they are confronted with additional impairment they did not realize they had. It appears that some polio survivors can never reach a state of safety from negative sequelae of the original disease. Some researchers estimate that 25% to 30% of polio survivors will experience post-polio stress syndrome (Cunningham, 1986).

Neuromuscular disease. The initial shock and subsequent coping with the devastating effects of and impairment attendant to neuromuscular diseases and disorders bring on crises of enormous impact to both survivors and their loved ones. We are referring to neuromuscular conditions such as multiple sclerosis (MS), amyotropic lateral sclerosis (ALS, commonly known as "Lou Gehrig's disease") (Rabin, 1985), and myasthenia gravis (Wilson, 1972). Some neuromuscular diseases such as MS may take years to render a survivor completely disabled. Others, such as ALS and myasthenia gravis, may cause total disability quite rapidly. Since there is no known cure for such diseases, a positive diagnosis has the effect of changing the survivor's life immediately and permanently. Because there is no known cause, persons with neuromuscular diseases appear to be randomly stricken, making prevention virtually impossible. Rabin (1985) described the evolving emotional stages that a person with severe neuromuscular disease may experience. These stages may include (1) shock, denial, and disbelief; (2) recognition that the condition is indeed real, personal, and serious; (3) anger; (4) bargaining, rationalization, or hope that a cure will soon be found; (5) depression and despair; and (6) acceptance.

Congenital disabilities. Physical disabilities that stem from prenatal causes, very early childhood conditions, or diseases present a variety of special categories of physical limitation. Young children whose hearing or sight is severely impaired, for instance, require specialized medical care, and the initial crisis intervention must include both the children and their families (Glick & Pellman, 1982; Holzhauser, 1986). Severe physical handicaps in infancy frequently represent traumatic crises for parents and challenging health care problems for medical and other caregivers (Dickman, 1985; Russell, 1985). Roy (1985) profiled seven children who were wheelchair users as a result of congenital conditions. The children in his study were described as leading difficult but active, positive, and enjoyable lives despite varying degrees of serious neuromuscular conditions attributed to congenital arthrogryposis, hemolyphangioma, cerebral palsy, spina bifida, and muscular dystrophy.

Congenital physical conditions may present problems that can be effectively overcome during infancy or early childhood. Or they may call for lifelong special care and have implications for parents, schools, medical caregivers, and others associated with the survivor (Doyle, Goodman, Grotsky, & Mann, 1979). Russell (1985) has extensively researched and documented the special challenges, needs, resources, and care needed to help physically impaired children, and Doyle et al. (1979) have provided comprehensive guidance for helping parents and caregivers respond to the needs of children with disabilities. Upon the discovery of serious physical disabilities in young children, parents may have to deal with emergent emotional stages in their children quite similar to those experienced by adults upon learning that they have a severe neuromuscular condition (Dickman, 1985; Russell, 1985).

Alzheimer's disease. Alzheimer's disease, which usually occurs in people after age 65, is now known to strike as early as age 20. It is a progressive, irreversible neurological disease that, according to Lollar (1986a), results in untold thousands of handicaps per year and causes 150,000 deaths per year (p. 16). According to Frank (1985), approximately 2 million older Americans have Alzheimer's disease, and it is projected that by the year 2000 more than 4 million older citizens will have the disease. The crises attributable to Alzheimer's and other similar diseases, which impair physical and/or mental functioning, constitute a combination of untold pain and suffering for survivors and their families, and, at this writing, represent an insoluble dilemma for the medical world. Any person or family with this kind of physical condition and impairment may become the client of the crisis worker. Early on, Alzheimer's clients may go through emotional stages such as denial, bargaining, depression, and despair. As the disease progresses, clients apparently lose (or cease to manifest) these particular emotional states (Frank, 1985, pp. 5–6).

Object loss. Schoenberg (1980) defines *object loss* as the "actual or threatened loss of any significant object, whether an intimate person, an aspect of self-concept, a limb, a valued possession, money, status in society, health, youth—any impoverishment or disengagement of bonding to a love object, whether tied by tendrils or by shackles" (p. 9). The loss of one or more limbs typifies the kind of physical object loss that produces emotional crisis. "Normal" mourning and "pathological" mourning of lost objects are distributed along a spectrum from least to most grief producing (Ellard, Volkan, & Paul, 1974, p. 187). Parkes (1970) identified four phases that people normally experience in the period of mourning and readjustment following object loss: numbness, yearning to recover the lost object, despairing disorganization, and behavioral reorganization (pp. 187–201). The extent and kind of crisis that people manifest in relation to object loss depend on the individual's personality, the nature of the loss, the relationship between the person and the lost object, and the individual's cultural values (Schoenberg, 1980, p. 9).

Spinal cord injury. In this chapter we will focus mainly on the crisis following spinal cord injury (SCI) because it is highly representative of severely limiting conditions. Also SCIs usually occur in youthful, healthy, vibrant, physically active people in a sudden and devastating manner. These factors make it even more appropriate to study SCI as a severely limiting physical condition.

Riggin (1976) defined SCI as "an illness or accident which causes trauma to the spinal cord portion of the central nervous system and which results in paralysis of two or more extremities with the loss of voluntary movement below the level of injury, including the voluntary use of excretory and sexual functions" (p. 7). Crisis intervention with SCI survivors usually occurs during the early part of their treatment.

According to Kleinfield (1979), SCIs have caused thousands of persons to become either paraplegics or quadriplegics. Depending on the nature and extent of the injury and the immediacy and quality of medical care, some individuals experience varying degrees of return of their previous motor controls (Nasaw, 1975; Willis & Willis, 1974); some individuals experience no return (Cox-Gedmark, 1980; Eareckson, 1976). Many SCI clients, whether they attain motor recovery or not, undergo severe crises; then they finally find ways to cope, readjust, and carry on their lives as survivors (Cox-Gedmark, 1980; Eareckson, 1976; Helms, 1978; Kleinfield, 1979; Levitt & Guralnick, 1985; Moore, 1986; Nasaw, 1975; Willis & Willis, 1974).

Other serious physical disabilities. Many different physical disabilities may leave the survivor in a state of crisis: leukemia, physical injury (as from an accident or assault), disease, severe diabetes mellitus, epilepsy, stroke, cancer, and a host of other conditions may become realities of life.

DYNAMICS OF SCI

The dynamics of SCI people are unique because all of their injuries produce neurological impairment. Nevertheless, SCI survivors are representative of the whole category of physically limiting conditions addressed in this chapter because the common cause of the initial crisis in physically limited people is impairment of motor control and physical mobility. The impact of altered neuromotor functioning and physical immobility requires reorganization of recoverers' options as well as their view of themselves. The fact of the injury calls for others in the environment, at least initially, to contribute enormously to the survivor's coping with the physical, emotional, social, psychological, and vocational problems generated by the impairment. To facilitate our understanding of the SCI survivor's prospects, we will take a brief look at the characteristics of injured people, the stages or emotional states they typically experience, and the impact of psychosocial, cultural, and personal dynamics. In this chapter we prefer to refer to persons with spinal cord injury as *people, recoverers, survivors, individuals, clients,* or *wheelchair users* rather than *impaired, disabled,* or *patients* because the latter terms carry negative connotations of helplessness and dependency.

Characteristics of SCI Survivors

General statistics. Pierce and Nickel (1977) reported that upward of 10,000 spinal cord injuries, resulting in paraplegia or quadriplegia, occur in the United States each year and that about 200,000 paraplegics and quadriplegics were living in the United States in 1977. They also estimated that about 70% of all SCIs were sustained in either motor vehicle or sports accidents. They speculated that a careful check of water for depth, submerged objects, and other dangers in a pond or pool each time before diving in, could prevent some 30% of all SCIs each year and that the wearing of seat belts in automobiles would result in another 20% reduction (p. 1). Furthermore, an estimated 10% of all injured persons sustain further serious damage after the accident because of improper handling or inadequate diagnosis (pp. 1–2).

High risk among young males. Although all segments of the population are subject to SCI and are represented among the injured, males between the ages of 15 and 40 who are actively engaged in many outdoor physical activities are at a greater risk than any other age group (Gunther, 1969, p. 94). Young males probably spend more time in moving motor vehicles, especially motorcycles, and engage in more risk-taking activities, such as diving, than any other group. Thus, young males stand a greater probability of sustaining severe injuries than the remainder of the population.

Increasing mean age. Young males have traditionally received more SCIs in wars than any other segment of the population. However, the war-related SCI population's mean age has been steadily increasing probably because those injured in past wars are getting older, with no new current wars to produce injured veterans. Eisenberg and Tierney (1985) reported that older SCI military veterans have been steadily increasing their use of health care resources and that more research is needed to assess the health needs of these veterans as well as the effects of various treatment modalities.

Short-term and long-term aspects. SCI people go through short-term and long-term reactions to their injuries (Burke & Murray, 1975). Readjustment and recovery progressions and mechanisms must also include short-term and long-term responses and treatments (pp. 78–80).

Stages or Emotional States

The progression from the initial SCI crisis to long-term coping varies from person to person. A great many physical and emotional stages, phases, or reactions may be expected in SCI persons. Caregivers and families should understand that these stages and emotions are normal, may occur in an erratic or fluid or regressive manner, may be exhibited over a long or short period, and require caregiver responses of strength, consistency, and understanding (Moore, 1986).

Burke and Murray (1975) view the stages or emotional states of SCI people as occurring in two different time frames: immediate and long term. The immediate reactions survivors may feel are anxiety, depression, denial, grief, mourning, and somatic fears. Long-term reactions may include overdependency, underdependency, aggression, and somatic complaints (pp. 78–80).

DeLoach and Greer (1981), taking a developmental view of the changing states through which severely disabled people pass, note that not all the emotional states are negative. Most recovering individuals finally achieve a state called *stigma incorporation*, which is similar to self-actualization. Whenever a state of stigma incorporation is achieved, the SCI recoverer is normally able to recognize that many positive things accrued from the disablement (pp. 214–221). The progression from what DeLoach and Greer refer to as *stigma recognition* to stigma incorporation requires time, and the latter state is accompanied by the development of stress-resolution strategies with a reality base (p. 221).

Naughton (1963) simply combined the several emotional states through which SCI persons typically pass under three broad stages: loss of self-esteem, despair, and readjustment (pp. 135–138). Pierce and Nickel (1977) also incorporated SCI emotional states into three phases, which they labeled (1) the *preshock* and *shock* phases, (2) the *defensive retreat* phase, and (3) the *acknowledgment* phase (pp. 300–302).

It should be emphasized that survivors do not necessarily exhibit all the phases or emotional states in a linear progression. Undoubtedly each person experiences reaction to the injury differently. There may be rapid thrusts forward and then regression to a previous phase. The point is that the reactions of SCI persons tend to evolve from the depths of depression and despair toward adjustment and coping. The understanding and support of caregivers and family are needed to encourage and expedite forward movement toward adjustment (Eareckson, 1976).

Psychosocial and Cultural Dynamics

Social attitudes. Society has shown widespread ignorance of and discrimination against the physically limited, including SCI recoverers (Kleinfield, 1979). Societal ignorance and discrimination constitute major factors in impeding the readjustment and rehabilitation of the physically limited because

(Kleinfield estimates) there may be as many as 50 million Americans who have some sort of physical handicap.

The interpersonal view of SCI recovery (Naughton, 1963) represents what those individuals around the recoverer hear and see the recoverer saying and doing and how people interpret the recoverer's behaviors within the social milieu (p. 135). The attitudes of each person on the medical/caregiving team and each family member may have the effect of depersonalizing and infantilizing the recoverer, thereby retarding the progress of rehabilitation (Moore, 1986). Their attitudes may also reinforce the recoverer's positive self-image, as well as serving as symbols of success and independence in a social and psychological sense (Moore, 1986; Pierce & Nickel, 1977, pp. 310–311). Social attitudes, then, are key ingredients in the lives of SCI people. DeLoach and Greer (1981) reported that social interaction may be a source of considerable stress for the SCI person, but that social interaction can also bring much personal fulfillment (pp. 228–249).

What people believe about recoverers affects them in many ways. Gunther (1969) proposed that collective attitudes, especially of those in close proximity to the recoverer, have an impact on the recoverer's progress. He listed three major dynamics that affect the rehabilitation process: (1) the collective attitudes and emotional responses of attending medical personnel, (2) the individual's own history of personal and developmental experiences, and (3) social role and social environmental factors (family, friends, vocational, organizational) (pp. 100–102).

Role of the family.   Members of recoverers' families usually require time to conceptualize, adjust, and integrate the newly injured family member's status and prospects into their own view of the future. Therefore, another key factor in SCI recovery is the education of significant family members and their inclusion in the care of the survivor. The reason why family understanding is so important to the adjustment process is that an SCI profoundly alters the lifestyle and roles of every member—the injured, siblings, spouses, children, and parents. Crisis intervention, education, and counseling with family members may supply them with the understandings they need to cope with the new situation and provide effective supports for the recoverer (Pierce & Nickel, 1977, pp. 303–306). Riggin (1976) found that SCI recoverers expressed concerns about who would help to take care of them after their hospitalization. They indicated preferences for close family members (p. 85). Hathcock (1986) agrees with the Riggin findings but cautions that wheelchair users do not want to be overprotected and that they should be held accountable for doing all those things they are capable of doing by themselves.

Substance abuse.   Drug and alcohol abuse and other complications have become serious social factors among SCI survivors (Bedbrook, Beer, & McLaren, 1985, pp. 69–77). Substance addiction has emerged as a formidable problem for medical, social, and family caregivers, as well as for survivors themselves. Extreme caution must be used in prescribing and administering pain-controlling drugs for SCI people. Cull and Hardy (1977) report that the rehabilitation of paraplegics who have become addicted to drugs is practically impossible (p. 136). Pierce and Nickel (1977) also express concern that SCI clients, to a greater extent than clients in general, abuse and use illegal drugs within the hospital setting. They cited the policing and control of illegal drug traffic as a major problem in treating SCI clients (p. 299). Ruge (1969) speaks of both alcoholism and drug addiction as constituting a rather common problem among quadriplegics (p. 135). Riggin's (1976) SCI clients reported to her that they used LSD and smoked pot while they were in the hospital following their injuries (p. 75).

Caregivers may be surprised to learn that SCI clients they are attempting to help are abusing drugs. They may even be oblivious to the fact that their clients feel the need to acquire and take illegal substances. Drug abuse is of special concern to workers attempting to help SCI clients because the addiction itself mitigates against successful treatment. The diagnosis of drug abuse is important to the crisis worker because it is necessary, whenever possible, to control the abuse so that counseling or crisis intervention techniques are more likely to be successful.

We do not wish to imply that the blame for drug abuse lies solely with the SCI person. It has been suggested by Riggin (1976), Cunningham (1986), Hathcock (1986), and Moore (1986) that the alleged high incidence of drug abuse may be initially rooted in the medical establishment's handling of prescription drugs. Cunningham further suggests that part of the problem may be one of educating medical people about the whole area of pain management among SCI people. As one example, she notes that to view every muscle spasm and every pain as a catastrophe and to react by overmedicating to ensure that it does not happen again may be overresponding in a way that is eventually harmful to the SCI person. Cunningham (1986) suggests that our cultural view of pain, along with our institutional tendency to try to eradicate all pain, may be a societal value that works to the detriment of SCI people. She also points out that, during the decades of the 1960s and 1970s, the SCI population tended to be predominantly young, active, risk-taking males— many of whom might have experimented with and used drugs regardless of whether they became SCI survivors or not.

Vocational and social mastery. Positive social interaction, remunerative employment, recreation, and participation in sports represent the kinds of cultural involvement that society and SCI recoverers equate with success (Harris, 1963, p. 141). For most survivors themselves, successful rehabilitation must be accompanied by some tangible degree of successful vocational and social mastery. Bedbrook (1986) examined in depth the necessity of vocational and educational adjustment. Apparently, the concept of career development as a continuous lifelong process applies to all people, including SCI recoverers. What this means for crisis workers and other caregivers is that vocational and social mastery may involve special forms of life adjustment in SCI clients. But some level of mastery is of vital importance to their adjustment.

Personal and Psychological Dynamics

Predisposing factors. Sutton (1973) has shown that there are a number of personal factors that affect the rehabilitation, readjustment, and attitude of the SCI client (p. 150). A person's (1) age, (2) sex, (3) social situation, (4) personality, (5) preexisting disease, and (6) associated injuries may influence recovery. Young males who, prior to their SCI condition, had poor social histories, difficulties in keeping a job, criminal misdemeanors, recurrent bronchitis or other respiratory troubles, cardiac disability, or hypertension tended to have adjustment problems. Any personal condition, according to Sutton (1973), that results in the client's being uninterested, uncooperative, or unmotivated becomes an important dynamic in the care of that person (p. 151). What these personal factors mean to the crisis worker is that crisis intervention must focus on the whole person. One worker alone may not have the required expertise to help the client. A multidisciplinary thrust may be needed more with problematic clients than with those who have histories of positive personal and social attainment. Clients with strong and positive personal traits will be more amenable to motivation and recovery. Those with weak and negative traits are apt to need special help from medical and nursing staff, orderlies, counselors, physical therapists, and other helpers. Clients must come to the point where they are personally ready to participate in their own rehabilitation. As long as they resign themselves to being passively waited on hand and foot, their movement toward resolution of their crisis as well as their total readjustment will be greatly impeded (Sutton, 1973).

Personal shock effect. The initial SCI trauma is often sudden, shattering the established personal goals and preinjury self-concept of the client. Such catastrophic shock effect requires time to allow the client to integrate the injury into a new reality. Those persons around the client must understand the shock effect and allow ample time and space for the client to come to grips with the emergent conditions (Pierce & Nickel, 1977, pp. 299–305). Intervention should be structured so that survival needs of the client are met first (p. 302), but this priority does not mean that caregivers should ignore behaviors such as withdrawal or suicidal ideation. To the contrary, defenses or unusual coping mechanisms indicate that clients are using whatever behaviors they can to protect themselves. Caregivers should be sensitive to and accept unusual behavior and attitudes and help the client to channel all behaviors— even exaggerated ones—in healthy directions (p. 300).

Personal view. The SCI client's self-perception (view from within) is more important than society's view (Naughton, 1963). The *self-view* refers to what the client truly feels and believes about his or her prospects, "what has happened to his [or her] self-esteem in terms of the personal characteristics he [or she] values at that stage in his [or her] life" (p. 135). Bedbrook (1986), Cull and Hardy (1977), Pierce and Nickel (1977), and Riggin (1976) have identified a positive self-concept, self-image, or self-esteem as being of fundamental importance to the readjustment and rehabilitation of SCI clients. The value of such a personal view by clients should be kept in mind at all times by those persons whose role is the encouragement and facilitation of positive growth on the part of SCI clients.

Client motivation.   Motivation of the SCI client to achieve as high a degree of self-sufficiency as possible rests largely within the person. Gunther (1969) referred to client motivation as the primary intangible factor influencing recovery (p. 101). The crucial power of the client's own indivisible will or enthusiasm is necessary if satisfactory recovery or rehabilitation is to be accomplished. A basic goal of the motivated client is ultimately to become capable of achieving as much mastery over the SCI condition as possible. This means that clients must somehow come to grips with the conflict between dependence and independence (Bedbrook, 1986; Moore, 1986; Pierce & Nickel, 1977; Riggin, 1976). Client motivation lies at the root of what Pierce and Nickel (1977) refer to as the development and maintenance of maximum social functioning and the maintenance of life skills (p. 315). DeLoach and Greer (1981) have described such client motivation in terms of developmental changes in the individual's self-states—which can result (given time and appropriate supports) in a transformation or "metamorphosis" within the individual (pp. 214–221). Achievement of such metamorphosis is equated to the attainment of optimal motivational level in recoverers.

Sexual dynamics.   Sexual concerns, including sexual functioning (especially in SCI males under 40), are of great interest and importance to both client and worker (Burke & Murray, 1975, pp. 61–65; Sutton, 1973, pp. 162–164). Males are typically reluctant to discuss the issue of sexuality during early phases of their treatment. But such reluctance should not be interpreted by caregivers as signifying lack of interest on the part of clients. Sexuality is usually a very important concern of both male and female SCI clients (Betts & Rosen, 1969, pp. 180–181; DeLoach & Greer, 1981, pp. 65–99; Sutton, 1973, p. 163).

According to Burke and Murray (1975), the degree of possible sexual functioning and the accompanying sensations are individual matters subject to each SCI client's particular spinal cord injury (pp. 61–62). DeLoach and Greer (1981) report that both society and caregiving professionals have long been ignorant and misinformed about the sexual functioning and capabilities of both SCI males and females. Their studies indicate that many SCI persons experience satisfactory sex lives and that nearly all of them successfully engage in some degree of normal and/or alternative sexual behavior (pp. 69–72). Since most clients are concerned but sensitive about their sexuality, they are unlikely to volunteer information about their troubled feelings and difficulties (Ruge, 1969, p. 181). Caregivers may need to introduce the subject. Riggin (1976) demonstrated that males in SCI groups offer support, safety, and comfort to each other in introducing and discussing sexual concerns. Support groups are a way of affording clients the chance to explore various sensitive issues such as their sexuality.

Suicidal dynamics. The rate of suicidal ideation, contemplation, gesture, and/or attempt is higher among SCI persons than among other categories of crisis clients or the population as a whole (Pierce & Nickel, 1977, p. 299). Burke and Murray (1975) report that SCI clients' actual rate of commission of suicide is no higher than that of the normal population (p. 82). Riggin (1976) found that clients' verbalizations about suicide were manifested repeatedly in both individual and group therapy sessions (p. 72). Ruge (1969) characterizes clients' suicidal ideation and behavior as a desperate reaching out for support, attacking themselves rather than the environment as the source of their distress (p. 100). Crisis workers and other caregivers must, of course, interpret all suicidal behaviors as important—to be taken seriously. Actions that ensure the client's safety (such as continued hospitalization or referral for psychiatric treatment), helping the client develop a sense of self-worth, and affording the client opportunities to form meaningful relationships with others are some of the immediate interventions that caregivers may elect.

INTERVENTION STRATEGIES

Crisis intervention with SCI survivors is often difficult and complex because of the unique nature of their injuries and because a great number of medical and other caregiving procedures are involved in providing for physical survival needs. Crisis intervention can occur only if the body is alive and responsive. The client's psychological, emotional, and social needs can normally be attended to only after the basic survival and safety needs are met. As we view it, crisis intervention may not be needed by every SCI client. Cull and Hardy (1977) include both physical medicine and rehabilitation in the total treatment of SCI clients. Rehabilitation includes physical therapy, occupational therapy, use of special equipment, recreational therapy, rehabilitation nursing, and individual and group counseling, in addition to physical medicine interventions. We believe that crisis intervention strategies may be needed and/or provided at any time during the recovery process.

In actual crisis intervention with SCI clients, the fundamental relationship skills and strategies described in Chapter 2 are applicable. Crisis workers intervening in the lives of SCI persons expect that each person in every crisis category is unique. The crisis worker who responds as if no two clients and no two client crises were ever alike will be right on target. That is not to say that similarities do not count. Nor is it to say that the category of SCI clients is not unique or special. What we are saying is that a basic body of important helping skills and strategies is generic and pervades the broad spectrum of crisis intervention practice.

Therapeutic Modalities

From our research into crisis intervention with SCI persons and our interviews with survivors, we have concluded that caregivers for these clients should be prepared to use a wide variety of systems of counseling (Brammer, 1985, pp. 90–114; Cormier & Hackney, 1987). The indications from recoverers, for example, Hathcock (1986) and Moore (1986), are that effective crisis workers would be advised to rely heavily on counseling systems such as Glasser's (1984) control theory, Glasser's (1965) reality therapy (RT), and Ellis's (1962, 1982) rational-emotive therapy (RET). These systems are particularly applicable to the life situations of SCI clients because the physical and social realities of the injuries and conditions generated by traditional health care systems tend to strip clients of their own rationality and control. Control theory, RT, and RET provide the kinds of strategies needed by SCI clients to regain some degree of autonomy and control.

Control theory. William Glasser's (1984) control theory is an ideal system for clients and their caregivers. It is based on Glasser's set of five powerful and basic needs (pp. 5–18):

1. the need to survive and reproduce
2. the need to belong—to love, share, and cooperate
3. the need for power
4. the need for freedom
5. the need for fun.

Control theory has great applicability to SCI clients because it focuses directly on putting the control into the person. Glasser's position is that everything we *do, think,* and *feel* comes from inside us. Every behavior we emit is not, as many people assume, a response to persons or events in our environment. Each behavior is, instead, our best attempt to control or gain control of others or the world around us. For example, Glasser asserts that we do not suffer from depression. Rather, we depress ourselves to gain some kind of control. He says that this depressing is counterproductive and, in the long run, destructive. We do not suffer from anxiety or migraine headaches; rather, we choose to engage in "anxiety" or "headaching" to gain some degree of control over some person or situation. The essence of control theory for SCI clients is that they can intentionally control their lives in positive and healthy ways. Through control theory, people can learn to take relatively full charge of all areas of their lives: marital and other relationships, raising children, mobility, alcoholism and addictive tendencies, diseases, personal problems, disabilities, psychosomatic illness, weight management, career development, and job satisfaction. According to Moore (1986), the key issue in SCI recoverers' lives is *control.* Glasser's (1984) control theory fills the bill and should be required reading for every caregiver as well as every recoverer.

Reality therapy. Reality therapy (RT) (Glasser, 1965) has a great deal of usefulness and appeal to SCI survivors and their caregivers because it emphasizes independence, success identity, and fulfilling one's needs in effective and responsible ways. According to Hathcock (1986), one bane of the existence of SCI survivors is that of dependency. Caregivers using RT focus on the needs of SCI survivors in the here-and-now. Some of the primary goals of survivors are (1) to feel worthwhile to themselves and others, (2) to attain some degree of success each day, (3) to fulfill their needs in responsible ways (that do not deprive others of the ways and means of fulfilling their needs), (4) to evaluate or make value judgments regarding their own behavioral effectiveness, and (5) to make no excuses for their failings or shortcomings. RT's strengths add up to helping SCI survivors face their problems, their strengths, their potentials, and the environment in a realistic and scientific manner and to plan and live their lives as effectively and independently as possible.

Rational-emotive therapy. SCI survivors, as well as other populations of clients, are susceptible to their own irrational beliefs about their life situations and the external events affecting them. Rational-emotive therapy (RET) (Ellis, 1962, 1982) helps clients to detect and dispute their own irrational beliefs about external events. It assists them scientifically to analyze their perfectionistic tendencies, their self-defeating behaviors, their emotions and thought patterns, and their skill deficits. RET enables clients to develop ways to dispute their self-defeating thoughts and behaviors and to plan more effective response patterns. RET is also recognized as a proven therapy for assisting clients to overcome addictive tendencies, as many SCI survivors need to do (Ellis, 1987). RET uses powerful cognitive and behavioral alternatives in individual therapy and it exerts strong social-influence pressures in group therapy to assist people in breaking addictive habits. Thus, RET techniques may be employed by SCI survivors for fully accepting themselves and the assets they have, taking steps to overcome external adversities, and gaining both insight into and power over their physical and environmental debilitations.

In the remainder of this section on intervention strategies we will refer to and occasionally draw upon the case of Paul, an SCI recoverer and amputee. We will focus on four aspects of intervention: assessment, individual counseling and/or crisis intervention, group counseling and/or crisis intervention, and environmental supports. The overall objective in working with Paul is to place as much control in his hands as possible—to nurture in him independence, realistic and rational thinking, and his intentional choice of positive action steps. In some difficult clients, only small incremental steps may be observed. Nevertheless, small positive steps *are* steps. Elements of control theory, RT, and RET are used to illustrate much of the intervention work done with Paul.

―――――――――――――― *CASE OF PAUL* ――――――――――――――

Paul Ramirez, single, age 25, is classified as a "totally disabled" veteran whose military career was interrupted by an automobile accident at the age of 23. His injury resulted in the amputation of his right leg just above the knee, considerable internal bodily injury, skull fracture, broken arms, and permanent spinal cord injury (paraplegia). He now has normal use of his upper body—torso, arms, shoulders, and head. For the first year following the accident, Paul remained in military hospitals. During that time he received an enormous amount of medical treatment; he was given a disability discharge; and he was supplied with a wheelchair and a specially equipped van. He was also provided with rehabilitation counseling. However, Paul began drinking heavily and started using both prescription and illegal drugs excessively. As a result of his continuous "high," the counseling was ineffective.

During the past year, Paul has alienated his family (mother, father, and two sisters) and he has had constant difficulties getting along with Veterans Administration (VA) personnel, rehabilitation counselors, and people in educational institutions. He has continued to drink and use drugs. He presents himself as an angry, embittered, defensive, frightened, and somewhat paranoid individual. He denies that he has a drinking or a drug problem. He exhibits mood swings from depressed and withdrawn to demanding and aggressive states. His family sees him as vacillating between overdependent martyr and underdependent tyrant. He says he is planning to get a job and also continue his education. But, so far, no employment or schooling opportunity has proved lasting or acceptable to him. Paul's family views him as rejecting or driving away his best sources of help. He views many of the caregivers and professional helpers as incompetent, threatening, or untrustworthy. Right now he is resigned to facing a world that he avows has too many unresponsive, uncaring, and uncooperative agency personnel—even though he has been the beneficiary of an abundance of excellent human and technical resources and expertise. He says he doesn't know how much longer he can stand "being jacked around like a yo-yo."

Paul's assets are his superior intelligence, an unusual amount of determination, his articulateness in both written and spoken communication, an ability to learn easily, persevering parents (despite the adversities, they persist in their love, understanding, support, and belief in him), and his great physical stamina.

Assessment

As we stated in Chapter 2, assessment is an ongoing process during crisis intervention. With SCI clients, the continuous and ongoing assessment is unusually complex because it involves so many dimensions: medical, physiological, psychological, social, vocational, familial, recreational, personal or attitudinal, and environmental. Any unilateral concept of assessment must therefore be rejected by the crisis worker or other case managers. The research clearly validates a multidisciplinary approach to assessment of SCI client needs, including the crosscommunication and pooling of information by different specialty team members (Bedbrook, 1986; Bedbrook, Beer, &. McLaren, 1985; Cull & Hardy, 1977; Judd & Burrows, 1986; Meinecke, 1985).

Prior to initiating intervention strategies, the crisis worker should be able to answer a number of salient questions about the SCI client: What are the status and needs of this client's medical and physical being? What about psychological or emotional status and needs? What social factors are acting on the client? What is the outlook for the person's vocational development? How does the client's family fit into the complex picture? What are the leisure and recreational needs of this individual? What personal or attitudinal factors does this client possess and how will these factors affect intervention outcomes? What environmental constraints and needs must be considered to ensure that intervention strategies are appropriate?

How do we get answers to these questions? According to Ruge (1969), some of them can be gleaned from reading the client's charts. Some can be discovered through observations by medical and other professional personnel. *"Most of this vital information, however, can be learned by sitting down and talking with the patient"* (p. 101). (Italics in original.) We agree with Ruge. An enormous amount of assessment data is available to the worker who has the desire and the skill to listen to and hear what clients need from clients themselves.

Evaluation of injury and prognosis.   An integral aspect of assessment involves the early determination of the extent of the physical injury and trauma—both to the spinal cord and to the other bodily components—affecting the person's functioning (Hathcock, 1986). Injuries such as skull fractures, internal bodily trauma, broken or crushed bones, amputations, cuts, burns, torn tissue, abrasions, and serious bruises must be considered in the early prognosis of the client's treatment and recovery. As the case data indicate, Paul Ramirez sustained multiple physical injuries, which necessitated a variety of treatment procedures in inpatient and outpatient programs at military and VA hospitals. The following dialogue, which takes place during the early or acute phase of Paul's treatment, depicts one aspect of his varied health care. He had been placed in an acute care spinal injury unit which is widely known for successfully treating serious and difficult SCI cases. To preserve the anonymity of that facility, we have assigned it the fictitious name of "Glenwood."

Paul: They sent me to the Glenwood unit because here they are a lot better equipped to treat spinal cord injuries. I wish they could have sent me here earlier, but they said I was so bunged up I couldn't be moved. That's what *they* said! The team of doctors, physical therapists, and other medical staff met with me and told me I needed to be at Glenwood.

CW: So, you're here at Glenwood because of a decision by the medical team over there, and you look like you're feeling pretty confident about being here now.

Paul: Yeah, I sure am. In some ways they were pretty good over there, but they treated me like a piece of meat! I think wheelchair users are treated like animals. Like our brains have been injured and we can't think. They shuttle you around like sheep—not like humans! Over here, they are equipped to get you moving. It's sometimes painful, but they really know what they're doing, like in the mat room— that's what we call the PT room or exercise spa. That mat room is the best thing about Glenwood. But the whole place—the whole staff—is better here.

Getting SCI survivors to the right place at the right time is a critical element in early intervention. According to Moore (1986), the decision regarding appropriate location, staff, and physical facilities rests upon an accurate assessment of survivors' injuries, needs, abilities, and potential for recovery.

Medication and drugs. Hathcock (1986) noted that an assessment of a survivor's needs and the effects of medication and drugs should be made early in the treatment plan and the survivor's drug regimen and consumption should be monitored by the medical staff. Since pain management is an important aspect of many SCI survivors' treatment, care must be taken to ensure that the appropriate types and dosage of drugs are prescribed and administered.

Paul: I could get anything I wanted. And I did!

CW: You mean you used too many drugs—and got hooked?

Paul: I got used to them. I've got them all—morphine, Demerol®, Valium. You name it! Even though I don't need them to kill the pain, now, I take them every day.

Paul's situation confirms Bedbrook, Beer, & McLaren's (1985) admonition that pain control and drug consumption by SCI clients are important and complex aspects of their care. Early assessment and intervention procedures to prevent drug abuse should be a standard strategy of the caregiving team. We emphasize again that every survivor's needs for medication are unique to that person's injury and bodily requirements, and the management of medication and drugs is the exclusive purview of the attending physician.

Equipment needs. A wide variety of equipment, technology, prostheses, mechanical devices, and environmental modifications may be needed to enable SCI people to attain satisfactory mobility. The early evaluation of personal needs with regard to affording optimal control (for example, physical mobility) is, according to Moore (1986), an important aspect of crisis intervention. The very act of appraisal of equipment and environmental needs can be a strategy that encourages survivors. Cull and Hardy (1977) stated that assessment of neurophysiological deficits and the available selection of equipment affording independence are of great importance as initial guidelines for starting SCI treatment programs. They further stated that such assessment "should reflect the maximum level of functioning that can be envisioned" for the survivor (p. 225).

While he is still undergoing inpatient treatment at the Glenwood facility, Paul Ramirez confirms Cull and Hardy's recommendation.

Paul: They were in here this morning talking to me about a permanent wheelchair. What the fuck do they think they're doing? They act like they think I ought to be out on the street tomorrow! The VA will probably be in here before you know it—to cut off my disability check and send me out to hunt for a job! If the VA and these clowns over here who are masquerading around as doctors are so concerned, why can't they find out what's causing this hurting in my elbow and shoulder that they butchered up! Or give me something strong enough to kill this pain! They're acting like they want me to be out on my own next week! Can't they look at me and see the shape I'm in? They put me through hell! And now what the fuck do you want?

CW: What I'm trying to do is to help you to be able to gain a little control over what happens to you here. You seem to be feeling pressured to do something you're not ready to do, and you seem to have a lot of anger and resistance. What do you suppose this angering you're choosing to do is getting for you?

Here, the worker is using a control-theory strategy of pointing out to Paul that he is choosing to be angry—that he is "angering"—and that this is a sign that he can exert self-control.

Paul: You're as bad as they are! What the hell do you mean, I'm angering? They're making me angry! It's them that's doing it! You're worse than they are!

CW: What I'm trying to do is to help you discover that you're choosing to be angry and to help us figure out what your angering means. Maybe there's strength in your choosing to anger that can be used to get you what you want rather than turning them off toward you. You do have choices—even angering is choosing. Just because you're injured physically doesn't mean you're powerless! *They* can't really make you angry. Only *you* can make you angry!

The worker is using RET to dispute Paul's negative and irrational thinking and to try to show him that he is causing his own self-defeating consequences.

Paul: What difference does it make? They're still treating me like I'm a lot stronger than I am, and I resent it! I'm tired as hell of being jacked around! Tired as hell of you yelling at me, too!

CW: I'm really glad you can express it. That's a lot better than suppressing it. But what is it about them talking to you about a wheelchair that makes you so angry? And what does it cause them to do when they see you so hostile about it? Or, what does it protect inside you, when faced with it, that you knowingly or unknowingly can't stand to face?

The worker is employing a combination of control theory and RET to try to get Paul to question his behavior and thinking and to perhaps get a glimpse of the fact that what he's doing might be self-defeating.

Paul: I don't know. All I know is that nobody really cares about what's going on with me. They just do their jobs—like this is just another factory or business. How do they know how I feel? Hell, they don't care!

CW: Paul, I hope you keep on questioning every phase of your treatment. And I hope you keep on angering and expressing every bit of concern you have, because that's the only way they or I can know, from you, the world's best expert on your feelings, how you're doing. What I'm trying to do right now is to understand, as completely as I can, how you feel and what you need—and, Paul, I'm seeing that you're pretty angry and hostile about the lack of personal attention.

Paul: Yeah. It really ticked me off when they suddenly bopped in here with all that wheelchair stuff this soon. How do they know what I'm ready to do, when I don't even know myself? You're all acting like idiots.

CW: What do you want to see happen to you now?

Paul: Well, I don't know. Yes, I do too! I want to know that they know exactly what they're doing with my treatment, and I want to be treated like a human being— with feelings and with a future.

CW: So what you're wanting is to have some say—to have some control over your life. What I'm trying to do is to help you to get us to begin generating the kind of treatment that's best for you, and to start shaping your own future right now. You *do* have a choice!

The crisis worker is attempting to use elements of various counseling systems, including control theory, to accomplish several interventional goals: to begin to assess Paul's needs, to educate him, to empower him to begin to take control of his own life, and to defuse, but not shut off, some of his anger. Although Paul is a negative and somewhat difficult client, the worker's strategy produces, later in the interview, some apparently positive results.

Paul: Yeah. I think I see it a little bit differently now. I don't want to be dependent the rest of my life! And it's true that nobody, including me or the doctors, knows how much progress I might be able to make in the future. So they've got to not restrict me—they've got to assume that I have the potential for doing almost anything I want to at some time in the future.

CW: So what you want is for them to calculate on the safe side for you—not on the too-restrictive side. You really don't want to wind up any more dependent than you absolutely have to. And you want to have a part in assessing what you need and how far you can go and how soon you can do it.

Paul: Precisely! If they'll play it straight with me, I'll play it straight with them. If they don't, they're going to hear from me! I have no intention of being a docile or a model patient.

It is not the worker's goal to placate, control, or change Paul or make him a compliant client. The main objective is to involve Paul in the assessment of his own needs. Some secondary objectives are to keep the channels of communication open and to provide Paul with the encouragement and education needed to generate, inside himself, the power to control his emotions and his behaviors.

Multidisciplinary assessment.   No one professional has all the answers for appraising the needs of SCI people (Harris, 1963; Pierce & Nickel, 1977; Ruge, 1969). Not only should medical and psychological specialists be involved but also persons with expertise and experience in many fields, such as electronics and mechanics, should be sought. As examples, Harris (1963), in the 1960s, and Wilson (1972), in the 1970s, documented how electronics as well as mechanics may play a vital role in helping quadriplegics and paraplegics attain varying degrees of mobility—even quadriplegics who can move only a few muscles. Paul Ramirez's case demonstrates the value of multidisciplinary assessment.

Paul: Shit! You'd think that Winston Churchill's war cabinet had met to discuss my case. You'd think my getting ready to leave Glenwood was the invasion of Europe! I thought a van was a van, and that you just ordered a special van. All of you imbeciles must have gourds for heads!

CW: What we're trying to do is make sure the van is right for you in every detail. We want every accessory on it to serve at your command and at your choice. That's why just anyone's van would not be right for you. Now's the time for all of us, including you, to make sure that vehicle serves you and only you. What are the aspects about the van and about the process of tailoring the van for you that will help us to learn and enable you to better carry on your life?

Paul: Well, now I will concede that they are considering my capabilities. I can see that even the nurses and the physical therapists have some opinions that help. I know that, whether it's a van or anything else, the input of a whole lot of people will get better results than just one person doing all the deciding.

CW: How can you use what you've learned to make sure you get what you need in other important aspects of your life now and in the future?

The crisis worker's response is an open-ended question, which is typical in the use of control theory, RT, and RET with SCI clients. Such questions are valuable for clients because they focus on the client's central issues and need of forward movement—providing what we call *directionality* and *intentionality* to the client. They also tend to preclude defensive thinking and responding by clients such as Paul, who might otherwise focus on negative aspects of the past or on all the things they cannot do now.

We cannot overemphasize the wisdom of consulting across disciplines when examining the needs of SCI clients. The fact that a wide diversity of specialization is brought to bear on the assessment of clients' needs is of enormous value to clients. Such a team appraisal is in itself a valuable intervention strategy.

Control. Determination of the degree of control, autonomy, freedom, independence, or personal space that is possible for SCI survivors is what Moore (1986) calls an important assessment question. Paul Ramirez's greatest internal threat seems to be the feeling of vulnerability to the lack of or the loss of control.

Paul: I don't trust these nerds! They're liable to just send me off in that van and say, "Good riddance!" They probably don't give a red cent what happens to me, just as long as they get me out of here!

CW: Paul, where's your proof that that's what their motives are? Look at how they went about getting and tailoring all your equipment especially for you, including your new van. They haven't abandoned you so far. Where's your proof that they intend to do all this doom and gloom stuff to you?

The worker is using RET to challenge and confront Paul. Ellis (1962) uses confrontational methods to call clients' attention to certain self-defeating beliefs and statements. Such beliefs and statements tend to cause clients to assume that (1) difficult problems are usually catastrophic; (2) distasteful or unwanted events are usually awful; and (3) one must not accept one's own attainments to be anything except perfect at all times. In confronting clients with these beliefs, Ellis refers to them in RET language: (1) catastrophizing (what clients are doing to reflect their irrational beliefs); (2) awfulizing (also reflecting their irrational beliefs); and (3) perfectionism (what clients believe about what their own performance should be). One objective in using RET strategies with Paul is to get him to think more scientifically and rationally about his own thinking and behaving.

Paul: Hell! I know I'm probably overreacting. But I'm scared they're not aware of how vulnerable I'm going to be out there.

CW: You're really frightened at the thought of not knowing what's going to happen to you. But there's a difference between just being afraid and apprehensive about what's out there and creating a catastrophe out of it, in your mind, before it even happens. Where's your proof that it will be a catastrophe? It's also possible that it could prove to be the most liberating and exhilarating and triumphant experience you've ever had! Don't you see how your negative fears and awfulizing literally predispose you to panic and they literally create your negative pictures in your mind's eye—when there's absolutely no scientific proof whatsoever that anything bad is going to happen?

The worker continues to use RET to dispute Paul's irrational thinking and to respond in a didactic, educative, and persuasive way—to reindoctrinate him and to try to get him to reindoctrinate himself. A secondary aim is to get him to stop devaluing others and almost everything they do.

Paul: Yeah, since you put it that way, I can see that I'm my own worst enemy in this.

CW: Yes! And what are the mental images and signals that you can get hold of, any time you find yourself catastrophizing like this, to literally take charge of your own life so that your negative, self-defeating thoughts don't trap you into expecting failure rather than success?

The worker is not attacking Paul personally. To the contrary, even though the worker is vigorously disputing Paul's faulty thinking, Paul is probably feeling supported because the worker is not dealing with extraneous issues or issues introduced by the worker. Paul's autonomy and control are not questioned. Rather, these dimensions are emphatically supported by the worker because the worker keeps insistently pursuing the goal of fostering forward movement in Paul. The worker does not get angry, defensive, or punitive with Paul.

The use of assessment techniques to discover better ways to keep the client's control and autonomy in central focus is right on target. Such use of assessment, according to Ellis (1987), helps clients to find out how to take charge of their own changing life situations in positive ways and helps them to take the first step in their quest to overcome life's adversities. Such a rational and scientific view of assessment is particularly applicable to SCI recoverers.

Psychological, educational, and vocational assessment. According to Guidubaldi, Kehle, and Murray (1979), multifactored evaluation of handicapped persons usually includes assessments of "ability levels in cognitive, social-emotional, academic, perceptual-motor and self-help domains" (pp. 245–246). Some, but not all, SCI clients require assessment of their emotional, educational, and career needs quite early in their rehabilitation programs. Hathcock (1986) indicates that the need for assessment of depression or other debilitating conditions, for instance, varies among individual recoverers' personalities and situations. Some individuals rarely feel depressed and experience little difficulty in dealing with their depression. Others are depressed a great deal and frequently need help in coping with depression as well as other negative feelings. Some people need very little assistance with their educational and vocational planning. Others, however, experience a great deal of stress over their career development. The appraisal of the psychological, educational, and vocational needs of SCI clients yields important information upon which to base intervention and treatment decisions. Paul Ramirez's case provides a relevant example. In the following dialogue, the initials by which Paul identifies specific tests he has taken are (1) MMPI, Minnesota Multiphasic Personality Inventory; (2) PCDP, Personal Career Development Profile; and (3) ACT, American College Testing Program, normally administered as one of the college admissions tests to prospective freshmen.

Paul: They gave me a bunch of tests and then didn't use them—as far as I know. They gave me the MMPI and the PCDP. And I got my ACTs for them from home, which I took back in high school. But shit, it didn't amount to anything around here, not to this bunch of dummies! What a bunch of klutzes they have around here!

CW: You're disappointed that they didn't use these tests to evaluate your situation and to help you. What you want is some real help, starting with these test scores. How do you propose going about making sure those test scores go to work helping you right now?

The worker uses an RT type of questioning technique to try to get Paul to take responsibility for what he wants to do in the here-and-now.

Paul: There you go again! You're a worse klutz than they are! Tell me this, wise guy—why in hell did they give me the tests if they didn't intend to use them to help me? I may need to know what that MMPI said about my psyche. If I'm crazy, I need to know it. Even if I'm a little nutty, I need to know it! I may need to know what that PCDP said about my career and my job interests. I get as mad as a hornet at the way they go about keeping what we need a secret from us.

CW: You're not only angry at the staff, but you're also disappointed because you did not receive the test information you need and deserve. What I suggest you and I do right now is to figure out a way for you to obtain and use the profiles of those tests—and any other evaluative information you need to make some sound decisions for your future.

The worker remains nondefensive, attempts to obtain Paul's cooperation, and offers to assist him in taking one small, positive, forward, action step. The use of the "what" and the "how" questions as open-ended queries with clients is typical of workers employing RT techniques.

The use of self-report test data by itself is only a small part of assessment.

However, if such data are available, they should be used to enhance and increase the information base upon which decisions affecting SCI clients are made.

Legal needs. According to Burke and Murray (1975), every effort should be made to ensure that SCI clients are aware of their legal rights (p. 83). Hathcock (1986) also affirms the importance of giving each individual access to competent legal assistance whenever it is needed. Survivors may have a need for the assessment of their legal requirements solely because of the status change brought on as a result of their injuries. Whether the recoverer deals with a divorce, litigation resulting from the injuring accident, or a problem over insurance, finances, child custody, or property, an attorney who is an advocate of the person's unique requirements is needed. Attorneys should certainly be equipped by both experience and attitude to serve the special interests of recoverers.

Paul: My lawyer says he can get my van fixed or force them to get me another one. The lift doesn't do like it is supposed to do. And the computerized climate control broke down. It was supposed to have a 36-month warranty on the climate control, and they say they won't fix it. They are really jacking me around. And here you are, poking your damn nose in my business again!

CW: Paul, the real issue here is not my nose poking. The important issue is your using your power of persuasion to get your own transportation in order. What you want is for your van to be dependable and serviceable—as it is supposed to be. How can you make sure that your attorney understands what you need and is committed to serving your best interests?

Paul: Hell, he knows what I need! He looks at me as a person, not as a handicapped person. He doesn't just see a wheelchair when he looks at me, like some jerks I could name!

CW: You feel secure and valued by him, and you're confident that he will represent you well. What you really want to do is to *solve* the van situation. How can you make sure you get your van fixed right—and do so in a way in which you don't have to choose to be angry at the staff or anyone else?

The worker uses an RT question to get Paul to think about getting what he needs in responsible ways—implying that Paul can choose to be something other than angry.

Not every recovery will experience legal problems. For those who do, a valid assessment should be made by an attorney who is conversant with the unique needs and circumstances of SCI survivors.

Response to challenge. According to Hathcock (1986), some SCI recoverers are motivated by a challenge and some are not. An assessment is needed to determine how recoverers view challenge. If a person is discouraged by a challenge, caregivers will want to look for ways to help that person take risks and develop techniques for dealing with challenge. If an individual thrives on challenge, appropriate challenges should be provided.

CW: Paul, it seems to me that you're one of those individuals who have definitely negative and positive attitudes and reactions to a challenge. On the one hand, you seem to experience some kind of pleasure or some kind of high over a challenge. On the other hand, you seem to be afraid to risk the unknown. What would be so bad if you tried something and it flopped? You seem to shoot yourself in the foot, so to speak; then, you either kick yourself or blame others. What are you doing when you're turning your anger on yourself or toward others who are trying to help you?

Paul: You're so damned judgmental! Hell, if I really want to do something, I'll show you! I'll find a way to do it. Just don't tell me I can't do something.

CW: You sound quite sure about that. But that's not the way you generally come across. How can you use that kind of optimism whenever you find yourself vilifying other people but needing to think positively, take risks, or face some challenge that's scary but that you really would like to conquer or surmount?

The worker uses RET to confront Paul's behavior, not Paul personally. The aim is not to try to change Paul totally, but to make one small advance toward getting him to begin to accept himself and others and to view the world rationally.

To some extent, Paul explores and examines his risk-taking needs and behaviors. The RET techniques appear to be somewhat facilitative in helping him to understand how he deals with life's challenges.

Paul: Yeah. That discussion did give me some insight into the way I deal with challenges. That should help me in the future. But I'll tell you right quickly—nobody's going to walk on me!

CW: The main issue is not whether they are trying to walk on you. The main thing right now is: What are the internal signals and flags you can use to ensure that you can pay more attention to what you want and what you need without getting mad and lashing out at others? What internal flags can you begin to use right now?

Paul: Yeah. I guess I do need to work on that some.

The crisis worker attempts to help Paul realize that he can be his own decision maker and guide—without attacking others.

For some clients, assessment of their potential for responding to challenge is easy. For others, it may be more difficult. However, recoverers are their own best experts on how they feel. We believe that the best technique for assessing how clients face a challenge is to ask the clients—and then listen and use control theory, RT, or RET to empower the clients to use their own thinking. This strategy should enable them to meet their own challenges—as independently of help from others as possible.

Internal needs. Recoverers often have a keen sense of their inner organism's physical and emotional state. Caregivers should listen to and place importance on SCI recoverers' sensory phenomena, intuitions, and concerns about their inner well-being. Hathcock (1986) points out that often the SCI person is keenly sensitive to and aware of inner effects of drugs and of nutrition (or the lack of it), the damaging effects of unhealed or infectious tissue, nuances in the neuromuscular functioning, and other factors that have a direct bearing on healing, recovery, and overall wellness. Paul confirms some of Hathcock's advice that caregivers pay particular attention to the client's own inner assessment.

Paul: At one time, they were determined to classify me as a quadriplegic. They said, according to my charts and readouts, that I'd have little or no returns to my upper limbs. But I could tell, I could sense, a tingling. I could somehow sense an inner healing or growth potential in my upper body which they didn't detect. I somehow knew I'd get more returns. Now, I have a lot of confidence that I'll get even more.

SCI people such as Paul know a lot about their physical and emotional condition. The recoverer's own sense of his or her bodily needs is an important aspect of assessment. If recoverers are lethargic and willing to sit back and let others make all the decisions for them, caregivers should find ways to get recoverers moving on their own behalf. Helping SCI clients to know and sense a great deal about their inner condition and needs should be regarded as one important goal in the assessment process.

Individual Counseling and/or Crisis Intervention

The strategies used in assessment are equally valuable in individual counseling and crisis intervention. Caregivers whose role is to help SCI recoverers should remember that the multidisciplinary approach is a cornerstone of intervention (Bedbrook, 1986; Bedbrook, Beer, & McLaren, 1985; Cull & Hardy, 1977; Gunther, 1969; Harris, 1985; Meinecke, 1985; Pierce & Nickel, 1977). For the medical team, attending to the acute physical and safety crisis is paramount (Harris, 1985). Once the survivor's medical and safety needs are stabilized, a host of concerns must be faced by the survivor and the caregiving support persons (Bedbrook, 1986; Cunningham, 1986; Sutton, 1973).

It is not always feasible or even desirable to separate crisis intervention from assessment or rehabilitation (Bedbrook, 1986) because the various aspects of recovery are interdependent (Cull & Hardy, 1977; Pierce & Nickel, 1977). All of the physical, psychological, social, recreational, sexual, vocational, and other personal needs of any client population are among the requirements of SCI people (Cunningham, 1986; Hathcock, 1986; Lollar, 1986b; Moore, 1986; Sutton, 1973). The issues and problems may seem to be somewhat more urgent or magnified in the SCI population. Although any of the unique needs may be seen as being within the purview of the crisis worker, the overall goal of SCI recoverers is not to be a special population. Rather, they are more concerned with living their normal daily lives (Lollar, 1986b; Zola, 1982). This is the central focus of individual counseling and/or crisis intervention strategies with SCI recoverers, and it is a core issue in the counseling and crisis intervention with Paul Ramirez. The brief excerpts of dialogue concerning Paul's case are not necessarily presented sequentially. The various segments were selected from early, middle, or late intervention sessions to serve to illustrate specific concepts or helping strategies.

Physical and safety needs first.   Newly injured persons frequently have so much pain and so many urgent physical complications that attention to the immediate physical and safety needs come first.

Paul: I was worried about my military career, my family, and my plans to marry my girlfriend. But those things faded into the background because I was in so much pain and I was so spaced out on drugs. I had operations on my arm, on my head, on my body, and on my leg—where it was amputated. I was so out of it most of the time that I didn't worry too much. It didn't matter that much to me then.

CW: Now that your physical safety is no longer critical, what are your main concerns?

The worker affirms that safety, Step 2 of the crisis intervention model, comes first; then the worker sets the stage for Paul to begin to examine his chief concerns, which have been overshadowed by the physical injury.

Caregivers should be sensitive and knowledgeable enough to defer pushing clients to deal with the noncritical concerns until they have achieved sufficient equilibrium in physical condition and safety to ensure that SCI clients are ready to move on (Hathcock, 1986).

Physical therapy.   According to Bromley (1976), appropriate physical therapy is an important aspect of treatment and crisis intervention with SCI recoverers. Even though recoverers themselves may feel that they are not yet ready, the requirements of their attending physicians must be taken seriously and carried out. Paul expressed such a concern during an early interview, when he was a newly injured recoverer.

Paul: Oh, no! I don't want to do it. I would if I could. I want to wait until I'm healed a little more. You get out of here—right now!

Physical therapist: I'm not going to ask you to run any foot races. You've got to start sometime. I'll see to it that you have just the right amount of movement. We're going down to the mat room, even if we do nothing but watch today. I won't absolutely guarantee that you won't feel any physical stress at all. But I assure you that this will be a good thing for you. It will help you to gain courage.

Paul: Well, all right, then. I guess I have to go, but I don't trust you. I want to make progress. But I guess I wanted more time.

Physical therapist: I know you want to make progress, and that's what I'm here for. The first step! We'll do it a step at a time. A little bit every day. That's how you'll make the progress that you want to make.

Paul was an ambivalent client who was both fearful and desirous of improving. The physical therapist was sensitive, supportive, and firm in carrying out the physical therapy component of Paul's medical regimen. Later, Paul could understand and verbalize the importance of early physical therapy.

Paul: It was a little painful to get up and get started so soon. But even though it hurt, it did turn out to be one of the best things for me. Getting up and getting moving ended up giving me a sense of personal control, which was just as important as the physical wellness it promoted. Physical therapy was, and still is, one of the most vital parts of my treatment.

Clarifying feelings. One of the most important strategies crisis workers have for helping SCI clients is listening to them and helping them clarify their own feelings (Cormier & Hackney, 1987). Moore (1986) points out that unless the worker can help clients to clarify their feelings, clients may not come to understand that they have choices. Paul is no exception.

Paul: I'm sick and tired of being treated like a piece of meat! I want to be treated like a full-fledged human being. And you're no better than all the others!

CW: You're angry about the dehumanizing and patronizing way you're being treated, and what you want is to be recognized and treated like the person you are. What can you do now to take the first step toward receiving the treatment you want?

Paul: I guess I can tell the head nurse to stop so many visitors from coming in here and gawking at me—like I'm a freak or an animal in a zoo.

CW: You're feeling irritated and uncomfortable about being on display—like an object everyone is dropping by to see—and you'd like to have more control over how many visitors you have and when you have them. What, in addition to telling the head nurse what you want, do you intend to have happen, starting right now, with regard to your visitor situation?

The crisis worker is attempting to clarify Paul's feelings and, at the same time, use rational techniques to provide both forward movement and inner control in the client. The main focus in the worker's strategy is to facilitate positive thinking and acting on the part of Paul—to open up his own forward movement.

Control. Probably the most important issue in the lives of SCI survivors, as well as with all other people, is that of control or loss of control (Cormier & Hackney, 1987; Ellis, 1987; Glasser, 1984; Hathcock, 1986; Lollar, 1986b; Moore, 1986; Nasaw, 1975; Willis & Willis, 1974). By virtue of the fact that SCI survivors land in health care institutions for their initial treatment and much of their follow-up, they may experience a marked loss of control. Glasser (1984) reminds us that the "most difficult place to retain control over your life is in a hospital" (p. 221). He also advises that one should never relinquish total control or responsibility over one's health or one's life. Moore (1986) says that feeling a sense of control or autonomy is the top priority for SCI recoverers. After two years as a recoverer, Paul is asked about and reflects upon the need for control.

Paul: It's essential that wheelchair users not be stripped of all their control over their lives.

CW: What should the caregiving staff do?

Paul: They should allow wheelchair users to express their feelings openly—about the patronizing and dehumanizing situations or any other things that need changing in the hospital. They should listen to what the survivors want—give them some say in how treatment is carried out. I think survivors would have a healthier perspective if they thought they could influence what happens to them.

CW: Just because you're in a hospital doesn't mean you're helpless. What can you do to control how hospital staff members respond to you?

Paul: I can tell them I'll not stand for any more of that crap. I can say how I want to be treated.

CW: Right! But tell me, Paul, what is this "crap" you're telling me people are giving you?

Paul: Well, staffers who take care of spinal-injured people should not impose their philosophical or religious beliefs on survivors. Some well-meaning staff members want to impose their brand of religion—prayer, conversion, or any kind of religious teaching—on people. That was one of the worst things that happened to me and to many others I've spoken to. They should keep their religious dogma to themselves—that imposes on the freedom and control of people. Now, I won't stand for it! Some of the wheelchair users let them get away with it. It's a crying shame, too.

CW: So you do have considerable control. What other positive areas of your life can you control?

The worker is using RET to get Paul to dispute his own irrational and exaggerated beliefs and to indoctrinate himself into thinking and expecting that empowerment to control his environment rests within himself.

Some of the other aspects of control involve privacy and dignity. Moore (1986) describes the need for privacy as a need for space or a need for some quality time alone—to think and meditate. Brammer (1985) cites the need for "centering," meaning having a time and place to get in touch with and develop one's own inner awareness or inner peace (p. 109). Hathcock (1986) recommends that SCI people have the freedom and capability to relax, as well as to generate their own diversion. Every survivor's relaxation requirements may not be the same. But the institution should see to it that survivors have some control over the kind, amount, and structure of their own relaxation activities. Hathcock also cites physical activity, relaxation therapy, reading, music, drugs, hypnosis, TV, and video as examples of options to assist in relaxation.

Depression and suicide.   Caregivers must be prepared to face problems of depression and suicide among SCI people. Cox-Gedmark (1980) and Judd and Burrows (1986) remind us that helpers should acknowledge the reality of depression and suicidal ideation, assure the client that these feelings are normal and that it is all right to talk about them, and make use of the full range of crisis intervention strategies (such as those described in Chapters 2 and 3) to ensure that clients get safely past the periods of depression and suicidal ideation. Paul Ramirez is asked whether he felt suicidal during his treatment.

Paul: Yeah. Nearly two years ago. Right after I was injured.

CW: What pulled you through?

Paul: Diversion. Whenever I'd get to thinking about it, I'd go right then and watch movies or cable TV or listen to music.

CW: If you lapsed back into suicidal thoughts right now, what would you do to counteract them?

Paul: I'd do something—anything concrete, just to get me up and get me moving around and actively thinking.

Hathcock (1986) confirms Paul's advice. He states that many clients, especially early in their treatment, have suicidal ideation and that they may be diverted from depression and suicidal thoughts by focusing on taking care of their children, parents, spouses, or other loved ones, as well as by engaging in any meaningful and concrete physical or mental activity. Judd and Burrows (1986) recommend that professional therapy, on a long-term treatment basis, be provided for SCI clients who manifest continuing suicidal tendencies.

Success. Moore (1986) and Lollar (1986b) identify success itself as a valuable, positive, intrinsic reinforcer in SCI clients. The idea that success begets success is no less true for SCI recoverers than for any other group of people. Moore (1986) recommends that caregivers capitalize on the success phenomenon by recognizing, nurturing, and taking advantage of any and every small degree of success. Even if an SCI recoverer is able only to take a digger and plant one small plant or roll a bowling ball down the lane one time, the recoverer can regard these achievements as successes and build upon them for further attainment. Recoverers themselves should be allowed to discuss their successes openly, and caregivers should value and appreciate such discussions. Very early in his treatment, Paul provides a prime example.

Paul: It was the first time I was alone in the mat room. I was down on my stomach, and I knew I had to get up by myself. I was determined to get up by myself. At first I thought I was helpless and couldn't do it alone. I didn't think it was possible, but I somehow rolled myself over and actually pushed myself up! I actually pushed myself up!

CW: What did that do for you?

Paul: I felt like I had won a victory! I knew right then that I could and would survive!

Hathcock (1986) classifies performance in public as a success-producing activity. SCI recoverers may have a great amount of stage fright prior to any type of public demonstration, display, or performance. But they may derive an enormous amount of stimulation and self-confidence through such individual or group efforts. SCI recoverers who have experienced successful performance in public describe the effects as giving them a tremendous "high"— one of the most therapeutic activities a person can experience.

Returning home. A major stressor and stress period for recoverers is returning home—making the transition from inpatient status to outpatient status (Bedbrook, Beer, & McLaren, 1985; Meinecke, 1985). Many times SCI survivors find that the attitudes of family members toward recoverers have changed since the injury. Family members may exhibit any one or a combination of behavioral, attitudinal, and emotional responses: fear, blame, ignorance, condescension, anger, neglect, disregard, disrespect, reluctance to communicate, and reluctance to touch physically. Many times, as a result of consequences brought about by the injury, drastic changes, such as separation and divorce, occur. The additional family stresses compound an already difficult and complicated recovery situation for the SCI survivor. For some SCI clients, dealing with the family is a greater stressor than dealing with the effects of the injury (Hathcock, 1986). Paul expresses some difficulty upon returning home.

Paul: When I got home my dad started hassling me about lots of things, including my doing drugs. I knew right then it wasn't going to work. I knew that I had to get a place of my own. I mean, don't get me wrong! I love my family. But it's a bigger hassle being around them than being in the hospital.

CW: How are you fulfilling your needs to be independent and to relate to your father at the same time?

Here, the worker uses an RT-type question as an open-ended way to encourage Paul to focus on the here-and-now, as well as on fulfilling his needs in positive and responsible ways.

According to Moore (1986), education, training, and reading can play positive roles in helping clients successfully return home, as well as engaging in other normal phases of life. Not only clients but also family members can profit through receiving education and training on what to expect and what to do to adjust. Moore notes that video tapes of SCI recoverers doing things are very helpful in facilitating family and survivor discussions and expectations. Video tapes showing SCI survivors at work, playing sports, and living normal lives are reported to be effective. Moore (1986) also advocates bibliotherapy as an important adjunct in helping recoverers returning home, as well as their families receiving them. It is equally important for every member of the family to understand and accept the fact that all the recoverer needs is to live as normal a life as possible and that each family member should have an optimal amount of control. Special counseling programs for recoverers' parents (Prescott & Hulnick, 1979), children (Kennedy & Bush, 1979), or whole family (Cormier & Hackney, 1987, pp. 217–238) may be helpful in paving the way for SCI persons to return home. However, regarding returning home, Hathcock (1986) admonishes both survivors and families to be sensitive, respectful, and aware that SCI persons do not want to be smothered— and stresses that SCI people should be expected to be responsible for doing everything they are physically capable of doing.

Individual differences. We cannot overemphasize the concept of individual differences in working with SCI people. Recoverers have the same emotional and situational problems as everyone else. Each person is unique; therefore, each recoverer is unique.

Paul: This place is too damn regimented!

CW: How is it too regimented for you?

Paul: The way they do their meals. Why can't they understand that I don't want to eat everything they want me to eat? I don't even want to eat *when* they want me to eat. I've never seen a place try to force so much conformity on you as they do around here!

Moore (1986) alludes to the need to attend to individual differences. She says that sometimes caregivers subconsciously attempt to mold all SCI clients into one group—apparently to make them into what caregivers preconceive them to be. But SCI people differ from one another as much as other people do: they progress and regress; they may go from positive to negative; they may get past their denial, anger, and depression at one time and later find themselves right back again. If caregivers try too hard to shape survivors into one homogeneous type, survivors may respond with resentment, guilt, ambivalence, withdrawal, or anger. A thorough knowledge of and belief in the concept of individual differences are requisites for beginning to work with SCI people. It is essential that caregivers adapt and model strategies, attitudes, and behaviors that reflect a knowledge of and belief in the uniqueness of each person.

Group Counseling and/or Crisis Intervention

The basic need to belong—to share, to cooperate, and to love—is pervasive among all people (Glasser, 1984). Glasser believes that this need to belong is as important as the need to survive, saying, "Most people who commit or attempt suicide describe incredible loneliness as the reason" (p. 9). We find that this fundamental need to belong is a central concern of all SCI recoverers. This section on group counseling and/or group intervention is predicated upon the great amount of research that indicates group techniques to be among the most effective and necessary strategies for helping SCI people (Corey, 1985; Corey & Corey, 1987; Glasser, 1984, pp. 9–10; Harris, 1963, pp. 141–144; Ohlsen, 1970; Riggin, 1976).

Group supports. According to Moore (1986), the case against isolation in crisis intervention with SCI people—especially the newly injured—cannot be put too strongly. In fact, group support is a vital factor in promoting the psychological well-being of all SCI recoverers (Riggin, 1976). One of the greatest mistakes in the early treatment of SCI people is to keep them in a room alone, isolated and immobile (Moore, 1986). The interaction with other recoverers, whether it be in a formal group or in everyday activities (such as physical therapy, recreational therapy, occupational therapy, or leisure time) is helpful. The therapeutic value of group supports is also enhanced through interaction in both formal and informal groups composed of recoverers in varying stages of rehabilitation (Riggin, 1976). Newly injured people receive positive moral support, reassurance, and hope from people who have been through the process and have had several years' experience in successfully controlling their lives. Staff members who are themselves SCI survivors provide an enormous amount of help to SCI clients. Health care units serving SCI clients would do well to employ SCI survivors as regular staff members (Hathcock, 1986).

Group therapy. Riggin (1976) found that group therapy was valued by a great majority of military veterans who were paraplegics and quadriplegics. Group therapy expands and enhances recoverers' views, perceptions, alternatives, and potential. Many times SCI people lack the experience to make a smooth transition from their able-bodied to their SCI lifestyles. Also, for many of them, some topics are too sensitive to be dealt with anywhere except in a group of trusted peers. Examples of such problems are substance addiction (Ellis, 1987; Riggin, 1976, pp. 74–80), sexual functioning (Cull & Hardy, 1977, pp. 54–86), and suicidal ideations or plans (Riggin, 1976, p. 72).

Caregivers who conduct group therapy with SCI clients should be trained and experienced in conducting such therapy and should be endowed with the attitudes, values, and other personal attributes to enable them to establish rapport and work effectively with SCI clientele. We recommend that group therapists working with this special population use a combination of skills derived from different therapeutic modalities. Especially appropriate are person-centered relationship skills (Brammer, 1985, pp. 21–39; Cormier & Cormier, 1985, pp. 11–42; Cormier & Hackney, 1987, pp. 35–64; Rogers, 1980), rational-emotive skills (Ellis, 1962, 1982, 1987), control skills (Glasser, 1984), and reality skills (Glasser, 1965). These systems of counseling and psychotherapy, though not the only applicable modalities, provide caregivers with the strategies that SCI clients need to (1) understand others and be understood, (2) develop self-esteem, (3) develop trusting relationships, (4) focus on immediate and fundamental human needs in the here-and-now, (5) examine alternatives, (6) scientifically and systematically plan appropriate and rational action steps, (7) gain control over their lives, and (8) engage in appropriate lifelong personal and career development.

Both Hathcock (1986) and Moore (1986) advocate various group modalities that effectively empower recoverers to gain autonomy and control over their own lives. We believe that group therapy with SCI clients functions best with more than one group leader. Cunningham (1986) has indicated that caregivers who are themselves SCI survivors are of great therapeutic value to recoverers. We maintain that SCI survivors who are trained in group therapy and who have the characteristics of genuineness, empathy, and acceptance are of great value as leaders or coleaders of SCI groups. Health care agencies would do well to avail themselves of staffers who possess these qualifications.

Physical and recreational activity. According to Hathcock (1986), group and individual activities that involve physical exercise and recreation should be an integral part of the regimen of SCI clients. Cull and Hardy (1977) place great importance on recreational activity, whether recoverers are active or spectator participants. They view recreation as drawing from human endeavors "such as the arts and crafts, music and rhythmics, drama, literature, the sciences, vigorous physical activities, individual sports and team sports, plus the passive appreciation of all of the aforementioned in leisure" (p. 281).

Survivors of all sorts of physical disability attach great importance to physical and recreational activities (Cunningham, 1986). Some of the printed space appearing in the bimonthly news magazine *The Disability Rag* (1987) is devoted to sports, recreational, and physical activities. Most of the articles are written by physically limited survivors who are proactive in educating and sensitizing the public to the rights, capabilities, and dignity of *people* who happen to be handicapped. The *Rag* depicts SCI people as engaging in virtually every phase of human activity in their communities.

Recreation fulfills both individual and group needs. Cull and Hardy (1977) recommend recreation for wheelchair users, and they contend that "the individual becomes a participant in recreation and is not a patient or a client, thereby allowing for more normal reciprocities between people and people, and people and things" (p. 281). Even though physical exercise, recreation, and sports are considered to be essentially group endeavors, they are ultimately self-motivating, self-fulfilling, and self-evaluating within the individual. Whether wheelchair users are children (Roy, 1985) or adults (DeLoach & Greer, 1981), recreation and physical activities play an important and vital part in their lives. We have not encountered one SCI recoverer who spoke against physical activity, exercise, and recreation.

Family supports. Any program of group counseling and/or crisis intervention involving SCI recoverers would be enhanced by an organized and intentional focus on successful transition from the health care institution to the home—including working with families strategically (Cormier & Hackney, 1987, pp. 230–233; Pierce & Nickel, 1977, pp. 305–306; Riggin, 1976, pp. 77–78). The reason why the group is such a powerful and effective proving ground for returning home is that no one survivor can think of or know all the problems, pitfalls, and complexities that will face any particular recoverer or family. Ideally, "returning-home groups" should contain a variety of survivors and family members.

In the past, too much emphasis has been placed on the recoverer and too little attention has been paid to preparing and educating the family. Hathcock (1986) pointed out that group counseling/consultation/education for family members is needed to prepare them for facing their own problems of working through the recovery and readjustment period immediately following the return home of the SCI family member. Both recoverers and family members must be prepared to cope with the changes in behaviors, emotions, and attitudes on the part of everyone in the household. It is too late to wait until the recoverer gets home and then discover that everyone is exhibiting negative attitudes and behaviors. If caregivers are proactive in their preparation for the "returning-home transition," many problems and misconceptions can be avoided.

The systematic intervention strategies described by Cormier and Hackney (1987) provide a sound basis for caregivers to help families improve their communication and adjustment patterns and to better prepare them to understand and accommodate the changes that have been brought about as a result of the family member's recovering status. Moore (1986) has suggested that one of the most valuable "returning home" strategies is to schedule a structured showing of the motion picture *Coming Home*, starring Jon Voight and Jane Fonda, followed by a discussion attended by the recoverer, significant family members, and the caregiving staff.

Sexual concerns. SCI recoverers experience a great deal of concern over matters of their sexual needs—sexual acceptance, sexual performance, and sexual satisfaction (Cull & Hardy, 1977, pp. 54–86; Green & Sloan, 1986; Pierce & Nickel, 1977, pp. 171–185; Riggin, 1976, p. 79; Ruge, 1969, pp. 180–181; Sutton, 1973, pp. 162–164). Riggin (1976) found that SCI recoverers were reluctant to discuss sexual matters except in a group—and then, only after a great deal of trust and rapport had been established among both group members and leaders. Moore (1986) asserts that all SCI clients, regardless of age or sex, are vitally concerned with their own sexuality. She recommends dealing with sexual concerns within the educative group format using these strategies: (1) conducting matter-of-fact discussions in groups, where experienced recoverers can educate the less experienced ones, (2) using videotaped examples of SCI persons engaging in sexual activities, and (3) facilitating honest and open interactions to allow each group member to obtain forthright answers to his or her concerns. Moore advises caregivers to be prepared, by both training and attitude, to deal directly with the sexual concerns of their clients. It goes without saying that workers who deal with the issues of human sexuality in SCI groups must themselves be comfortable about their own sexuality and sexual concerns.

Career and vocational implications. Another important concern of SCI recoverers that can be dealt with effectively and efficiently in groups is the whole area of career development (Brolin & Gysbers, 1979; Sinick, 1979). We believe that career development for everyone is a continuous, developmental, lifelong process. If caregivers can understand that career development applies to SCI recoverers as well as it does to everyone else, they can use the group as a means to help clients begin to formulate ideas, options, and action steps toward their own career development. We believe that career-development plans offer an effective means for moving from a state of crisis to noncrisis, and many researchers seem to agree (Burke & Murray, 1975, p. 84; Cull & Hardy, 1977, pp. 87–99, 203–223; Pierce & Nickel, 1977, pp. 205–224, 319–326; Ruge, 1969, pp. 171–178). Intervention strategies in groups are enhanced by having facilitators who have training and skill in modern career development and by the inclusion, within groups, of SCI recoverers who are themselves currently successful in and enjoying their careers. Moore (1986) has indicated that the involvement of persons who have experienced their own transitions from crisis to vocational adjustment has a profound effect on newly injured recoverers. Caregivers would do well to use both the power of the group and the expertise of experienced recoverers in providing for their SCI clients a window on the future. This can be a remarkably effective group intervention strategy.

There are many fields of endeavor in which survivors can enter and succeed. Lollar (1986b) gives an account of a young athlete who at age 17 broke his neck in a water-skiing accident. Prior to the accident, the young man had planned to pursue a career in athletics. After the accident, he redirected his energies and became a highly successful broker. Lollar reports that many people, both currently employed and retired, are eager and willing to help SCI survivors learn and get into careers. There are many sources available to assist SCI people in their quest for suitable careers, among them educational institutions, the government, the private sector, and the retired sector.

Problems of substance addiction. The addictive use of alcohol and drugs has long been a formidable problem in the lives of SCI recoverers (Bedbrook, Beer, & McLaren, 1985, pp. 69–77; Cull & Hardy, 1977, p. 136; Pierce & Nickel, 1977, p. 299; Riggin, 1976, p. 75; Ruge, 1969, p. 135). Coping with addiction is perhaps the most difficult of all problems that recoverers face. Most hospitals have alcohol and drug (A and D) units with the facilities and the trained staff to deal with addictive problems. Also, most communities have a variety of resources, such as Alcoholics Anonymous (AA) and A and D specialty units. Unless crisis workers are well trained and experienced in A and D care, the procedure of choice is to refer SCI clients for expert medical care for their A and D problems. It is generally conceded that the treatment of addiction can best be accomplished in groups. But just any group will not do. Whenever an addictive problem is detected, we recommend that the caregiver immediately refer the SCI client for medical evaluation and, if needed, specialized medical treatment.

Environmental Supports

The sections on assessment, individual counseling, and group intervention with SCI recoverers have touched on many of the important implications for environmental supports. We are defining appropriate environmental supports as those physical facilities, equipment, apparatus, and staff actions that will enable survivors safely and successfully to get through the three stages of treatment, which Cull and Hardy (1977, p. 174) identify as acute, intermediate, and final:

Acute stage—limiting the survivor to life-saving treatments and procedures

Intermediate stage—curtailed treatments, procedures, and activities because of orthopedic or other medical constraints

Final state—medical and orthopedic stability, allowing survivors to fully participate in all aspects of their treatment programs.

Stimulation. Hathcock (1986) states that it is essential that all SCI recovery phases be physically and psychologically stimulating. From the acute stage through the final stage, exercise and physical therapy spaces and equipment should afford balanced degrees of stimulation and privacy. At times, clients may need space in which to meditate, think, and achieve psychological centering in privacy. At other times, more of an atmosphere of community recreation may be desired. Paul Ramirez expresses a sense of frustration over what he believes to be an inadequate support system.

Paul: I'm glad they're finally sending me to Glenwood. I hate it here! These idiots either leave me in my room to rot or they wheel me down to the recreation hall and park me in that pandemonium! Man, I need some time by myself some of the time—just to be me!

CW: So you're a little angry because what you're wanting is some private quality time—in a place conducive to meeting your private needs. How can you go about getting that quality time for yourself?

Paul: Well, I can't—not here. That's one of the good things about going to Glenwood. I know I'll be better off there.

CW: How can you start right now to plan your actions so that even here, before you get to Glenwood, you can acquire quality time for yourself?

The worker is using control theory to predispose Paul to expect to take action for himself whenever, in the future, he finds himself in need of private time.

The procedures and facilities of the health care unit should be rewarding to clients and should allow them, as they progress, increasing opportunities to observe and communicate with other survivors, as well as providing quality private time when they need it. Moore (1986) advocates providing experienced SCI survivors on the staff and in facilities such as physical therapy rooms. She also recommends that staff personnel be selected for their acceptant and flexible attitudes as well as their technical training. Staff personnel should certainly be suited to working with SCI recoverers. She also suggests that clients be given information on a variety of treatment hospitals and facilities and be given choices of locations for their continued treatment and rehabilitation. For instance, if the facility of choice is in another state, she suggests that the client be transferred to that site whenever it is medically safe to do so.

Staff attire. Moore (1986) states that the way staff personnel dress affects the way clients feel and respond. Traditional hospital attire, for example, connotes power and authority over clients and may keep them from gaining a feeling of autonomy. It may instead contribute to an attitude of learned help-lessness. Moore says that in facilities where doctors, nurses, physical thera-pists, counselors, and other workers dress in street clothing, a more rehabili-tative atmosphere is transmitted to clients.

Nutrition and food service. Recovering SCI people are sensitive to their food and food services. Hathcock (1986) notes that SCI recoverers, more than most other populations, require a nutritional regimen that will promote reha-bilitation. He says that we cannot take it for granted that inpatient facilities will automatically prescribe and provide appropriate nutrition for the indi-vidual. He enjoins all recoverers to learn about, become proactive in, and take a great deal of responsibility for attending to their own nutritional require-ments.

Paul: I know now not to assume they'll feed you right.

CW: What have you learned, so that you can ensure that you get a proper diet in the future?

Paul: I've learned that I've got to take care of my own body and its nutritional re-quirements. I was aghast when I asked my physician what I should eat! He told me to eat anything I wanted. That's dumb. I asked him because I really wanted to know. What a nut! What if I decided I only wanted to eat pie because that's what I like? That really ticked me off! That's when I started studying nutrition. I knew right then I'd better learn to take care of myself!

For survivors to obtain their body's uniquely needed balance of foods and fluids, they should be knowledgeable and should have choices. This means that they need nutritional education as well as access to food services that provide a balanced variety and flexibility both in choices and in eating times.

Use of prescription drugs. Moore (1986) cautions against the overuse of drugs in the treatment of SCI survivors. She admonishes caregivers to be es-pecially careful about administering drugs for the sole purpose of keeping people quiet. Her reasons are that (1) clients need to experience the full im-pact of recovery—to subvert this experience is to risk dependency, delay, or even addiction; (2) it denies the client the right to work through the normal stages of recovery; (3) it may engender compliance—and thereby thwart the vocal client who has valuable feedback and suggestions for the health care unit; and (4) it may deny clients the right to individuality of expression and behavior.

Decision making. Moore (1986) contends that SCI survivors should be in-cluded in discussions pertaining to their particular case decisions. She says that it is detrimental to survivors' morale for the hospital or medical staff to discuss their cases in the hallway or anywhere within sight of survivors. An incident in Paul's case confirms Moore's contention.

Paul: You should have heard them! They were out there in the hallway talking about the instability of my vertebral column at the lesion site. They had been in my room and they congregated out in the hall, just behind the open door. At first they were whispering. That really scared me. Then they got louder. I'd hear them say, "He'll not be able to . . . " and stuff like that. I had just been injured, too! That was bad, man—real bad! Besides being scared as hell, I was also mad as hell!

According to Moore (1986) case discussions should be conducted either in the survivors' presence (with survivor participation invited) or in private spaces designated for such discussions. In the instance Paul describes, it would have been better for the staff to discuss the case in complete privacy, then designate one of the physicians to explain the medical prognosis to Paul and invite him to ask questions and/or make comments.

SUMMARY

In discussing crisis intervention strategies with individuals experiencing severe physical limitations, we concentrated on spinal cord injury recoverers as a representative population. We believe that the kinds of problems and interventions that apply to this population generalize, to a great extent, to most of the other groups facing physically handicapping or limiting conditions.

Some of the commonalities of survivors and recoverers of severe physical limitations are that (1) they are like everyone else in that their main objective is to live their lives as normally as possible, (2) an overriding issue in their daily lives is *control* of their own lives—gaining as much autonomy, independence, and self-sufficiency as possible, and (3) their basic needs, like the needs of all other people, include (a) the need to survive, (b) the need to belong—to love, share, and cooperate, (c) the need for power—to feel that one has power, (d) the need for freedom, and (e) the need for fun—renewal and recreation. The ways in which SCI persons go about achieving their objectives, dealing with their life issues, and fulfilling their needs differ as much among themselves as they do among individuals in all other populations.

The concerns of survivors and recoverers are similar to human concerns everywhere. Some problems are exacerbated because of limitations such as immobility. The facilitation of coping with the problems calls for special environmental, attitudinal, and organizational responses and considerations. By and large, the physically limited can make their own way whenever the physical, attitudinal, and social hurdles are removed from their paths.

We have dealt with four major aspects of crisis intervention: assessment, individual intervention strategies, group intervention strategies, and environmental supports. A large number of procedures, techniques, and interventions are available to caregivers, institutions, families, and clients themselves for helping survivors get past their own crisis phases and get on with their lives. The most important ingredients that caregivers can bring to the crisis intervention scene are a genuine concern and caring for clients, an understanding of the dynamics and needs of clients, and the ability to allow clients to decide and be as responsible for themselves as possible.

REFERENCES

Bedbrook, G. M. (1986). *Lifetime care of the paraplegic patient.* Harlow, Essex, U.K.: Churchill Livingstone.

Bedbrook, G. M., Beer, N. I. E., & McLaren, R. K. (1985, April). Preventive measures in the tertiary care of spinal cord injured people. *Paraplegia, 23*(2), pp. 69–77.

Betts, H. B., & Rosen, J. (1969). Rehabilitation. In D. Ruge (Ed.), *Spinal cord injuries* (pp. 167–182). Springfield, IL: Charles C Thomas.

Brammer, L. M. (1985). *The helping relationship: Process and skills* (3rd ed.). Englewood Cliffs, NJ: Prentice-Hall.

Brolin, D. E., & Gysbers, N. C. (1979, December). Career education for persons with handicaps. *Personnel and Guidance Journal, 58,* 258–262.

Bromley, I. (1976). *Tetraplegia and paraplegia: A guide for physiotherapists.* Edinburgh: Churchill Livingstone.

Burke, D. C., & Murray, D. D. (1975). *Handbook of spinal cord medicine.* New York: Macmillan.

Corey, G. (1985). *Theory and practice of group counseling* (2nd ed.). Pacific Grove, CA: Brooks/Cole.

Corey, M. S., & Corey, G. (1987). *Groups: Process and practice* (3rd ed.). Pacific Grove, CA: Brooks/Cole.

Cormier, L. S., & Hackney, H. (1987). *The professional counselor: A process guide to helping.* Englewood Cliffs, NJ: Prentice-Hall.

Cormier, W. H., & Cormier, L. S. (1985). *Interviewing strategies for helpers: Fundamental skills and cognitive-behavioral interventions* (2nd ed.). Pacific Grove, CA: Brooks/Cole.

Cox-Gedmark, J. (1980). *Coping with physical disability.* Philadelphia: Westminster Press.

Cull, J. G., & Hardy, R. E. (Eds.) (1977). *Physical medicine and rehabilitation approaches in spinal cord injury.* Springfield, IL: Charles C Thomas.

Cunningham, D. (1986, October 28). Polio survivors: Perspectives and problems (audiotaped interview, Cassette Tape No. 6-1). Memphis: Center for Independent Living.

DeLoach, C., & Greer, B. G. (1981). *Adjustment to severe physical disability: A metamorphosis.* New York: McGraw-Hill.

Dickman, I. R. (1985). *One miracle at a time: How to get help for your disabled child—from the experience of other parents.* New York: Simon & Schuster.

Disability Rag, The. (1987, January/February). Bimonthly news magazine. Published by *The Disability Rag,* Box 145, Louisville, KY. Copyrighted by The Advocado Press, Inc.

Doyle, P. B., Goodman, J. F., Grotsky, J. N., & Mann, L. (1979). *Helping the severely handicapped child: A guide for parents and teachers.* New York: Thomas Y. Crowell.

Eareckson, J. (1976). *Joni.* New York: Bantam Books.

Eisenberg, M. G., & Tierney, D. O. (1985, December). Changing demographic profile of the spinal cord injury population: Implications for health care support systems. *Paraplegia, 23*(6), pp. 335–343.

Ellard, J., Volkan, V., & Paul, N. L. (1974). *Normal and pathological responses to bereavement.* New York: MSS Information Corporation.

Ellis, A. (1962). *Reason and emotion in psychotherapy.* Secaucus, NJ: Lyle Stuart.

Ellis, A. (1982). *Rational-emotive therapy* [Film]. New York: Institute for Rational-Emotive Therapy.

Ellis, A. (1987, January). Employee assistance training workshop: A rational-emotive approach. New York: Institute for Rational-Emotive Therapy.

Frank, J. (1985). *Alzheimer's disease: The silent epidemic.* Minneapolis: Lerner Publications.

Glasser, W. (1965). *Reality therapy: A new approach to psychiatry.* New York: Harper & Row.

Glasser, W. (1984). *Control theory: A new explanation of how we control our lives.* New York: Harper & Row.

Glick, F. P., & Pellman, D. R. (1982). *Breaking silence: A family grows with deafness.* Scottdale, PA: Herald Press.

Green, B. G., & Sloan, S. L. (1986, June). Penile prostheses in spinal cord injured patients: Combined psychosexual counseling and surgical regimen. *Paraplegia, 24*(3), pp. 167–172.

Guidubaldi, J., Kehle, T. J., & Murray, J. N. (1979, December). Assessment strategies for the handicapped. *Personnel and Guidance Journal, 58,* 245–251.

Gunther, M. S. (1969). Emotional aspects. In D. Ruge (Ed.), *Spinal cord injuries.* Springfield, IL: Charles C Thomas.

Harris, P. (Ed.). (1963, June). *Spinal injuries: Proceedings of a symposium held in the Royal College of Surgeons of Edinburgh.* London: Morrison & Gibb, Ltd.

Harris, P. (1985, February). Acute spinal cord injury patients—who cares? *Paraplegia, 23*(1), pp. 1–6.

Hathcock, J. (1986, November 12). Perspectives on spinal cord injury and multiple amputations (Audiotaped interview, Cassette Tape No. 6-3). Memphis: Memphis State University, Department of Counseling and Personnel Services.

Helms, T. (1978). *Against all odds.* New York: Thomas Y. Crowell.

Holzhauser, G. K. (1986). *Making the best of it: How to cope with being handicapped.* New York: Ballantine Books.

Judd, F. K., & Burrows, G. D. (1986, February). Liaison psychiatry in a spinal cord injury unit. *Paraplegia, 24*(1), pp. 6–19.

Kennedy, K. M., & Bush, D. F. (1979, December). Counseling the children of handicapped parents. *Personnel and Guidance Journal, 58,* 267–270.

Kleinfield, S. (1979). *The hidden minority: A profile of handicapped Americans.* Boston: Little, Brown.

Levitt, P. M., & Guralnick, E. S. (1985). *You can make it back: Coping with serious illness.* New York: Facts on File Publications.

Lollar, M. (1986a, September 28). Stranger in the mirror: What we know about Alzheimer. *Mid-South, The Commercial Appeal Magazine,* Memphis.

Lollar, M. (1986b, December 7). Trading in spirit: Paralyzed while skiing, an athlete redirects his energy. *Mid-South, The Commercial Appeal Magazine,* Memphis.

Marx, J. L. (1974). *Keep trying: A practical book for the handicapped by a polio victim.* New York: Harper & Row.

Meinecke, F. W. (1985, April). Some thoughts about neurological recovery in spinal cord injuries: A philosophical review. *Paraplegia, 23*(2), pp. 78–81.

Moore, B. (1986, November 5). Crisis phase of recovery in spinal cord injury (Audiotaped interview, Cassette No. 6-2). Memphis: Memphis State University, Department of Counseling and Personnel Services.

Nasaw, J. L. (1975). *Easy walking.* Philadelphia: Lippincott.

Naughton, J. A. L. (1963, June). Psychological adjustment to severe physical disability. In P. Harris (Ed.), *Spinal injuries: Proceedings of a symposium held in the Royal College of Surgeons of Edinburgh* (pp. 135–138). London: Morrison & Gibb, Ltd.

Ohlsen, M. (1970). *Group counseling.* New York: Holt, Rinehart & Winston.

Parkes, C. M. (1970). "Seeking" and "finding" a lost object: Evidence from recent studies of the reaction to bereavement. *Social Science Medicine, 4,* 187–201.

Parkes, C. M. (1972). *Bereavement: Studies of grief in adult life.* New York: International Universities Press.

Pierce, D. S., & Nickel, V. H. (Eds.). (1977). *The total care of spinal cord injuries.* Boston: Little, Brown.

Prescott, M. R., & Hulnick, H. R. (1979, December). Counseling parents of handicapped children: An empathic approach. *Personnel and Guidance Journal, 58,* 263–266.

Rabin, R. (1985). *Six parts love: One family's battle with Lou Gehrig's disease.* New York: Scribner's.

Riggin, O. Z. (1976). *A comparison of individual and group therapy on self-concept and depression of patients with spinal cord injury.* Unpublished doctoral dissertation, Memphis State University, Memphis.

Rogers, C. R. (1980). *A way of being.* Boston: Houghton Mifflin.

Roy, R. (1985). *Move over, wheelchairs coming through: Seven young people in wheelchairs talk about their lives.* New York: Clarion Books (Houghton Mifflin).

Ruge, D. (Ed.). (1969). *Spinal cord injuries.* Springfield, IL: Charles C Thomas.

Russell, P. (1985). *The wheelchair child: How handicapped children can enjoy life to its fullest.* Englewood Cliffs, NJ: Prentice-Hall.

Schoenberg, B. M. (1980). *Bereavement counseling: A multidisciplinary handbook.* Westport, CT: Greenwood Press.

Sinick, D. (1979, December). Career counseling with handicapped persons. *Personnel and Guidance Journal, 58,* 252–257.

Sutton, N. G. (1973). *Injuries of the spinal cord: The management of paraplegia and tetraplegia.* London: Butterworths.

Warren, M. P., & Kirkendall, D. (1973). *Bottom high to the crowd.* New York: Walker & Company.

Whipple, L. J. (1980). *Whole again.* Ottawa, IL: Caroline House Publishers, Inc.

Willis, J., & Willis, M. (1974). " . . . *But there are always miracles.*" New York: Viking Press.

Wilson, D. C. (1972). *Hilary: The brave world of Hilary Pole.* New York: McGraw-Hill.

Zola, I. K. (Ed.). (1982). *Ordinary lives: Voices of disability and disease.* Cambridge, MA: Apple-Wood Books.

■ Classroom Exercises: Case of Janice

The case of Janice is representative of thousands of people who have experienced a crisis of loss resultant from spinal cord injury. Even though Janice's sudden physical impairment was unique to her and to the many persons responsible for helping with her care, her experience contained many elements that were common to or similar to those of other survivors—from polio survivors to amputees to other spinal cord injury persons.

Janice Mitchell, age 18, finally had to confront the fact that she would probably be a paraplegic the rest of her life. She had an accident at the swimming pool during the summer, shortly after her graduation from high school. She underwent a great deal of medical treatment and physical therapy before her doctors and her parents conceded that she could expect no further returns of her former neural functioning. Janice herself experienced periods of denial, grief, anger, bargaining, guilt and self-blame, depression, and finally acceptance before becoming somewhat reconciled to a life of paraplegia.

In high school, Janice had been an outstanding competitor in both swimming and tennis. She was also an honor student in her academic subjects. She was awarded an academic scholarship at a large state university. She had planned to be a member of the women's swim team at the university.

Following her medical treatment and release from the hospital, Janice began her long, hard task of readjustment. She decided to get ready to attend classes on her academic scholarship.

Now, Janice is planning to matriculate at the university, starting next semester. She hopes to use the several weeks remaining prior to enrollment in the university to get adjusted to a wheelchair and to become acclimated to a whole new way of life without the use of her legs. She has limited but functional strength in both arms and hands. But she still finds herself occasionally lapsing into a state of despondency and depression, even though she is continuing her physical therapy daily. She has periodic episodes of withdrawal, anger, self-recrimination, and self-pity. She has recurring dreams in which she vividly experiences walking and swimming again, only to awaken and feel depressed over the dream. What Janice wants to do is to get herself accustomed to her new condition so she can get on with her education and her life. But, right now, she feels stuck in her crisis of stress, loss, and grief. She appears to be receptive to working on overcoming her negative feelings and defenses.

Janice's assets are that she is capable; she is an effective academic achiever; she generally has a positive outlook on life; her parents are supportive, loving, and understanding; she is career oriented; she has an unusual amount of physical and mental stamina; and she thrives on a challenge.

Counseling Simulations in Small Groups

Each group of five or six persons undertakes a crisis intervention task related to the case of Janice:

> Group 1—*Assessment* of Janice's case
> Group 2—*Individual* counseling and/or crisis intervention with Janice
> Group 3—*Group* counseling and/or crisis intervention with Janice
> Group 4—*Environmental supports* for Janice.

If there are more than four groups, some groups will have the same topic. Each group conducts a simulated crisis counseling session: one member takes the role of Janice, another member takes the role of the crisis worker, and the remaining members take the role of observers. Observers will observe the simulation and then develop written plans for the case management of Janice's counseling and crisis intervention. For example, Group 1 observers will write plans for *assessment* while the simulated crisis counseling session is being enacted, and Group 2 observers will write plans for *individual counseling and/or crisis intervention* while the simulated crisis counseling session is being enacted.

All groups simulate the counseling sessions at the same time, allowing enough space between groups to avoid distractions. At the conclusion of the enactment of the counseling sessions, observers within each group will consolidate their written plans and report them to the small group. In the remaining time, representatives from the various groups report to the whole class on the observers' findings for all four intervention topics related to the case of Janice.

Counseling Simulation in a Large Group

In a variation of the first exercise, one pair of participants conducts a simulated crisis counseling session in a fishbowl arrangement (encircled by the remaining group members). Use only one of the four topics. All the remaining members are observers.

Reviewing Simulations on Tape

Conduct crisis counseling simulations as described in the first exercise. Videotape (with sound) each group enactment. The instructor will select the tapes judged to have the greatest educational impact, and, at a later time, replay those video sessions to the whole class. Use the video replays as a basis for classroom discussion. A particularly valuable learning exercise is to identify, prior to viewing the videotapes, the most effective strategies portrayed and explain why each identified strategy is effective.

CHAPTER 7

Post Traumatic Stress Disorder

BACKGROUND

The popular press, professional journals, and the media have raised the public consciousness about what stress in our daily lives can do to us both psychologically and physiologically. The Type-A individual is characterized by a frenetic work pace, heart attack, maladjustive compensatory behavior, and an early grave. This chapter is about a far lesser-known aspect of stress that also affects a great many people. Although it is not as glamorous, almost anyone who experiences it will surely at some time become a candidate for crisis intervention.

Psychic trauma is a process initiated by an event that confronts an individual with an acute, overwhelming threat (Freud, 1917/1963). When the event occurs, the inner agency of the mind loses its ability to control the disorganizing effects of the experience and disequilibrium occurs. The trauma tears up the individual's psychological anchors, which are fixed in a secure sense of "what has been" in the past and "what should be" in the present (Erikson, 1968). When a traumatic event occurs that represents nothing like the security of past events, and the individual's mind is unable effectively to answer basic questions of "how" and "why" it occurred and "what" it means, a crisis ensues. The event propels the individual into a traumatic state lasting for as long as the mind needs to reorganize, classify, and make sense of the traumatic event. Then and only then does psychic equilibrium return (Furst, 1978).

Susceptibility to severe psychic disorganization as a result of traumatic events appears to be a product of several factors. A person's genetic, constitutional, and personality make-up, state of mind, psychological development, social support system, and the content, intensity, and duration of the event all seem to be contributors to the severity of the trauma (Furst, 1967; Kelman, 1945; Moses, 1978). If the individual is able effectively to integrate the trauma into conscious awareness and organize it as a part of the past (as unpleasant as the event may be), then homeostasis returns, the problem is coped with, and the individual continues to travel life's rocky road. If the event is not effectively integrated and is submerged from awareness, then the chances for the initiating stressor to reemerge in a variety of symptomological forms months or years after the event become a high probability. When such crisis events are caused by the reemergence of the original, unresolved stressor, they fall under the category of delayed or posttrauma stress disorders (PTSD).

PTSD is a newborn compared with the other crises we have examined, at least in regard to achieving official designation as such. To understand why this is so, read the following description of an imaginary computer built about 1966. The computer is called the 11-Bravo.

> **11-Bravo:** Military service computer. Basic mother board installed at Ft. Leonard Wood, Parris Island, and other military programming facilities. Subroutines installed for specialized combat modes at Ft. Benning, Little Creek, and other specialized military programming facilities. Set to run basic and specialized offensive combat files on command. Activated Republic of South Vietnam 1966-1974. Alternate, nonfunctional hacker programs not designed for this computer were emplaced in some 11-Bravos at destination. Surplused after one year run time Southeast Asia. *Warning! Some 11-Bravos have not been deactivated and remain combat operational!* If your family has come into possession of an 11-Bravo that refuses to run on standard civilian mode, take it to the nearest Vietnam Veterans Center immediately for reprogramming.

Our mythical 11-Bravo (military parlance for a combat infantryman) is the major reason that PTSD finally found its way into the third edition of the *Diagnostic and Statistical Manual of Mental Disorders* (DSM-III) of the American Psychiatric Association (1980) as a classifiable and valid mental disorder.

Historical Precursors

However, PTSD has been in existence for a long time. Probably the first written account of a person who suffered at least the acute version of this disorder was that of Samuel Pepys, the noted diarist of 17th-century England. His diary's account of the Great London Fire of 1666 and his agitated mental state long after the fire would admirably fit diagnostic criteria for the DSM-III (Daly, 1983). Historically though, the antecedents of what has been designated as PTSD first came to the attention of the medical establishment in the late 19th and early 20th centuries. Two events serve as benchmarks.

First, with the advent of rail transportation and subsequent train wrecks, physicians and early psychiatrists began to encounter in accident victims trauma with no identifiable physical basis. Railway accident victims of this type became so numerous that a medical term, *railway spine*, became an accepted diagnosis. Psychologically, the synonymous term *compensation neurosis* came into existence for invalidism suffered as a result of such accidents (Trimble, 1985, pp. 7–10). Concomitantly, Freud formulated the concept of *hysterical neurosis* with trauma cases. He documented symptoms of warded-off ideas, denial, repression, emotional avoidance, compulsive repetition of trauma-related behavior, and recurrent attacks of trauma-related emotional sensations (Breuer & Freud, 1895/1955).

Second, the advent of modern warfare in World War I and World War II, with powerful artillery and aerial bombardment, generated terms such as *shell shock* and *combat fatigue* to attempt to explain the condition of traumatized soldiers who had no apparent physical wounds. Various hypotheses were proposed to account for such strange maladies (Trimble, 1985, p. 8), but Freud (1919/1959) believed that the term *war neurosis* more aptly characterized what was an emotional disorder that had nothing to do with the prevailing medical notion of neurologically based shell shock.

The United States Medical Service Corps came to recognize combat fatigue in World War II and the Korean War as a treatable psychological disturbance. The treatment approach was that combat fatigue was invariably acute and treatment was best conducted as quickly and as close to the battle lines as possible. The idea was to facilitate a quick return to active duty. The prevailing thought was that time heals all wounds, and that little concern needed to be given to long-term effects of traumatic stress. Such has not been the case (Archibald, Long, Miller, & Tuddenham, 1962). Indeed, a notable proponent of establishing the Vietnam Veterans Centers, Dr. Arthur Blank, ruefully commented that when he was an army psychiatrist in Vietnam he felt there would be no long-term difficulties for veterans (MacPherson, 1984, p. 237).

Contemporary Precursors

Although PTSD can and does run the gamut of natural and man-made catastrophes, it was the debacle of Vietnam that clearly brought PTSD to the awareness of both the human service professions and the public. Through a combination of events and circumstances unparalleled in the military history of the United States, veterans who returned from that conflict began to develop a variety of mental health problems that had little basis for treatment in the prevailing psychological literature. This combination of events and circumstances, which will be discussed at length in this chapter's section on dynamics, had insidious and long-term consequences that were not readily apparent to either the victims or human service professionals who attempted to treat them.

Misdiagnosed, mistreated, and misunderstood, military service personnel became known to a variety of social service agencies that included the police, mental health facilities, and unemployment offices (MacPherson, 1984, pp. 207–330; pp. 651–690). The sheer weight of their numbers and their inability to function in a civilian society made them outcasts in their own country. The worst part of the problem was that onset was not spontaneous or directly attributable to any wartime stressor but was delayed, in many cases for months and even years after the veteran came home.

DYNAMICS

Diagnostic Categorization

PTSD is a complex and diagnostically troublesome disorder. The *Longman Dictionary of Psychology and Psychiatry* (1984) and the DSM-III provide an encapsulated review of the problem. This is Longman's definition of PTSD (Goldenson, 1984, p. 573):

> An anxiety disorder produced by an uncommon, extremely stressful life event (e.g., assault, rape, military combat, flood, earthquake, death camp, torture, car accident, head trauma, etc.), and characterized by (a) reexperiencing the trauma in painful recollections or recurrent dreams or nightmares, (b) diminished responsiveness (emotional anesthesia or numbing), with disinterest in significant activities and with feelings of detachment and estrangement from others, and (c) such symptoms as exaggerated startle responses, disturbed sleep, difficulty in concentrating or remembering, guilt about surviving when others did not, and avoidance of activities that call the traumatic event to mind.

The first diagnostic description of PTSD as an identifiable malady occurred in 1980. The DSM-III lists the following diagnostic criteria (p. 238):

A. Existence of a recognizable stressor that would evoke significant symptoms of distress in almost anyone.
B. Reexperiencing the trauma as evidenced by at least one of the following:
   (1) recurrent and intrusive recollections of the event.
   (2) recurrent dreams of the event.
   (3) sudden acting or feeling as if the traumatic event were reoccurring, because of an association with an environmental or ideational stimulus.
C. Numbing of responsiveness to or reduced involvement with the external world, beginning some time after the trauma, as shown by at least one of the following:
   (1) markedly diminished interest in one or more significant activities.
   (2) feeling of detachment or estrangement from others.
   (3) constricted affect.
D. At least two of the following symptoms that were not present before the trauma:
   (1) hyperalertness or exaggerated startle response.
   (2) sleep disturbance.
   (3) guilt about surviving while others have not, or about behavior required for survival.
   (4) memory impairment or trouble concentrating.
   (5) avoidance of activities that arouse recollection of the traumatic event.
   (6) intensification of symptoms by exposure to events that symbolize or resemble the traumatic event.

Conflicting Diagnoses

Given the wide variety of behaviors that characterize the disorder, it is not uncommon for those who suffer from PTSD to have companion diagnoses of anxiety, depressive, organic mental, and substance use disorders (American Psychiatric Association, 1980, p. 237). Further, because of presenting symptoms, PTSD may be confused with adjustment, paranoid, somatoform, and personality disorders. A variety of other problems that militate against a correct diagnosis include (1) resistance by the examiner to DSM-III criteria as valid, (2) adverse interactional styles in the claimant, (3) lack of corroboration of the stressor, (4) inability of the claimant to discuss the event, (5) exaggeration and falsification of data, (6) idiosyncratic disorders not related to the stressor, (7) intercurrent stress from other sources, (8) deviant social behavior, (9) a need for "either/or" judgments by the examiner, and (10) the reciprocal impact of the event on the examiner (Atkinson, Henderson, Sparr, & Deale, 1982).

Because of the symptomotology presented, Vietnam veterans with PTSD could be and in most instances were viewed by human service professionals as being inadequate personality types or having long-term character disorders. Very few of the symptoms of PTSD are unique to the disorder. Thus, accurate diagnosis requires careful examination of the sequencing and relationship of presenting problems prior to and after the trauma. Diagnosis of the problem is confounded even more because onset from the time of the stimulating trauma is so variable. For both human service workers and people closely related to victims, the disorder is hard to understand, particularly the delay of onset (Scurfield, 1985, pp. 221–226). Thus, diagnosis and treatment of PTSD are complicated because there are few "pure" cases and few symptoms are unique to the disorder (Atkinson, Sparr, & Sheff, 1984).

Premorbidity

Not only does such variability cause difficulty in diagnosis and give clinicians pause to question whether there really is a PTSD event, but also those who have close interpersonal relationships with victims wonder whether the person is not suffering from some other inherent or preexisting malady. Although there are undoubtedly some people who are more predisposed to stress than others, there is little evidence to suggest that PTSD is activated because of some preexisting psychopathology (Wilson, Smith, & Johnson, 1985, pp. 142–172).

Several years ago the collapse of a concrete walkway in a crowded hotel gave us a prime example of how one event may suddenly produce PTSD symptoms. Biographical data gathered following the Kansas City Hyatt Regency Skywalk disaster revealed that few survivors had character disorders prior to the event. Yet many were suffering from a variety of presenting symptoms six months after the event itself (Wilkinson, 1983). Probably the best summing statement about who will and who will not manifest PTSD was made by Grinker and Speigel (1945) in their study of World War II veterans. They concluded that no matter how strong, normal, or stable a person might be, if the stress were sufficient to cross that particular individual's threshold, a "war neurosis" would develop. In short, susceptibility to PTSD is a function of several factors: genetic predisposition, constitution, personality make-up, past life experiences, state of mind, phase of development at onset, and the content and intensity of the event (Furst, 1967; Kelman, 1945; Moses, 1978).

Physiological Responses

PTSD is not "just in the head." Several studies conducted on traumatized individuals have found that a variety of measurable physiological responses occur. Selye, a researcher in human stress responses, found that adrenalin and adrenal cortical hormones were released into the subject's system at a significantly increased rate (Brende & Parson, 1985, pp. 78–79). Askevold's (1977) study of Norwegian merchant mariners in World War II showed impaired memory, concentration, and concrete thinking plus a variety of somatic complaints that included vertigo, uncontrolled sweats, impotency, dyspepsia, dyspnea, and somatic pain. Bower (1981) found PTSD to be associated with poorly controlled or integrated cerebral functioning with abnormal suppression of right-hemisphere functioning when psychic numbing, intrusive flashbacks, and nightmares were occurring with the subject. Bower also found that victims who demonstrated hypervigilance, aggressive behavior, and character pathology conversely had suppressed functioning of the left hemisphere. These changed physiological states are important because they not only cause the individual extreme physical and psychological duress but also imply why people do not "get over" PTSD.

Affective State Dependent Retention

Changed physiological functioning because of traumatic stimuli is important as a building block to Bower's (1981) hypothesis of *affective state dependent retention*. Bower has proposed that since the traumatic event was stored in memory under completely different physiological (increased heart rate, higher adrenal output) and psychological (extreme fright, shock) circumstances, different mood states will markedly interfere with recollection of specific cues of the event. Therefore, the important elements of the memory that need exposure in order to promote anxiety reduction are not accessible in the unaroused state (Keane, Fairbank, Caddell, Zimmering, & Bender, 1985, p. 266) and can only be remembered when that approximate state is reintroduced by cues in the environment (Keane, 1976; Weingartner, Miller, & Murphy, 1977). Thus, the notion that a victim of PTSD can "just forget" or adopt a "better, more positive attitude" does little to effect change in the victim (Keane et al., 1985, p. 266). This proposal has important implications for treatment, particularly with respect to returning the individual to as close an approximation to the event as possible.

Incidence

If PTSD has been with us for so long, what made it finally surface with such profound impact? Quoted in MacPherson (1984, p. 224) Blank states "Long term presence of stress reactions is not unique. They isolated that with World War II veterans. What is unique, however, about Vietnam veterans and stress is the long term persistence in large numbers." The numbers of returning Vietnam veterans that were having some kind of personality disorder went far beyond what statistics would predict. Although a definite number can't be given, various surveys have indicated that approximately half of the 3 million service personnel who served in Vietnam have severe psychological problems (Figley, 1978). Polls taken on selected samples of veterans indicated that from 44% to 61% still have symptoms indicating PTSD and 17% are fully classifiable as PTSD cases (DeFazio, 1978; Fischer, Boyle, & Bucuvalas, 1980). A best estimate indicates about 800,000 veterans of Vietnam who manifest symptoms of PTSD including estimates ranging from 33% to 60% of all combat veterans (Brende & Parson, 1985, p. 1).

Residual Impact

People's basic assumptions about their belief in the world as a meaningful and comprehensible place, their own personal invulnerability, and their view of themselves in a positive light account to a great extent for their individual manifestations of PTSD (Figley, 1985, pp. 401–402). Even in the most well-integrated people, who have excellent coping abilities, good rational and cognitive behavior patterns, and positive social support systems, residual effects of traumatizing events linger.

An outstanding example of such residual effects is the experience of a retired Marine captain who had seen extensive field duty as a combat infantryman in Vietnam in 1968. The anecdote he related typifies the residual effects in an individual who is psychologically well integrated, is securely employed in a professional job, has a tightly knit, extended family support system, and on the whole enjoys life and has a positive outlook on it.

Chris: I had just gotten home from work late one summer evening. The kids had decided to camp out in the woods down by the creek. A thunderstorm was rolling in and I decided I'd better go down and check on them to see if they were packed in for the night. It had started to rain pretty heavily and there was a lot of thunder and lightning. I pulled on a poncho and got a flashlight, crossed the road, and went into the woods. I don't suppose it was 200 yards to where the kids were camped. Now, I'd grown up running those woods, so I knew it like the back of my hand. However, once I got into the woods things kinda went haywire. I immediately thought, "Get off the trail or you'll get the whole platoon zapped." I slipped off the path and became a part of the scenery. Every sense in my body went up to full alert. I was back in Nam again operating with my platoon and I was on a natural, adrenalin high. Time and place kinda went into suspended animation and I eased through the woods, kinda like standing off and watching myself do this, knowing it was me, but yet not me too. The last thing I remember before walking into the clearing where the kids had their tent set up was that we could have ambushed the hell out of that place. I don't harp and brood on Nam, put it behind me after I got out of the Corps, but that night sure put me in a different place than central Indiana, July 1984. I just couldn't believe that would ever happen. It's a bit unnerving.

Trauma Type

Catastrophes, when viewed by the public, tend to fall into one category: bad. However, one of the interesting phenomena of PTSD is that there is a marked distinction between natural and man-made catastrophes. Acts of God create far fewer victims of PTSD than do man-made ones. This effect is even more pronounced when the disaster directly affects the social support system of the family. Children of murdered parents, holocaust survivors, hostages, raped women, and victims of incest are all strong potential candidates for PTSD. In their study of 26 incest victims, Donaldson and Gardner (1985) found that all but one met clear diagnostic criteria for PTSD (p. 361).

Like Samuel Pepys, survivors of uncommissioned man-made disasters such as the breaking of the Buffalo Creek dam and commissioned trauma like the Chowchilla bus kidnapping clearly carry high potential for PTSD. (The Buffalo Creek disaster occurred when a coal company retainer dam broke during a series of heavy rainstorms. The resulting flood wiped out the residents living in the Buffalo Creek, West Virginia valley causing death, injury, and severe property damage. The bus kidnapping occurred when a Chowchilla, California school bus carrying elementary and secondary school children was hijacked at gunpoint. The children were taken from the bus, driven to a buried semi trailer, and locked in it.) What makes these events so particularly terrible is that they would seem to be tragedies that should not have happened, responsibility for them can be quickly placed, and they clearly violate accepted standards of human justice (Figley, 1985a, pp. 400–401). Thus, there exists in any man-made catastrophe the likelihood of posttrauma psychological problems.

Vietnam: The Archetype

Although the subject matter of this chapter relates to catastrophes of all these types, it is still Vietnam and its survivors who best manifest what the chapter is about. This is true not only because of the large numbers presenting the problem but also because the conditions necessary to activate PTSD are nowhere more clearly evident. In a comparative analysis of PTSD among various survivor groups, Wilson, Smith, and Johnson (1985) isolated a number of variables that were hypothesized as predisposing to PTSD: degree of life threat, degree of bereavement, speed of onset, duration of the trauma, degree of displacement in home continuity, potential for recurrence, degree of exposure to death, dying, and destruction, degree of moral conflict inherent in the situation, role of the person in the trauma, and the proportion of the community affected. They compared these variables in a variety of trauma groups: Vietnam combat veterans, victims of rape, auto accident, armed robbery, natural disasters, divorces, life-threatening illness of a loved one, family trauma, death of a significant other, and multiple trauma, and a control group. Outcomes were significant for veterans on seven of the ten dimensions, with rape victims being a distant second. When the data were transformed to fit precise PTSD dimensions, all stressor categories were significant, but combat veterans were even more significantly different from all other stressor groups (pp. 142–172). In plain words, the data suggest that one could not experience a catastrophic event more likely to produce PTSD than Vietnam.

Why did this occur? Although any war could be construed to produce many PTSD symptoms, the rules of war got changed in Vietnam. First, the average age of the soldier in Vietnam was 19.2, as opposed to 26.0 in World War II (Brende & Parson, 1985, p. 19). Whatever basic training might program into our mythical 11-Bravo computer, a 19-year-old psychologically immature soldier was not mentally prepared for the psychic trauma that awaited him in Vietnam (MacPherson, 1984, pp. 62–63).

Hypervigilance. In Vietnam, there was no front line and no relief from constant vigilance. A 365-day combat tour was exactly that. In comparison to World War II troops who might be in acute combat situations and then be pulled off the line, Vietnam "grunts" spent extended periods of time in the field, and even when they were in a base camp resting for another "hump" in the "bush," they had to be alert for rocket attacks and combat assaults on their position. Hypervigilance became an iron-clad rule of survival. Listen to Billie Mac, a composite character of many combat veterans we have interviewed, who will be followed throughout this chapter:

Billie Mac: I was 18 when the plane set down at Da Nang. The crew chief told us to hit the ground running because Da Nang was under a rocket attack. I was scared stiff. Well, Da Nang was heaven, rockets and all, to what later happened. It got a lot, lot worse than that.

Lack of goals. No territory was ever "won," so there was no concrete feeling of accomplishment. There was a feeling of betrayal by combat troops over a war that had no fixed goals for winning and a command structure that was waging a war of attrition, with "body counts" being the primary way of judging whether a mission was successful (Lifton, 1974; MacPherson, 1984, p. 58).

Billie Mac: We swept that one village at least a half dozen times. Sometimes we'd dig in and dare the NVA to hit us and they did. We lost a half dozen guys in that pesthole. For what? For nothin'. We gave it up and they moved right back in.

Victim/victimizer. It further compounds the virulent psychological milieu of Vietnam that veterans, unlike most individuals who suffer from PTSD, played two roles—that of victim and that of victimizer. The physical nature of the enemy could not allow a soldier to distinguish friend from foe, nor could vigilance be relaxed around women or children because of their potential lethality. Because the enemy was Asian and had extremely different cultural values from Americans, it was relatively simple to dehumanize the killing or the maiming of them, particularly when troops saw such things done to their comrades. The nasty way guerrilla war is fought brought out brutality on both sides, and incidents that would normally be considered morally repugnant were committed in the name of staying alive and getting even (Lifton, 1974). Shifts of role from victim to aggressor could occur in seconds (Brende & Parson, 1985, p. 96).

Billie Mac: I couldn't imagine killing a kid or woman. That was true until our medic tried to take care of a kid covered with blood. We all thought he was wounded. When John went over to the dink, he opened up his arms and had a grenade. Blew him and the medic away. Kill them after that? You bet!

Bonding, debriefing, and guilt. The way the armed services filled units had much to do with lack of a support system within the service itself. Personnel replacements were parceled piecemeal into units. Although this method put rookies with veterans, it was not the best way to bond a unit together. The rotation system also took its psychological toll. Each person did a 365-day tour. "Thirty-two days and a wake-up" or a "one-digit midget" became the watchword for being close to the end of a one-year tour in Vietnam. The stress of being "short" caused men to become very self-preservative and immobilized. Units as a whole were never moved out of combat, and a man who entered combat singly returned singly without benefit of debriefing time. The war was essentially fought in patrol and platoon actions. It was a loner's war, and the soldier who fought alone went home alone (MacPherson, 1984, pp. 64–65). One day a man might be sweating out an ambush in the jungle and two days later be sitting on his front porch back home.

It is no great surprise that returning soldiers who had no transition period from Vietnam to the United States were viewed as "different" and "changed" by their relatives (Brende & Parson, 1985, pp. 48–49). Such rapid transitions out of life-threatening situations, both for rest and recreation and for DEROS (Date of Expected Return from Overseas), left many with survivor's guilt (Speigel, 1981). They were glad to be out of Vietnam, but felt guilty of betrayal for leaving comrades behind or took responsibility when they were away from their units and friends were hurt or killed (MacPherson, 1984, p. 237).

Billie Mac: It was inside of a week from jungle to home. My folks thought it was pretty weird because I put my fatigues on and slept in the woods. I just couldn't take being confined in that house. I had to be able to move. I kept thinking about the guy who took my place as squad leader, Johnson. He was a screw-off. I knew he was gonna get somebody wasted. I needed to be there, but I sure didn't want to be. I immediately got drunk and stayed that way for a long time.

Civilian adjustment. The rapid change from intense alertness in order to preserve one's life to trying to readjust to a humdrum society made many question where the "real world" was. Further, the returnee's basic belief system would be quickly jarred when, upon his arrival home, he would be greeted with insensitivity and hostility for having risked his life for his country (Brende & Parson, 1985, p. 72). Veterans would quickly find that for all the ability they showed in making command decisions of life-or-death importance and the authority they had over expensive equipment in Vietnam, the onus of having been there relegated them to civilian jobs far below their capabilities (MacPherson, 1984, p. 65).

Billie Mac: Any job I could get stunk. They were all menial and they acted like they were doing me a favor. Hell! I'd made a lot bigger and smarter decisions than anybody I ever had as a boss.

Substance abuse.   The ease with which soldiers could obtain alcohol and drugs to numb themselves and escape mentally from the reality of Vietnam had severe consequences, both in addiction upon return and in the public's growing misconception that veterans were all "drug-crazed baby killers" and were to be shunned because they were too erratic and undependable (Brende & Parson, 1985, p. 72; MacPherson, 1984, pp. 64–65, 221–222).

Billie Mac: Yeah, I drank. Yeah, I shot kids. I drank mainly to try to forget about shooting kids. Anybody who hadn't been there could never understand.

Attitude.   The time period served in Vietnam seems to be highly correlated with PTSD. Historically the war can be divided into trimesters. Anyone serving in Vietnam during the last two trimesters, from the time of the Tet offensive to the wind-down in the war, would have, from a psychological standpoint, a much greater reason to question the purpose of being there than those who had served early on. The prevailing attitude of "Nobody can win, so just concentrate on surviving" cynicism was in direct opposition to the "Save a democracy from the perils of communism" idealism of the first trimester (Laufer, Yager, & Grey-Wouters, 1981).

Antiwar sentiment.   The impact of the antiwar sentiment veterans met on their return home cannot be minimized. It is unique to the Vietnam war and found its focal point in returnees. Veterans were spurned immediately on their arrival in the United States, suffered prejudice on college campuses as they came back to school, were left out of jobs because of antiwar sentiments, and were disenfranchised from government programs through low G.I. bills and government disavowal of physical problems associated with Agent Orange. Perhaps worst of all were the comparisons their fathers made—men who had fought the "honorable" fight of World War II and could not understand the problems their sons suffered in a war that was not black or white but was a dirty shade of gray (MacPherson, 1984, pp. 54–58).

Billie Mac: I tried to talk to my old man about it. He'd been in WW II on Okinawa. Hell, he might as well have been in the Revolutionary War for all he could understand about Nam. He finally got so mad that he told me I was nuts and no damn good. He didn't mean that, but I'll never forget it.

All these factors came together in a sort of generic problem for veterans trying to make meaning out of a situation that was life threatening and generally considered pointless (Williams, 1983). To survive such a situation called for imposing psychological defense mechanisms that made for a fertile breeding ground for PTSD.

Denial/Numbing

As individuals attempt to cope with catastrophes, they become passive (immobile and paralyzed) or active (able to cope) with the situation. Individual reactions fall into three major groupings: momentary freezing, flight reaction, and denial/numbing. In the prolonged stress of a combat situation, denial/ numbing is the most common response and allows the soldier to cope and live with the experience in three ways: by believing he is invulnerable to harm, by becoming fatalistic, or by taking matters into his own hands, becoming extremely aggressive. Any of these proactive stances allows the victim to get through the trauma and cope with it without losing complete control (Figley, 1985a, pp. 406–408). Typically, survivors of trauma will let down these defense barriers and will have acute stress disorders immediately after the trauma, but will recover. For those who do not, continued emotional numbing and repression can have severe consequences.

Billie Mac: Looking back on it, I can't believe how callous I became. SOP [standard operating procedure] was, "It don't mean nothin', screw it, drive on." This would be right after a B-40 round had blown your buddy's brains all over you. You had to put it behind you to survive. Fifteen years later I have survived, but I wake up to the sound of that incoming round.

Submerging emotions out of conscious awareness does not mean that they are summarily discarded. The price is that emotional numbing left in place and not relieved can generalize to other aspects of one's life and result in later psychological difficulties (Wilkinson, 1983). Shunted into the unconscious for a long time, trigger events in the form of everyday stressors can pile up and cause emotional blowouts when the individual is least prepared for them (Figley, 1985a, p. 408).

Billie Mac: I can't stand the sound of a chopper. Every time I hear one, I want to run. I get the feeling that every time I hear the 5 o'clock traffic chopper, it's gonna circle in, pick me up, and take me to a hot LZ [landing zone].

What the individual needs most is to bring these thoughts into conscious awareness and come to grips with them so they can be resolved. Yet, rather than confronting the intrusive and threatening material, the individual is more likely to deny its existence and use a variety of avoidance responses to escape from the situation (Horowitz, Wilner, Kaltreider, & Alvarez, 1980).

Intrusive-Repetitive Ideation

The other major symptom of PTSD is intrusive-repetitive ideation (Horowitz & Solomon, 1975). Intrusive-repetitive thoughts become so problematic for the individual that they begin to dominate existence. Intrusive thoughts generally take the form of visual images that are sparked by sights, sounds, smells, or tactile reminders that bring the repressed images to awareness (Donaldson & Gardner, 1985, pp. 371–372).

Billie Mac: That day at the village when Al got it keeps coming back. I don't go fishing in the bayou any more. It smells and looks like Nam, and every time I'd go I start thinking about that village.

Accompanying emotions of guilt, sadness, anger, and rage occur as the thoughts continue to intrude into awareness. To keep these disturbing thoughts out of awareness, the individual may resort to self-medication in the form of alcohol or drugs. Use of alcohol and drugs may temporarily relieve depressive, hostile, anxious, and fearful mood states (Horowitz & Solomon, 1975), but what usually occurs is a vicious cycle that alternates between being anesthetized to reality by the narcotic and experiencing elevated intrusion of the trauma with every return to sobriety. The ultimate outcome is increased dependence on the addictive substance as a method of keeping the intrusive thoughts submerged (LaCoursiere, Bodfrey, & Ruby, 1980).

Billie Mac: The drinkin' is no damn good, I know that, but try going without sleep for a week and knowing every time you nod off that horrible nightmare's gonna come. Then it starts popping up in the daytime and you drink more to keep it pushed back.

Family Support

Natural disasters leave so few emotional scars because such disasters often strike intact social support systems simultaneously. In natural disasters that affect the whole community, everyone becomes a survivor. Family members help each other through the horror of the disaster and there is no blaming the victim (Figley, 1985a, p. 409). One of the keystones for bridging the gap between traumatic events and a return to adequate and wholesome functioning is a strong support system that is most generally based within the family. But when the trauma is intrafamilial and takes the form of child and spouse abuse, those who are most traumatized are most generally the ones who are denied the most social support within the family. Those who should provide the most comfort are the ones who are inflicting the most pain (Figley, 1985a, p. 411).

For Vietnam veterans, social support systems were lacking. The perceptual and cognitive alterations and distortions that accompanied a veteran's return home took place for both the veteran and the family. Issues of sex, responsibility, and fidelity emerged early between victim and family (Brende & Parson, 1985, pp. 46–47). For the veteran, dependency issues arise that tend to alienate and push away those on whom the veteran would be most dependent while in transition from the shock of the traumatic event. Whereas hypervigilance and pervasive suspiciousness were mandatory for survival in a combat zone, they no longer fit at home. This fact makes little difference, given the response sets the individual has internalized.

Further exacerbating family relationships is the ingrained tendency to "not feel." Whereas the individual would like to be able to demonstrate feelings of caring and love, experience has taught the victim that exposure of feelings is foolhardy because it invariably makes the victim vulnerable to further pain. These concepts strike at the very heart of what sustains family life—trust. The response of family members is to feel misunderstood, unloved, fearful, and angry. The response is reciprocal and plunges all members deeper into a vortex of family discordance. For veterans, the battle has moved from the field to within themselves and spills over into the rest of the family.

From a family-system perspective, if children, parents, or spouses attempt to regulate the continuing warfare in which the victim is engaging, they will be worn down and out by the effort. The victim may also become so dependent on the stabilizing person (usually the spouse) that the victim's needs breed resentment in anyone else who demands time and effort (usually children). The outcome of this spiral is what the victim may fear most from the support system—rejection. Feelings of guilt, numbing, anger, and loss plague the victim, and the spiral continues ever downward into more inappropriate behavior patterns and ultimate disintegration of the family.

Vietnam veterans are not the only victims bothered with such difficulties. Victims of incest report behavioral and emotional changes involving difficulty with friends, school failure, teenage pregnancy, drug abuse, suicide attempts, sexual acting out, hysterical seizures, intense guilt, rage, anger, and low self-esteem (Donaldson & Gardner, 1985, p. 359). The same is true for rape victims who, if children, may have parents who are psychologically unable to provide support for them, or, if adults, may have a spouse who is unable to respond in supportive ways (Notman & Nadelson, 1976).

Maladaptive Family Responses

Danieli (1985, pp. 299–304) has categorized families of PTSD victims into four distinct types. Although the research was conducted on Jewish families that were victims of the holocaust, the types are generically representative of what those who work with PTSD victims are likely to find. In our own experience, the first three types are characteristic of families of Vietnam veterans and the third type is particularly characteristic of those who have been sexually traumatized or suffered abuse.

Victim. Families of the victim type operate from a closed system, having little interaction with outsiders. A high priority is put on physical, nutritional, and material needs. Security is the watchword. Joy and self-fulfillment are regarded as frivolous. All questions concerning the family's well-being are seen as life-and-death matters. There are no adequate outlets for anger, and there is a lot of survivor guilt. There are overprotection of and overinvolvement with all members of the family, which lead children to have problems in establishing meaningful relationships in general and marital relationships in particular. Children get the message that they are not to outdo their parents, and as a result often unconsciously destroy their successes and accomplishments. Children are often used as mediators in such failing families, yet they are generally powerless to effect any meaningful changes.

Fighter. In families of the fighter type, weakness and self-pity are not permitted. Admonitions to build and achieve are predominant. Pride in one's work and accomplishments are given high family status. Relaxation and pleasure are superfluous. Although there is a great deal of mistrust of and little socialization with outsiders, aggression in the form of achievement and standing up for one's rights is encouraged. The avoidance of any dependence on others and the utter contempt for it in themselves and others are barriers to forming any positive peer or marital relationships. Problems of sharing or delegating responsibility are also viewed as an act of dependence. In order to be seen as adequate, children must assume a "hero" identity, oftentimes placing themselves in risky or dangerous situations to prove their worth.

Numbing. The numbing response to trauma engulfs the whole family. Silence is pervasive and emotions are depleted. The family system consumes its energy by engaging everyone in protecting everyone else. Children are left to their own devices in the business of growing up and often look outside the home for role models and mentors. Since numbing is modeled for the children, they adopt the behavior, with the result that they appear less intelligent and capable than they are. Because the family is immersed in the victim role, children are not the central focus and generally believe themselves not to be worthy of attention. Carried over into their adult lives, the response invariably causes them to seek out relationships in which they are "mothered" by the spouse. Because of their inability to assume responsibility, they generally have problems establishing close relationships with their own children or even wanting to have children.

Those who make it. People who make it are persistent and intent on achieving success. They tend to deny their background and particularly the horrifying experiences they have been through. Children of these families respond bitterly to finding out, usually indirectly, about the problems their parents suffered. These families also experience a great deal of denial and are much like "numb" families. The accomplishments of the survivor of the trauma are paramount in the family. Although proud of parental achievements, children feel a good deal of emotional distance from their parents. Parents in this group often use their influence and money to "ease the path" and thus deny children the logical consequences of their actions.

Maladaptive Patterns

Summed dynamically, PTSD involves five common patterns.

Death imprint. First is a death imprint. Particularly in young victims, the sense of invulnerability is vanquished and is replaced by rage and anger at one's newfound mortality (Lifton, 1975). For veterans in particular, there is a continuing identity with death. The normal boundary between living and dying is suspended. It is not unusual for veterans to describe themselves as already dead. The only way they have of testing the boundary between life and death is to seek sensation, even if it means danger and physical pain (Brende & Parson, 1985, p. 100). Combined with rage reactions, sensation-seeking behaviors put victims squarely on a collision path with law enforcement agencies, employers, and families.

Billie Mac: After every law officer in Mississippi started chasing me, I ditched the car and ran into a woods. They even had bloodhounds after me. I slipped through them like a sieve. It was crazy, but for one of the few times since I've been back I really felt alive. I'd done that a hundred times on patrol.

Survivor's guilt.   Second is the guilt of not being killed when others were. Guilt comes in a variety of forms: guilt about surviving when others did not, guilt over not preventing the death of another, rejection by others for not having somehow been braver under the circumstances, guilt over complaints when compared with others who have suffered more, and guilt that the trauma is partly the victim's fault (Frederick, 1980). Most commonly, guilt takes the form of intrusive thoughts such as, "I could have done more, and if I had he/she'd still be here," or, "If I had just done this or that, it (the trauma) wouldn't have happened." Dynamically, the basis of these thoughts may be relief that the other person was the one to die or the victim was lucky to get off so lightly (Egendorf, 1975).

Billie Mac: I was the only one in my outfit to get out of Tet without a scratch. I wonder why. Why me out of all those people? I've screwed my life up since then. Why did I deserve to get out clean when all those other good men didn't?

Desensitization.   Third is desensitizing oneself to totally unacceptable events and then trying to return to a semblance of normalcy in a peaceful world. Feelings of guilt and fear over pleasurable responses to physical violence to others may occur. These feelings may become so acute that the victim conceals firearms for protection against imagined enemies but is simultaneously terrified of the guns and what might happen because of the violence that continuously seethes below the victim's calm outer appearance. These strong bipolar emotional currents that flow back and forth within the individual lead to hostile, defensive, anxious, depressive, and fearful mood states that find little relief (Horowitz & Solomon, 1975).

Billie Mac: I don't hunt anymore. I hate it. Yet this one guy who was my boss didn't know how close he came to getting killed. I was within one inch of taking him out, I was so hot. It would have been a pleasure, the guy was such an ass.

Estrangement.   Fourth is the feeling that any future relationships will be counterfeit, that they mean little or nothing in the great scheme of things. As the individual attempts to ward off reminders of the experience, severe interpersonal difficulties occur. Because of the vastly different experiences they have undergone, PTSD victims become estranged from their peers and truncate social relationships with them because "they don't understand," and indeed "they" do not. The result is that the individual becomes more isolated from social support systems and develops secondary symptoms that range from neurosis to psychosis (Horowitz & Solomon, 1975).

Billie Mac: I was sitting at my dad's watching TV when Saigon fell. I went nuts and trashed the house. What the hell was it all for? That really cooked it with my old man. I moved out after that and haven't said anything to him since.

Emotional enmeshment.   Fifth is a continuous struggle to move forward in a postholocaust existence, but with an inability to find any significance in life (Lifton, 1975; Lifton, 1973, pp. 191–216). Emotional fixation, particularly for veterans, has disastrous effects on family life. Sent to Vietnam as adolescents, and exposed to prolonged trauma that the majority of the population will never experience, these victims cannot bring themselves to engage in equitable relationships with their families and friends, nor can their families begin to understand their aberrant behavior (Brende & Parson, 1985, pp. 116–117).

Billie Mac: I can't believe what I've done to my kids. I love them more than anything in the world. At times, I'm the greatest dad in the world, coach the little league team, take them everywhere. The next minute I'm all over them. I've knocked them around in a rage and that scares hell out of me. I'm some kind of Jekyll and Hyde and my kids are afraid of me.

Children and PTSD

For children who suffer trauma, much less is known about PTSD. However, case reports of kidnapping (Senior, Gladstone, & Nurcombe, 1982; Terr, 1979), abuse (Green, 1983), animal attack (Gislason & Call, 1982), tornado (Bloch, Silber, & Perry, 1956), and murder of a parent (Eth & Pynoos, 1985) suggest that PTSD is a valid disorder for children. Terr's (1983) in-depth four-year follow-up on children who were victims of the Chowchilla, California, bus kidnapping in the late 1970s substantiates that PTSD does occur with children, although dynamically in somewhat different form. The victims of this trauma were a group of 26 elementary and high school children who were kidnapped together with their school bus, were carried about in vans for 11 hours by their kidnappers, and were buried alive in a truck trailer.

Denial.   Terr (1983) found that the children still had specific feelings of traumatic anxiety over the event after four years. When asked to speak about it, children generalized their anxiety from the event to statements like, "I'm afraid of the feeling of being afraid." Unlike combat veterans, who might boast about harrowing experiences, the children were profoundly embarrassed by their experience, were unwilling to talk about the event, and shied away from any publicity. They generally voiced feelings of being humiliated and mortified when asked about their experience. Whereas eight of fifteen children

dren overcame their fear of vehicles such as vans and buses, they still reported occasional panic attacks triggered by unexpected sudden confrontation with stimuli such as seeing a van parked across the street from their house and vaguely wondering if some of the kidnappers' friends had not come back for them.

Eighteen of the children were found to employ suppression or conscious avoidance of the trauma. Parents often aided them in this endeavor, although the two children whose parents encouraged them to talk about the experience were still not spared its residual effects. Their typical response was that they hated the feeling of helplessness they experienced and needed to feel in control of the situation.

All the children could remember almost every second and minute of the contents of the event. However, they were able to remember few, if any, of the emotions or behaviors they experienced during the ordeal (Terr, 1983). The work production of adults may seriously decline after such an event, but Terr (1983) found very little decline in the children's school performance, although Eth and Pynoos (1985, p. 44) believe that continuous intrusion of a traumatic event, evolution of a cognitive style of forgetting, and interference of depressed affect with mental processes very definitely influence school achievement.

Intrusion. Terr (1983) found that intrusive thoughts did not repeatedly enter the children's conscious thoughts; however, sleep brought very different problems. Whereas a few reported daydreams, the children had nightmares through which ran many repetitious themes of death (Pruett, 1979; Schetky, 1978; Terr, 1983). The children believed these dreams to be highly predictive of the future and made comments like this: "I'm 11 now but I don't think I'll live very long maybe 12, cause somebody will come along and shoot me" (Terr, 1983). Adolescents in particular are brought face to face with their own vulnerability and, in the case of those who have experienced the murder of a parent, report that they will never marry or have children because they fear history will be repeated (Eth & Pynoos, 1985, p. 48).

Reenactment. The play of these children is very distinctive because of its thematic quality, longevity, dangerousness, intensity, contagiousness to siblings, and unconscious linkage to the traumatic event (Bergen, 1958; Maclean, 1977; Terr, 1981). The clearly prevalent dynamic is a continuing reenactment of their plight during the trauma (Eth & Pynoos, 1985, p. 42). This thematic play can be characterized as burdened, constricted, and joyless (Wallerstein & Kelly, 1975). For adolescents, reenactment may take the form of delinquent behavior that is similar to that of their adult counterparts (Eth & Pynoos, 1985, p. 47). Delinquent acts ranging from truancy, sexual activity, and theft to reckless driving, drug abuse, and obtaining weapons are typical of traumatized adolescents (Newman, 1976).

Physical responses. Physiologically, approximately half the children of the Chowchilla kidnapping manifested physical problems that could be construed to be related to the trauma of being held prisoner without food, water, or bathroom stops (Terr, 1983). In young children, regression may occur and previously learned skills such as toilet training may have to be retaught (Bloch, Silber, & Perry, 1956).

Displacement.   A great deal of displacement of affect occurred, with emotions about the event being shifted to a related time, an associated idea, or another person—particularly the interviewing psychiatrist. Prior to the follow-up interviews, children displayed a variety of displaced behaviors, including the belief by one of the children that the psychiatrist had placed notes posing questions about the kidnapping in her school locker (Terr, 1983).

Transposition.   One of the most profound changes occurred in transposition of events surrounding the trauma. Events that happened after the trauma got changed to having happened before the trauma (Terr, 1983). Also, there was a general belief that those events were predictive of what was about to happen to them (Ayalon, 1983). Children attempted to resolve their vulnerability and lack of control by saying they should have listened to the omens and "shouldn't have stepped in the bad luck square" (Terr, 1983). Such distortions of time have become part of the child's developing personality and are attempts to take personal responsibility and even feel guilty for events over which they had no control.

Terr's (1983) study indicates that whereas children behave differently from adults in their attempt to resolve the traumatic event, they are no more flexible or adaptable than adults after a trauma, and it would be erroneous to assume that they "just grow out of the event." Further, these children did not become toughened by their experience, but simply narrowed their sphere of influence in very restrictive ways to control their environment better.

INTERVENTION STRATEGIES

The crisis intervention strategies used with clients suffering from PTSD are drawn heavily from the six steps in crisis intervention and related concepts found in Chapter 2. Special emphases are integrated into the intervention to attend to the unique needs of PTSD clients. The cases, dialogues, and exercises incorporate and apply both the fundamental skills described in Chapter 2 and the special emphases which pertain to PTSD.

Assessment

Although the MMPI has been found to differentiate veterans from controls on clusters of problems dealing with intimacy and sociability (Roberts, Penk, & Gearing, 1982; Merbaum, 1977) and indications are that PTSD victims have elevated scores on the Beck and Zung Depression Scales (Keane et al., 1985), no paper-and-pencil test currently predicts PTSD across trauma types. The structured interview probably remains the best diagnostic device for determining if a victim has PTSD. Figley's very comprehensive Structured Interview for PTSD (Figley, 1985b, pp. 424–438), although specifically aimed at Vietnam veterans, could be adapted to almost anyone who is suspected of having PTSD. Exclusive of combat-related questions, the interview covers the kind and degree of PTSD symptoms the client is suffering, along with associated features such as depression, anxiety, substance abuse, legal problems, relationship problems, premorbid adjustment, and a mental status exam. However, the survey is somewhat lengthy and not likely to be used by an intake interviewer unless PTSD symptoms are clearly pronounced.

Exploratory interview. Any intake interview should allow the client full range to describe current problems without interference by the interviewer. The interviewer should carefully consider what the client is saying about the problem in comparison with the PTSD criteria listed in the DSM-III. Symptoms should be carefully gleaned for their frequency, duration, intensity, and pervasiveness. Masking but indicating symptoms of PTSD also include substance abuse, violence and aggression, domestic problems, bad employment records, paranoid ideation, auditory or visual hallucination, magical thinking, delusions, and autonomic arousal. Virtually all PTSD victims will report variations on a theme of chronic anxiety and depressive symptoms including sleep and appetite loss, anhedonia, guilt, and suicidal ideation (Keane et al., 1985, pp. 269–277). The interviewer should, with great sensitivity, attempt to discern if there are functional relationships between these symptoms and antecedent events.

A clear distinction between individuals with character disorders and those suffering from PTSD is their affiliative responses. In general, victims of PTSD avoid interpersonal relationships, as opposed to exhibiting the ingratiating gregariousness of a sociopath. PTSD victims have few close friends, prefer being alone, and discuss few intimate details of their lives. Unexpected contact with other people or stimuli reminiscent of the traumatic event may make victims extremely "jumpy" and "edgy" (Keane et al., 1985, p. 270).

Thus, during an intake interview, the wise human service worker will attempt to elicit any biographical data that may uncover distant traumatic events. The human service worker should never dismiss a report, no matter how trivial it may seem, of involvement in a catastrophic situation (Scurfield, 1985, pp. 238–239). Because PTSD victims may be very reluctant to talk about the trauma they have been through, human service workers should attempt to obtain background information from relatives, co-workers, and any other persons who have personal knowledge of the victim. The personal history is particularly important when substance abuse is involved, because if PTSD is not identified, all the efforts of the worker will not ameliorate the substance-abuse problem. The watchword for the interviewer is to be suspicious that presenting symptoms may be masking PTSD, and the human service worker attempting to formulate an initial diagnosis would do well to mentally check off presenting problems against DSM-III criteria for this disorder.

We cannot emphasize the foregoing recommendation too strongly, especially for those clients who present themselves in a depressed state. Our own clinical experience with such clients has uncovered many who have suffered sexual abuse as children. We are coming more and more to believe that, until ruled out, PTSD should be a suspected causative agent. However, getting at it may prove extremely difficult, particularly on account of the severe social taboos associated with talking about incestuous and abusive relationships. Therefore, in an initial assessment, even though the interviewer may have a strong hunch that repression of a traumatic event is causing the problem, the causative agent should never be exposed, interpreted, or even guessed until a high degree of trust has been built (Scurfield, 1985, pp. 238–239).

Children. For children, exploration of a traumatic event may best be achieved by having them use various play media (Gumaer, 1984). Eth and Pynoos (1985, p. 37) propose having children draw their feelings of the event and tell a story about it. James and Myer (in press) report that for very young children, the use of puppets may serve to establish a bridge of trust between the human service worker and the child and reduce the threat of relating traumatic experiences to an adult. By using play media, the child will often alert the human service worker to current means of coping and ways of defending against the trauma (Eth & Pynoos, 1985, p. 37).

Phases of Recovery

Brende and Parson (1985, pp. 185–186) have compiled the work of Wilson (1980), Figley (1978), and Horowitz (1976) to construct five phases of recovery in the PTSD victim. These phases directly parallel treatment approaches, and each has its own crisis stage.

1. *The emergency or outcry phase.* The victim experiences heightened "fight/flight" reactions to the life-threatening situation. This phase lasts as long as the survivor believes it to last. Pulse, blood pressure, respiration, and muscle activity are all increased. Concomitant feelings of fear and helplessness predominate. Termination of the event itself is followed by relief and confusion. Questions about why the event happened and what its consequences will be dominate the victim's thoughts.

2. *The emotional numbing and denial phase.* The survivor protects psychic well-being by burying the experience in subconscious memory. By avoiding the experience, the victim temporarily reduces anxiety and stress symptoms. Many victims remain forever at this stage unless they receive professional intervention.

3. *The intrusive-repetitive phase.* The survivor has nightmares, volatile mood swings, intrusive images, and startle responses. Other pathological and antisocial defense mechanisms may be put into place in a futile attempt to rebury the trauma. It is at this point that the delayed stress becomes so overwhelming that the victim is propelled to seek help or becomes so mired in the pathology of the situation that outside intervention is mandated.

4. *The reflective-transition phase.* The survivor develops a larger personal perspective on the traumatic events and becomes positive and constructive, with a forward- rather than backward-looking perspective. The victim comes to grips with the trauma and confronts the problem.

5. *The integration phase.* The survivor successfully integrates the trauma with all other past experiences and restores a sense of continuity to life. The trauma is successfully placed fully in the past.

Neat and orderly progression for the PTSD victim through these stages is the exception rather than the rule. What is more likely to occur is a precipitative crisis far removed in chronological time from the event itself and then a continuing series of crises that escalate until the victim voluntarily seeks help or is forced to seek it. Once intervention occurs, a cyclic pattern of avoidance, recall, recovery, and more avoidance continues until the core issues that gave birth to PTSD are resolved (Figley, 1985a, pp. 402–404). The human service worker can expect a series of crises as this process unfolds.

Initiating Intervention

As disequilibrium from the trauma subsides, some form of reorganization takes place. The reorganized state is either adaptive or maladaptive, and it is important to intervene before maladaptive reorganization occurs (Scurfield, 1985, p. 239); otherwise treatment may become much more difficult (Horowitz, 1976, p. 123). In the best of all possible worlds, treatment for the psychological problems associated with the catastrophe would begin immediately after its occurrence. Processing of a stressful event in an ideal manner would allow the victim to perceive the event correctly and objectively, translate perceptions into a clear meaning, relate the meaning to enduring attitudes about life, decide on appropriate action to be taken, and, finally, revise attitudes, memories, and beliefs to fit a new developmental direction made necessary by the experience (Horowitz, 1976, pp. 112–114). Generally, people refuse early intervention because they either see the event as too difficult to deal with or believe that people of good character ought to be able to cope with such events on their own without outside intervention. It is these two faulty assumptions that get victims into the delayed part of the disorder, where most of the treatment population will emerge.

Another problem compounding treatment is the various personality types of victims. The paranoid victim will play out an accusation theme, which leads to more and more compartmentalized, defensive, fearful, and angry behavior. The hysterical victim will have uncontrollable experiences of dread and anxiety. The obsessional personality type will continuously ruminate about whether or not correct action was taken (Horowitz, 1976, p. 114).

Acceptance

If we have been relentless in stressing the need for excellent listening and responding skills, congruence, empathy, and genuine positive regard for the client, it is because our experience teaches that these are absolute musts in crisis intervention. Nowhere does this axiom hold more clearly than in the case of PTSD victims. Not only are they essential in enabling the human service worker to make a clear and adequate assessment, but also, given the variety of negative and conflicting emotional baggage the victim brings to the session, it is absolutely paramount that the human service worker provide an accepting atmosphere so that the victim can start to recount and encounter the trauma. The human service worker must walk a tightwire here, both reflecting the fears and anxieties of the victim in a helpful and understanding way and also gently probing to uncover the events that precipitated the current problems. This must be done carefully, for premature discussion about the traumatic event would be insensitive and likely lead to verbal and psychological shutdown by the victim (Brende & Parson, 1985, p. 163).

However, as soon as is feasible, the human service worker should attempt to reflect the client's feelings about the traumatic experience and establish a foundation for mutual understanding (Walker & Nash, 1982). Disclosure of the trauma is difficult for the PTSD victim, because recounting what has happened may be horrifying and socially unacceptable. Also, open-minded acceptance of the client's story may be extremely difficult for and repugnant to the human service worker, but if therapeutic progress is to be made, nothing less will do (Brende & Parson, 1985, p. 178).

Billie Mac: (Thinking to himself.) If I tell about killing that kid what will the counselor think? A baby killer, that's what! Yet, it's bugging the hell out of me. (Slowly tells the counselor about the incident.)

HSW: (Stating personal feelings.) I know how hard it was for you to talk about that. A part of me wonders how you or anybody could ever kill a child. However, I understand how scared you were, wondering whether he had a grenade, what a moral quandary that put you in, and the guilt and anguish you feel as you recall the incident.

Risks of Treatment

It is also incumbent upon the human service worker to state clearly the risks inherent in treatment. It may be hard to make such statements and to propose a poor prognosis, but it is a safe bet that the victim will silently have pondered many of the same questions. After the initial crisis has passed, and the victim is back to a state of at least semiequilibrium, the human service worker should convey clearly the following risks, as outlined by Brende and Parson (1985, pp. 168–174):

1. There may be only partial recovery; there are no magical cures for this tenacious and pernicious problem.
2. Because of the continuing nature of the crisis, either long bouts with hospitals or weekly trips to the therapist are required and play havoc with keeping a job.
3. As catharsis of the event occurs, it is inevitable that the victim gets worse

before getting better. Fear of a psychotic breakdown may occur as the victim learns more about the disorder.

4. As the struggle to find oneself goes forward, personality change may put heavy burdens on interpersonal relationships as significant others see a very different person emerge from the therapeutic experience.

5. Psychic pain may become almost intolerable as the victim reexperiences disturbing memories and emotions that, as they are voiced, may cause rejection by friends and professionals alike.

6. Because of the numerous self-constraints placed upon volatile emotions, the victim may fear that giving vent to those emotions will lead to uncontrolled anger and result in physical harm to others. Because of the hurt suffered, it will also be very difficult for the victim to give up the idea of revenge on both real and imagined perpetrators of the traumatic event.

7. Because of the compartmentalized and constricted lifestyle that follows the trauma, the victim will safeguard against change and may have extreme difficulty following directions and doing what others may suggest, no matter how reasonable and proper. Giving up such maladaptive self-reliance will put the victim at the mercy of others, a seemingly intolerable situation.

8. A great deal of pain will result from coming to accept the world as it is with all its frailties and injustices. In attempting to gain reentry into such an imperfect world, the victim is in danger of losing patience with it and falling back into the vortex of PTSD.

9. Correlative with accepting the frailties of the world is also the acceptance of one's own set of infirmities; bad memories may return; relationships may not always be excellent; others may obtain better jobs for no legitimate reason. Acceptance of oneself, including the guilt, sorrow, and regret that goes with it, is the sine qua non of getting through PTSD, but it may be an extremely difficult and fearsome task that will call for far more courage than surviving the catastrophe itself.

The Veterans Center

In view of the risks, what kind of help can a victim of PTSD expect, and where? Because of the large numbers of victims and the agitation and subsequent legislation to fund help for them, let us turn to the Vietnam veteran and the many Vietnam veterans centers scattered throughout the country for a working treatment model. Veterans centers provide a variety of services to their constituents, covering all kinds of readjustment counseling. They do crisis intervention, do referral and follow-up on medical disabilities, assist with legal problems, upgrade less-than-honorable discharges, consult with police departments and parole officers, and provide job placement and vocational counseling (Brende & Parson, 1985, pp. 210–211). Since 1979, veterans centers have served 300,000 men and women and have performed outreach services to 60,000 more (Brende & Parson, 1985, p. 113). Most important, the centers and their staff members have been in the forefront in developing therapeutic approaches with PTSD cases.

A key component of the veterans center's attack on PTSD is its multimodal approach, and from this standpoint it probably has material, professional, financial, and other resource advantages, particularly its alliance with VA hospitals, that other mental health facilities lack. However, its therapeutic approach can be instituted with almost any type of PTSD victim, can be used in any setting, and would seem to have particular utility with victims of rape, incest, and child abuse (Donaldson & Gardner, 1985, p. 373). The principal initiating components of this treatment approach are the "rap" or self-help and support group tied in with individual therapy from counselors at the center. From what is now known about PTSD, the combination of group and individual therapy appears most efficacious.

Group work is helpful because of the shared experience, mutual support, sense of community, reduction of stigma, and restoration of self-pride it fosters. Confrontation by peers is more acceptable than confrontation by professionals because it is reality oriented (Scurfield, 1985, pp. 247–248). Groups also serve an educative function. One of the first jobs of the human service worker in the veterans center is educative in nature. PTSD victims coming to seek help for the first time are scared. Although they have been able to overcome some tremendous physical adversities, the psychological ones they now face are confusing and frightening. The terrifying nature of PTSD calls for clearly delineating what is happening and why. Answers to questions of victims such as "What are common PTSD symptoms?" "Why do victims use drugs?" "What are definitions of words like 'secret,' 'conscience,' 'anger,' 'helplessness,' 'love,' and 'trust'?" "How long will it take to get better?" "Am I crazy?" "What do I do in this situation?" "Will I ever be as I was before this happened?" help build a cognitive anchor for the victim.

Individual therapy is used to buttress the supportive atmosphere of the group and to deal specifically with crises idiosyncratic to the victim's life. In both group and individual therapy, it is important for two reasons that therapists working with the victim keep in close touch with one another (Brende, 1981). First, engaging in both kinds of therapy has the potential to result in therapeutic drainage. Important issues brought up in one setting may not be transferred to the other (Ohlsen, 1970, p. 122). Second, because of the distinct possibility of transference and countertransference issues, it is extremely easy for the individual therapist to get trapped psychologically with such emotionally volatile groups and lose objectivity. Cotherapists that work closely together in planning and coordinating activities are highly beneficial (Brewi, 1986).

Rap Groups

Rap groups were started for veterans in 1970 by Robert Lifton and Chaim Shatan in New York City. Lifton and Shatan were human service professionals who had become disaffected with the Veterans Administration's constant refusal to acknowledge that many Vietnam veterans were suffering from combat-induced psychological problems. An outgrowth of Veterans Against the War, a protest movement, the rap groups were a vehicle for those men who felt that they could not make sense out of their experience and found common ground with other men who were experiencing the same problems (Egendorf, 1975). Rap groups became the members' own therapy groups, without the benefit of professional psychotherapy. Indeed, the rap group was probably started as a reaction to human service professionals who had done a generally poor job with veterans in the first place. The veterans' experience with the formal structure of therapy merely augmented their existing anger toward authority (Lifton, 1978; Shatan, 1978). The outcome of this dilemma was that professionals finally came to recognize the success of rap groups and integrated them into more traditional formats (Walker, 1983).

The human service worker who works with such groups needs some special qualifications. Distrust and suspicion are strong in the early stage of such groups, and human service workers can be expected to be tested over and over again until they have proven themselves to be congruent and trustworthy (Gressard, 1986). Our own experience shows this to be true regardless of whether or not the human service worker has had experiences similar to those of the victim.

Veterans groups are conducted with veterans as leaders because of the defensiveness and hostility with which most veterans view professionals who have not undergone the Vietnam experience. This is problematic because of the shortage of human service workers who meet both professional and experiential qualifications of victims. As a result, it is advisable to use a veteran as a coleader (Gressard, 1986). One could extrapolate this notion to group work with other kinds of trauma victims. The problem is that such professionals are often not readily available for the particular kind of trauma event with which the human service worker is dealing. Therefore, the Vietnam Veterans Center of Memphis has published a list of 12 rules of the road for establishing credibility of nonveterans who work therapeutically with veterans (Memphis Vietnam Veterans Center, 1985).

1. He has the experiential knowledge you don't have; you have the clinical and technical knowledge he doesn't have. Together you can forge a working alliance.
2. Make your desire to understand come across so that considerable experiential gaps are bridged.
3. Realize that the veteran wants you to help him help you understand. In the process, he recreates and reexperiences the sources of the problems and you, by providing the therapeutic climate, gain an in-depth understanding of the Vietnam experience.
4. A female therapist serves as a role model, i.e., a woman who can understand and accept the victim for what he is, which has important effects on the veteran.
5. Clinical experience and expertise with Vietnam veterans is built over time—as

your understanding and technical expertise grows, you will be accepted in the group and accepted as the leader despite your lack of direct experience.

6. As a nonveteran, you can challenge the defense of exclusivity, i.e., as one who wasn't there can't understand, thus serving to break through his feelings of isolation and "contamination."

7. Your military combat naivete often helps the veteran to explore and express himself. In his effort to help you understand, he uncovers areas of conflict.

8. At the same time, because of your naivete, you must guard against becoming too involved in Vietnam problems and memories thereby "triggering" situational stress which may need immediate attention and treatment.

9. Realize that moral conflicts will probably be raised for you personally as stories unfold; guard against any display of emotional revulsion to a vet who describes real atrocities. Be nonjudgmental and objective.

10. Guard against overidentification with the vet or hero worship, or you will blunt your problem-solving ability.

11. Expect to need controls and to have to clearly enforce them for your sake and the vets—don't try to do therapy with a vet who is drunk or "stoned," refuse to be a party to long tirades on the phone, bar all weapons and mean it.

12. Heed the signs of burnout: thinking or talking too much about your clients to others, finding yourself having combat-like nightmares, etc. Step back and evaluate whether you may be too immersed in trying to do too much for too many.

One further admonition is necessary for any human service worker who would work with such victims. Frick and Bogart (1982) identified one of the stages that veterans go through as "rage at their counselor." This stage is important as part of coming to terms with authority and nonveterans. Human service workers need to deal with such anger by owning their mistakes in being insensitive to issues, accepting and reflecting the victim's anger while at the same time not being defensive, containing impulsive responses after being attacked, owning their own anger, and not becoming discouraged and giving up when attacked.

Therapeutic Sequence

The chronology of events that occurs, while elastic, operates in the following manner. Once a PTSD client is stabilized, the human service worker suggests participation in the group. No demands are made of the individual (Brewi, 1986). The human service worker issues an invitation something like this:

HSW: We've got some guys that meet on Wednesday night to talk about many of the problems you're trying to deal with now. I think you've got a lot in common with them and believe it might be helpful for you to meet them. They've all been in Nam and are trying to come to terms with their experiences there. You don't have to talk if you don't want to, that's up to you. You'll probably feel a lot of different emotions, and some of those aren't going to be too pleasant. However, all of the guys you'll meet have been feeling a lot of the same kinds of things even though they may have different kinds of problems that brought them into the vet center. From that standpoint they all know what you're going through, and while it may get tough, they'll support you and not pass judgment. I'd really like to see you come in.

Once the individual agrees, he comes to the group, which meets for an hour and a half. The group is composed entirely of Vietnam veterans. The first item is that individuals are asked to introduce themselves by name and unit. This structured event is not just for the purpose of getting into war stories; it also serves to move men psychologically back in time to the starting point of their trauma and to cement the "we-ness" of the group. After introductions, anything on anybody's mind is fair game for conversation.

The group will be composed of "veterans" who have been through many such sessions and "greenhorns" who are at their first meeting. As in any other group, there will be some problem members who are monopolizers, some who are hostile and acting out, scapegoats, socializers, and a constellation of other typical group members (for a complete description of problem clients, see Ohlsen, 1970, pp. 164–192). Occupationally, members will range from lawyers, doctors, carpenters, and electronic technicians to the unemployed, parolees, and hospitalized substance abusers. Topics range from problems of day-to-day living to the government, families, the war, and how all these problems affect them.

The leaders at the Memphis center are two social workers and a clinical psychologist, all with combat time in Vietnam, but they are not group therapists in the truest sense of the word. They are more like participatory members who have been endowed with the task of keeping the group within loose guidelines concerning time, monopolizing the group, facilitating support and responses from the other members, and, in a few extreme instances, acting as empathic but firm sergeants-at-arms. As leaders they must be willing to keep a low profile while group members interact. Their leadership role is subtle rather than directive and requires an infinite supply of patience as the group struggles toward resolution of its problems. If therapy in a classical sense of the word is to occur, it happens much later in the game. A clear distinction of the rap from the therapy group is that trauma and its expiation are the main focus and not life adjustment. Life-adjustment problems represent another stage in the crisis of this malady and are handled later. The group is large, ranging from 12 to 24 members. The typical rap group will start something like this:

HSW: Hi, everybody. We've got some new people here and because they don't know everybody I'd like you all to introduce yourself and your unit. I'm George McClellan, 25th division, infantryman, Nam 69–70.

Joe: Joe LaDue, First Air Cav, gunner, Nam 67–68.

Ralph: Ralph Novicki, SEALS, Nam 68.

Billie Mac: B. M. Anson, First Marines, infantryman, Nam 68.

Skeeter: Skeeter Schmidt, Rangers, 69–70 Nam.

Lamont: Lamont Stokes, 101st Airborne, radio operator, Nam 70.

(Introductions continue around the group).

HSW: Has anybody got anything that's hot?

Joe: That poem that George read really hit me last week. I sure wish I could put words together like that. Although I still hate what the NVA did, I can respect them as people individually.

A rather lively discussion takes place regarding the poem, whose main theme is that whatever side a soldier is on, he has the same hopes and fears. Some men have resolved their hatred for the North Vietnamese and others have not. The men loosen up and wheel into other issues. One issue is expressing feelings.

Lamont: Hey! Whatcha mean it's too tough to talk, why not put some of that stuff you feelin' down in here?

Joe: I dunno. What've I got to say?

Lamont: Hey, turkey, we listen to everybody in here, don't we!

Joe: Well, yeaah, but. . . .

Ralph: No "buts" about it. Why doncha give it a try?

Typically, when one member attempts to do something positive in his life, members leap to his support, sometimes pushing, sometimes cajoling, sometimes confronting, but the support and caring are always there. Another generic problem surfaces, the inability to find a job, particularly for those men who are undergoing therapy.

Lamont: I tell you all I am by God sick of it! I put my butt on the line for this country, I ain't never done nothin' wrong, went to church, enlisted and all that shuck. I hurt like hell from the shrapnel still in me. They say I got no problem over to the VA. It's in my mind. Like hell, it be in my legs. I'm no good at workin', can't keep a job, 'cause my legs, can't get no help from them. I'd like to show them what I could do with an M-60.

Billie Mac: (Pushes Lamont to tell specifically what happened and then responds.) Man, I hear that, but if you get off like you are now you're gonna wind up in jail or worse, and I can tell you that's no place to be. I was so down when the wife left that I went off. Oh, yeah, I foxed the cops, but I still wound up in jail. Talk to George or Gene, they've got some clout over there, they can straighten that out.

Lamont: It ain't just the VA, man, it's this whole country that's haywire.

HSW: So the anger goes way beyond the VA, and while we can help you with that, sounds like there's something more eatin' at you.

Billie Mac: Yeah, Lamont! What's stickin' in your craw? You been chewin' on somethin' the last two weeks. What you mad about, man?

Lamont: I dunno. I really dunno. Man, I just get so uptight sometimes I think I'm gonna blow sky high and that scares me pea green, man!

Ralph: (Gently.) We've all been there, and know how tough it is; you knew it'd get worse before it got better, we all told you that. It's hell. You been talkin' to your counselor?

Lamont: Yeah, I been talkin' to Gene. But it just seems like the more stuff comes up, the worse my leg feels.

Because of the mutual support and resources within the group, lots of suggestions are given about how Lamont can grapple with his emotional turmoil. Lamont's anger is a common thread that runs through many members: anger toward the establishment and particularly toward the VA. Ralph's comments offer no great insight, but they are therapeutic in that they are accepting and understanding of the rage and the trauma Lamont feels. Skeeter, a new member of the group, who has been silent throughout the meeting, finally speaks up in a quiet, trembling voice. He is a doctor, with clean-cut good looks, dressed neatly and conservatively, and on first appearance would seem to have everything going for him. That is anything but the case.

Skeeter: I don't know what kind of help I can get here. I'm a doctor. I'm about to lose my license to practice. I'm also in trouble with the law. I wrote a bunch of bogus prescriptions to subsidize my own coke habit. My wife has cleared out with the kids, says she can't take it any more. I'm a nervous wreck. I've been coming here for six weeks talking to George. They dried me out at the VA. He finally talked me into coming to the group. I thought I could handle things. The damn dreams are getting worse. I don't know that anybody can help me with this. Christ, I wasn't much in Nam and now I'm nothing here. (Wipes tears from his eyes.) I can't handle anything. (Holds head in his hands and returns to silence.)

Skeeter is a very erudite man. However, as he tries to find a starting place to talk, his sentences are strung together in disjointed fashion; to admit his problems to this group, men like those he led as a Ranger Captain in Vietnam, is getting close to rock bottom. George has pushed for him to come into the group for quite a while with little success. One might guess that this man, who is so distinctly different from other group members in speech, dress, and occupation, would be greeted with something less than enthusiasm, particularly since he was an officer and most of the group were not.

Ralph: If you could survive for a year in the Nam in the Rangers you can survive this. I mean nobody's poppin' at you with an AK-47.

Skeeter: I don't know, it's like it's all coming undone and I can't stop it.

Lamont: You stayin' off the nose dust and the pills since dryin' out?

Skeeter: Yeah, but I dunno about that either—whether I can go on.

Lamont: You've been off for ten weeks ever since the VA cleaned you out and you come here, I'd say that's somethin'. Do it one step at a time. You livin' and you clean. I was savin' this, but I'm gonna say it now. Look at me, man, how screwed up I am, but it's been a year and I ain't been on that crap. (General applause and some derisive but good-natured cat-calls. Lamont smiles.) You think you no better than me, well, that's a crock. You here now and that took guts, so you got a lot of help. We wiped you officers' noses in Nam, so what's the difference now? (General laughter from the group.)

Lamont, who has been vitriolic in ventilating his feelings, switches roles and becomes a support person to Skeeter. In mutual help groups like this, such role shifts are common and the need to become a helper rather than a beneficiary is extremely important (Silverman, 1986). It is indicative of the progress that members of mutual help groups can make toward becoming integrated with the mainstream of living. George, the leader of the group, recognizes this shift and wisely lets Lamont carry the dialogue. George's major contribution, besides summing what has been said, is to reinforce Lamont for his role shift.

HSW: What I hear everybody saying is that while those are some stiff problems, that they've been there, and know what you're going through. You're also doing something right now, even though you may not think so. You've taken three steps in your own right. Going to the VA, coming in here to see me, and then coming into this group. I don't think it could be said any better than Lamont said it. We're here to help each other, and that's what it's all about, man. It makes me proud to be a vet. Thanks, Lamont.

Lamont: (Smiles sheepishly.) Aw, man, don't be layin' that shine on me.

Ralph then begins a long-running commentary about a friend who is a mercenary and now is MIA in Afghanistan.

Billie Mac: Well, that's tough. But from what you're saying, you could have saved him, Superman, and now you're taking a guilt trip on that. Ain't we been here before?

Ralph: If I just wasn't stuck in this wheelchair. How could he have done such a stupid thing? No way he couldn't take out a tank on his own and that's how I hear he got it.

Joe: Wheelchair or not, you can't do a thing for him. If he's gone he's gone. I'm not sure what it is for you, feeling guilty, cause you've talked about that before with guys who bought it in Nam, angry because what happened to you to get you in that chair, sorry he got it, or what. You talk about all that crap like it still goes on and don't do much about it now. What about you, man, and your future? We ain't in no war and you ain't gonna go to one unless it's the Handicapped Olympics War.

A general heated discussion ensues, which ranges from losing one's buddies to the rightness of Vietnam and government support for it and whether Joe has any right to pick on Ralph in the manner he has.

Joe: Hey, man, you know me better than that! I love you, you big dumb ape, and that's why I said that to you, 'ceptin' you don't wanta hear that about livin' past time when you know that's the truth.

Confrontation is not unusual in these groups. Probably more than in most mutual help groups, at times a great deal of heated discussion and confrontation go on. Although this is not an encounter group, the members are not shy about calling some pretty straight shots. Such confrontations may initially meet with little acceptance or even with hostility, but the underlying trust that has been built up enables such hard-hitting statements to be made with little interference from the leaders.

As the group session closes, each member is given the floor to speak on what has personally occurred for him during the meeting. No one else is allowed to respond to his comments. Summing statements include both reflections about the impact of the discussion on oneself and reinforcing comments to others. Finally, the group rises, joins hands, and has a silent moment of meditation. One of the authors, who has been a practitioner in the helping professions for 20 years, found, in visiting this group, one of the most moving moments of his professional life. The emotionally positive high voltage that flowed through the locked hands of some very tough men was both touching and powerful, and it conveyed far better than words the caring and support each man felt for his comrades.

As each man speaks of his experiences, the human service worker continues to educate the group about what occurs with the disorder. The men learn that traumatic experiences can produce psychological maladjustment in anyone. They come to understand that intrusive imagery, startle responses, rage, anger, and unresolved grief are common and continuing occurrences. They come to see the fear of losing control as a by-product both of training and of closely guarding emotions to keep from experiencing the full onslaught of the disorder and realize that it does not mean they are crazy. Although some of the symptoms may never go away, they see men who have gotten better and learn that the condition is amenable to treatment. At the very least, with work, the disorder can be controlled or reduced in severity and frequency of occurrence. Finally, the men are reinforced over and over by leaders and their peers for being strong enough to have experienced what they did and be in the group talking about their problems.

Evidence seems to suggest that victims who have suffered other types of catastrophic intrusion into their lives can profit from support groups such as the veterans center uses. Donaldson and Gardner (1985) report that incest victims quickly gain an intense sense of relief in coming together with other victims in mutual support groups. Typical comments are, "No one else understands, but I can come out of the closet here." A Vietnam veteran, when asked where he could be found six months hence, said, "Six months from now . . . come here on Wednesday night 'cause these are the people that care about me." When asked why this was so important, the veteran said, "I don't have to explain anything to anybody here, what it was like, or how I felt if I don't want to, but if I do, they all understand 'cause they been there."

Defining these groups at a deeper level is Foulkes's (1948) comment that such support groups can reinforce each other's normal reactions and break down each other's pathological reactions because they collectively constitute the very norm from which the individuals deviate. As such, members of the veterans rap group have what one member called very good "crap detectors": "We can smell it immediately when somebody isn't coming clean with us."

Combat Group

Once a given evening's session has ended, the group is split in two. Some of the men go into what is called the combat group and the others go into the life-adjustment group. Participation in either of the two groups depends on the member's stage of recovery.

Because Vietnam veterans are both victims and victimizers, the combat group serves as a cathartic agent. The group is built along the lines of the small squad units that operated in Vietnam. Each member is asked to re-count combat experiences there and reflect upon its impact on him both then and now. The group's purpose is best summarized in the statement of Ralph:

Ralph: I was a SEAL, and this country didn't make anybody better at the jobs of in-terdiction, murder, mayhem, and efficiently slaughtering the enemy than us. As soon as I arrived in the country, they took us out in the bush and got us blooded. I waited on the trail and we ambushed a group of VC. I mean this wasn't long-range stuff, this was up close and personal. I killed an old man with a Bowie knife. Cut his throat and got his blood all over me. He was the first of many. Sure, he was carrying an AK-47 and I have no doubt that he would have offed me, but I still can't get that old guy out of my mind. I don't know why, but he's the guy I dream about.

Unlike the free-wheeling rap group, with its laissez-faire attitude, the com-bat group is designed specifically to dig up buried emotions. The leaders make conscious attempts to weld the experiences generated by combat into what is happening "here and now." Given Horowitz's (1976, p. 115) premise that no stress response syndrome is ever a matter of a single conflicted train of ideational and affective responses, the twists and turns over various con-tent and time frames are probably appropriate and to be expected as the men hopscotch between Vietnam and their contemporary world. Free associ-ation is encouraged, and one monologue leads into another. The leader en-courages as much detail as possible, seeking clues to long-buried guilt and anger. Such clues may give the human service worker material to use in indi-vidual sessions with clients.

For some men, speaking of what has happened to them is extremely difficult. Billie Mac, who has been silent for many weeks in the combat group, finally gets up and, protesting that he has never written anything longer than a postcard, reads the following:

Where Did B. M. Go?

What happened to B. M.—the boy from Mississippi—happy-go-lucky, not a care in the world, who loved life, sports, the sunshine, the rain . . . and everything in the used-to-be-beautiful world. Everyone told B. M., "Go to school. Play sports. Go to college. Make everyone proud of you. B. M., you are one of a kind!" But B. M. de-cided to do for his country. B. M. wanted to go to war and fight to win . . . to serve his country . . . to make everyone proud of him. B. M. went to war, B. M. killed, mas-sacred, mutilated, burnt, hated—a hate that was like a drunk hate—tore his own heart out a little at a time, time after time.

B. M. fought and survived a war that one hundred twenty seven warriors that went with B. M. didn't. B. M. hated and was cold and mean. B. M. didn't care whether he came home or not. B. M. looked at everyone around him and wondered why the people hated him. Why they were scared of him . . . why they feared the warrior from Vietnam who went to a fight they were scared to fight.

B. M. wanted to love . . . to be loved. It seemed like the world was completely dif-ferent from him and didn't have the same ideals about life and love.

B. M. became a drunk. He drank to forget the war, the brave warriors who had given their lives in Vietnam, to forget the people that he was living around. To these people B. M. was a cold-blooded murdering S.O.B.—a baby-killing M.F.

B. M. had been taught all his life, "Thou shalt not kill, love thine enemy." B. M. lost his morals. B. M. killed his enemies. B. M. cut the heads off some of his enemies. B. M. cut the ears off and mutilated them. B. M. lost his soul. B. M. is lost to God, to the world—and that B. M. can't be forgiven. He has committed an unforgivable sin to man and God's will. People can say, "Ask God to forgive you, B. M." But B. M. can't forgive himself and can't ask for forgiveness. B. M. feels that if he dies he is going to hell. B. M. has accepted that as part of his life. B. M. has accepted that feeling like someone took his heart out and stomped it into the ground. B. M.'s life is full of hurt and pain. There is not a day in his life that he doesn't feel hurt or hurt the ones he loves.

B. M. just wants to be loved . . . to love himself again; to get rid of that hard feeling deep down inside of his heart. B. M. wants to have peace of mind, to be at peace with himself and his heart. Is it too much for him to ask, to seek, to search for? Is death what it will take for B. M. to finally find peace within himself?

Why can't B. M. get out of all these depressing moods he stays in . . . and cries about nothing when he is driving down the road.

Sometimes B. M. thinks he is a crazy S.O.B. Maybe the people are right. Why can't B. M. keep a job? Because B. M. was a fuckup after he got back from Vietnam. His vengeance and his screwed up attitude keep him in trouble. B. M. would get so much on his mind and B. M. would keep putting it back inside. The more he put it back, the worse his depression would get until it would erupt in a rage of vengeance, which would always wind up hurting himself or the people he loved. People would say, "Don't worry, B. M., things will get better. We will help you. Now help yourself." If B. M. knew how to help himself, he wouldn't be in the shape he is in. Even the government deceived B. M. They told B. M., "Don't worry, B. M. You go and fight this war for your country and if anything happens we will take care of you." B. M.'s response to this is, "Fine! I will do all I can for my government and my country." But give me my heart and soul back. Make me sleep at night. Make me quit crying. Take this depression away. Help me find a job and help me feel alive again. Give me back what you took from me. B. M. is what you took and I want myself back. I've done everything you wanted of me, so just give myself back to me.

I wish I could give back the lives I have taken from the world, but I know that I can't. I would if I could and I am the one that will have to live with that in my heart throughout eternity.

Upon completing his reading of this cathartic statement, B. M. runs from the group sobbing, goes to the bathroom, and vomits.

B. M. vividly and dramatically illustrates the anguish of PTSD in his writing: anguish from both an intra- and interpersonal standpoint, of guilt he feels within himself for his moral travesties and rage at the travesties visited on him by an impersonal government and an uncaring society; anguish over what he was and is and how he is now attempting to resolve and reintegrate these two vastly different people that were and are B. M. Billie Mac continuously uses his nickname, pointing over and over to himself, but in the third person. Only in the last paragraph does his plea change clearly to subjective, first-person, owning statements. Even these statements are couched in terms of magical thinking—wish fulfillment. This is typical of the kind of self-condemnation that an individual who is both victim and victimizer experiences.

This excruciating piece of writing is an initiating step in the long process that moves from self-condemnation to what Lifton (1973) calls *animated guilt.*

Animated guilt enables the victim to start taking responsibility for past actions and start to experience new degrees of personal liberation. B. M.'s first step, though small, is significant. The self-destructive behaviors of 15 years are starting to give way.

This rather dramatic example of journal writing was done voluntarily, but when clients in a crisis situation will not talk about their experiences, sometimes suggesting that they write down their feelings can be a way of breaking the impasse (Gilliland, James, Roberts, & Bowman, 1984, pp. 287–294). After Billie Mac returns to the group, the human service worker pursues the idea of keeping a journal (Pearsons, 1965).

HSW: B. M., everybody thought that was great. Could you do some more of that? I mean write those feelings down whenever.

Billie Mac: I dunno. I mean, I just couldn't sleep and I just set down and started in. That was terrible.

Chorus from the group: You're wrong! George wasn't kidding! That was tough! I wish I could have done that! That was great, terrific!

By putting down their thoughts in their own words and then hearing them, victims place the terrible memories at a safe enough psychological distance that they and the human service worker can analyze them (Cienfuegos & Monelli, 1983). Journal writing gives the human service worker a catalyst for encouraging the kind of free association necessary to open the crystallized defenses of the victim who might otherwise never open up and explore the traumatic event (Progoff, 1975).

Yet, as catharsis takes place within the combat group, one may hypothesize as to the extent of the rehashing of old battles fought. For these very tough men, trained to the very best of their ability, the combat experience did not happen 20 or more years ago. It is as if they just got off the plane and back into the "world" yesterday. The vivid detail of combat situations gives one cause to wonder if indeed this is old-war-story time or really is something therapeutic.

It is easy to see in some of these men a great deal of ambivalence concerning combat. While suffering horrible events, they were also on an all-time adrenalin high. They agonize over their present situation but continuously retreat into the days when they rose to the sound of gunfire. While they protest that they love their families and wish to change their ways of behaving toward them, one wonders if they love the call of battle even better.

An alternative hypothesis may be advanced. For these men, the combat group is a psychological detoxification process. Addicts who are just coming out of detoxification know full well the agony of not being able or not wanting to remember what happened to them. To come to grips with the buried trauma that helped produce that dependence may be an awesome task. First, as stories are continuously repeated, individuals move from the content of the episode to the emotional baggage that shields the true horror of the event from awareness. Long-buried guilt over what the victim did or did not do begins to emerge. Details that start one way slowly shift until the focus is on the affective reaction of the individual while the event was occurring. Much as the children of the Chowchilla bus kidnapping played "abduction" games over and over again in an attempt to sort through the traumatic event, patience and time are necessary to allow the adult victim to sort through the content of the trauma. As this occurs, the emotions that the altered content preserves begin to see the light of day.

Life Adjustment

As the guilt and horror of the combat situation are resolved, the men are moved into the life-adjustment group, which may be the more difficult one, and another crisis ensues. It is not enough to bring to light hidden traumatic experiences. The key is to integrate past experiences, to find meaning and new ways of coping, making atonement not only for oneself but for others, and find new directions in life (Brende & Parson, 1985, pp. 199–201). The group at this point will diminish and absences will increase. The reason is twofold. First, threatening material will again be covered. Second, action and behavioral change now become mandatory. Moving from the insight gained about what happened in the past to taking that insight and applying it to present time is a giant step, and one that is guaranteed to be rife with crisis. What is now called for is to get on with the business of living. At this juncture, intervention will take many forms, depending on what the particular problems are that the individual faces. Such problems range from serious substance abuse to obtaining saleable vocational skills. Most of these problems will be referred to human service workers who are skilled in dealing with the individual's particular problem. The life-adjustment group will serve as a common base in which members can trade success stories and receive reinforcement and encouragement for their efforts.

However, one thread will usually run through the circumstances of all men at this stage. That thread is of vital importance and must be rewoven into the fabric of their lives. It is their family. Whereas any of these men could fight in a barroom brawl and give a good account of themselves, wrestling with the close intimacy of interpersonal problems and the intrapsychic strain under which that puts them is quite another story, particularly with regard to reconciliation with and atonement to family members.

The veterans center also makes available a support group for the women close to these men. The group is both educative and cathartic in nature and provides a forum for the women as they struggle to make sense out of what the men in their lives have been going through and what is yet to come. The women's group runs concurrently with the rap group. For any victim who has PTSD, the ripple effects that spread out to their family reach far and wide. As strange as it may seem, while families may be stressed to the limit in adapting to the PTSD victim, they do try to adapt, at times in pathological ways. As the victim changes, the family may be in for a rude awakening and not be able to make parallel changes. This problem is clearly evident in the section on dynamics and in what our composite veteran, Billie Mac, has to say.

When families reach this stage, they are usually referred to family system specialists for conjoint therapy. For this group, to get through the crisis of re-learning how to be effective members of their families and society will call for the same kind of courage that propelled them into the veterans center in the first place, although this time it may be much more difficult because they will be working with the people whom they need and have hurt the most.

Individual Intervention

Stress reduction. Individual therapy goes hand in hand with group work. From crisis stage to crisis stage, a multimodal therapeutic approach is used (Scurfield, 1985, p. 250). In the first phase of recovery, the emergency or out-cry phase, the major problem is to get the victim stabilized; this means reducing the anxiety and physical responses associated with the trauma. Meditation, relaxation, and biofeedback may be used (Kolb & Mutalipassi, 1982).

In relaxation training and meditation the human service worker teaches the victim how to relax body muscle groups systematically and to focus calmly on mental images that produce psychic relief of body tensions and stress (Benson, 1976; Wolpe, 1958). Victims learn how to exercise self-control over many of their stresses and anxieties and dampen debilitating physiological responses.

HSW: OK, Billie Mac. Just imagine that you are lying on the beach with that soft warm sand, the calm breeze blowing gently over you, the gentle lapping of the cool, crystal-clear water, and just easily focus your attention on that scene. Now just notice the difference in your body too. Notice the difference between how your muscles feel when they are tense and relaxed. Starting with your legs, just tense them up, feel how your muscles tighten up. Now relax them, and just feel that tightness drop away. Notice the difference and the really pleasant feelings that occur when your muscles are just hanging loose and flaccid. Continue to picture the scene on the beach as you work your way up your body, alternating between tensing and relaxing your muscles. Notice as you continue to do this how you can change the way your body feels and what you can focus on in your mind's eye.

Extinguishing intrusive images. Once the victim has learned how to relax, other therapeutic strategies such as systematic desensitization, thought stopping, flooding, implosion, and Gestalt techniques may be employed (Black & Keane, 1982; Fairbank & Keane, 1982; Keane & Kaloupek, 1982; Marafiote, 1980; Parson, 1984; Scurfield, 1985).

The human service worker continues to work slowly through the relaxation exercises and the mental imagery, continuously reinforcing the client for being able to shift to calm, relaxed scenes and away from the intrusive, anxiety-producing images. Practice for the victim in this and the other techniques to be covered in individual therapy is important. We recommend that sessions be audiotaped so that the victim may practice the procedures at home on a daily basis.

Once the victim has learned how to relax, the second phase of intervention occurs, coincident with the victim's emotional numbing and denial phase of recovery. This phase is concerned with bringing to conscious awareness the traumatic event and the hidden facts and emotions about it that the victim denies (Brende & Parson, 1985, pp. 191–192). A favorite phrase of the Vietnam infantryman, "Screw it, it don't mean nothing," aptly characterizes this stage and what has to be done. In a gentle but forceful way, the human service worker guides the victim, in the here-and-now of the therapeutic moment, to reexperience in the fullest possible detail what occurred in the traumatic experience so that submerged feelings are uncovered and ultimately expunged (Scurfield, 1985, p. 245). While deeply relaxed, the victim is asked to reexperience the terrible events of the trauma, with the injunction that at any time the memories can be switched off and the victim can return to the pleasant image of the beach.

HSW: Now go back to the village and tell me what is happening.

Billie Mac: (Lying down, relaxed, eyes closed.) The point man all of a sudden comes under fire and gets popped. I see him get hit. He's lying in the open across a ditch about 100 meters from the tree line. It's really getting hot, a lot of fire from concealed bunkers. They're using him as bait. This goes on for about five minutes, I guess. All of a sudden I decide to go and get him. Me and some other guys just get up and run across the open field to the ditch. We're getting all kinds of fire and out of five of us, only me and Al make it to the ditch without getting dinged. The point man is only about five meters from me, but I can't get at him. (Billie Mac breaks into a sweat with slight tremors.) I finally spot where the concealed bunker is that's making it so hot for us. I've got a LAW [light antitank weapon] and I get a bead on the bunker and zap it. At about the same time there's an explosion right next to me, a B-40 grenade, I guess, and that's all I remember until I wake up on the medivac chopper. (Breaks into profuse sweating and major tremors.)

HSW: All right, just shift out of that scene and back to the beach and just relax. Notice the cool water, the warm sand, the gentle breeze, and just let your muscles relax. (Billie Mac noticeably relaxes and, with continued directives from the human service worker, returns to a calm, relaxed state.)

Although the account of the combat situation is fearsome in its intensity, the human service worker suspects that it alone is not responsible for the traumatic reaction. Billie Mac was in many such situations, but this village is the focal point of his nightmares and intrusive thoughts. The human service worker suspects that there is more here than what Billie Mac is revealing, and seeks to slowly peel away the psychological walls that defend the trauma from awareness. The human service worker believes that the recounting of the combat situation, despite having psychological value as a defense mechanism, is probably not historically accurate. The victim has left out certain traumatic parts of the story and the human service worker's job becomes one of trying to fill in the gaps (Horowitz, 1976, pp. 117–118). Having built a very strong rapport and mutual trust with the victim (Keane et al., 1985, p. 291), the human service worker probes into the situation and actively seeks to interpret and clarify the content of the client's story with respect to its potentially overwhelming effect (Scurfield, 1985, p. 245).

HSW: Go back to the village and the ditch right before you take out the bunker. What do you see?

Billie Mac: I see the point man, he's alive, but bad off.

HSW: What are you thinking?

Billie Mac: I've got to get him, but I can't, the fire's too heavy.

HSW: What do you feel?

Billie Mac: Scared, I um . . . I can't seem to do anything . . . the rounds are really coming. . . .

HSW: What's happening around you?

Billie Mac: Al keeps yelling, "Take the bunker out with the LAW!"

HSW: Then what?

Billie Mac: I . . . can't . . . do it . . . it . . . I'm terrified. (Starts to shake uncontrollably.)

HSW: Stay right with that, Billie. I'm right here.

Billie Mac: Al grabs the LAW, stands up and fires it and—Oh, my God! Get down! Oh, Jesus, the B-40 got Al. He's gone. His blood's all over me. . . . I killed him. It was my job and I couldn't do it and I killed Al. (Breaks into uncontrollable sobbing and shaking.)

HSW: It's OK! Just erase that scene from your mind and slide back to that warm quiet beach. Just put yourself out of the fire fight and back to that beach and relax, just focusing that soft sand in your mind.

As the victim breaks through the defenses that have allowed him to numb and shield the actual events from awareness, the full force of the reality of the incident floods over him, along with the overwhelming feelings of fear, guilt, remorse, and terror that accompany the event. As these thoughts come into awareness, they give the human service worker a much clearer picture of the how and why of Phase 2 (denial and numbing) and those of Phase 3 (intrusive-repetitive thoughts). The human service worker, using tolerable doses of reminiscence of the event, seeks to push forward into full awareness what the true scene at the event was and not what the victim's mind has fantasized it to be.

HSW: Now shift out of the scene at the beach and go back to the village. The B-40 has just gone off and Al is gone. What happens next?

Billie Mac: I can't remember . . . I don't know . . . I passed out.

HSW: (Gently.) Yes, you can. Just think a moment and picture the scene.

Billie Mac: Oh, God! You've got to get the point man now, Al took the bunker out and died doing it. You've got to go get him. I'm up and running, the fire is terrible, it's only 20 feet to him but it's like a mile, I'm so damn scared. (Breath coming in rapid, ragged gasps.) I've got him and am dragging him back to the ditch. Bullets are kicking up all around me, I'll be cut in two. He weighs a ton. I get to the ditch and roll him and me into it. I turn him over and . . . Oh, Mother of Mary! He's dead. Why, oh why, didn't I get there sooner? I could have saved him. You puke-faced coward. (Starts uncontrolled sobbing.)

HSW: (Very calmly.) You are OK. Just shift out of that scene and back to the beach. Just take all the time you need to relax and erase that scene from your mind. Just let the cool breeze blow over you, smell the clean salt air and enjoy that feeling of being completely relaxed. (Time passes, and Billie Mac becomes noticeably more relaxed.) Now I'm going to count up from one to ten and when I reach ten you'll be fully alert and refreshed.

The human service worker does this and brings Billie Mac back to present time. The worker then processes the events of the imagery session with Billie Mac. At this point, the worker uses a more psychodynamic approach, actively intervening in the situation through clarification and interpretation of what the client says.

HSW: So it's not just that terrible fight at the village, but more what you didn't do. You feel as if you were a coward there, and that cowardice cost the life of your friend. It's almost as if all these years you'd been trying to atone for that in the only way you know how. That is, by doing things that would almost guarantee that you die too. The brushes with the law, the uncontrollable rage that winds up in knock-down, drag-out fights, the DWIs, and the suicide attempt.

Billie Mac: I don't know. (Sobbing.) I feel so terrible about it. How could I have frozen? It would have been better if I had got killed rather than live with this.

HSW: Yet you did act. You went after the man, and you couldn't know whether a minute or two would have saved his life. It seems as if that minute or two of indecision has caused 15 years of terrible retribution that you can never pay off. I'd like to suggest that it has been paid with interest and now the time has come to pay the balance. Are you willing to do that?

Billie Mac: (Shakily.) I guess . . . although I don't know how much more I can take.

HSW: Remember! We've made it this far. Trust me and yourself. Together we can pull through this.

Even if the human service worker is right on target with his interpretation, getting Billie Mac to integrate the material and also allowing him to reconcile himself to the event are much more difficult matters. Although it can be extremely traumatic for the client, the human service worker will attempt to encourage the client to experience the full range of emotional responses that he felt at the time of the event, as well as how he tried to make sense of it (Donaldson & Gardner, 1985, p. 370). This marks the fourth phase of the crisis, the reflective-transition phase (Brende & Parson, 1985, p. 192). The human service worker will do this by combining behavioral techniques of flooding and thought stopping.

Flooding. In flooding (Stampfl & Levis, 1967), the fear-evoking stimuli are presented continuously. The rationale is that if the victim is literally flooded with anxiety-provoking stimuli for several periods of from one to two hours, the client will discover that there is no basis for fear. Continuously flooding the client causes the stimuli generating the anxiety to be imploded; that is, repeating the response without reinforcement will cause the tendency to perform that response to diminish. As the victim reenacts the trauma, the human service worker puts in the missing pieces of the puzzle and ferrets out all conditioned stimuli buried in memory. The result is that no noxious components of memory will be left to recondition debilitating responses (Keane et al. 1985, p. 265). This technique is a very serious therapeutic endeavor and should not be undertaken by neophytes until they have received supervised training.

Under no circumstances do we believe that flooding should be used with children, up to approximately sixteen years of age. Rather, we would propose that children be taught how to relax and slowly be desensitized to the trauma (Wolpe, 1958) or that a person-centered approach utilizing various play media be used to let the child slowly work through the trauma (Eth & Pynoos, 1985; Gumaer, 1984).

Thought stopping. Thought stopping is a simple but powerful device that allows the victim, with help from the human service worker, to change debilitating, intrusive thoughts to self-enhancing ones. The human service worker initially sets the scene and builds the images until the fear-evoking stimuli are at maximum arousal, and then shouts "Stop!" and replaces them with positive, self-enhancing thoughts (Williams & Long, 1979, p. 285). The human service worker tells the victim that at the point when the intrusive scene is most terrifying, the human service worker will slam a book sharply on the table and state in a firm voice, "Stop! Shift back to the beach!" The victim will be passive throughout the procedure, with the human service worker setting and enhancing the scene. An audio tape of the session is made, and the client is given the assignment of listening to the tape and then using the procedure whenever the intrusive images occur.

HSW: Now erase the beach scene and come back to the village. You're in the ditch. Bullets are snapping angrily over your head. Smell the stench of that ditch, feel death all around you, eagerly licking its chops. You can almost see the grim reaper there. Feel the frightening aspect of that scene. You'd like to run away, but there's nowhere to run. Oh, what a fool you were to ever make the dash out here in no-man's-land. Look back and see your squad members shot up, contorted in pain, with the blood and dirt covering them. Peek over the ditch and see the point man, he's in terrible pain, screaming for help, but there's a blizzard of fire coming from the bunker. It's certain death to stick your head above the dike. Feel the conflict. You want to do something, you know you've got to take the bunker out, but you are paralyzed. You can smell the fear in you, sweating out of your pores. Look at Al, he expects you to do something, you're the squad leader, but you can't. Feel Al's stare. Listen to him yelling, "Take the bunker now, man." Your fingers are glued to the LAW. Feel Al grab the LAW. Watch him as he stands up in that dreadful hail of death and fires the LAW into the bunker, and in the next instant see the explosion and the dirt fly as the B-40 round hits and Al disappears in the flame and smoke. Smell the smoke of cordite and the sheared copper odor of blood. Enhance those images—hear, smell, feel, see, taste that terrible moment. It's all there now as it really was. (Billie Mac is writhing in the reclining chair.) NOW STOP! (Slams book down on desk.) Shift away.

Billie Mac: (Screaming.) I can't do it!

HSW: Yes, you can! Just slide out of that and into that soft warm sand. Stay with that beach scene, smell the salt air, the cool breeze, and know that you can do that any time you want. Notice the difference in how your body feels, what goes through your mind. Just enjoy that feeling of knowing you can move into that scene.

This sequence is repeated over and over until the victim is able to switch volitionally from the intrusive image to the relaxing one with ease.

Gestalt techniques.   The Gestalt techniques of reaching into the victim's past and bringing to conscious awareness what Gestalt practitioners call "unfinished business" is particularly helpful in draining the pustulant affect that infects the event (Scurfield, 1985, p. 246). For Billie Mac this technique will take a different twist and will be the last part of the crisis, that of making atonement, penance, and restitution (Horowitz & Solomon, 1975).

HSW: The empty chairs in front of you represent various people. Al, the point man, other members of your squad that got hit on that day in the village. I want you to tell them what you felt about what you did. I may move to one of the chairs or have you take their place. Right now I want you to imagine Al in that chair over there. What are you going to say to him?

Billie Mac: I'm . . . so sorry. I froze. I shouldn't have done that. I killed you and I can't ever forget that.

HSW: (Takes the chair of Al.) Hey, man, what about that time at Chu Lai, and the A Shau valley? You didn't freeze then. You saved my bacon then. Remember how I froze. You didn't say squat. You think you're perfect?

Billie Mac: You were my best friend and I let that happen. It was my job. (Sobs.)

HSW: (As Al.) You think you got a corner on the market. Everybody was scared. I just did it. You gave me back my life a half dozen times. I'll never forget that. You did well by me, buddy. I got no regrets.

Billie Mac: Jesus, I miss you, I loved you so damn much.

HSW: (As Al.) Then remember the good times we had. That R & R in Bangkok, when we took the town apart. Those are the parts I remember. I love you too, buddy, but it's time we were done with that village. There's no forgiving to be done. You did your part plenty. It's time for you to say good-bye to me. (The HSW gets up and goes over and takes Billie Mac into his arms and hugs him. Billie Mac weeps, releasing a flood of emotion.)

For each man in the squad, the scene is replayed. Sometimes Billie Mac takes the role of the other man, and sometimes the human service worker does. Each piece of unfinished business is slowly and patiently worked through until Billie Mac has reconciled accounts with each person who was there on that terrible day. Clearly, Billie Mac goes through a painful but necessary grieving process that must take place if he is to put the event behind him (Brende & Parson, 1985, p. 105). As Billie Mac makes atonement for that day long past, and the trauma is expunged, the human service worker seeks to pull him to the present time and help him move forward with his life. Intensive intervention slacks off and the victim may then go through a series of booster sessions on an "as needed" basis, with a minimum of a booster session once a month for three to four months (Balson & Dempster, 1980). This point marks the fifth, or integration, phase of the crisis.

One way survivors move from the tightly wrapped intrapersonal world of agony they have lived in to a more self-actualized and healthy interpersonal focus is to use their experience to help other victims (Lifton, 1973, pp. 99–133). Listen to two veterans, one a volunteer and one a professional in the human service field.

Jim: I'm in the group not because of what happened in Nam. I'm pretty much through that. A year's worth of the VA and some excellent help from other people got me over being nuts. I'm here because I owe those folks and maybe, I'm not sure how, to pay some back for what I got.

George: Why did I become a social worker at the vet center? Because I'd been in Nam, hassled with my own stuff, and thought I knew something about it and could help other people. Frankly, I think I've done about all I can here, and I believe I'm ready to start something else professionally. I'm going back to school and would like to concentrate on working with kids.

For both of these men, the ghosts of PTSD are exorcised. They have integrated all aspects of the traumatic experience, both the positive and the negative. They know pretty clearly who they were before, during, and after the event. They have accepted responsibility for their own actions, as imperfect as those actions may have been at the time, and have made atonement for any guilt they carried (Scurfield, 1985, p. 246). George, in particular, manifests a forward view. Trauma changed his life dramatically. He grew from it and became a human service worker who dealt with the very problem he had conquered. He is now ready to move forward into other areas of human service. He has become more than a survivor. He has become a full-fledged member of the human race again, and though it may seem a meaningless platitude to some, he is a better person for it.

SUMMARY

Posttraumatic stress disorder (PTSD) has multiple symptoms and for that reason is often confused with a variety of other disorders. Its basis is found in maladaptive adjustment to a traumatic event. The disorder is both acute and chronic. In its chronic form it is insidious and may take months or years to appear. Its symptoms include, but are not limited to, anxiety, depression, substance abuse, hypervigilance, intrusive-repetitive thoughts, sleep disturbance, poor social relationships, suicidal ideation, and denial and numbing of the traumatic event. Both natural and man-made disasters may be responsible for PTSD, but it is far more likely to occur in victims who have been exposed to some man-made disaster that should have been prevented and is beyond accepted moral and societal bounds.

PTSD has probably been in existence as long as humankind has been rational enough to personalize the disasters that assail it. However, it was the debacle of the Vietnam War that brought it enough publicity to become a classifiable malady. The psychologically virulent milieu that was Vietnam became a ripe breeding ground for trauma, which found its way back to the United States in an estimated 800,000 service personnel who have PTSD or related disorders.

Slow to recognize the disorder, human service professionals did little to ameliorate problems returning veterans suffered. Self-help groups were started by veterans when they had no other place to turn. Through lobbying efforts by such men as Dr. Arthur Blank, funding for Vietnam veterans centers was set up throughout the United States. Along with other mental health professionals who had been grappling with the problems of veterans and other victims of trauma, staffers at the centers began developing treatment approaches for PTSD. Most notable of the techniques have been the rap groups developed at the veterans centers, which are a combination of support and therapeutic catharsis groups. Continuing treatment includes both group and individual intervention that is multimodal in nature.

We hope that Vietnam and its dark legacy have passed from the scene and that such mass mental health problems are a one-time occurrence for this country. However, investigation of PTSD has taught us that many other trauma victims do not just "grow out" of their trauma and that time doesn't heal all wounds. Victims of trauma, especially of those types that originate in familial or severe sexual abuse, are prime candidates for PTSD. Bringing PTSD into the light of day has also disclosed many victims who were previously unknown to the mental health profession or were thought to be suffering from other kinds of disorders.

If PTSD has taught the human services one thing, it is that no traumatic experience should ever be dismissed in a cursory manner and that any initial assessment of a crisis client should investigate the possibility of a traumatic event buried somewhere in the client's past. Assessment and intervention are particularly difficult when the traumatic event is of a familial or sexual nature. A great deal of finesse and skill is necessary to uncover and treat such problems because of clients' reluctance to talk about socially taboo subjects or the feeling that a person, especially a man, should have the intestinal fortitude to bear up under the trauma. From what we now know, the latter assumption is patently false; under the right circumstances, anyone can fall victim to PTSD.

Interest in both cause and cure of PTSD has initiated a tremendous upsurge in research in the past few years. An excellent, comprehensive summary and discussion of PTSD may be found in the Brunner/Mazel Psychological Stress Series (Figley, 1978, 1985b; Figley & McCubben, 1983; McCubben & Figley, 1983). For any human service worker who would like more first-hand information from practitioners, the Vietnam veterans centers scattered throughout the United States are an excellent resource.

REFERENCES

American Psychiatric Association (1980). *Diagnostic and statistical manual of mental disorders* (3rd ed.). Washington, DC: Author.

Archibald, H. C., Long, D. M., Miller, C., & Tuddenham, R. D. (1962). Gross stress reaction in combat—a 15 year follow-up. *American Journal of Psychiatry, 119*, 317–322.

Askevold, F. (1977). War sailor syndrome. *Psychotherapy Psychosomatics, 27*, 133–138.

Atkinson, R. M., Henderson, R. G., Sparr, L. F., & Deale, S. (1982). Assessment of Viet Nam veterans for posttraumatic stress disorder in Veterans Administration disability claims. *American Journal of Psychiatry, 139*, 1118–1121.

Atkinson, R. M., Sparr, L. F., & Sheff, A. G. (1984). Diagnosis of posttraumatic stress disorder in Viet Nam veterans: Preliminary findings. *American Journal of Psychiatry, 141*, 694–696.

Ayalon, O. (1983). Coping with terrorism. In D. Meichenbaum and M. Jaremko (Eds.), *Stress reduction and prevention.* New York: Plenum.

Balson, P., & Dempster, C. (1980). Treatment of war neurosis from Vietnam. *Comprehensive Psychiatry, 21*, 167–176.

Benson, H. (1976). *The relaxation response.* New York: Avon.

Bergen, M. (1958). Effect of severe trauma on a 4-year-old child. *Psychoanalytic Study of the Child, 13*, 407–429.

Black, J. L., & Keane, T. M. (1982). Implosive therapy in the treatment of combat related fears in a World War II veteran. *Journal of Behavior Therapy and Experimental Psychiatry, 13*, 139–165.

Bloch, D. A., Silber, E., & Perry, S. E. (1956). Some factors in the emotional reaction of children to disaster. *American Journal of Psychiatry, 113*, 416–422.

Bower, G. H. (1981). Mood and memory. *American Psychologist, 36*, 129–148.

Brende, J. O. (1981). Combined individual and group therapy for Vietnam veterans. *International Journal of Group Psychotherapy, 31*, 367–378.

Brende, J. O. & Parson, E. R. (1985). *Vietnam veterans: The road to recovery.* New York: Plenum Press.

Breuer, J., & Freud, S. (1955). Studies on hysteria. In J. Strachey (Ed. and Trans.), *The standard edition of the complete psychological works of Sigmund Freud* (Vol. 2, pp. 1–10). London: Hogarth Press. (Original work published 1895.)

Brewi, B. (Speaker) (1986). *Crisis intervention with the Vietnam veteran* (Cassette recording No. 9). Memphis: Department of Counseling and Personnel Services, Memphis State University.

Cienfuegos, A. J., & Monelli, C. (1983). The testimony of political repression as a therapeutic instrument. *American Journal of Orthopsychiatry, 53*, 43–51.

Daly, R. J. (1983). Samuel Pepys and post-trauma stress disorder. *British Journal of Psychiatry, 143*, 64–68.

Danieli, Y. (1985). The treatment and prevention of long-term effects and intergenerational transmission of victimization: A lesson from holocaust survivors and their children. In C. R. Figley (Ed.), *Trauma and its wake: The study of post-trauma stress disorder* (pp. 295–313). New York: Brunner/Mazel.

DeFazio, V. J. (1978). Dynamic perspectives on the nature of combat stress. In C. R. Figley (Ed.), *Stress disorders among Vietnam veterans* (pp. 36–37). New York: Brunner/Mazel.

Donaldson, M. A., & Gardner, R., Jr. (1985). Diagnosis and treatment of traumatic stress among women after childhood incest. In C. R. Figley (Ed.), *Trauma and its wake: The study of post-trauma disorder* (pp. 356–377). New York: Brunner/Mazel.

Egendorf, A. (1975). A Vietnam veteran rap group and themes of post-war life. *Journal of Social Issues, 31*, 111–124.

Erikson, E. (1968). *Identity, youth, and crisis.* New York: Norton.

Eth, S., & Pynoos, R. S. (1985). Developmental perspective on psychic trauma in childhood. In C. R. Figley (Ed.), *Trauma and its wake: The study of post-trauma stress disorder* (pp. 36–52). New York: Brunner/Mazel.

Fairbank, J. A., & Keane, T. M. (1982). Flooding for combat-related stress disorders: Assessment of anxiety reduction across traumatic memories. *Behavior therapy, 13*, 499–510.

Figley, C. R. (Ed.). (1978). *Stress disorders among Vietnam veterans.* New York: Brunner/Mazel.

Figley, C. R. (1985a). From victim to survivor: Social responsibility in the wake of catastrophe. In C. R. Figley (Ed.), *Trauma and its wake: The study of post-trauma stress disorder* (pp. 398–416). New York: Brunner/Mazel.

Figley, C. R. (Ed.). (1985b). *Trauma and its wake: The study and treatment of post-traumatic stress disorder.* New York: Brunner/Mazel.

Figley, C. R., & McCubben, H. I. (Eds.). (1983). *Stress and the family: Vol. 2. Coping with catastrophe.* New York: Brunner/Mazel.

Fischer, V., Boyle, J. M., & Bucuvalas, M. (1980). *Myths and realities: A study of attitudes toward Vietnam era veterans.* Washington, DC: Lou Harris Associates.

Foulkes, S. H. (1948). *Introduction to group analytic psychotherapy.* London: Heineman.

Frederick, C. (1980). Effects of natural vs. human-induced violence: Evaluation and change. Minneapolis Medical Research Foundation, Inc./NIMH, Mental Health Services Development Branch. *Special issue: Services for Survivors,* pp. 71–75.

Freud, S. (1959). Introduction to psychoanalysis and the war neurosis. In J. Strachey (Ed. and Trans.), *The standard edition of the complete psychological works of Sigmund Freud* (Vol. 5). London: Hogarth Press. (Original work published 1919.)

Freud, S. (1963). Introductory lectures on psychoanalysis XVII. In J. Strachey (Ed. and Trans.), *The standard edition of the complete psychological works of Sigmund Freud* (Vol. 16). London, Hogarth Press. (Original work published 1917.)

Frick, R., & Bogart, M. L. (1982). Transference and countertransference in group therapy with Vietnam veterans. *Bulletin of the Menninger Clinic, 46,* 429–444.

Furst, S. S. (1967). A survey. In S. S. Furst (Ed.), *Psychic trauma.* New York: Basic Books.

Furst, S. S. (1978). The stimulus barrier and the pathogenicity of trauma. *International Journal of Psychoanalysis, 59,* 345–352.

Gilliland, B., James, R., Roberts, G., & Bowman, J. (1984). *Theories and strategies in counseling and psychotherapy.* Englewood Cliffs, NJ: Prentice-Hall.

Gislason, I. L., & Call, J. D. (1982). Dog bite in infancy: Trauma and personality development. *Journal of the American Academy of Child Psychiatry, 21,* 203–207.

Goldenson, R. M. (1984). Post-trauma stress disorder. *Longman dictionary of psychology and psychiatry.* New York: Longman.

Green, A. (1983). Dimensions of psychological trauma in abused children. *Journal of the American Academy of Child Psychiatry, 22,* 231–237.

Gressard, C. F. (1986). Self-help groups for Vietnam veterans experiencing post-traumatic stress disorder. *Journal for Specialists in Group Work, 11,* 74–79.

Grinker, R. R., & Speigel, J. P. (1945). *Men under stress.* Philadelphia: Blakiston.

Gumaer, J. (1984). *Counseling and therapy for children.* New York: Free Press.

Horowitz, M. J. (1976). *Stress response syndromes.* New York: Aronson.

Horowitz, M. J., & Solomon, G. F. (1975). A prediction of delayed stress response syndromes in Vietnam veterans. *Journal of Social Issues, 31,* 67–80.

Horowitz, M. J., Wilner, N., Kaltreider, N., & Alvarez, W. (1980). Signs and symptoms of post-trauma stress disorders. *Archives of General Psychiatry, 37,* 85–92.

James, R. K., & Myer, R. (in press). Puppets: The elementary counselor's right or left arm. *Elementary School Guidance and Counseling.*

Keane, T. M. (1976). *State dependent retention and its relationship to psychopathology.* Unpublished manuscript, State University of New York at Binghamton.

Keane, T. M., Fairbank, J. A., Caddell, J. M., Zimmering, R. T., & Bender, M. E. (1985). A behavioral approach to assessing and treating post-trauma stress disorder in Vietnam veterans. In C. R. Figley (Ed.), *Trauma and its wake: The study of post-trauma stress disorder* (pp. 257–294). New York: Brunner/Mazel.

Keane, T. M., & Kaloupek, D. G. (1982). Imaginal flooding in the treatment of post traumatic stress disorder. *Journal of Consulting and Clinical Psychology, 50,* 138–140.

Kelman, H. (1945). Character and the traumatic syndrome. *Journal of Nervous and Mental Disease, 102,* 121–153.

Kolb, L. C., & Mutalipassi, L. R. (1982). The conditioned emotional response: A sub-class of the chronic and delayed stress disorder. *Psychiatric Annals, 12,* 969–987.

LaCoursiere, R. B., Bodfrey, K. E., & Ruby, L. M. (1980). Traumatic neurosis in the etiology of alcoholism: Vietnam and other trauma. *American Journal of Psychiatry, 137,* 966–968.

Laufer, R., Yager, T., & Grey-Wouters, E. (1981). Post-war trauma: Social and psychological problems of Vietnam veterans in the aftermath of the Vietnam War. In A. Egendorf, C. Kadushin, & R. S. Laufer (Eds.), *Legacies of Vietnam* (Vol. 1). Washington, DC: U.S. Government Printing Office.

Lifton, R. J. (1973). *Home from the war: Vietnam veterans—neither victims nor executioners.* New York: Simon & Schuster.

Lifton, R. J. (1974). "Death imprints" on youth in Vietnam. *Journal of Clinical Child Psychology, 3,* 47–49.

Lifton, R. J. (1975). The postwar war. *Journal of Social Issues, 31,* 181–195.

Lifton, R. J. (1978). Advocacy and corruption in the healing profession. In C. R. Figley (Ed.), *Stress disorders among veterans* (pp. 209–230). New York: Brunner/Mazel.

Longman dictionary of psychology and psychiatry. (1984). New York: Longman.

Maclean, G. (1977). Psychic trauma and traumatic neurosis: Play therapy with a four-year-old boy. *Canadian Psychiatric Association Journal, 22,* 71–76.

MacPherson, M. (1984). *Long time passing: Vietnam and the haunted generation.* New York: Doubleday.

Marafiote, R. (1980). Behavioral strategies in group treatment of Vietnam veterans. In T. Williams (Ed.), *Post-traumatic stress disorders of the Vietnam veteran* (pp. 49–70). Cincinnati: Disabled American Veterans.

McCubben, H. I., & Figley, C. R. (1983). *Stress and the family: Vol. I: Coping with normative transitions.* New York: Brunner/Mazel.

Memphis Vietnam Veterans Center. (1985). *The nonveteran helper.* Unpublished pamphlet of the Memphis Vietnam Veterans Center.

Merbaum, M. (1977). Some personality characteristics of soldiers exposed to extreme stress: A follow-up of post-hospital adjustment. *Journal of Clinical Psychology, 33,* 558–562.

Moses, R. (1978). Adult psychic trauma: The question of early predisposition and some detailed mechanisms. *International Journal of Psychoanalysis, 59,* 353–363.

Newman, C. J. (1976). Children of disaster: Clinical observations at Buffalo Creek. *American Journal of Psychiatry, 133,* 306–312.

Notman, M., & Nadelson, C. (1976). The rape victim: Psychodynamic considerations. *American Journal of Psychiatry, 133,* 408–412.

Ohlsen, M. M. (1970). *Group counseling.* New York: Holt, Rinehart & Winston.

Parson, E. R. (1984). The reparation of the self: Clinical and theoretical dimensions in the treatment of Vietnam veterans. *Journal of Contemporary Psychotherapy, 14,* 4–56.

Pearsons, L. (1965). *The use of written communications in psychotherapy.* Springfield, IL: Charles C Thomas.

Progoff, I. (1975). *At a journal workshop.* New York: Dialogue House Library.

Pruett, K. R. (1979). Home treatment for two infants who witnessed their mother's murder. *Journal of the American Academy of Child Psychiatry, 18,* 647–657.

Roberts, W. R., Penk, W. E., & Gearing, M. L. (1982). Interpersonal problems of Vietnam combat veterans with symptoms of post-traumatic stress disorder. *Journal of Abnormal Psychology, 91,* 444–450.

Schetky, D. H. (1978). Preschoolers' response to the murder of their mothers by their fathers. *Bulletin of the American Academy of Psychiatry and Law, 6,* 45–47.

Scurfield, R. M. (1985). Post-trauma stress assessment and treatment: Overview and formulations. In C. R. Figley (Ed.), *Trauma and its wake: The study of post-trauma stress disorder* (pp. 219–256). New York: Brunner/Mazel.

Senior, N., Gladstone, T., & Nurcombe, B. (1982). Child snatching: A case report. *Journal of the American Academy of Child Psychiatry, 21,* 579–583.

Shatan, C. (1978). The emotional content of combat continues. In C. R. Figley (Ed.), *Stress disorders among Vietnam veterans* (pp. 43–52). New York: Brunner/Mazel.

Silverman, P. R. (1986). The perils of borrowing: Role of the professional in mutual help groups. *Journal of Specialists in Group Work, 11,* 68–73.

Speigel, D. (1981). Vietnam grief work under hypnosis. *American Journal of Clinical Hypnosis, 24,* 33–40.

Stampfl, T. G., & Levis, D. J. (1967). Essentials of implosive therapy: A learning-theory-based psychodynamic behavioral therapy. *Journal of Abnormal Psychology, 72,* 496–503.

Terr, L. C. (1979). Children of Chowchilla: Study of psychic trauma. *Psychoanalytic Study of the Child, 34,* 547–623.

Terr, L. C. (1981). "Forbidden games": Post-traumatic child's play. *Journal of the American Academy of Child Psychiatry, 22,* 221–230.

Terr, L. C. (1983). Chowchilla revisited: The effects of psychic trauma four years after a school-bus kidnapping. *American Journal of Psychiatry, 140,* 1543–1550.

Trimble, M. R. (1985). Post-traumatic stress disorder. History of a concept. In C. R. Figley (Ed.), *Trauma and its wake: The study of post-trauma stress disorder* (pp. 5–14). New York: Brunner/Mazel.

Walker, J. I. (1983). Comparison of "rap" groups with traditional group therapy in the treatment of Vietnam combat veterans. *Group, 7,* 48–57.

Walker, J. I., & Nash, J. L. (1982). Group therapy in the treatment of Vietnam combat veterans. *International Journal of Group Psychotherapy, 31,* 376–389.

Wallerstein, J. S., & Kelly, J. B. (1975). The effects of parental divorce: Experiences of the preschool child. *Journal of the American Academy of Child Psychiatry, 14,* 600–616.

Weingartner, H., Miller, H., & Murphy, D. L. (1977). Mood-state-dependent retrieval of verbal associations. *Journal of Abnormal Psychology, 86,* 276–284.

Wilkinson, C. B. (1983). Aftermath of a disaster: The collapse of the Hyatt Regency steel skywalk. *American Journal of Psychiatry, 140,* 1134–1139.

Williams, C. C. (1983). The mental foxhole: The Vietnam veteran's search for meaning. *American Journal of Orthopsychiatry, 53,* 4–17.

Williams, R. L., & Long, J. D. (1979). *Toward a self-managed life style* (2nd ed.). Boston: Houghton Mifflin.

Wilson, J. P. (1980). Conflict, stress, and growth: Effects of the war on psychosocial development. In C. R. Figley & S. Leventman (Eds.), *Strangers at Home.* New York: Praeger.

Wilson, J. P., Smith, W. K., & Johnson, S. (1985). A comparative analysis of PTSD among various survivor groups. In C. R. Figley (Ed.), *Trauma and its wake: The study of post-trauma stress disorder* (pp. 142–172). New York: Brunner/Mazel.

Wolpe, J. (1958). *Psychotherapy by reciprocal inhibition.* Stanford, CA: Stanford University Press.

■ Classroom Exercises: Case of Ann

Ann Wotachek is a 44-year-old woman who is currently enrolled in a graduate human service program at a state university. She has been an excellent but quiet student throughout her academic coursework. She is now in her last semester and is currently enrolled in a practicum experience at a local family-services facility that deals largely with child abuse. A phone call from the on-site supervisor to her practicum coordinator reveals that Ann is having trouble with her clientele.

Specifically, Ann becomes very defensive and hostile toward any parent whose child may have been abused. She becomes overly sympathetic with the child and is not effective in her intervention. The problem has progressed to the point that she becomes argumentative with her on-site supervisor over whether parents should even be treated or not. Ann's angry contention is that parents should immediately be jailed.

When she meets with her university supervisor, careful probing leads her supervisor to believe that Ann herself was abused in some way as a child.

Reflection of this hunch brings a tearful and cathartic response from Ann. She reveals that she was raped by a stranger when she was 9 years old, beaten severely, and left for dead. She survived the ordeal, only to be blamed by her mother for what happened.

Further exploration indicates that Ann has many unresolved feelings of guilt and rage over the incident of 35 years ago, particularly in regard to her mother's vindictive response to the trauma. Her one attempt at marriage failed within 6 months of the wedding and she refuses to talk about it at all. She has no male friends, has not dated since her marriage 20 years ago, and has only one female friend. She states that she is extremely lonely but feels so alienated that she just can't make friends. Any relationship with a man is absolutely out of the question. She reveals that she has been in therapy before and that it has done absolutely no good. Ann oscillates between depression and inappropriate verbal rages. At present, she is extremely depressed because she feels that her last chance at making something of herself is about to meet with failure. Yet in almost the same breath she attacks the supervisor because he questions whether she should continue in the same practicum setting.

Ann also indicates that she has had trouble sleeping at night ever since she started the practicum. Her sleep disturbance is due to nightmares about her mother, now dead, who is accusing her of being sexually promiscuous. Her supervisor suspects that she is a victim of PTSD and suggests that she get in touch with a local therapist who specializes in cases of sexual abuse. Somewhat reluctantly, Ann agrees to go.

Using Gestalt Techniques to Resolve Unfinished Business

With the class divided into pairs, one person assumes the role of Ann or, if male, the role of a sexually abused boy. The other person, enacting the interventionist's role, places an empty chair opposite the victim. The chair will contain the victim's mother. The victim will conduct a conversation with the mother about the traumatic event. The interventionist may feel free to have the victim change chairs and assume the mother's role. The interventionist may also feel free to sit in the chair and assume the role of the mother or sit in the client's chair and have the victim be the mother.

The focus in this exercise is on release of feelings. The interventionist should steer away from analysis of content and concentrate on the emotional issues of the role play. Consistent and timely processing of feelings is important. After the victim has spoken to the empty chair and vice versa, the interventionist should pose a processing question on the order of, "How did you feel when you said that?" After approximately ten minutes, the partners switch and repeat the process. Whenever both partners have concluded their Gestalt enactments make sure that they verbally disassociate themselves from the roles they have played. When the role play is finished, return to a large group circle and discuss what happened. Questions to be discussed may include

1. How contrived did the exercise feel?
2. Did the role play become more realistic as it progressed?
3. What makes this an effective technique to use with victims of PTSD?
4. How do your own feelings come into play as you assume the role of Ann?
5. What alternatives can you think of that would get at the anger Ann feels toward her mother?
6. Is it important to get at such feelings, or should the interventionist concentrate on the symptoms that are currently hindering Ann's performance?

An admonition to the instructor is important in this exercise. It has been our experience that one or more class members may have had a real-life experience similar to that expressed by the character. The instructor should circulate among the pairs and keep a sharp eye out for members who become highly agitated or depressed during the exercise. Individual deprogramming or referral to a mental health professional may be necessary for those who have had such experiences, and experience a traumatic reaction to the exercise.

The Interventionist's Role in Support Groups

As a supplementary activity, read the articles in *The Journal of Specialists in Group Work, 11(2),* May, 1986. This special issue is entirely devoted to the support-group concept. After reading the issue, discuss the following questions:

1. What should the role of a human service professional be in the support group?
2. Does the human service worker have to "be one" in order to be effective in such groups?
3. How do support groups fit in with overall intervention?
4. What kinds of support groups do you know about that operate in your geographic locale?
5. How does one go about getting into such groups?

CHAPTER 8

Substance Abuse

BACKGROUND

"Wine is a mocker, strong drink is raging" (Proverbs 20:1). "At the last it biteth like a serpent, and stingeth like an adder" (Proverbs 23:32). These Biblical verses depict the continuing saga of drugs and addiction with which humankind has struggled over the ages. Efforts to treat the problem of substance abuse go back at least to the Romans, who attempted aversive conditioning of drunkards by placing spiders in the bottom of wine cups (J. W. Smith, 1982, p. 875).

Whole economies have been founded on drug use. The United States of American has been no shirker in this regard. The discovery that an acre of corn could be made much more saleable by turning it into alcohol played a dominant role in developing the economies of colonial New England and the early American frontier. How striking the demand for and the problem of alcohol became in colonial America is eloquently described by Asbury (1950, pp. 3–19), who documented the prodigious gallonage manufactured, the drunkenness extant in the population, the belief that alcohol could cure everything from hangnails to consumption, and its use to alleviate a hard and drudgesome life.

In 1785, nearly everyone in the United States would have thought the idea of abstinence to be ludicrous, but by 1835 a temperance movement "demonizing" alcohol was in full swing (Levine, 1984). The effort to "keep a devil out of the mouth of America" culminated in the Volstead Act and ratification of the Eighteenth Amendment to the Constitution, which brought prohibition to the country in 1920 (Asbury, 1950; Edwards, 1985). What this "Noble Experiment" did was allow the rampant growth of organized crime by providing a thirsty public with bathtub gin, Canadian whiskey, and moonshine. The Twenty-First Amendment repealing prohibition in 1933 is a large legislative memorial to the futility of trying to prohibit a drug, and in a social perspective it has much to say about what a society believes to be good or evil.

In view of contemporary issues of drug abuse, it seems that we do not learn the lessons of history very well. The expansion of smuggling, underground drug factories, and rising domestic cultivation of illicit drugs continues. The illicit drug trade is so lucrative that conservative estimates rank it only behind Exxon, the nation's largest corporation, in profits of some $80 billion a year (W. F. Smith, 1982). The New York City special narcotics prosecutor calculated the drug trade in New York City alone to be a $45-billion-a-year business that retains 10,000 full-time and between 100,000 and 300,000 part-time employees. These figures rank illegal drug distribution only behind the retail and manufacturing industry as New York City's biggest employer (Goode, 1984, p. 51).

Legal drugs are also big business. The total retail amount spent on alcoholic beverages in the United States in 1983 was estimated at $60 billion (Olson & Gerstein, 1985, p. 18). Considering these figures, it is not too difficult to understand why economic motivation was one of the forces that helped repeal prohibition. An assessment of how bad the correlative problem of substance abuse is gets lost and submerged in the exponential numbers that are attached to it. Two-thirds of the adult population use alcohol regularly, and 10% of those may be classified as alcoholic (Goode, 1984, p. 4). Per-capita consumption of all intoxicating beverages in 1984 was 38.67 gallons (U.S. Department of Commerce, 1986). What makes this statistic astounding is that one-third of the population drinks 95% of the output (Olson & Gerstein, 1985, p. 13).

Drug abuse is especially important in the social context of what various special interest groups think should be done about it. Big business, law enforcement, the judiciary, religious organizations, human service providers of all types, the medical establishment, legislatures, journalists, educators, family members of alcoholics, and survivors of victims of DWI vehicular homicides—all have a vested interest in either providing, controlling, or eradicating intoxicants. Whereas every one of these principals may agree that abuse is a problem, reaching a unified decision on how to handle the problem is about as likely as winning the grand prize in the state lottery.

Sociocultural Determinants

The society and the cultural background of an individual seem to have a great deal to do with what kinds of pharmacological and extrapharmacological effects will occur with use of addictive substances. Taking alcohol as an example, at a 0.40% blood alcohol content (BAC) most people pass out, and that is generally construed to be the LD-50 level—the level of intoxication at which about half of the people will die from an overdose (Goode, 1984, p. 62). Physiological outcomes are much the same for everyone having that BAC. However, psychological outcomes are very different as the user progresses to a 0.40% BAC level. Whereas one person with a BAC of 0.10% may want to fight a whole motorcycle gang, another may be the caricature of the garrulous, happy drunk, and another may sit stone-faced and bother no one.

It is a chemical fallacy that a specific dose of drug *Z* will invariably cause effect *A* in a user. What does seem to be true is that set and setting have a great effect on the behavior of the drug user. "Set" may be defined as the mental and emotional state of the user, including expectations, intelligence, personality, feelings, and so on. "Setting" refers to the social and physical environment of the user at the time of use. It may be defined as immediate surroundings, such as a living room as opposed to a bar, or, in a broader context, may be the legal and religious perspective of the country (Goode, 1984, p. 35).

Set and setting define which situations are appropriate for drug use and which are not. Nowhere is this more clear than in the fallacious belief that alcohol automatically releases inhibitions. In a comprehensive study of a number of tribes who have very different beliefs about what is appropriate and inappropriate behavior, MacAndrew and Edgerton (1969) found that people would not automatically lose their inhibitions and violate norms due to ingestion of alcohol unless the particular culture permitted it. Further, when a member of one culture was placed in a different cultural setting, that person might act in extraordinary ways when drinking that were very different from his own societal norms (Heath, 1985, p. 470).

Alcohol: Number One

Considering all the drugs with which to demonstrate crisis intervention procedures with drug abusers, we debated long and hard as to which to choose. The choice of potential abusive agents available today is much like a cafeteria menu. In attempting to compose a generic drug abuser for this chapter, we were tempted to select one of the more glamorous forms of drugs. Cocaine addiction fell high on the list because of the high publicity it has received, its fast addiction time, its potential physical and psychological outcomes, the tremendous cost, vigorous attempts by law enforcement to stop it, and its lethality (there are few old cocaine addicts because they just do not live that long). However, after much discussion, we believe that alcohol is still the best abusive agent to depict what happens in the crisis of addiction. There are several reasons for our choice.

1. *Duration.* Alcohol has a clear history in the United States, both in its use and in attempts to contain it. Starting with the temperance movement in the 19th century, followed by the founding of Alcoholics Anonymous (AA) in the 1930s and the birth of the National Institute of Alcohol Abuse and Alcoholism (NIAAA) in 1971 to coordinate the federal government's attempt to provide research, public education, and treatment (Costello, 1982, p. 1197), alcohol continues to play a great role in how our society attempts to deal with drug abuse.

2. *Alcohol is legal.* There are only limited conditions under which one can go to jail for possession. Even for people caught under those conditions, the social acceptability of alcohol plays an important part in determining punishment.

3. *Widespread use.* Given that alcohol is legal, figures support the con-

tention that it continues to be the most abused drug. From 7% to 10% of the population (10 to 18 million) may be diagnosed as alcoholic, and they in turn may implicate another 45 to 75 million family members in their disorder (Costello, 1982, p. 1197; Goode, 1984, p. 70). Comparing this figure with an estimate of 500,000 heroin addicts in the United States makes it apparent that a typical drug addict is an alcoholic (Goode, 1984, p. 54).

4. *Financial cost.* Because of lost time from the job, splitting of families, expenditures on the substance, hospital care, education, law enforcement, judicial, and correctional expenditures, the indirect financial cost of the disorder may be greater than that of any other public health issue (Costello, 1982, p. 1197). Estimated dollar amount due to lost job time alone ran above $20 billion in the early 1970s (Berry & Boland, 1977).

5. *Psychological cost.* If one believes only a part of the literature on codependency, adult children of alcoholics, and family systems, the psychological trauma that afflicts members of an alcoholic's family is appalling. Family members left in the wake of an alcoholic's slide into chronic abuse represent a tremendous pool of maladaptive psychological dynamics and coping mechanisms that reach beyond the family into the total fabric of society (Ames, 1985). Olsen (1987) reports that 38 million children are adversely affected by their alcoholic parents.

6. *Physical health.* Although physical ramifications of continued alcohol abuse may not be nearly as sudden and shocking as those of overdoses of "crack," PCP, heroin, cocaine, or amphetamines, continued and chronic abuse of alcohol leads to a wide variety of physical health problems that include but are not limited to delirium tremens, liver and pancreatic disease, Korsakoff's syndrome, reproductive and sexual dysfunction, poor fetal development, endocrine disturbances, gastrointestinal irritation, respiratory failure, heart disease, reduced immunity, cancer, and malnutrition (Pattison & Kaufman, 1982a).

In absolute terms, alcohol leads the list of acute physical problems associated with drug overdose. Emergency room reports of the early 1980s indicate that 19% of emergency admissions were due to use of alcohol alone or in combination with other drugs and fatal overdoses of alcohol accounted for 17% of emergency room deaths related to drug abuse (Drug Abuse Warning Network, 1983). These data *do not* include chronic conditions, accidents, or assaults related to alcohol abuse.

7. *Crime.* The high cost of illegal recreational drug use inextricably links these drugs to crime involving theft. Whereas these drugs are notoriously tied to agitated and violent behavior (particularly in those who are coming off depressants and need another fix or are pumped up on stimulants), alcohol is still a major contributor to violent behavior that is responsible for many assaults and murders (MacDonald, 1961; Pernanen, 1976; Shupe, 1953). Further, and contrary to popular opinion, property crime offenders also have high percentages of alcohol use (Collins, 1980; Shupe, 1953).

8. *Accidents.* About one-half of all highway deaths in the United States and Canada are alcohol related (Canadian Commission of Inquiry into the

Nonmedical Use of Drugs, 1973, pp. 393–395; National Commission on Marijuana and Drug Abuse, 1973, pp. 28–32). Highway deaths involving alcohol have been responsible for the loss of more American lives than all those lost in all the wars in which the United States has fought (Goode, 1984, p. 60). In single-car accidents involving fatalities, 70% of male and 40% of female drivers had BACs of 0.10% or higher (Ray, 1983). Haberman and Baden (1974) found that one-third of victims of falls and pedestrian fatalities had BACs of 0.10% or higher. Victims of drowning (41%), fire (58%), stabbing (68%), and firearms (40%) all had BAC levels of 0.10% (Goode, 1984, p. 61).

9. *Alcohol is a drug.* There is no biochemical aspect of alcohol that is different from what most would consider drug use. The difference between alcohol and all other drugs is the arbitrary definition of society, which does not see people who drink as drug users (Goode, 1984, pp. 5, 55).

10. *Polyuse.* The addiction picture in the United States is changing. Very few "pure alcoholics" exist. Most persons who become addicted today use a variety of other drugs in addition to alcohol (Maxwell, 1986, p. 6).

11. *Controversy.* Controversy surrounds the issues of both the etiology of alcoholism and its treatment. One of the most significant issues about alcoholism is defining exactly what it is. Is it clearly a disease, or is it "dis-ease" with one's ability to cope? Treatment issues spin off this controversy and pit AA and recovering alcoholics against professionals in the field of medicine, psychology, sociology, and anthropology. Alcoholism is one of the few health problems about which beliefs are so embedded in the popular health culture and so strongly held that they influence both patients and practitioners. As a result, a number of models have developed to explain its existence.

Models of Addiction

Very few programs for treatment of chemical dependency adhere to any one model of addiction. What one is likely to find is a treatment program that uses a compilation of many models. Currently there is no single, clear-cut model or treatment approach based on theory or research that holds sway over another. The debate over the efficacy of these models continues and serves to define competing schools of thought rather than facilitating agreement among proponents. The best that can be said about this current state of affairs is that the field of chemical-dependency treatment is in a preparadigmatic period: one in which all the facts that could possibly pertain to the development of a given science are likely to seem equally relevant (Shaffer, 1986). It is our position that each one of the models has worthwhile components. Accordingly, we take an eclectic approach and hold that at present *no one model is better than another and each has utility in treatment.*

Disease model. In the disease model of addiction, drug use is seen as an aberrant condition afflicting otherwise healthy people, and exposure to the drug leads to physiological addiction. Through a sequence of internal events, alcoholics lose control of their drinking behavior (Jellinek,

1960). With increased use, more and more alcohol is needed to meet physiological needs. When use ceases or is reduced, the drug reaches too low a level for the tolerance that has been created, the person goes into withdrawal, and physiological craving leads to continued use (Oetting & Beauvais, 1986). Jellinek (1946, 1952) postulated that certain types of alcohol users could be classified as ill and were suffering from a progressive disease that could be divided into phases. The World Health Organization's (1952) and the American Medical Association's (1956) acceptance of a diagnostic framework for alcohol abuse as a disease has lent much to the credibility of the disease model.

Genetic predisposition model. The genetic model proposes an inherited and transmitted predisposition to become a substance abuser (Cadoret & Gaith, 1978; Cotton, 1979; Goodwin, 1979; Schuckit & Rayses, 1979; Vaillant, 1983; Vaillant & Milofsky, 1982). Research from these studies found that adopted children of an alcoholic parent, monozygotic twins of an alcoholic parent, and children from multiproblem families with an alcoholic parent were four to five times as likely to become an alcoholic as children from comparable groups who had no alcoholic parents.

Gateway model. The gateway model proposes an orderly progression from one drug to another and particularly applies to young people as they move into heavier and heavier drug use (Dupont, 1984; Hamburg, Kraemer, & Jahnke, 1975). Only after trying beer will the person move to whiskey, then to marijuana and pills, and finally move on to PCP, cocaine, and heroin (Oetting & Beauvais, 1986).

Prescriptive model. Cases fitting instances of the prescriptive model are rather rare. It includes self-prescription and physician-prescription users who are using alcohol and other drugs as tranquilizing agents to relieve acute or chronic pain symptoms (Blume, 1973; Pattison & Kaufman, 1982b, p. 11).

Psychoanalytic model. Certain pathological personality traits established early in childhood predispose the individual to alcoholism (Barry, 1974; Zwerling, 1959). Spotts and Shontz (1980) traced the obsession with a particular drug to specific flaws in early development and demonstrated how the action of that drug meshed with the resulting personality.

Behavioral learning model. Drinking is caused and maintained by the association of alcohol intake with positive rewarding experiences. Habituation is progressively strengthened by repetitive use of alcohol to combat anxiety and alleviate stress (Pattison & Kaufman, 1982b, p. 12).

Sociocultural models. Sociocultural models examine factors external to the individual. The environment is a chief contributing factor and is inclusive of demographic and ethnographic variables such as race, age, socioeconomic status, employment, education, social norms, religion, crime rates, belief systems, consumption rates, drinking behavior, and so on. All of these may be considered as possible determinants of alcoholism. In its emphasis on environmental factors this approach empirically challenges the disease model (Heath, 1978; Lukoff, 1980).

Lifestyle model. The rewards of living in an altered state of consciousness outweigh all other costs of a destructive, drug-dependent lifestyle. For the people described by the lifestyle model, a drug-free existence is no existence at all (Pattison & Kaufman, 1982b, p. 12).

Peer-cluster model. Drug use is linked to small groups of people, including pairs such as best friends or boyfriend-girlfriend, who share beliefs, attitudes, values, and rationale for drug use. Drug use plays an important role in group membership and identification (Oetting & Beauvais, 1986).

Psychosocial model. A constellation of factors involving an individual's personality, environment, and behavior are interrelated and organized so as to develop a dynamic state designated as *problem-behavior proneness.* These variables define both the personal problems and the social environments that may underlie involvement with drugs—the greater the level of drug use, the greater the level of deviance (Jessor, Chase, & Donovan, 1980; Jessor & Jessor, 1977).

The Model Controversy

The major division of thought segregates the disease model from all the other models, which propose chemical dependency as something other than biologically based. At the center of this controversy have been the treatment principles of AA, funding by the NIAAA, and third-party payments by health insurance companies.

AA. One of the abiding principles of AA has been the insistence that there is a permanent change in the alcoholic's biochemistry and that willpower and insight as the essential forces for change are useless. The disease model communicates hope and implies that only one part of the alcoholic is disabled. It is psychologically efficacious because it reduces the guilt, confusion, and self-doubt about moral worth and lack of willpower that might otherwise plague the alcoholic (Stuckey & Harrison, 1982, p. 871).

For AA the disease basis of alcoholism may be compared with diabetes. Certainly diabetes is a permanent condition, but by watching their diet, diabetics can contain their level of blood sugar within normal limits. The analogy is clear that if the alcoholic remains abstinent, then his or her body will not be affected. Just as there is no such thing as an ex-diabetic, there is also no such thing as an ex-alcoholic. Thus, in the disease concept, the alcoholic is always "recovering" (Bissell, 1982, p. 811). This concept has been collectively systematized in AA's 12-step program to recovery (Stuckey & Harrison, 1982, p. 866).

Model's shortcomings. Neither alcoholism as a disease nor alcoholism as an illness is well defined in health professions (Chrisman, 1985, p. 15) and, 40 years after Jellinek's first proposal that specific types of alcoholism fit a disease model, what that disease is remains vague and uncertain (Ames, 1985,

p. 24). A true disease model must also reject the influence of situational factors on alcohol consumption (Peele, 1986), and there is a growing body of knowledge questioning the appropriateness of a disease model, which would imply orderly progression of symptoms, concepts of physiologically based craving, loss of control, and the choice of abstinence as the only acceptable goal of treatment (Marlatt & Donovan, 1982, p. 560).

Finally, the view that persons who have been chemically dependent and then drink moderately for a number of years are only temporarily postponing a full-scale relapse is no more valid than that of persons who abstain for an equivalent period of time and then relapse. It would seem that either abstinence or nonproblem drinking can be maintained over long periods of time, and neither outcome precludes the possibility of relapse (Sobell & Sobell, 1978, pp. 19–20).

Competition. There may be another reason for the number of conflicting views of what alcoholism is and how to treat it. Since the advent of the NIAAA and the provision of money for research, education, and treatment, the field of drug abuse treatment has grown exponentially. Because AA had been the principal actor until the NIAAA arrived on the scene, it would prove little for others to attempt entrance into the abuse field singing the same theoretical song and playing the same treatment tune as AA. Therefore, to obtain recognition, other theoreticians proposed alternate approaches to the disease model. No research evidence exists to support this cynical view. Nevertheless, our subjective view, based on numerous dialogues with experts in the field, is that there is some truth to this controversial viewpoint.

Insurance. Until the time that treatment of substance abuse became a paying proposition, few professionals cared to be bothered with it. The field was left largely to the volunteer efforts of AA. Those individuals within AA had seen all too clearly the ineptitude with which professionals had attempted to handle them or dismissed their abuse problem outright. However, with the advent of third party payments from insurance companies to health care providers for the treatment of drug addiction, hospitals and health care professionals became highly interested in the problem as witnessed by a dramatic increase in the number of drug dependence units throughout the country. We find it intriguing that most "cures" in such units take twenty-eight days, the exact time span covered by many insurance programs. As a result, it is not surprising that when professionals entered the field they and their theories were greeted with suspicion and hostility by AA (Rosenberg, 1982, pp. 802–809).

Given this controversy, it is little wonder that clinicians do not endorse the findings of researchers, and this situation further impedes efforts at teaching and training in addiction fields (Shaffer, 1986). This is a sad state of affairs. We would hope that movement toward rapprochement, which now appears to be under way between more moderate elements in the field, will continue and will result in a systematic, eclectic paradigm of theory and treatment that uses the best of all models and discards the worst. It is from this complex, conflicted, commingled, and convoluted perspective that we present this chapter.

DYNAMICS

Definitions

Many definitions are coined in an attempt to adequately describe those who get into trouble with drugs. To facilitate the reading of this chapter, we list the following commonly used terms in alphabetical order.

Abuse. The chronic, recurrent misuse of chemicals (Lawson, Ellis, & Rivers, 1984, p. 37). Abuse occurs when there is a pathological use of the substance and a minimal duration of disturbance of at least one month. "Pathological" may be variously defined as referring to intoxication throughout the day, inability to cut down or stop use, restriction of use to certain times of the day, need for daily functioning, and physical complications arising from intoxication. "Duration" refers to signs of disturbance occurring throughout the month and sufficiently frequently for a pattern of pathological use to become apparent (American Psychiatric Association, 1980, pp. 163–164).

Addiction. A cellular change that occurs with the increased use of most depressant drugs. The primary clinical features are the development of tolerance and the development of withdrawal symptoms upon the removal of the drug (Lawson, Ellis, & Rivers, 1984, p. 37).

Alcoholism. A highly complex condition characterized by preoccupation with alcohol and loss of control over its consumption such as to lead to intoxication if drinking is begun; by chronicity; by progression; and by a tendency to relapse. It is associated with physical disability and impaired emotional, occupational, and/or social adjustment as a result of persistent use (Shearer, 1968, p. 6).

Chemical dependent. Any person who has a dependence on drugs such that the substance governs his or her life to the extent that it severely impairs the ability to function psychologically and/or physically (Lawson, Ellis, & Rivers, 1984, p. 37). Currently the "in" term for a person receiving treatment for a drug problem.

Codependent. Any significant person in the chemical dependent's life, such as spouse, parent, lover, or child, who is enmeshed in the chemical dependency (Maxwell, 1986, p. 7).

Dependence. Physical dependency is the inevitable result of the pharmacological action of some drugs, given sufficient time and dosage quantity. Psychological dependency occurs in users who have a strong urge to alter their state of consciousness through the use of a chemical. This mental state may be the only factor involved, even in cases of the most intense craving and perpetuation of compulsive abuse. These two types of dependency may occur independently or in combination with one another (Lawson, Ellis, & Rivers, 1984, p. 37).

Drug. A psychoactive substance that has a direct and significant impact on the processes of the mind with respect to thinking, feeling, and acting. The term *drug* is a cultural artifact and a social fabrication because it denotes something that has been arbitrarily defined by certain segments of society as a drug (Goode, 1984, p. 15).

Enabler. A codependent who, by first rejecting and then tolerating the chemical dependency, furthers its progression in the dependent. Maintenance of the relationship is more important than the problem of chemical dependency (Maxwell, 1986, p. 103).

Habituation. The degree to which one is accustomed to taking a certain drug. A habituated user can and will take more of a drug than a first-time experimenter (Goode, 1984, p. 33). Defined in regard to an addictive/dependent state, it is imprecise and ambiguous (Pattison & Kaufman, 1982b, p. 9).

Misuse. Use of a chemical with some adverse physical, psychological, social, or legal consequence (Lawson, Ellis, & Rivers, 1984, p. 37).

Use. The intake of a chemical substance into the body with the goal of somehow altering one's state of consciousness (Lawson, Ellis, & Rivers, 1984, p. 37).

These definitions do not nearly convey the power that chemical dependence holds over people. The comments of two chemical dependents we know paint a striking picture of what being addicted and chemically dependent really means:

> Federal correctional incarcerate (alcohol and cocaine addict): Think of the best sex you ever had! Man! Think how great that feeling was! I mean the best and greatest! Well, that ain't nothin' compared to shovin' that spike in your arm and getting that first rush. That's why I do it.
>
> University professor (recovering alcoholic): When you get stressed out, there may be a number of things you do to get over it. You may go out and jog, pray, meditate, have a fight with your wife, chop wood, and so on. The problem with that is the payoff is variable. It may or may not work. When I get stressed out I drink. *My* way works *all* the time and *every* time. It's invariable. I know what will happen before I do it. It is absolutely dependable in taking the pain away. Beat that!

Defense Mechanisms

Drug abusers offer examples of all of the defense mechanisms one might find in a text on abnormal psychology. Gordon, a recovering alcoholic we will follow throughout the rest of this chapter, is a composite, displaying these maladaptive defense mechanisms.

Denial. Alcoholism is often called the "disease of denial" (Lawson, Ellis, & Rivers, 1984, p. 36). Denial is the emotional refusal to acknowledge a person, situation, condition, or event the way it actually is (Perez, 1985, p. 5). Addicts are deniers par excellence of the reality of their situation.

Gordon: Real men handle their problems. I'll handle mine. I've had a lot of problems lately. Sure I like a drink. Do a lot of business that way. Most of my friends drink. I get loaded every once in a while, but so would you if you had the pressures I do right now.

Displacement. Alcoholics find many targets on which to unload their problems. Displacement is the ventilation of hostility on a person or object, neither of whom deserves it (Perez, 1985, p. 6).

Gordon: Yell at my wife? You betcha. Always griping at me for not being at home. Hey! I provided a great living, then when I really needed her support because of the pressure at work, she'd just whine more.

Fantasy. Alcoholics use fantasy to escape from a variety of threatening circumstances and emotions. They escape boredom with the job, anxiety in coping with relationships, and frustration over career progress by retreating to a drug-induced euphoria. That euphoric state is far more rewarding than the real world and one to which the alcoholic feels compelled to return again and again (Perez, 1985, p. 6).

Gordon: Having a drink takes the edge off. I mean, you can just relax and put it out of your mind for a while—the job, the old lady, everything. I can really get it together and plan the next big project.

Projection. Alcoholics often attribute motives within themselves to significant others. Sensitivity, suspiciousness, and hostility toward others are outward manifestations of the distancing, estrangement, and lack of communication that characterize the alcoholic (Perez, 1985, p. 6).

Gordon: Amy never did love me. Oh, she loved the house, the club, and the private schools for the kids, and all that. I finally figured that out and told her that straight to her face!

Rationalization. Alcoholics make all kinds of excuses to support their addiction and their felt inadequacies of acting and behaving (Perez, 1985, p. 6).

Gordon: By God! I had severe back problems from doing the engineering on that sorting machine. Hell! Even the doctor gave me a prescription for the pain. That machine made this company. It had to get finished. What's wrong with taking a couple of pops at midnight? It made my back quit aching. I got it done.

Intellectualization. Alcoholics speak in generalizations or theoretical terms in an impersonal manner and thereby remove themselves from hurtful feelings (Maxwell, 1986, p. 65).

Gordon: They say I drink too much. Well, I've done some extensive reading on the subject and I certainly don't fit the category of a drunken bum. What do they know, anyway? They're not doctors.

Minimizing. Alcoholics play down the seriousness of the situation (Maxwell, 1986, p. 64).

Gordon: This is just temporary. I got a little out of line. No problem. I'll just have to watch things a little closer.

Reaction formation. Reaction formation occurs as a defense to perceived threat and is one of the worst defense mechanisms employed because it distances dependents from their true feelings. Addicts constantly fear rejection and go out of their way to find it—even if it is not there (Perez, 1985, p. 11).

Gordon: Those kids of mine, too. The little ingrates. Gave them everything. Lisa just stares at me. Mark even said I didn't love him because I missed a lousy soccer game. He sure didn't miss his personal computer I got him. No time for the old man 'cause he was too busy himself. That kid never loved me. Always took up for his mom.

Regression. Alcoholics are often immature and narcissistic, with resulting behavior similar to that of emotional prepubescence. The behavior is intended to manipulate, control, and get one's way. Temper tantrums, sulking, and pouting are all common forms of regression (Perez, 1985, p. 6).

Gordon: There was no use talking to her, so I just clammed up. Wouldn't support me in the business. Me apologize? She's the one who ought to apologize! I'm not saying one word to her until she does.

Repression. Alcoholics deal with threatening and hurtful events by burying them in unconscious memory (Perez, 1985, p. 7). When sober alcoholics repress the dependency needs and angry feelings that accompany them, and they remember nothing of the personality and behavior changes that occur when they are intoxicated (Zimberg, 1982, p. 1002).

Gordon: Warnings about my job performance. No way! They just dropped it on me one day. Things were fine up to that point! The same with the family. No warning! No nothing! They just up and leave. I never touched a hair on their head!

These defense mechanisms are far different from those of the average neurotic. They may be extremely intrusive into others' lives: grossly inconvenient, inexcusable, objectionable, and socially undesirable. The chemical dependent's defenses are sometimes primitive and regressive. They may personify the alcoholic as a self-centered and dependent person. Unlike the neurotic, some alcoholics suffer no discomfort and may not be motivated to change. The two major components of a sociopathic personality can dominate here. The chemical dependent can have no conscience and is sometimes excessively egocentric (Perez, 1985, p. 9). Arrogance, grandiosity, and omnipotence at the expense of others are the kinds of personality traits that sometimes predominate in alcoholics (Goodwin, Crane, & Guze, 1971; Guze, Goodwin, &

Crane, 1969; Guze, Tuason, Galfield, Stewart, & Picken, 1962; Maxwell, 1986, pp. 64–70) and there is indication of these traits in prealcoholics (Loper, Kammeier, & Hoffman, 1973).

> *Depression.*   Enmeshed in the hostile and angry feelings of the alcoholic is depression (Hoffman, 1970; Kristianson, 1970; Speigel, Hadley, & Hadley, 1970). Alcoholics perceive that they are beset by an uncaring world. When floods of guilt come pouring through the walls of abusers' defenses, they are overwhelmed by an inability to take any kind of reasonable control over their lives and undo the damage they have done to themselves and significant others. The cyclical battering alcoholics take between having no conscience and having an overpowering one is draining and leaves little psychic energy for anything but depression when they start sobering up.

In a worst case scenario, the defense mechanisms of most chemical dependents serve one goal and one goal only. They support, nurture, and help feed the one god in the addict's life—the drug. Nothing else matters. The drug becomes an ultimate and demanding taskmaster. No service is given to anything else until its needs are fulfilled! Feeble attempts to control it are hallmarked by guilt and remorse, but those feelings are niggardly in comparison with the urge to get "fixed" (Stuckey & Harrison, 1982, p. 868).

> *Gordon:*   I can't understand how things got this way. We used to have a great family. Yeah! I hate thinking about it. When I get to thinking about it, I feel rotten. Well, you can't function on the job with that kind of cloud hanging over you, so I'd have a drink and I'd feel better. Four or five and you can forget it all. But what else was I to do under all that?

Enabling and Codependency

When a family is enmeshed in addiction, the crisis is compounded, and a strange phenomenon occurs. In an attempt to keep the family in equilibrium, members will first reject and then begin to tolerate the addict. To keep the family in homeostasis, various members unconsciously assume roles that not only keep the system on an even keel but also enable the addict to fall further into the addiction (Ford, 1987, pp. 16–17; Perez, 1985, p. 19).

The marital relationship becomes highly competitive, with the alcoholic's dependency needs counterbalanced by the spouse. Being forceful, blunt, active, and domineering are ways that the spouse seeks to retake control of the situation. However, neither alcoholic nor spouse gains dominance, and this continuous warfare results in each blaming the other for the family's problems (Kaufman & Pattison, 1982a, p. 667). By attempting to maintain the system, even though it is extremely pathological, family members become codependents. They also manifest many of the *maladaptive* and *unconscious* defense mechanisms that their addicted counterparts have.

Defense mechanisms.   We have used the responses of Amy, Gordon's wife, to illustrate these defenses, which immobilize the family system.

Suppression. Codependents may suppress the problems the addict brings to the family by maintaining a "stiff upper lip" and not allowing their emotions to surface (Maxwell, 1986, pp. 78–79). This is a defense of quiet desperation and is based on the hope that some miraculous change will occur in the dependent.

Amy: I made a commitment when I got married that it was for keeps. He was probably an alcoholic when we got married, but a contract is a contract. In sickness and health and all that.

Disassociation. For those who disassociate themselves from the problem and repress it, their perception of events is drastically altered by putting the problem aside. Disassociation means distancing the problem emotionally and sometimes geographically (Maxwell, 1986, p. 80).

Amy: When it got really bad I'd make sure the kids were busy doing something and then I'd throw myself into the club work. That kept my mind off of his problem. The best two weeks of my life every year would be going back home to my parents. I'd take the kids and we could get away.

Repression. Repression of events takes disassociation a step further. By burying hurtful events in unconscious memory, codependents avoid having to grapple with the terrible feelings that accompany those events (Maxwell, 1986, p. 82).

Amy: I mean he's horrible all the time when he's bombed, but what he actually says I'm not real sure. He's real nasty, but I can't quite put my finger on what he actually does.

Seeking therapeutic assistance may be another form of escape for codependents. A lot of catharsis may occur in therapy, but little real change is considered because it would also mean that the codependents would have to face reality and make some serious changes away from the maladaptive coping patterns that they have established (Maxwell, 1986, p. 82).

Amy: If somehow he could just change. I don't know, maybe you could talk him into coming here. I know that I at least get a little peace of mind from coming to these sessions.

Intellectualization. Codependents use intellectualization to keep themselves distanced from the hurtful affect. In attempting to keep the system in balance, they are obsessive-compulsive in planning and attending to details. They spend a great deal of time thinking about and attending to the problem without ever feeling much about it. By compulsively paying attention to the many details of these events, intellectualizers order their outward world but do nothing about their inner turmoil (Maxwell, 1986, pp. 83–84).

Amy: It's exhausting, but I've figured out when he's really going on a bender. So I plan activities down to the last detail to keep everybody busy and out of his way. The parties are the worst because I've got this whole ritual laid out so that he won't get angry. It really takes some planning to keep things in balance then. By putting together a stepwise plan I can keep it down to a dull roar.

Displacement. By displacement, a codependent moves feelings off the focal point of the problem, the addict's behavior, and moves it to less frightening and hurtful subject matter (Maxwell, 1986, p. 86).

Amy: I've been reading about this new vitamin therapy, and I'm really concerned Gordon's going to get sick because he's so run down. I've been giving him all kinds of good information on this and even got him an appointment with this M.D. who practices holistic medicine.

Reaction formation. As the alcoholic becomes more and more and more irresponsible, a typical reaction for the codependent is to become more and more responsible. In actuality, this assumed responsibility for the family is focused directly on the alcoholic. The only safe way for the codependent to stay in the relationship is to give in and submerge the anger he or she feels. Reaction formation is ideally suited to this situation because alcoholics, no matter how much they express their independence, are among the neediest people in the world. Taking over for the alcoholic, codependents "save" the marriage and the family by behaving in ways exactly opposite to their internal feelings about the situation. Instead of expressing their true feelings toward the addict's behavior, the codependents appear to accept it (Maxwell, 1986, pp. 88–90).

Amy: The family has to keep going. That's why I'd take those plans for him when he couldn't make the plane and call in sick for him. I know he said some terrible things to me and the kids, but he really didn't mean them. He wouldn't act that way when he was sober.

By denying their own needs, reaction formation forestalls indefinitely the codependents' ability to change the situation. This defense overextends the codependent in every conceivable way and can lead to physical or emotional breakdown. In the latter stages of alcoholism, codependents may resort to the very immature defenses of passive aggression and hypochondriasis (Maxwell, 1986, pp. 88–90).

Passive aggression. By being late, forgetting, starting arguments and then leaving, overspending, and the implied threat of suicide the codependent keeps everyone in a state of uproar (Maxwell, 1986, pp. 91–94).

Amy: I don't know what's come over me. I've watched the money so carefully over the years. Gordon's still getting a paycheck, but I just can't seem to get bills paid and we're getting duns from creditors.

Hypochondriasis. The defense of hypochondriasis converts anger into physical complaints. This is an extremely effective punishment of others because no matter how much consolation they receive, codependents obtain attention by this defense mechanism, and they don't give it up without a struggle (Maxwell, 1986, pp. 94–95).

Amy: (Weeping.) I'm sorry for breaking down like this. It's just with everything else

I keep getting these terrible migraines. They knock me flat for a day at a time, and then I get behind and can't handle all the other stuff and wind up bawling.

Children.   Children of alcoholic marriages may be cast into roles vacated by the alcoholic. The eldest son may assume many of the responsibilities abandoned by the alcoholic father, placing himself in overt competition with the father (Pattison & Kaufman, 1982a, p. 667).

Amy: I had to ask Mark to start doing a lot of things. He really became a good little Mr. Fixit—taking care of the car and plumbing and stuff because the house was really getting run down and we couldn't afford to have it done. Gordon hit the ceiling over that, but he never would do anything about it. He'd just bitch and then go in the den and have a drink.

Daughters of alcoholic fathers may blame their mothers for the problems in the family. They may erroneously assume that if the mother were more loving and affectionate, father would not drink (Kaufman & Pattison, 1982a, p. 667).

Lisa: Dad drinks and I hate it. But I think sometimes Mom could be more loving. All she ever does is get in a huff and then they have a fight.

Children who issue out of this nightmare of pathological dynamics will leave home as soon as they can, but they take a great deal of this emotional baggage with them in the form of their own defense mechanisms, which, while serving to numb them while they were living at home, may have caustic effects in their own lives as they attempt to form interpersonal relationships as adults (Kaufman & Pattison, 1982a, p. 667). Because of the pathological basis for living within the alcoholic family system, these children are at risk for serious emotional illness as *adult children of alcoholics* (Burk, 1972; Mik, 1970; Miller & Jang, 1977).

Lisa: I hate it. I'm getting out of here in one year. I'm sorry for Mom, but I can't take it. I may go to college, but if I have to get married to get out of here I will!

To summarize, a codependent feels unworthy, guilty, inadequate, and subservient. A codependent loses his or her identity and becomes a fixer, appeaser, people pleaser, manipulator, and finally a victim. The codependent does not believe he or she can get well until the dependent gets well. To that extent the dependent and codependent are one and the same. The dependent is preoccupied with alcohol and the codependent is preoccupied with the alcoholic (Maxwell, 1986, pp. 98–100).

Amy: My world revolves around him. I even go to those damn parties where all I can look forward to is getting insulted by him. I never do anything right. Yet he sure as hell couldn't cut it without me. He puts out this big macho image when he couldn't even wipe his nose.

The typical response to the chemically dependent person is first to reject and then to tolerate the objectionable behavior. This marks a person as an enabler (Maxwell, 1986, p. 103). In the early phases of enabling there is denial and rationalization that the behavior will improve, and the enabler takes responsibility and assumes guilt for the alcoholic. In the middle phases the enabler becomes hostile, disgusted, and pitying and becomes preoccupied with protecting and shielding the alcoholic. In advanced phases, the enabler's feelings of extreme hostility, withdrawal, and suspicion become generalized to the total environment. In the final phases, responsibility for and quarreling with the alcoholic become all encompassing. Outside interests and maintenance of self are disregarded in all-consuming attempts to keep the system and the alcoholic stabilized (Kaufman & Pattison, 1982b, pp. 1022–1024).

Each of these phases is for naught. Chemically dependent persons listen to nothing. They respect only action, and only when that action threatens to interrupt their dependency in some way. Only when enablers decide to stop rescuing dependents and let them start to suffer the natural consequences of their actions will there be any change in the dependent's behavior (Stuckey & Harrison, 1982, p. 870).

Multivariate Diagnosis

Although we agree with Maxwell (1986, p. 33) that treatment approaches to drug abuse should be based on dealing with the abuse first, we also believe that certain components that treat individually of particular persons in particular settings must be used. A therapeutic approach for a 45-year-old housewife who anesthetizes herself in front of the soap operas with a pitcher of martinis every afternoon may be quite different from one for the 16-year-old who has been doing street drugs with his peer group (Lawson, Ellis, & Rivers, 1984, p. ix). Not only do setting events contribute to how treatment is carried out but also the particular kinds of personality constellations, demographics, learning history, ethnicity, social support systems, term of abuse, sex, age, and drinking systems determine the behaviors of the alcoholic and dictate specific treatment (McCrady, 1982, p. 682).

Our own theoretical approach, backed by a great deal of reported research (Pattison & Kaufman, 1982b, p. 13), is that alcoholism is a multivariate construct and implies the following (pp. 13–14):

1. There are multiple patterns of use, misuse, and abuse that may be denoted as a pattern of alcoholism.
2. There are multiple interactive etiological variables that may combine to produce a pattern of alcoholism.
3. All persons are vulnerable to the development of some type of alcoholism problem.
4. Treatment interventions must be multimodal to correspond to the particular pattern of alcoholism in a specific person.
5. Treatment outcomes will vary in accordance with specific alcoholism patterns, persons, and social contexts.
6. Preventive interventions must be multiple and diverse to address diverse etiologic factors.

INTERVENTION STRATEGIES

Transcrisis and Transcrisis Points

Crisis in a substance abuser's life rarely manifests itself as a one-time occurrence. The abuser's life is characterized by both transcrisis and transcrisis points. Typically, transcrisis points erupt in a series of what may appear to be single crises from time to time. In this chapter, we deal with both the transcrisis and these transcrisis points which abusers manifest.

Generally the transcrisis is related to the whole problem of addiction. Transcrisis points are related to the recurrent crises in the abuser's everyday life which seem to erupt in spontaneous ways whenever the person encounters stressors and which are rarely identified as being rooted in the greater underlying transcrisis of addiction.

In this chapter we portray crisis workers dealing with both the transcrisis and transcrisis points. The conceptual framework contained in the six-step model explained in Chapter 2 applies to all phases of substance abuse work. In addition to the six-step method, effective intervention with abusers almost always requires clients to become highly involved in a number of other methodologies including treatment groups such as those associated with family systems therapy, AA, or comparable specialized treatment groups. It is from the vantage point of both transcrisis and transcrisis points and a broad variety of intervention strategies that we deal with crisis work with addictive clients.

Assessment

The assessment of chemical dependence is a complex task, but it is critical in formulating differential diagnoses, specific outcome goals, and valid treatment modalities (Kaufman & Pattison, 1982b, p. 1091). The DSM-III of the American Psychiatric Association (1980) devotes an entire section of 16 pages to substance abuse disorders (pp. 163–179). This includes diagnoses that refer to maladaptive behavior associated with more or less regular use of the substances. Acute and chronic systemic effects are found under substance-induced organic mental disorders and include another 34 pages of disorders (pp. 128–162). Clearly, the reason for allotting this large amount of space to substance abuse is the large part it plays in much of the mental health business that occurs in the United States.

Psychometrics. A wide variety of personality tests have been used in attempts to characterize an alcoholic personality (Knox, 1976). A prototype is the MacAndrew Alcoholism Scale, which contains 49 items extracted from the Minnesota Multiphasic Personality Inventory. The MacAndrew has been somewhat successful in predicting alcoholism (Knox, 1980). The Alcohol-Use Inventory is another psychometric device that has demonstrated utility in measuring the psychological, social, marital, and family factors affecting alcohol use (Wanberg, Horn, & Foster, 1977). A major problem with these and other personality tests, though, is that they are unstable over time. The alcoholic may have very different scores and configurations prior to and after detoxification (Knox, 1976). These and other tests have general use in determining personality types of abusers, but no absolute pattern of personality has yet been found that covers all types of alcoholism (Mendelson & Mello, 1979).

Direct psychometric methods are related to alcoholic behavior and use. Prototypical are the Michigan Alcohol Screening Test (MAST), which asks questions about alcohol consumption and drinking behavior, and the Alcadd Test, which measures drinking in terms of regularity, preference over other activities, loss of control, rationalization of use, and emotionality (Ornstein, 1976). Problems with self-report measures such as these are the veracity of the respondent and acknowledgment of the severity of the problem (Knox, 1982, p. 58).

Diagnostic intake. A comprehensive clinical assessment of a chemical dependent will cover biological and psychosocial components of the problem and will include a complete medical workup. Whatever the diagnostic system used, one question overrides all others, and that is: Does the diagnosis help the individual and does it provide information necessary to treatment (Lawson, Ellis, & Rivers, 1984, p. 44)? Toward that goal, one of the better intake formats we have seen is the Continuous Data Questionnaire (CDQ) (Poley, Lea, & Vibe, 1979). Combined with a complete medical workup and psychometric measures, the CDQ provides an extensive and intensive profile of the client. The CDQ specifies treatment stage, alcohol use, work/education background, family system, social-recreational-community involvement, adjudication, personality and emotional development, physical and sexual health, motivation, and a comprehensive section for intake worker's conclusions.

The CDQ accomplishes a number of important tasks. First, it monitors a client at many points in the treatment process. Second, it is not concerned with drug issues to the exclusion of other problems. Its comprehensiveness allows the worker to obtain information on a variety of areas that may need remediation. Third, the CDQ gives a historical perspective on the client before and during treatment that will enable the therapist to make an excellent analysis of what treatment goals need to be established and how those goals are being met. In sum, the CDQ or a similar intake device is of critical importance in providing the worker with a road map of the treatment process.

Assessment by the worker. We believe that the worker's ability to retrieve, analyze, and synthesize clinical information is crucial to making a valid assessment and subsequent treatment decisions. An initiating interview to determine drug abuse is unlike many other exploratory interviews because the defense mechanisms of the chemical dependent will be granite hard, and the worker must be aware that these defenses will do all they can to safeguard the abuser's secret.

Analysis starts by monitoring the verbal defenses of the client. Hedging, minimizing, seduction, changing the subject, projecting onto significant others, and refusal to speak directly about oneself in the here-and-now are defenses all clients may manifest. However, these are extremely pronounced in the alcoholic. For example, ruminating on past drinking episodes and drinking friends should not be viewed as innocent, idle nostalgia, but rather suggests that the person has not learned to fill the social void in his or her life left by giving up the abusing agent and while physically detoxified is not psychologically detoxified (Perez, 1985, pp. 34–37).

Behavioral assessment includes such simple procedures as noticing whether there is alcohol on the client's breath. Chewing peppermint or gum and heavy use of cologne or perfume may be attempts to mask alcoholic odors. Physical appearance of an alcoholic may include facial puffiness, a red nose, sudden weight gain, a glazed look or a hunted, fearful aspect, shaking, rigid attending and listening or a very casual, laid-back approach (Perez, 1985, pp. 34–37). Having conducted the intake assessment, the worker should write a summary in narrative form that includes all the points we have discussed in the CDQ. The following case write-up of Gordon is typical.

Intake Analysis and Summary of Gordon Brand

Chemical use.   Gordon Brand was seen after initial admission for polydrug overdose. Stage of treatment is initial assessment. The date is March 15, 1987. The client is a 42-year-old male Caucasian who was brought to St. Polycarp by the paramedics for treatment of a drug overdose. BAC was 0.37% on admission with evidence of Quaalude® ingestion. Gordon was comatose on entry and was in intensive care for three days. Preferential drug is alcohol. Over the past three months, Gordon reports consuming a bit less than a pint of whiskey per day, although this quantity is subject to scrutiny because of client's defensive responses. Drinking is continuous and Gordon does not remember when he was last abstinent. Drinking has been with peers from work and alone at home. Lately drinking has been mostly by himself. Valium was prescribed by Gordon's family physician for "stress" and Gordon has used it rather extensively for a number of years, especially when he was trying to "cut down" alcohol use. His only experience with Quaaludes was immediately prior to admission, and he maintains this was a "terrible mistake" and will not use them again.

His social drinking behavior includes the three-martini lunch, stopping at a local bar after work, and numerous parties that are social/business in nature. His ability to control alcohol use is rated by himself as neither difficult nor easy and the seriousness of his problem is probably underrated because of his extensive and intensive denial system. Gordon's wife is an occasional user of alcohol, but tends more to abstinence.

Educational and vocational background. Gordon is a college graduate with a degree in mechanical engineering and a master's in business administration. He is employed as director of internal operations by United Tectonics. His income is approximately $80,000 a year, with numerous perquisites. He reports no absences from work due to alcohol or drug-related problems, but does report he has missed approximately 20 days of work in the last two months due to "intestinal problems" and generally feeling "unwell." His best estimate of being late to work is 10 times during the last month. He indicates he is moderately satisfied with his job, but says he would be extremely satisfied if the company president "would get off his back and leave him alone." He rates his job performance as quite good and says it would be excellent if he were not currently ill.

He is not sure how much money he owes at present because "that was always his wife's job," but believes besides a house note of $1750 and two car notes of $850 he pays "about $1500 a month on credit cards." Cost of drinking is "peanuts." He is not sure how much outstanding debt he has, but vaguely remembers his wife saying something about bills being overdue.

Family status. Gordon currently resides with his wife and children in an upper-middle-class subdivision and has lived there for the past 8 years. He relates that he used to love his wife a great deal, but now gets along poorly with her. He maintains that he gets along moderately well with his children, Lisa and Mark, although "they side with their mother on most things." Prior to the last two months he often (several times a week) did things with his family. He believes his family is very important to him but is extremely angry that his wife is not more supportive. He also feels he is extremely important to his family, but states this in economic terms: "All I'm good for is to bring home a paycheck." He does not handle arguments with his wife well and "clams up" after initial exchanges. His dealings with his children are much the same, and he reports, "They don't listen to me and are rebellious."

Social involvement. He reports having many business acquaintances, but no real friends. Gordon has been involved with a number of charitable and service organizations in the community, until the last couple of years, when he got so involved in work that he could not do those things any more. He enjoyed service activities, particularly with the Boys' Club. His recreational pursuits are "tinkering" around in his shop at home, fishing and hunting, and reading military history.

Judicial involvement. Aside from being found by the police passed out in his car, he has no prior arrest record. He reported one domestic disturbance call when he and his wife were arguing, but smoothed that over with the officer who responded to the call.

Health. His physical and mental health have been average to poor. He last saw a doctor about six months ago and was told that he had the beginnings of major health problems, "something to do with his guts and stress," but he is not quite sure what it was. He has been taking an antacid for the problem. He has "fallen down" on his eating habits because of both stress and a nervous stomach and only occasionally eats regular, well-balanced meals. He averages about 5 to 6 hours' sleep a night and uses alcohol and Valium to help him get to sleep, particularly when he is under stress. He has never been in the hospital for other than minor medical problems. He has never considered suicide, but states it is not the worst thing in the world. His sexual health is poor. He has no strong sexual urges, has not had or cared to have sex in a long time, and had been very unsatisfied with his sex life, but now is neither satisfied nor unsatisfied.

Gordon presented the appearance of a man coming out from addiction. After he had been stabilized for his overdose he slept for the better part of three days. His withdrawal symptoms were severe enough that he was given phenobarbital to ease the pain of withdrawal. His appearance is sallow and wan. He is overweight and his muscle tone is poor, with his flesh sagging over his body. As he sits in the intake interview he has a hunted look to his eyes and is constantly wringing his hands when he is not chain smoking. His agitation is further demonstrated by pitched up and accelerated speech patterns.

Personality profile. His personality and emotional development are rated moderately low in responsibility to self and others, very low in self-worth and general feeling of well-being, high on anxiety and depression and neither high nor low on initiative, sociability, assertiveness, and hostile aggression towards others. He is more tense than relaxed, more critical than tolerant, more depressed than happy, more nervous than calm, more unfriendly than friendly, more unforgiving than forgiving, and much more sickly than healthy. The MacAndrew supports this self-analysis and the MAST indicates he is a heavy alcohol abuser.

Motivation. He is ambivalent about changing. Although he can articulate goals, they are generally nonspecific, such as "straightening things out at home and work." His rating of present attempts to accomplish these tasks is very unsuccessful and he rates as moderately important a goal to stop abusing alcohol "for a while." His most desirable use of alcohol would be to drink socially, "because drinking alone really isn't all that good and probably helped get me here in the first place." He believes no one is interested in his problems "except to get on my back."

Corroboration. Follow-up includes checking with Gordon's employer, wife and doctor. Their story is a good deal different from what Gordon reports. Mr. Fredricks, the president of United, indicates that Gordon was one of his best employees until about three years ago, when his drinking got steadily worse and his performance declined. At first, Mr. Fredricks said nothing about the drinking, because Gordon still had a performance rating that was superior to those of most other members of the staff—drunk or sober. Later,

Mr. Fredricks gave him some fatherly advice about his problem, which Gordon ignored. Three months ago, the advice turned into a warning about absences and poor performance. Mr. Fredricks now feels that unless Gordon dries out and takes care of his problem, termination is imminent. Mr. Fredricks also agreed that Gordon had been such a valuable employee that the company would pick up any cost for treatment that insurance did not cover. The employer agreed to support and coordinate efforts with the hospital. Analysis of employer cooperation in regard to chemical dependency treatment is excellent.

Gordon's wife Amy supports his employer's analysis of the problem. His drinking has steadily escalated to the point that the family has become completely dysfunctional. She and the children are terrified of Gordon when he is drunk, which is most of the time. He has become an isolate from his family and only relates to them when he wants something. Any mention of his drinking causes severe arguments and then a period of sullen hostility. Amy also reports serious financial problems, saying that they are behind on the house and car notes and owe credit card accounts of $7000. Two months ago Gordon got drunk, became violent, and threatened her. The police intervened in the situation and Gordon left the house. She threatened to obtain a restraining order on Gordon, but relented after he promised to remain sober and be the husband and father he used to be. He kept his vow for two weeks, then he started drinking even more heavily. She states that she is near a nervous breakdown and has a number of physical complaints that are probably due to the stress of trying to deal with Gordon for so many years. She is "sick" of it and is thinking of filing for divorce. She did agree to come to the hospital for an interview if Gordon agreed to treatment. General analysis of the home situation is that it is extremely poor and may not be redeemable.

A call to Gordon's doctor indicated that he had given Gordon a severe upbraiding six months ago about his drinking and stated that he would no longer give him prescriptions for Valium. He had recommended at that time that Gordon seek immediate inpatient treatment for severe alcohol abuse. He also told Gordon that he was having liver, pancreas, and intestinal problems due to alcohol and that if he kept drinking he was going to be in critical trouble in short order. Gordon became hostile and told his family doctor of 15 years that he "didn't know what he was talking about and wasn't much good if he couldn't give him some tranquilizers for the stress he was experiencing."

Conclusions. General analysis of interviews with Gordon, his boss, wife, and doctor is that Gordon shows clear signs of chemical dependency (alcohol) across physical, psychological, and social components of his life. He denies that he has a problem with alcohol and has put in place strong defense mechanisms to shield him from the reality of the situation. He is in extreme peril of losing his job, family, and quite possibly his life. He is in need of immediate inpatient treatment. Recommendations after staffing with the chemical dependency unit were

1. that Gordon be apprised of the seriousness of his physical condition
2. that Gordon be apprised of the options of keeping his job
3. that Gordon be apprised of the perilous state of his marriage
4. that Gordon fully experience the crisis he is in and that workers gain his agreement to undergo treatment in the chemical dependency unit
5. that if he agreed to undergo treatment, his family be contacted with the proposal that they also undergo treatment as codependents
6. that if he agreed to treatment, particular goals be established for a comprehensive rehabilitation plan
7. that controlled drinking is not an option due to the seriousness of his physical problems and the failure of his previous self-managed attempts to quit.

The Workers

Carolyn and Ray, two counselors on the treatment staff of St. Polycarp, were assigned to Gordon. They can be loosely described as the good-guy/bad-guy team. Carolyn is a recovering alcoholic who is direct, assertive, and confrontive. At times she uses self-disclosure about her own dependency so that the client can't get away with saying, "Nobody knows the trouble I've seen." She has a high degree of credibility even though, as residents on the unit say, "She's meaner than a snake when you try and con her." She is also a good model. The alcoholic can look at her as a peer and say, "If she can get through this, so can I," and, "Here is a tough, competent person who has been where I am, and if that's true, then there's hope for me" (Graham, 1986).

Ray is more nondirective and unconditionally accepting. His stock in trade are the basic skills of empathic listening and responding. His job is to build a healthy, trusting relationship and focus on the client's positive attributes, to promote faith in the client, and to help the client to come to his or her own self-realizations about the problem. Ray is also a model in that he is a professional who is not an alcoholic. Clients cannot reject treatment on the basis that "they're just a bunch of burned-out boozers here."

Another reason that Carolyn and Ray operate as a team is that drug users are the most manipulative group of clients we know. Clients may con one person, but they will have a much more difficult time conning two people. Carolyn and Ray run constant perceptual checks with one another. One of them might be wrong, but the two of them together seldom are. Teaming is also a support mechanism for the workers. Working with drug addicts is one of the toughest jobs in therapy. By acting as a team they have far less chance of burning out (Parker, 1986).

The two workers manifest to the highest degree the points Brill (1981, pp. 61–70) makes in regard to what it takes to be a world-class chemical dependency worker:

1. need to be aware of their own underlying biases about drug use and users

2. should understand their own personal needs and feelings regarding power and dependency prior to becoming involved in the field

3. must possess skill in communication and in fully accepting a wide range of behaviors and personalities

4. must be trained in a number of treatment modalities

5. must be able to deal with challenges by clients who are adept at intimidating, testing, challenging, rationalizing, provoking, and trapping therapists

6. must be prepared to deal with dishonesty, cover-ups, illegal activities, and other forms of deviant behavior

7. must develop skill in dealing with a continuing saga of client crises, which tends to put workers in a bind between rejecting the client and assuming responsibility for solving the crisis, thereby engendering dependency

8. must be prepared to confront an unmotivated family support system in which treatment is often a long, drawn-out process (characterized by relapses, regressions, and dashed hopes for a rapid cure)

9. must find ways to deal with clients who cannot tolerate success—for any one of a variety of reasons, some drug users engage in self-defeating behaviors whenever an important attainment becomes imminent

10. must be competent in dealing with drug users even if their clients relapse and come to a treatment session high on drugs

11. must learn and practice ways to deal with resistant clients who are sent by a court, parole officer, or other authority

12. should be aware that drug users will employ seductive tactics: tell the worker what the worker wants to hear; present a pleasant, agreeable front; imitate the worker's favorite jargon; diagnose themselves and corroborate what the worker has been saying; confirm that they have made great progress as a result of the worker's help where all others have failed—all of which usually mask the client's underlying rage and hostility

13. must deal with clients who want to talk only about drugs and their drug exploits, to the exclusion of any meaningful work in solving their problem

14. must realize that many clients will drop out of treatment when it seems that the treatment is beginning to be effective; that the irregular and inconsistent pattern of contact is endemic to drug users; that clients tend to disengage from treatment when things are going well and return when there is a new crisis.

Crisis Points

Clients who are addicted will have used drugs to shield themselves from all kinds of hurtful feelings, thoughts, and behaviors. Once this shield is taken away, all the problems will tend to converge like an accordion, and clients will be assailed from all sides at once. The very reasons that the alcoholic drank in the first place will return in condensed, magnified, and more powerful ways. Each instance will present a crisis point for clients. As a result, the whole therapeutic inpatient treatment program may be seen as transcrisis in nature. Successfully jumping one hurdle generally means getting ready immediately for the next one and the next one after that.

Motivation

The first crisis to be dealt with is getting the client motivated to dry out. Working with a "wet" person is impossible, because all the person is interested in is getting "fixed" (Parker, 1986). To get the person to detoxify means creating enough of a crisis that the person voluntarily agrees to stay. The best way to do this is by attacking the client's vulnerable points. For Gordon, there are two: his job and his health.

Carolyn: Hello, Gordon. I'm Carolyn and this is Ray. We're from the chemical dependency unit and we'd like to talk with you.

Gordon: Well, that's fine, but I don't know why you're talking to me. I made a dumb mistake and took some pills I shouldn't have, but that won't ever happen again.

Carolyn: Maybe not. But from your intake interview and the problem that got you here, we think you very seriously need to consider coming over to the chemical dependency unit.

Gordon: I really need to get out of here and get back to my job. It's hanging by a thread as it is.

Ray: We understand how concerned you are about your job. We've talked to your employer, Mr. Fredricks, and he understands the situation. He's willing to support you if you go into treatment.

Gordon: (Angrily.) I'll bet! That S.O.B. used to be my best friend. He'll use me being a drunk to give me the axe. That's all the excuse he'd need.

Carolyn: He may be the biggest S.O.B. in the state. But he cares about you and has offered you a choice. He believes that if you don't seek help from us, then you're not going to have a job at all. He also said you'll have your same job when you finish treatment. I have him outside and I want you to hear it with your own ears.

(After a lengthy conversation, Mr. Fredricks leaves.)

Gordon: He really means it. My God! No job. What'll I do?

Ray: Look at it this way. You know you've got some pretty severe physical problems. What difference will a few days make? You meet your commitment to your boss, and you're also someplace where your physical problems can be monitored. It's a no-lose deal.

Gordon: I'm no drunken bum!

Ray: We understand that, but I'm wondering if this statement rings true that drinking at times produces results you dislike.

Gordon: Yes. I could say that.

Ray: Seems like it would be worth your time to find out a bit more about that. What's a few days' difference one way or the other?

Gordon: I've never been in the hospital before, this is the first time.

Ray: I understand how scary that must have been, waking up and not knowing how you got here in the first place. I also know you're smart enough to know when something's haywire.

Gordon: But going into a dryout ward. It's like I can't handle my problems.

Ray: I'd guess that going into treatment would seem like a sign of weakness, but I'd like to point out that if anything else was wrong with you it would be a sign of mature and healthy thinking to get it taken care of, wouldn't it? You have a serious illness here that needs help.

Carolyn: If you had cancer, would you try to do surgery on yourself? You do want to get better in regard to your health problems, don't you? The doctor told you how serious your physical problems are, didn't he? That you have liver, pancreas, and severe intestinal problems and that if they're not taken care of you will most likely die. Do you believe he's putting you on, or is that what you want? Notice your hands right now. They're shaking so hard you couldn't hold a pencil and write your name.

Gordon: I can too.

Carolyn: Go ahead and do it then. (Hands Gordon the pencil and paper.)

Gordon: (Attempts to write down his name and produces an illegible scrawl that wobbles across the page.)

Carolyn: In all honesty, is that your typical signature?

Gordon: (Voice breaks.) I . . . no, it isn't. I'm . . . I'm sick.

Carolyn: Yes, you are! That's why we're concerned about you and want you to come into the program.

Gordon: (Downcast but still defiant.) OK. I'll give it a try, but I'm not promising anything. If I don't like it, I'll leave.

Ray: That's all we ask. Now let us tell you in general what your treatment is going to be. We want you to know what's going to happen so you can help us plan what'll be most effective for you.

The human service workers are creating a crisis. They are not above putting the client in a corner to get him to stay and will do all they can to motivate him to do so. Very few clients will be self-motivated to change their abusing behavior (Lawson, Ellis, & Rivers, 1984, p. 67). Outside motivation must often be used. In this case it is Gordon's job and his health. For most male alcoholics, their job is critical, and it is the last part of their environment to suffer. There are two major reasons for this. First, to lose one's job is to admit failure to handle the problem. A job is at the core of one's self-esteem, and to lose that is to admit that the chemical dependent has hit rock bottom. Second, without a job, there is no money to keep up one's supply of the addictive substance (Parker, 1986; Trice & Beyer, 1982, pp. 955–956).

Balancing confrontation about poor job performance is an empathic and genuine concern for Gordon's health that specifically tells him that someone now cares what happens to him. The confrontation is firm, but not blaming (Huberty & Brandon, 1982, p. 1082). The information reported is factual and not judgmental. By alternating between the two approaches, the workers seek to set the stage for Gordon through a combination of fear for his life and hope through treatment.

While creating the crisis, the workers avoid directly confronting or accusing Gordon of being an alcoholic. Early attempts to make clients confess to their addiction will likely lead to very defensive behavior. Although the word *manipulate* has an ugly connotation, in a sense all therapists manipulate their clients to positively increase the chances of successful therapy (Lawson, Ellis, & Rivers, 1984, p. 77). The facts of Gordon's case indicate that he is in serious, if not lethal, trouble. The first ten days of treatment are going to be the most difficult, and throughout this time, one of the workers' major tasks will be to keep Gordon from leaving against medical advice (Parker, 1986).

Detoxification

Once Gordon has agreed to go into the unit, he is transferred to a private room close to the nurses' station and completes his detoxification. Important to this process is that being "undrunk" should not be confused with being detoxified. Detoxification is a very serious medical process, depending on how badly addicted the alcoholic is. Although the procedure may seem to run counter to the goal of detoxification, Gordon is given phenobarbital to allow him to avoid the severe pain accompanying withdrawal. Detoxification is not a character-building experience, so there is no need for him to hurt while going through it. About three days are necessary to get the effects of alcohol out of his system. During that time, Gordon is allowed to sleep as much as possible, eat a well-balanced diet, and watch TV. If he is up to it, other clients who have gone through detoxification will come in and talk with him. The others do not come to proselytize, but to let him know that as tough as it is, they made it through this preliminary crisis stage and so will he (Parker, 1986).

Henry (another patient): Hi! My name's Henry Schultz. I'm another patient here. Ray thought you might be up for some company.

Gordon: Man. I'm glad to talk to somebody. This is tough, I guess I was strung out.

Henry: It is tough! I went through it three weeks ago. I guess you could use a drink, huh?

Gordon: Brother, could I!

Henry: Yeah, I know. That's not gonna get easier for a while either, they make you come face up to it here. It's no piece of cake, but they really care about you. I just wanted to tell you I'm here if you want to talk. I'm not gonna tell you not to drink or judge you about what you've done and nobody else will either. I've gotten into AA in a big way, and it's really been a help.

Gordon: I don't know about that, spilling your guts and all. I don't think I could do that.

Henry: I thought the same thing. Lay my soul bare in front of a bunch of drunks, no way! But it's easier than you think. Especially when you meet the people. Hell!

There's all kinds of people in it, some big shots, little shots, but all of us are not-so-hot shots when it comes to drinking.

(The conversation continues for a good bit, with Gordon asking all kinds of questions about treatment and about Henry's drinking problems, and guardedly discussing himself.)

This initial dialogue with one of the other clients is important because it safely lets Gordon consider what the possibilities for recovery are, provides a peer as a resource, gives him a role model, and establishes at least one relationship within the therapeutic community (Parker, 1986).

Treatment Goals

After Gordon's assessment and detoxification, but prior to going into treatment, Carolyn and Ray carefully go over treatment goals with Gordon. His treatment plan contains a comprehensive set of goals. Each was developed from his assessment plan, which identifies a specific debilitating condition, a goal to alleviate that condition, and a set of specific objectives for attaining the goal. Here are two sample goals.

1. *Gordon's drinking goal.*

Condition: Excessive consumption of alcohol. Gordon has difficulty meeting the demands of his work and social responsibilities without drinking.

Goal: Eliminate the consumption of alcohol.

Objectives: Gordon will

a. eliminate the intake of alcohol both during working hours and after working hours every day, including the weekend

b. express his feelings and choose positive coping behaviors, which he will employ to deal with stress-producing persons, events, or situations

c. demonstrate for 28 days of inpatient treatment and 6 months' aftercare that he is able to cope successfully with persons, events, and situations at work and at home that trigger anxiety and avoid the use of alcohol to reduce that anxiety

d. use the group and St. Poly's staff as a source of support and strength in attaining the goal of eliminating alcohol consumption by actively participating in group, helping other people attain their goals, and committing himself to accepting help and support from others in working on his own goals.

2. *Gordon's emotional and social goal.*

Condition: Gordon either withdraws from interaction or inappropriately acts out with others, including his own family, when he is stressed.

Goal: Emit appropriate emotional and social responses while in the presence of others who may produce stress, including his own family.

Objectives: Gordon will

a. engage in nondrug conversation with a staff member at least twice each day and with a peer at least three times each day during inpatient treatment

b. carry on at least one nonargumentative discussion with each family member (Amy, Mark, Lisa) during each visit during inpatient treatment

c. during aftercare, carry on at least two nonargumentative discussions per day with Amy and at least one such discussion per day with both Mark and Lisa

d. engage in a minimum of one social activity (game room, gym, horseshoe pit, lake area, dancing, etc.) during inpatient treatment

e. engage in a minimum of two social activities (in absence of alcohol) with his family during 6 months of aftercare—activities to be planned by family as a group.

The comprehensive treatment goals were the basis for implementing group therapy. Each client's personalized goals were written on butcher paper and posted in the treatment room during each group session. These treatment goals served as immediate and constant reinforcers as the group worked on recovering from their chemical dependency.

Groups

The format for our demonstration of intervention procedures will be the treatment group. There are a number of reasons why groups are preferable in treating addiction. First and foremost, the relationship skills of chemical dependents are typically wretched. Chemical dependents desperately need positive social interaction to replace isolated self-involvement with their chemical seducer (Lawson, Ellis, & Rivers, 1984, p. 122). Belonging, acceptance, affection, social interaction, nonuniqueness, equality, and development of a new self-concept are all relationship needs that can best be met by the treatment group (Dinkmeyer & Muro, 1979). Specific outcomes of the treatment group (Corey & Corey, 1977; Ohlsen, 1970) include

1. learning more effective social skills
2. gaining support for new behaviors by reality testing in a safe environment
3. encouragement of experimentation and risk taking through modeling by others
4. re-creation of the world outside, with all its diversity and problems
5. providing opportunity for honest feedback by peers rather than "know-it-all" professionals
6. learning through emotional closeness of others
7. having a safe environment to self-disclose about threatening issues and being accepted by others while doing so
8. productive tension that propels and promotes change
9. increased focus on here-and-now events rather than past activities
10. making an emotional investment not only in oneself but also in other members.

Inpatient treatment at St. Polycarp consists of several kinds of group work: group therapy, group education, multiple-family therapy, AA group meetings, community groups, and aftercare groups. Usually there will be from six to ten members in the group. The group will be a heterogeneous mix of sex, age, and race. This mix occurs by design, because the staff wants the unique problems of each member to surface. Addicts have severe blind spots for their own defenses but not necessarily for each other's. Thus, the diversity of members should allow them to be able to see through the defense mechanisms of their peers, confront these blind spots, and help their peers accomplish treatment goals (Ohlsen, 1970, pp. 109–110). For brevity's sake we will introduce four representative members of Gordon's group.

Alice is a 55-year-old Caucasian housewife who had been finishing off her afternoon in an alcoholic haze of martinis. Her children have left and she is now an "empty nester." Her husband and children had denied her drinking until she was involved in an auto accident, left the scene, and was picked up DWI. She was remanded to St. Polycarp by a judge.

Liz is a 35-year-old Black nurse. She was in charge of ICU. She burned out on the job and was caught raiding the pharmaceutical cabinet. She yo-yos between depressants (alcohol and pills) to take the pain of the job away and amphetamines to get her "up" for her job. She is on suspension and in danger of losing her job and her license.

Manuel is a 24-year-old suspended bank guard whose father died an alcoholic when Manuel was 11. His Chicano background dictates a macho image that says, "I take care of and handle everything," including alcohol and pills—which he did not handle. He is single and has used alcohol and pills since he was a teenager.

Ruth is a 41-year-old Caucasian who was sexually abused repeatedly by her stepfather when she was a teenager. She married at 18, had two children, and was divorced at 23. She has worked as a bookkeeper for a construction company for the past ten years. She has had several short, fruitless liaisons with men. She has been an alcohol abuser since her teenage years. She got drunk, took some sleeping pills, and turned the gas on in her apartment. The paramedics brought her to St. Polycarp.

Relationship Skills

Session 2. Despite Gordon's stated desire and willingness to interact positively with other clients and to work on his own addiction in the group, this initial dialogue shows typical difficulties during early developmental phases of the group. Gordon's long history of denial and lack of communication of feelings, trust, and personal needs carries over into the early group sessions.

Gordon: Nothing against the rest of you here, but I really don't understand the reason for putting me in here with such heavy abusers. Ray, how was I chosen for this group anyway?

Ray: You don't see yourself fitting in?

Liz: Yeah, Gordon, you think your boozing's different from ours. Looks to me like you're Mr. High and Mighty and we're a bunch of gutter bums.

Alice: Afraid we've got your number? Still denying what you are. Boy, have you got something to learn!

Carolyn: What I see happening here is basically a lack of trust in this group. That's not only an important issue for here but for outside as well. What I want to do is turn on the video and go back over the introductions and the individual goals you'd all set for yourself that we did in our first session. They may help us all begin to see this group as a unified whole with common needs.

As Brill (1981, p. 129) indicates, during the initial phases, the group leader should provide support and structure, setting the stage for group members to develop trust and cohesiveness. The video tape is important to this endeavor and will be used throughout the sessions. The use of video taping is a powerful tool for assessment, feedback, and therapeutic purposes, catching in pictures and words the dysfunctional defense systems the clients build for themselves (Brill, 1981; Hay & Nathan, 1982; Sobell & Sobell, 1978).

Responsibility

Treatment schedule.   Gordon is going to be very busy with his day once he comes out of detoxification. Gordon will be up at 7:00 every morning. He is responsible for getting his room clean, showering, and dressing. Before breakfast he will meet with his small group and read and discuss the daily passage from the *Twenty-Four Hours a Day* book (Alcoholics Anonymous, 1985). From 9:00 to 10:30 every morning he will be in a small group. This group will deal with value clarification, assertion training, enabling behavior, anger, and a variety of other topics that fuel the fires of alcoholism. From 10:30 to 12:00 Gordon will be in a small therapeutic group that will look specifically at each member's maladaptive coping skills and defense mechanisms. After lunch, from 12:30 to 1:30 he will be in an occupational therapy group that will allow him to use his hands as well as his mind. From 1:30 to 2:30 he will be in a physical therapy group to get his body back in shape. Both of these afternoon activities are for the specific purpose of teaching him to substitute positive addictions for the negative one of alcoholism. He will then be allowed time for a shower and a bit of leisure. From 3:30 to 4:30 he will learn about the AA "Big Book" (Alcoholics Anonymous, 1976). From 4:30 to 5:30 he will have an individual session with his counselors to review his progress, set goals, and obtain homework assignments. After dinner, from 6:00 to 8:00 he may either be in a family therapy session, attend an AA meeting, listen to a speaker on addiction, or view an educational video tape. After this he will have reading and journal writing to complete. By 11:00 he will be dead tired and ready for bed.

Cramming the day with all these activities fills two purposes. First, a great deal of learning needs to take place in the short time available. Each activity is designed to furnish part of this reeducation process. Second, there is usually very little structure in the lives of chemical dependents. The therapeutic community and its activities teach them to live responsibly. By being on time, taking care of their rooms, and completing their assignments, they reengage in responsible living and relearn to make commitments and keep them (Parker, 1986).

Session 3. Clients learn to retake control over their lives, but this is not always easily done. Listen to Gordon as he confronts responsibility.

Gordon: What gripes me is they treat you like kids around here. Do this, go there, learn that!

Alice: Do you know why we're supposed to do that? It's because we need to know those things if we're going to be any good when we get out.

Gordon: That's fine, but I'm an adult and I can read this on my own.

Liz: Have you? And if you did, could you get anything out of it?

Gordon: I don't know who you are to talk about responsibility. They nailed you for raiding the pharmacy cabinet, didn't they?

Carolyn: When you unload on Liz, that's a neat way of getting the load off your back. If you could make us as angry at you as you feel toward everybody else, then you'd be justified in telling us all to buzz off.

Gordon: She asked for it. We're talking about all the Mickey Mouse stuff like cleaning up your room and so forth. If that's helping me with my drinking problem, I'll kiss your foot.

Manuel (Gordon's roommate): Maybe if you'd paid more attention to the Mickey Mouse stuff and not the booze you wouldn't be here now. Every morning I got to say something about living in a pig sty. If you were that sloppy I'm surprised you still got that big buck job.

Gordon: Oh! Now it's my work. I'll have you know I carried my load at work and I sure as hell don't see what making my bed's got to do with getting back on track.

Ray: When the others say those things to you, it's hard to believe you aren't responsible. Hence, you react angrily to them. While you were highly responsible and capable in the past, it's tough and hurts to be confronted with the fact that you're having trouble keeping up now.

Gordon: That's not right, I . . .

Ruth: Then what is right, Gordon? Sure it's not fun. It's not supposed to be a vacation. You've got 24 more days here. You haven't been responsible for a long time is what the others are saying, and now you pull the same thing with us.

Gordon: What do you want from me? You all sound just like my wife.

Ray: It's the same old tune you're hearing from them, and it makes you angry when you have to take on responsibility, so you'll show them.

Manuel: If he can't even get his bed made, he's not showing me much.

Gordon: I'll show you all!

Carolyn: It's not a question of showing them anything. It's a question, I think, of having the courage to show yourself.

Gordon: I don't know. It scares the hell out of me. I'm not sure what I can do anymore.

Ray: When you say it that way, I think we all understand. It's not just the simple things like making a bed or reading the assignment. It's the scary feeling of doing something you haven't done for a long time and wondering whether you'll fail again.

If Gordon can find enough fault with the treatment center, the staff, or their practices, and get them to respond in the same kind of manner, he will be "justified" in his stance and also justified in returning to alcohol. This rebellious attitude is met by the therapist with empathy and some interpretation. Confrontation would be inappropriate and would place the locus of control too far outside the client—it would put control of his sobriety into the hands of someone else (Wallace, 1978, p. 38). When he answers the other group members in caustic ways, the workers respond empathically to the persons attacked, and when Gordon is attacked, the workers respond in supportive ways to him, casting hypotheses about how he feels now and how it may generalize to others who have attacked him (Ohlsen, 1970, pp. 116–129). By not reinforcing such dependent behavior, but reinforcing Gordon when he takes responsibility on his own shoulders, the workers provide a model for reassuming independence (Blume, 1978, p. 71).

Alice: (Weeping.) I know it sounds silly, but that damn wood sculpture I've been working on in art therapy is terrible. I can't get it right. It's just like everything else in my life.

Gordon: Ah, look, Alice. I used to do that as a hobby. If you wouldn't mind I could maybe give you a hand. I know how frustrating that can be.

Manuel: Hey, man! That's the first time you ever said you'd do anything for anybody. You feelin' OK?

Gordon: It's no big deal.

Ray: Yet I think Manuel's got a point. It's good to see you care about Alice. Offering to help her says you're taking on responsibility for someone else, something you haven't been able to do in a long time. Now if we can just get you to make Manuel's bed. (General laughter, Gordon included.)

Denial

In adults a rigid, nonmodifiable, and repeated use of denial is a defense that is usually associated with psychotic disorders and addiction. As long as it is intact, the client cannot feel concern with doing anything constructive about his or her illness (Maxwell, 1986, p. 176). It is the glue that holds a shattered self-esteem together. The most difficult task of the worker is to lessen the denial and encourage increased self-awareness and disclosure while at the same time keeping anxiety at minimal levels (Wallace, 1978, p. 32). In the treatment of alcoholism, two levels of denial exist. The first is the denial of the presence and magnitude of a drinking problem (Blume, 1978, pp. 68–69). Continued denial specifically associated with drinking is a poor prognosis, and the chemical dependent who continues to use denial is not likely to stay sober.

The second level is denial of long-standing life problems. While it may sound antithetical to recovery, denial of serious life problems other than drinking is an appropriate defense mechanism early on in treatment. This is so because those are the stressors that probably triggered drug use in the first place. To break down defenses in these areas would put more stress on the system, increase anxiety, and set the client up for failure (Chalmers & Wallace, 1978, p. 262).

Confrontation.   As Adler (1956, p. 396) says, "It is not enough to be a friend of mankind, a benevolent counselor. Such counseling simply makes life agreeable for the client; the counselor praises the client, all the time believing that the counselor will arrive at results through the charm of his or her personality." When heavy denial and its defensive consorts are encountered, confrontation is probably the most potent and dangerous weapon the worker has (Lawson, Ellis, & Rivers, 1984, p. 125). The use of confrontation as a therapeutic technique needs to be carefully considered. Putting a resisting and denying client on the "hot seat" is a questionable practice for a variety of reasons. First, other clients may viciously attack the client and in the process force compliance or make a scapegoat of the client. Second, focusing only on the one client may permit other members in the group to become less involved. Third, dependent clients are excellent at seducing others into taking responsibility through advice giving (Ohlsen, 1970, pp. 127, 168).

The purpose of confrontation is not to vent personal frustration, impose belief systems contrary to those of the client, or act in punitive ways (Lawson, Ellis, & Rivers, 1984, p. 101). Critical in the confrontation is the worker's emotional astuteness and competence in determining the correct moment to confront (Perez, 1985, p. 164). A main ingredient in successfully confronting a client is trust, which is essential for the confrontation to carry the most therapeutic weight.

A principal characteristic of confrontation is its challenge. The challenge is embedded in a question so that an immediate feeling response is evoked. A second characteristic of confrontation is that it is direct and action oriented. The client is constantly placed in new roles and situations calling for a response. Explored in a sensitive, perceptive manner, these new roles and situations enable a client to be aware of discrepancies between behaviors and intentions, feelings and messages, and insights and actions (Dinkmeyer, Pew, & Dinkmeyer, 1979, p. 110). Confrontive statements can be hooked to reflective and interpretive statements. They also are generally connected with an owning statement, one that says clearly that "I," the counselor, own this. If the client denies the statement, then the confrontation is redirected: "OK, if that's not you, then what is you?" Confrontations are generally made in the form of a demand and are linked to alternatives. Confrontation catches a client in a contradiction and asks the client why he or she behaves in such a contradictory manner. Used judiciously and altered to fit the dilemma, confrontation can be extremely helpful in jarring clients out of old response patterns (Shulman, 1973, p. 198). There are five major areas of confrontation:

1. experiential: a response to any discrepancy perceived by the worker
2. strength: focused on the client's resources, especially if the client does not recognize them
3. weakness: focused on the client's liabilities or pathology

4. didactic: clarification of misinformation or lack of information
5. encouragement to action: pressing the client to act on his or her world in a constructive manner and discouraging a passive attitude toward life.

Experiential, strength, and encouragement should be used most frequently, with much less reliance on exploiting the client's weaknesses (Lawson, Ellis, & Rivers, 1984, p. 103).

Session 5. Confrontation is always used in relation to behaviors and never used to attack a client's personhood. Many confrontations will be paradoxical, enlarged to farcical dimensions, and have humor attached so that the client may clearly see the ridiculousness of the behavior called to question.

Gordon: It's easy for you to say I shouldn't go drinking with the guys after work. You just can't do that and stay on the inside track.

Carolyn: (Catching the discrepancy.) So if you don't do what they want, you're out. Yet the very act of continuing to drink has almost put you out. Do you see the discrepancy there?

Gordon: Yes, but I've got to be a team player. Can't let those young sharks get ahead.

Manuel: (Calling the question.) Ahead of what?

Carolyn: (Creating an exaggerated image.) Picture this, Gordon. You're a little minnow swimming around in a martini glass with all these big hungry fish circling you, but you're so goofy from that vodka ocean that you swim right into their jaws. How does that fit?

Gordon: (Chuckles.) OK. I'll accept that. If only there was some way to get out of that double bind.

Ray: (Proposing action.) What would happen if you did exactly the opposite of what you've been doing? That is, just turn that martini lunch down. Become one of the sober sharks instead of the drunken minnows? How could you do that?

Gordon: I don't know. (Lamely.) Then I wouldn't be a regular guy.

Ruth: (Drawing the paradox.) Yeah. You've been a regular guy, all right. That's with a three-martini lunch. Why don't you put a half-dozen down? Then you'd be Superman. I thought I was Superwoman when I did that crap and you see me now.

Gordon: (Sullenly.) Now, wait a second! I didn't mean that. (Turns to Carolyn.) That's not true. How can she say that? We're supposed to be helping each other. How can you let her attack me?

Carolyn: (Redirecting.) Then what did you mean? (Placing a demand with a reflection.) I understand how that hurts, but I also believe that when you try to get me to support you and imply that I'm a lousy counselor if I don't, I'd just be playing into that game of "poor me." What will you do instead? (Proposing alternatives.) You have some choices. You can sit and sulk, you can be dependent and ask me to take your part, or you can use your considerable strength and make a clear assertive statement back. Which will it be?

Alice: (Creating an image.) See how you get yourself. You want to be so darn independent, yet you continuously say, "Come and hold me, look what a poor child am I." I get this picture of a big baby in a crib and it's full of empty bourbon bottles and you nestled in there.

Gordon: By God that isn't true. I'm not a baby. Life's been a bitch.

Carolyn: (Commiserating overbearingly.) Yep! Life's that way. It's rotten, cruel and unusual punishment. Wouldn't it be wonderful to make everybody responsible for your drinking put on hair shirts and roll around in cinders. That would pay them back for all the harm they've done to you.

Gordon: People just don't understand me, and that includes all of you. I'm gonna leave this stinkin' place.

Carolyn: (Avoiding a trap.) I'd not like to see that happen, but what they're doing is confronting your own ways of fooling yourself and attempting to get you to see the strengths you've got. If I get them off your back, you don't have to be responsible. If I don't, you leave and I'm at fault. Either way you'd have an excuse for continuing to blame somebody else. (Attributing the projection.) It seems as if you'd like me to get into the same kinds of double binds you put yourself in. (Owning.) So if you believe I'm not much of a counselor because of that, it's certainly your privilege.

Gordon: (Rocks back in chair.) I do that? Damn! I guess maybe I do.

Some of the responses may seem to put Gordon on the hot seat, but the other members are willing to own that they too have been where Gordon is now. The confrontations point to the affective, cognitive, and behavioral discrepancies in Gordon's life, not to the totality of Gordon, the person. The confrontations are exhortations to action. The group is pushing Gordon to make changes in his life, particularly in regard to the way he denies and defends his drinking behavior.

Mental Sets

According to Ellis (1987), it is not the event itself that causes us to feel and act in certain irrational ways, but our belief about that event that gets us into trouble. By starting to think "insane" thoughts about what people or events "should," "ought," "must" do or be to make it a perfect world, chemical dependents become victims to their irrational thoughts about the event. By putting such irrational statements up in the billboard of their minds, chemical dependents can easily fall back into hurt, rejected feelings and manifest these feelings in behavior designed to pay back the persons or events that intrude into their self-centered universe. It is extremely important to catch chemical dependents as they begin to build these billboards, because this kind of thinking is what starts a chain of events that can ultimately build up to another drinking episode. The key to stopping this "insane" thinking is teaching the person to recognize the cues that appear antecedent to the negative feelings and subsequent bad behavioral outcomes. Once these cues are picked up, then new, rational statements can be manufactured to replace the old, debilitating ones that underlie beliefs.

Session 7. A videotape of session 6 was used as the focus for group therapy in session 7. Session 6 had examined the events and behaviors that brought each client to St. Polycarp. The group viewed excerpts of session 6 that were selected by the group leaders to vividly re-create and model each individual's unique addictive situation and to stimulate and to uncover each member's defense mechanisms. Clients first portrayed themselves; then, after a discussion of defense mechanisms chemical dependents commonly use, members exchanged roles and attempted to model what the other's defenses appeared to be.

Manuel: Man, those were tough. Liz played me to a T! I also thought Alice really hit Gordon's nail on the head too!

Ray: How he first rationalizes, and then when things really get hot, regresses.

Gordon: Before I saw that video tape I would never have believed it! But there I was. Rationalizing my drinking by telling myself I was "sick" when I couldn't make it to work because I was hung over or still smashed. Boy, was that sad! And then with my doctor about my health. Just throwing a fit. Alice role-played me so well, it was as if she'd been there. It made me sick to watch that. What a jerk!

Ruth: What about that preadolescent stuff, "I'll take my ball and go home," see how Liz did that with the doctor routine. It was just like yesterday with the family therapy. I didn't know whether that was your mother or wife, the way you were manipulating her and sulking like a kid who didn't get any candy.

Gordon: (Angrily.) What do you mean, acting like a kid? Why don't we take a look at how you act around that teenager of yours?

Liz: Look at what you just did, Gordon. You're regressing right now!

Alice: That video tape didn't lie. Don't you see how you get into that? It's weird that you can see the rationalizing, but kick up your heels when we call you on the regression.

Carolyn: Remember the work we did on cueing in our verbal and nonverbal behavior the other day. Notice what feelings you get when your defense mechanisms kick in and what thoughts go through your head to get that going.
(Gordon looks at videotape again.)

Gordon: (Sheepishly.) Maybe I was acting like a kid. Maybe I wasn't connecting that stuff you call cueing to my real life.

Carolyn: Right here we have a good example of how you might begin to use that cueing. When Ruth confronted you just a minute ago, what messages went through your mind to cause you to react angrily and then attack her—rather than looking at yourself?

Gordon: The first thing that flashed through was, "You're just like my wife." She's always implying I'm not capable of acting like an adult. She makes me crazy when she does that.

Carolyn: Using Gordon as an example, what cues did we teach you all to recognize and what did we learn to do to counteract our irrational thinking as well as our behavior?

Ruth: First off, Gordon needs to recognize that as one of those stop signs you were talking about. Any time that he relates to the old ways he behaved toward Amy and hears, "I'm not good enough," he needs to see that as a warning sign that he's kicking in a lot of that old dependent, put-down crap.

Manuel: He also could change "she" to "I" 'cause it's really him and his beliefs about what she said. He allows that to happen.

Alice: He could make an assertive statement out of it, like, "I understand how you might feel that way, but right now I'm feeling like I'm behaving pretty straight with you and it hurts me that you'd feel I haven't changed."

Cueing provides Gordon with psychological stop signs. These are not easy to see, especially when, in the heat of the moment, it is all too easy to revert to years' worth of programmed thinking. Cueing is like any other new skill and will take much practice and feedback before the client is able to "rewire" his or her thinking.

Carolyn: I want you all to list out your cues for those predicaments that make you crazy, angry, depressed, and so on in your logs. Then let's work on building new belief statements. Monitor yourself as we work together and see if you can catch yourself before others do. If you feel a bit odd when you put those new statements in and say them, then you're on the right track.

If clients cannot catch the insane messages they send themselves, then other physiological or affective responses may work as cues. Sweating hands, a lump in the throat, and a palpitating heart may be good physical cues. The flush of anger, the chagrin of embarrassment, and the gloom of despair may be good affective cues.

Setting Events

Sobell and Sobell (1978) have done significant work in demonstrating how setting events reinforce the desire to drink. In their therapeutic experiments they have rigged elaborate sets that include complete taverns. Subtly but surely, settings and the events that occur within them provide powerful cues to respond in particular kinds of ways. Returning to a world that is filled with potent environmental cues to drink strains the newfound coping skills of the recovering alcoholic to the limit and can create another crisis point.

Putting chemical dependents in role plays and imaginal sets in groups will work effectively in helping them recognize and manipulate environments that are powerfully reinforcing of their chemical dependency. By learning how to use cognitive restructuring (McMullin & Giles, 1981), imaging (Neisser, 1976), coping thoughts (Cormier & Hackney, 1987), emotive imagery and covert modeling (Cormier & Cormier, 1985), and stress inoculation (Meichenbaum, 1985), clients are able to armor themselves against the negative setting events that they will inevitably encounter.

Session 10. The group has constructed and role-played a setting event that portrays Gordon getting into his car after a very stressful day at work, which has been interrupted by phone calls from home saying that Mark has been suspended from school because he was found with a marijuana cigarette in his possession. Gordon watches as Manuel plays the part.

Manuel: (As Gordon, talking to himself as he guns the car out of the company lot.) Jesus Christ! Everything was supposed to be better. If this is better, screw it! Work sucks! The president is on my back again. Produce! Produce! Produce! That's all I hear. And now Mark! I suppose that's my fault too. Amy sure laid that one on me while going nuts over the phone. That's what I got to look forward to when I hit the door. Hey, there's the Olde English Inn coming up over the hill. My favorite water-ing hole, those dark oak booths and overstuffed chairs. Man, do they make a mean Manhattan in there. I can just smell that aroma. I'll bet some of the old crowd's still there too, and Roxie, my favorite bartender. They sure never gave me any flak. Glad to see me. It's happy hour too! Man, are my hands sweating, I'm shaking too. I've got to settle down. Two for the price of one. To hell with it. I'll just have one and go. It'll take the edge off before I hit the door and have to deal with Amy and Mark. (Manuel turns the car into the inn.)

Ray: OK! Now, that's not a pretty scene, but we know that there are going to be times just like that. The world isn't perfect, and you're going to run into problems like that, feel those lousy emotions, and those tempting places like the Olde English Inn are going to be there just waiting for a day like that. What are you going to do, Gordon?

Gordon: All right. Let me put my plan into action. My positive self-statements will be, "I don't care how rough it's been at work, I did a helluva job today. The boss al-ways gripes like that around the end of the month so don't take it personally." My stress inoculates will be a number of things. First, I'll put Mozart on the tape deck, that's calming and reminds me of being on the banks of Lake Zurich just watching the sailboats glide by. Yeah, I'm already relaxed. Behaviorally, I can practice my breathing skills, just taking deep easy breaths and letting all that stress flow right out my nose. While I'm doing that, I can see my jogging shoes and sweats waiting for me by the back door at home.

I can replace my negative thoughts about home by saying, "I would have come in and blustered and stormed around and grilled Mark, generally raised hell and then sulked. That didn't do a damn bit of good except get me stressed out even more. I know I can think clearer and more rationally after I've worked out. I'll ask Amy to go for a jog around Audubon Park. I can feel that sweat pouring out of my body, clean-ing it out. I can feel my body, hard, lean, coordinated, just like a fine machine, just rolling along, eating up the miles. That'll feel good."

Now here comes the Inn over the hill. I'm starting to think how easy it'd be to just turn in there. I can feel my hands getting sweaty, and my throat's dry. I put my thought stopping into gear, "STOP THAT! Switch. Think what your sagging, pulpy body was after you got through with a bout in there, turkey! You couldn't stumble to the john without gasping for air. God, were you ever a sorry sucker."

To cue myself to how good I now feel, I'll flex my leg and feel that hard thigh muscle, a great tactile cue to remind me how far I've come, and I'm not giving that up. Reviewing my self-talk, I can say, "Yeah, Roxie and the inn were a great place to get quietly smashed, but that was then. Looking at the place in broad daylight, it's shopworn, and I've got real oak in my study instead of that fiberboard, ersatz stuff in there. Ha! I'll bet the boys look a little shopworn too after today. Further, I never really liked that sweet smell of a Manhattan, always covered it with a cigarette. I don't want that crap. There's nothing like a V-8, and only 10 calories too. Then what I want is to get out and run."

I also know that after I get back from jogging I can use all the communication skills I've learned here. No ranting and raving. It's a bitch about Mark, but I don't need to catastrophize over it. I can handle that, and I'll take the time to handle it.

My family's the most important thing in the world to me, and I'm not just paying lip service to it, I'm living it! Press the accelerator down and go on by with no regrets.

By taping and practicing these new mental images over and over with the assistance of the workers and the group, Gordon learns how to use a wide variety of positive coping mechanisms to get by this potentially dangerous environmental set. This is not a one-shot exercise. It will take Gordon a great deal of practice to reprogram himself to ignore those old cues that set him up to drink.

Family

The attitudes, structure, and function of the family system have been shown to be perhaps the most important variables in the outcome of treatment. If the system changes from enabling to more adaptive behavior, it may sustain improvement and change in the alcoholic (Kaufman & Pattison, 1982a, p. 669). However, this is easier said than done because, paradoxically, if the alcoholic makes a commitment to stop drinking, the maladaptive family may become so threatened that it does everything in its power to reinstitute the homeostasis of alcoholism. In the case of Gordon, several hypotheses support this idea. If his drinking ceased, one or more family members might attempt to sabotage his sobriety; Amy might undermine the treatment to ensure that Gordon's drinking recurred so she could retain control. The drinking may represent a cover to distract attention from underlying relationship conflicts. Gordon's alcohol use may have been a stabilizing rather than a disruptive influence on the family's lifestyle and represented attempts to deal with family issues that could not be confronted during sober periods.

From the perspective of the codependent, the vehemently denied but enabling statement translates into something like, "If I get you fixed, then I can let go, and you can take care of me and I won't have to be responsible ever again! But I can't really risk that, because I really want the power of control, without having to take responsibility for that power." The threat of disturbing such a tenuous family equilibrium creates a crisis of substantial proportions, and it is one of the most difficult situations with which the worker must deal.

At St. Polycarp, members of the family are not allowed to see the client for the first ten days of treatment. The only interaction between the staff and the family in this early stage is to obtain a social history. Families are kept away from the chemical dependent for fear that they may try to sabotage treatment efforts in a bid to return the recovering addict back to his or her addiction (Parker, 1986).

Amy: (On the telephone.) Carolyn, I know you said that we wouldn't be allowed to come see Gordon until we first came together in family therapy, but his folks have flown in from Chicago and I was wondering if we couldn't just bring them out for a while. He sounded pretty good when I talked to him on the phone. The kids really miss him, too.

Carolyn: I understand how his parents must be concerned, but as I told you when we took the social history, these first few days are critical to Gordon's assuming responsibility for getting well. As I told you then, it's awfully easy to fall back into old ways of behaving. You wouldn't want the work we've done so far to come undone, would you?

Amy: Well . . . of course not. But what will I tell Gordon's parents?

Carolyn: Tell them the truth. That Gordon's been dependent on other people a long time. He's got to handle this himself for a bit longer.

The worker lays a guilt trip on Amy. This may be construed as manipulation of the rankest type, but the chances for sabotage are too great, even though the client's family may have badgered the client to go into treatment in the first place. Indeed, if Amy feels that Gordon is getting better, this may cause a great deal of anxiety for her. If she has been a "supermom," she may be afraid that in his newfound strength Gordon may usurp her place in the system. Alcoholics may also play this game by complaining that their family really needs them (Parker, 1986).

Fourth day.

Gordon: Look, I've got the booze out of my system. I really need to get out of here.

Carolyn: We discussed that when you agreed to come into the program. You'll see your family with me next week in therapy.

Gordon: (Adamant.) My family really needs me! By God! You don't want me to see them. Just because you don't have a family, trying to stick it to me. (Sarcastic.) Hell, you couldn't get a man again if you were covered with gold dust!

Carolyn: (Calmly.) It would be neat if you could blame me for all that's gone on in your family over the years, but it won't wash. They also needed you when you were a drunk for the last four years.

Gordon: (Pleading, promising, and whining.) Look. I've really learned my lesson this time. I haven't even wanted a drink since I've been at St. Poly's.

Carolyn: (Assertively.) I don't listen to that. I don't need any promises, and you don't need to make any. We operate like AA, one day at a time. This is the fourth day you've been sober. Tomorrow we'll work on five. That's the way it is.

Gordon: (Screaming.) Listen you cold, merciless bitch. I can leave here any damn time I want to.

Carolyn: (Calmly and calculatedly.) If screaming is your way of getting me to cave in, that won't work either. If you leave against medical advice, and that's what it is, you are signing your death warrant. Is that how you will help your family?

Gordon: (Whining.) You don't trust me.

Carolyn: You're right about that. You haven't earned my trust yet. You can earn it by doing your level best in this program. Show me you want to stay sober and that'll go a long way toward it. Leave and you'll end up dead inside of a year. I want you to clearly understand, physically dead. So if you've become so responsible, make the choice. If you stay here I'll do everything in my power to help you get back to your family in good shape. If you leave there's nothing I can do for you. So choose.

The worker experiences a wide range of the client's manipulations. She turns Gordon's ploys against him in calm, factual, and confrontive ways. She will not take on any of the client's responsibility for getting well other than to say she'll work with him, nor will she accept any of the client's residual emotions that he tries to project onto her. The worker is not above painting a very grim picture for the client's future when he threatens to leave. Her primary mission is to keep him in treatment, and Carolyn will use her considerable manipulative skills to do that when necessary.

Family options.   Families like Gordon's have three options: (1) keep doing what they have been doing, and nothing changes, except for the worse, (2) detach and emotionally distance themselves from the alcoholic, and changes may occur for the better, or (3) separate and physically distance themselves from the alcoholic, and changes may also occur for the better. Although paradoxical to what one might assume to be the closeness and caring the alcoholic's support system ought to demonstrate, choices 2 or 3 are the most supportive ways significant others can act toward an alcoholic. The alcoholic must understand that significant others will no longer tolerate the addictive behavior and the harm that it does to them. While such choices undoubtedly may breed crisis, this in no way means the people in the support system have given up. Choices 2 and 3 indicate that the family members will become responsible for themselves rather than trying to change the alcoholic. If the family can say, "We prefer that you not kill yourself, but we won't let you kill us, so you must make a choice as we have," this is an excellent start on the road to recovery (Kaufman & Pattison, 1982b, p. 1026). Even if both codependents and dependent agree to change, there should not be explicit or implicit assumptions that family ties will be fully reconstituted. While long-term nurturing of all system members is ideal, such positive interactions will not happen overnight. Each individual member first has to get intimate with himself or herself before trying to do so with the alcoholic. Any attempts to reassume responsibility for the alcoholic, no matter how well intended, have a high probability of enabling and promoting a relapse (Maxwell, 1986, p. 209). Avoidance of enabling behavior and assumption of responsibility are difficult as Gordon's first family therapy session shows.

Family therapy session.   The primary task of the worker in the family is to detect and penetrate the defense systems the family has set up to keep things stable. Almost without exception, alcoholic families will have real trouble expressing feelings and communicating with one another (Maxwell, 1986, pp. 205–206). By keeping a low profile in the beginning, the worker lets the pathology of the family emerge (Parker, 1986). As Carolyn sits quietly, Gordon, Amy, Lisa, and Mark exchange stilted pleasantries and defensive comments, punctuated by long, awkward silences. As soon as the worker obtains an adequate assessment of the family's dynamic interaction, she becomes involved.

Amy: Now, I don't want you to worry about anything. I talked to your boss and he assured me the company is behind you 100 percent.

Gordon: That's great!

Carolyn: Amy, I'd like you to notice what you just did. You decided to take care of Gordon. What about your own feelings about carrying the load?

Amy: I just didn't want him to worry about his job. I know how much he's put into it.

Carolyn: Yes, but what about your feelings?

Amy: It just seems to me that Gordon should concentrate his efforts on getting better, don't you think?

Carolyn: Do you see what you're doing? I've asked you twice to speak to your feelings. Yet each time, you take responsibility for Gordon. You talk about him and not yourself. You pose a question that asks for my agreement. And you shift to events rather than dealing with your feelings. How does that strike you, Gordon?

Gordon: Er, I don't know. I guess Amy ought to express how she feels.

Carolyn: How do you feel?

Gordon: I think we probably don't do enough talking about our feelings.

Carolyn: That's right, but how do you feel?

This short exchange graphically demonstrates the tremendous difficulty the two adults have in expressing feelings to one another. They adroitly shift off this topic in a variety of ways. One very subtle way to avoid direct confrontation about feelings is to send a messenger. Of course, the messenger has to be very careful how the news is delivered, otherwise he or she may get psychologically murdered in completing the task.

Amy: Lisa, tell your father what Grandpa and Grandma had to say.

Lisa: Ah, they said they were real sorry they didn't get to see you, and hoped you get well. They'd have really liked to stay and come here today, but Grandpa had to get back to Chicago for a meeting.

Carolyn: I wonder why you asked Lisa to tell Gordon that. My guess is that's a touchy subject about his parents leaving. Does your mom often ask you to do that?

Lisa: You bet! You do that all the time, Mom. Whenever you've got something you think'll cause a ruckus, you always send me to tell Dad 'cause you think he'll take it from me. Then I'm the bad guy. I hate it!

Carolyn: So you see, there's another way of getting around dealing with feelings. Send somebody else and let them deal with it, because feelings are risky, scary, and hard to handle.

Amy: Lisa has always been the apple of her dad's eye. She's always had a way with him.

Carolyn: Excuse me for picking on you right now, Amy, but what were you just doing?

Amy: I was talking about Lisa and her relationship with her dad.

Carolyn: That's right! You were talking *about* her, not *to* her. What would happen if you said that straight out? You might risk getting a feeling response back.

Lisa: Mom, you wouldn't like that. You always tell me to bear up when I try to talk to you about my feelings, and that goes for you too, Dad! Mom, you're too worried about what's going on with Dad's drinking to care about me, and Dad, you're too worried about getting a drink to listen, and if it wasn't booze it was work. Is it any wonder this family's screwed up?

Carolyn: Great, Lisa! Lisa's raised some pretty hot issues. Any feelings about them?

Gordon: (Looking at Carolyn.) I guess I just didn't realize I wasn't being the father I could be to her. I didn't realize I was doing that. I'm sorry.

Carolyn: Gordon, do you want me to be your messenger to Lisa?

Gordon: No!

Carolyn: Then don't tell me, but tell her that.

Amy: Well, I just know Mark doesn't feel that way. A real little trooper. He's kept a stiff upper lip through all this, kept up his grades and done everything around the house, plus made his own spending money mowing yards.

Carolyn: Amy, it is interesting that you find it difficult to feel for yourself, yet can tell others how they feel and even answer for them. What I'd like to do now is give each one of you an assignment for next time that specifically gets at what problems I see with communication in this group. Mark, since you didn't say anything today, I want you to write a letter to each member in the family telling each how you feel about him or her. Lisa, I'd like you to wear a big paper heart next time, and every time somebody doesn't respond directly to you or speak to their feelings, I'd like you to tear a piece of your heart off. Amy, in the codependency group I want you to solicit direct, feeling responses from people. I'll give you the questions to ask. Gordon, I want you to write down some of the feelings you had in here today into a script, and then take it back to the group and we'll role-play it on the video tape.

The major task is teaching all the family members to express their feelings in an open and honest way. Debilitating communication patterns are pointed out over and over to all family members who engage in disruptive communications. It is noteworthy that no mention is made of Gordon's drinking by anyone except Lisa. This conspiracy of silence still continues even after Gordon is in a chemical treatment unit and the whole family is in therapy for the problem. As Parker (1986) says, "There's a big, pet, pink rhinoceros [alcoholism] sitting there in the middle of the family, but everybody circles around it as if it didn't even exist, and it just keeps getting bigger and bigger and taking up more space." This problem will need to be reflected by the worker, for the sooner the alcoholism is brought into the open, the quicker the family can start building a new communication system.

Another issue is Mark, who has remained silent throughout the session. Invariably there is someone who can be extremely helpful in changing the system (Kaufman & Pattison, 1982b, p. 1031). Mark may have a great deal to do with changing the family network. Lisa is also a potent member of this system. The worker early on acknowledges her strength and reinforces her for clear, directional feeling responses—a rarity in this family. Finally, to facilitate communication, tasks may be assigned within the session as homework.

Session 17. As the masking behaviors that support the codependency are stripped away, it may be expected that more and more radical attempts are made to restore the old system. A very traumatic experience from a multiple-family session that occurred the day before session 17 illustrates this dramatically. Ten minutes before the end of the multiple-family session, Amy announced that she was so distraught she was thinking of suicide. This threw things into an uproar and necessitated an individual suicide intervention with Amy that lasted two hours after the group session. Gordon, who had been attempting to deal with some of his feelings with Amy, was paralyzed and shocked into submission. This therapeutic material was immediately brought back to the group.

To help Gordon deal with this ploy, an "alter ego" exercise was videotaped. An alter-ego routine is done by having members of the group stand behind each seated role player and verbally state the potent (but unspoken) self-thoughts and self-talk that they perceive to be going on inside the role player's head.

Carolyn: (Role-modeling Amy.) Gordon, I understand you wanted to talk to me about what happened in the family session yesterday.

Ruth: (Taking the role of Carolyn's alter ego [Amy], standing behind Carolyn, with her hands resting gently on Carolyn's shoulders.) I don't like this one little bit. But I really got him, the bastard.

Gordon: (Avoiding eye contact and stammering.) Yes . . . I was disturbed about the way you brought up the suicide stuff . . . without me knowing about it.

Ray: (Taking the role of alter ego of Gordon, standing directly behind Gordon, with his hands resting gently on Gordon's shoulders.) This is scary as hell! I'd like to kill her myself. I'm struggling like crazy to stay straight and she pulls that number. I want to tell her what I really feel about that. But I can't. I've got to protect her and me, so don't run your mouth. But I'm feeling betrayed too! Why am I feeling so paralyzed?

Carolyn: (Role-modeling Amy.) Dear, I really didn't mean it the way it looked, it just came out. I couldn't help it. They said to get our feelings out. This whole mess is . . . I just want you to get well and for us to be just like we used to be . . . right after we were married.

Ruth: (As alter ego of Carolyn [Amy].) I've got to cover this up, put it back on him. Let him wallow in it and see what he's done to me. It's payback time.

Gordon: (Looking Carolyn straight in the eyes.) Look, I feel lousy about what I've done in the past. But there's nothing I can do about it now. When you pull that kind of stunt it's just the past all over again. It hurts like hell when you do that. What I want to do is cut through all that phony baloney we've put on each other. I don't feel like it was ever anything but that. What I'm concerned about is right now. I'm scared to death I'm not gonna cut this, and I need you to understand that. I don't believe I'll break, whatever happens. You don't have to act helpless or self-destructive to keep me in line or earn my love. You've got that already and you'll have more of it, the better both of us get. By the way, you still haven't talked about how you feel.

Group: (Cheers.) All right, Gordon! Way to go!

Ray: (As alter ego of Gordon.) Holy cow! I don't believe I did that. I spilled the beans, told her how I felt. I thought I'd throw up, I was so scared, but I didn't. Maybe I have got what it takes to get out of this. I feel good. I really feel *good!* (Breaks from role.) How did that go, Gordon?

Gordon: (Smiling from ear to ear.) That's the first time in years, maybe ever, I said stuff like that. And you alter egos are right. I do feel good. If that had happened before I came here, it'd be a sure bet I'd have started drinking. There may be something else that sets me off, but I don't believe it'll be from keeping my feelings shut up now.

Ray: Could you now do that with Amy?

Gordon: It'd still be scary, but yes. I think, no, I *feel* like I can.

By bouncing submerged feelings off Gordon, the alter egos attempt to make crystal clear what the hidden messages are that drive the codependent and dependent. Given the opportunity to bring these agendas into the open, dependents and codependents can construct self-enhancing, positive, feeling-based, coping statements that untangle the snares and traps they set for one another. Although difficult and risky, constructing these kinds of statements is absolutely necessary to forming new and equitable relationships in a drug-free family system.

Aftercare

At St. Polycarp the aftercare program requires that the client attend meetings two evenings a week for at least six months following dismissal from inpatient treatment. To address the issues of codependency and enabling activities, workers attempt to ensure that all significant family members also participate (McCrory, 1987). The objectives of aftercare are (1) to provide ongoing education and information needed to maintain sobriety, (2) to create an environment in which natural and healthy social-influence patterns reinforce positive behaviors and self-esteem, (3) to establish an ongoing group of caring, accepting, empathic, genuine, trusting individuals who serve as an extended family, among whom the individual can always feel safe and understood, and (4) to serve as the first line of safety any time a crisis occurs. The aftercare safety line may need to extend to one of the most difficult crises the drug dependent faces—the euphoria that often accompanies recovery.

Euphoria. Maxwell (1986, p. 229) refers to recovery euphoria as a reaction formation. Gordon used euphoria as a highly sophisticated defense to replace the immature defenses that he had used during his active chemical dependency. Almost immediately after he left inpatient treatment, Gordon changed to a rabid proselyte. He made AA and being the completely responsible parent and husband his whole life. He became an all-knowing, all-responsible, didactic, forceful autocrat who smothered his family, directing the life of Amy, Mark, and Lisa. Although he was overbearing, his family was so afraid that confronting his behavior would send him back to drinking that they walked on eggshells. In fact, when such reaction formations occur, family members may resent the dependent's sober behavior so much that they secretly wish he or she would return to drinking. Only through some tough family aftercare was Gordon's overdose of perfectionism and righteous recovery brought under control.

Carolyn: Gordon, a moment ago you described how frustrated you have been because Mark clams up and withdraws from you, and you also spoke to the fact that now Lisa seems to be even more resentful of you than when you were drinking. Notice how Mark is slumped back in his chair and Lisa is sitting with arms and legs crossed as you discuss how exasperated you are.

Gordon: I can't understand it. Dinner is supposed to be our time together. Right after I got out of inpatient treatment we were really communicating. But that's all changed lately. They've started shutting me out again. I love them and I want what's best for them. I just want to make it up to them for being the lousy dad and husband I was for so long. Why are they locking me out?

Carolyn: Mark, what are your feelings as your dad is relating his frustration?

Mark: (Shedding tears.) I'm mad at him . . . because nothing I say is right and everything I do is either wrong or not good enough.

Lisa: Yeah. I wish sometimes you were drinking again. At least then you left us alone.

Amy: Gordon, the kids are finally saying what we've all been feeling at home. Your personality is so overpowering since you quit drinking that none of us can come up to your standards. And AA, as good as it is, has become the center of our universe. Don't misunderstand, I don't want you to drink again, but there's just got to be something in between. We're worn out. We just need a normal life. We don't need you as Superman. Lord knows, I pulled that long enough.

Gordon: I don't know what to say. I just wanted to make things up to you. I don't know what to do!

Carolyn: This whole thing you're experiencing is not uncommon. As problematic as it is, it's a good sign and sort of a stage of development on the road to recovery. Understand it for that and we can work on it just like we have the other hot spots that have come up.

Blind spots.   Carolyn keyed in on Gordon's euphoria and took steps during the aftercare session to help the whole family deal with the issue. Such euphoric responses should be carefully monitored in aftercare settings because they may literally drive significant others to return to enabling behavior.

Further, zealous immersion in programs such as AA is also fraught with peril. For some people, organizations such as AA no longer fulfill a support function, but rather become a platform for airing the recovering chemical dependent's self-indulgence. Based on the premise that the recovering alcoholic now knows all the answers and will gladly tell them to anyone who will listen, this presumptive stand may indicate that the individual has lost perspective on what the essence of a support group is about and is building up to drink. In short, the rules of the road that the individual rigidly espouses to others no longer hold for the individual, and this self-centered view may become a lethal one in regard to drinking. Upon the first sign that others may not share the recovering chemical dependent's viewpoints, the person may fall from these dizzying heights, become depressed and angry, and have a relapse.

To summarize the major task of aftercare, if the dependent, aside from performing his or her jobs inside and outside the home, is concentrating almost solely on maintaining chemical freedom, he or she is doing about all that needs to be done. If codependents, aside from jobs inside and outside the home, are focusing on themselves rather than on the dependent, then they are doing all that needs to be done (Maxwell, 1986, p. 234).

In family therapy session, six months after inpatient treatment.

Gordon: One thing strikes me now. I guess I went 180 degrees in the other direction. I was as rigid in my abstinence as I was in my drinking. I was so damned afraid that I'd fall off the wagon, and I think everybody else around me was too, that if I didn't go hog wild in trying to be the best recovering alcoholic there ever was, and the best father and husband there ever was, I'd go right back to being a drunk. The truth is I was still scared to death and so was everybody else. It's taken some time, but I now realize that I'm just about average. I sure keep going to the AA meetings and I'm ready to help anyone else, but I don't have to stand out on a streetcorner looking for drunks. I'll probably always need a support group, and while that bugs me at times, I know there are things that bug everybody else, and that's OK. I guess I'd rate myself as an average father and husband. We still have problems, and I guess that doesn't make me much different from any other guy. And the best part about that is it feels just fine.

SUMMARY

The crisis of addiction is unique among all crisis categories. It is full of complexities, controversies, and contradictions. The prognosis for cure is poor because the condition is beset with multiple transcrisis points. A person may appear to be cured, only to relapse later into a drug episode more severe than before.

We have summarized several models of addiction, which attribute the problem to inherited, environmental, social, biological, chemical, or psychological causative factors. It appears that each of the models is partially correct and partially incorrect in ascribing causality.

In terms of dynamics, it seems that there are many types and degrees of addiction. The most prevalent and puzzling dynamic revolves around the concept of psychological denial. The chemical dependent tends to deny adamantly that there is addiction and to deny that any problem exists related to the addictive behavior. Family, friends, and even bosses frequently become a part of the denial system and unknowingly contribute to the addict's difficulties by becoming enablers. The treatment and rehabilitation of clients is enormously complicated when significant others reinforce the narcissistic and sociopathic behavior of the chemical dependent by abetting the dependency.

The stabilization of an addictive crisis is difficult in that it usually requires, first, that the dependent become aware that he or she needs help and second, that the person have some motivation to seek help. To that end, reasoning with the dependent about the problem is generally useless. Most often, direct confrontation and the generation of a crisis of significant proportions by some significant other such as an employer or spouse are the only ways to propel an abuser to treatment.

It is clear that a multimodal approach is needed to help addicted persons through the crises they face. Competent medical supervision and counseling are needed from the detoxification phase through aftercare. Group counseling is a primary operating mode because peers who are themselves recovering addicts are highly effective in breaking down denial systems of fellow chemical dependents. Extensive use is made of family, friends, employers, and support groups such as Alcoholics Anonymous, to supplement what professional caregivers can do for clients.

At present, there is no known permanent cure for chemical dependents. Following stabilization, clients must work and practice coping skills for the remainder of their lives to prevent a relapse.

REFERENCES

Adler, A. (1956). *The individual psychology of Alfred Adler: A systematic presentation in selections from his writing,* (pp. 384–410.) H. L. Ansbacher & R. R. Ansbacher (Eds.), New York: Harper & Row.

Alcoholics Anonymous (1976). *Alcoholics Anonymous* (3rd ed.). New York: Anonymous World Services, Inc.

Alcoholics Anonymous (1985). *Twenty-four hours a day.* Garden City, MN: Hazeldein.

American Medical Association (1956). Hospitalization of patients with alcoholism. *Journal of the American Medical Association, 162,* 750.

American Psychiatric Association (1980). *Diagnostic and statistical manual of mental disorders* (3rd ed.). Washington, DC: Author.

Ames, G. M. (1985). American beliefs about alcoholism: Historical perspectives on the medical–moral controversy. In L. A. Bennett & G. M. Ames (Eds.), *The American experience with alcohol: Contrasting cultural perspectives* (pp. 23–40). New York: Plenum.

Asbury, H. (1950). *The great illusion: An informal history of prohibition.* Garden City, NY: Doubleday.

Barry, H. (1974). Psychological factors in alcoholism. In B. Kissin & H. Begleiter (Eds.), *The biology of alcoholism: Clinical pathology* (Vol. 3, pp. 53–108). New York: Plenum.

Berry, E. R., & Boland, J. P. (1977). *The economic cost of abuse.* New York: Free Press.

Bissell, L. (1982). Recovered alcoholic counselors. In E. M. Pattison & E. Kaufman (Eds.), *Encyclopedic handbook of alcoholism* (pp. 810–820). New York: Gardner Press.

Blume, S. (1973). Iatrogenic alcoholism. *Quarterly Journal of Studies on Alcohol, 34,* 1348–1352.

Blume, S. B. (1978). Group psychotherapy in the treatment of alcoholism. In S. Zimberg, J. Wallace, & S. B. Blume (Eds.), *Practical approaches to alcoholism psychotherapy* (pp. 63–76). New York: Plenum.

Brill, L. (1981). *The clinical treatment of substance abusers.* New York: Free Press.

Burk, E. D. (1972). Some contemporary issues in child development and the children of alcoholic parents. *Annals of New York Academy of Science, 197,* 189–197.

Cadoret, R. J., & Gaith, A. (1978). Inheritance of alcoholism in adoptees. *British Journal of Psychiatry, 132,* 252–258.

Canadian Commission of Inquiry into the Nonmedical Use of Drugs (1973). Ottawa: Information Canada.

Chalmers, D. K., & Wallace, J. (1978). Evaluation of patient progress. In S. Zimberg, J. Wallace, & S. B. Blume (Eds.), *Practical approaches to alcoholism psychotherapy* (pp. 255–279). New York: Plenum.

Chrisman, N. J. (1985). Alcoholism: Illness or disease. In L. A. Bennett & G. M. Ames (Eds.), *The American experience with alcohol: Contrasting cultural perspectives* (pp. 7–22.) New York: Plenum.

Collins, J. (1980). *Alcohol use and criminal behavior: An empirical, theoretical, and methodological overview.* Research Triangle Park, NC: Research Triangle Institute.

Corey, G., & Corey, M. S. (1977). *Group process and practice.* Pacific Grove, CA: Brooks/Cole.

Cormier, L. S., & Hackney, H. (1987). *The professional counselor: A process guide to helping.* Englewood Cliffs, NJ: Prentice-Hall.

Cormier, W. H., & Cormier, L. S. (1985). *Interviewing strategies for helpers: Fundamental skills and cognitive behavioral interventions* (2nd ed.). Pacific Grove, CA: Brooks/Cole.

Costello, R. M. (1982). Evaluation of alcoholism treatment programs. In E. M. Pattison & E. Kaufman (Eds.), *Encyclopedic handbook of alcoholism* (pp. 1179–1210). New York: Gardner Press.

Cotton, N. S. (1979). The familial incidence of alcoholism. *Journal of Studies on Alcohol, 40,* 89–115.

Dinkmeyer, D. C., & Muro, J. (1979). *Group counseling: Theory and practice.* Itasca, IL: F.E. Peacock.

Dinkmeyer, D. C., Pew, W. L., & Dinkmeyer, D. C., Jr. (1979). *Adlerian counseling and psychotherapy.* Pacific Grove, CA: Brooks/Cole.

Drug Abuse Warning Network (DAWN) (1983). Data from the Drug Abuse Warning Network statistical series, Quarterly Report, Provisional Data Series G, No. 12 (July–September). Rockville, MD: National Institute on Drug Abuse.

Dupont, R. L. (1984). *Getting tough on gateway drugs.* Washington, DC: American Psychiatric Press.

Edwards, G. T. (1985). Appalachia: The effects of cultural values on the consumption of alcohol. In L. A. Bennett & G. M. Ames (Eds.). *The American experience with alcohol* (pp. 131–146). New York: Plenum.

Ellis, A. (1987, January). *Employee assistance training workshop: A rational-emotive approach.* New York: Institute for Rational-Emotive Therapy.

Ford, B. (1987). *Betty: A glad awakening.* New York: Doubleday.

Goode, E. (1984). *Drugs in American society.* New York: Knopf.

Goodwin, D. W. (1979). Alcoholism and heredity. *Archives of General Psychiatry, 36,* 57–61.

Goodwin, D. W., Crane, J. B., & Guze, S. B. (1971). Felons who drink. *Quarterly Journal of Studies on Alcohol, 32,* 136–148.

Graham, D. (Speaker). (1986). *Denial, dependency, and codependency in drug treatment programs.* (Cassette Recording No. 8-1). Memphis: Department of Counseling and Personnel Services, Memphis State University.

Guze, S. B., Goodwin, D. W., & Crane, J. B. (1969). Community and psychiatric disorders. *Archives of General Psychiatry, 20,* 583–591.

Guze, S. B., Tuason, D. W., Galfield, D., Stewart, M. A., & Picken, B. (1962). Psychiatric illness and crime with particular reference to alcoholism: A study of 223 criminals. *Journal of Nervous and Mental Disease, 134,* 512–521.

Haberman, P. W. & Baden, M. M. (1974, March). Alcoholism and violent death. *Quarterly Journal of Studies on Alcohol, 35,* No. 1, Part A, 221–231.

Hamburg, B. A., Kraemer, H. C., & Jahnke, W. (1975). A hierarchy of drug use in adolescence: Behavioral and attitudinal correlates of substantive drug use. *American Journal of Psychiatry, 132,* 1155–1163.

Hay, W. M., & Nathan, P. E. (Eds.). (1982). *Clinical case studies in the behavioral treatment of alcoholism.* New York: Plenum.

Heath, D. B. (1978). The sociocultural model of alcohol use: Problems and prospects. *Journal of Operation Psychiatry, 9,* 56–66.

Heath, D. B. (1985). American experience with alcohol: Commonalities and contrasts. In L. A. Bennett & G. M. Ames (Eds.), *The American experience with alcohol: Contrasting cultural experiences* (pp. 461–480). New York: Plenum.

Hoffman, H. (1970). Depression and defensiveness in self-descriptive moods of alcoholics. *Psychological Reports, 26,* 23–26.

Huberty, J. D., & Brandon, J. C. (1982). Nonmedical alcohol detoxification. In E. M. Pattison & E. Kaufman (Eds.), *Encyclopedic handbook of alcoholism* (pp. 1076–1085). New York: Gardner Press.

Jellinek, E. M. (1946). Phases in the drinking history of alcoholics. *Quarterly Journal of Studies on Alcohol, 7,* 1–88.

Jellinek, E. M. (1952). Phases of alcohol addiction. *Quarterly Journal of Studies on Alcohol, 13,* 673–684.

Jellinek, A. M. (1960). *The disease concept of alcoholism.* New Haven, CT: Hillhouse Press.

Jessor, R., Chase, J. D., & Donovan, J. E. (1980). Psychosocial correlates of marijuana use and problem drinking in a national sample of adolescents. *American Journal of Public Health, 70,* 604–613.

Jessor, R., & Jessor, S. L. (1977). *Problem behavior and psychosocial development: A longitudinal study of youth.* New York: Academic Press.

Kaufman, E., & Pattison, E. M. (1982a). The family and alcoholism. In E. M. Pattison & E. Kaufman (Eds.), *Encyclopedic handbook of alcoholism* (pp. 662–672). New York: Gardner Press.

Kaufman, E., & Pattison, E. M. (1982b). The family and network therapy in alcoholism. In E. M. Pattison & E. Kaufman (Eds.), *Encyclopedic handbook of alcoholism* (pp. 1022–1032). New York: Gardner Press.

Knox, W. J. (1976). Objective psychological measurement and alcoholism: Review of the literature, 1971–72. *Psychological Reports, 38,* 1023–1050 (Monograph Suppl. 1-V38).

Knox, W. J. (1980). Objective psychological measurement and alcoholism: Survey of the literature, 1974. *Psychological Reports, 47,* 51–68 (Monograph Suppl. 1-V47).

Knox, W. J. (1982). The professionals: The issue of alcoholism. In E. M. Pattison & E. Kaufman (Eds.), *Encyclopedic handbook of alcoholism* (pp. 795–801). New York: Gardner Press.

Kristianson, P. A. (1970). A comparison study of two alcoholic groups and control group. *British Journal of Medical Psychology, 43,* 161–175.

Lawson, G. W., Ellis, D. C., & Rivers, P. C. (Eds.). (1984). *Essentials of chemical dependency counseling.* Rockville, MD: Aspen Systems Corp.

Levine, H. (1984). The alcohol problem in America: From temperance to alcoholism. *British Journal of Addiction, 79,* 109–119.

Loper, R. G., Kammeier, M. L., & Hoffman, H. (1973). MMPI characteristics of college freshman males who later became alcoholic. *Journal of Abnormal Psychology, 82,* 159–162.

Lukoff, I. F. (1980). Toward a sociology of drug use. In D. J. Lettieri, M. Sayers, & H. W. Pearson (Eds.), *Theories on drug abuse: Selected contemporary perspectives* (NIDA Research Monograph No. 30). Rockville, MD: National Institute on Drug Abuse.

MacAndrew, C., & Edgerton, R. B. (1969). *Drunken comportment.* Chicago: Aldine.

MacDonald, J. (1961). *The murderer and his victim.* Springfield, IL: Charles C. Thomas.

Marlatt, G. A., & Donovan, D. M. (1982). Behavioral psychology approaches to alcoholism. In E. M. Pattison & E. Kaufman (Eds.), *Encyclopedic handbook of alcoholism* (pp. 560–577.) New York: Gardner Press.

Maxwell, R. (1986). *Breakthrough: What to do when alcoholism or chemical dependency hits close to home.* New York: Ballantine.

McCrady, B. S. (1982). Marital dysfunction: Alcoholism and marriage. In E. M. Pattison & E. Kaufman (Eds.), *Encyclopedic handbook of alcoholism* (pp. 673–685). New York: Gardner Press.

McCrory, J. (Speaker). (1987). *Aftercare and co-dependency in drug treatment programs.* (Cassette Recording No. 8-4). Memphis: Department of Counseling and Personnel Services, Memphis State University.

McMullin, R. E., & Giles, T. R. (1981). *Cognitive behavior therapy: A restructuring approach.* New York: Grune & Stratton.

Meichenbaum, D. (1985). *Stress-inoculation training.* New York: Pergamon Press.

Mendelson, J. H., & Mello, N. K. (Eds.). (1979). *The diagnosis and treatment of alcoholism.* New York: McGraw-Hill.

Mik, G. (1970). Sons of alcoholic fathers. *British Journal of Addiction, 65,* 305–315.

Miller, J. D., & Jang, M. (1977). Children of alcoholism: A 20-year longitudinal study. *Social Work Research, 13,* 23–29.

National Commission on Marijuana and Drug Abuse (1973). *Drug abuse in America: Problems in perspective. The technical papers of the second report of the National Commission on Marijuana and Drug Abuse.* Washington, DC: U.S. Government Printing Office.

Neisser, U. (1976). *Cognition and reality: Principles and implications of cognitive psychology.* San Francisco: W. H. Freeman.

Oetting, E. R., & Beauvais, F. (1986). Peer cluster theory: Drugs and the adolescent. *Journal of Counseling and Development, 65,* 17–22.

Ohlsen, M. (1970). *Group counseling.* New York: Holt, Rinehart & Winston.

Olsen, M. (1987, March 17). *Life quest: Hidden addicts, the nature and impact of addictive behavior* [Documentary]. ABC Television Network.

Olson, S., & Gerstein, D. R. (1985). *Alcoholism in America: Taking action to prevent abuse.* Washington, DC: National Academy Press.

Ornstein, P. (1976). The Alcadd Test as a predictor of post-hospital drinking behavior. *Psychological Reports, 43,* 611–617.

Parker, C. (Speaker). (1986). *Alcoholic inpatient treatment.* (Cassette Recording No. 8-2). Memphis: Department of Counseling and Personnel Services, Memphis State University.

Pattison, E. M., & Kaufman, E. (Eds.). (1982a). *Encyclopedic handbook of alcoholism.* New York: Gardner Press.

Pattison, E. M., & Kaufman, E. (1982b). The alcoholism syndrome: Definitions and models. In E. M. Pattison & E. Kaufman (Eds.), *Encyclopedic handbook of alcoholism* (pp. 3–30). New York: Gardner Press.

Peele, S. (1986). The "cure" for adolescent drug abuse: Worse than the problem? *Journal of Counseling and Development, 65,* 23–24.

Perez, J. F. (1985). *Counseling the alcoholic.* Muncie, IN: Accelerated Development.

Pernanen, K. (1976). The biology of alcoholism. In B. Kissin & H. Begleiter (Eds.), *Social aspects of alcoholism* (Vol. 4, pp. 42–57). New York: Plenum.

Poley, W., Lea, G., & Vibe, G. (1979). *Alcoholism: A treatment manual.* New York: Gardner Press.

Ray, O. (1983). *Drugs, society, and human behavior* (3rd ed.). St. Louis: C.V. Mosby.

Rosenberg, C. M. (1982). The paraprofessional in alcoholism treatment. In E. M. Pattison & E. Kaufman (Eds.), *Encyclopedic handbook of alcoholism* (pp. 802–809). New York: Gardner Press.

Schuckit, M. A., & Rayses, V. (1979). Ethanol ingestion: Differences in blood acetaldehyde concentrations in relatives of alcoholics and controls. *Science, 203,* 54–55.

Shaffer, H. (1986). Observations on substance abuse theory. *Journal of Counseling and Development, 65,* 26–28.

Shearer, R. J. (1968). *Manual of alcoholism of the American Medical Association.* Washington, DC: American Medical Association.

Shulman, B. (1973). *Contributions to individual psychology: Selected papers of Bernard Shulman.* Chicago: Alfred Adler Institute.

Shupe, L. (1953). Alcohol and crime. *Journal of Criminal Law and Criminal Political Science, 44,* 661–664.

Smith, J. W. (1982). Treatment of alcoholism in aversion conditioning hospitals. In E. M. Pattison & E. Kaufman (Eds.), *Encyclopedic handbook of alcoholism* (pp. 874–884). New York: Gardner Press.

Smith, W. F. (1982, Summer). Drug traffic today—challenges and response. *Drug Enforcement,* pp. 2–6.

Sobell, M. B., & Sobell, L. C. (1978). *Behavioral treatment of alcohol problems: Individualized therapy and controlled drinking.* New York: Plenum.

Speigel, D., Hadley, P. A., & Hadley, R. G. (1970). Personality test patterns of rehabilitation center alcoholics, psychiatric inpatients and normals. *Journal of Clinical Psychology*, 26, 366–371.

Spotts, J. V., & Shontz, F. C. (1980). A life theme theory of chronic drug abuse. In D. J. Lettieri, M. Sayers, & H. W. Pearson (Eds.), *Theories on drug abuse: Selected contemporary perspectives* (NIDA Research Monograph No. 30, pp. 59–70). Rockville, MD: National Institute on Drug Abuse.

Stuckey, R. F., & Harrison, J. S. (1982). The alcoholism rehabilitation center. In E. M. Pattison & E. Kaufman (Eds.), *Encyclopedic handbook of alcoholism* (pp. 865–873). New York: Gardner Press.

Trice, H. M., & Beyer, J. M. (1982). Job-based alcoholism programs: Motivating problem drinkers to rehabilitation. In E. M. Pattison & E. Kaufman (Eds.), *Encyclopedic handbook of alcoholism* (pp. 954–978). New York: Gardner Press.

U.S. Department of Commerce, Bureau of Census. (1986). *Statistical Abstract of U.S.* (106th ed.). Washington, DC: U.S. Government Printing Office.

Vaillant, G. E. (1983). *The natural history of alcoholism: Causes, patterns, and paths to recovery.* Cambridge, MA: Harvard University Press.

Vaillant, G. E., & Milofsky, E. (1982). The etiology of alcoholism: A prospective viewpoint. *American Psychologist*, 37, 494–503.

Wallace, J. (1978). Critical issues in alcoholism therapy. In S. Zimberg, J. Wallace, & S. B. Blume (Eds.), *Practical approaches to alcoholism psychotherapy* (pp. 31–46). New York: Plenum.

Wanberg, R. W., Horn, J. L., & Foster, F. M. (1977). A differential assessment model for alcoholism: The scales of the Alcohol Use Inventory. *Journal of Studies on Alcohol*, 33, 512–543.

World Health Organization (1952). Expert committee on mental health alcoholism subcommittee. Second report. (World Health Organization Technical Service Report No. 18). In H. Milt (Ed.), *Basic handbook on alcoholism.* Fairhaven, NJ: Scientific Aids Publication.

Zimberg, S. (1982). Psychotherapy in the treatment of alcoholism. In E. M. Pattison & E. Kaufman (Eds.), *Encyclopedic handbook of alcoholism* (pp. 999–1010). New York: Gardner Press.

Zwerling, I. (1959). Psychiatric findings in an interdisciplinary study of 46 alcoholic patients. *Quarterly Journal of Studies on Alcohol*, 20, 543–554.

◼ Classroom Exercises: Addictive Behaviors

All of us have addictions, whether they be drinking alcohol, eating chocolate, gambling on blackjack, buying plaid sport coats, overspending on credit cards, or reading the sports page at breakfast. Anything that we start out wanting and not necessarily needing, but end up either psychologically or physically craving, may be considered addicting. Such addictive behaviors may be as simple as not being able to pass the candy bar machine to attending every Memphis State basketball game—no matter what!

With the class divided into pairs, each person discusses a behavior around which the person seems to plan his or her life (at least in small part). For example, one of the authors of this book does just fine without coffee and cigarettes in the morning until he gets to work. Immediately upon hanging his coat up and setting his brief case down, he picks up his cup and heads for the coffee pot. Nothing, and we mean absolutely nothing, happens until that first cup of coffee goes down along with a cigarette. It's all downhill after that, and he consumes numerous cups of coffee and cigarettes until he goes home from work. There, he drinks no more coffee, but does put away some antacid.

Each student will isolate such a behavior and then commit to refraining from that behavior for one day. Keep a one-day journal listing your thoughts, feelings, and behaviors as you sweat out the day in abstinence. At the next class meeting, report on the difficulties you faced in forgoing your addiction for a day. This exercise should give individuals a small bit of empathy for the person who has a serious chemical dependency.

Denial

Once you have discussed in class what addictive behavior does to you, separate again into pairs. One person takes the part of the interventionist and the other that of the client. Role-play for about ten minutes. The client will engage in denial that the addiction is a problem, using any of the defense mechanisms described in this chapter. The interventionist's task is to crack the denial system of the client by using the confrontational skills listed in the chapter. Audio tape the role play and then reverse roles. Each member will listen to and critique the role play in regard to both denial and confrontation of the denial. Return to the large group and discuss what each member learned from the experience. Questions may include the following:

1. How difficult was it for the worker to confront the client?
2. What kinds of feelings did both client and worker have as they carried the role play forward?
3. Did the worker confront the specific addicting behavior, the defense used to shield it from awareness, or the total personhood of the client?
4. Did the worker feel insecure or threatened while attempting the confrontation?
5. Did the client feel threatened, or was he or she able easily to fend off the worker's attempts to break down the denial?

Psychological Blind Spots

Assume that for people to become addicted to drugs they must have psychological "blind spots" that keep them from becoming aware of their addictive tendencies and shield them from acknowledging the harmful effects of their addiction, both to themselves and to their loved ones. In small groups, each person is to identify, write down, and then share with the group what might be some of the blind spots they have with respect to the addiction discussed in the first exercise. As if they were significant others in the person's life, the other members of the group brainstorm and expand upon these blind spots. Finally, the group will devise strategies for convincing the person that he or she has the blind spot and needs to take preventive steps that would safeguard against letting a habit turn into a full-blown addiction.

CHAPTER 9

Sexual Assault

BACKGROUND

There is abundant evidence to suggest that crises resulting from sexual abuse are different in nature, intensity, and extent from other forms of crisis (Burgess & Holmstrom, 1985; Finkelhor, 1979, 1984; Williams & Holmes, 1981). How the crisis affects an individual victim depends on many variables. Age, race/ethnicity, family background, cultural and religious mores, community attitudes, type of abuse experienced, length of time and intensity of victimization, attitudes about sex roles, attitudes of family and support persons following disclosure/discovery of the abuse, and effects of police or legal proceedings following disclosure/discovery of the abuse all influence the trauma of a sexual assault (Williams & Holmes, 1981). Crisis intervention with victims of sexual abuse incorporates the basic principles of the six steps discussed in Chapter 2.

One victim may appear to take sexual assault in stride, whereas another person subjected to a similar experience virtually falls apart. One individual may work through the crisis rather quickly, and another may suffer varying degrees of debilitation for a long period of time. Many victims experience long-term residual effects, which Burgess and Holmstrom (1974, 1979) and Burgess (1985) have delineated as *rape trauma syndrome.* Frazier and Borgida (1985) have reported that many psychologists now classify rape trauma syndrome as a particular example of posttraumatic stress disorder, as defined in the DSM-III of the American Psychiatric Association (1980). (Chapter 7 in this book contains a more comprehensive coverage of posttraumatic stress disorder.) Our thrust in this chapter is to help the client deal with the crisis itself, not the ensuing disorder—to help the client to restore functional equilibrium. Therefore the role of crisis workers may be limited to detection, crisis intervention, and referral of clients with rape trauma syndrome and other long-term problems related to sexual abuse. Specialized medical, psychiatric, or psychological treatments are needed in these cases.

Any person may at one time or another be the victim of sexual abuse (Molmen, 1982, p. 12). Although the majority of victims are children and females under 30 (Amir, 1971; Bass & Thornton, 1983), sexual assault victims have been identified among males and females from every segment of the population—children, adolescents, adults, and older adults (Williams & Holmes, 1981).

For many years the phenomena of rape and other forms of sexual abuse received attention mainly as crimes. They were largely the purview of law enforcement and the legal system. The predominant societal response was punitive—directed at the attacker. Because of increased public awareness through consciousness raising by the media, the feminist movement, and a host of writers such as Amir (1971), Brownmiller (1975), and A. B. Davis (1985), public concern has shifted to helping the victims of sexual abuse.

Programs, centers, and agencies for helping victims of sexual abuse have been established in most cities. Telephone hot lines and rape crisis centers are now within reach of the majority of the population. Listings of resources and agencies to assist victims throughout the country have been compiled by a number of persons, such as Bass and Thornton (1983), Benedict (1985), Grossman and Sutherland (1983), and Townley (1985). Victims can also acquire information and assistance through crisis hot lines, community mental health centers, or emergency line 911. In most cities, persons needing help can look in the telephone directory under "Rape" or call the local number of the Department of Human Services. Almost any practicing nurse, psychologist, social worker, certified counselor, or other human services worker can refer victims and their families to appropriate sources of assistance.

Definition of Rape

There are many definitions of rape. Some are based on legal constructs; some are derived from other sources. We prefer to use Benedict's (1985) definition of rape as "any sexual act that is forced upon you" (p. 1). Brownmiller (1975) distinguishes between most legal definitions and what she refers to as a "woman's" definition. The legal definition of rape as "the forcible perpetration of an act of sexual intercourse on the body of a woman not one's wife" (p. 380) is seen as much too narrow and protective of the male-supremacy philosophy. Brownmiller's preferred definition from a woman's perspective is that rape is "a sexual invasion of the body by force, an incursion into the private, personal inner space without consent—in short, an internal assault from one of several avenues and by one of several methods [that] constitutes a deliberate violation of emotional, physical, and rational integrity and is a hostile, degrading act of violence" (p. 376). That definition appears to encompass the whole scope of rape, as well as other forms of sexual abuse/misuse.

In this chapter we have used Benedict's definition of rape because it is both simple and it encompasses the whole scope of sexual abuse/misuse. Brownmiller's more comprehensive definition is included because it provides a valuable perspective in addition to Benedict's definition.

Literature on Rape and Sexual Abuse

Recent research and writings can be of enormous value to crisis workers who deal with sexual abuse victims. We have organized and abstracted the literature on rape by incorporating it into seven fundamental assumptions, which we have derived from the findings of representative sources. These fundamentals contain the threads that are woven into a conceptual network throughout the chapter.

1. *Rape is not sex.* The preponderance of research and literature give credence to the declaration that rape, incest, sodomy, digital or object penetration of the vagina or anus, forced oral sex, forced fondling, forced masturbation, and other forms of sexual abuse or misuse are acts of aggression, violence, force, or the willful exercise of power, dominance, or control over other persons, rather than expressions of sexuality (Benedict, 1985, pp. 5–12; Burgess, 1985; Carnes, 1983; Colao & Hosansky, 1983; Fortune, 1983; Geiser, 1979, pp. 14–19; Hursch, 1977; Janosik, 1984, p. 268; Katz & Mazur, 1979; O'Brien, 1983; Sussman & Bordwell, 1981; West, Roy, & Nichols, 1978).

2. *Rape is an uninvited act.* There is overwhelming evidence that victims seldom invite or provoke sexual assault. Victims do not ask for or deserve the various negative feelings or emotions that result from rape and other forms of sexual abuse/misuse. These emotional responses may include a feeling of fear of death or serious injury, panic, terror, degradation, humiliation, helplessness, violation, being overwhelmed, shame, guilt, anger, denial, blame, betrayal, disbelief, loss of control, rage, loss of self-esteem, and immediate or delayed trauma. In the case of sexual assault, the victim's ensuing negative emotions are brought on directly by the act of sexual abuse itself (Benedict, 1985; Brownmiller, 1975; Burgess & Holmstrom, 1974, 1985; A. B. Davis, 1985; Ellis, 1983; Frazier & Borgida, 1985; Geiser, 1979, pp. 26–31; Grossman & Sutherland, 1983).

3. *Rape may happen to anyone.* Contrary to common opinion, victims of rape and other forms of sexual abuse/misuse include persons of all ages, races, cultural backgrounds, social groups, and sexes and sexual preferences (although most rapes are committed on the persons of females)—from young children through older adults. Most of the recorded rapes of men have occurred in penal institutions, although such assaults may occur anywhere. Men are more reluctant to report rapes than are women (Bass & Thornton, 1983; Benedict, 1985; Burgess, 1985; Colao & Hosansky, 1983, p. 17; Russell, 1982; Williams & Holmes, 1981).

4. *Rapists come from every segment of society.* People who rape and commit other forms of sexual abuse/misuse have been identified in every stratum of society—from judges to messenger boys, from weaklings to muscular types, from vagrants to corporate executives, from husbands and fathers to strangers, from known friends or relatives to unknown intruders (Benedict, 1985, pp. 9–10; Burgess, Groth, Holmstrom, & Sgroi, 1978; Burgess & Holmstrom, 1979; Greer & Stuart, 1983; Groth & Birnbaum, 1979; Hursch, 1977;

Kempe, 1984; Medea & Thompson, 1974, pp. 29–36; Rada, 1978; Russell, 1982; Sanford, 1980; Sussman & Bordwell, 1981; Townley, 1985, pp. 80–91).

5. *The incidence of sexual assault has been underreported.* The literature describes rape and other types of sexual offense as being a widespread social problem of epidemic proportions. That statement is based on *reported* levels of assault. What is more disturbing is that the literature consistently estimates that "fifty to ninety percent of all rapes or attempted rapes go unreported" (Sussman & Bordwell, 1981, p. 15). The research indicates that suspects are apprehended in about 5% of the cases and that prosecutors obtain convictions in less than 3% of these cases. Most of the reports on rape and sexual assault record only specific age categories. Most instances of incest and molestation are never reported. The vast majority of crime survey reports do not report child sexual abuse of persons under the age of 12 (Bass & Thornton, 1983; Benedict, 1985, pp. 186–192; Brownmiller, 1975, p. 175; Geiser, 1979, pp. 9–10; Medea & Thompson, 1974; Sussman & Bordwell, 1981, p. 15; Townley, 1985, p. 24).

6. *Nearly all perpetrators of sexual abuse/misuse are men; most victims are women and children.* Sexual assault and abuse/misuse in all their many forms are predominantly male crimes. Most research indicates that males between the ages of 18 and 35 inflict 99% of the sexual assaults in the United States (Plummer, 1984, p. v; Medea & Thompson, 1974; Townley, 1985, p. 162).

7. *The recovery of victims of sexual assault/abuse/misuse is enhanced by the empathic help and understanding of the persons close to them.* Whether the victim's support persons be family, friends, associates, medical or legal personnel, crisis workers, or long-term therapists, the important ingredients in the helping relationship are acceptance, genuineness, empathy, caring, and nonjudgmental understanding. The literature uniformly supports treating the victim as a positive, recovering survivor who deserves empathy and support—not as a person who is suspect and blamed for being stupid enough to get raped. The fact is that the assault is considered a crime caused by a violent attacker. The victim emerges alive and should be admired, encouraged, accepted, and helped to recover as soon as possible (Benedict, 1985; Colao & Hosansky, 1983; Gil, 1984; Grossman & Sutherland, 1983; Groth & Stevenson, 1984; James & Nasjleti, 1983; Karpel & Strauss, 1983; Knopp, 1982; Mayer, 1983; McCombie, 1980; Renshaw, 1982; Sanford, 1980).

DYNAMICS OF RAPE AND SEXUAL ABUSE

Psychosocial and Cultural Dynamics

Rape is a complex phenomenon. Sussman and Bordwell (1981) have vividly demonstrated that each rapist's reasons for assault are individual. Yet the vast majority of rapes have to do with the power relationships between men and women (p. 12). Somehow the contemporary sociocultural milieu produces some males who feel such absence of power and control in their lives that they develop a need to "take it" (control). These males come to believe that it is a "right" (p. 5) and proceed to rationalize and justify their behavior even though doing so invades and takes by force the very essence of another person's life and body. The rapist's justification for committing this ultimate act of humiliation and degradation comes down to forcing the victim to submit. Since most victims are females and children, it is largely a concept of adult male supremacy, even though adult males are themselves sometimes raped. The notion of male supremacy has its roots deep in our cultural history, which has, for centuries, equated property rights of men to the access to and control of the bodies of women, children, and others who are perceived as dependents (Brownmiller, 1975).

Social factors. In the Western world aggression and domination are portrayed as accepted male characteristics, while peacefulness and submission are deemed appropriate for females. These attitudes and values are woven into our social fabric. Brownmiller (1975) and others have documented a part of the history of rape as a psychosocial means by which the victors in wars reward themselves and humiliate their vanquished foes. The wholesale rape and killing of helpless women and children represents the ultimate vulnerability and defeat of a people. It likewise represents the ultimate humiliation and subjugation of a person. Whether it is inflicted on hundreds, as reported in war, or on one person, the purpose is quite similar—the use of unrestrained power to force the vanquished into total submission.

Finkelhor (1979) reports that sexual deviance and victimization are more likely to emerge in families characterized by a high degree of social isolation. Such deviance has been observed in isolated Appalachian families as well as in some cities and suburbs. In fairly self-contained communities, the tolerance of sexual deviance, such as incest, may be passed on from generation to generation (pp. 25–26). Finkelhor also identifies role confusion and fear of abandonment as sources of the sociopathology of child abuse (pp. 26–27). He concurrently reports a positive correlation between the isolated circumstances of those in extreme poverty and the incidence of incest and sexual abuse.

Societal attitudes about rape have long impeded victim advocacy. In recent years, improved communications, wider reporting, and better research information have tended to improve the lot of the victim. However, additional negative dimensions have been added, such as the complicating effect of the automobile (increased mobility), the accelerated maturation rate of children and adolescents, population concentration in urban centers, emergence and acceptance of violence in the visual media, greater amounts of personal leisure time, and more discretionary money to spend. These are only a few of many factors that have altered and confounded our social milieu and made sexual assault easier (Amir, 1971; Brownmiller, 1975).

Cultural factors. Our cultural heritage has apparently lagged behind our technological and social patterns. Despite factors such as industrialization, population mobility, birth control, the feminist movement, employment of women outside the household, smaller families, higher divorce rates, single-parent families, blended families, relaxed moral codes, and higher economic standards of living, our attitudes about sex, sexuality, and sexual assault have been slow to change (Williams & Holmes, 1981). One example of this cultural lag is the persistent belief that rape is a crime committed for sex (Benedict, 1985; Brownmiller, 1975). The list of myths about rape is long, and these myths are only the tip of the iceberg of problems contemporary culture faces in dealing with rape and other forms of sexual abuse/misuse (Benedict, 1985).

Personal and psychological factors.   The personal and psychological factors unique in men affect both their decision to assault and the way the assault is carried out. The factors unique in women tend to affect their responses to rape and their recovery process. The male offender

1. acts hostile, aggressive, condescending, and domineering even though he often feels weak, inadequate, threatened, and dependent
2. believes he should act strong, courageous, and manly
3. lacks the skills to make his point in society
4. may be *angry*—the angry rapist is likely to use more violence and force than is needed to compel the victim to submit and is likely to threaten, beat, and revile the victim
5. may need to exercise *power*—the power rapist is likely to use the assault situation to prove to himself and to the victim that he is powerful, omnipotent, and in total control
6. may show *sadistic* patterns—the sadistic rapist frequently uses extreme violence, and often mutilates or murders the victim

(Amir, 1971; Groth & Birnbaum, 1979; Williams & Holmes, 1981).
The female victim

1. fears for her life
2. may respond by exhibiting no emotions—appearing unaffected
3. feels humiliated, demeaned, and degraded
4. may suffer immediate physical and psychological injury as well as long-term trauma
5. may experience impaired sexual functioning
6. may blame herself and feel guilty
7. may experience difficulty relating to and trusting others—especially men
8. may experience fantasies, daydreams, and nightmares—vividly reliving the assault or additional encounters with the assailant—or may have mental images of scenes of revenge
9. may feel intense anger or hatred toward the assailant
10. will never be the same, even though most victims, over time, develop ways to recover, cope, and go on with their lives
11. may be fearful of going to the police or a rape crisis center
12. may be reluctant to discuss the assault with members of her family, friends, and others because of the risk of rejection and embarrassment

(Amir, 1971; Benedict, 1985; Williams & Holmes, 1981).

Myths of Rape

The social and cultural myths of rape have received much attention in the literature on sexual abuse. Many writers and rape crisis centers have compiled long lists of the myths. Eradicating these myths is an important part of helping victims to recover, helping families and associates to understand and offer appropriate support, and helping the professions (mental health, medical, educational, legal) to provide the services that victims (and their families and friends) and abusers (and their families and friends) need. Benedict (1985, pp. 5–12) has incorporated society's most prevalent and harmful myths into five broad categories.

1. *Rape is sex.* The notion that rape equals sex is perhaps the most destructive myth of all. If we believe that rape is sex, then it follows that rape doesn't hurt (physically or psychologically) any more than sex. We can even believe that the victim enjoys and is erotically stimulated by it. The fact is that rape is no joke or tongue-in-cheek matter! Rape is violence, torture, and a life-threatening event. It is utterly humiliating. It is robbery of another person's essence by personal assault. Whether the rape is done by a stranger, a date, a family member, a famous person, or a tramp—rape is *wrong, inexcusable,* and a *horrifying* crime (Sussman & Bordwell, 1981).

2. *Rape is motivated by lust.* Groth and Birnbaum (1979) believe that the motivation for rape is most likely to be power, anger, revenge, control, frustration, or sadism. Benedict (1985) reports that some men may come to associate sex with violence, thereby viewing victims not as human beings but as objects of prey and viewing sex as an act of power (p. 8).

3. *Rapists are weird loners.* No such contention can be supported by the research. Rapists come from every walk of life (Amir, 1971; Medea & Thompson, 1974, pp. 29–36). The rapist could be the man next door, a charming businessman, a laborer, a relative, a transient, or anyone else.

4. *Women provoke rape.* Sussman and Bordwell (1981) have clearly shown that what the victim does prior to the rape has little, if anything, to do with the rapist's decision to assault. Although most rapists deny that they are rapists, rationalize that women provoke it, or deny that the sexual assaults are rape, there are virtually no documented cases in which women have lured men into raping them. It is true that many women are unlucky enough to be in the wrong place at the time of the assault or are otherwise out of reach of assistance. However, being vulnerable is never a cause or a reason to be raped.

5. *Only bad women are raped.* This myth is one of the most blatant examples of a "blame the victim" attitude (Brownmiller, 1975). This myth is taken to mean that, if the woman has a "bad" reputation, the rape is justified. Brownmiller's point is that a person's alleged reputation has nothing to do with whether she deserves to be raped. Rape is rape! Whether the victim is a professional hooker or a minister should make no difference. Neither deserves to be assaulted and both are entitled to equal protection and treatment.

It is not easy or simple to eradicate or even to refute these five myths in society at large. Even when people mentally come to understand the fallacies of the myths, many individuals hold negative residual attitudes, derived from the myths, which color their language, beliefs, and behavior. Evidence of this crops up everywhere—from our jokes and cartoons to our judicial decisions. It is essential that crisis workers dealing with victims of sexual assault free themselves of these myths prior to working with clients. It is also necessary that we, as a society, reeducate and reorient ourselves concerning these myths if we are ever to break the cycle of injustice that we have perpetrated in the whole area of sexual abuse/misuse (Benedict, 1985).

DYNAMICS OF SEXUAL ABUSE OF CHILDREN

Recent Historical Dynamics

According to Finkelhor (1984), several factors have contributed to the emergence of child sexual abuse as a problem for society. Resolution of the problem has been championed by the women's movement, the children's protection movement, and a coalition of groups with successful experience in promoting social issues (p. 3). It has recently been established that the sexual abuse of children is a worldwide problem and not one confined to the United States (pp. 5–6). The rate of abuse has grown with the advent of widespread divorce, remarriage, and easy conjugal pairings and dissolvements (increasing the amount of exposure of children to stepfathers, boyfriends, and lovers of children's mothers) (p. 7). Rapid change in sexual norms has accompanied an erosion of traditional, externalized sexual controls, aided and abetted by popular pornography, portraying children as sex objects (p. 8). The sexualization of life, which has become prevalent in the media, has led to new, increased, and heightened expectations. Such expectations, faced by many men who were locked into situations in which they felt a sense of sexual deprivation, led to the abuse of children by men seeking alternatives for their sexual gratification (p. 9). An additional factor proposed by Finkelhor (1984) is that women have become less willing to live in subservient, passive, childlike roles. Some men, threatened by the assertiveness of women, have turned to children as compliant sex partners (p. 9).

Phases of Child Sexual Abuse

The dynamics of rape apply to the whole scope of sexual abuse/misuse. There are some additional dimensions that crisis workers should consider when dealing with situations involving children. According to Murphy (1985), reporting on the dynamics of sexual abuse developed by Sgroi (1982), the behavior of the abuser may be traced through five phases: (1) engagement, (2) sexual interaction, (3) secrecy, (4) disclosure, and (5) suppression. These phases apply to both intra- and extrafamilial abuse, providing the crisis worker with a basis on which to identify and follow the case movement from stage to stage. The Sgroi model also enables the worker to view and understand abuse from the abuser's point of view. Murphy (1985) has applied

Sgroi's concepts to child sexual-abuse treatment, including the treatment of abusers.

Engagement phase. The abuser's objective in the engagement phase is to get the child involved in sexual activity with the abuser. Both access to the child and opportunity (privacy) are needed if the abuser is to be successful. Therefore, if we were looking for possible instances of unreported abuse, we would identify times and situations when the abuser and the victim were alone together. We must also look for different strategies that two different types of abusers (child molesters and child rapists) may employ (Murphy, 1985, p. 1).

Molesters tend to use *enticement* and *entrapment* to get the child engaged in sexual activity. *Enticement* may include deceit, trickery, rewards, or the use of adult authority to tell the child in a matter-of-fact way that the child is expected to participate. *Entrapment* is used to manipulate the child into feeling obligated to participate through traps, blackmail, and so forth. Molesters may make pornographic pictures or video tapes and convince the child that there is no other choice than going along with the secret activity and may also seek to impose guilt by making the child feel responsible for the abuse (Murphy, 1985, p. 1).

Child rapists use *threat* (particularly the threat of harm) or the imposition of superior physical *force* to engage the child in the abusive activity. Typically, the rapist will threaten to kill or injure the child or someone dear to the child or threaten to commit suicide himself, convincing the child that he or she will be blamed for the rapist's death if the child resists or reports the rape. In using superior force, the rapist may simply overpower the child, restrain the child by tying him or her, give the child drugs or alcohol, or physically brutalize the child into submission (Murphy, 1985, p. 1).

The vast majority (about 80%) of abusers use the first two strategies—enticement and entrapment. The strategies or categories of engagement by abusers are used to identify the dynamics, not the type, of sexual activity. Abusers tend to repeat their engagement patterns and show little tendency to move from nonviolent to violent strategies. Molesters are apt to consistently entice or trap their victims, whereas child rapists tend to use threat or force almost exclusively. The strategy used by the abuser is an important issue in treatment because victims typically wonder throughout their lives why they permitted it to happen (Murphy, 1985, p. 1).

Victimized children do not normally conceptualize the total picture: that they have been overpowered, manipulated, deceived, coerced, or entrapped into the sexual activity (Murphy, 1985, p. 2). They will probably need help in sorting out and getting past the crippling aspects of the abuse. Victims may have difficulty placing the full blame and responsibility on the abuser and absolving themselves of their previous assumption that they contributed to the abuse.

Sexual abuse at an early age may result in severe psychological and behavioral repercussions in later stages of life and, unless it is resolved, will continue to haunt and debilitate the individual in numerous facets of life (T. B. Davis, 1985). (This phenomenon is clearly portrayed in the case of Pearl, which follows later in this chapter.) The way victims deal with themselves and others may change as a result of their perception of the abuse. The sooner the victims can deal with the issues, the better are their chances of recovery. But they must be allowed time to deal with it. They must not be forced to deal with their sexual abuse until they are ready (Bass & Thornton, 1983, pp. 15–22; Colao & Hosansky, 1983, pp. 135–162).

Sexual interaction phase.   Types of abuse may include (blatant or surreptitious) masturbation (the abuser may masturbate prior to making physical contact with the child), fondling, digital penetration, oral or anal penetration, dry intercourse, intercourse, forcing or coercing the child into touching the abuser's genitals, forced prostitution, and pornography. Children may be coaxed into cooperation, not consenting, because abusers—as adult authority figures—often command, engage, or enlist cooperation from the victim. Children lack the maturity, experience, and age to be able to consent, but they may cooperate because of their subservient status (Murphy, 1985, p. 2; Plummer, 1984, p. 145).

Secrecy phase.   Abusers communicate to children that others must not discover the sexual activity. The objective of abusers is to continue the activity. This necessitates avoiding detection and maintaining access to the child while continuing the abuse. The techniques for maintaining the secrecy may involve incorporating "rules" or "games," implicating the child in the activity, and setting the child up to be responsible for keeping the secret (Bass & Thornton, 1983; Murphy, 1985, p. 2).

Disclosure phase.   Sometimes the abuser is discovered accidentally. At other times the abuse is disclosed intentionally by the child or someone else. Intentional disclosure is usually made by the victim. Frequently intentional disclosure enormously complicates the abuse because parents and others refuse to either face it or believe it. Accidental discovery may come as a result of such consequences as pregnancy, VD, sexual acting out, promiscuity, and physical trauma. The way the abuse is disclosed can affect the child's self-esteem and reaction to treatment. For instance, disbelieving adults sometimes respond by blaming and punishing the child—and allow the sexual abuse to continue (Molmen, 1982, pp. 35–36; Murphy, 1985, p. 2).

Suppression phase.   The suppression phase may begin as soon as disclosure takes place. Suppression may be attempted by the abuser, the victim, parents, other family members, professionals, the community, or an institution. There are many reasons for suppression: fear of publicity; fear of reprisal; to protect the reputation of a family, an abuser, or an institution; to avoid prosecution; to avoid responsibility; to protect the child; to avoid embarrassment; to avoid the kinds of confrontation and intervention required to deal effectively with the difficult and sensitive situation; and fear of getting involved.

Survival phase.   On the basis of our own experience and the reports of a number of other writers, we have added a sixth phase, the survival phase. It is during this phase that we recommend implementation of strategies for helping the child and the family to respond to and recover from the abuse as much as possible. Phase 6 includes stopping the abuse, providing needed medical and psychological treatment for the child, and helping the significant others close to the child to overcome the trauma, fear, anger, and despair caused by the abuse (Benedict, 1985; Grossman & Sutherland, 1983). It also involves preventing further abuse (Bass & Thornton, 1983; Colao & Hosansky, 1983; Plummer, 1984; Townley, 1985) and prosecuting and/or getting counseling for the abuser (Benedict, 1985). There appears to be a growing need for facilities to care for child sexual-abuse victims and their families. According to Carter (1986), only 20% to 25% of abused children are receiving any treatment or protection. She reports that additional treatment centers are needed for detecting and treating children who are victims of both physical and sexual abuse (p. 42).

In summarizing the dynamics of child sexual abuse, it appears that abusers and pedophiles—adults who have an abnormal sexual desire for children—are able to carry on their activities because children are largely powerless and vulnerable and because families and society are reluctant to face and deal with the realities of the abuse. Child sexual abuse is an area that is beginning to receive considerable public attention. The abuse should be stopped. Child victims should be helped to recover. Abusers should be identified, stopped, punished, and treated. Child sexual abuse/misuse and other forms of abuse and neglect are complex problems that require concerted efforts to solve. We have dealt with some of the other forms of child abuse and crisis in Chapter 7.

INTERVENTION STRATEGIES

Rape and other forms of sexual assault cover a broad spectrum of abuse and require a wide variety of intervention strategies for crisis workers. The conceptual basis for the intervention strategies is the six-step model which was discussed in Chapter 2. We have identified five cases, more or less representative, through which we have illustrated various kinds and stages of crisis work. Because of space limitation, we have confined our interventional time frame to two phases: (1) from the moment of the assault until 24 hours have elapsed and (2) from the start of the second day following the assault until the end of the first three-month period. This does not mean that all sex abuse crises end in three months (Benedict, 1985; Williams & Holmes, 1981). Most crisis situations do occur during that time frame. We assume that most of the counseling that extends beyond three months is within the framework of long-term counseling or health care. We are aware also that rape crisis centers and programs, although engaged primarily in crisis intervention, do not make such a time-limited distinction. Workers in these centers will gladly talk with a victim even if the assault occurred many years ago.

We will present five cases from which to illustrate a variety of intervention strategies. The sexual-assault abstracts of Susie, Nadine, Hazel, Pearl, and Jeanette will be followed by segments of worker/client dialogue and crisis intervention strategies from the perspectives of both immediate and postassault effects.

CASE OF SUSIE

Susie, age 8, is the middle child in the family. She, her brother, age 11, and a 5-year-old sister live with her mother and stepfather, whom her mother married nearly two years ago. Susie's mother, Allene, and father divorced when the youngest child was about 1 year old. Susie's stepfather started off by fondling her. This went on for several weeks. Although she was bewildered, scared, and intimidated, no one else knew about the activity. Recently, while everyone else was out of the house, her stepfather raped her. He threatened to kill Susie, Allene, and her sister if she told anyone. The following morning Susie confided in her brother who, in turn, told Allene what had happened. Allene found Susie's bloody undergarments, took Susie to the hospital, and had the stepfather arrested. Susie's mother, Allene, plans to file for divorce as soon as possible and she plans to prosecute him.

CASE OF NADINE

Nadine, age 16, married John when he came home from sea for the holidays. They went away for a two-day honeymoon. Nadine was a virgin and she was quite naive and frightened about sex. On their wedding night, John raped Nadine. During all the subsequent nights of John's two-week leave, Nadine submitted, but each time it was unwanted sex on her part. She didn't feel she had the right or the power to protest. Early this morning, John left to return to his ship for a six-month voyage at sea. Nadine's girlfriend advised her to contact the YWCA Rape Crisis Center today. Nadine feels devastated and worthless and blames and hates herself for what has happened to her.

CASE OF HAZEL

Hazel, age 19, is a physical education major in her junior year in college. She rooms with another woman, Wanda, her same age, who is also a physical education major. As Hazel entered her apartment building alone at 3:30 P.M., she was confronted by a person in his late teens who put a knife to her throat, forced her into her apartment, and raped her three times—first in the vagina, then in the anus, and finally forcing her to suck his penis. He continually cursed her, threatened her, promised to come back, and said he knew where to find her and that he would kill her if she reported him. Hazel feels devastated, humiliated, and filthy, and blames herself for not fighting back. She has always prided herself on her physical strength, self-sufficiency, independence, and positive outlook. Now she says she feels like a stupid pushover.

─────────────────── *CASE OF PEARL* ───────────────────

Pearl was sexually abused by her biological father regularly from ages 8 through 15. For 20 years she suppressed all memories and emotions related to the abuse, which had included fondling, digital penetration, and intercourse. Now, at age 35, she has regained her memory of the abuse and is experiencing severe symptoms of delayed rape trauma syndrome. Her marriage is breaking up; her career is in shambles; her communications and relationship with her three children are adversely affected by her own personal turmoil; her rage toward her father and her anger toward her mother have robbed her of her self-respect and her affection toward her parents, who live across town from her. Her only daughter, a middle child, has recently reached her eighth birthday, and Pearl is deeply obsessed with her daughter's safety. Pearl feels a great deal of guilt, shame, remorse, and loss of self-esteem. For several years she has been experiencing suicidal ideations, and, since the recovery of her memory of the abuse, these ideations have seriously intensified.

─────────────────── *CASE OF JEANETTE* ───────────────────

Jeanette is a 50-year-old teacher. She has been living alone in a small house since the younger of her two children went away to college two months ago. Jeanette was divorced seven years ago. When she returned home from the store at 9:30 P.M. last evening, she was met, as she emerged from her car in her driveway, by a gunman in his middle twenties. She dropped a small bag of groceries and some items from her purse as she was abducted at gunpoint and forced into the gunman's car, which was parked on the street. Jeanette was beaten, driven away to an isolated area several miles from her home, raped, beaten again, robbed, and abandoned, bleeding and bruised, with her clothing in shreds. She was weak and dazed, but was able to find her way to the nearest house, where she called for help. Now Jeanette is experiencing physical and emotional trauma. She is amazed at herself for being alive, because she believes the attacker meant to kill her.

The First 24 Hours

From the moment the victim of sexual assault is freed from the assailant, the first 24 hours is a critical period. Since each victim's experience is unique, each person's response is also unique. Crisis workers must be prepared to be open, to understand, and to respond to a wide variety of individual differences in clients. A sampling of segments from our five cases will reflect some of the important considerations for crisis intervention during the first 24 hours following the assault, or from the moment the victim presents the assault as a crisis problem.

Immediately following the assault, the most important need the victim experiences is to feel and be safe again. Hazel clearly expresses this need.

Hazel: Now I'm scared to death to go back there. I've got to get back out there and find my roommate. She doesn't even know it yet. I'm scared for either one of us to stay there tonight.

CW: Hazel, it's really important that you're in a place where you feel safe tonight. Where can you go, perhaps with your roommate, where you can feel safe, comfortable, and in control again?

Hazel: Well, my mother picked me up and took me to the hospital. I was planning to stay at home—my parents' home—tonight if I can get Wanda to come with me. I'm sure she'll want to come with me. My mother was a dear. She was so understanding. I knew she would be. My dad's a problem, though. He met us at the emergency room. He's so mad! He's eager to find that guy and kill him! He's more concerned about catching that guy than about how bad I was hurt. He's pressuring me to go to the police right now! Gee, I'm not sure I'm ready for that.

CW: You've done the right thing, calling your mother and getting yourself to the hospital. Most of all, you've survived a horrible crime that you in no way caused. Now it is important for you to feel safe, and your mother is probably your best source of support right now. And any police reporting should be your decision. I hope you don't get pressured into reporting when you don't want to or before you're ready. I'm sure that your father is having a difficult time with it. But if and when you do want to report it to the police, we'll go with you if you want us to. In fact, we'll be with you during any police or legal hearings concerning the rape if you so desire. If you do decide to report it, it is best to report it as early as possible and certainly within 24 hours—for gathering evidence and giving the police a chance to pursue it while it's fresh.

Hazel: They gathered evidence at the emergency room. I also got the preventive injections for VD and the antipregnancy pill which they offered. I'd die if I came up pregnant! The nurse, she was real good. She told me all about the evidence. I'm just not ready for the police today. Maybe tomorrow. I just want to go get cleaned up. I feel filthy all over—inside and out. Filthy, slimy, dirty. Ugh! I just want to find Wanda, go home, and put it as far away from me as possible today. I do feel sort of uncomfortable about putting Dad off, though.

CW: This has been one *hell of a day* for you. You've never before felt this violated and demeaned. I can imagine how hurt and upset and confused you must feel. Right now, I'm concerned that what *you need* gets attended to. I want to do whatever I can to help.

Hazel: Well, like I said, I just want to get clean and comfortable and get somewhere safe where I can get myself together again before I'm hassled by Daddy about going to the police.

CW: I certainly see your point. I'm so thankful that you're here and alive! The most important thing now is for you to get your feet back on solid ground again. I'll be happy to talk with your father whenever you want me to—tonight, tomorrow, or any time. Maybe you'd like me to talk with him by myself now and together with you tomorrow, or not at all, or however you'd like. I can see that the thought of confronting your father right now is really bothering you.

The segment with Hazel reflects the need not only for immediate safety and control but also for freedom from pressure from others. Hazel has already experienced too much emotional stress and physical pain today. She should not be pressured, doubted, blamed, or lectured at any time concerning the assault.

In cases where there is physical injury, the victim will need immediate medical evaluation and care. Susie's mother, Allene, deals with that and several other important concerns.

Allene: This has been a horrifying ordeal. I've stayed in the room with Susie all night. She's sleeping comfortably now. She's under sedation. I won't know the extent of her physical damage until all the tests are in. I'm afraid it's pretty bad, though. It's been a living hell. A nightmare!

CW: You've certainly been through a lot in the last few hours. And you've done a remarkable job of taking care of Susie. Your concerns about her injuries are certainly justified. You're obviously a very good mother who has suddenly been thrust into this—nothing you or Susie did caused it. It was perpetrated upon her and you. Our unit is here to assist you in any way we can. We want to provide someone to be with you and Susie, if you need us, during these critical hours of your hospital stay, as well as providing aftercare and follow-up counseling if needed.

Allene: I appreciate it. Everything happened so fast! I don't know how I managed without falling apart. It's like a wild dream—an ugly nightmare. I don't know how I'll handle it when the dust settles. I'm so mad—I could just kill him! I feel like I've been raped too. There's so much on me right now. I don't know if I'm capable of bearing up under all that's got to be done. Damn, damn, damn that man! Excuse me, I shouldn't blow up like that.

CW: That's all right. You have a perfect right to be angry and to say it. It's good that you care enough to be upset, and it's good to see you direct your anger at him—the real cause of Susie's hurt and your anger. Both of you deserve better treatment than he gave you, and no child asks to be raped.

Allene: That's right. I trusted him! And he took advantage of her. She was helpless— a helpless child. I've got to show her where I stand on this. First, I'm going to take good care of her, and then I'm going to send that louse to jail for good!

Allene shows a variety of legitimate concerns. The crisis worker permits her to express her anger, isn't threatened by Allene's outburst, encourages her to keep owning and expressing her feelings, and lets her know that neither she nor Susie was to blame for the assault. That strategy is important in letting Allene know that she can be in control and that the worker believes in her, without the worker's jumping in and expressing the anger for her.

In some assault situations, the victim assumes the fault was all hers, and it is difficult to get her to focus and place the responsibility on the attacker. Nadine shows intense self-blame as she talks with a female crisis worker at the rape crisis center.

Nadine: It was like a horrible dream. He must think I'm awful. I was nothing but a big crybaby. He may never come back. I don't know what I was thinking about when I married him. I didn't even think about the sex part of it. I only imagined the romantic part of it. I was so shocked that first night! When it really dawned on me the first time that he was really going to do it—stick that thing in me. God! What an idiot and a dope I am! I begged and begged him not to do it so fast—not right then. I pleaded with him to give me a little time to get used to the idea. He just said no. He just said I'd have to get used to it sooner or later, and that it would have to hurt the first time to feel good later. Finally, he was on top of me and I felt like I was going to die. I said, "Oh, please don't, I'm going to scream." And he said, "Don't scream." And he held his hand over my mouth, and he . . . he raped me! I wanted to die, right then. I was a bloody mess. I guess I got what I deserved.

CW: I noticed you called it "rape," which is exactly what it was. Even though you were married to him, it was still rape. I also noticed you seemed to mostly blame yourself—you're somewhat reluctant to place any of the blame on him.

Nadine: Well, I wish he had been more gentle and certainly more understanding. But it was his right. I belong to him now. It was stupid *me* that married him! I didn't have to do it. So, in a way, I deserved what I got, didn't I?

CW: I can see why you may believe that. But just because you married him doesn't mean he owns your body and can use you sexually against your will. No, I don't think you deserved that, and I certainly don't think you're stupid. I do think it took a great deal of courage for you to come in here to talk about it. You're entitled to your own feelings and you're entitled to decide when and how you wish to have sex, even with your husband. I'm so glad you're here now, and I want to assure you that we want to help you get through this difficult time and to figure out what choices you have and what you want to do.

Nadine: (Sobbing.) I didn't want it that way. (Long pause—sobbing continues.) I just wanted—I just needed to be held. First to be treated gently. (Sobbing continues.)

CW: Do you want me to hold you now? I don't want to impose it on you, if you don't want it, but I can see you really did miss just being held and comforted.

Nadine: (Still sobbing—moves to and embraces the crisis worker.)

CW: (Responds by embracing Nadine, as long as she wishes.)

The crisis worker is sensitive to Nadine's emotional needs as well as to her personal autonomy. She does not want to cause Nadine any additional emotional stress. But she senses that Nadine needs the comfort, assurance, and trust of both words and physical contact. She verbally asks Nadine whether she wants to be held. Recovering rape victims are unusually sensitive to emotional and physical overtures from others. The crisis worker is correct in not taking Nadine's preference for granted.

There are situations in which the most helpful and appropriate immediate response from a crisis worker is empathy and assurance that the victim is still alive. Jeanette's rape was a case in point.

Jeanette: I spent most of the night in the emergency room. It was horrible—the rape. I don't know how I came out alive and without any broken bones. He intended to kill me. Part of the time I was in a daze. I don't know what came over me.

I must have blanked out. I don't know how long I lay out there alone after he left me. I certainly didn't fight back or protest.

CW: Jeanette, I'm so proud of you for the way you handled it. You did whatever it took to stay alive. You saved yourself, and that took courage. Whatever you did, whether it was blanking out or offering no protests, was right, because it preserved your life, and that's the important thing right now.

Jeanette: Well, that's probably a good way to look at it. Right now, I'm tired—exhausted. I thank the Lord I'm here. I feel like I'm in a sort of twilight zone. Maybe part of me did die. I'm feeling so alone and vulnerable.

CW: So you're needing rest and comfort now. After what you've been through, I can see how you would be feeling like you're in a twilight zone. My concern for you right now is that you'll be able to get some rest in a safe and comfortable place. Where would you feel safe in resting the rest of today and tonight?

Jeanette: I don't know. Home, I guess, but . . . (Pause, with apprehensive look.)

CW: But you'd like someone there with you whom you really trust and feel comfortable with. Who might that be in this locale?

Jeanette: Well, my sister. I'd want her there with me. She's the only one I can think of. I don't think I can go into that driveway by myself today. There's no way I'd go there after dark by myself.

The crisis worker's intuition is right when she guesses that the place of safety and comfort for Jeanette would be her own home, but that the frightening part would be getting past the place in her driveway where she was abducted. The crisis worker is also correct in reassuring Jeanette for her actions, which brought her out alive.

An important issue for rape victims is control. Jeanette has experienced an emotionally draining loss of control to the attacker, and she needs to be reassured that that loss of control is neither total nor permanent. She did what she had to do to survive, and that took courage. It is important to her for others to recognize her and give her credit. Whatever small amount of control she has, she can build upon that as a basis for beginning her long journey toward recovery. Also, the crisis worker does not impose on Jeanette a place for resting or an accompanying person of trust and understanding. These immediate choices are both derived from Jeanette and are undoubtedly more appropriate than any of the choices the crisis worker might have generated or insisted that Jeanette take.

Autonomy and control are important factors in the recovery of assault victims. Frequently victims find family members, friends, spouses, lovers, and others who tend to disallow the victim's expression of emotions or who tend to respond negatively toward the victim. Pearl experienced a great feeling of being discounted by others, some of which she expressed to the crisis worker with whom she talked.

Pearl: I was seeing this male therapist, and he was supposed to be good. But I could see that he didn't know a thing about women who had experienced childhood rape by their fathers. I could tell by his looks that he didn't want me to be angry. It was like he thought I'd be angry at him or something. He must have been threatened by my hatred of my father's forcing sex on me all those years.

CW: You want to be able to express whatever anger you feel toward your father and you don't appreciate someone else trying to restrain you.

Pearl: Right, because I've held it in so long it has about destroyed me. I wanted to just let it out at last. I wanted to stamp my feet, rant, rave, and holler at the top of my voice.

CW: Do it now, if you like.

Pearl: I appreciate your invitation, but I'll have to wait and see if I work up to it; that is, if I feel like doing it again, like I felt with him.

CW: Well, Pearl, any time you feel like it, just rant and rave all you want to, because you truly deserve it, after holding it back for so long.

Pearl: Actually, I haven't been very conscious of it until recently. It was apparently buried deep inside me until all this hell broke loose. I think the reason I kept it so deep inside me for all those years was that I really felt guilty. I really believed that it was all my fault. I believed that I somehow seduced my father all those years. I know now that that's not so, but I still feel depressed and down on myself.

CW: Like you somehow let it happen or encouraged it to happen, so you're still feeling that heavy load of guilt even though the thinking part of you is questioning it. You're wanting to deal with it more effectively than you have done in the past.

Pearl: It's all so complicated. I just can't seem to turn it around and feel good about myself. I'd like to put it behind me and live for me!

The interview with Pearl continues. The crisis worker's assessment is that Pearl will probably need long-term therapy with an expert female specialist who is competent in dealing with delayed rape trauma syndrome in adult victims of childhood incest. Pearl is exhibiting some fairly typical symptoms. Furthermore, the crisis worker knows that Pearl needs more time and expertise than the rape crisis center can offer, so the worker makes a mental note to make an appropriate referral. The crisis worker is not surprised when, during the same interview, Pearl expresses some additional feelings that are typical of adults victimized by childhood incest.

Pearl: I've never liked my mother much. Now I think I hate her.

CW: You hate her for not being sensitive enough to pick up on the incest and protect you.

Pearl: Well, she was so weak! And she had so many problems of her own. I tried to tell her what Daddy was doing, but she either didn't want to believe or wouldn't believe it, and she wound up putting it all back on me. I kept thinking, hoping she'd figure out what was happening. But she didn't. Maybe she was just plain stupid.

CW: It's hard for you to understand or to forgive your mother, and it is painful for you to realize now that you were just a little girl who was brutalized by her father and that you were helpless and wronged and didn't have a choice in the matter. You're also having a hard time absolving yourself of the guilt.

Pearl: I guess I was made to feel so bad when I did try to confront it. Even as an older child, before it stopped, I tried to confront it again—with my father and with my mother separately. All I got was denial and putdowns. "You're imagining things." "It really wasn't sex he was doing to you." "You are lying again." "You are growing up to be a temptress or a whore." "You are nothing but a rotten, mean, bad girl—you aren't fit for anything else." I guess I finally decided I was really bad and that I deserved the treatment I was getting.

The crisis worker again realizes that Pearl's recovery will probably require more help than can be provided in a few brief sessions. The case of Pearl demonstrates several fairly typical characteristics of delayed rape trauma syndrome, especially in adult victims of childhood incest. It also shows some typical responses of crisis workers who come into contact with such clients.

Victim's needs. The case summaries we have presented identify several important needs that victims of sexual assault have manifested over the years. These needs closely parallel Benedict's (1985) findings and should prove helpful to crisis workers and to abuse victims themselves. In the first 24 hours, the victim

1. wants to be in a safe and comfortable place
2. prefers to have someone with her whom she trusts and feels close to
3. needs to get clean, bathed, and have a change of clothing as soon as possible
4. needs to be free of pressure from others to report the rape, go for counseling, go to the police, etc.
5. needs medical evaluation and care
6. may need to go for preventive medication for venereal disease and pregnancy
7. may need her emotional needs cared for today.

Support-person services. The case summaries also bring to light several considerations that should benefit those persons close to victims who are in a position to serve as support persons. These considerations may also benefit crisis workers. Support persons may assist the victim in the first 24 hours by

1. showing her genuine empathy and concern
2. assuring her that she is believed—not discounting her story
3. letting their words and behavior show her she is valued
4. offering her comfort, a place to stay, or to hold her (ask her first)
5. assuring her that she is not blamed and that she did not cause the assault
6. letting her know that others are proud of her for being a survivor
7. staying with her as long as she needs someone
8. refraining from pressuring her to take certain actions—let her make choices at her own pace
9. permitting her to express a full range of emotions, such as showing anger, rage, ranting and raving, and stamping her feet, and restraining themselves from jumping in and expressing emotions for her
10. listening to her without judging, protesting, butting in, asking diverting

questions, quizzing, blaming, doubting, laughing, manipulating, minimizing the assault, denying the seriousness, etc.
11. letting her tell the full story.

From Second Day to Three Months Following the Assault

A wide range of needs, differences, characteristics, and strategies are inherent
in crisis intervention with victims of sexual assault from day number 2
through three months afterward. Of course, each victim and each case is different. Many rape victims experience residual effects the rest of their lives.
But generally speaking, by the three-month mark, most victims are out of the
crisis phase. Many victims consider themselves "recovered" in anywhere from
nine to thirty-six months, depending on the severity of the assault, the victim's background, and the victim's coping mechanisms and resources. The
victim/worker segments illustrate various stages of crisis intervention occurring between the second day and three months following each assault.

Medical treatment and advice are one of several important aspects of crisis
intervention with sexual assault victims. Hazel's case illustrates that point.

Hazel: I still can't believe I'm having this trouble. I never had it before. I have sore
throats; I can't eat; and I'm even nauseated half the time. I washed out my mouth a
million times the first two days after it happened. I know my mouth and throat are
clean—that I got all of his old stuff out. But still, the thought of it just chokes me up
and aggravates me.

CW: So you're feeling like it's a carry-over in your mind. How does that square with
your medical tests? How can you be sure that's it?

Hazel: Well, my doctor says I'm OK. I have also gotten negative reports on my VD
tests, but I'm still getting intense itching in my vagina and pain in my anus area,
but the doctor says there's nothing wrong in either place.

Hazel's symptoms are not unusual. It often requires a long period of time
to get back to normalcy following a rape like the one that was forced upon
her. A variety of physical and psychological symptoms, related to the sexual
assault, can be expected in many victims.

Each case of sexual assault is unique, and the effects of the assault on
clients of varying coping abilities, backgrounds, and family situations can be
expected to differ. Allene's concerns over Susie form quite a contrast with the
problems that Hazel has experienced, even though both of them express concerns that are quite real to them and that are fairly typical of recovering victims.

Allene: Well, Susie seems to be back in good, radiant health now. But our life is hell.
That man is still out. His trial has been put off again. I'm afraid he might even come
around again. I've heard some things about how bold he is in parading around. But
I wouldn't have believed some of our friends, and even some of my own relatives.
They either shun us or are afraid to be around us. I wouldn't have believed it until
it happened.

CW: You're disappointed in their reactions toward you and your children—when you need them most, they're not there. Now is when you need them!

Allene: That's right. They could be so much help now—staying with the kids while I work, helping all the children readjust, helping us get settled in another apartment.

CW: I can see that you need support persons now more than ever, and you'd like help from relatives—but they aren't helping now. How would you like to come and visit our family support group? They're there to help. They know what you're going through, and I believe that someone there might help you out.

Allene brings out a problem that is quite common. Many people are uncomfortable being around victims—especially families experiencing known or suspected child abuse. It is not an issue that can be forced. Probably a better option is something on the order of the crisis worker's suggestion: ask someone who has experienced it, understands it, and has recovered, to lend a helping hand. If support groups are available, they can be ideal sources of help. Crisis agencies, such as rape crisis centers, can usually put victims in touch with such help.

Nadine has experienced some problems that are different from Allene's. Nadine's problems are recurrent and quite common among victims of rape.

Nadine: I was much better. I thought I was about over it. Then I started having all this trouble sleeping. I got depressed and just stayed in bed.

CW: You felt that your recovery was coming along fine. Now, the rape is haunting you again, and you're still looking for ways to cope with it.

Nadine: I am, but I feel like I'm going backward. I'm having nightmares. They're exaggerated. But it's him, right there over me again. About to rape me again. Sometimes he's distorted. Sometimes the whole nightmare's distorted. Then, when I do sleep at night, I have these flashes, during the day. Just all of a sudden, it flashes right in front of me, just as plain as day.

CW: And these are nearly all images of your husband; it's always him overpowering you and you being unable to resist and being really scared.

Nadine: (Nods.) Like I'm paralyzed.

CW: What do you make of this? What does it seem to mean to you now?

Nadine: It means I'm scared, I guess. I'm dreading the thought of him coming home again. It means I'm thinking about it a whole lot. I don't know what's going to happen.

CW: What do you want to see happen?

Like Nadine, many rape victims experience dreams, nightmares, flashbacks, and depression. Most victims are troubled by these experiences and expend considerable energy attempting to deal with them. One excellent coping strategy that the crisis worker later suggested to Nadine is to get involved in a support group of recovering rape victims.

Some rape victims find that their assault adversely affects their work performance and their normal sexual functioning. Jeanette's case exhibits both problems and even more.

Jeanette: I've never missed school or even wanted to. But, the last few weeks, I've taken sick leave when I wasn't really sick. I just don't know.

CW: It sounds like you're surprised at yourself and a little worried too; that you'd hoped the rape wouldn't affect you that badly. But it sounds like you have a suspicion that it has.

Jeanette: Or I'm just using it as an excuse! But, then there's the other area—my sex life. I haven't been up to trying sex again at all. My boyfriend, the only one I have sex with, has been understanding and caring. But I know he must be bewildered. We're both afraid to discuss it. I think he still wants sex. But then I've wondered, maybe he doesn't want me sexually any more. Like I'm spoiled goods. But I don't know. We just don't talk about that.

CW: Your sex life concerns you. You don't want to be pushed into sex just yet. But you're wondering how he feels, and what you'd really like to be able to do is to discuss it with him.

Jeanette: Yes, but I'm afraid to, or I don't want him to think I'm pushing him.

CW: What would you like to have happen with regard to your sex life?

Jeanette: I guess I'd like to have him say, "I understand. I still want you sexually. But I can wait until you're ready. For now, I just want to hold you and love you and caress you and not push you into intercourse until you are ready." I guess that's about what I'd like to hear him say.

Jeanette's fears about resuming sex and about discussing it with her lover are typical. It is a sensitive area for anyone. Men are perhaps more sensitive about rejection, but women are more sensitive about being pushed into resuming sexual activity too soon after being assaulted. Decisions in this delicate area run the risk of adversely affecting sexual activity permanently. In cases like Jeanette's, referral for sex therapy is a good idea if the problem persists after about six months. The important thing for the crisis worker and the spouse/lover to know is that the woman must not be pushed into resuming sex too soon.

Pearl's rape trauma syndrome shows some usual and some unusual patterns. Some of them are characteristic of adult reaction to childhood incestuous encounters and some are more characteristic of reactions to rape after attaining adulthood.

Pearl: I used to have nightmares. But I got out of them. Lately, I've had them again. I've had crying spells. I've been depressed. I've had mood swings. God! I've had mood swings! It's a wonder anybody can stand me. I have had tantrums. Bad ones, over some little thing—over nothing, really. And I've had phobias. Some really silly phobias.

CW: What do you make of these now?

Pearl: That I want attention, I guess. Maybe that I want to clear this stuff up—once and for all. I'm tired of fooling with it.

CW: Why now? What's different now, that makes you want so desperately to get things settled now?

Pearl: Well. Hmmm. Maybe I don't want my daughter to have my kind of life. Or maybe I want to live a better life, through her, by making sure she grows up without sexual abuse. She's 8. The same age I was when I was first raped by my father. God! What a life!

Pearl identifies an important dynamic in her life. But it is not an issue that the crisis worker can easily help her cure. Again, the crisis worker feels that Pearl needs expert therapy, preferably with a female therapist. Such a specialist is located in Pearl's city, and Pearl agrees to see her.

In the case of Pearl the dialogue excerpts are taken from one lengthy crisis intervention session. We mention this in order to clarify the crisis worker's assessments that Pearl will require referral for expert therapy in addition to being a one-time client in crisis intervention. There is no delay in referring Pearl. The referral issue is reiterated to emphasize the fact that almost all adult victims of childhood sexual abuse who are seen in crisis intervention also need prolonged therapy to enable them to successfully cope with their deep-seated traumas.

The crisis worker recognizes that Pearl is experiencing several of the delayed sexual-abuse symptoms or traumas that many adult victims of childhood abuse exhibit. According to T. B. Davis (1985), women who repress until adulthood their feelings and memories of childhood incest or sexual abuse frequently have recurring and debilitating problems of adjustment. Examples of delayed symptoms that are frequently displayed are withdrawal or reclusiveness, fearfulness of getting emotionally close to men, seductiveness, promiscuity, lack of sustained physical and emotional stamina, extreme vacillation in heterosexual relationships (cannot live with men and cannot live without them), low self-esteem, and suicidal ideations.

Although crisis workers normally refer victims exhibiting delayed sexual abuse symptoms, it may be helpful for workers to recognize some of the lifestyles and patterns that may develop in women who have repressed long-term feelings related to abuse. Some typical lifestyles and patterns are (1) getting stuck or trapped in a rut and being unable to make decisions, take initiative, and make progress because of constantly reliving the trauma, (2) exhibiting self-defeating behaviors, then engaging in self-blame, (3) taking on perfectionistic attitudes and applying them to herself—she can never be good enough, must make *sure* everything is going to be perfect, no task she does is ever adequate, and (4) doubting whether she is capable or adequate enough to do what she wants to do and, consequently, cannot afford to take risks. Patterns such as these constantly keep the victim in a state of turmoil and rob her of her happiness and productivity.

The symptoms of delayed sexual abuse syndrome are difficult to diagnose because the victim is usually experienced and skilled at masking the behaviors. The treatment of such victims is exceptionally difficult. It is recommended that victims be referred to female therapists who specialize in treating victims of delayed sexual abuse syndrome because the dynamics of this type of disorder mitigate against successful treatment by male therapists (T. B. Davis, 1985).

A strategy that has been most successful in helping victims of delayed sexual abuse syndrome is to get the victim into a support group of recovered and recovering victims. It appears that a group of victims who have successfully learned to cope with this particular delayed trauma can be more effective in helping victims who are stuck than most of the other strategies. Probably the best treatment is to provide a combination, placing the victim both with a support group and with a specially trained female therapist (T. B. Davis, 1985).

Victim's needs. The case summaries have helped us to identify some needs of the typical sexual assault victim and infer several others. Indications are that the victim

1. may need continuing medical consultation, advice, or treatment; she may experience soreness, pain, itching, nausea, sleeplessness, loss of appetite, etc.
2. may have difficulty resuming work; the added stress of the rape may create too much stress in the workplace
3. needs to have people reach out to her, listen to her, and verbally assure her—not shun her or fear continuing to relate to her
4. needs the acceptance and support of family and friends
5. may have difficulty resuming sexual relations and needs understanding without pressure
6. may exhibit unusual mood swings and emotional outbursts, which others will need to understand and allow
7. may experience nightmares, flashbacks, phobias, denial, disbelief, and other unusual effects
8. may go into depression, which may be accompanied by suicidal ideation.

Support-person services. Support persons can be of optimal help during this phase of recovery. They may assist victims of sexual assault by

1. understanding and accepting the victim's changed moods, tantrums, etc., and allowing her the freedom to act them out
2. being available, but not intruding—while supporting the victim through encouraging her to regain control and to recover her life
3. ensuring that she doesn't have to go home alone (without overprotecting her)
4. realizing that recovery takes a long time and lots of hard work
5. allowing her to make her own decisions about reporting the rape and prosecuting the assailant
6. leaving it up to her to decide whether she wants to change jobs or places of residence
7. responding to her in positive ways, so that she does not sense that the crisis worker blames her for "letting it happen" or that the crisis worker feels she is not capable of taking care of herself

8. allowing her to talk about the assault to whomever she wishes, whenever she wishes, but not disclosing the assault to anyone without her prior consent

9. showing empathy, concern, and understanding without dominating her

10. recognizing that she will likely suffer from low self-esteem (finding ways to show her she is genuinely valued and respected)

11. recognizing that her hurt will not end when the physical scratches and bruises are gone—that her emotional healing will require a long time

12. trying to find ways to help her trust men again—assisting male associates (friends, co-workers, brothers, and her father) to show tolerance, understanding, and confidence. It is detrimental to her for male support persons to exhibit and express myths about rape. Typically, men have more difficulty understanding rape than women.

13. trying to find ways to encourage female co-workers, friends, sisters, and her mother to believe in her and not avoid her or avoid talking with her openly about the rape

14. including her children, if she has children, in all considerations concerning help toward emotional recovery

15. referring her to sexual assault support groups for victims and family members. Support groups can be of enormous help. Many YWCA Rape Crisis Centers and National Organization for Women (NOW) chapters have support groups.

16. realizing that the victim's husband, partner, or lover may develop symptoms similar to those of the victim (nightmares, phobias, rage, guilt, self-blame, self-hate, etc.) and may need help similar to that needed by the victim herself

17. (for husband or lover) giving her time to recover, free from pressure, before resuming sexual activity; letting her know he is still interested in her, still desires her, but that former patterns of sex life will be resumed at her own pace. It is important to talk this out openly with her, to clear the air for both parties.

SUMMARY

Sexual abuse affects all segments of society. Individuals from every developmental age, sexual, and racial/ethnic group and sociocultural stratum have been represented among victims. Infants, children, teenagers, adults, and the elderly: no age group is free from risk. The vast majority of sexual assaults are perpetrated upon women and upon children of both sexes. Sexual abuse/misuse may occur in many forms: unwanted or forced penile, digital, or object penetration of the vagina, anus, or mouth; fondling; forced or entrapped prostitution; pornography; obscene phone calls; or any forced, unwanted, tricked, or entrapped sexual activity.

Rapists and other sexual abusers are nearly always males who come from all walks of life. Most abusers appear to perceive victims as objects of prey rather than as persons. Abusers display a variety of pathologies. They usually assault, not out of lust or desire for sexual gratification, but out of a perceived need to control, exert power over, punish, vanquish, defeat, hurt, destroy, degrade, or humiliate others. Typically, abusers deny, minimize, and/or rationalize their behavior to the extent that they themselves rarely define their attacks as abuse. Instead, they usually charge that the victim asked for, deserved, or caused the abusive activity.

In recent years the public has become more aware of the phenomenon of rape and other forms of sexual abuse, and increased awareness appears to have ushered in a greater sensitivity to and advocacy for the rights and needs of victims. The helping professions have provided many additional programs for assisting victims: crisis intervention, research, counseling, medical services, long-term mental health care, new laws and legal advocacy, more vigorous efforts to prosecute offenders, and more sympathetic and proactive news media. However, much remains to be done in the arena of sexual assault. There remains a pressing need for society at large to understand better the dynamics of sexual abuse and the needs of victims and their families. There is a great need for society to overcome a number of long-standing myths about rape and other forms of sexual abuse. There is a need for better reporting and improved police and legal responding. There is a need for victims to accept counseling and not to blame themselves. And, finally, there is a need for victims' families, friends, and co-workers to be willing and able to respond to victims with openness, genuineness, acceptance, understanding, and respect, all of which are key attitudes or conditions for nurturing recovery from the debilitating trauma and effects of sexual assault.

REFERENCES

American Psychiatric Association. (1980). *Diagnostic and statistical manual of mental disorders* (3rd ed.). Washington, DC: Author.

Amir, M. (1971). *Patterns in forcible rape.* Chicago: University of Chicago Press.

Bass, E., & Thornton, L. (Eds.). (1983). *I never told anyone: Writings by women survivors of child sexual abuse.* New York: Harper & Row.

Benedict, H. (1985). *Recovery: How to survive sexual assault—for women, men, teenagers, their friends and families.* Garden City, NY: Doubleday.

Brownmiller, S. (1975). *Against our will: Men, women, and rape.* New York: Simon & Schuster.

Burgess, A. W. (Ed.). (1985). *Rape and sexual assault: A research handbook.* New York: Garland.

Burgess, A. W., Groth, A. N., Holmstrom, L. L., & Sgroi, S. M. (1978). *Sexual assault of children and adolescents.* Lexington, MA: Lexington Books.

Burgess, A. W., & Holmstrom, L. L. (1974). Rape trauma syndrome. *American Journal of Psychiatry, 131,* 981–986.

Burgess, A. W., & Holmstrom, L. L. (1979). *Rape: Crisis and recovery.* Bowie, MD: Robert J. Brady Co.

Burgess, A. W., & Holmstrom, L. L. (1985). Rape trauma syndrome and post traumatic stress response. In A. W. Burgess (Ed.), *Rape and sexual assault: A research handbook* (pp. 56–60). New York: Garland.

Carnes, P. (1983). *The sexual addiction.* Minneapolis, MN: CompCare Publications.

Carter, K. (1986, January 3). Pediatrics: Chicago hospital converts vacant unit into cost-effective child abuse ward. *Modern Healthcare, 16,* 42–45.

Colao, F., & Hosansky, T. (1983). *Your children should know: Teach your children the strategies that will keep them safe from assault and crime.* New York: Berkeley Books.

Davis, A. B. (1985, November 10). Fears follow sex abuse victims. *The Commercial Appeal*, Memphis, Section G, pp. 1–3.

Davis, T. B. (1985, October 10). Adult females who have been victimized by childhood incest and sexual abuse: Assessment and treatment techniques (Lecture). Counseling Psychology Seminar, Department of Counseling and Personnel Services, Memphis State University.

Ellis, E. (1983). A review of empirical rape research: Victim reactions and response to treatment. *Clinical Psychology Reviews, 3*, 473–490.

Finkelhor, D. (1979). *Sexually victimized children.* New York: Free Press.

Finkelhor, D. (1984). *Child sexual abuse: New theory and research.* New York: Free Press.

Fortune, M. M. (1983). *Sexual violence: The unmentionable sin.* New York: Pilgrim Press.

Frazier, P., & Borgida, E. (1985). Rape trauma syndrome evidence in court. *American Psychologist, 40*, 984–993.

Geiser, R. L. (1979). *Hidden victims: The sexual abuse of children.* Boston: Beacon Press.

Gil, E. (1984). *Outgrowing the pain.* Palo Alto, CA: Consulting Psychologists Press.

Greer, J. G., & Stuart, I. R. (Eds.). (1983). *The sexual aggressor: Current perspectives on treatment.* New York: Van Nostrand Reinhold.

Grossman, R., & Sutherland, J. (1983). *Surviving sexual assault.* New York: Congdon & Weed.

Groth, A. N., & Birnbaum, H. J. (1979). *Men who rape: The psychology of the offender.* New York: Plenum.

Groth, A. N., & Stevenson, T. M. (1984). *Anatomical drawings for use in the investigation and intervention of child sexual abuse.* Newton Center, MA: Forensic Mental Health Association.

Hursch, C. J. (1977). *The trouble with rape.* Chicago: Nelson-Hall.

James, B. J., & Nasjleti, M. (1983). *Treating sexually abused children and their families.* Palo Alto, CA: Consulting Psychologists Press.

Janosik, E. H. (1984). *Crisis counseling: A contemporary approach.* Monterey, CA: Wadsworth.

Karpel, M. A., & Strauss, E. S. (1983). *Family evaluation.* New York: Gardner Press.

Katz, S., & Mazur, M. (1979). *Understanding the rape victim.* New York: Wiley.

Kempe, R. S. (1984). *The common secret: Sexual abuse of children and adolescents.* New York: W. H. Freeman.

Knopp, F. H. (1982). *Remedial intervention in adolescent sex offenses: Nine program descriptions.* New York: Safer Society Press.

Mayer, A. (1983). *Incest: A treatment manual for therapy with victims, spouses and offenders.* Kalamazoo, MI: Learning Publications, Inc.

McCombie, S. L. (1980). *Rape crisis intervention handbook.* New York: Plenum.

Medea, A., & Thompson, K. (1974). *Against rape. A survival manual for women: How to avoid entrapment and how to cope with rape physically and emotionally.* New York: Farrar, Straus & Giroux.

Molmen, M. E. M. (1982). *Avoiding rape: Without putting yourself in protective custody.* Grand Forks, ND: Athena Press.

Murphy, W. D. (1985, October). The dynamics and phase of sexual abuse (Mimeographed, 3 pages). Sexual Abuse Treatment Project, Department of Human Services, University of Tennessee, Memphis.

O'Brien, S. (1983). *Child pornography.* Dubuque, IA: Kendall/Hunt.

Plummer, C. A. (1984). *Preventing sexual abuse: Activities and strategies for working with children and adolescents.* Holmes Beach, FL: Learning Publications, Inc.

Rada, R. T. (1978). *Clinical aspects of the rapist.* New York: Grune & Stratton.

Renshaw, D. (1982). *Incest: Understanding and treatment.* Boston: Little, Brown.

Russell, D. E. (1982). *Rape in marriage.* New York: Macmillan.

Sanford, L. T. (1980). *The silent children: A parent's guide to prevention of child sexual abuse.* New York: McGraw-Hill.

Sgroi, S. M. (1982). *Handbook of clinical intervention in child sexual abuse.* Lexington, MA: Lexington Books.

Sussman, L., & Bordwell, S. (1981). *The rapist file: Interviews with convicted rapists.* New York: Chelsea House.

Townley, R. (1985). *Safe and sound: A parent's guide to child protection.* New York: Simon & Schuster.

West, D. J., Roy, C., & Nichols, F. L. (1978). *Understanding sexual attacks*. London: Heineman.

Williams, J. E., & Holmes, K. A. (1981). *The assault: Rape and public attitudes*. Westport, CT: Greenwood Press.

■ Classroom Exercises

Invited Presentation by Outside Consultants

Your instructor may invite into the classroom the director and a counselor from a rape crisis center or experts from an alternate source. The presentation should be announced ahead of time so that you have sufficient time to read, discuss, and prepare questions for the visiting consultants. The consultants may bring along a brief film or video tape on sexual assault, as well as pamphlets and materials describing the services and operation of the center they represent. Consultants typically prefer to make a brief presentation so that a large block of time is reserved for responding to students' questions and concerns.

Counseling Simulations in Small Groups

The instructor constructs one-page scenarios of one or more sex-abuse-victim situations. The five cases in this chapter may be used as models for developing the scenarios. A realistic source is recent newspaper accounts of rapes and sexual assaults. The class is divided randomly into task groups, which will conduct their own crisis intervention sessions simultaneously, rather than before the whole class. One person enacts the role of victim and one the role of crisis worker, and the remaining persons are observer/evaluators. Only the victim in each group is given a copy of a sexual-assault scenario. The victim will need a few minutes to read and get into the mood to enact the role. Then the victim and crisis worker enact a crisis intervention session.

For a specified length of time, the victims are interviewed by the crisis workers in the groups, with the observer/evaluators taking notes. The instructor will circulate around the room, briefly looking in on each group as it engages in its crisis intervention session. The crisis worker in each group is instructed to be as facilitative and helpful as possible, incorporating the strategies suggested in this chapter into the six-step crisis counseling model learned in Chapter 2.

Whenever the instructor calls "time" to conclude the crisis intervention sessions, a few moments should be reserved for observer/evaluators to provide constructive feedback to their respective groups. Some suggested guidelines for observer/evaluators are these questions:

1. What verbal responses and nonverbal behaviors did the crisis worker exhibit that appeared to be most helpful to the victim?
2. What verbal responses and nonverbal behaviors (if any) appeared to be the least helpful or to elicit negative responses from the victim?

After each observer/evaluator has had an opportunity to provide constructive feedback in the respective groups, each task group is allowed a brief period of discussion and a period for the "victim" to disassociate from the role. The "victim" can "derole" by taking a moment to tell other members of the task group, "This is the reason I am not the person I portrayed in that scenario" or make a similar statement of disengagement from the role played. The exercise should be concluded by providing an opportunity for one observer/evaluator from each group to share a one-minute summary statement (of that particular group's experience) with the entire class.

CHAPTER 10

Hostage Crisis: Negotiation Strategies

BACKGROUND

The following news brief appeared in the Memphis *Commercial Appeal* ("Insurance for Hostage Victims") on November 23, 1985:

> An insurance company has come up with a new policy. If you are worried about being taken hostage you can get an insurance policy for one million dollars that will pay off if you do not survive the incident. A one hundred thousand dollar reward will also be paid for information leading to the capture of the hostage takers—dead or alive.

The horrifying tragedies that take place a continent away from us, or in social institutions such as penitentiaries that are psychologically a continent away, make splashy headlines. Most of us assume that being taken hostage will happen to the other guy, certainly not us. Yet, if you had been a prison guard in the Attica, New York, penitentiary in 1971, a health care worker in a variety of settings from a Granite City, Illinois, Community Mental Health Center to St. Jude Children's Research Hospital in Memphis, Tennessee, a traveler on any number of commercial airline flights that were hijacked in the 1970s or 1980s, a customer or employee in a recent bank holdup, or a tourist on the *Achille Lauro* cruise ship in 1985, you might have been exceedingly wise to take out such an insurance policy.

Hostage taking has been with society throughout recorded history; however, its upsurge since the 1970s has been exponential. Why is this so? Although it may seem otherwise, hostage taking is a crisis event that is instigated by the weak and powerless. Such disenfranchised individuals consider it a feasible response for two reasons.

First, with the advent of instantaneous electronic media coverage, dramatic news events from around the world can be broadcast live into every home via television. Through the media, the hostage takers thus gain a far wider platform to air their grievances or make their demands than they could possibly expect to obtain by any other means. A hostage situation is the height of real-life drama and gives the hostage takers power to command attention they would otherwise never have.

Second, hostage takers obtain power by the seeming randomness of their acts. No one can be sure if and when he or she may be taken hostage. Every venture into public holds the threat of becoming a victim in a hostage incident. Faith in the government to protect the populace becomes shaken, because there can never be enough police to guard every train station, bus depot, bank, airport, and shopping center every minute against those who may wish to take hostages. Further, hostage taking puts powerful law enforcement agencies at the holders' mercy. Governments cannot exert their superior force against the hostage takers out of fear that they may hurt the hostages—the very people who make up the system and those whom their agencies are sworn to protect.

Hostage negotiation, at least in the United States, can be traced back to 1973, when the Federal Bureau of Investigation (FBI) began research into, and training for, negotiation of hostage situations in order to combat the upsurge of aircraft hijackings. In 1974, the Los Angeles Police Department, which was encountering terrorist activity by the Symbionese Liberation Army, instituted an in-house hostage recovery team patterned after that of the FBI. Since that time, virtually every metropolitan area police department and national security force around the world has had personnel undergo hostage negotiation training.

Although hostage negotiation has many components of crisis intervention that would seem particularly appropriate to the skills of mental health professionals, negotiation has remained primarily the dominion of the police. The following definition of hostage taking shows why: "Hostage taking is a criminal act which consists of taking hold of one or several persons, in order to use them, by threatening their well-being to the end of exerting a constraint upon a third party" (Crelinsten, 1976, p. 23). The definition portrays three principal actors in the scenario of a hostage taking: the hostage (A), who is the means by which the hostage taker (B) gains something from a third party (C) (Crelinsten, 1976, p. 23). This triangular aspect of a hostage situation makes it different from other crisis situations described in this book, in which the human service worker deals primarily with one other individual, the victim. Here, the rules of crisis intervention are changed, for it is the victimizer with whom the crisis interventionist is dealing.

Although perhaps the most dramatic variety, political terrorism is a small part of the overall hostage scene. To bring the issue up close and personal, the human services worker is likely to meet individuals who have had their lives radically altered in what they may feel are very negative ways by human service agencies. The rise of the American health care system as a bureaucratic institution has led people to feel uncared for and ignored in times of emotional stress, particularly when they do not seem to have the ability to find coping mechanisms or resources on their own (Turner, 1984, p. 177).

People who have butted their heads against human services systems that seem little concerned with the needs of recipients and very much entangled in yards of bureaucratic red tape may feel angry enough to take matters into their own hands. Just as hostage taking is a political act for terrorists too weak to cause revolution, it is, in the health care setting, a feeling act from people too weak to change what they believe to be grave injustices perpetrated on them by that system (Turner, 1984, p. 172).

Between terrorists and emotionally distraught people who are angry with the health care system lie a wide range of individuals who, under the right circumstances and conditions, will take hostages to make their particular point or obtain access to some perceived goal. Such goals may range from political, personal, and financial power to drugs, money, and escape.

Hostage taking may be premeditated and deliberate or incidental and reluctant, but it is usually precipitated by the volatile eruption of some preexisting crisis event (Bahn, 1980, p. 151). Thus, hostage taking arises from many situations, of which these are examples (Hassell, 1976, pp. 108–111):

1. As a result of stress, in many cases aided by heavy use of alcohol, a domestic dispute arises. This dispute escalates to include threats of violence or actual violence between relatives, usually a husband and wife or boyfriend and girlfriend.
2. Response time by the police in answering an armed robbery in progress is so fast that the hostage taker is trapped at the scene and thus takes hostages to assure an escape.
3. The mentally deranged individual, who out of fear for his or her own life or because of some "message," takes hostages for protection.
4. Convicts who take hostages to address grievances about prison conditions.
5. The least common situation, at least in the United States, is the terrorist organization which uses hostages as a tool of political or financial power to force concessions from a nation, corporation, or powerful individual.

To think that anyone, particularly the human service worker, is immune to this phenomenon is to be the proverbial head-in-the-sand ostrich.

We want to underscore that whereas this chapter may be seen as belonging more aptly in a spy novel by Robert Ludlum, it is a very serious business—one of which human service workers, from police officers and prison guards to social workers and psychologists, need to be aware and one they are likely to face. There are two reasons for our admonition. First, if you should ever become a hostage, you can take rudimentary steps to stay alive. Second, if initially you are cast in the role of negotiator, you should be able to keep the situation contained.

This chapter will not make one a skilled negotiator. To become a negotiator takes a great deal of training. What this chapter will do is give you the basic knowledge to survive a hostage situation or to keep the situation at a reasonable level of stability until help arrives. What is now known about hostage situations is no guarantee of survival or safety from physical and/or psychological trauma. Yet there are some basic rules that will greatly increase your own or others' chances of survival.

DYNAMICS

Although hostage negotiation units were created with the terrorist in mind, most use of negotiation units has been occasioned by domestic quarrels, mental illness, or aborted robberies (Gettinger, 1983, p. 24). As such, the crisis that arises is always within the context of a law enforcement operation (Miron & Goldstein, 1978, p. 5).

At the onset of a hostage taking, the responding law enforcement agency's first objective is to contain and stabilize the scene. Since time is on the side of the law enforcement agency, the longer the situation remains stable, the higher the probability that the event will end peaceably. Maintaining control is a critical factor in any crisis situation. Hostage situations are no different. As a result, whoever controls the source of stimulation in the hostage situation also gains control of the response and the situation itself (Lanceley, 1981, p. 30). It is through negotiation that control is established and shifted from the hostage to the police negotiator. If sufficient calm and order can be restored to the situation to bring it to a standoff, and then it is further constricted so that alternatives finally are reduced to one way out—the authorities' way—then the negotiator has accomplished the task (Miron & Goldstein, 1978, p. 6).

Yet, for a positive outcome to occur, certain general dynamics of hostage takers need to be understood. First, hostage takers should be viewed as individuals who have reached an acute level of frustration. Second, the taking of hostages should be viewed as an attempt at problem solving. Third, hostages are seen in most cases as merely pawns in a larger game and are used as bargaining chips throughout the negotiation process. Finally, the taking of hostages is an attention-seeking behavior to attract an audience, for without an audience the hostage taking is meaningless (Schlossberg, 1980, pp. 113–114).

Dynamically, there are two general classifications of behavior that may be observed in hostage takers: instrumental behavior and expressive behavior. Instrumental behavior has some recognizable goal that the perpetrator seeks to have fulfilled. Those engaging in expressive behavior seek to display their power. Of the two, the latter is the more difficult to understand, for such action appears to the casual observer to be senseless. There would seem to be no way that the perpetrators can gain anything except their own or others' destruction (Miron & Goldstein, 1978, p. 10). However, as an expressive gesture, such action is extremely powerful and indicates to the world at large that, although by drastic means, the perpetrators are able for a short while to take matters and destiny into their own hands. These dynamics combine variously to generate a number of categories of hostage taker. Along with the specific typologies go recommendations on how to deal with them.

Typologies

If the negotiator can ferret out characteristics and identify the particular type of hostage taker, then the negotiator can make a valid assessment of the situation and construct appropriate psychological and behavioral responses. Researchers vary on the number of typologies that exist. However, the following types seem to cover most situations:

1. The fleeing felon
2. The mentally disturbed
   a. the paranoid schizophrenic personality
   b. the depressive personality
   c. the inadequate personality
   d. the antisocial personality
3. The estranged person
4. The institutionalized individual
5. The wronged person
6. The religious fanatic
7. The political terrorist

Miron and Goldstein (1978, pp. 96–97) have developed a table that prescribes intervention techniques to be used with each type. With criminal types who are engaging in instrumental behavior, a rational, problem-solving approach that seeks a compromise in concrete terms is proposed. With psychotic, emotionally disturbed types who are engaging in expressive behavior, emphasis is on emotional techniques that use reflection of feelings and restatement of content. With terrorists who are "emotionally rational," a mix of the two basic techniques is best suited.

Fleeing felons.   The felon who is attempting to flee the scene of a crime is the most common type of hostage taker. These hostage takers are usually career criminals, but they are not the most successful in their field. Characteristic of the felon is a lack of premeditation and generally poor planning in commission of the crime. The hostage taking is a desperate move: interrupted in the commission of the crime, the felon, in order to assure his or her own safety, reactively seizes a bystander. The hostage is seen as a passport to freedom or, at worst, some sort of shield against immediate harm (Cooper, 1976, p. 106).

From a negotiations standpoint, felons are the easiest to deal with because they are capable of rational thinking. More important, they do not generally have a cause for which they are willing to die. A rational, reality-oriented approach is recommended. The discussion should be factual. The disclosure of facts about the situation gives rise to problem solving on the part of the hostage taker, leading to the eventual realization that surrender is his or her best option. In favor of the negotiator, the fleeing felon is one of the most likely to fall into the Stockholm syndrome (Fuselier, 1981a), which we will describe shortly.

HT (Hostage taker):   I want out of this bank with the money, transportation to the airport, and a plane waiting to take me to South America, and I'm taking three hostages with me. I want that plane waiting in 30 minutes or somebody gets killed.

Neg (Negotiator):   I can't make those guarantees right now. You know I'll have to buck that up the line, so let's be reasonable about that time limit. What do you say?

The mentally disturbed.   Mentally disturbed hostage takers suffer from various kinds of psychological maladies. A mentally disturbed person may or may not be in touch with reality. This individual will likely be a loner, acting in obedience to some intensely personal, often obscure impulse (Cooper, 1981, p. 57), and may believe that taking hostages will carry out some sacred mission or prove that he or she can do something important (Fuselier, 1981a). In the case of the mentally disturbed, the most difficult task for the negotiator is predicting behavior. There are four major diagnostic categories of mentally disturbed hostage takers that the negotiator is likely to encounter.

The paranoid schizophrenic personality. Paranoid schizophrenics are out of touch with reality. They are easily recognized by their false system of beliefs and especially by their hallucinations or delusions. They often take hostages in order to carry out what they believe is a "master plan" or to obey "orders from some special person or deity" (Fuselier, 1981a). These psychotic individuals are frustrated; they want something and cannot get it. Paranoid schizophrenics are conflicted and have difficulty coping with even minimally stressful situations. The result is aggressive and creative thinking. The combination of frustration and conflict produces a tremendous amount of anxiety. Excessive anxiety tends to make such individuals extremely sensitive and volatile.

Good negotiating strategy calls for reducing anxiety and at the same time attempting to create a problem-solving climate (Maher, 1977, pp. 64–65). The best approach is to accept the paranoid schizophrenic's statements as true. Although the negotiator should not agree that he or she also hears the same voices or shares the beliefs of the psychotic, the negotiator should not try to argue or convince the psychotic that he or she is wrong (Fuselier, 1981a). Empathic understanding of the beliefs of the paranoid and reflection of the disturbed individual's feelings are appropriate responses.

HT: The radio messages keep coming, even though I've told these people to shut their radios off. They're driving me crazy!

Neg: It must be really exasperating that they won't do what you tell them, particularly when all you want is peace and quiet.

The depressive personality. Hostage takers who are depressed seem to be in an incapacitated mental state. They are very confused people who identify themselves by their inability to make a firm decision. They may be characterized by slow, subdued speech, a negative outlook on life, and demands that are intermingled with references to death. Their hostages are frequently persons known to them. Depressed individuals are very unpredictable and are extremely dangerous. Often they are suicidal and may initiate a hostage taking in order to force the police to shoot them (Strentz, 1984, p. 185).

Persons suffering from depression have difficulty making decisions. In these cases, a problem-solving approach would most likely be futile. With the depressive, the negotiator must be firm and manipulative.

HT: I just don't know what to do, it's just a mess.

Neg: The mess will just get worse if you keep putting yourself deeper in this hole. Send the children out and we'll talk about you.

If the individual is suicidal, the negotiator needs to extract a commitment, no matter how tenuous, to keep the person from acting out a threat, and if possible change the subject to get the person's mind off the action he or she is about to take. In the following dialogue, the negotiator attempts to shift the hostage taker's focus away from suicidal ideation and onto more effective communication. Negotiations in this case involve applying in a very paced way the intervention procedures described in the chapter on suicide (Chapter 3).

HT: I wonder if you'd see that the picture albums get to the kids?

Neg: I'd be willing to help in any way I can, but I want you to agree to not do anything until we get all these other issues settled. By the way, would you mind speaking into the phone a little louder? My hearing isn't all that good and we must have a bad connection.

Inadequate personality. The inadequate personality usually displays a good deal of narcissistic, attention-seeking behavior. Many times this is an individual who has attempted a crime and has been caught in the process. Since the hostage-taking incident may be the high point of the person's life, the inadequate personality tends to stretch the situation for all it is worth. Identified by key phrases such as "I'll show them who's boss" and "Now they'll see what I can do," this hostage taker basks in the limelight of the situation. Such pronouncements are indicative of a low self-image. Therefore, the motivation for taking hostages may be to prove that the inadequate type can succeed at something. Yet, in the same instant, inadequate types may appear contrite and apologetic for their behavior. Initially, the inadequate personality type may state demands with considerable conviction and then turn around and provide the negotiator with several options (Strentz, 1984, p. 185). Negotiators need to be aware of and seize those options.

The primary strategy of the negotiator is to present problem-solving alternatives so that the hostage taker will not feel that he or she has "failed again." Playing up to this hostage taker's ego and helping the person to find a face-saving alternative is an excellent tactic. Inadequate personalities have a need to prove themselves to some "significant" others. The "I'll show them" statements are indicative of this need, and their true meaning ultimately may be the murder of the hostages if their egos are not handled with extreme care.

HT: I want a personal interview with the news director of Channel 3 right now. I've got some things I want to say. You do that and I'll let them go.

Neg: I understand how important it is to you to get on television. You let those people go now and I'll see that you get on the 10 o'clock news.

Antisocial personality. The antisocial personality repeatedly comes into conflict with society and is incapable of having significant loyalty to individuals, groups, or social values. Antisocial types tend to blame others and offer rationalizations for their behavior (American Psychiatric Association, 1980, pp. 317–321). The antisocial personality who takes hostages is generally engaged in an expressive act unless the individual is caught in the middle of a felony. The antisocial type is likely to dehumanize the hostages and should be considered extremely dangerous to them because the person will manifest little feeling for their well-being. Although antisocial personalities have not internalized ethical values, they do understand their effect on others and are therefore potent adversaries. Although persons of this type lack emotional depth, they may display a wide range of skillful emotional overlays in place of true emotional responses (Lanceley, 1981, pp. 31–32).

The only concern of these hostage takers is for themselves. Therefore, the negotiator should be aware that this type has no compunction about doing anything to anybody. If at any point this hostage taker feels that hostages are a burden, they will be killed. The profound egocentricity of the antisocial type requires constant stimulation. A primary objective in the negotiation process is to keep the holder's attention and avoid having him or her turn attention to the hostages as a source of stimulus.

This person is not only street wise but also police wise, so trickery is not a good idea. Also, the negotiator should avoid references to jail or hospitalization because antisocial types are likely to become highly agitated if they feel that they are going to lose their freedom or it is insinuated that they are crazy. Finally, the inflated ego of the antisocial type makes formation of the Stockholm syndrome highly unlikely (Fuselier, 1981a).

HT: Don't give me that crap about "more time." You get that car in here or I start doing some fun things to this little 6-year-old, and her mommy gets to watch.

Neg: I know you're mad about the car, but you know I gotta go through procedures. I understand you could work the kid over, but I wonder if you've thought about the good that'll do you in the long run. It's your hide you're dealing with, too! So let's work on that side of it.

Estranged person. Invariably the estranged hostage taker will know the hostage, who will probably be a spouse or lover. The estranged hostage taker is experiencing a breakdown in his or her interpersonal relationships. These breakdowns lead to domestic quarrels and, in turn, the escalating nature of the quarrels and the feared loss of the significant other lead the estranged person to commit the hostage taking event. (Alcohol often provides the liquid courage necessary to carry out the hostage taking.) The estranged hostage taker seeks to coerce the maintenance of the relationship through forceful action. The most distinctive feature of this kind of hostage taking is its intensely personal nature and the unique purpose of the hostage taker in attempting continued domination over the significant other (Cooper, 1981, pp. 27–28).

As in any other domestic dispute, the negotiator should be extremely careful of this volatile situation and use empathic listening and responding skills to their fullest. With this type, the negotiator must contend with the highly personal nature of the hostage taking and the continued denial of reality. Intrinsic to intervention is the negotiator's ability to keep denial from turning into despair. The key to resolution is that the estranged hostage taker needs to be shown a graceful way out (Cooper, 1981, p. 28).

HT: It's not my fault. I've done everything she asked and then she still jilted me. If I can't have her, nobody will.

Neg: She really hurt you, then. I can start to see why you feel you had to do this. I'm wondering, though, if she can't see now just how strongly you feel. Perhaps you've made your point to her. You certainly have to me!

Institutionalized individual. Institutionalized hostage takers are inmates who have a grievance, usually about conditions within the system in which they are confined. The only other reason for taking hostages is to obtain a passport to freedom. Hostage takings of this sort are usually deemed instrumental acts that are planned to produce concrete changes in the institution (Maher, 1977, p. 65). Only in a very few instances do inmates perpetrate a hostage situation as a desperate expressive act to obtain revenge. However, given the mix of violent individuals in most correctional settings, the situation, if not contained immediately, can become exceedingly dangerous for both hostages and other inmates. If rapid response by law enforcement cannot be accomplished, then the situation is treated as if the negotiator were dealing with mentally "normal" criminals (Fuselier, 1981a).

HT: We want to see the warden and we want these 25 demands met and they ain't negotiable.

Neg: And I want to see and hear that the hostages are all right before we talk about any demands.

Wronged person. The wronged hostage taker is dissatisfied or aggrieved by the system at large or a particular bureaucracy. Wronged individuals may be identified by the "crosses" they bear and the paranoia associated with their beliefs. These hostage takers feel so grossly discriminated against by the "establishment" that they seek to remake society to their own satisfaction (Cooper, 1981, p. 10). Targeted hostages are those who for some reason (such as race, sex, religion, or job title) provoke the hostage taker to displays of uncontrolled rage and action. The hostages thus become the scapegoats on whom the hostage taker avenges all the real and imagined wrongs he or she has suffered.

Aggrieved or wronged individuals are high on the list of potential candidates with whom the human service worker may become involved—if not as a negotiator then as a hostage. Aggrieved individuals feel that no one in a position of responsibility will redress the terrible wrongs that have been done to them. After exhausting a variety of acceptable options within the system and still receiving no redress, these individuals may do something dramatic (Turner, 1984, p. 178).

Associated with this type of hostage taking is the high priority attached to publicity, for the hostage taker is usually motivated to make the public aware of the "wrongs" imposed by the particular authorities in question. If the law enforcement agency allows for media involvement, a close cooperative relationship between the two must exist. The media should not be allowed to operate as freelance negotiators. However, proper involvement of the media can enhance the opportunity for the release of the hostages if the hostage taker perceives that a "wrong" will be made "right" by a public airing (Gladis, 1979).

HT: The doctors, nurses, the administrators, the psychologists, the social workers, they're all at fault. She wouldn't have died if they'd done their job. Everybody thinks this is such a hot-shot hospital. It's really Murder Incorporated, and people need to know the truth.

Neg: I realize what a terrible shock her death was, and how you trusted all those people. Yet you believe they let you down and should be exposed for the incompetent blunders they've made. Would you be willing to make a deal? If I can set it up so you can read that prepared statement you've got about the hospital, will you let those people out?

Religious fanatic. Religious fanatics have the same inflexible and uncompromising attitude in their beliefs as political terrorists. But, unlike political terrorists, religious fanatics do not usually take hostages for offensive purposes. Rather, hostages are seen as sacrificial lambs that must be made to pay for the "sins" of the unrepentant. The taking of the American embassy in Iran in 1979 is a classic example of this situation. The hostage takers are unwilling to talk with those who are in a position to negotiate because they are not in the business of negotiation. What they are in the business of is atonement. Therefore, their demands are such that they are invariably impossible to meet—at least for a considerable time into the future.

Because religious zealots do not consider themselves accountable to anyone except their own deity, negotiations are very difficult and invariably call for outside help by someone whose nationality, religion, or some other attribute does not cast them in the "devil" category (Maher, 1977, p. viii). Hostages are subject to the religious and moral whimsy of such fanatics and may expect a long, arduous, and dangerous experience. Thus, the religious fanatic who is a hostage taker poses a particular problem to the negotiation process because such an individual must either die for the cause or relinquish it (Cooper, 1981, p. 45). As has been demonstrated over and over again in the Middle East, the former is more likely than the latter. In nearly every case of hostage taking by a religious fanatic, some sort of face-saving gesture will be required if the situation is to be resolved (Cooper, 1976, p. 104).

HT: This is God's will. If I allow you to pack me off to jail like a common thief, no one will believe in our holy cause.

Neg: What if we consider setting a low bond, maybe even self-recognizance? That way you wouldn't have to go to jail, and both your honor and your cause would be untarnished.

Political terrorists.   Terrorism is a political act ordinarily committed by an organized group, involving death or the threat of death dealt out randomly to noncombatants (Schreiber, 1978, p. 20). Its targets are not particular individuals but institutions that represent the power of the state. In a head-to-head confrontation with the government in power, the terrorist would invariably lose. From a strategic standpoint, terrorism always issues out of weakness. What makes the terrorist so threatening is the ability to strike at any place or any time. It is impossible for the state to guard every busy intersection, department store, power plant, and transportation facility. The state's vastness and its mission to protect all facets of public life are its major weaknesses when confronted with terrorism.

To be effective, terrorist activities must appear to be random in nature so that no one feels safe any place or any time. If the terrorist organization can breed such fear, then the populace starts to lose faith in the government's ability to take care of them. This is exactly what the terrorists want as a preliminary to exercising their own political demands.

Reduced to basics, terrorism is a form of communication that takes the form of a threat against innocent people. The whole idea of a terrorist act is to let the world know who did what to whom. Without an audience or the means to get a message to that audience, the act would be meaningless. Therefore, above all other forms of hostage taking, terrorists must have media exposure. The message is always "Take warning, notice us, we are mad as hell and won't take it anymore. We are deadly serious and you must meet our demands" (Schreiber, 1978, pp. 17–18, 113).

Hostage takings employed by political terrorists are well-designed, premeditated undertakings that are orchestrated by a political machine much larger than the hostage takers themselves. The political machine is a quasimilitary regime, and the hostage takers are seen merely as soldiers of the cause. The hostage takers and their projects are always subordinated to the goals of the organization (Cooper, 1981, p. 5). As such, the "soldiers" are expendable and generally know it.

How, then, can such people be recruited into the organization? To generate such allegiance calls for extreme commitment and sacrifice. The terrorist must believe enough in the cause to die willingly for it, and must further believe that he or she is making the world, or at least his or her part of it, a better place to live (Maher, 1977, pp. 65–66). This belief must be ingrained to the point that for the greater good, a few dozen bodies scattered around the Vienna or Rome airport are seen as a small price to pay to wake the world up to the problems the terrorist regards as all pervasive.

To carry out acts of violence against innocent people takes a great deal of righteous anger and zeal. Terrorists must feel that the cause is so just that they would willingly die for it. A perfect catalyst for making the political terrorist into a dedicated soldier willing to pay any price for the accomplishment of the organization's goal is to mix in some religious fervor. To be promised and believe that one will go to heaven for carrying out such terrible actions is extremely potent. For the true believer, no greater reward can occur. However, the only way to obtain that reward is to die! The hostage taker with these beliefs becomes a very dangerous individual.

While carrying out their missions, terrorists shaped by that blend of influences have extremely heightened emotional responsiveness that often edges on hysteria (Schreiber, 1978, p. 42). Therefore, in hostage undertakings, the zeal of the terrorists must always be tempered by someone in control who can obtain the maximum leverage from the event. To obtain the greatest results, the leaders must achieve the right combination of what may seem like unreasonable violence and coldly calculated goals. For even the most disciplined organizations this does not always happen. Too many times, in the heat of the moment, with the controlling organization of the terrorists far removed from the actual scene, things go awry. Therein lie the hope and despair of the negotiation process.

From the negotiator's standpoint, the fact that the organization's goals are paramount is a plus. It means that the terrorists can be reasoned with, provided that two conditions are fulfilled. First, the terrorist must be convinced that there is something to reason and bargain about. Second, the terrorist must trust the person who is doing the negotiating (Schreiber, 1978, p. 99).

An effective negotiator in terrorist hostage takings invariably means a disinterested third party who manifests the same characteristics as those who negotiate with religious fanatics. Having a third-party negotiator would also seem to be important to those invested with the responsibility of seeing the hostages safely freed. If events go sour, blame does not tend to fall so heavily on the responsible party. Of more importance, third-party negotiators are not so highly subject to the demands of public opinion, which create pressure on a government to capitulate to the demands of the hostage takers.

In dealing with terrorists, any negotiations should be directed to the topmost leadership of their quasimilitary network. Negotiators should attempt to convince the hostage takers that their point has been well made, their demands have been well heard, and killing the hostage would simply serve to discredit them in the eyes of the public (Fuselier, 1981a).

HT: I tell you in the name of all freedom-loving peoples and all that is holy, we will kill these infidel running dogs.

Neg: You have acquitted yourselves heroically in the name of your people and your mission. Yet if you kill those people you will be no better in the eyes of the world than those who have done such to you. Consider this with your leaders.

Stages of a Hostage Situation

Throughout the entire hostage episode, emotions of both parties move on a curve that oscillates between desperation and euphoria. As the episode is protracted, the cycle tends to dampen and retreat from both emotional extremes (Schreiber, 1978, p. 50). It is within this context that the following stages should be examined. There are four stages to a hostage situation: alarm, crisis, accommodation, and resolution (Strentz, 1984, pp. 189–194). The stages will be examined as they apply both to the hostage taker and to the hostage.

Alarm.   The alarm stage is the most traumatic and dangerous. Whatever the type of hostage takers, in this first stage their emotions are running exceedingly high, their reason may be diminished, and they may be extremely aggressive in their reaction to any perceived threat. To force their will upon the hostages, the general belief of the hostage takers is that hostages must be terrorized into submission. Therefore, hostage takers may be inclined to harass, abuse, or even kill anyone who seems to be interfering with their attempts to consolidate their position (Strentz, 1984, p. 190).

For the unprepared individual who suddenly becomes a hostage, the alarm stage is traumatic in every aspect. A previously tranquil situation now becomes a life-and-death one that pivots every minute. For the victim, defenseless and confused, the nightmarish experience takes on an unreal aspect. For many, denial of the reality of the situation sets in, particularly when those from whom they expect help seem to be doing nothing.

Effective coping at this early stage means immediately putting into place a strong will to survive and not succumbing to panic. Any sign of panic may cause the perpetrators to overreact to a highly charged situation and dramatically diminish the chances of survival (Strentz, 1984, p. 196). Hostages should disregard any notion of being a hero. Untrained, unarmed, and poorly conditioned civilians can best secure survival by maintaining low profiles (pp. 201–202) and staying calm and alert (Miron & Goldstein, 1978, p. 92).

Crisis.   The crisis stage marks the beginning of reason for the hostage takers. However, there is still a great deal of unpredictability and danger as they try to consolidate their position. Initial attempts at negotiation at this stage may be marked by outrageous demands and emotional diatribes by the hostage holders. Because of fear of assault by the authorities, hostage takers may move hostages to a more secure area or enlist their cooperation in making the area they are in more secure (Strentz, 1984, p. 191).

For the hostage, the crisis stage is the most critical because it sets the tone for the remainder of the situation. Hostage–captor interaction at this stage can either enhance or reduce hostages' chances of survival. Although denial by hostages may still be in place as a defense mechanism, the decision to face reality and engage in normal behavior generally provides some emotional relief and mental escape (Strentz, 1984, p. 203). If a hostage is in a position of responsibility, he or she cannot afford to lose emotional control. Dignified, nonthreatening behavior is the watchword. Hostages who are in positions of responsibility have to be very careful that they do not intimidate their captors. If their captors have inferiority feelings to begin with, they may see defiance as an attempt by the hostage to humiliate them. In particular, verbal humiliation is a precipitator of violence (p. 203).

At this stage hostages may start to experience three problems: isolation, claustrophobia, and/or the loss of a sense of time. Individuals who are isolated will have to come to grips with the fact that the only human contacts they have may be extremely hostile toward them. Claustrophobia can take its toll even if the individual is not isolated and confined to a small cell. An airliner can become a very tight place if all the windows have been covered and hostages are required to remain strapped into their seats. A problem that becomes very important is the loss of sense of time. By this stage, captors have usually removed personal items, including watches, from the hostages. Sense of time becomes very important to someone held captive who is hoping for rescue. Asking for such small favors as information about time or date puts hostages completely at the mercy of their captors. Hostage takers use such requests to good advantage in earning compliance from their captives (Strentz, 1984, p. 197). The message is, "We can do with you what we want. There is no hope other than what we give you!"

Accommodation.   The accommodation stage is the longest and most tranquil. This stage can go in one of two distinct directions, depending upon the type of hostage taker. The mentally ill may talk at length in highly emotional ways about their problems, using the situation to gain attention, and finally wind down to the point of willingness to surrender after they have had their say. The criminal caught in the act will spend the time bargaining for freedom. Terrorists will take the time to identify and segregate hostages according to their value to them. In each case, the holders may begin to temper their demands as they too begin to feel the stress of captivity (Strentz, 1984, p. 192).

For the hostage, the accommodation stage is marked by time dragging by. Boredom, punctuated only by moments of terror, is the hallmark of this stage. The crests and troughs of emotions that have occurred until this point are likely to induce fatigue in the hostage and hostage taker. If this stage becomes protracted, then there is a likelihood that what is known as the Stockholm syndrome, named after an aborted bank holdup in Sweden during which one of the hostages fell in love with her captor, will come into operation (Strentz, 1984, p. 198).

The Stockholm syndrome is possible if three conditions are met: extended period of time, not being isolated from one's captor, and positive contact between captor and captives (Fuselier, 1981b). The phenomenon comprises the three following elements (Strentz, 1984, p. 198):

1. Positive feelings are generated toward the hostage taker from the hostages.
2. Negative feelings are generated toward the authorities by the hostages.
3. Positive feelings are generated toward the hostages by their captors.

Evidence would seem to support the idea that this is not a well-gauged ploy on the part of the hostage to ensure survival. The phenomenon is probably an automatic, unconscious emotional response to the trauma of being taken hostage (Strentz, 1979, p. 2). Rather, it would seem that as people are thrown together, both captor and captive start to respond to one another on more personal terms. If this occurs, it becomes very hard to regard one another as faceless entities to be despised and used. Familiarity with each other provides a fertile ground for identification with the other's problems, hopes, fears, and outlook on life. If such positive identification by a hostage is reciprocated by the holder, the hostage's chances of survival go up considerably (Ochberg, 1977). During this stage it is not uncommon for hostages to feel that the authorities are the chief cause of the problem and that if they would only go home the siege would end (Strentz, 1984, p. 200).

The hostage can make use of this phenomenon. In as genuine a way as possible, the hostage should seek to build a positive relationship with his or her captors. The easiest way to do this is to be as real a person as possible by attempting to share the more personal aspects of one's life and attempt to elicit the same from the holders. If hostages make attempts to gain familiarity with the hostage takers, they would probably be wise to avoid political discussions with them, since such discussions accentuate differences between captor and captive (Miron & Goldstein, 1978, p. 92).

A captive who is a well-integrated individual may boost hostage morale by exploiting perceived weaknesses in the captors, although this is an extremely dangerous ploy if it backfires. The approach takes strength of character and is not generally recommended unless captives are isolated for a long period of time with only their own resources on which to fall back. In a protracted situation, hostages must take care of their physical needs. Eating and exercising are musts. Hostages should take whatever food is offered. Even if it is possible to do only flexibility exercises, they should be done on a regular basis (Strentz, 1984, p. 204).

Resolution. In the resolution stage the hostage takers will have become fatigued as the long hours or days have taken their toll. The high expectations that they held early on will become dashed as perpetrators find that they have lost most of the bargaining chips. At this stage, the skill of the negotiator is paramount. Whether there is a positive or negative resolution to the situation will depend on the ability of the negotiator to skillfully bring closure to the situation (Strentz, 1984, p. 193).

In particular, it is important to understand the difference between the behavior of a hostage taker who is planning to surrender and one who is planning on committing suicide (see the chapter on suicide, Chapter 3, for such cues and rituals). Inadequate personality types are a high risk for the latter response. They may see surrender as just another in a long list of failures, whereas suicide may seem to be a positive solution. The problem with suicide is that the hostage taker may not have enough courage to accomplish the act on his or her own. To force the issue, the hostage taker may engage the police by failing to heed their instructions, firing at them, or firing at a hostage (Strentz, 1984, pp. 193–194). If the hostage taker gives any cues at all during this final stage, the negotiator should be prepared to move immediately into a suicide prevention mode. Whatever the type, and however long and arduous the incident, the trained negotiator takes a purposeful and dignified approach to the surrender of the perpetrator.

If force has to be used, there will be a lot of confusion and noise. This is intentional on the part of the rescuers as a diversion. Hostages need to lie down if possible, or sit tight. Hostages should also keep their hands plainly visible by locking them behind their heads so that the rescuers clearly know who is a hostage and who is not. Hostages need to be calm and alert and follow orders of their rescuers explicitly (Strentz, 1984, pp. 205–206).

In the resolution stage, reaction of the hostages will be mixed, both toward the takers and toward their rescuers. Although relieved to be freed from the terror they have experienced, hostages may be hostile toward their rescuers and believe that the authorities were in the main responsible for having caused the trauma. Despite their recognition that their captors put them through a living hell and held the hostages' lives in their hands, hostages tend to feel that they in some way owe their holders for having given them their life back (Strentz, 1984, pp. 200–201).

Survivors of a hostage situation indicate that a variety of physical and psychological problems, ranging from paranoia about repeat occurrences and survival guilt to posttrauma anxiety attacks, may appear a long time after the incident. Survivors need to be aware that resolution of the situation may not necessarily mean the end of their problems associated with being taken hostage (Strentz, 1984, p. 201).

Characteristics of a Negotiator

Who should negotiate? Hostage takers will always seek to bargain at the highest level of authority within the hierarchy of the responding agency. It is strongly suggested that the agency in charge of negotiations not permit this for two reasons. First, that person probably does not have the negotiating skills required. Second, the negotiator's rank should be low enough to function as a buffer. Creating a buffer position allows a climate for flexibility in decision making, which is imperative in problem-solving situations. Therefore, the best bet is a negotiator who appears to be essentially a pawn and a conduit having little autonomy in the area of policy (Schreiber, 1978, pp. 102–103; Maher, 1977, p. 14).

If at all possible, negotiators should be available that can be matched with the hostage takers in race, sex, socioeconomic background, religious beliefs, and so on (Lanceley, 1981). Further, on any negotiating team there should be two negotiators available in case one wears out or engenders the enmity of the hostage takers (Maher, 1977, p. 38). Since negotiation strategies are based on psychological principles, a controversial issue is the use of psychologists, psychiatrists, or other mental health professionals as negotiators.

There are a number of arguments against using mental health professionals as negotiators. First and foremost, hostage negotiations are a law enforcement operation and therefore should be dealt with in terms of immediate resolution of conflict rather than in terms of therapy. Second, the use of mental health professionals supplants the use of a negotiating-team approach, particularly if decisive physical action needs to be taken, and allows for a division of responsibility. Third, a mental health professional may not be nearly as wise in the use of street psychology as a person who has lived in and experienced the milieu of the hostage taker. Fourth, identification of the negotiator as a mental health professional may make hostage takers extremely agitated if they conclude that the authorities believe them to be mentally deranged (Maher, 1977, p. 9).

Yet a mental health professional, by virtue of training and personality characteristics, fits many of the criteria Miron and Goldstein (1978, pp. 93–94, 137–166) propose for selection of a negotiator. (Indeed, the case study in this chapter involves a psychologist as the negotiator and has a successful outcome, although because of the setting and the psychologist's reputation he may have been the best and only option.) The resolution of this dilemma has been to make a psychologist a member of the negotiating team in a consultative capacity (Maher, 1977, p. 9). As a consultant, the psychologist serves as a resource person, adviser to the negotiator, intelligence gatherer, debriefer of victims and witnesses, and post hoc evaluator of the total response effort (Powitzky, 1979). Particularly as a consultant to the negotiator, the psychologist should

1. constantly assess the mental status of the hostage taker, as well as that of the negotiator
2. not become directly involved in the negotiations, thereby remaining as objective as possible
3. recommend techniques, approaches, or responses that will help resolve the situation

(Fuselier, 1981b).

It should be understood that the only responsibility of the negotiator is to conduct all verbal interactions with the hostage taker to the successful conclusion of the situation (Fuselier, 1981b). To discharge such an awesome responsibility, the ideal negotiator will possess special characteristics. The following list is compiled from Miron and Goldstein (1978, pp. 93–94) and Maher (1977, pp. 17–18).

1. interpersonal sensitivity and empathic understanding
2. intellectual ability to deal with cognitive complexities
3. tolerance for ambiguity
4. positive self-concept
5. low authoritarianism
6. interviewing experience
7. past experience in stressful situations
8. verbal skills
9. flexibility, especially under pressure
10. firm but not overpowering manner
11. nonargumentativeness
12. nonsusceptibility to slurs about personhood

13. belief in the power of verbal persuasion
14. mature appearance
15. calm presence of mind
16. good physical condition
17. background in psychology, especially abnormal and social behavior
18. freedom from values associated with ethnic, racial, or religious background
19. street wisdom
20. familiarity with ideology of perpetrator if perpetrator is a terrorist
21. conciliation, compromise, and bargaining skills

All these attributes may sound as if the negotiator must be a combination of Freud, Martin Luther King. Jr., and Superman. However, that is not the case. In fact, adequate personality testing, good law enforcement experience, and intensive training can produce many qualified candidates in any large law enforcement agency. What does not fit for a negotiator is the converse of the characteristics listed. Anyone who is high on authoritarianism, believes in physical force, power, and toughness, is rigid and inflexible, and works from a macho orientation has no business being a hostage negotiator (Miron & Goldstein, 1978, p. 94).

INTERVENTION STRATEGIES

Because hostage takings epitomize crisis conditions, the hostage negotiator is very much like an eclectic counselor who must have a variety of techniques to fit different and constantly changing situations. The only difference is that the negotiator is dealing with a victimizer rather than the victim, and the main object of the negotiator's attention is invariably holding a weapon.

The six-step crisis intervention model in Chapter 2 provides the nucleus of the concepts and skills needed by negotiators to successfully intervene in hostage crises. Assessing the motives and emotional status of the hostage taker is an extremely important and delicate task because people's lives are generally at stake. Negotiators must be competent in listening and relationship skills because the hostage taker cannot be tested or evaluated in any normal way during the period of the emergency. Understanding and assessing the degree of mobility/immobility that the hostage taker feels is of particular importance because the negotiator needs to decide how directive, collaborative, or nondirective to be. Examination of alternatives available is critical to the outcome of the negotiation. The negotiator will want to get the hostage taker to consider options other than killing the hostages. The intervention strategies in this chapter are designed to help the negotiator deal with the difficult crisis of hostage taking. A variety of techniques are provided to enable the negotiator to offer the hostage taker honorable alternatives to hurting or killing people.

The following intervention procedures have been compiled from a number of sources. They represent procedures that would be universally recognized by hostage negotiation teams and can be considered to be constants in the negotiating process. Yet each hostage situation is an entity unto itself and cannot be reduced to any formula that works for all cases. Therefore, the successful negotiator, like other crisis interventionists, will be creative but will follow procedure, take risks but proceed with caution, have empathy but believe in justice, and have patience but move decisively. There is no recipe for operating on these continuums. Thus, the successful negotiator possesses a combination of experience, training, knowledge, and artistry, and the following guidelines should be perceived in that light.

Safety

As in all other law enforcement operations, safety is the foremost consideration. In a hostage situation, inner and outer perimeters are secured around the hostage scene and a command post is established in the inner perimeter. This is the first step in the strategy of containment and negotiation. Containing and stabilizing the scene prevent the scope of the event from expanding (Schlossberg, 1980).

Information

The most important information the negotiator needs to know, as quickly as possible, is who the hostage taker is, to obtain a profile. Who are his or her close friends, relatives? Does he or she have children, spouse, girlfriend, boyfriend? What kind of criminal record? How many arrests and for what? Is there a psychiatric record? Has the hostage taker ever been committed? Is he or she currently obtaining professional help? What is the professional's name, and is the professional available?

What kinds of specialized skills does the hostage taker have? What does the person know about weapons, explosives, electronics? Can the person fly, drive, operate special equipment? What kinds of special affiliations? Does the hostage taker belong to a religious order? sects? gangs?

What are the individual's deviations? sexual preferences? Does the person use drugs, alcohol? What are his or her immediate problems?—money? love life? parole problems? addiction? All of these pieces make up the puzzle of who the hostage taker is and perhaps will give the negotiator a clue to a positive solution (Miron & Goldstein, 1978, pp. 92–93).

The next piece of information to be determined is just who the hostages are. Are there really hostages? If so, how many, how old, and what sex are they? What is their current emotional state? Are they intelligent? Do they have potential for aggression? Does anybody need medical assistance or have special requirements? Are they related to their captor or complete strangers (Miron & Goldstein, 1978, p. 93)?

The last piece of initial information needed concerns the hostage site itself. What are safe observation positions? What are the safest approach and escape routes? Are there telephones or other means of communication present? What amount of space, number of rooms, obstacles, ventilation, and so on, compose the site? What is the access to food, water, toilet facilities?

Stabilization

As information about hostage taker, hostage, and site is being gathered, the initial tasks of the negotiator are to contain and stabilize the situation (Miron & Goldstein, 1978, p. 95). These initial minutes are the most critical for the hostages, and what the negotiating team does now will determine whether the situation is safely resolved (Turner, 1984, pp. 179–180). The negotiator's first goals are to calm the perpetrator and build rapport with him or her (Miron & Goldstein, 1978, p. 95). A low-keyed counseling approach that emphasizes reflective listening skills, letting the hostage taker know that the negotiator understands how strongly he or she feels, is an excellent opening strategy (Mirabella & Trudeau, 1981).

Neg: From what you're saying, you really feel angry at them. I understand how frustrated you are at the housing authority folks. It's as if they haven't heard a thing you've been saying.

It is important that the negotiator stay calm, especially during these opening gambits (Schreiber, 1978, p. 103). By tone of voice, choice of words, facial expression, and gestures the negotiator models a calmness that will, one hopes, transfer itself to the hostage taker. Reassurance is part of the attempt to keep the situation tranquil (Miron & Goldstein, 1978, p. 97).

Neg: (Sits down, takes off coat, lights a cigarette in view, but not in the same room or within reach of hostage taker.) It doesn't seem like we're going any place for a while, so just take your time and tell me what it is you want. I'm sure we can reach a mutually agreeable solution.

The negotiator needs to allow the hostage taker the opportunity to ventilate feelings (Miron & Goldstein, 1978, p. 98). Ventilating provides a number of positive outcomes. The perpetrator's continued talking permits the negotiator to identify the person's mental state and personal problems and to assess the general atmosphere of the situation (Maher, 1977, p. 36). It is also very difficult for the hostage taker to remain emotionally charged and at the same time present lengthy discourses and answer questions about his or her problems to the negotiator (Miron & Goldstein, 1978, p. 98). One of the best ways to keep the perpetrator engaged is to ask open-ended questions.

Neg: I'm not sure I understand what you're really peeved about. How would you like them to set up the tenant grievance procedure with the housing authority? What would you see your role as being in that?

At the same time the negotiator must be careful not to intrude into the psychological space of the hostage taker (Maher, 1977, p. 36). Interpretive statements about the causal dynamics that motivate the hostage taker may generate hostility and increased agitation. To suggest that some personal inadequacy is at the root of the hostage taker's problem is unwise. The following type of statement is *not* suggested.

Neg: So it's really going way back to those inadequate feelings you had as a child. Your mother and father always put you down, so now you're really trying to show them how potent you are when in fact you really know that it isn't so.

Under no circumstances should the negotiator try to provoke the hostage taker. Arguing, demeaning remarks, outright rejection of demands, and sudden surprises have no place in the dialogue. Any signs of increased agitation or aggression in the hostage taker should be monitored carefully. Disjointed and speeded-up speech, flared nostrils, flushed cheeks, restlessness, pounding or shaking of fists, and so on, are all indicators that the negotiator needs to cool the situation down. One of the best ways to accomplish this is to distract the hostage taker by asking questions totally irrelevant to the situation or suggesting something contrary to what the perpetrator thinks the authorities might want (Miron & Goldstein, 1978, pp. 98–99).

Neg: You said you were interested in pro basketball and the Knicks in particular. Think they've got a chance against the Celtics tonight?

Neg: Well, if you think we're all infidel, godless swine, I guess that's your right. If you feel like you've got to let people know about your feelings, then maybe you ought to go on the radio. (The negotiator and the media have previously worked out the conditions under which this would happen.)

By trying to see the problem through the hostage taker's eyes, the negotiator tries to build rapport with the perpetrator. Using owning or "I" statements is one way the negotiator can establish a relationship with the hostage taker. Genuine and noncontrived self-disclosure about the negotiator's own life as it seems to apply to the conversation is a useful way of establishing the relationship and instigating reciprocal disclosure on the part of the hostage taker (Maher, 1977, p. 41).

Neg: I can sure understand that. I put in long hours, do good work, and still catch hell from the boss even though somebody else screwed up the job. It sure seems like the department isn't very damn grateful for all the effort I put out. Is that about the way you feel about your job?

Pacing the dialogue in a slow and purposeful manner is a key component in the negotiations and works in favor of the authorities. Although hostages may become depressed and question the handling of the situation as time drags by, delay is to their benefit. By not rushing, the negotiator allows the relationship to develop. Also, time wears down the resources of the hostage takers faster than it does those of the authorities. Lack of sleep, hunger, thirst, and unrelenting tension focus the hostage taker on the calm reasonableness of the negotiator and aid and abet the problem-solving process (Miron & Goldstein, 1978, p. 99; Maher, 1977, p. 13).

Eleven hours into negotiations.
Neg: Man! I'm getting tired. Gonna get a cup of coffee and pump some caffeine in my body. How about taking a break off the heavy stuff and just talk some basketball for a while. Maybe if you want some coffee we could talk about that. (The coffee will have some strings attached.)

Finally, a good negotiator, like a good therapist, is excellent at restating the hostage taker's ideas back to him. This technique serves to clarify both to the hostage taker and to the negotiator what is really being said. It also builds rapport with the hostage taker because he or she is assured of being listened to very carefully. The hostage taker's words mean something and count for something with the negotiator (Miron & Goldstein, 1978, p. 102).

Neg: OK! Let me see if I understand you correctly. You want to read your manifesto over the radio but you're worried that they'll ask you some questions you don't want to answer right now. You're also concerned that they'll try to keep your attention diverted so we can pull something on you. Is that about it?

Persuasion

The ultimate mission of the negotiator is to persuade the hostage taker to give up without harming anyone. There are a number of guidelines to which the negotiator should adhere in accomplishing this task. Persuasion should start with agreement with some of the perpetrator's ideas. Agreement in principle tends to soften the hostage taker's resistance to later negotiations (Miron & Goldstein, 1978, p. 103).

Neg: I agree with you. The scandalous conditions in public housing need to be aired, and you've done your research well.

The negotiator should start by negotiating smaller issues first, such as foodstuffs, medicine, cigarettes, and ways of communicating (Miron & Goldstein, 1978, p. 103). However, the negotiator should make it clear from the start that the hostage taker gets nothing without giving something in return (Maher, 1977, p. 13).

Neg: I'll see about getting the lights turned back on, but I want some indication that the people are all right.

The less attention paid to the hostages in the dialogue the better. Continuous reference to hostages may exaggerate the hostage taker's sense of importance, turn his or her attention obsessively to them, and steer the dialogue away from resolution (Maher, 1977, p. 12).

Neg: Yes. I understand you'll start shooting one every 30 minutes if we don't comply with your demands, but what I'm not clear about is how you particularly want the transportation provided.

There is one exception to this rule, and that is an attempt by the negotiator to foster the Stockholm syndrome. Any action the negotiator can instigate to emphasize the human qualities of the hostages to the hostage taker should be considered. Most people have difficulty inflicting pain on another unless the victim remains dehumanized (Strentz, 1979, p. 10). Thus, flag words like "hostage" should never be used (Fuselier, 1981b). The negotiator should attempt to make the captives appear as human as possible.

Neg: I wonder if you could check on Mr. Smith and see how he's feeling. We understand from his wife that he has a heart problem. Also as a good-faith gesture we'd like you to let Mrs. Jones speak to her children. They don't have a father and they're pretty scared.

If at all possible, the negotiator should try to convince the hostage takers that their hostages are actually useless (Schreiber, 1978, p. 111). At points like this, closed questions are better than open-ended ones because they force "yes" or "no" answers and do not allow for a lot of philosophizing or emotional diatribe (Miron & Goldstein, 1978, p. 101).

Neg: How in the world are you going to make your escape with all those people, anyway? Seems to me like the old folks and kids are just going to slow you down. Besides that, you can't keep an eye on everybody at once when you're moving. Do you agree?

At some point in the negotiations there comes a time when the most powerful argument can be made to the most telling effect (Schreiber, 1978, p. 112). When that time comes, the negotiator must clearly and with conviction not only state what the facts are, but give his or her conclusions (Miron & Goldstein, 1978, p. 103). There are some things that absolutely cannot be negotiated: firearms, exchange of hostages, and, most generally, drugs (Maher, 1977, p. 67). If drugs are part of the negotiation package, the effects should carefully be evaluated by a physician before they are ever made a bargaining tool (Maher, 1977, p. 39).

Neg: As a total package you've got to realize that it's unacceptable. The guns are not acceptable, for instance. However, there are some parts of the package I believe can be negotiated. Think about it! The rest of the package is a good one and we can make a deal on it.

Under most circumstances, friends, relatives, family, clergy, and other associates should not be brought to the scene. This is particularly true if the hostage taker asks for them because he or she may want to kill them. If people such as these could help, the perpetrator would probably not be in this situation in the first place. If bringing such people to the scene becomes an absolute must, then the negotiator also needs to know clearly what their feelings are and needs to be close enough that he or she can hear what's going on (Maher, 1977, pp. 14–15, 67).

Neg: If we brought your wife down here, what could she do different? You already said she never understands you. Why have her come?

The negotiator should argue both sides of any point. By presenting both sides, the negotiator is more likely to be taken seriously by the perpetrator. Further, the negotiator should argue against one or more unimportant aspects of the authorities' position as a way of showing how fair and open-minded the negotiator is (Miron & Goldstein, 1978, p. 104).

Neg: I can understand why you don't like having the area outside the building dark. I know it makes you nervous when you can't see what's going on. However, think about it from our side. The cops are just as nervous as you. What's to keep you from taking a shot at them if they're silhouetted? By the way, that letter you quoted to me that you want to read to the housing authority sounds pretty good and doesn't seem all that unreasonable to me. I can't see why the mayor is taking such a hard line in not letting you read it to the media.

A combination of delaying compliance, minimizing counterarguments, and promoting active listening with the perpetrator are excellent techniques when negotiations get down to the finish. In delaying compliance, the negotiator proposes that the perpetrator not make up his or her mind immediately, think it over, and see if he or she will not see it the negotiator's way at some future point. Immediately, the negotiator should follow up by offering weakened counterarguments to the proposition. Such counterarguments compromise and weaken the captor's own arguments. Finally, passive listening does little for the problem-solving process. Active listening should be used. The perpetrator should be asked to think about his or her position and what the consequences might be (Miron & Goldstein, 1978, pp. 103–104).

Neg: You've heard what the offer is. I know it's not everything you wanted. I know that reading that letter to the media is nonnegotiable, but what if I could get them to guarantee it right after you give up? The TV crews are all here and I don't think the city administration could get away with just hustling you off. I believe I could get authorization for you to do that. Why don't you roll it around for a while and see how it comes out? There's no rush.

Although it may seem irrational to do so, the negotiator should agree reluctantly with demands that may in reality benefit the authorities' position because these points may then be used to garner further concessions down the road (Miron & Goldstein, 1978, p. 106).

Neg: OK. If you really want a car instead of a bus, we'll see what we can do, but that's going to take some more time and I don't think my boss is gonna like it. (The situation is beneficial to authorities because fewer hostages have the possibility of being moved.)

The negotiator should refrain from making suggestions unless absolutely necessary. This tactic keeps the hostage taker in a decision-making process (Fuselier, 1981b). The perpetrator is then the one who has to make movement. Offering suggestions may also speed up time factors, which may not be advantageous to the negotiator (Miron & Goldstein, 1978, pp. 106–107).

Neg: You're the guy who's in control. You'll have to decide what to come back with. I'm just the go-between.

Two positions the negotiator must take which may seem in opposition to the goal are keeping the hostage taker's hopes alive and realizing that the hostage taker may have to be allowed to escape. The perpetrator must feel up until the time that all hostages are released that he or she has not undertaken the seizure in vain and that there is some hope of escape. One way of sustaining this assurance is by continuously reinforcing the hostage taker every time that he or she gives in on a point (Miron & Goldstein, 1978, pp. 105–107).

Neg: Personally, I really respect you for letting the old people and children go. I know that wasn't easy, but you did get agreement on your transfer conditions to the airport.

Neg: All right! We're agreed. The Barangan government has agreed to give you asylum and has provided the plane to take you to their country. As soon as you step inside the Baranga National Airliner, the last hostage at the foot of the ladder walks away. You clearly understand that if anything happens to that last hostage, that airliner, no matter who's on it, does not leave the airport. If anything bad happens, I have been instructed to tell you that we are not in the least concerned about what protests the Barangan government might have.

NEGOTIATING WITH JAMES

The scene is the diagnostic unit of a large penitentiary. Ricardo Cuervo, a psychologist, has just stepped out of his office. He almost runs into an officer escorting an inmate to some part of the unit. The inmate asks him in a rather abrasive manner, "Who are you?"

Ricardo responds civilly, "Do you need to see me?"

The response of the inmate is curt: "No! I ain't crazy!"

Ricardo reenters his office and thinks, "Something is wrong with that picture!" Stepping back out into the hall, Ricardo sees what was bothering him. First, the officer and inmate are standing still outside his door. There is no reason for the officer and the inmate to be together in the educational unit. Second, the inmate is a half step in back of the officer and pressing against his back.

The officer's face looks like he has seen a ghost, and he shouts, "Do what he says, he's got a shank!" (A shank is a prison-manufactured knife.) Ricardo does not know it yet, but he is about to become a hostage.

The inmate immediately says in a low, menacing voice, "Do what I say or he gets it right now!"

As Ricardo moves down the hall in front of the two, another psychologist happens along and becomes part of the procession. Before they are halfway down the hall, another corrections officer and a secretary are commandeered by the inmate. The inmate casts back and forth, looking for a sanctuary, and finally hustles his entourage into a small office of the secretary to the director of Social Services. The office is approximately 8' by 12' and has a doorway leading to the director's office. The office secretary, Sandra, is at once seized by the inmate, and the director, alarmed at what he sees taking place out of the corner of his vision, opens the adjoining office door. He is promptly taken captive by the inmate, who now threatens to kill the secretary if anyone does anything. Seven people are now the hostages of James Worthington, a convicted murderer of a clerk who was killed in a convenience store holdup.

Worthington, with a firm grip on Sandra, and the shank pressed below her rib cage, is at the side of the outer door, with a peripheral view of the hallway. Two others, the original corrections officer and Delphinia, another secretary, are in front of Sandra's desk, situated three or four feet from the door to the hallway. The rest of the hostages, including Cuervo, are behind the desk, sandwiched between it and file cabinets, away from the door to the director's office. This is the setting as the hostage situation, which is to last three hours, begins.

Ricardo: What do you want?

James: (Very aggressive, labile, agitated, with eyes glazed and bulging and rigid posture.) You shut the hell up. I know I'm gonna die today. This is it!

Sandra: (Screaming.) Don't hurt me! I'm afraid! Please put the knife away.

Officer: (Arms waving in a random motoric way.) Yeah, what do you want?

James: (Becomes violently agitated and yanks the woman tighter to him and screams.) Shut up, Goddammit! I'm goin' out today and I'll take every one of you with me. You think I give a shit about you.

(At this point a crowd and a lot of confusion invade the hallway. It is apparent that a riot alarm has been set off. A number of custodial officers attempt to get in the doorway.)

James: (Shouting at the top of his lungs.) Tell those bastards not to come in here or the woman dies, NOW!

Chorus from hostages: Stay out! He's got a knife! He means business! He'll kill her!

James: (Screaming, with menacing gestures.) I'll stick her, I mean it.

In these early moments of the alarm stage, the hostages, including Ricardo, make a big mistake by pushing the panic button. The screaming of the secretary and motoric movements of the officer are highly agitating to the hostage holder. The attempts by the psychologist to find out what the problem is are miscalculated. The demeanor of the hostage taker is such that whatever is wrong is not going to be solved at the moment. The hostage taker is engaging in expressive behavior and the instrumental response of the psychologist and the officer are not going to help but merely agitate James. Compounding James's agitation is the confusion in the hallway. The situation out there is far from contained. A custody captain comes to the door and tries to persuade James to throw out the knife.

James: I can't take it any more—I've had enough of this bullshit!

Captain: (In a commanding voice.) Don't hurt the females.

James: If I'm gonna die, I might as well take as many of these mothers with me as I can.

Captain: (In a more subdued voice.) Tell me what the problem is, let's see it we can resolve it.

The captain's initial assessment is by the book. He responds in an instrumental way to the hostage taker by trying to find out what his goal is. Most incarcerated individuals are engaging in instrumental behavior when they take hostages and have clear-cut motives and demands. However, whatever has happened to James, it is plain that this is the wrong approach at this moment. Dr. Harold Deacon, director of psychology, is now on the scene outside the doorway. Although not trained as a hostage negotiator, Dr. Deacon offers his services to the captain.

Captain: Doc Deacon is out here and would like to talk to you.

James: I told you I ain't nuts. I don't wanta talk to no shrink.

Dr. Deacon makes a quick assessment of the hostage holder's behavior and responds in an empathic, expressive mode. The vehemence of James about his mental status tells Dr. Deacon that he is going to have to be very careful. Denial of diminished mental capacity by the hostage taker is a clue that he may be an antisocial type. If so, this extremely dangerous type of hostage taker must be handled in an expressive mode, but responses will have to be made very carefully and continually keep the focus on the perpetrator and away from the hostages.

Dr. Deacon: Sounds as if you're pretty angry and nobody's listening to you.

James: That ain't the half of it, Doc.

The response by James gives Dr. Deacon two clues. First, he responds by acknowledging Dr. Deacon's reflective statement. The acknowledgment indicates that the hostage holder has a lot of angry feelings that need ventilating. Second, "the half of it" indicates that the holder does have some kind of agenda, but that there is more of an affective than cognitive basis to it at the moment. The dialogue continues for a few minutes as the holder angrily ventilates and Dr. Deacon responds in a deep empathic manner. Finally, Dr. Deacon takes a risk, one that probably would be seen as tactically unsound in most hostage situations.

Dr. Deacon: I'm really having trouble hearing from out here in the hallway. I wonder if I might step into the room?

James: No!

Dr. Deacon: I understand how you feel, but I really am having a hard time hearing you.

James: Well, OK! But I'm not coming out.

As Dr. Deacon enters the room, the original corrections officer taken by James, arms waving wildly, bolts out the door. James is unable to stop the officer because of his hold on Sandra. He immediately flies into a rage.

James: Come back here, you sonofabitch. You tricked me, Doc. Now I'm gonna cut her good.

This foolish, panic-stricken move by the officer is exceedingly dangerous. Although he makes good his escape, he immediately jeopardizes the other hostages. The hostage holder, fearing he may lose control of the rest of the hostages, will invariably feel he has to reassert his power over them in very aggressive ways. Dr. Deacon will have to respond quickly with a statement designed to restore some equilibrium to the situation.

Dr. Deacon: Hold it! That was stupid. But I'm here now. You've got me, the director of psychology. Frankly, I'm a helluva lot more valuable than he is. So relax. You've come out ahead in the deal.

James: (Still highly agitated.) OK! OK! I got you, it's cool. That jerk was driving me nuts anyways, wavin' his arms around like some freak.

In one respect, the officer's escape helps the situation. His uncontrolled behavior heightens the tension of the hostage taker. The officer's inability to get control of himself puts the hostages in harm's way, given the high degree of emotional strain that James is experiencing. His departure allows James to divert his attention from controlling the hostages to concentrating on what Dr. Deacon is saying.

Generally, going into the room would be unwise because it gives up another person to the situation. However, Dr. Deacon's assessment is that as James continues to ventilate, his voice has toned down, his lability tends more towards rational than irrational behavior, and he is not swearing as much. Further, Dr. Deacon wants to be able to see clearly the nonverbal behavior of the hostage holder and measure it against verbal behavior presented. Dr. Deacon is having a hard time hearing, and although he uses the fact as a ploy to get into the room, it is something the hostage taker can accept as reasonable.

It is now about 30 minutes into the situation. At approximately this point, a special hostage negotiator for the prison system arrives at the scene and takes up residency outside in the hallway with the custody captain. Dr. Deacon is inside the room, face to face with James.

Dr. Deacon: Something's really hurting. I wonder if you could help me understand why you're so angry.

James: (Slowly, but with increasing speed and vitriol, opens up.) They wouldn't let me go to my grandfather's funeral. Gave me some jive talk that he wasn't on no relative list in my jacket. The social worker never even come back and give me an explanation after I asked him. No respect, man! None at all! Then last week, Furdy, down in metal shop, says I got me an attitude, says he's gonna lay me up for six months without pay. Sent my ass up to the PCC [Prison Classification Committee], which lays a lot of shuck on me—six months with no pay. Man! How they expect me not to have an attitude, the time hard enough without that? Those be unjust, unrighteous people, man! They don't listen to nothin'. I may be a con, but I deserve some respect, they really piss me off, man! Well, look at me and them now. I got seven hostages. Who's got the respect now? They damn sure gonna kill me when this is done so I might as well take as many with me as I can. Particularly that sucker over there. (Points to the director of Social Services.) He sat there this morning on the PCC and didn't say jack, didn't listen to a word I said. (Turns menacingly to director of Social Services.)

Dr. Deacon: (Seeks to get James's focus of attention off the hostage and back to his feelings about the problem.) It doesn't have to be that way. Nobody's going to hurt you. (Rapidly but clearly restates the hostage taker's problems and feelings about the administration's response to them.)

Deacon's restatement seeks to affirm and clarify for James that at least someone in the administration is now listening to him. He also seeks to affirm that James is still in good shape, that nothing irreparable has happened. It is extremely important that James understand he still has options at this point and that doing harm to the director will severely limit those options for him. The key feeling seems to be loss of respect. Dr. Deacon's assessment is that James is not overly angry with what happened as much as with how it happened. These pieces of information allow Dr. Deacon to further assess James and classify him into two other categories of hostage taker. The information also confirms for Dr. Deacon the negotiation approach he has taken with James and gives the psychologist information on areas he will need to pursue.

What Dr. Deacon hypothesizes from James's diatribe is that he feels both wronged and inadequate. Dr. Deacon needs to reinforce at any opportunity the respect James feels he has lost. He can also use this information to set up a problem-solving situation based on restoration of James's lost self-esteem to resolve the situation. Further, Dr. Deacon obtains two pieces of concrete information, the grandfather's death and the confinement to his cell with no work, pay, or privileges, that make James feel he has been unjustly dealt with by the authorities. The combined weight of these two problems, plus James's impulsivity, has pushed him over the edge. Somehow or another, Dr. Deacon needs to make the "wrong" done James "right."

Dr. Deacon has another piece of information, which is alarming. The hostage taker has an axe to grind with one of the hostages, the director of Social Services. For the moment, all Dr. Deacon can do is hope to take attention and heat away from the director by refocusing attention to the problem.

Another tactical error may have been made at this juncture. Dr. Deacon has no background data other than what he has ascertained from his brief encounter with the hostage taker. Had he been able to take the time to find out who the holder was, a psychological profile would have indicated that James Worthington is a man of above-average intelligence with a history of antisocial behavior that is heavily flavored with impulsive acting out and some deep-seated feelings of inadequacy. Also Dr. Deacon does not know why James is incarcerated. The fact that the offense is murder, combined with the personality attributes of James, casts an ominous shadow over the negotiations. However, a positive factor is that Dr. Deacon has had many years of experience in this business and is probably as good as anybody in the field at making rapid and accurate assessments about personality traits and what is likely to happen to those traits behaviorally in stressful situations in the penitentiary. In short, whereas he does not personally know James, he is both "head" and "street" smart to convicts.

Dr. Deacon also understands from James's rapid mood swings and emotional outbursts that James is on the borderline of having a psychotic break. Those swings need to be contained and stabilized. James manifests characteristics of a variety of hostage taker types, but such a construct is not uncommon. There are few textbook types when it comes to personality configurations. Dr. Deacon is aware of this and will have to pace himself in response to the dominant typologies that flux and flow in James. Until he can get James back to some semblance of equilibrium with each of the typologies he sees, little progress can be expected toward resolution of the situation.

James: I don't want to talk to anybody here. (To Cuervo.) You, get me the governor on the phone. Or the commissioner of corrections.

Cuervo: I'd be glad to try, but I don't know the number.

James: (Shouts out the door.) Hey, I wanta talk to the governor or the commissioner. Somebody get 'em on the line.

Neg: (Outside the room.) They're not available. Tell me what you want and deal with me. Let's see what we can work out.

James: Screw you, I want the governor.

Although the negotiator is technically right in keeping the negotiations contained, his response creates a problem. Dr. Deacon has effectively taken over the negotiation role in the eyes of the hostage taker. For better or worse, Dr. Deacon is the controlling factor and the professional negotiator is now relegated to a backup role. Too many hands in the kitchen will spoil the soup. Dr. Deacon immediately picks up on this and regains control.

Dr. Deacon: James, it seems like what we have going can be solved between us. Whatever needs to be done, I'll see that it gets done.

James: You'll just say I'm crazy. Think I'm crazy?

Dr. Deacon: No, I don't think you're crazy. I believe you're under a lot of stress and feel like no one would listen to you to the point that you had to do something that would get some attention. I can't imagine anyone not being under a lot of stress given all that's happened to you and what's going on right now. I'd be willing to go up before a judge or the institutional administration and go to bat for you.

James: They'll say I was crazy and I couldn't stand that, just puttin' me down, when I got some real, legitimate gripes.

Dr. Deacon: I meant what I said. You're not crazy. I appreciate where you're coming from. There's a helluva lot of pressure going on inside you right now and what I offered is an honorable way out for any man, but you have to give up your weapon and walk out if you want that from me.

Cuervo: Dr. Deacon's right. Anybody would feel the stress, I know I do.

James: You shut up! The doc's doin' the talkin.'

Even though Cuervo is also a psychologist, his reinforcement of Dr. Deacon does not help the situation. James sees Cuervo and the others as only one thing, bargaining tools. Cuervo and the other hostages would best be advised to be quiet and unobtrusive in the situation. Cuervo realizes this fact immediately and quickly gets the point across to the other hostages.

Meanwhile, Dr. Deacon has used James's question about being crazy as a wedge. He goes on to give James a plausible, rational reason that speaks directly to James's wounded pride. He is giving James a way out with some honor attached to it and in the bargain is saying that James has an ally. He is also saying that part of the bargain will be no violence. What's more, he is shifting attention away from the hostages to James's own well-being. Notice that no time limit is put on dropping the weapon, but Dr. Deacon states this as a logical prerequisite to the things that need to happen for James. It is now about one hour into the situation. Although James is still making some erratic emotional swings, he is much calmer than before.

In general, the crisis stage has passed and the accommodation stage has commenced. Dr. Deacon has seated himself on the edge of the desk, rolled up his shirt sleeves, loosened his tie, and put his hands in his pockets. At this point a subtle change occurs in James. He pulls a six-page letter from a back pocket and asks Dr. Deacon to look it over.

Dr. Deacon: I'm frankly amazed. This is a precise, articulate, well-written letter that clearly spells out specifics of your complaints. You've obviously thought this out carefully. It surely isn't the typical jailhouse crap I see. This is good information to support your case.

James: (Flicker of a smile, head up.) You really think so, Doc? Would you read it out loud to those guys out there?

Dr. Deacon has won a major victory here. The letter from James is well written, and Dr. Deacon can legitimately state that. By reinforcing James, he allows the hostage taker to regain some of his lost self-esteem. Dr. Deacon reads the letter, and it is decided that a copy of the letter should be made to give to the administration and the commission. James has calmed down quite a bit.

In response to a calm plea from Sandra that he is hurting her, James apologizes, tells her he does not want anything bad to happen to her, and loosens his grip, pulling the knife away from her rib cage. His action is another positive sign. If James were a full-blown antisocial personality, it is doubtful that such action would be forthcoming.

The one major expressive problem still centers on the director of Social Services, who continuously receives threatening and vicious statements from James. It seems that the director is the focal point for all of James's frustrations. Dr. Deacon decides that there must be a resolution to this problem before anything else can be accomplished.

James: Heeey, Mr. Dye-rec-tore! How you feel now, baby? You ain't so noncommitted now, are you, sucker? How'd you like to get your big fat ego punctured with this? (Waves knife around.)

Dr. Deacon: Well, my guess is that you're scaring the hell out of him, and if that's your intention you're doing a fine job.

James: Hey, Doc, I just want to make him feel like I did when he was sittin' up there this mornin' playin' God with me.

Dr. Deacon: What you're saying is, he made you lose your self-respect and you hurt because of that. Why don't you ask him how he feels now?

Dr. Deacon takes a big risk here. He interprets what the feelings of James are and attributes the causality of those feelings directly to the hostage. What the hostage says will determine a lot about how the hostage taker reacts. However, Dr. Deacon knows the capabilities of the director of Social Services and believes that the bet is a good one. In any event, Dr. Deacon stands ready to assume the role of mediator if the responses of the director are unacceptable to James.

Director of Social Services: James, I don't know what else to say but that I'm sorry you feel like I wasn't paying attention to you this morning. I sure wish you'd had the letter and read it, because that would have made a difference. I don't know if you believe I'm sincere or not, but I feel bad about it, particularly since some of these people might get hurt for something I did that could have been straightened out without all this.

Dr. Deacon: James, he said that pretty straight. How do you feel about that?

James: (Visibly calmer.) Yeah, man, well, we all make mistakes and yours was a big one.

Director of Social Services: Well, I'd say from what's happened, you're right.

James: How do I know I'll be safe if I let these people go?

It is now more than two hours into the situation. This is the first time that James has talked about letting people go and voiced a concern for his own well-being. It is a critical point in the situation that must not be missed. If Dr. Deacon can capitalize on it, the resolution stage is at hand.

Dr. Deacon: What's of most concern to you?

James: That I stay alive. I want to be transported to another institution. I don't want any of the guards to get up my backside here. I also want some guarantees that when I do go out of here, that I don't get worked over.

Dr. Deacon: I can't guarantee any of that, but let's pass it on to the captain. None of it sounds unreasonable. I can understand your concerns.

Dr. Deacon makes no promises, but he owns his feelings about James's position and further increases the bond between himself and the hostage taker. A good deal of negotiation now takes place about the possibility of a transfer, statements to the press, some new demands, how the transfer will take place, recriminations, how the hostages will be released, and a variety of other subjects. The exchanges proceed with Dr. Deacon serving as the conduit between James and the captain and professional negotiator.

Captain: We can do that. I got the OK from the commissioner. We could move you to Starkton.

James: How do I know I can trust you?

Captain: James, you and I have had dealings before, right, man? Did I ever run a game on you? Tell you I could do something and didn't? If I could do it, it got done. Isn't that right?

James: Doc, what do you think about that? Is he runnin' a game on me?

Dr. Deacon: I believe him, but how's that square with you? Is he right?

James: Yeah, man, I guess that's right. But what about all those other dudes?

Dr. Deacon: Look, I'll be willing to walk out of here with you and ride over to Starkton and see you get settled in over there. With me around there's no way that any of the officers would risk working you over.

James: OK. Let's work out the details.

When James checks the situation out with Dr. Deacon, it is a good indication that a bond of trust between the two has been established. Dr. Deacon serves as James's perceptual check throughout the negotiations but is careful to allow James to continue to feel that he is the person with ultimate responsibility. Final details are worked out between the captain, Dr. Deacon, and James. The women are let go first. The captain and negotiator come into the room and the other men are ushered out. James is given some paper and a pencil to write down some more statements he has to make to the media. To get the paper and pencil, he relinquishes the knife. Once his statement is finished, James is transported to another institution, with Dr. Deacon going along to be sure that he is safe.

In this hostage situation, although it took place in a penitentiary, James typifies the kind of emotionally overwrought person with whom human service workers are likely to come in contact in the course of their work. Although a professional negotiator appeared on the scene, the initial moments were critical. The arrival, willingness, and capability of Dr. Deacon during the crisis stage had a great deal to do with the successful resolution of the situation. Even though Dr. Deacon had no formal training in hostage negotiation, he was able to use his considerable therapeutic and crisis intervention skills to resolve the situation. A professional negotiator, particularly in smaller communities with few resources, may not always be available. We are categorically in favor of using trained negotiators. However, when such experts are not on staff, the skills that human service workers like Dr. Deacon bring to the situation may be the best and most expert available. At such times, like it or not, the human service worker becomes a negotiator.

SUMMARY

With wide-ranging access to the media as a format to air a variety of grievances, hostage taking has increased tremendously since 1970. A great deal of publicity surrounds terrorist hostage takings, but the human service worker is more likely to become involved with a variety of hostage-taker types who have little to do with worldwide political agendas.

Although hostage taking is certainly a crisis-oriented problem, it is unlike other crisis situations in that it is invariably a law enforcement operation and one that deals much more closely with the victimizer than with the victim. The art of crisis resolution in hostage taking is the art of negotiating and calls for experience, courage, physical stamina, guile, creativity, street smartness, and a variety of other attributes. Not every human service worker possesses qualities compatible with a negotiator's role.

Hostage takers come in a variety of types. Perpetrators of such events may be psychotic, be suffering from estrangement, feel they have been wronged, extol religious zealotry, believe fanatically in a political movement, or be dissatisfied with conditions in an institution, or they may have been caught in the middle of a crime. Understanding which type the hostage negotiator is dealing with is of critical importance because subsequent negotiating strategies will differ by type. In general, all hostage takers are engaged in either instrumental or expressive behavior or some combination of the two. Instrumental hostage takers are after a very clear, concrete goal. Expressive hostage takers are in pursuit of power.

A variety of negotiating techniques are available. These techniques range from the typical active listening and responding skills that most other crisis interventionists would commonly use to some very sophisticated and, perhaps, somewhat devious methods. One of the more famous techniques may be the attempt of the negotiator to try to generate the Stockholm syndrome in the hostage takers. The end point of all these techniques is to wear the hostage takers down enough that they will be willing to give up the hostages without further violence. In all hostage situations, time is most clearly on the side of the negotiators. Therefore, it is imperative that hostage negotiators proceed slowly and with patience.

For hostages, it is clear that keeping a low profile and staying psychologically and physically alert are the best initial moves in the early stages of this crisis situation. Panic and displays of emotional instability are to be avoided at all costs. If the situation becomes extended, hostages may attempt, in careful and congruent ways, to convey personal aspects of their lives to their captors. Becoming a person rather than a bargaining chip in the eyes of one's holders makes it very difficult for them to dehumanize the hostage to the point that he or she can be easily killed. Resolution for the hostage does not necessarily occur when the perpetrators are taken into custody and the hostages are freed. Poststress trauma may be associated with this crisis and call for extended psychological intervention.

REFERENCES

American Psychiatric Association. (1980). *Diagnostic and statistical manual of mental disorders* (3rd ed.). Washington, DC: American Psychiatric Association.

Bahn, C. (1980). Hostage taking—the takers, the taken, and the context. *Annals of the New York Academy of Sciences, 347,* 151–156.

Cooper, A. (1976). Panelist's report. In R.D. Crelinsten, D. Laberge-Altmejd, & D. Szabo (Eds.), *Hostage-taking: Problems of prevention and control* (pp. 101–107). Montreal, Canada: Universite de Montreal.

Cooper, H. (1981). *The hostage-takers.* Boulder, CO: Paladin Press.

Crelinsten, R. D. (1976). The study of hostage taking: A systems approach. In R. D. Crelinsten, D. Laberge-Altmejd, & D. Szabo (Eds.), *Hostage-taking: Problems of prevention and control* (pp. 21–26). Montreal, Canada: Universite de Montreal.

Fuselier, G. N. (1981a). A practical overview of hostage negotiations. *F.B.I. Law Enforcement Bulletin, 50* (Pt. 1), 2–6.

Fuselier, G. N. (1981b). A practical overview of hostage negotiations. *F.B.I. Law Enforcement Bulletin, 50* (Pt. 2), 10–15.

Gettinger, S. (1983). Police response to hostage situations. In J. T. O'Brien & M. Marcus (Eds.), *Crime and justice in America: Critical issues for the future* (pp. 209–220). New York: Pergamon Press.

Gladis, S. D. (1979). The hostage terrorist situation and the media. *F.B.I. Law Enforcement Bulletin, 48,* 10–15.

Hassell, M. (1976). Panelist's report. In R. D. Crelinsten, D. Laberge-Altmejd, & D. Szabo (Eds.),

Hostage-taking: Problems of prevention and control (pp. 108–114). Montreal, Canada: Universite de Montreal.

Insurance for hostage victims. (1985, November 2). *The Commercial Appeal,* Memphis, p. 2.

Lanceley, F. J. (1981). The antisocial personality as a hostage taker. *Journal of Police Science and Administration, 9,* 28-34.

Maher, G. F. (1977). *Hostage: A police approach to a contemporary crisis.* Springfield, IL: Charles C Thomas.

Mirabella, R. W., & Trudeau, J. (1981). Managing hostage negotiations: An analysis of twenty-nine incidents. *The Police Chief, 48,* 45–47.

Miron, M. S., & Goldstein, A. P. (1978). *Hostage.* Kalamazoo, MI: Behaviordelia.

Ochberg, F. M. (1977). The victims of terrorism: Psychiatric considerations. *Terrorism, 1,* 147–168.

Powitzky, R. J. (1979). The use and misuse of psychologists in a hostage situation. *The Police Chief, 46,* 30–33.

Schlossberg, G. (1980). Values and organization on hostage and crisis negotiation teams. *Annals of the New York Academy of Sciences, 347,* 113–116.

Schreiber, J. (1978). *The ultimate weapon: Terrorists and world order.* New York: Morrow.

Strentz, T. (1979, April). The Stockholm syndrome: Law enforcement policy and ego defenses of the hostage. *The Law Enforcement Bulletin,* pp. 1–11.

Strentz, T. (1984). Hostage survival guidelines. In J. Turner (Ed.), *Violence in the medical care setting* (pp. 183–208). Rockville, MD: Aspen Publications.

Turner, J. (1984). Hostage incidents in health care settings. In J. Turner (Ed.), *Violence in the medical care setting* (pp. 171–181). Rockville, MD: Aspen Publications.

■ Classroom Exercises: Case of Mr. X

We have deviated a bit from our usual case approach because no one particular type of hostage taker predominates in all situations. We have constructed two hostage settings for the following exercises.

The setting is a human services agency. The only information available is that there is a man with a gun who has locked himself in a suite of offices on the second floor of the five-floor building. Eyewitnesses who have escaped from the scene describe the man as dressed in casual clothes, polite but very firm in giving directions and commands. One of the eyewitnesses thinks that she has seen him some place before today, but she's not exactly certain where that was. There seem to be about six hostages in the second-floor area, but nobody knows just exactly how many clients and staff were there when the takeover occurred. Neither does anyone know for sure whether any hostages have been hurt, although they think not, even though several shots were fired and there was a lot of shouting in the initial minutes of the takeover. The police have contained the scene and have the telephone number of the second floor. An action news team from Channel 5 has just arrived, and a fairly large crowd is beginning to gather. As the principal negotiator, you have just arrived on the scene.

Simulated Negotiations with Mr. X

You will need two rooms for this activity and a telephone connection between the two. Tape recorders and/or video tapes should be available in each room. Roles to be played are those of a hostage taker, four hostages, two negotiators, and a psychological consultant. The rest of the class, half in each of the two rooms, will be responsible for taking observational notes during the process. A nice way of handling observation is to assign certain members to monitor each of the actors in the role play.

Mr. X, the hostage taker, will have to decide which of the typologies, as outlined in this chapter, he will portray. He is not to tell anybody his type. Participants will have to decide on the basis of the hostage taker's actions as the drama unfolds, what his typology is. The main objective of the hostage taker should be to get what he wants from the situation. What he wants, of course, depends on what his typology is, and it is one of the missions of the negotiation team to find that out.

The hostages themselves should be portrayed as people in the crisis stage of the hostage situation. Things are starting to settle down, but there is still a lot of confusion. Hostages are advised to act on their own resources, using whatever skills and knowledge they have available. They must follow, to the best of their ability, the directives of the hostage taker. The one thing they cannot do is escape. The main objective of the hostages is to stay alive.

The negotiators are to act in coordination with one another, but only one negotiator is allowed to speak on the telephone at any time. The instructor may wish to rotate available class members in the role of negotiators. The negotiators are also on their own resources, but have the opportunity to consult with one another and the psychologist who is on the scene. The psychologist will not engage in any direct dialogue with the hostage taker, but will be available at all times to speak with the negotiators. The ultimate objective of the exercise is to get everyone, including the hostage taker, out safely.

Although it is impossible to draw out the exercise to the duration of a typical hostage situation, we recommend taking at least 45 minutes for the exercise. Upon completion of the exercise all role players will be called upon to verbally disassociate themselves from the parts they played. They will do this in front of the entire class. Questions to be discussed by the class following the disassociation activity are:

1. What typology would you say the hostage taker was?
2. How did he demonstrate that?
3. How do you think the negotiators handled the situation?
4. What negotiating techniques did they use?
5. Can you specifically identify some of them?
6. At what points were the negotiators able to get the hostage taker to give in on some of his demands?
7. At what points did the negotiators have problems?
8. What were those problems?
9. What might the negotiators have done differently when they encountered problems?
10. How was the psychologist used?
11. Do you believe the psychologist was useful?
12. What else should the psychologist have done?
13. How did the hostages feel as they went through the experience?

14. How did they feel toward their captor?
15. How did they feel toward their rescuers?
16. How did they feel about their fellow hostages?
17. How did they feel about themselves after the seige was over?

An excellent additional assignment is to divide the class according to whether they were with the hostages or the negotiators. Discuss what their perceptions were and how they might have been different if they had exchanged rooms. The audio or video tapes may be used to demonstrate what went on in each of the rooms and will add an objective perspective to what may become some very stimulating interchanges as various people defend their actions.

──────────────── *CASE OF MS. Y* ────────────────

You have been called to make a home visit in response to a request for assistance from one of your clients. As you arrive at the home, you are met at the door by a strange woman who immediately confronts you with an automatic weapon and demands that you come into the house. Ms. Y is exceedingly angry and agitated. In her first few minutes of rambling rather incoherently from subject to subject, you gather that your role has become something between that of a hostage and that of a negotiator. There are signs of violence in the house. Furniture is overturned and broken, and you notice what you believe are signs of blood on the carpet. You do not see any of the family members present.

Simulated Negotiations with Ms. Y

With the class divided into dyads, one person will be the hostage taker and one person will be the human service worker. Again the typology of the hostage taker is unclear and must be determined as the role unfolds. The human service worker must try to determine what has happened to the family, attempt to extract himself or herself from the situation, and convince the hostage taker to surrender. Use an audio tape recorder as you go through the dialogue. Spend about 30 minutes doing the exercise. When you have finished, go back and process the session by listening to the tape with your partner. Consider these questions from the point of view of the human service worker as you process the tape:

1. What was the typology of the hostage taker?
2. How did your guess as to type affect your response patterns?
3. Were you more instrumental or expressive in your negotiation approach?
4. What impact did playing a dual role of being both hostage and negotiator have on you?
5. What could you have done or have said differently if given an opportunity to engage in an instant replay?
6. What statements seemed to work really well for you?

After you have finished with your dyad, reassemble as a total class and discuss your role plays. The instructor may want to write on a blackboard all the really good points hostage/negotiators were able to make, under what circumstances, and with what types of perpetrators. In another column, the instructor may note all the blunders that were made. The instructor should carefully monitor these role plays. As participants become involved, they tend to lose their inhibitions. Hostage takers in particular may start to act out in some overly aggressive ways. Such actions should be supervised carefully. Other people in the building should also be warned about what is occurring so no one becomes alarmed and calls the police. (That actually happened in our department!) Under no circumstances should real weapons be used in the role play.

CHAPTER 11

Personal Loss: Bereavement, Grief, and Separation

BACKGROUND

To be human in the world as we know it is to experience loss. Some obvious major losses precipitate emotional trauma in individuals, which result in crisis. Some losses are relatively minor, cause no crisis, and are not so obvious; yet minor losses may also exact an emotional toll that the individual can ill afford to pay. Examples of major losses are the death of a loved one, the breakup of a close relationship, separation, and divorce. Some not-so-obvious or minor losses are loss of job, loss of money, moving to a different residence, illness (diminished health), changing schools or teachers, being robbed, and attainment of success (loss of striving) (Colgrove, Bloomfield, & McWilliams, 1976, p. 2).

Recovery from a major loss, such as the death of a child, parent, or spouse, may require several years. Reconciling oneself to minor loss, such as breaking a favorite dish or a wall hanging, may require only a few moments or hours (Colgrove, Bloomfield, & McWilliams, 1976, p. 16). During our normal growth and development, we experience many minor losses and a few major ones. But, according to Freeman (1978), the inevitable coping with numerous losses, which we must learn to do, plays an important role in our emotional development (p. 16).

The objective of this chapter is to provide a general survey of ways in which crisis workers may help clients understand and cope with losses. The concepts and skills described in the six-step model in Chapter 2 undergird the helping strategies we recommend for workers to use in helping people experiencing a crisis of personal loss. There are many helpful interventions available to crisis workers whose clients present problems of grief and bereavement (Osterweis, Solomon, & Green, 1984, pp. 215–279; Rando, 1984, pp. 75–117; Schneider, 1984, pp. 207–271). Crisis workers may prepare themselves to assist grieving clients by remembering that *all* crises can eventually be reformulated within a context of growth (Schneider, 1984, pp. 207–227). "Reformulated within a context of growth" refers to the healthy resolution of grief by bereaved individuals—attaining the ability to abstract meaning from a previously totally destructive event and emerging with greater strength, self-trust, and sense of freedom than they had before (p. 208).

The ultimate growth toward coping with loss occurs when the griever comes to grips with his or her own mortality (Rando, 1984, pp. 2–7). The final loss—death—is the conclusive stage in our development (Schoenberg, 1980, pp. 24–28). All living things go through stages of birth, growth, and death. All human losses—great or small—are increments in the journey through life. As Buscaglia (1982) so dramatically put it in *The Fall of Freddie the Leaf*, ". . . no matter how big or small, how weak or strong. We first do our job. We experience the sun and the moon, the wind and the rain. We learn to dance and to laugh. Then we die" (p. 16).

Loss can be great or small, but it is always personal. Coping with loss—overcoming, healing, and recovering—is also personal. Since no one else can overcome, heal, or recover for a person, the development of strategies for helping an individual cope with loss is perhaps the most difficult interventional area crisis workers encounter. Crisis workers should come to terms with their own mortality and be currently past their own periods of grief before entering into the role of caregiver to clients suffering from debilitating losses (Rando, 1984, pp. 430–444).

DYNAMICS

Cultural Dynamics

Denial of death. According to Rando (1984), each culture develops its own beliefs, mores, norms, standards, and attitudes toward death. Groups with differing backgrounds within a culture have vastly different attitudes toward death. But Rando states that "For all societies there seem to be three general patterns of response: *death accepting, death defying,* or *death denying*" (p. 51, italics added).

Kübler-Ross (1975) writes that our culture seems to believe that "death has become a dreaded and unspeakable issue to be avoided by every means possible" and that it may be "that death reminds us of our human vulnerability in spite of our technological advances" (p. 5). Becker (1973) documents how the fear or denial of death in the United States constitutes a fundamental factor in human behavior. His contention is that much of what people do in terms of cultural and scientific advancement is designed to avoid facing the finality of death. Becker further asserts that human beings have an innate fear of death, which leads them to try to transcend death through erecting hero systems and symbols. These systems and symbols may be observed in many shapes and forms—from monuments to presidential libraries, to tombstones, to this book! They may be manifested even in the choice of one's profession. Kübler-Ross (1981) reports that there have been studies indicating that doctors tend to "choose medicine as a career because of an inordinate fear of death. And medicine is dedicated to defeating death" (p. 128). One wonders whether other helping professionals might be similarly motivated in the choice of their careers. We can only speculate about the influence on people of the fear and denial of death, but it appears that the effect is both pervasive and powerful.

Historical progression. Schoenberg (1980) describes how societal mores and attitudes toward life, death, and dying in the United States have changed over the years. As the country shifted from a rural to an urban orientation and lifestyle, there has been a shift from a death-defying culture to a death-denying culture (pp. 51–56). Whereas farm families (children and adults alike) usually came in contact with birth, life, and death of animals as well as people, individuals in the cities rarely encountered dead animals or dead people. People in rural communities cared for their own dying relatives and friends. They prepared the corpses for burial and dug the graves by hand. They laid out the bodies of the dead in the parlor and commemorated the lives of the departed; then they buried them in the family or community cemetery. That is quite a contrast to the way funerals are managed today.

Schoenberg (1980) indicates that the denial of death generates negative attitudes and fears related to the death milieu, which may result in immobilizing traumas (p. 63). Such immobility tends to keep people from viewing death as the normal and final stage of life and reduces their adaptive energy needed to accept and cope with irrevocable loss (p. 18). Levitt and Guralnick (1985) contend that the death-denial practice is outmoded and that, in cases of dying patients who must cope with and plan for their own deaths, it cheats them of their right to know (pp. 235–237). The position of Levitt and Guralnick is that family members and physicians cannot decide without bias whether dying persons should be told the truth and that the patients themselves are the ones who ought to decide whether they are ready to know the truth about their illness or condition. The practice of withholding the truth about a patient's terminal illness is only one example of a negative outcome of the denial of death.

Schoenberg (1980) states that death education is needed to help people understand their feelings and beliefs about loss of loved ones, so that living can be more adaptive and enjoyable. As long as our cultural denial of death remains strong and pervasive, death education will be mainly an innovation for the future (p. 55).

The social organization of bereavement as well as the social reaction to the loss of loved ones has changed partly because of shifts in age-specific mortality patterns (Osterweis, Solomon, & Green, 1984). In former times, adult life expectancy was short and infant mortality was high. Epidemics and famines frequently wiped out large numbers of people. Communities were small and close knit. Death was taken personally by everyone in the community and mourning rituals were community-wide events (pp. 199–200).

In modern times, the bereavement process has tended to become standardized because of laws, regulations, and the development of specialists who carry out the laws and regulations. Death usually occurs in a hospital or nursing home. Frequently the deceased is an older individual who has been out of the mainstream of community activity for a number of years; as a result, deceased persons are not as widely known as they were in their younger years. Mourning has tended to move out of the home and into funeral parlors and hospital chapels. Laws affecting the role of funeral directors and the policies of employers have influenced the ways society mourns. Workplaces have established rules governing the time employees may take off from work following the death of a close family member or loved one. Many institutional constraints on behavior have tended to impose social uniformity upon the previously diverse patterns of grief and bereavement. Today, grief that follows a death has become institutionalized (Osterweis, Solomon, & Green, 1984, pp. 201–202).

The sociocultural changes that occurred between the 1930s and 1980s brought important changes in reliance on such helping roles as physicians, nurses, psychologists, social workers, counselors, rehabilitation specialists, and related workers (Schneider, 1984, p. ix). Changes in divorce rates, career development, aging patterns, birth-control and child-rearing practices, marriage stability, population mobility, and information dissemination have greatly affected people's lives—including the way society views and deals with stress, loss, and grief.

Neurophysiological Dynamics

Recent research indicates that certain neurophysiological healing powers may affect the way specific individuals respond to and deal with the crisis of loss. Ornstein and Sobel (1987) summarized several recent studies that indicate that the human brain, in addition to rational cognition, serves to maintain the body's health. The brain apparently controls the body's immune system and is able to come to its rescue if it becomes immobilized by the stress that can result from grief and bereavement. The brain counteracts the emotional and physical devastation that accompany grief and bereavement by releasing "several powerful neurohormones, including catecholamines, corticosteroids, and endorphins." These alter the immune function and fortify the body to develop its own adaptive physiological responses to the grief and bereavement (p. 50). The research suggests that persons with a strong sense of belonging may have minds that are better adapted to preventing disease. It is further suggested that individuals may use their minds to strengthen their immune systems, thereby enabling them to overcome and cope more effectively with the devastation brought about by personal loss.

Conceptual Approaches to Bereavement

The human response to loss has been a subject of interest and study for many years. Theoretical perspectives have been developed during this century by individuals representing a wide range of disciplines. Of eighteen models of response to bereavement we have studied, we will summarize two. The first is the Kübler-Ross (1969) model, which is probably the most popular and best-known system. The second is the Schneider (1984) model, which is the most comprehensive system we have seen. These two models or systems provide a representative view of the theoretical or conceptual dynamics of the human response to loss.

The Kübler-Ross model. In her five-stage model, Elisabeth Kübler-Ross (1969) outlines the human reactions or responses that people experience as they attempt to cope with their own imminent deaths. Her concepts have also been applied to the process of grief and bereavement following most personal losses.

1. *Stage 1 is denial and isolation.* The typical response to the first awareness of one's own terminal condition may be something like, "No, it cannot be me. There must be a mistake. This is simply not true." Kübler-Ross (1969) regards initial denial as a healthy way of coping with the painful and uncomfortable news. She states that "denial functions as a buffer after unexpected shocking news, allows the patient to collect himself and, with time, mobilize other, less radical, defenses" (p. 35). During this stage the patient may generate a temporary protective denial system and isolate himself or herself from information or persons that might confirm the terminal condition. Or the patient may become energetic in garnering proof and support from others that death is not going to occur.

2. *Stage 2 is anger.* The second stage is characterized by a "why me?" pattern. Persons in this stage cannot continue the myth of denial, so they may exhibit hostility, rage, envy, and resentment in addition to anger. Kübler-Ross reports that families and staffs find it quite difficult to deal with people during the anger stage (p. 44). The patient's anger is a normal adaptation. It is a desperate attempt to gain attention, to demand respect and understanding, and to establish some small measure of control. The patient's anger should not be taken personally by staff or family members. Such expressions of anger and hostility toward other people, the world, or God appear to be typical ways that patients use to try to cry out for love and acceptance.

3. *Stage 3 is bargaining.* During the third stage, patients bargain with physicians or bargain with God for an extension of life, one more chance, or time to do one more thing. This is another period of self-delusion, hoping to be rewarded for promises of good behavior or good deeds. It is a normal attempt to postpone death. Rather than brushing aside the patient's bargaining, the sensitive caregiver should listen to the concerns that underlie the behavior. The patient may need to deal with guilt or other hidden emotions.

4. *Stage 4 is depression.* Whenever the medical condition, the physical proof, bodily appearance, and evidence of the senses force the patient personally to admit that the prognosis is, indeed, terminal, a sense of loss ensues. Most patients are confronted with many losses as a result of impending death: career, money, loved ones, and possessions, in addition to life itself. It

is normal for depression to set in. Kübler-Ross (1969) identifies two kinds of depression in the terminally ill: (1) reactive depression and (2) preparatory depression (p. 76). The first is a reaction to the irrevocable loss; the second is an inner emotional preparation to give up everything. Patients in preparatory depression should be responded to with love, caring, and empathy, using few or no words. Attempts by caregivers to cheer the patient up will only interfere with the person's preparatory grieving.

5. *Stage 5 is acceptance.* Patients who have traveled through the previous four stages may reach the point at which they are tired, weak, finished with their mourning, reconciled to their loss, and acceptant of their situation. This stage is characterized by a quiet, peaceful resignation. It is not a happy stage. It is a time in which patients draw into themselves. It is a time when patients do not need conversation or large crowds. Family members and caregivers should show love and support by simply being present, sitting in silence, holding the patient's hand, or calmly responding to the patient's needs or requests. Patients in the fifth stage should be provided with treatment to make their lives as pain free and comfortable as possible.

The Kübler-Ross model does not purport to be applicable in every detail to every patient. It is a general conceptual framework that Kübler-Ross developed over years of research, study, and practice. The model was developed for the purpose of providing ways for dying patients to teach caregivers and families how they feel and what they need.

The Schneider model.   John Schneider (1984) developed a comprehensive eight-stage model, which he calls "The Process of Grieving." It is a holistic, growth-promoting model designed to nurture as much personal growth as possible within a context of stress, loss, and grief. Schneider's concept of losses "include internal events, systems of belief, and the processes of growth and aging as well as the easily recognized losses, such as death and divorce" (p. x).

1. *Stage 1 is the initial awareness of loss.* The initial impact of a loss is generally a significant stressor causing a threat to the body's sense of homeostasis (Schneider, 1984, p. 104). The holistic dimensions of this initial awareness stage typically include physical, behavioral, emotional, cognitive, and spiritual dimensions. Shock, confusion, numbness, detachment, disbelief, and disorientation are only a few of a variety of behaviors, emotions, or feelings that the individual may experience as a normal adaptive response to the realization that a significant loss has occurred.

2. *Stage 2 is characterized by attempts at limiting awareness by holding on.* Holding on means concentrating one's thoughts and emotional energy, for a period of time, on whatever positive aspects of the loss one can recognize and making use of whatever inner resources or hopes one has to immediately stave off immobility and disequilibrium. Holding-on strategies are normal processes that the individual adopts in order to try to use coping behav-

iors that have worked in the past to cope with loss, frustration, stress, and conflict. This stage has the effect of providing time to put the present loss into perspective, renew energies, and limit feelings of helplessness and despair (Schneider, 1984, pp. 120–122). Some of the behaviors, emotions, and feelings accompanying holding on are muscular tension, sleep disturbance, independence, replacement search, belief in internal control, yearning, ruminations, euphoria, bargaining, and guilt.

3. *Stage 3 is characterized by attempts at limiting awareness by letting go.* Letting go is described by Schneider (1984) as recognizing one's personal limits with regard to the loss and the turning loose of "unrealistic goals, unwarranted assumptions, and unnecessary illusions. This stage enables people to separate themselves from dependency or attachment to the lost person or object, paving the way for future adaptive behaviors and attitudes" (pp. 137–138). A few of the characteristic behaviors, emotions, and feelings that may occur during letting go are depression, rejection, disgust, anxiety, shame, pessimism, self-destructive ideation, cynicism, forgetting, and hedonism. During Stage 3, people may decide to give up their formerly held ideals, beliefs, and values.

4. *Stage 4 is awareness of the extent of the loss.* Schneider (1984) describes the awareness stage as the one most readily recognized as mourning—the most painful, lonely, helpless, and hopeless phase through which the loss sufferer goes (pp. 161–162). The individual may experience a flooding of consciousness, feelings of deprivation, and extreme grief and feel defenseless in coping with the reality of the loss. A few of the typical behaviors, emotions, and feelings observed in sufferers are exhaustion, pain, silence, aloneness, preoccupation, sadness, loneliness, helplessness, hopelessness, absence of future time, existential focus, emptiness, and weakness.

5. *Stage 5 is gaining perspective on the loss.* The normal function of the perspective-gaining stage is described by Schneider (1984) as reaching a point of accepting that what is done is done and providing the bereaved persons with a time to make peace with their past. This gaining of perspective may take two forms: "1) discovering the balance of the positive and negative aspects of the loss, including how the bereaved has grown as well as what is permanently gone; and 2) gaining perspective on both the extent and the limits of responsibility for the loss, the bereaved's own and that of others" (p. 190). A few of the typical behaviors, emotions, and feelings that people experience during the stage of gaining perspective are patience, solitude, acceptance, forgiveness, openness, reminiscence, healing, and peace.

6. *Stage 6 is resolving the loss.* Schneider (1984) states that "grief has been resolved when the bereaved can see and pursue activities unconnected with the loss without it being a reaction against (letting go) or identifying with (holding on) the lost person or object" (p. 205). Stage 6 is a time of "self-forgiveness, restitution, commitment, accepting responsibility for actions and beliefs, finishing business, and saying goodbye" (p. 206). Some characteristic behaviors, emotions, and feelings of Stage 6 are self-care, relinquishing, forgiveness of self and others, determination, and peacefulness.

7. *Stage 7 is reformulating loss in a context of growth.* Schneider (1984) views the reformulation of loss as an outgrowth of resolving grief. When grief is faced and experienced through to resolution, it may provide the motivational impetus for personal growth by reminding people of their "strengths and limits, mortality, and the finiteness of the time they have" (p. 226). The reformulation stage of grief focuses on "1) discovering potential rather than limits; 2) seeing problems as challenges; 3) being curious again; and 4) seeking a balance between the different aspects of self" (p. 226). Some of the observed behaviors, feelings, and emotions accompanying Stage 7 are enhanced sensory awareness, assertion, spontaneity, patience, joy, integrity/balance/centeredness, recognition of illusions, joy, curiosity, and increased tolerance for pain.

8. *Stage 8 is transforming loss into new levels of attachment.* The stage of transformation is an integration of the physical, emotional, cognitive, behavioral, and spiritual aspects of the person—as an integral part of the process of reformulation to higher levels of understanding and acceptance of the loss. Transformation does not end the cycles of loss and grief; but the process makes it possible for people to approach life "with greater openness and the willingness to surrender more readily the necessity of structure in life" and release energies that create new strength (Schneider, 1984, p. 248). It is perhaps ironic that, out of life's greatest loss, there may emerge a reformulation and transformation that produce a greater capacity for growth than before. The transformational stage is accompanied by such behavioral, feeling, or emotional dimensions as awareness of interrelationships, unconditional love, creativity, wholeness, deep empathy, end of searching, and commitment.

In summary, the Schneider model of grief integrates people's physical, cognitive, emotional, behavioral, and spiritual manifestations. The model can be applied to pathological issues as well as to the potential for personal growth of all people. The dynamics of this model serve as a comprehensive backdrop for the crisis worker who wishes to view each client and each crisis situation as unique and to deal with each person as a "whole" person.

Types of Loss

People may encounter many different types of loss that produce stress, trauma, and/or grief. We have identified several types that crisis workers may encounter. It is not our purpose to provide crisis intervention techniques for dealing with every specific type of loss. What we want to show here is that loss covers a broad scope and that certain fundamental helping skills and strategies apply in a generic way to helping individuals suffering from loss.

Death of a spouse. The death of a spouse is one of the most emotionally stressful and disruptive events in life. It is experienced by more than 80,000 people each year (Shucter, 1986). There are many more women survivors (widows) than men (widowers), and the bereaved spouse typically faces a number of problems and stages of bereavement alone (Kübler-Ross, 1969). In addition to the immediate shock and stress, many survivors face serious personal, emotional, economic, social, career, family, and community problems (Johnson, 1977; Osterweis, Solomon, & Green, 1984, pp. 71–75; Rando, 1984, pp. 144–149).

Shucter (1986) identifies six dimensions in the spousal grief process: (1) emotional and mental responses to the loss, such as shock, anger, or guilt, (2) ways of coping with the pain of bereavement, (3) ways of continuing a relationship with the deceased, (4) changes in how people function socially, at work, and medically, (5) changing relationships with family and friends, and (6) the changing identity of the survivor. Typically the loss of a spouse is an emotionally overwhelming event, ranked on a life-event continuum as the most stressful of all human losses (Osterweis, Solomon, & Green, 1984, p. 71). Facing a completely new and unfamiliar set of problems alone, during a period of intense bereavement, constitutes enormous adjustment problems for most surviving spouses.

Death of a child.   The death of a child is a major life crisis for parents (Edelstein, 1984; Hansen & Frantz, 1984, pp. 11–26; Kübler-Ross, 1983; Kushner, 1983; Wass & Corr, 1985). Every parent is unique in terms of needs, history, personality, coping style, relationship to others, social concerns, and family situation. Therefore, every parent suffers the loss of a child somewhat differently. The death of a child is traumatic for parents, whether it occurs as stillbirth or sudden infant death syndrome (SIDS) or follows accident or illness in adolescence or young adulthood (Osterweis, Solomon, & Green, 1984, pp. 75–79). It is equally traumatic for aged parents to lose their children who may be middle-aged or older. Regardless of the ages of parents or children, the death of a child is always a major loss. Although infant mortality is much lower today than it was in earlier years, even today infants sometimes survive only a few days. Children occasionally die as a result of accident, disease, abuse, congenital causes, and violence. The child's age, suddenness of death, circumstances of the death, and family situation affect the bereavement and adjustment of parents, family, relatives, and friends (Rando, 1984, pp. 367–415).

Bereavement following a suicide.   Death as a result of suicide is accompanied by numerous negative cultural messages and meanings. Therefore, the loss of a loved one because of suicide is doubly stressful (Edelstein, 1984, p. 21; Rando, 1984, p. 150). Grieving loved ones left behind by a suicide may refer to themselves as "victims" because, in addition to the emotional stress of the death itself, the survivors must also deal with burdens such as social stigma, guilt, blame, a search for the cause or meaning, unfinished business, and perceived rejection wrought by the suicide (Rando, 1984, pp. 151–152).

The "real victim" of suicide is said to be not the body in the coffin but the family and other loved ones (Hansen & Frantz, 1984, p. 36). Osterweis, Solomon, and Green (1984) report that survivors of the death of a loved one by suicide are thought to be more vulnerable to physical and mental health problems than grievers from other causes of death (p. 87).

The nature and intensity of the survivor's bereavement depend on various factors, such as the survivor's cultural values, survivor's relationship with the deceased, age and physical condition of the deceased, the nature of the suicide, and the survivor's personality characteristics and mental health (Osterweis, Solomon, & Green, 1984, p. 88). According to Stone (1972), seven emotional states may constitute a typical adaptation pattern in the bereavement process in the surviving loved ones of death by suicide. These states, which resemble stages of the Kübler-Ross model, are shock, catharsis, depression, guilt, preoccupation with the loss, anger, and reality (p. 27).

Bereavement during childhood. An essential dynamic in understanding childhood grief is that the emotions and reactions of children differ from those of adults because of developmental considerations (Osterweis, Solomon, & Green, 1984, pp. 100–101). Individuals from infancy through adolescence suffer from the loss of a significant loved one, such as a parent or sibling (Parkes, 1972, pp. 178–179; Schoenberg, 1980; Wass & Corr, 1984). But their cognitive, affective, and behavioral responses must be approached not in terms of adult perspectives but in terms of each child's understanding and developmental stage (Rando, 1984, pp. 157–162). Children are especially vulnerable during periods of major loss because their inexperience and their undeveloped personalities can easily lead to confusion and misinterpretation of events. Such childhood misinterpretation can lead to the development of pathological disorders in adulthood. Since children's personalities are growing and absorbing social stimuli at a very rapid and concentrated rate, care must be taken to provide reassurance and support during family bereavement. They may ask the same questions over and over about the loss, not so much for the factual information but for reassurance that the adult view is consistent, that the story has not changed, and that the grieving adults and children are safe. Children need to hear, over and over again, the simple, truthful, reassuring words of adults who are relatively secure and who show genuine concern for the children's feelings (Osterweis, Solomon, & Green, 1984, p. 100).

Some people believe that children should be shielded and protected from exposure to death and loss. The research suggests, however, that bereaved children will make healthier adjustments to loss if they are confronted with the loss truthfully and actively (Osterweis, Solomon, & Green, 1984, pp. 99–127; Rando, 1984, p. 155; Schoenberg, 1980, pp. 151–154). Even though children during the bereavement process may exhibit behavioral responses that adults may interpret as "not caring" or "not understanding," children should be permitted to proceed with mourning at a level and pace appropriate to their development. They should be permitted to mourn in an environment of reassurance and unconditional love. Schoenberg (1980) has pointed out that the lack of grieving in children may later produce psychological disturbance as well as physical problems (p. 200).

Bereavement during adolescence.   Hansen and Frantz (1984, pp. 36–47, 62–72) describe adolescents who are in bereavement as needing to be included (involved) in the family's grief, while at the same time needing periods of privacy. Many times the adolescent may feel excluded, for example, at the sudden death of a grandparent. Other bereaved family members may erroneously assume that the adolescent's perceptions of events are the same as those of the adults. At such times adolescents may not know how to behave like their adult counterparts because they do not have a sufficient understanding of death, of the circumstances of the death, or of the appropriate mourning role. Adolescents may feel a deep sense of pain, fear, guilt, helplessness, and grief, yet they may not know how to express or feel comfortable in expressing these emotions. Adolescents in grief need to be given understanding, information, and private time. They need opportunities to be included in discussions, planning, mourning, and funeral and commemorative activities (pp. 62–67).

Adolescent bereavement is complicated and exacerbated by the pressures of modern society and the special developmental needs of adolescents themselves. The stress, pain, and grief associated with living through the teen years make adolescence a difficult developmental stage. Gardner (1970) points out that adolescents cannot mature if they believe others hold the solutions to all their questions. The fear and anxiety generated by normal adolescent ambivalence (of childlike dependency versus independently standing alone) make the developmental tasks between the ages of 12 and 21 particularly difficult for both teenagers and parents (p. 169). Hurlock (1978) identifies several characteristic pubescent attitudes and behaviors, such as antagonism, aggression, boredom, withdrawal, and fault finding (p. 248).

Ohlsen (1970) identifies 13 unique needs of teenagers, such as a need for identity, self-understanding, independence, communication techniques, and social skills (p. 198). Ivey (1986) shows that the traditional view of development (as a linear progression) does not adequately apply to dealing with adolescents. He views movement through each of the different life stages of development as holistic stages of transformation. Thus, the focus in counseling and therapy of an individual should be holistic and, in the case of adolescents, attend to even small changes and nuances in their attitudes and behaviors.

The adolescent stage itself appears to be difficult for parents to handle. Experience of loss and grief may cause additional stresses on both parents and adolescents. Periods of bereavement may be further complicated in a large number of teenagers who experience problems related to social deviancy.

One recent study reported by Gelman, Raine, Jackson, Katz, Weathers, and Coppola (1986) shows that approximately one-third of all adolescents get through the pubescent or "awkward" years without a hitch; another third get into occasional difficulty; and one-third experience major troubles. Further, mental health professionals report that teenage problems are worsening (p. 52). The dramatic increase in society of substance abuse, sexual abuse at home, violent behavior, divorce, separation, remarriage, teenage rebelliousness and crime, runaways, and truancy leaves many parents and adolescents terrified, with feelings of helplessness, and in a state of shock (pp. 53–54).

Adolescent behaviors can be destructive, not only to the teenager but also to other family members—sometimes destroying the whole family structure (Hansen & Frantz, 1984, p. 36). The stress and grief associated with problems in the teenage years confront parents and adolescents alike with the loss of love, support, and security of the family. Even when there is no death involved, the feelings of loss and grief are profound and painful for both adolescents and adults and often require intervention from outside the family to help avoid further traumatic experiences.

Separation and divorce. About 50% of all marriages end in divorce (Schwed, 1986, p. C7), and this breakup in marriages is an epidemic that is ripping the United States apart (Pauley, 1986). It is devastating to adults and children alike. The crisis of separation and divorce often places children in untenable positions, causing them to feel confused, insecure, fearful, trapped, angry, unloved, and guilty. The adult parties are also adversely affected. According to Johnson (1977), the most common experience that marriage partners have regarding separation is intense and disturbing fear and emotional turmoil. Such fear and turmoil are described in the following passage (Johnson, 1977, p. 50):

> The feeling of being overwhelmed by unfamiliar, unexpected, and frightening emotion is normal; the fear of being totally unable to meet new and even old responsibilities is normal; the fear of losing complete control is normal. While a very few of those who experience these fears do succumb to serious emotional difficulties, the overwhelming majority do not; and in most, if not all, cases of mental breakdown, the central precipitating cause is fear itself.

Separation is almost always experienced as a loss. Even when the separation is desired and sought, it precipitates a sense of frustration, failure, loss, and mourning. Johnson (1977) says that experiencing the facing and mourning of the loss, rather than denying it, can be both healing and constructive (p. 55).

Schneider (1984) reports that persons suffering from loss due to divorce or widowhood "show significant and consistently higher vulnerability to almost every major physical and mental disorder, particularly to heart disease" (p. 19). The phenomenon of separation and divorce is a widespread and complex contributor to loss in today's world. Colgrove, Bloomfield, and McWilliams (1976) advise that surviving and healing, following such loss, begin by recognizing and facing the loss immediately and doing the mourning now (pp. 1–2).

Death of a pet. Bereavement over the death of pets has become a phenomenon of concern in recent years (Downs & Walters, 1986; Nieburg & Fischer, 1982). Downs and Walters reported that more and more people seem to be forming strong bonds of affection and attachment to their pets. They did not rule out the possibility that people are now more likely to acknowledge the bonds that have always been there. Perhaps fewer people are ashamed to admit that pets are considered members of the family and that death of a pet has always been a severe blow. When pets die or suffer terminal illness and have to be "put to sleep," the owners may suffer grief, guilt, and other emotional reactions similar to those experienced at the death of human family members. Even when the death of a pet does not constitute a devastating event, it is nonetheless an emotionally sobering time. The death of a pet may provide a naturally occurring opportunity for adults in the family to introduce children to the concept and experience of death and dying (Koocher, 1975; Nieburg & Fischer, 1982; Schoenberg, 1980, pp. 203–204).

Bereavement in the elderly.   The elderly generally experience more losses than their younger counterparts: loss of relatives and friends; loss of job, status, and money; loss of bodily functions and abilities; and loss of independence and self-respect (Freeman, 1978, p. 116). The most profound and devastating loss that the elderly may encounter is the loss of a spouse (Schoenberg, 1980, pp. 211–214). It is not known whether age, as such, affects the cognitive and behavioral aspects of adult bereavement. It does appear that advancing age tends to correlate with a decrease in coping strategies. But it is not known whether this decrease is related to one's greater awareness of impending death, decrease in physical stamina and function, or other factors (Schoenberg, 1980, pp. 221–223).

Schoenberg (1980, p. 230), summarizes four conclusions that may be drawn from the literature on bereavement and age:

1. The elderly present more somatic problems than psychological problems.
2. There is no indication that the intensity of grief varies significantly with age.
3. A small amount of evidence suggests that grief among the elderly may be more prolonged than among younger people.
4. Elderly people tend to be lonelier and to have far longer periods of loneliness than their younger counterparts.

From a developmental standpoint, bereavement among the elderly is compounded by decreases in sensory acuity, general decline in health, and reduced mobility. Having a lower income and fewer support persons available to them than in their younger years also represent changes that may affect them. With the relative numbers of elderly continuing to increase, as people live longer, crisis workers and other caregivers face an ever-increasing need to study gerontology. Certainly the elderly must be both understood and prized by those who help them in their times of grief, as well as in other adjustment concerns.

INTERVENTION STRATEGIES

This section on crisis intervention focuses on the types of grief we have identified. One case example and intervention techniques for each type of grief are presented.

Intervention strategies for helping people who are suffering major losses may include, at one time or another, all the known systems of counseling and other techniques of assisting. The concepts and skills which are basic for these strategies are found in the six-step model in Chapter 2. Both long-term and short-term grief work are applicable. Assistance may be provided for an individual, a family, a staff, or a group of close friends. An example of long-term intervention was the case of two parents who were grieving over the suicide of their only child. The long-term intervention included couples' counseling, referral for psychiatric evaluation, and weekly meetings with a support group called Compassionate Friends. An example of short-term intervention occurred when a crisis worker met for only one session with a group of employees of a bookstore to assist them in their grief over the loss of one of their fellow employees.

Intervention may be done by an individual crisis worker, counselor, or other caregiver, by a group of workers, or by an interdisciplinary team. Intervention with a family in grief following the sudden death of a member in an automobile accident, for example, may be enhanced by a multidisciplinary team consisting of the attending physician, a psychiatric nurse, a counselor or psychologist, and a chaplain. Osterweis, Solomon, and Green (1984) and Rando (1984) have documented strong cases for the interdisciplinary approach to helping, care, and intervention in the lives of sufferers from grief, dying, death, and bereavement.

The Crisis Worker's Own Grief

Schneider (1984) reminds us that "it is not possible to be a facilitator of the growth aspects of bereavement if the helper is not also experiencing growth in relation to personal losses" (p. 270). Both Rando (1984) and Schoenberg (1980) challenge caregivers to come to grips with their own personal and professional attitudes toward death, grief, and bereavement before venturing into helping relationships with clients who are in grief.

According to Rando (1984), there are several reasons why caregivers should ensure that their own grief and attitudes about grief are not allowed to intrude upon their helping relationships with others (pp. 430–435). Rando's position does not contradict Schneider's. The knowledge and perspective gained from one's own growth following grief should serve as a quiet reservoir of strength for workers. But the worker's own grief experience should not be projected or imposed on clients.

Emotional investment in the client. A certain degree of emotional investment in clients is normal and needed. Overinvestment in those whom they help may require crisis workers to expend an inordinate amount of energy on their own grief responses in cases of dying and bereaved clients.

Bereavement overload. If the worker forms close bonds with several clients, the emotional load may involve too many risks and grief responses on the part of the worker. A series of client losses may cause the worker to experience bereavement overload or burnout. Workers can deal with their own bereavement overload provided that they are aware of it while it is happening to them and that they act upon their internal signals to get help and/or take steps to effect their own renewal before several client losses get them down.

Countertransference. Sometimes crisis workers who are engaged in grief work with others find that such work awakens their own feelings, thoughts, memories, and fantasies about losses in their own lives. Workers who experience such countertransference will be severely impaired in helping others. To deal with countertransference, caregivers who regularly work with loss-related clients should be involved in continuing support systems, such as supervision, peer support groups, case discussion staffing, and personal-development activities. A one-shot remediation will not suffice. An ongoing, proactive, preventive self-awareness and stress-management program is essential.

Emotional replenishment. Caregivers in the area of grief and bereavement work must take special care to minister to their own emotional needs. To do this, caregivers need support systems to provide for their physical, emotional, and psychological wellness; they themselves need to have regular access to empathic listeners for the purpose of sharing their own feelings; and they need the reinforcement from others that they, the caregivers, are valued. The knowledge that they are helping clients is not sufficient in itself. Emotional replenishment involves both taking care of oneself internally and having environmental supports from significant others—a supervisor, friends, family, colleagues—and meaningful physical and emotional activities.

Facing own mortality. Work with clients who are dying and/or grieving brings risks of many stressors. One of the important aspects of such work is that it may arouse existential anxiety over one's own death. Support groups, supervision, in-service training, and reading are suggested for coping mechanisms. Spiritual-growth activities are worthwhile alternatives for many caregivers.

Sense of power. Caregivers, like all other people, need a sense of power or control. Working with clients in dying, grief, and bereavement may cause workers to identify vicariously with the losses of their clients. Such identification may result in a sense of loss of power or control on the part of workers. Strategies for preventing feelings of loss of power are essentially the same as those recommended for dealing with countertransference.

Tendency to rescue. Crisis workers may have selected their respective professions because they have an inner need to "rescue" or save people from distress. It is essential that workers relinquish the rescue fantasy. Continuing education, supervision, and crisis-worker discussion groups are effective ways to help workers give up the notion of rescuing and fixing their clients.

Requisites for Working with Grievers

The listening, responding, and relationship skills we presented in Chapter 2 are applicable in dealing with all types of human loss. Crisis workers, caregivers, and other helpers must be personally ready to help people who are grieving and be secure enough within their own lives to be free of threat or need to control the grieving process in others. The requisites for working with dying patients (Rando, 1984) provide some additional considerations if we replace the word *dying* with the word *grief*. The prerequisites for crisis workers and caregivers would then be (p. 271):

1. a personal confrontation with grief in the sense of having begun to come to grips with one's own grief, grieving, and philosophy of grief
2. an understanding of the grief process and an appreciation for the total experience of the grieving person
3. effective listening skills and the ability to respond appropriately (this attending behavior will be nonverbal as well as verbal)
4. a commitment to giving part of oneself to the grieving person and to working with the griever's family when appropriate
5. a knowledge of one's own personal limits, knowing when there is a need to get away from grief, and establishing mechanisms for averting burnout.

Cases Dealing with Types of Grief

Death of a spouse.   Stuart Wynn, a machinist, age 44, his wife Kate, a bookkeeper, age 42, and one daughter, Anne, a high school senior, age 18, were a stable, middle-class family living in a quiet middle-class neighborhood in a large city. On her way to work one morning aboard a city bus, Kate Wynn suffered a severe stroke and was taken by ambulance to a hospital emergency room. A neighbor, who was also aboard the bus Kate was riding, phoned Stuart at work, and Stuart rushed to the hospital. Kate was placed in an intensive care unit but never regained consciousness after the stroke. She lived only 24 hours, leaving Stuart and Anne stunned and in a state of grief. As far as Stuart knew, Kate had been in good health and had had no medical history to indicate that she might have a health problem.

The case of Stuart is an example of immediate short-term crisis intervention. The first intervention session was a very brief meeting that included only the crisis worker and Stuart. The second meeting, approximately 20 minutes later, was also a short-term intervention session that featured a meeting between Stuart and his daughter and a multidisciplinary team consisting of the crisis worker, the attending physician, a psychiatric nurse, and the hospital chaplain. These initial short-term sessions were aimed at providing

1. empathic understanding and acknowledgment of the special problems related to Kate's sudden death
2. assurance to Stuart and Anne that all appropriate emergency medical measures had been attempted in efforts to save Kate

3. emotional support for both Stuart and Anne by the worker and by the other members of a multidisciplinary team
4. time alone with Kate's body prior to its being picked up for autopsy
5. referral resources that Stuart needed immediately to make arrangements for the funeral, notification of kin, and other matters
6. information about autopsy rights and procedures, in case Stuart requested it (which he did)
7. contact with the family minister, at Stuart's request.

Intervention strategies provided and issues explored with Stuart during the days and weeks immediately following Kate's burial were these:

1. *Individual counseling and intervention.* Issues of loneliness and bereavement related to Kate's absence. Implications for regaining equilibrium and going on with his life. Emotional supports for Anne. Identification of functions and roles in the family that were previously carried out by Kate and that must be reevaluated or reassigned. Review of either Kübler-Ross's or Schneider's stages of grief and assurance that Stuart would, in time, reformulate the loss. Grief work regarding the new identity—without Kate. It was now "I," "Stuart," instead of "us"—"Stuart and Kate." Identifying and dealing with Stuart's areas of vulnerability created by Kate's death. Assessment of ways to remember and use the positive strengths of Kate's life in a healthy and growth-promoting way for both himself and Anne.

2. *Spouse-survivor support group work.* Assess overall implications of Stuart's widowerhood, such as loss of social connections. Group-generated alternatives available to Stuart and others who had recently experienced the death of a spouse. Suggestions and guidance from the support group on Stuart's responses and single-parenting role with regard to Anne, his 18-year-old daughter. Referral to other groups, organizations, and institutions offering assistance and support appropriate for Stuart's particular situation. Group focus on ways to cope with the loneliness and other emotions brought on by the absence of one's spouse.

During the first contact with Stuart at the hospital, on the afternoon of Kate's sudden death, the crisis worker met individually with Stuart. The following segment illustrates a part of the first intervention session with Stuart.

CW: (Holding Stuart's hand.) Stuart, I realize your wife's death has been sudden and overwhelming to you. I want you to know that I am here to help you with whatever you need done. (Silence. Still holding Stuart's hand.) I'll be with you and assist you in whatever way I can. (Silence. Still holding Stuart's hand.)

The crisis worker's assessment is that Stuart's emotional status is one of shock, denial, or disbelief.

Stuart: This is so unreal! I just can't believe she's gone. It's such a sudden blow to me. Right now my main thought is Anne—our daughter. She just got here. I guess right now what I want is to make sure she's OK. I want to find out if she wants to see her mother before they take her away from the hospital.

CW: So you're needing to talk with Anne—and it's pretty urgent that you see her right away. Let's see if we can find her.

A few moments later.

Stuart: (Accompanied by Anne.) We want to be with Kate—to be alone with her some before they take her away. Can you arrange for us to do that?

CW: Yes, we'll arrange for that right now.

Stuart: One other thing. I'm afraid we're going to be in a pretty heavy way after we've seen her. Could you arrange for us to sit in the chapel a while after we get back? And is there a chaplain around who could be with us for a few moments?

CW: I'll phone Chaplain Myer again. He's aware of Kate's death and he said he'd be available any time, if you want him. I'll go with you and leave you alone with Kate's body and then, when you're ready, I'll go with you to the chapel. Do you want the chaplain to come now and go with us?

The work with Stuart was immediate and intense. During the first hour, provisions were made for a brief individual session with Stuart, private time for Stuart and Anne in the hospital chapel, and a multidisciplinary team session with Stuart and Anne. Definite provisions for follow-up work were established for helping Stuart and Anne during the following days and weeks. The crisis worker's immediate concern was to deal with Stuart's initial phase of grief, which corresponded with Kübler-Ross's (1969) first stage of denial, isolation, shock, and disbelief. The worker's primary goal was to help Stuart, an hour at a time and/or a day at a time, deal with the loss of Kate.

The worker kept in mind that as time evolved, the emergent stages of anger, bargaining, depression, and acceptance would need to be faced. But, for the moment, the short-term intervention focused on Stuart's need to deal with his first stage of grief. The worker was also sensitive to allowing Stuart to become aware of his own loss. There was never a thought or attempt to try to manage, defer, speed up, or otherwise intrude upon Stuart's grief process. Short-term grief work, in Stuart's case, was more a supportive way of being than overtly doing. Initial grief work is as much attitude on the part of caregivers as it is behavior.

Death of a child.   Brad Drake, age 34, a rural postal carrier, and his wife Helen, age 30, had twin sons, Herbert and Hubert, age 6. Late one afternoon, while Brad was doing the chores at the barn behind their house and Helen was preparing supper, Hubert attempted to cross the highway in front of their house and was struck by an automobile. The parents rushed Hubert to the hospital 22 miles away, but the child was pronounced dead on arrival. The death of Hubert left them feeling a deep sense of grief, hurt, bewilderment, guilt, powerlessness, psychological immobility and vulnerability, and searching for answers and meaning.

Approximately two weeks following Hubert's burial, Brad and Helen together sought counseling. The crisis worker saw them together immediately following the intake interview. The worker decided that crisis intervention could provide three interrelated but equally important things for Brad and

Helen: (1) facilitate the release of their grief energy, (2) reassure them that their feelings were normal, and (3) put them into communication with other grieving parents. These goals of intervention, described by Hansen and Frantz (1984, pp. 21–22), formed the basis for starting grief work with Brad and Helen Drake. The intervention strategies with the Drakes provided

1. empathic understanding and acknowledgment of Brad and Helen's grief related to Hubert's sudden death
2. an opportunity for both parents to talk about their grief, about Hubert, about Hubert's accidental death, about the good times and feelings Hubert had brought into their lives, and about their feelings since Hubert's death
3. a chance to shed tears, which both Brad and Helen did
4. exploration of previously unidentified and unspoken anger and guilt
5. assessment of the family's needs related to grief work and tentative plans for continuation of the work begun during the initial session.

The case of Brad and Helen is an example of long-term intervention. The strategies provided and issues explored with Brad and Helen during the days and weeks following Hubert's burial were as follows:

1. *Couple counseling and intervention.* The impact of the death on the twin brother, Herbert, and appropriate parental handling of Herbert. Continuation of grief work through talk, tears, expressions of guilt and anger, reminiscence and commemoration of Hubert's life, redirection of energies toward the family and creative work together, and a regular exercise program. Reassurance of Brad and Helen that they were not going crazy. Affirmation that they were the best parents they could be; that their parenting should not be blamed for the accident. Assessment of family problems and potentials. Assessment of marital relationship following the death of Hubert and exploration of ways to cope with the effects of the bereavement on the marriage. Reassurance of Brad and Helen that the grief and pain will continue for a long time and that this is normal; that they'll always have memories of the loss; that they will, in time, let go of the pattern of holding onto their grief and move on; that there is no set timetable for them to finish their grieving.

2. *Parent-survivor and support group work.* Involvement of Brad and Helen in a group whose common focus is the loss of a child. Group-supported talk, reminiscence, sharing, grief, tears. Making contact with other bereaved parents for mutual support by phone in addition to group meetings. Bringing parents together so that the newly bereaved can be helped by parents who are further advanced in the grieving process than Brad and Helen.

3. *Reading and media helps.* Provision of books and other reading material, films and other audiovisual material about bereavement in children and youth, as well as in parents. (The booklet *Death education: A concern for the living*, by Gibson, Roberts, and Buttery [1982], is a good source.) Putting the parents in touch with interventional supports such as parental self-help bereavement groups (Bordow, 1982; Dickens, 1985; Schiff, 1977).

The first crisis intervention session with Brad and Helen was rather emotionally low keyed, compared with later sessions, because both parents were still in a stage of denial and isolation. The crisis worker noted that they exhibited signs of being physically and emotionally drained; they vacillated between moping and benign circumspection, but showed no indication of movement to later stages of anger, bargaining, or depression. The crisis worker's goal was not to facilitate their advancement to a later stage of grief; rather, the aim was to understand their current inner concerns and to provide them with opportunities to identify and express their immediate and deep feelings openly.

CW: I sense that you are both feeling drainage of your emotional energy—like you're stuck there and cannot seem to move on.

Brad: Yes. Stuck is the word. But I need this time. I don't want to rush or be rushed. (Silence.) I guess we're in unknown and uncharted territory.

CW: It is very important not to hurry yourself or to be hurried.

Helen: We've just about stopped talking about it. We've become two lonely recluses in the same house. That worries me.

CW: Helen, what would you like to be doing right now, instead of being stuck and isolated?

Helen: I'd like to be more open. I'd like to know what's going on with Brad, and I'd like to be able to share feelings—even though they may be sad.

The worker was attempting to respond in a way that would allow both parents the autonomy to experience their current state of bereavement and, at the same time, encourage them to open up and provide mutual support. Open communication was viewed as important in terms of their grief as well as their relationship. The worker was successful in helping both of them share their concerns, which, in turn, enabled them to move on to other issues of importance to them.

Brad: We just don't know where to turn. We take our religion seriously and we've talked to our minister. That doesn't seem to help us. I keep on asking, "Why, why, why?"

Helen: We know the story of Job and such as that. We know tragedy strikes anywhere and anybody. Still, we don't know—we can't see—that a God of love or a God of justice can condone or permit the life of a good and innocent child like that to be snuffed out. I'm amazed at myself for talking like that. But my words are nothing compared to my thinking since this happened. I'm thinking I may be going insane or something.

CW: Helen, I am sure you're not going insane. You're responding in a way that makes perfect sense to me. You have both lost the most important and precious gift a mother and father can lose. It is natural and normal for you to experience unusual feelings and grief. You're doing a very good thing by talking openly about your thoughts and feelings. That's why I'm glad you came and reached out to me today. Nobody can erase your hurt or bring your son back, but I will be here with you, trying to help as best I can, in your time of need.

Later in the same session, the crisis worker has facilitated their release of grief energy and suggested that they contact a local, ongoing support group.

Brad: I'm glad we came today. We would like to come in again. The group of parents you spoke about is a good idea. I think we need that now, and we are going to need it more.

Helen: We didn't know about Compassionate Friends. I'll call them this afternoon. It's good to know that such a group exists. It sounds like a wonderful thing.

CW: I think you will both be glad you discovered Compassionate Friends. I'm truly glad you came, and I'll look forward to seeing you again. Here's my card, in case you want to call me. And don't forget your books.

Helen: Thank you, so much. It sounds like the books you recommended, especially the ones by Carol Staudacher and Harold Kushner, will be especially timely for us.

Helen was referring to Staudacher's (1987) paperback book titled *Beyond grief* and Kushner's (1983) paperback titled *When bad things happen to good people.* The two books combine to represent comprehensive guidelines for surviving the death of a loved one. They are appropriate for both the bereaved and the helping professional because both volumes are readable, objective, positive, comforting, and professionally written. The crisis worker was employing a strategy of bibliotherapy (Ellis & Abrahms, 1978, p. 123), which is an effective way of providing information, reinforcement, and supports through reading and other media that pertain to specific client concerns. The worker was also providing verbal and nonverbal warmth and understanding and attempting to model open communication to encourage them to strengthen their own mutual supports at home. The worker kept the focus on their current concerns, not intruding or imposing extraneous demands on them.

The fact that Brad and Helen returned for follow-up grief work, made a commitment to become involved in a support group, and accepted relevant reading material indicated to the worker that the objectives for intervention were being attained. The worker continued to meet with Brad and Helen while they were also attending the parent support group. The support group provided discussions, resource persons, and readings on several aspects of grief and bereavement, such as the major phases of grief (Tatelbaum, 1980), psychological perspectives (Smith, 1985), and individual and social realities (Stephenson, 1985). Brad and Helen reported that the readings helped them to discuss their loss more openly—both in the group and at home.

Bereavement following a suicide. Leah Nichols, age 54, manager of a branch bank, returned home from work Friday evening and discovered her son, Ronnie, age 24, dead from a gunshot wound. Ronnie had left a suicide note where he had apparently killed himself in his bedroom. Leah's husband, a college professor, had been dead (of heart failure) about a year, and she and Ronnie had lived in the family home. Ronnie's other siblings, Brenda, age 31, Richard, age 27, and Larry, age 22, were married and living in cities scattered about the region. Ronnie had been a warm, friendly, loving, and lovable person who had never married or dated much. He was highly sensitive and was given to mood swings from deep depression to euphoria. He had expressed suicidal ideations since his elementary school years and had been under psychiatric care since his adolescent years. But in recent months he had appeared to be gaining in maturity and had gotten off his medication. Ronnie was employed at a local bookstore, where he was regarded as friendly and dependable. Everyone who knew him liked him. Leah's grief was heavy and painful, but she felt she should set a controlled and circumspect image for the other three siblings and other friends and relatives.

Intervention strategies provided and issues explored with the Nichols family during the days and weeks immediately following Ronnie's suicide were these:

1. *Individual counseling and intervention.* Assessment of the impact of Leah's having lost her husband to heart failure and a son to suicide in such a brief time frame. Opportunities for Leah to release her grief energy. Assessment of Leah's medical and psychological vulnerability. Brief therapy for siblings when appropriate and needed.

2. *Family systems therapy.* Facilitate the family's release of grief energy. Focus on the value and impact of Ronnie's life as well as his death. Exploration of and dealing with residual guilt among family members. Group search for meaning and understanding of Ronnie's suicide. Assessment and addressing of anger, blame, rejection, unfinished business, and stigma encountered by family members. Facilitate family decisions and actions to commemorate Ronnie's life. Help family members to become reconciled to the fact that Ronnie chose death and help family members reformulate his death within a context of their own growth.

Individual crisis counseling following Ronnie's suicide was provided for Leah. The individual follow-up grief work with Leah Nichols dealt with a good many issues that are common in suicide work: denial, guilt, bargaining, and depression. The issue of Leah's martyrdom came out during an individual session approximately three weeks following Ronnie's funeral.

Leah: My kids think I'm holding back. They say I'm too stoic, too unaffected, or too aloof. They think my lack of showing emotions is not normal—not healthy.

CW: What do you think?

Leah: I don't know. I guess I believe somebody has to keep the lid on—keep a steady head during all this. I haven't wanted to trouble any of them with my problems. Their daddy's death, then Ronnie's. They've had enough without me dumping my grief on them.

CW: What are you saying, at a deep level, below the surface, right now?

Leah: I guess I am saying I'm hurting and that I have a need to weep, to feel the impact of the loss of Ronnie, too. I guess my actions have looked pretty cold and strange to them. I guess I've been trying to protect them—to keep them from hurting.

CW: What will it do for you to keep them from hurting?

Leah: Make me a martyr, I guess. I don't know what else it could be.

The crisis worker was not attempting to steer Leah to any particular conclusion. Rather, the questioning strategy, a combination of techniques from reality therapy, rational-emotive therapy, and Gestalt therapy, was used to help Leah home in on her own world. This crisis intervention technique would be ineffective if the worker were trying to analyze or identify pathology in Leah's behavior. Diagnosing, prescribing a cure, and managing Leah's recovery for her would have also been inappropriate.

Leah: I really had no notion I was playing the martyr when I came in here today. The kids could see something I couldn't see. I'm too close to it, I guess.

CW: What do you want to see happen now?

Leah: I want to get rid of it. I don't need it. The kids don't need it. I want to put it behind me.

CW: How are you going to put it behind you?

The worker continued to use reality therapy techniques (Glasser, 1965) to ascribe autonomy and responsibility to Leah. Leah's stability and mobility were assessed to be excellent. She had the power and the motivation to take the lead, on her own, and to exercise independent judgment and choices. Individual counseling with clients following a suicide may make use of any therapeutic modality that is appropriate for the client. The interview with Leah featured several different modalities, under an overall umbrella of the six steps in crisis intervention described in Chapter 2.

Group work was also used in the case of Leah. At approximately the same time as the individual session with Leah, the manager of the bookstore where Ronnie had worked requested a session between the crisis worker and the entire bookstore staff. The manager said that the employees were having a hard time becoming reconciled to Ronnie's suicide. One group session was conducted. Every employee of the bookstore attended and participated in the group session. The crisis worker facilitated the crisis group work by using the following format, with the employees sitting in a circle in a conference room:

1. The worker made a brief introduction, outlining the purposes and structure of the meeting.
2. Starting with the bookstore manager, each participant was given an opportunity to verbalize how he or she wished to remember Ronnie and to identify his most positive attribute.
3. During the second round, each employee was given an opportunity to take care of unfinished business with Ronnie and to verbally say good-bye to Ronnie.
4. The crisis worker summarized the content and feelings that the group had expressed. Then the crisis worker ended the session by (a) affirming the legitimate grief expressed by the group, (b) absolving the group of guilt and responsibility for Ronnie's death, (c) honoring the attributes and memory of Ronnie's life by a period of silent meditation, asking all persons present to imagine themselves saying good-bye and letting go of Ronnie, and (d) giving permission for each person to end the stage of acute grief at the conclusion of the meeting.

The crisis worker used a format that is useful in many crisis group settings—especially in a group whose concern is loss and grief. A variation of this group technique would be appropriate with a variety of groups representing a family, a fraternal group, the employees in a workplace, a school group, or a church group (any group dealing with a loss-related crisis).

What the worker did with the bookstore staff, in relation to Ronnie's suicide, was to tap into the power and cohesiveness of the group to nurture group restoration of the equilibrium of individual members. The worker's assessment was that the group norm was stuck in a stage of denial, isolation, and guilt. The group session was a powerful one. Although it appeared to the crisis worker that each member was ready to let go of Ronnie and move on toward positive growth, the worker invited members to come in for individual follow-up. In this case, none was requested.

Bereavement during childhood.   Elmer and Irene Kirk, ages 36 and 38 respectively, were spending all the time, energy, and money they could get in their attempts to cope with the terminal illness of their son Charles, 5 years old. After a year of being in and out of the children's research hospital, Charles sensed that he did not have long to live, but Elmer and Irene were attempting to make Charles's remaining days as happy and meaningful as Charles's physical condition would permit. Their only other child, Corine, age 8, felt sad, bewildered, lonely, and neglected.

The whole family was consumed with grief the day Charles died. In addition to grief, Corine suffered from guilt. She felt guilty because she had dared to wish within herself for several months that Charles's illness would just end and get it over. Somehow Corine believed that her wish had contributed to the death of her brother. She also felt guilty because she was alive and didn't deserve to live as much as Charles.

Intervention strategies provided and issues explored with the Kirk family during the days and weeks immediately prior to and following the death of Charles were the following:

1. *Individual counseling and intervention.* Assessment of Corine's concept of death. Ensure that Corine has opportunities to participate actively and learn about the medical facts relating to Charles's terminal illness in a truthful and realistic manner. Use child-centered counseling approaches in helping Corine deal with and refute her guilt feelings related to her brother's death: child-centered approaches to include the use of puppets, art work, sand play, and psychodrama. Assessment of the impact of Charles's death on both parents and Corine. Include Corine in the funeral plans and commemorative activities. Provide opportunities for each family member to release grief energy. Assessment of the impact of Charles's illness and death on the marriage and provision of individual therapy for Elmer and Irene as needed.

2. *Family systems therapy.* Assessment of the family's stress level and coping resources. Provide opportunities for the family together to explore the important issues related to Charles's death: the meaning, the good times and memories, guilt, blame, anger, rejection, and unfinished business. Focus on

Corine: ensure that she knows that she is loved and that the time and energy that Elmer and Irene have devoted to Charles in no way diminished their love and devotion to Corine. Discussion of feelings openly and honestly, keeping in mind the developmental capacity of Corine. Ensure that all family members have permission to mourn openly. Assume that Charles's death will have a lasting impact on Corine and will be manifested through her play, her fantasy life, and her relationship to both Elmer and Irene.

Crisis intervention strategies with children are different from strategies employed with adults because children are not miniature grownups. Children respond to counseling or teaching in a different way from adults. Typically they learn more through concrete, tactile, enactment, and model-observation modes than through listening to lectures.

A number of versatile child-centered approaches are available and appropriate for use in crisis intervention:

1. Puppets can help children use a total range of abilities for learning and communicating ideas (touching, talking, hearing, seeing, enacting, sharing) (James & Myer, in press).
2. Art work is effective in allowing children alternative modes of expression, so that they are not bound only to the written or spoken word (Gumaer, 1984).
3. Sand play provides creative and participatory modes, wherein children are not bound to written or spoken communication, are less inhibited, and are more prone toward creative self-expression (using sand as a safe and familiar medium) (Vinturella & James, in press).
4. Psychodrama allows children to observe, enact, self-disclose, question, experience, and learn in a protected environment (Gumaer, 1984).

Using puppets in crisis counseling with Corine, the worker was able to help her dispute her irrational and magical belief that her covert wish had caused her brother's death. During two previous sessions with the crisis worker, Corine had developed a great deal of trust in the worker and considerable facility and ease in using the raggedy puppets. At the third session, there were five puppets: Raggedy Ann, Raggedy Billy (Raggedy Ann's dying brother), Raggedy Mom, Raggedy Dad, and Raggedy Doctor.

CW: (Holding Raggedy Billy and Raggedy Mom—Raggedy Billy speaking.) Mommy, Mommy, Ann said I'm dying because she had bad thoughts—she wished I would die, so you and Daddy could leave the hospital and come back home.

CW: (Holding Raggedy Billy and Raggedy Mom—Raggedy Mom speaking.) Oh, Billy! Wishing someone is dead can *never, never* make it happen! Your sister Ann has a perfect right to wish for this hurting and sickness to end. She is so lonesome for Mommy and Daddy and for you, too. It's normal for her to wish this sickness were ending. But Ann should never feel bad or guilty just because she wished something. Remember, *wishing* doesn't make it happen!

CW: (Holding Raggedy Billy and Raggedy Mom—Raggedy Billy speaking.) Mommy, I wish I could see my sister Ann. I'd like to tell her it's OK.

CW: (Holding Raggedy Billy and Raggedy Mom—Raggedy Mom speaking.) Oh, Billy, my dear son (Smack—Raggedy Mom kisses Raggedy Billy.), I love you and I love Ann. Here comes your sister now. Why don't you talk to her? She's in the hospital to visit you.

CW: (Holding Raggedy Billy and Raggedy Mom—turning toward Corine, Raggedy Billy speaking.) Hi, sister Ann. I'm glad you came to the hospital to see me. I wanted to tell you how much I love you and how much I will miss you when I die. I want you to know that you should not worry about the wishes and thoughts you had. My disease is making me die. Your thoughts cannot make me or anyone else die. I want you to know it's all right. I love you, Mom loves you, and Daddy loves you. We will always love you.

Corine: (Holding Raggedy Ann and Raggedy Dad—Raggedy Ann speaking.) I'm sorry. I wish you wouldn't die. I'm very, very sorry. I hope you don't die.

CW: (Holding Raggedy Billy and Raggedy Mom—Raggedy Mom speaking.) Oh, Ann, we all hope he doesn't die. But I'm afraid he will. Then we will all be sad together. We will miss him. But we will have to learn to live without Billy when he's gone. We will still love him. But we will have each other and love each other. We will never blame you or ourselves for his death. His death will be caused by his sickness, not by your thoughts or wishes nor by my thoughts or wishes.

The segment is an example of puppet dialogue in child-centered crisis counseling. The crisis worker was using a variety of theoretical approaches: rational-emotive, behavioral, and Gestalt therapies. Though the segment cannot reveal all the preparatory work and dialogue that preceded and followed this brief encounter, it provides some idea of how versatile and effective puppetry can be. The crisis worker was focusing on only one dimension of bereavement during childhood—Corine's guilt feelings. But there are few, if any, dimensions of childhood bereavement that cannot be effectively dealt with through play media.

Corine's grief work could have been processed with equal effectiveness by a crisis worker skilled in using art work, sand play, or psychodrama. Any concern or issue related to childhood grief may be approached through child-centered methods. What we want to emphasize is that intervention with children must be handled differently from adult intervention and that it is absolutely necessary for crisis workers who help children to be highly trained and knowledgeable in child-centered counseling techniques.

Bereavement during adolescence. An accident following the prom in early May resulted in the deaths of four Cedar Grove High School students: Phil, age 16, the driver of the car, Jerry, age 17, Lucille, age 16, and Velma, age 17. The whole school and the entire community were distraught with grief and sadness. The families were in a state of shocked bereavement. A group of seven classmates at school, representing the four youngsters' closest friends, appeared to be stuck in their grief. Even after the commemoration program in the auditorium was concluded, the group did not feel they could resume their school activities or daily lives without further grief work. Shirley, Lee,

Peggy, and Bryan, all 17, and Eddie, Sheila, and Cynthia, all 16, requested the help of the school counselor in reaching some understanding and resolution of their feelings of anguish and grief.

These were the intervention strategies provided and issues explored with the adolescents by the school counselor during the days and weeks immediately following the burial of the four teenagers killed in the automobile accident after the prom:

1. *Individual counseling and intervention.* Assess individual stress levels. Provide individuals a safe place to release stress energy. Help adolescents feel comfortable in expressing how they feel. Provide death education for adolescents.

2. *Group grief work.* Provide an atmosphere for the seven adolescents in a group to deal with the deaths of their four classmates in particular and with the area of death and dying in general. Provide for group sessions and projects that commemorate the deceased classmates. Group exploration of unfinished business through written or role-playing exercises. Provision for students to deal with the deaths outside the group within the school environment. Exploration of appropriate group contact and activity involving the families of the deceased.

In cases of sudden death, grief, and bereavement among adolescents, a great deal of shock, vulnerability, remorse, and other emotions will quickly emerge. Because most adolescents lack experience dealing with the death of their peers and because social influence is powerful and pervasive in a setting such as a high school, the use of adolescent group grief work is an ideal strategy for controlling distortions and rumors and for helping young people release grief energy and begin to resolve their feelings of loss.

The Cedar Grove High School counselor was attentive to the feelings of fear, shock, powerlessness, and emptiness that many students manifested. The counselor believed that a group would be an appropriate setting for the students to share their feelings of grief and vulnerability. The group grief work was also perceived to be an appropriate activity in which the school could nurture learning and provide appropriate modeling for handling real-life bereavement and commemoration. The counselor, meeting with the group in the group guidance room, served as the crisis worker. She met with several grief work groups during the days immediately following the deaths of the four students. Each group, though different in composition, shared a common theme of needing to deal with the deaths of their classmates. The counselor set the tone by introducing the topic and encouraging members to share their emotional responses to the loss. Later during the session, after the release of students' grief energy, the counselor began to use structured techniques to help them sharpen their memories and focus on reality.

CW: I really appreciate all of the expressions of your feelings you've given so freely. Before the session began today, I asked Peggy to go by the yearbook office and pick up a copy of this year's *Wildcat.* I also asked her to pick up some leftover photographs that the yearbook staff did not use. Peggy, would you like to share some of them with the group?

Peggy: I put filing cards in the pages of the annual that I thought we'd like to look at. Oh, and I've got some great shots of Lucille, Jerry, and Velma. I only found one of Phil, and that was in a group. But Phil's class picture is in there (pointing toward the yearbook), and all four of them look so real and so alive and so happy in the activities section.

The students in the group showed a great deal of interest and released a great amount of stress energy while examining the photographs of the deceased students. Later in the session, the group discussed death in general, the impact of death on the living, and their own deaths. The counselor was able to use another technique that is sometimes effective in group grief work: the epitaph exercise. Each group member was given four index cards and was instructed: "If you were given the responsibility for writing the epitaphs for Phil, Jerry, Lucille, and Velma, write down the exact words on the cards that would appear on their gravestones." The group shared their epitaphs and discussed them.

Eddie: I thought Cynthia's was really good when she wrote—about Jerry—"Here lies the Will Rogers of Cedar Grove," because he really did like everybody. (Students nod in agreement.)

Shirley: I almost cried when I wrote Velma's, and then I did when Sheila read Velma's. I just felt like I couldn't stand it. It's so true. I'm really going to miss that girl. (Students nod in agreement. Long period of silence; thoughtful look on all faces.)

CW: I think what we've done is to write down, in the briefest form, what we want to remember most about each of our beloved classmates.

Before the session ended, the counselor led the group in identifying the positive contributions that each of the deceased students had made and in verbalizing their good-byes to each of their departed classmates. The counselor was attempting to use the power and social influence of the group setting to enhance the emotional impact upon each member and to prepare each member to say good-bye, let go of the deceased, and to begin to get ready to go on living.

Separation and divorce. When Don Nakamura, age 32, an automobile salesman, came home and announced to Hattie, age 30, that he wanted a divorce, it shattered Hattie's world. The marriage had been going downhill for a long time, and during the preceding months Don had been staying out nights. Nevertheless, Hattie, a licensed practical nurse, wanted to patch things up and to have a child. But Don was adamant and Hattie finally reluctantly admitted that the marriage was over. She was still distraught, with feelings of grief, guilt, worthlessness, and failure. Hattie felt that her life was meaningless. She didn't want to face life alone; she was stuck in grief and felt that she was doomed to live the remainder of her life unfulfilled, without a husband or a child, because no decent man would ever want her. She felt like a complete failure and blamed herself for not succeeding in the marriage. Hattie found herself frozen in a state of tears, grief, remorse, guilt, depression, and self-pity.

Intervention strategies provided and issues explored with Hattie during the days and weeks immediately following Don's announcement to her that he wanted a divorce were as follows:

1. *Individual counseling and intervention.* Assessment of Hattie's lethality level. Assessment of her coping skills and resources. Provision of a safe atmosphere for her to talk it out and cry. Assessment of available support persons. Consideration of her feelings of worthlessness, fear, failure, guilt, anger, depression, self-pity, and unfulfillment. Use of rational-emotive, reality therapy, cognitive-behavioral, and other therapeutic modalities to help Hattie identify and successfully refute her negative and self-defeating beliefs and self-statements. Reprogramming her internal sentences and developing positive action steps that she can own, practice, and carry out independently of a helping person.

2. *Support group work.* Identify divorce self-help groups for Hattie to use as supports. Assess her social needs on a time continuum from the present forward for several years. Use the self-help group to assist her in making realistic plans for her personal and social adjustment to her new situation.

3. *Referral resources.* Assess Hattie's need for legal, vocational, and financial assistance. If necessary, identify specific referral persons for her to contact immediately. (While interviewing her, carefully assess statements reflecting her present autonomy and ability to attain her goals. For example, dependence on her husband's attorney, banker, or accountant may not serve her best interests. Many newly estranged wives find that they need a different attorney, banker, and accountant from the ones used by their spouses and that their vocational-development needs must be severed completely from those of the husband. Often this is a sudden and difficult switch. Therefore the worker must be sensitive, supportive, realistic, and assertive because Hattie is so vulnerable during this phase of her separation.)

The abrupt termination of relationships by separation is frequently accompanied by emotional responses found in other types of personal loss such as death. People who experience the loss of separation may exhibit shock, disbelief, denial, anger, withdrawal, guilt, and depression. Each person responds in unique ways. Some individuals will cry for several days. Some will verbally ventilate for days on end—to anyone who will listen. Some will go into a state of withdrawal, described by one person like this: "When he came in and told me he was leaving, packed his clothes, and left, I got in the bed and didn't move. I intended to stay there until I died."

The loss by separation may be the result of severance of a marriage, a lover relationship, a gay or lesbian relationship, a business partnership, or any other close personal attachment. Helping people overcome the emotional and behavioral results of the loss of a relationship requires crisis intervention skills similar to those needed in other types of grief and bereavement.

In the case of Hattie, the client presented herself for crisis intervention several days after she had stayed in bed with the intention of crying and grieving herself to death. Hattie truly wanted to die after Don told her he was permanently leaving. At first her denial was so profound that she thought to herself, "This can never be. I will never be a divorcee. My parents must never know. My friends must never find out." Hattie did not talk to anyone about Don's leaving for several days. There was denial: "He really isn't leaving for good. He will be back. We will work things out." There was guilt: "What did I do to cause this? I must have been a terrible wife. I shouldn't have been so blind to his needs. If I just died in an accident, he could go on and marry the other woman and no one would ever have to know." There was anger: "I've a good mind to find her and pay her back for all the misery she's caused me."

Hattie experienced several stages of grief before she brought herself to the point of presenting her problem to the crisis worker.

CW: Well, Hattie, what brings you to see me today?

Hattie: My whole life is a wreck. It's really a mess. The main thing is that my marriage is breaking up. Well, I guess it has broken up. My husband's gone. Been gone over a week. I guess you could say that the marriage is down the tubes.

CW: You're feeling rather hopeless about the marriage. What has happened today, in relation to your marriage breakup, to impel you to come in right now?

Hattie: Well, I was tired of lying around feeling sorry for myself—thinking about killing myself or harming my husband's girlfriend. My intuition told me that neither one of those acts would solve anything, so I've come in here looking for better answers.

CW: Hattie, I'm really glad you decided to come today. What I want to find out first is whether you are in danger of suicide now. Are you still strongly contemplating suicide? Do you have a means at hand to do it? And how close are you to suicide now?

The crisis worker's first concern was Hattie's immediate safety. It appeared from her verbal and nonverbal cues that she was hopeful and stable enough to have some mobility. The fact that she came to present her problem was another positive factor. Then, when Hattie told the worker that she didn't have a definite plan or a definite means to kill herself, the worker proceeded with other steps in the crisis interview. At one point, Hattie appeared to be in a stage of "holding on," which Schneider (1984) described as having elements of anger, bargaining, and denial.

Hattie: I just can't believe this is happening to me. My whole world has caved in on me. This is simply horrible. I just can't stand it. I just don't know what I'm going to do without him.

CW: You're truly feeling terrible about the breakup of your marriage. But what I believe you're meaning is that this situation is causing you a great deal of hurt and causing you to make some major shifts in your life. But it seems to me you enormously complicate matters when you convince yourself, inside your head, that this is the most terrible catastrophe that could possibly happen to you. *Telling yourself* that you can't stand it and *believing* that it's horrible and that you're terrible seem to be an exaggeration that is getting in the way. That is different from telling yourself that it is very bad, and you hate it, but that you didn't cause it and that this isn't the end of the world—even though it may make your life very difficult for a while. You see where your catastrophizing, exaggerating, and awfulizing color your thinking and get in the way of your clearly and objectively assessing not only what has happened but also what your real options are, don't you?

Hattie: Well, yes. Since you put it that way, I guess I have come down harder on myself and on the problem than is necessary. I know it isn't really horrible, but I feel, at the time, that it's horrible and awful.

CW: Then your *believing* it's horrible and awful is the real culprit, isn't it? There is a difference between your beliefs and how things really are.

Hattie: You're right! It helps just to look at it differently, even though it doesn't solve my big mess.

CW: You're right. It doesn't solve it. But we can objectively examine it and together begin to figure out options you can choose if we know on the front end, even though you're grieving over your hurt, that we are not dealing with a world-shattering catastrophe.

The crisis worker was intervening by using elements of rational-emotive therapy described in Ellis and Grieger (1977). The worker was attempting to dispute the client's irrational beliefs about the separation and help her begin to direct her emotional energy toward the real issues. Hattie was an intelligent person who quickly responded to the rational ideas presented. But, as is typical in such cases dealing with the emotional state during loss, the worker knew that repetition, practice, support, and encouragement would need to be provided. A person in Hattie's state must have far more than just a one-shot session using RET to get her beyond her crisis and back to a state of equilibrium.

In addition to using RET as a crisis intervention strategy, the crisis worker also used a self-managed behavioral technique (Williams & Long, 1983) to help Hattie expend her grief energy over a period of several weeks. What Hattie did was to make a series of sound tapes—alone, at home—in a sequential and systematic manner. The purposes for making the tapes were (1) to serve as a mechanism for self-catharsis, (2) to present to the crisis worker her full story, (3) to clarify, in her own mind, the stages of grief she was going through, and (4) to document her progress on a set of cassette tapes that might be provided for other women to use in similar cases of loss. Hattie worked regularly and diligently on the self-taped sessions. The cassettes were quite useful to the crisis worker. But the main value of the behavioral plan was providing Hattie the purpose and the experience of doing it. She described in detail both her feelings and her actions throughout several stages: shock and disbelief, denial, anger, withdrawal, guilt, depression, searching, and resolution.

Hattie made eight cassette tapes. She reported that the most valuable and helpful aspect of the sound-taping activity was that of listening to her own tapes, which she found herself doing over and over. Hattie kept the cassettes with the stated intention of continuing to listen to them. But she later reported that after her crisis subsided, she didn't need to listen to them any more.

Death of a pet. The Thompsons, Hollis, age 36, Faye, age 33, and their adopted daughter, Dawn, age 4, were grieving over the death of Tinfoil, their aged terrier. Tinfoil was like a member of the family. He had been a faithful companion to the Thompsons since they were newlyweds; he had been the affectionate and protective playmate of Dawn from the day the Thompsons got her through the adoption agency.

The veterinarian told the Thompsons that Tinfoil's medical condition made it necessary to terminate his life.

These were the intervention strategies provided and issues explored with the Thompson family during the days and weeks immediately following the death of their pet:

1. *Individual counseling and intervention.* Assessment of the levels of grief, guilt, and stress in each—Hollis, Faye, and Dawn. Assessment of Dawn's understanding of the death of the pet. Provide a period to grieve and release grief energy. Follow-up play therapy and ceremonial events as outlets for Dawn (Schoenberg, 1980, pp. 203–204).

2. *Group work.* Provide an opportunity for the family to talk about Tinfoil's death in a realistic, factual, and honest manner. Use the death of the pet to help Dawn begin to develop her concept of death, free of misinformation. Provide opportunities and activities for the family to commemorate the life of the pet and to reformulate the death of the pet within a context of growth.

Schoenberg (1980) has suggested that families use ceremonial events and play therapy to help deal with their grief following the death of a pet (pp. 203–204). Ceremonial events open up opportunities for discussion, sharing of feelings, and explanations to children. Play therapy provides opportunities for children to have healthy experiences and to take an active role in the family's grief work. Workers using play therapy techniques employ both objects of play and the process of play to enable children to think about, talk about, and develop positive attitudes about issues or events that might be too threatening or too complex for them to understand through abstract didactic instruction. Examples of play therapy objects which might be used are dolls, sand boxes, and a variety of toys. Some examples of the use of the process of play might be taking a trip, attending a funeral, and visiting the hospital. In the case of the Thompsons, both play therapy and ceremonial events were used.

Faye: We had a small funeral in the back yard. I helped Dawn invite a few of her close friends to the funeral, and our next-door neighbors mailed us a sympathy card. Hollis and Dawn dug Tinfoil's grave and we had a simple but beautiful graveside service. There were flowers and friends, and we paid tribute and said good-bye to him. It was a good thing for our family and for the friends who came. The funeral and our family discussions provided a good background later on for Dawn's play therapy. We even had another small ceremony when we put Tinfoil's collar on the bulletin board in Dawn's room. We're still grieving somewhat over his death, but it has been a learning experience for all of us, and I think Dawn will have a realistic and healthy view of death, loss, and grief as a result of these activities.

Such experiences as those described by Faye are undoubtedly "learning experiences" for adults as well as children. There are many other strategies that could be used to assist people who have lost a pet. For instance, where children are involved, puppets, art work, sand play, photographs of the pet, and modeling clay are only a few of the play therapy techniques that might be used to stimulate discussion. Also, variations on ceremonial events may be developed to fit the needs of each specific situation involving loss of a pet. The strategies used in dealing with the loss of pets are aimed at the same goals as those used in any human loss: helping the grievers wind down their various stages of grief in healthy and growth-promoting ways.

Bereavement in the elderly.   Rosa and Robert Kizer, ages 82 and 85 respectively, had been living in a nursing home for four years. Robert had been there more than a year when Rosa had to join him. Robert had become immobile at the age of 73 following a stroke. Their three living children resided in other states and were busy with their own families, so Rosa placed Robert in the nursing home when he was 80 and she was no longer able to care for him because he required 24-hour nursing care. Robert's physical condition continued to deteriorate during his stay at the nursing home until he could not speak or move his body. He could turn his head a little and nod or shake his head for yes and no, and could swallow some liquid foods—but his eating had to be managed skillfully to avoid choking him. By this time Rosa was no longer housed in Robert's room because of the specialized care he required. Rosa was quite mobile, physically, but her memory lapses kept her from assuming any role in caring for Robert. Rosa was in the dining room eating breakfast when one of the medical staff members came and requested that she come to Robert's room because they couldn't rouse him. When Rosa arrived at the room a staff physician met her and informed her that Robert had apparently died in his sleep.

Intervention strategies provided and issues explored with Rosa during the days and weeks immediately following the death of Robert were these:

1. *Individual counseling and intervention.* Assessment of Rosa's level of grief and coping ability. Provision of opportunities for Rosa to release her grief energy. Assessment of Rosa's physical and mental capacities to cope. Assessment of her children's ability to help. Examine her economic, medical, legal needs. Use of therapeutic strategies such as person-centered therapy, reminiscence techniques, and validation therapy to help Rosa feel calm and se-

cure, and to remember vividly that she is a worthwhile person and that she and Robert have had worthwhile lives.

2. *Group work.* Groups within the nursing home. Support groups.

3. *Referrals.* Medical. Religious. Organizations. Legal assistance. Rosa's church; her children; senior citizens' agencies.

Rosa Kizer continued to live in the nursing home following Robert's death. Her grief was alleviated by several factors: she was physically mobile, she had lots of friends in the nursing home and in the community, she was an outgoing person with an optimistic outlook on life, and she was visited regularly for several weeks by a crisis worker who used reminiscence and validation therapy techniques (American Association of Retired People, 1986). Even with the positive factors she had going for her, Rosa experienced periods of denial, isolation, loneliness, fear, anger, bargaining, and depression. The crisis worker's goal was to help Rosa through the various stages of grief, to achieve a satisfactory degree of reconciliation with and acceptance of Robert's death, and to begin to establish her postcrisis life as a worthwhile person.

Rosa: A lot of times I just mope around. Some of the time I get to feeling sorry for myself. Then, sometimes I forget and find myself walking down to Robert's room before I remember that he isn't there any more. My life seems so meaningless without him.

CW: (Holding Rosa's hand and gently caressing the top of her hand and forearm.) You're really missing him and you're also having trouble remembering. What would you like to recall most?

Rosa: Oh, I'd like to recall the times when all of us were at home and healthy. When the kids were home. But that seems so far away in the past.

CW: Rosa, I'd like to know what it means to you to vividly remember the good times in your life—like when your family was together.

The crisis worker was relaxed, talking in a soft and caring tone, and gently caressing Rosa. The worker had taken special care to arrive at Rosa's room at the exact appointment time (many older clients are very sensitive about people promising to come to see them, then arriving late). In facilitating Rosa's reminiscing, the worker was careful not to appear pressed for time or anxious to leave and go on to the next patient. (The "hurried and harried" behavior of caregivers gets on the nerves of many elderly clients and causes them to lose confidence in the caregiver.) The worker was careful to nurture Rosa's trust, which is absolutely necessary for helping people through validation therapy or reminiscence techniques.

Rosa: We lived out on the mountain then. Goodness gracious me, we had such a good time! All of us worked hard then, but we played hard and enjoyed life too. (Long pause. Rosa is smiling.)

CW: Take just as long as you wish to think about life out on that mountain—just as vividly and clearly as you can get it in your mind. Just relax and take as long as you wish. Just take your memories back there and get hold of those good feelings you have about those good times.

Rosa: (Long pause.) Yes, yes! What a beautiful place and a beautiful time in life. We lived on the ridge overlooking a deep, green valley. Had such beautiful children. Grew about everything we ate. Yes, those were the times that warm one's heart. That was a glorious time. A sight for sore eyes! (Long pause.)

CW: It sounds wonderful! It sounds like it warms your heart right now, just remembering it clearly and telling me about it so clearly.

The crisis worker's objective was to get Rosa into touch with her vivid memories of real occurrences in her past, which she could recall, identify with, describe, and feel worthwhile about. The worker also wanted to feel and show genuine respect for and interest in Rosa's memories and descriptions. Such genuineness on the part of an interested listener is a good catalyst for sharing and validating one's own past. The worker assured Rosa that he appreciated the shared journey into her past and that he respected her for it and wanted to continue to do more on the next visit. Rosa was also encouraged, through cognitive-behavior techniques (Cormier & Cormier, 1985; Meichenbaum, 1985), to think about the past between visits and to be prepared to bring other important and memorable events into open expression. The worker reminded Rosa that she had the power, in her mind, to imagine and to go back and experience many healthy and happy times, and then to return in her mind to her room and feel a real sense of pride in her own private history of accomplishments.

Interviews were a small part of the overall individual work with Rosa. The support group, containing other elderly people who had recently experienced loss, was another important intervention strategy. The techniques for working with the elderly do not have to be highly formal, structured, or complicated. All intervention should be done by workers who live and model relationship skills (Cormier & Hackney, 1987; Egan, 1982) such as empathy, genuineness, acceptance, respect, warmth, and sincere caring in a relaxed and nonhurried way.

SUMMARY

In this chapter we have outlined the major components of the dynamic stages of grief and death depicted in the models developed by both Kübler-Ross (1969) and Schneider (1984). We have also identified several types of loss, presented typical cases, and discussed strategies that crisis workers may use in counseling and intervention. A global perspective that may be drawn from the chapter is that crisis workers must be prepared to respect the privacy, individuality, and autonomy of the bereaved and to avoid the imposition of their own values upon the persons they seek to help.

Every human being will, at one time or another, suffer personal loss. During our lives most of us will encounter numerous people who are experiencing bereavement or grief as a result of some personal loss. What may be clearly perceived as a personal loss ranges from a devastating occurrence, such as the death of a spouse or a child, to what many people might view as an insignificant loss. In any event, it is an important loss if the individual perceives it as such.

Persons in helping roles are encouraged to make use of their personal assets, listening competencies, compassion, and skill at making referrals to assist the bereaved in coping, as best they can, with their own unique losses. Although the bereaved can never forget the loss and return to a state of complete precrisis equilibrium, they can be helped to reformulate their loss within a context of growth.

We have indicated how important it is for crisis workers to become competent in using referral resources as an intervention strategy. We are concluding this summary by listing several important sources. Most of the organizations and societies on this list have branches in many large cities. Local library information centers and crisis intervention agencies usually have information about how to reach these resources in your area.

1. American Euthanasia Foundation
   95 N. Birch Road, Suite 301
   Ft. Lauderdale, FL 33304
   This foundation develops and distributes "Mercy Wills."
2. The Compassionate Friends
   P.O. Box 1347
   Oak Brook, IL 60521
   Compassionate Friends is a nonprofit, nondenominational network of self-help support groups for parents who have experienced the death of a child. More than 300 local chapters throughout the United States offer emotional and physical support for bereaved parents and siblings.
3. Concern for Dying
   250 W. 57th St.
   New York, NY 10107
   This organization develops and distributes "Living Wills," conducts workshop sessions on death and dying, and provides educational materials on the right not to prolong life during terminal illness. It publishes a newsletter and has regional branches in various parts of the United States.
4. Crisis Telephone Hot Lines
   Located in major cities in the United States, telephone hot lines for crisis callers are usually open for calls 24 hours each day. Phones are usually answered by volunteers who have been trained in crisis intervention strategies and referrals. Crisis centers in the United States are similar to the Good Samaritans organization in England. They are nonprofit and usually receive funding from donations, local governments, and the United Way. The address of the national office is
   American Association of Suicidology
   2459 South Ash
   Denver, CO 80222

5. Hemlock Society
P.O. Box 66218
Los Angeles, CA 90066
This society supports voluntary euthanasia for the advanced terminally ill and the seriously incurably ill. It publishes a quarterly and other material on voluntary euthanasia.

6. Hospice Services
(See the Yellow Pages of the local phone book for hospice agency listings, services, and locations.) Hospice service agencies typically provide care at home for the terminally ill and bereavement counseling for seriously incurably ill patients and their families.

7. International Council for Infant Survival (Sudden Infant Death)
P.O. Box 3841
Davenport, IA 52808
This council comprises national, regional, state, and local groups. It develops and disseminates information for individuals and families who have lost a child to SIDS. It supports research on SIDS and publishes a newsletter and other materials related to the subject.

8. Mothers Against Drunk Drivers (MADD)
5330 Primrose, Suite 146
Fair Oaks, CA 95628
MADD is a confederation of nonprofit national, regional, and state branches, which serves as advocates of victims of drunk-driving accidents. They support law enforcement efforts and state and federal legislation for reform and better enforcement of laws related to drunk driving; they provide counseling for victims; and they develop and disseminate a newsletter and information for victims and their families on bereavement groups and other advocacy measures.

9. National Sudden Infant Death Foundation (SIDS)
Two Metro Plaza, Suite 205
8240 Professional Place
Landover, MD 20785
This national foundation has local groups throughout the United States that assist bereaved parents who have lost a child to SIDS. They support research and public information on SIDS; they work with families and professionals in caring for high-risk infants; and they publish a newsletter and other material related to SIDS.

10. Parents of Murdered Children
1739 Bella Vista
Cincinnati, OH 45237
This organization offers physical and emotional support for parents whose children have been murdered. It disseminates information pertaining to victims, survivors, the criminal justice system, and public awareness. It publishes a newsletter and has local branch groups throughout the country.

11. Society for the Right to Die
    250 W. 57th St.
    New York, NY 10107
    This society engages in educational, judicial, and legislative activities to protect the rights of dying patients. It publishes materials and focuses on protecting physicians, hospitals, and health care providers from liability threats associated with caring for patients who wish to die.
12. Telophase Society (Funeral)
    San Diego, California
    This is a private, for-profit society that provides services for cremation and burial at sea.
13. The Neptune Society
    San Francisco, California
    This is a society that provides advocacy and services for cremation and burial at sea.

REFERENCES

American Association of Retired People (AARP). (1986, September). Reminiscence: Thanks for the memory. *AARP News Bulletin, 27*(8), p. 2.

Becker, E. (1973). *The denial of death.* New York: Free Press.

Bordow, J. (1982). *The ultimate loss: Coping with the death of a child.* New York: Beaufort Books.

Buscaglia, L. (1982). *The fall of Freddie the leaf: A story of life for all ages.* New York: Holt, Rinehart & Winston.

Colgrove, M., Bloomfield, H. H., & McWilliams, P. (1976). *How to survive the loss of a love.* New York: Bantam Books.

Cormier, L. S., & Hackney, H. (1987). *The professional counselor: A process guide to helping.* Englewood Cliffs, NJ: Prentice-Hall.

Cormier, W. H., & Cormier, L. S. (1985). *Interviewing strategies for helpers: Fundamental skills and cognitive behavioral interventions* (2nd ed.). Pacific Grove, CA: Brooks/Cole.

Dickens, M. (1985). *Miracles of courage: How families meet the challenge of a child's critical illness.* New York: Dodd, Mead.

Downs, H., & Walters, B. (1986, May 15). *20/20 News Magazine* [Television program]. ABC Television Network.

Edelstein, L. (1984). *Maternal bereavement: Coping with the unexpected death of a child.* New York: Praeger.

Egan, G. (1982). *The skilled helper: Model, skills, and methods for effective helping* (2nd ed.). Pacific Grove, CA: Brooks/Cole.

Ellis, A., & Abrahms, E. (1978). *Brief psychotherapy in medical and health practice.* New York: Springer.

Ellis, A., & Grieger, R. (1977). *Handbook of rational-emotive therapy.* New York: Springer.

Freeman, L. (1978). *The sorrow and the fury: Overcoming hurt and loss from childhood to old age.* Englewood Cliffs, NJ: Prentice-Hall.

Gardner, G. W. (1970). *The emerging personality: Infancy through adolescence.* New York: Delacorte.

Gelman, D., Raine, G., Jackson, T., Katz, S., Weathers, D., & Coppola, V. (1986, January 20). Treating teens in trouble: Can the psychiatric ward fill in for the family? *Newsweek.*

Gibson, A. B., Roberts, P. C., & Buttery, T. J. (1982). *Death education: A concern for the living* (Fastback No. 173). Bloomington, IN: Phi Delta Kappa Educational Foundation.

Glasser, W. (1965). *Reality therapy.* New York: Harper & Row.

Gumaer, J. (1984). *Counseling and therapy for children.* New York: Free Press.

Hansen, J. C., & Frantz, T. T. (Eds.). (1984). *Death and grief in the family*. Rockville, MD: Aspen Systems Corporation.

Hurlock, E. B. (1978). *Child development* (6th ed.). New York: McGraw-Hill.

Ivey, A. E. (1986). *Developmental therapy: Theory into practice*. San Francisco: Jossey-Bass.

James, R. K., & Myer, R. (in press). Puppets: The elementary counselor's right or left arm. *Elementary School Guidance and Counseling*.

Johnson, S. M. (1977). *First person singular: Living the good life alone*. Philadelphia: Lippincott.

Koocher, G. (1975). Why isn't the gerbil moving?: Discussing death in the classroom. *Children Today, 4,* 18–36.

Kübler-Ross, E. (1969). *On death and dying*. New York: Macmillan.

Kübler-Ross, E. (1975). *Death: The final stage of growth*. Englewood Cliffs, NJ: Prentice-Hall.

Kübler-Ross, E. (1981). *Living with death and dying*. New York: Macmillan.

Kübler-Ross, E. (1983). *On children and death*. New York: Macmillan.

Kushner, H. S. (1983). *When bad things happen to good people*. New York: Avon.

Levitt, P. M., & Guralnick, E. S. (1985). *You can make it back: Coping with serious illness*. New York: Facts on File Publications.

Meichenbaum, D. (1985, May). Cognitive behavior modification: Perspectives, techniques, and applications. Two-day workshop, St. Louis, MO. Evaluation Research Associates (Syracuse, NY 13217).

Nieburg, H. A., & Fischer, A. (1982). *Pet loss: A thoughtful guide for adults and children*. New York: Harper & Row.

Ohlsen, M. M. (1970). *Group counseling*. New York: Holt, Rinehart & Winston.

Ornstein, R., & Sobel, D. (1987, March). The healing brain. *Psychology Today*, pp. 48–52.

Osterweis, M., Solomon, F., & Green, M. (Eds.). (1984). *Bereavement: Reactions, consequences, and care*. Washington, DC: National Academy Press.

Parkes, C. M. (1972). *Bereavement: Studies of grief in adult life*. New York: International Universities Press.

Pauley, J. (1986, June 3). *Divorce is changing America* ["White Paper" documentary]. National Broadcasting Company (NBC) News.

Rando, T. A. (1984). *Grief, dying, and death: Clinical interventions for caregivers*. Champaign, IL: Research Press.

Schiff, H. S. (1977). *The bereaved parent*. New York: Crown Publishers.

Schneider, J. (1984). *Stress, loss, and grief: Understanding their origins and growth potential*. Baltimore: University Park Press.

Schoenberg, B. M. (Ed.). (1980). *Bereavement counseling: A multidisciplinary handbook*. Westport, CT: Greenwood Press.

Schwed, M. (1986, June 3). Hard numbers hit home in divorce documentary: A decade into epidemic, "bad news" is coming in (United Press International). *The Commercial Appeal*, Memphis, p. C7.

Shucter, S. R. (1986). *Dimensions of grief: Adjusting to the death of a spouse*. San Francisco: Jossey-Bass.

Smith, W. J. (1985). *Dying in the human life cycle: Psychological, biomedical, and social perspectives*. New York: Holt, Rinehart & Winston.

Staudacher, C. (1987). *Beyond grief: A guide for recovering from the death of a loved one*. Oakland, CA: New Harbinger.

Stephenson, J. S. (1985). *Death, grief, and mourning: Individual and social realities*. New York: Free Press.

Stone, H. W. (1972). *Suicide and grief*. Philadelphia: Fortress Press.

Tatelbaum, J. (1980). *The courage to grieve*. New York: Lippincott & Crowell.

Vinturella, L., & James, R. K. (in press). Sandplay. *Elementary School Guidance and Counseling*.

Wass, H., & Corr, C. A. (1984). *Helping children cope with death: Guidelines and resources* (2nd ed.). New York: Harper & Row.

Wass, H., & Corr, C. A. (1985). *Childhood and death*. New York: Harper & Row.

Williams, R. L., & Long, J. D. (1983). *Toward a self-managed life style* (3rd ed.). Boston: Houghton Mifflin.

■ Classroom Exercises

Simulated Counseling with Prepared Cases

To gain experience and practice in dealing with various bereavement situations, the class will work in small groups. Each group is assigned a different type of bereavement, selected from the following list:

Case of Wynn family (death of a spouse)
Case of the Drake family (death of a child)
Case of the Nichols family (bereavement of a family following suicide)
Case of the Kirk family (bereavement during childhood)
Case of Cedar Grove High School (bereavement during adolescence)
Case of Hattie (separation and divorce)
Case of the Thompson family (death of a pet)
Case of Rosa (bereavement in the elderly)

Through role taking of bereaved clients in the various cases, students will spontaneously generate dialogue and crisis intervention techniques in each group.

Each group will select one or more clients from their assigned case. Group members will take the roles of the client(s), the crisis worker(s), and observer(s)/evaluator(s). A specified time limit will be given for the crisis intervention sessions, to be conducted simultaneously within each group. The crisis intervention session will begin as soon as the clients have had time to review the data of their case. While the crisis workers process the case with the clients, the observers/recorders will make a tape recording of the session, take notes, and be prepared to report on the effectiveness of the crisis intervention and to make suggestions for improvement.

Whenever the crisis intervention sessions have been completed, observers/reporters will make their reports to members of their particular groups. The exercise will be completed by providing time in each group for a summarizing discussion.

Simulated Counseling with Class-Developed Scenarios

Replicate Exercise I, except that each group has the task of generating a realistic bereavement situation for the role-taking exercise instead of using one of the eight cases described in the chapter. Group members may draw upon their own knowledge and experience for creating realistic scenarios. All groups should be cautioned to (1) refrain from using recognizable persons, places, or situations and (2) maintain confidentiality by refraining from mentioning the scenarios outside the classroom, even though only parts of real situations may have been simulated. The facilitator or instructor should monitor the group simulations to provide supportive counseling, after the activities have been completed, to any individual who identifies with the scenario so completely that a state of personal crisis is induced—a situation that is rare but possible.

At the conclusion of the exercise, individual role players will be instructed to verbally disassociate themselves from the roles they enacted during the simulation. The disassociation will be done within each small group.

FOCUS ON IMPROVING THE CRISIS WORKER

Part Three deals with helping the crisis worker (the counselor, the helper, the human service worker, the caregiver, and the agency leader) to perform crisis intervention functions in a preventive or proactive mode of working and living. Our philosophy is that prevention of worker burnout is a way of life for both individuals and agencies; that continuous learning or training is a preferred means of acquiring and maintaining helping attitudes, skills, and competencies; and that individual crisis workers can control their own personal and professional development, thereby enhancing their personal functioning as well as their value to society.

Chapter 12, on human service workers in crisis, is written and documented on the assumption that workers can avoid burnout by attending to their own physical, psychological, and emotional wellness. Individuals can not only prevent burnout but can also choose to positively and constructively nurture their own lifestyles, physical stamina, mental health, and personal vibrancy.

Human Service Workers in Crisis: Burnout

BACKGROUND

"Burnout" is not just some currently-in-vogue "pop" term that is designed to elicit sympathetic responses at work or at cocktail parties. It is a complex individual–societal phenomenon that affects the welfare of not only millions of human service workers but also tens of millions of those workers' clients as well (Farber, 1983, pp. vii, 1). Put in economic terms, billions of dollars are lost each year because of workers in all fields who can no longer function adequately in their jobs. Signs and symptoms of burnout appear in turnover, absenteeism, lowered productivity, and psychological problems (Riggar, 1985, p. xv). Yet, if burnout has been discussed in all occupations, why should it be endemic to the helping professions?

The bulk of writing and research that has been done on burnout has come from the helping professions. This is so because the helping professions represent the essence of people-oriented work. In the very nature of the job, intense involvement with people is a given, and most generally these are people that are not at the highest levels of self-actualized behavior (Maslach, 1982, pp. 32–33). This is the core of the helping professions, making them not just some of the most challenging but some of the most stress-prone occupations. Thus, human service professionals must be able to tolerate a variety of complex problems that are generally couched in ambiguity, deal with conflict from both client and institution, and somehow meet a myriad of demands from the ecological framework in which they operate (Paine, 1982, p. 21). For the crisis worker, this is true many times over. Crisis center work settings are notorious for long and erratic hours, short pay, low-functioning clients, immediate deadlines, and interagency red tape, and those are only a few of the ecological stressors that assault crisis workers, making them prime candidates for burnout.

However, the question arises of whether burnout is really dynamically identifiable. Paine (1982, p. 11) and Maslach (1982, p. 29) report critics who propose that burnout is "part of the job," so if a human service professional "can't stand the heat then he or she ought to get out of the kitchen," because there "always has been stress on this job and always will be."

Such cursory dismissal of burnout does not consider the major personal, social, and organizational costs that accrue when job stress turns into crisis (Paine, 1982, p. 11). Burnout is connected to loss of job productivity, impairment of inter- and intrapersonal relationships, and a variety of health problems. Burnout is not just part of the territory; it has major ramifications for both individuals and institutions (Maslach, 1982, p. 39). It is a very real problem, with chronic occupational stress as a primary causal factor (Tubesing & Tubesing, 1982, p. 156; Paine, 1982, p. 16).

Definition

A historical definition of *burnout* places it as a child of the 1970s. The term comes from the psychiatric concept of patients who were burned out physically, emotionally, spiritually, interpersonally, and behaviorally to the point of exhaustion (Paine, 1982, p. 16). It was first coined as a workplace term by Herbert Freudenberger, who used it to describe young, idealistic volunteers who were working with him in altenative health care settings and who started to look and act worse than many of their clients (Freudenberger, 1974, 1975). Yet to define burnout adequately is not a simple task. To highlight this problem, Riggar's (1985) introduction to a comprehensive annotated bibliography on burnout lists 18 different definitions culled from the literature (pp. xvi–xvii).

A very broad definition depicts burnout as an internal psychological experience involving feelings, attitudes, motives, and expectations (Maslach, 1982, p. 29). Being burned out means that the total psychic energy of the person has been consumed in trying to fuel the fires of existence. This energy crisis occurs because the psychic demand exceeds the supply (Tubesing & Tubesing, 1982, p. 156). Occupationally, burnout occurs when past and present problems from one's job continuously pile up. The problems may come from a variety of sources: demanding and overbearing bosses, unending blizzards of paper work, jack-of-all trades and master-of-none job descriptions, tidal waves of clients and catastrophic dilemmas, and 18-hour work days. The problems may vary in degree and kind, but the result is a continuous and grinding negative interface between the person and the work environment (Riggar, 1985, p. xvi). From the worker's standpoint, no short or long term relief is forthcoming.

Stress and Burnout

Burnout does not mean that a person is just "stressed" by a job. Stress occurs when there is a substantial imbalance (perceived or real) between environmental demands and the response capability of the individual. Stress can have both positive and negative effects. Burnout occurs when the stress becomes unmediated and the person has no support systems or other buffers to ease the unrelenting pressure (Farber, 1983, p. 14). The outcome is a person affected in every dimension of life by unlimited combinations of symptoms. Such a description very adequately meets the crisis conditions of being in a state of disequilibrium and paralysis. Let us now look at three human service professionals who are experientially and professionally different, but by almost any definition are in the process of "burning out."

Elaine. Elaine is a telephone counselor at the local rape crisis center. She has been a volunteer at the center for eight months and has been one of the best crisis workers ever employed there, smart, vivacious, cheery, and full of boundless zeal and energy. The director had thought it one of the best days' work she ever did when she persuaded Elaine to become a volunteer. Lately, Elaine has become exceedingly curt and short-tempered with her clients and fellow volunteers and has progressed to the point that all her co-workers give her a wide berth. They no longer invite her to go with them for lunch or even dally long in the coffee room when she enters. They are frankly fed up with her complaints about work, clients, and life in general. Elaine responds by blaming them for being uncommitted and redoubles her efforts to be the greatest crisis worker in the universe. Her professional relationships continue a downward spiral.

Mr. Templeton. Mr. Templeton has worked at Central Junior High School for two years. In that time he has instituted some sweeping changes in the guidance program that was, before he came, notorious for running attendance checks and not much more. Mr. Templeton's counseling approach changed all that. Formerly, the last place that students would have gone for help with personal problems would have been the counseling office. By getting out and explaining what his job was all about to students, faculty, parent groups, civic organizations, and anybody else who would listen, and indeed, making good on his promises, Mr. Templeton has turned the guidance office into something akin to a land office during the California gold rush. His principal, previously unimpressed with anything the counselor did with the exception of keeping track of the substitute teacher list, would now fight a circular saw to keep the likes of Mr. Templeton around. What the principal does not know is that Mr. Templeton has fantasies about sending the entire ninth grade to an Outward Bound camp in the Sahara Desert.

He has not had a new idea about how to improve the counseling program in six months and is wondering if maybe that stockbroker's job that he so capriciously turned down last year was not such a bad idea after all. As he considers all this, he wistfully looks at his wristwatch, then at the ninth grader sitting across from him, and wonders whether she is in his office because of grade problems or a problem at home. She has been talking for 30 minutes and he cannot remember two sentences she has said.

Josh. Josh is a social worker at an outpatient clinic for a community mental health center. He has worked there for five years. His patient load resembles something on the order of bus traffic to Mecca. He has just received a memorandum from the director further increasing his caseload by 20%, along with a rather curt directive to move on some of those old cases and get them off the clinic rolls. Josh is sitting in his friendly local tavern quietly getting drunk and wondering how he is going to put 20 people out on the street with no support. He is also mulling over what response he will make to his wife who just this morning asked for a separation. Among the complaints she voiced, his job was prominent: the lousy pay for somebody with a master's degree, the long hours with no compensatory time, the emergencies in the middle of the night, and particularly forgetting he is the father of their two children and a husband to her. Josh stares across the bar and orders another drink. While waiting for his order, he swallows an antacid tablet for the dull, burning pain slowly working its way outward from the pit of his stomach.

DYNAMICS

Commitment

What do these three human service professionals have in common? They are alike in that they are all empathic, sensitive, humane, idealistic, and people oriented and have been highly committed and dedicated to their profession. However, like most other human service workers prone to burnout, they also tend to be overly anxious, obsessional, enthusiastic, and susceptible to identifying with their clients (Farber, 1983, p. 4). For each of them, one or more of the cornerstones of burnout have been laid (p. 6):

1. *role ambiguity:* a lack of clarity concerning rights, responsibilities, methods, goals, status, and accountability to themselves or their institutions
2. *role conflict:* demands placed on them that are incompatible, inconsistent, and inappropriate with values and ethics
3. *role overload:* the quantity and quality of demands placed on them have become too great
4. *inconsequentiality:* a feeling on their part that no matter how hard they work, the outcome means little in terms of recognition, accomplishment, appreciation, or success.

They have, for a multiplicity of reasons, gotten cognitively, affectively, behaviorally, and physically into psychological hot water (Watkins, 1983; Patrick, 1979). They are ineffective for their clients, their organizations, their associates, their families, and, most of all, for themselves. Yet dedication and commitment exist in all varieties of jobs. What makes the human service professional different from other professionals? Certainly the possibility of burnout exists in every high-pressure job.

Professional Reality

First of all, in the generic occupation of human service work, what is presented in graduate school and what the neophyte human service worker finds in reality are often radically different (Warnath & Shelton, 1976). Students have the advantage of being assigned only a few clients in a practicum. There are no quotas to meet. There are no worries about dozens of other clients desperately in need of service. The open-ended relationships that are taught by idealistic, "the-way-it-ought-to-be" professors allow for leisurely intellectual debate on problem resolution, as opposed to the "Dodge City on Saturday night" approach that occurs in most crisis centers. The reality of institutions is that they must show production. Whether that production is measured in terms of quantity of bed linen laundered or numbers of case files opened, funding rests on the ability of the human service organization to be accountable. For the beginning human service worker, the pressure to complete and close cases rapidly becomes apparent.

Another grim reality that quickly confronts workers on entry into the field is both their own and their clients' limited degrees of freedom. The nice, neat, ribbon-wrapped solutions given by their professors soon pale before the powerlessness they feel when confronted with a morass of agency policies and institutional expectations that may have little to do with personal needs of client or worker (Warnath & Shelton, 1976).

The steady, sequential, and developmental approaches taught in graduate school quickly fall by the wayside when the worker is faced with a client who is out of control, paralyzed, and in a state of disequilibrium. The problem is further compounded when the beginning worker becomes involved in phone counseling. With no facial or other physical cues to guide responses, generally no tracking mechanisms to gain feedback on attempts to resolve problems, and the inevitable graveyard shifts, a crisis line worker quickly becomes a candidate for burnout (Baron & Cohen, 1982). What these realities point to is that burnout is not an individual fault or defect, but rather a phenomenon that should be seen as specific to a profession (Savicki & Cooley, 1982). The nature of the profession of human service work in general and the more specific area of crisis intervention necessitates an understanding of the etiology of burnout as it occurs in the human service worker.

Assumptions

Carroll and White (1982, p. 45) have listed a number of assumptions that describe the dynamics of burnout:

1. All stressors can help lead to burnout.
2. Burnout is psychobiological.
3. Environmental factors other than work can be contributors.
4. A lack of effective interpersonal relationships exists.
5. Signs of burnout will occur, but recognition of them depends on the astuteness of the observer.
6. Symptoms sometimes appear fast, but most usually occur over time.
7. Burnout is process rather than event oriented.
8. Burnout varies in severity from mild energy loss to death.
9. Burnout will also vary in duration.
10. Burnout and resulting crisis may occur more than once.
11. Awareness varies from complete denial to full consciousness of the problem.

12. Burnout is infectious in that it puts additional stress on other workers.
13. Burnout is most severe among professionals who give care to emotionally distressed, indigent clients.
14. An organization is burned out when stress and frustration of the workers become so bad that they cannot get the job done.
15. Restorative and preventive measures have to be individually tailored because of the idiosyncratic nature of burnout.
16. No known personality trait or personality configuration in and of itself will cause burnout.
17. Burnout is not a disease and the medical model is not an appropriate analytical model.
18. Burnout should not be confused with malingering.
19. Burnout may lead to personal and professional growth as well as despair and trauma.

Myths

Typically, candidates for burnout and crisis believe a number of myths about themselves. These irrational statements are adapted from Albert Ellis's list of 11 insane thoughts people say to themselves (Patterson, 1980, pp. 68–70):

1. My job is my life, which means long hours, no leisure time, and difficulty delegating authority. Anxiety, defensiveness, anger, and frustration are the result when things do not go perfectly.

2. I must be totally competent, knowledgeable, and able to help everyone. Unrealistic expectations of performance, a need to prove myself, lack of confidence, and overriding guilt occur when I am not.

3. To accomplish my job and maintain my own sense of self-worth, I must be liked and approved of by everyone with whom I work. Thus, I cannot assert myself, set limits, say no, disagree with others, or give negative feedback. Therefore, I get manipulated by others in my work setting—including clients. Self-doubt, passive hostility, insecurity, and subsequently depression are the reward.

4. Other people are hardheaded and difficult to deal with, do not understand the real value of my work, and should be more supportive. Stereotyping and generalizing about specific problems and people occur and lack of creativity, wasted energy, and decreased motivation result. There is a defeatist attitude and a passive acceptance of the status quo.

5. Any negative feedback indicates there is something wrong with what I do. I cannot evaluate my work realistically and make constructive changes. There is a great deal of anger with critics, which may manifest itself in either passive or aggressive hostility, depending on the person toward whom the anger is directed. Frustration and immobilization are the outcomes.

6. Because of past blunders and failures, things will not work the way they must. Old programs are not carried to fruition, nor are new ones created. Stagnation and decay in the work setting are the result.

7. Things have to work out the way I want. Extra hours, checking up on staff members' work, inability to compromise or delegate, overattention to detail, repetition of tasks, impatience with others, and an authoritarian style characterize behavior.

Multiple Dimensions

Burnout is a multidimensional phenomenon, consisting of behavioral, physical, interpersonal, and attitudinal components. Behaviorally, it appears as a marked departure from the worker's former behavioral norm (Forney, Wallace-Schutzman, & Wiggers, 1982). Physically, human service workers wear out because of the extraordinary demands placed on their mental and physical resources, and they are drained below their former level of optimal and capable performance (Eastman, 1981; Hall, Gardner, Perl, Stickney, & Pfefferbaum, 1979). Interpersonally, burnout pervades the worker's life, not only on the job site but also in his or her other relationships and environments as well (Watkins, 1983). Attitudinally, burnout represents a significant loss of commitment and moral purpose to one's work (Cherniss & Krantz, 1983).

Symptoms of burnout. The symptoms of burnout when collated appear as all the evils of Pandora's box let loose. We have set them in a format for ready reference and gleaned them from a variety of sources. Undoubtedly they are not all encompassing. Certainly not all human service workers in crisis manifest all the symptoms listed. Yet, for the watchful observer, many will become noticeable, particularly if one looks back in time and ascertains if there have been any pronounced changes in the worker in regard to the presence or absence of the following physical, behavioral, interpersonal, and attitudinal descriptors of burnout. Table 12-1, in no particular order, typifies what we have found.

Levels of burnout. Burnout can be categorized by three levels: trait, state, and activity (Forney, Wallace-Schutzman, & Wiggers, 1982). At a trait level, it is all pervasive, encompassing every facet of the worker's life. The worker is completely nonfunctional in regard to person, place, and time. Trait level of burnout is extremely serious and calls for immediate intervention in the worker's life.

At a state level, burnout may be periodic or situational. A classic example is what occurs during the period of full moon at a crisis line center. At such times it seems as if every crisis-prone person in town took a signal from a lunar clock to go beserk. Although problematic, such crisis situations are relieved when the moon wanes, and the crisis line worker returns to some semblance of normalcy. However, over the long term, such state events contribute mightily to anticipatory anxiety, which, if not dealt with, can precipitate total burnout.

Finally, burnout may be activity based. Any activity that is performed over

Table 12-1. Symptoms of Burnout

Behavioral	Physical	Interpersonal	Attitudinal
Reduced quantity or efficiency of work	Chronic fatigue	Withdrawal from family	Depression
Use and abuse of alcohol and illicit drugs	Lower resistance	Compulsion to do all and be all at home	Feeling of emptiness
Increase in absenteeism	Maladies occurring at organ weak points	No mature interactions—keeping hidden agendas	Ranging from omnipotence to incompetence
Increase in risk taking	Colds and viral infections	Keeping everyone subservient	Cynicism
Increase in medication	Migraine	Feeling drawn to people less secure	Paranoia
Clock watching	Poor coordination	Reduction of significant others to status of clients	Compulsiveness and obsessiveness
Complaining	Ulcers	Breaking up of long-lasting relationships	Callousness
Changing or quitting the job	Insomnia, nightmares, excessive sleeping	Becoming therapeutically minded and overreacting to comments of friends	Guilt
Inability to cope with minor problems	Gastrointestinal disorders	No separation of professional and social life	Boredom
Lack of creativity	Facial tics		Helplessness
Loss of enjoyment	Muscular tension		Terrifying and paralyzing feelings and thoughts
Loss of control	Addiction to alcohol and/or drugs		Stereotyping
Tardiness	Increased use of tobacco and caffeine		Depersonalizing
Dread of work	Over- and under-eating		Pessimism
			Air of righteousness
			Grandiosity

and over at an intense level, as in encounter group counseling of substance abusers or serving as a chaplain to the grief stricken in a trauma center, will invariably wear the armor off the most emotionally bullet-proof crisis worker. A simple way of decreasing chances of burnout when the stressor is activity based is to change the routine. However, such change is not always easily accomplished or even recognized as needed.

Stages of burnout. Another way of characterizing the road to burnout is by stages. Edelwich and Brodsky (1982, pp. 135–136) have delineated four stages through which the typical candidate for burnout goes.

Stage 1: enthusiasm. The worker enters the job situation with high hopes and unrealistic expectations. As bright and shining as the worker's potential appears, if such idealism is not tempered by orientation and training programs that define what the worker can reasonably expect to accomplish,

Table 12-1. (continued)

Behavioral	Physical	Interpersonal	Attitudinal
Vacillation between extremes of overinvolvement and detachment Mechanistic responding	Hyperactivity Sudden weight gain or loss Flare-ups in pre-existing medical conditions: high blood pressure, asthma, diabetes, etc. Injury from high-risk behavior Missed menstrual cycle Increased pre-menstrual tension	Allowing clients to abuse privacy of home by calls or visits at any time No opportunity for or enjoyment in just being one's self Loneliness Loss of authenticity Loss of ability to relate even to clients Avoidance of close interpersonal contact Switch from open and accepting to closed and denying Inability to cope with minor interpersonal problems Isolation from or overbonding with staff Increased expression of anger and mistrust	Sick humor, particularly aimed at clients Distrust of management, supervisors, and peers Hypercritical attitude toward institution and co-workers

such a rose-colored view of human service work will inevitably lead to the stage of stagnation.

Stage 2: stagnation. Stagnation occurs when the worker starts to feel that personal, financial, and career needs are not being met. Awareness may come from seeing individuals perceived as less able moving up the career ladder faster, pressures from home to meet increased financial obligations, and lack of personal intrinsic reinforcement for doing the job well. Astute management policy will head off stagnation by providing clear access up the career ladder, higher pay commensurate with increased job responsibilities, reduced overtime, and a variety of other incentives that clearly say to the worker, "You're doing a good job here, you're moving up in the organization, and we appreciate it." If intrinsic and extrinsic reinforcement does not occur, the worker will move into the next stage, frustration.

Stage 3: frustration. Frustration clearly indicates that the worker is in trouble. The worker starts questioning the effectiveness, value, and impact of his or her efforts in the face of ever-mounting obstacles. Since the effects of burnout are highly contagious in the organizational setting, one person's frustration is likely to have a domino effect on others. Direct confrontation is necessary at this stage. One appropriate way of meeting frustration is to confront the problem head on by arranging workshops or support groups to increase awareness of the burnout syndrome and generate problem solving as a group. Workshops and support groups can make constructive use of discontent by bringing about changes within both the institution and the individual. Catching the problem at this stage may well lead back to a more tempered stage of enthusiasm. If the problem is not resolved, then the final stage, apathy, is reached.

Stage 4: apathy. Apathy is burnout. It is a chronic indifference to the situation and defies most efforts at intervention. Apathy is truly a crisis stage: the individual is in a state of disequilibrium and immobility. Further compounding this stage are denial and little objective understanding of what is occurring. At this point psychotherapy is almost mandatory if reversal is to take place.

Worker/Client Relationships

Maslach (1982, pp. 36–37) has stated that the only human service workers who burn out are the ones who are on fire. What Maslach is implying seems to fit well with the intense heat of the helping relationship. Between a very real dedicatory ethic and at times an insatiable need to assist everyone with any type of problem, the idealistic human service worker sees his or her job as a calling. In an imperfect world, such an idealistic outlook can lead to overinvolvement and identification with the client—often to the detriment of the worker (Pines & Kafry, 1978).

As the human service worker becomes more deeply enmeshed in the helping relationship, it becomes harder and harder to say no to the demands of the client because of the worker's strong need to be accepted and liked. At this point, the worker has started to take on responsibility for the client. The worker's overinvolvement with the client may be manifested in a variety of ways. Extending the session beyond its usual time limit, taking and responding to phone calls at home at all hours of the night, experiencing hurt feelings over client failures, attempting dramatic cures on impossible cases, becoming panic stricken when well-laid plans go awry, refusing to withdraw from the case when it is clearly beyond the worker's purview, and losing one's sense of humor over the human dilemma are some of the many indicators that the worker is not paying attention to his or her own needs or, frankly, to the client's (Van Auken, 1979).

Worker/client interactions have an exacerbating effect on burnout because of the perceived nonreciprocal relationship between the two. From the worker's side, the relationship is characterized by giving, supporting, listening, emphasizing—all of which require a great deal of investment and generally garner little positive feedback or even acknowledgment from the client. On the client's part, a great deal of defensiveness, sympathy eliciting, conflicted, angry feelings, and other inappropriate behaviors mark the relationship. Such attitudes and behaviors are particularly likely if the client has been forced to enter therapy (Savicki & Cooley, 1982). Initially, and perhaps into the foreseeable future, little positive interaction between worker and client occurs (Maslach, 1978).

Under these circumstances the helping relationship quickly comes to be seen by the worker as a chore, and the client may regress and act out as a way of announcing the client's awareness of the worker's apathetic attitude. As this psychological vortex continues, and the worker becomes even more overwrought and discouraged, termination of the therapeutic relationship by the client is the likely result (Watkins, 1983). Such negative reinforcement does little to mollify the worker's already bruised ego and leads further to a downward spiral into crisis. Faced with failure and mounting pressure to succeed, the worker is more and more likely to start taking on ownership of the client's problems.

Countertransference. At times emotional aspects of the client may agitate feelings, thoughts, and behaviors that are deeply buried within the worker's own personality. When confronted with their own shortcomings, fears, faults, prejudices, and stereotypes as mirrored by the client, human service workers may begin behaving in inappropriate ways. Workers may act in ways designed to meet their own needs and not the clients'. The result is that clients are made to fit neatly into the workers' preconceived patterns for the way things ought to be (Freudenberger, 1977).

This phenomenon goes under many names, including countertransference, shadowing, and reciprocal impact. Whatever the name, the result is the same: the worker finds it increasingly harder to cope with the client's problems (Forney, Wallace-Schutzman, & Wiggers, 1982). Compensatory measures range from "working harder" to doing everything in one's power to get rid of the client. The end point is that clients continue to make little, if any, progress, and the circular nature of stress makes the situation worse. Particularly hot, emotion-laden material such as physical and sexual abuse of children, terminal illnesses, and chronic, suicidal ideation are prime examples of content that may be exceedingly stressful to the worker because of strong feelings and experiences the worker may have about the problem (Daley, 1979). If the phenomenon of countertransference is not recognized and dealt with in positive ways, the human service worker ends up feeling guilty about having negative feelings toward the client and is not even sure why those feelings are occurring. Such feelings are antithetical to what the worker has been taught and put significant stresses on the worker.

Stress.   Stress in the helping relationship is inevitable; otherwise the relationship would not be therapeutic. However, under the best of conditions therapy can be a draining emotional experience for both the worker and the client (Mitchell, 1977, pp. 143–146). All too often, little success is experienced and stress is increased, not only for the client but also for the worker (Pines & Maslach, 1978). When done for long time periods without a break, such work can become self-consuming for the human service worker, and continued direct contact with clients can lead to dehumanizing them as mere computer numbers on the case roll (Spicuzza & Devoe, 1982).

Compounding this problem is the fact that a large caseload may erect significant barriers to creatively helping and providing individualized, indepth attention to each client. The human service worker who operates on a mass-production, assembly-line program receives little intrinsic reinforcement. Particularly in agency work, paperwork demands and accountability procedures may be seen as so much bureaucratic red tape designed to hinder, rather than aid, the worker and client. The result is that the agency's rules and regulations are seen as an affront to the professionalism and integrity of the worker (Maslach & Pines, 1977). Indeed, there must be some respite from the emotional highs and lows that characterize helping relationships. If there is not, the work begins to take on a dull, meaningless cast, having few intrinsic payoffs for the worker, and can quickly start to lead down the road to burnout and crisis (Watkins, 1983).

Culpability of Organizations

Much of the responsibility for burnout rests with the employing agency and its inability either to recognize or to do anything about organizational problems that lead to burnout (Shinn & Mørch, 1983, p. 238). Savicki and Cooley (1987) compared degree of burnout with work environment and found that those workers who scored highest on burnout indexes felt that they had little impact on procedural and policy issues, lacked autonomy within the guidelines of the job structure, were unclear about agency objectives, had a high intensity of work assignments over extended periods of time, were highly restricted in how they could deal with clients, and felt generally unappreciated by their co-workers or supervisors. These findings should not be construed as representing "gripes" of the respondents. Numerous other studies (Barad, 1979; Maslach & Pines, 1977; Pines & Kafry, 1978; Pines & Maslach, 1978) have substantiated findings that agencies that do not take pains to communicate clearly with and support their staff have high burnout rates.

In contrast, those agencies that did allow input into the mission of the organization, were flexible in providing instrumental and emotional support to workers, and had support groups to help workers solve problems associated with the high stress of their jobs had workers with lower indexes of burnout (Savicki & Cooley, 1987). These findings are also consistent with those of other studies (Barad, 1979; Pines & Kafry, 1978; Shinn & Mørch, 1983), which found equitable and supportive agency policies and practices to be one of the main determiners of whether there would be significant burnout of staff.

Private Practitioners

Agency workers do not have a corner on the market of feelings of inadequacy when it comes to worker/client relationships. The same is true of the private practitioner, only probably to greater degrees. The human service worker in private practice does not have to deal with the many institutional problems that assail agency workers. Yet the private practitioner has the potential for even greater problems with respect to the helping relationship. Too many cases that become too complicated, with few referral resources, can cause extreme isolation for the private practitioner. Although the aloneness that pervades a private practice is not the same as the isolation that agency workers sometimes impose on themselves when placed in high-stress situations, it can be more complete. Fenced off from other professionals by ethical and ecological boundaries, the private practitioner has few others with whom to discuss client problems. More important, there are few other individuals with whom they will discuss their own personal problems.

There is a variety of reasons for this state of affairs. First, so little is said about burnout that practitioners often attribute their experience to personal inadequacy (Maslach, 1982, p. 37). Second, such persons typically see themselves as sociable, talented, responsive, frenetic, and high achievers (Freudenberger, 1982, p. 178). In no way, shape, or form is such an individual likely to feel secure enough to own the fact that all is not going well in his or her professional or personal life. Third, given such a personality, human service practitioners tend to invest a great deal in the job as a means of finding a sense of fulfillment and identity. Competition and achievement serve as guiding values, which are highly correlative with the need to be seen as worthy and capable (Freudenberger, 1982, p. 178).

Private practice is clearly a business. As such, it promotes the continuing fear that there will be no clients or that there will never be enough no matter how successfully the business is going (Mitchell, 1977, pp. 145–146). Every client termination raises questions: "Will there be someone to take her place?" "Will he pass the word along that I did him some good?" The private practitioner who is moving toward crisis invariably answers these questions negatively and redoubles his or her efforts to increase client loads and effect cures.

Starting and maintaining a private practice also call for maintaining a public presence. Whether such a presence involves making speeches to the Rotary Club on stress and the businessperson, consultation with the oncology staff on death and dying at the local hospital, or giving a workshop on discipline for Parents Without Partners, the continuous pressure of need to be seen as active, abreast of current developments, and visible are part of the sales program that must constantly be maintained and upgraded.

Although the private practitioner is his or her own boss, being an independent businessperson also means being completely responsible for maintaining the practice. Long hours and difficult work periods are the rule rather than the exception. Because most clients work regular hours, private practitioners devote many evenings and weekends to their work. Usually there is no one to pick up caseloads, so vacations or even short respites are few and far between. The practitioner is caught in a double bind. First, lack of feeling in control is clearly associated with burnout (Freudenberger, 1977). Secondly, while continuously exerting and extending control, the private practitioner becomes extruded beyond all possible legitimate parameters of coping. The result is that the more the practitioner attempts to control the situation, the more out of control the situation is perceived and comes to be.

Self-Recognition of Burnout

Whatever the degree of burnout, human service workers and their organizations have a notorious blind spot. What they can detect in others and change by therapeutic intervention, they are generally unaware of in themselves. Further, they have extreme difficulty maintaining both the personal and professional objectivity to self-diagnose burnout or foster the discipline and devote the energy to integrate effective intervention strategies into their own lives (Spicuzza & Devoe, 1982). What is problematic about burnout is that its symptoms and causes are neither universal nor specific in nature (Forney, Wallace-Schutzman, & Wiggers, 1982). Recognizing burnout is not always easy. In a medical analogy, its presenting symptoms might look like anything from typhoid fever to a broken leg.

Nevertheless, whereas no formula can be applied to diagnose its onset or to treat it, the affliction does not have to be terminal (Forney, Wallace-Schutzman, & Wiggers, 1982). Indeed, given the variety of symptoms and dynamics presented, both preventive and curative measures can be taken. Before we delve into intervention, we want to be very clear that we agree with Watkins (1983) that no one, and we would go a step further and state that *absolutely* no one, who practices in the human service professions is immune to burnout. It is a dangerous malady that in its extremes can be vocationally or even physically lethal if not dealt with in assertive ways.

Further, it has been our experience that human service workers, like some of you who are reading this passage and are saying, "It'll never happen to me," are invariably the kinds of fellow professionals we end up treating. Or, in absence of treatment, become those who can no longer stand to ply the trade and quit. Or, at the extreme, become substance abusers or suicidal. In these circumstances, the outcomes range from bad to worse. Bad for the profession and worse for you, the professional. So read this chapter as if it applied to you, because it does!

INTERVENTION STRATEGIES

The six-step model of crisis intervention described in Chapter 2 provides the essential guidelines for helping human service workers who find themselves frozen in the emotional state known as burnout. Emphasis in the application of the six-step method will usually focus on the directive end of the continuum. Even though human service workers, who are themselves clients suffering from burnout, normally have an excellent knowledge of helping skills, they are likely to be blind to using the skills they know to get themselves out of the predicament. Therefore, the crisis interventionist who helps a burned out human service worker will have to proceed in a very directive manner while confronting the client's irrational beliefs, proposing definite alternatives, and getting the client to commit to specific action steps that will get the person out of the state of immobility.

The human service worker in burnout may not be the only entity that is incapacitated. The agency or organization as well may be vulnerable. Therefore, the intervention strategies may be as appropriate for use with the system as they are for helping the person. Whether the focus is on the person in burnout or on the system, the application of strategies in this chapter is based on a very directive, positive, and assertive use of the six-step model.

Assessment

Two instruments are important in determining burnout. The Maslach Burnout Inventory (Maslach & Jackson, 1981a) measures three symptom patterns associated with burnout. The Emotional Exhaustion scale assesses feelings of being emotionally worn out by work. The Personal Accomplishment scale measures feelings of competence and achievement with work. The Depersonalization scale measures unfeeling and impersonal responses toward clients. The scales may also be combined to produce a total frequency and intensity score for burnout.

The Work Environment Scale (Moos, 1981) measures ten different dimensions of an organizational component named *social climate*. Scales range across job commitment, support from co-workers and management, independence in decision making, efficient and planful approaches to tasks, performance pressure, role clarity, degree of control by management, variety and change in job, and physical comfort. Taken together, these two instruments provide a way of examining the degree of burnout in relation to environmental factors within the organization that may contribute to it (Savicki & Cooley, 1987). Combining these instruments with symptomology of burnout previously presented will yield a fairly comprehensive picture of how burned out the worker is and will dictate the degree of intervention necessary.

Counseling intervention for the human service worker suffering from burnout may best be considered in three distinct parts: intervention through training, intervention with the organization, and intervention with the individual. This threefold approach makes intervention for burnout unlike other forms of crisis that we have considered.

Intervention through Training

It would be a simple matter if all human service workers who are subject to burnout and crisis could be taught stress-management skills that would make them immune to the intolerable work conditions they sometimes face.

Whereas stress-reduction mechanisms are laudable and play an important part in reduction of burnout, stress-reduction techniques alone are hardly sufficient. Such an approach isolates only the work load. It does not consider a variety of other equal and contributing problems. Unresolved personal issues, organizational problems, and conditions outside the work setting are key components of the problem. Stress-reduction techniques as such deal with one symptom and are not, in and of themselves, preventive.

Early on in a human service worker's training, and on an ongoing basis when in practice, emphasis needs to be placed on the worker's attitudes of overinvolvement. At least a part of training should focus on increasing therapeutic detachment and moderating idealism (Warnath & Shelton, 1976). Beginning human service practitioners need to have their rose-colored glasses gently removed so they can see that their good intentions are doing neither themselves nor their clients much good. Most particularly, while in training, beginners need to examine thoroughly their limited insight into their own unresolved issues and conflicts. Otherwise, such issues and conflicts may become a major source of stress for human service workers once they have begun practice. Carroll and White (1982, p. 49) have criticized training programs for this and other inadequacies that turn out technicians who are specialized in one narrow field of the helping service professions but have serious deficits in the broad array of skills needed to function effectively and have not clearly identified significant, unresolved conflicts in their own lives. If such issues are not dealt with early on in training, the ugly dividends are likely to be returned multifold at some point on the job.

One of the best ways to avoid those results is to train workers in some of the principles that Kell and Mueller (1966) promote concerning the reciprocal impact of the therapeutic relationship. Gaining increased insight into one's own impact on the relationship and how the client's impact affects the worker's view of self and subsequent behavior can assist the worker in endeavors both within and outside the counseling relationship (Watkins, 1983). The idea of detached concern that manifests itself in basic therapeutic skills of empathy, unconditional positive regard, caring, and congruence reflects an optimal balance between overinvolvement and depersonalization. However, to get that job done and avoid traumatic problems is quite another matter, one that requires the worker to be ever vigilant toward the subtle nuances of the therapeutic moment, which can all too quickly escalate into a full-scale crisis for both client and worker.

Intervention with the Organization

The organization may also be considered as client. When an organization is in danger of burnout, it is not just one individual but all those who work in the organization who should be involved in restructuring working conditions. Indeed, one of the major criticisms of burnout intervention has been the lack of change in the total system (Carroll & White, 1982, p. 56). Particularly in human service work, failures are frequently observable and there is no clear way to define success (Daley, 1979). Further, any positive impact that the worker has on the environment receives little recognition (Freudenberger, 1977). Lack of positive reinforcement by the institution is not at all uncommon and fits neatly into an aversive management policy: "There is no such thing as burnout, only staff who don't work and have malicious motives toward the organization." As staff become increasingly burned out, they tend to fulfill management's negative predictions about them (Carroll & White, 1982, pp. 53–54).

Therefore, from an ecological standpoint, the organization needs to move away from piecemeal interventions and apply techniques that have general inputs to the total organization rather than just inputs focused on individuals (Paine, 1982, p. 25). Ideally, interventions should be multifaceted and take into consideration both individual and environmental issues in a balanced and sensitive fashion (Carroll & White, 1982, p. 53).

When the total organization is burned out, Freudenberger (1975) suggests shutting it down for a period of time. At the least, shutting down gives staff a bit of breathing room. However, this approach is generally not enough if it involves only changing the office decor, having an office party, or having a one-shot in-service training program, because no lasting change takes place. Short of closing down, which is probably a pragmatic impossibility, the organization has a number of options.

As a start, the administration can take the time to articulate clearly the mission of the organization. Cherniss and Krantz (1983) found that organizations that have a clear ideology of purpose have reduced burnout in staff because they minimize ambiguity and doubt about what kind of action is to be taken. Time should be devoted both to establishing positive co-worker and supervisory relationships and to reducing the rules, regulations, and paper blizzard that line staff face as they attempt to provide service to their clients (Savicki & Cooley, 1987). Improvement of job design, flexible hours, continuous supervision and training, intrinsic and extrinsic reinforcement, and emotional support are a few of many changes that will go a long way toward reducing burnout (Shinn & Mørch, 1983, p. 238)

Social support systems. Social support systems are critical to avoiding burnout, whether they be at home or in the workplace. Support systems act as buffers for the individual and help maintain psychological and physical well-being over time (Pines, 1983, p. 157). However, in the human service business, support systems are hard to establish because of chaotic work schedules that militate heavily against strong social ties (Farber, 1983, pp. 16–17) and allow workers little time to enjoy positive interaction with one another because the focus is constantly on trying to solve client problems (Maslach, 1978). Although it is easy to give lip service to having adequate supports, when workers are experiencing stress they cannot or do not make the effort to discriminate the various functions a support system can serve and are left with a vague feeling that they are not getting what they need, but are not quite sure what "that" is (Pines, 1983, p. 172).

Social support systems have six basic support functions: listening, technical support, technical challenge, emotional support, emotional challenge, and sharing social reality (Pines, 1983).

Listening. Periodically, all workers need someone to listen actively to them in an empathic manner without giving advice or making judgments (p. 158).

Technical support. When confronted with complex client problems, all workers need someone who can affirm confidence in their endeavors. Such a person must have the expertise to understand the complexities of the job and be able to give the worker honest feedback (p. 158).

Technical challenge. If workers are not intellectually challenged, they will stagnate. Intellectual contact with significant others stretches the worker in a positive way. Such challenges can come only from people who do not intend to humiliate or gain an advantage and who have professional expertise equivalent to that of the worker (p. 158).

Emotional support. Workers need someone to be on their side in difficult situations, even if the significant others do not necessarily agree totally with the workers. Professional expertise is not necessary for this function (pp. 158–159).

Emotional challenge. It is comforting for workers to believe that they have explored all avenues in attempting to resolve their problems. Support persons serve a valuable function when they question such assumptions and confront the worker's excuses. This function should be used sparingly, otherwise it may be construed as nagging (p. 159).

Sharing social reality. When workers become unsure of the reliability of their own perceptions about the reality of the situation, they need external validation. This function is especially important when workers feel that they are losing the ability to evaluate what is happening with their clients and with the organization (p. 159).

Although Maslach and Jackson (1981b) found that the support system of a spouse makes married workers less prone to burnout than their unmarried colleagues, it is impossible for one's spouse or close friend to fulfill all these tasks (Pines, 1983, p. 172). Clearly, the worker needs to have functioning support systems at the job site. How, then, might this occur if it does not happen spontaneously?

Support groups. Within the organizational structure, time should be set aside for formal, structured support groups. Structurally, a support group resembles a problem-solving discussion group. The goal of such a group is to build a sense of competence and help workers feel that they can deal with the stresses they encounter in their work situation. A support group is a safe place for workers to disagree and challenge feelings of helplessness. The group serves as a cathartic agent for releasing pent-up emotions related to the job. Once catharsis occurs, members can realistically examine feelings associated with job stressors. By providing feedback, the support group validates for members that they are not alone in their feelings and reassures them that they are not abnormal in their response to the situation (Sculley, 1983, pp. 188–191).

The immediate goal for support groups is solving problems that lead to stress and burnout. Discussion of personal issues outside the work setting violates the goal of creating staff effectiveness because it increases the vulnerability of the members. To attempt to turn the group into one that deals with personality deficits would shift the group to the realm of therapy, and workers would leave feeling less competent rather than strengthened by the experience (Sculley, 1983, p. 189). However, having norms that permit talking about stressful events, feelings of fallibility, anger, guilt, and depression and making suggestions to improve group functioning through problem solving and application of the criteria previously listed by Pines (1983) are priority issues for the group.

To do this effectively, a support group not only needs the support of the administration but also must have a consultant/facilitator who is sensitive to the issues involved and can walk a tightwire between allowing the group to vent feelings and keeping the group in a problem-solving mode. The consultant/facilitator also needs to be in a position to provide the administration with information from the group that will allow for effective organizational change without becoming a "snitch" in the process (Sculley, 1983, pp. 193–194). Sculley (1983, p. 190) lists the differences between therapy and support groups.

Table 12-2. Differences between Therapy and Support Groups

	Therapy	**Support**
Goal	Personality change	Staff effectiveness
Method	Interpretation	Problem solving
Clients	Patients	Professionals
Content	Intrapsychic	Work problems
Leader	Therapist	Consultant

Workshops on burnout.   For a deeper level of intervention, we would propose institution of workshops that deal with burnout of the organization, with everybody in attendance, particularly administrative heads. The involvement of administration is critical at this juncture. If workers do not have confidence that organizational leadership is concerned, and believe that no open lines of communication to their administrative supervisors are available, then little change is likely to result (Berkeley Planning Associates, 1977). Attendance of supervisors is crucial to ensure that everyone understands the sources of stress that occur in the work setting because the factors that cause burnout in administrators are very different from those for direct service staff (Savicki & Cooley, 1987). In particular, emphasis on the nature and quality of interpersonal relationships is a key component to ameliorating stress and burnout (Carroll & White, 1982, p. 50). We personally feel so strongly about the foregoing that we will not agree to do any workshops that propose organizational change unless all administrators agree to participate fully and for the duration of the workshop.

A comprehensive workshop should be designed to explore the individual symptoms of burnout, analyze personal, professional, and organizational sources of burnout, and culminate by forming personal contracts designed to counteract on-the-job disillusionment and stress (Baron & Cohen, 1982). Spicuzza and Devoe (1982) have proposed a mutual-aid group that would concentrate on cognitive strategies such as participant presentations, guest lectures, films, and reading assignments on causes of burnout, holistic health, alienation, isolation, organizational principles, and the art of effective management. Each of these strategies does help to raise cognitive awareness about burnout and what to do about it, but we believe that personal involvement is paramount. Therefore, we would propose that Baron and Cohen's (1982) initiating procedures be followed and combined with Spicuzza and Devoe's three-stage paradigm.

Stage 1. All participants complete Coffman and Katz's (1979) 32-item stress symptom questionnaire or the Maslach Burnout Scale (Maslach & Jackson, 1981a) and then score themselves. To ascertain the degree of culpability of the organization in causing burnout, the Work Environment Scale (Moos, 1981) should also be administered. Participants are then asked to write down what personal contributions to burnout they have engendered in themselves and others in the organization. These comments are collected anonymously and put down on newsprint. The total group then processes these ideas with a view toward problem resolution. Professional contributions to burnout— that is, the myths and fantasies that are fallaciously assumed to be true in the human service professions—receive the same treatment as personal contributions. Processing of myths about how human service workers must be omniscient and omnipotent demonstrate clearly how such myths can exert stress on the individual. Finally, in this opening stage, organizational factors that are contributors need to be examined in the same way. Within the realities of what may be done, environmental factors that make for a positive or negative work setting need to be carefully examined.

There is inherent risk in such groups, and although most human service workers would extol risk taking as a necessary component of the healing process, for them to engage in such behavior is quite another story. Taking a risk may be especially intimidating in a group composed of members of the same organization. In such instances self-disclosure may be seen as individual weakness and failure at the job. Another problem is fear of recrimination for saying things that could reflect negatively on co-workers. However, Spicuzza and Devoe (1982) maintain that risk taking is necessary if new ideas, new behaviors, and new and meaningful relationships are to be accomplished. To provide an atmosphere that is conducive to taking risks, we would propose that a group facilitator who is not a part of the organization be retained to lead the group.

An added caution is that this is essentially a problem-solving group. Therefore, although getting personal feelings out in the open is a vital component, this is not an encounter group, whose primary product is emotional catharsis. The leader should thus steer members' self-disclosure in a direction that profits both the organization and the individual.

Stage 2. At this point group members should feel safe enough to share some of their more deeply felt personal inadequacies in regard to their daily functioning. Relationships with clients, loss of empathy, guilt over therapeutic failures, absenteeism, drug and alcohol abuse, and family problems due to job stress are but a few of the many problems that may surface. Confidentiality and a no-recrimination clause are mandatory if the group is to make progress at this stage. It is extremely important that administrators understand and abide by these ground rules. As the group works its way through personal, professional, and organizational problems, members should gain increased understanding of themselves and their own situation within the organization. Under open and safe conditions, much of the mystique about burnout is removed. Members find they are not alone as others speak to the same kinds of problems. By cognitively and affectively understanding burnout, members obtain increased knowledge of alternatives to changing both themselves and the organization.

Stage 3. The group members are asked to write down and discuss the positive aspects of their work setting. By doing this, they gain a positive outlook, and the workshop does not degenerate into a gripe session. The third stage is behaviorally oriented; that is, members are asked to concentrate on development of skills and behavioral plans to disrupt the burnout syndrome. Lots of social reinforcement should be provided by the leader and other group members for individuals as they plan new and more effective coping behaviors. Typically, relaxation and assertiveness training, realistic goal planning, more effective time management, systematic reinforcement schedules, restructured organizational policies, role clarity, clearer channels of communication, job changes, time sharing, and alternative compensation procedures for case overloads and long hours are some of the contractual agreements that may come out of the program. Whatever agreements are reached, whether for the organization or for the individual, they should be put down on paper in contractual, performance terms. Regular follow-up on the progress of both organizational and individual performance contracts is vital if the procedure is to have lasting effects.

Although Spicuzza & Devoe and Baron & Cohen do not set a time limit on their programs, experience has taught us that such programs should be set up for approximately three half-day sessions and should be spread out over a period of three weeks. Adhering to this schedule gives participants time to digest material presented and also sustains interest for the return sessions. At the completion of the workshop, it may be suggested that support groups be formed to continue the work started. A program like this one should foster identification among members with regard to their shared problems and, over time, shape a positive environment that allows members to determine realistically what can be changed in their work environment (Savicki & Cooley, 1982).

Intervention with the Individual

Whereas workers who are at the frustration stage antecedent to burnout may well be helped by being involved in burnout groups, those at the more serious stage of apathy will not (Edelwich & Brodsky, 1982, p. 137). In such cases, individual counseling is more appropriate (Baron & Cohen, 1982). The following case illustrates many of the dynamics and intervention techniques that have been presented in this chapter. It should be clearly understood that neither symptoms nor intervention procedures are all inclusive. For example, Tubesing and Tubesing (1982, p. 161) have listed 36 possible intervention strategies that cover physical, intellectual, social, emotional, spiritual, and environmental components of burnout, and those are not comprehensive by any means. Each worker is idiosyncratic and will not have the same constellation of presenting problems. Further, workers may be at varying degrees of immobility and disequilibrium according to where they are in the apathy stage. Therefore, no two persons will be alike in resolution of the crisis. The case presented is that of a professional with many years of experience and a doctorate, but neophytes should understand that Dr. Jane Lee is genotypical of any human service worker. Her case clearly points out that no worker is immune to burnout, no matter how much experience or expertise that worker may have.

--------------------- *CASE OF DR. JANE LEE* ---------------------

Dr. Jane Lee is a striking, raven-haired 43-year-old woman with aquiline features, a low, melodious voice, aquamarine eyes that twinkle, and a smile that could serve as a toothpaste commercial. She is extremely witty and incisive of intellect, is widely read, and can talk as easily with truck drivers as she can with lawyers. At any social function people gravitate toward her. She seems to have been born with the natural empathy and easy familiarity that many people consciously work their whole life for, yet never quite obtain. Divorced for ten years, Jane has raised her only son and has been both mother and father to him while carrying on an exceedingly successful professional life.

Jane has a thriving practice in marriage and family therapy. She has a heavy client load and is clearing approximately $60,000 a year. She is seen by her peers as extremely capable, and her clients speak highly of her. Two of her areas of specialty are dealing with families who have suffered catastrophic illnesses and unraveling family dynamics of anorexics. Jane has been in private practice for eight years. Prior to entering private practice she worked in a community mental health facility. She was so skillful at therapy there that she rose to the directorship of the clinical program.

Jane graduated from a major university with a Ph.D. in counseling psychology and completed her internship in a VA hospital. She then successfully completed an American Association of Marriage and Family Therapists internship at a private clinic. She has written and published many articles on therapy for anorexics and the families of individuals suffering from catastrophic illnesses. She has also given many in-service programs and presentations at national human service conferences.

By any stretch of the imagination, Jane appears to be a highly competent, successful therapist and an exceptionally endowed woman overall. Her ability and demeanor have made her a role model that many women in her community aspire to emulate, not to mention some few men. As Jane sits down with the crisis worker, she is seriously considering driving her new Oldsmobile into a bridge abutment!

Jane: I came here today because of what you said to me the other night when we were having a drink. You pretty much have me pegged. I'm burned out even more than what you think, more than what I like to admit. Today I had a decision to make, whether to kill myself or come here. I came here but I'm not sure it's the right decision. If I killed myself it seems like it would just be over and done with. I've taken care of everything concerning Bobby, my son. He's practically through with college, and even though we're very close, I really think it'd be better for him if I were gone. He wouldn't have to put up with my lousy behavior, and believe me, it's lousy right now. There's enough insurance to get him finished up in school and he could sell the house. He's the only one that really matters besides my clients, and right now I'm not doing worth a damn with them. I'm probably hurting more than I help and I'm just not up to it any more, so much pain and so damn little I can do about it. The only thing I can think about now when I go into a cancer ward is how bad the patients smell. Whoever said, "You don't have to smell them, all you gotta do is help them!" sure wasn't in this end of the business. I'm also starting to behave like those screwed-up anorexics I work with, too. It's starting to seem pretty reasonable to me that they aren't eating. Why the hell should they? Why the hell should I? Just sort of fade away and look thin while you're doing it. At least I'd make a great-looking corpse. Anyway, the main reason I came over today was to see if you'd be willing to take my clients. I've thought this over and you've got what it takes. I think you could help them, and if you agree, I'll start talking to them about coming over to your practice.

CW: What you just said scares the living hell out of me. There's a part of me that wants to run right out of here because what you're saying is really hitting home with the way I feel at times. There's another part of me that wants to tie you up in log chains until you come to your senses. Finally, there's another part of me that cares for you so much that I'm angry that you've let yourself get into this predicament. Most of all, though, I'm glad I made that reflection the other night and it finally sank in. I've seen you going downhill for quite a while now. My guess is that you didn't even know it was happening or just laid another piece of armor plate over yourself and said something like, "I've got to gut this through, I can't let down, I just need to work harder," or some of that other irrational garbage I hear you unload on yourself. First of all, I won't even consider what you said about the clients until we agree on one thing and that is you don't do any harm to yourself until we talk this through. So I want an agreement both as your therapist and as your friend that we shake on that before anything else happens. I won't take no for an answer. If that's not acceptable, we'll negotiate it. No matter what, we're now in this together.

The crisis worker is in a difficult position as the client's friend, fellow professional, and now as a therapist dealing with another human being in crisis. Because the crisis worker knows the client, she feels free to make some initial owning statements that let the client know exactly how she feels about the situation without becoming sympathetic in the bargain, which she could easily do because she has felt much the same way at prior times in her professional life (countertransference).

The crisis worker also makes an initial assessment of the lethality level of the client. Her reflective statement to the client a few evenings earlier was not made for idle conversation. The crisis worker has seen a slow but steady change coming over Jane in the last three months, and as she thinks about it, she sees that it was coming a good while before that. Jane has been keeping a stiff upper lip, but there have been indicators that all has not been well lately. She has been rather cynical about clients, as evidenced by her comment about how they smell. She has been suffering a variety of physical maladies that have ranged from unending colds to some severe gastrointestinal problems ominous enough to indicate that surgery might be in the near future.

Her relationships with men have always been friendly, although at arm's length. However, in the past couple of social engagements that the crisis worker and Jane have attended, a pall of icy silence has hung in the air whenever a man was introduced to her. As the crisis worker continues to assess the situation, she further realizes that Jane has truncated relationships with most of her acquaintances and has done this lately with the crisis worker on at least two occasions. Their relationship has been characterized by an easy rivalry, good comradeship, and just generally a lot of good times together without ever engaging in one-upmanship.

Lately, though, the crisis worker has had the feeling that Jane has treated her more as a client than as a friend and has attributed some deeper psychological meaning to even the most innocent conversation. If Jane isn't doing that, she has been trying to direct the crisis worker in everything from approaches to clients to buying clothes. The crisis worker has had the uneasy feeling for quite a while that Jane was trying to remold her in ways to fit Jane's image of what she ought to be, and that is the exact opposite of how she would characterize their relationship over the years.

Finally, Jane's comments about getting things straightened out with her son and getting her professional affairs in order in regard to her clients lead the crisis worker to believe that Jane's lethality level is high and that she is serious about doing away with herself. The rather detached, mechanistic way that Jane has reported all this and her blank, hollow look are completely at odds with Jane's usual sparkle, which has been absent the past few months. Performing a quick synthesis of all this background data, what Jane is saying, and the depressed way she is looking and behaving, the crisis worker makes the assessment that Jane is not kidding about killing herself and that the threat must be taken seriously. The crisis worker immediately goes into a suicide prevention mode and seeks a commitment from the client not to do anything until they have talked. At the very least, the crisis worker has bought herself some time.

Jane has done one thing right. She has gone to a significant other and is using that trusted other to self-disclose in a very intimate way some of her most troubled feelings (Maslach, 1976; Watkins, 1983). The crisis worker can juxtapose her own positive outlook as a stabilizing influence against the jaundiced worldview that Jane currently has.

Jane: All right, I can agree to that. I know that's part of the procedure. Hell! I guess I knew you'd do that when I came in here. Maybe I'm only kidding myself about all this anyway, just a bit of the blues, feeling sorry for myself and all that crap.

CW: I'm glad you came here, for whatever reason, and I'm also glad you agree to our contract even though you know it's part of the program. I also don't believe that about having the blues, either. I think it's much more than that. I believe right now you're hurting quite a bit. I don't know why, I've got some ideas that I'd like to explore with you, but first I'd like to hear what you think and feel is going on in your life right now.

While the crisis worker is acknowledging her regard for Jane, she is also doing quite a bit more. First, she has made a decision that she is going to take a pretty directive stance with Jane for the time being. The worker balances between making emotional challenges to the client and listening closely and accurately to Jane's problems. She also knows that Jane is extremely astute at the business they are engaged in, as evidenced by her comment about the contract. She is not going to let Jane play the game ahead of her. Her analysis is that Jane is out of control right now. This is a tough decision for the crisis worker to make and is a crucial point in the assessment process. The crisis worker needs not only to respect and support the wisdom of the client's choices but also to perform a realistic assessment of the client's strengths and weaknesses (Tubesing & Tubesing, 1982, p. 160). Above all, the crisis worker needs to stay closely in touch with the client's needs in the present moment (Van Auken, 1979). The crisis worker is therefore going to take control of the situation and will not sit back in a passive mode.

Jane: I don't know. I've dealt with all kinds of problems in my life and right now there's nothing I can really put my finger on. In comparison to what is going on now, I can tell you that going through the divorce with Jeff, taking off on my own to finish up the doctorate, and fighting my way up the ladder in the agency and then finally making a decision to go out on my own while raising Bobby make what's happening to me now seem like peanuts.

CW: Right! Those were really tough times, and you went through those like Superwoman. But that was then, and we're right here, right now, and from the looks of it you don't much feel like you're Superwoman, or Supermouse even, and what's happening in your life surely isn't peanuts or we wouldn't be having this talk right now. So what do you feel like right now?

The crisis worker acknowledges how tough the client has been, but will not let her get stuck in the past. The crisis worker wants to find out what is happening right now. What is more important about this now than it was a year ago? Further, the crisis worker will not let the client denigrate the problem. It is interesting that if Jane were the counselor here, she would probably ferret out what she has just done, retreating into the past, in a second. The difference is that Jane has really become a client, and although she may endeavor to be her own therapist or perhaps even be critical of the crisis worker's attempts to do therapy, she is as blind to the way she talks, thinks, and behaves as any other client. Jane's being a therapist gives her no edge in dealing with her own problems. In fact, her own expertise may militate heavily against her.

Professionals of Jane's caliber don't come unglued. Or at least that's the irrational thought that goes through Jane's head. She must be capable at all times, otherwise who would want to come to her? Furthermore Jane has excellent insight into herself. It is inconceivable to her that something going on in her life could be causing her any emotional affliction without her really understanding what it was. Whether we construe this to be vanity or not, it is an all-too-common notion that professionals have about themselves.

Human service workers like Jane tend to be much like medical doctors who know full well the addictive qualities of morphine, yet believe that because they are M.D.s there is no way that the use of it will get out of control for them. Both Jane and the M.D.s wind up like any other person, and their astute insight and understanding of what happens to others does them little good in the end.

Jane: All I can tell you is I'm washed out. Some little things, really. Like I get dates and appointments all mixed up. Last week topped that all off. I saw 44 clients last week. I think I got about a dozen appointments mixed up. I had people piling in on top of people, and my appointment book was really screwed up. It was a madhouse, and some of the people got agitated. A couple wound up cussing me out, and I probably deserved it. Nothing like that ever happened before.

CW: Never?

Jane: Well, to a far lesser extent. I've been strung out before, but I could always get it straightened out.

CW: How?

Jane: About every three months things would start to get out of hand. I'd just sit back and say, "Janie, old girl, you've got to get out of here for a while." I'd just hop in the car and take off for a weekend in Chicago. Check into a hotel, take in a show, and eat some really special meals, and use about half the hotel's hot water washing the clients off of me. Seems like that would clear the cobwebs out of my head.

CW: When was the last time you did that?

Jane: (Wistfully.) About nine months ago.

CW: Why so long?

Jane: Well, I bought that new office and went in and remodeled the whole thing. I contracted a lot of the stuff, but spent a lot of time on it myself. I cut the contractor a deal. If I could work on it too, he'd reduce the price.

CW: So being the omnipotent individual you are, you threw out at least one thing that keeps you on an even keel. In fact, rather than getting away from the office, you've been spending almost all your time there. Let's see, we've got a couple of characters running around inside of Jane—Dr. Jane healer to the world and Jane the carpenter. Wonder who else is inside there?

The crisis worker is looking for a link between the past and the present. If Jane had some coping mechanisms in the past, what were they? What's different about the way she has coped in the past and what she is doing now? What the crisis worker is doing here is very different from letting the client just wallow in the past. She is specifically looking for coping mechanisms in the past that can be linked to the present and what is happening in the present to keep those coping mechanisms from being put into place. She is also beginning to build a character repertoire with Jane in the hope that Jane can start to see all the various aspects of herself that are now motivating her to do some of the things she does (Butts, 1986). To set the stage for the client's regaining control of her life, the crisis worker proposes a positive character in Jane.

CW: I also heard of a character that I'd call Janice. A person who knows when her stress bucket is full, and is practical and smart enough to get away from the crap that goes on at that office. Where have you stuck her?

Jane: Back up on the shelf with Janie?

CW: Who's Janie?

Jane: She's the gal who's a little crazy. Who can joke with her clients and get up in the middle of the night and go out and start seeding her lawn and sing Chuck Berry songs while she's doing it. (Embarrassed.) There's just no time for them right now. It's not just the new office, but I also needed another car, and since Bobby has changed schools there were a lot of added expenses in that. So I really needed to devote my time to building my caseload up to meet those financial obligations. If I can get through the next two years, I should have a lot of this behind me and can breathe easier.

CW: Well, I'm sure glad to hear you're planning on being around for the next two years, anyway. But that's not the question now, is it, because right now it sounds to me as if you're wrung out. You don't have any more energy to give, and you've set up on the wall a couple of people who are pretty important in recharging your batteries. Do you see how important they are and what it's cost you to do that?

The crisis worker is not yet making direct suggestions as to what Jane needs to do; however, she is hoping to raise Jane's consciousness to the fact that she has unconsciously changed her operating method. The crisis worker attempts to get her to recognize this by describing what these very positive characters have done for her and how there is a void in her life when they have been removed from it. By doing so, the crisis worker is attempting to marshal some very healthy defense mechanisms that have previously helped Jane cope well with the stressful life she leads.

Jane: I guess so, but I don't know how to get out of it.

CW: What will happen if you don't work on the office this next weekend?

Jane: The new plumbing isn't in. Clients wouldn't be able to use the bathroom. I'd also feel guilty for not working on it, the inconvenience and all.

CW: (Laughing.) Well, the first part of that problem is pretty easily handled. Call the porta-potty people. I can imagine a sign that says "The crap stops here" hanging from the door as clients walk in. (Jane starts to smile and giggle for the first time since walking in the door.) The other part of that is, who's the character laying a guilt trip on you? Tell me some more about her.

The crisis worker takes a little bit of a well-gauged risk here by injecting some humor into the situation. She does this because humor has been important in Jane's life, is helpful to her in coping, and turns her away from some of the cynicism she feels toward her clients and starts to allow her to laugh at herself a little. The value of well-placed humor cannot be overemphasized. Van Auken (1979) extols the injection of humor even into the most pathetic of situations. Getting a smile or a laugh from clients is a direct intrusion into the depressive thought processes and behaviors in which they are mired.

The crisis worker also starts to hammer a bit on Jane's guilt. Generally the crisis worker sees guilt as a pretty useless emotion, consumptive of energy that could be used in other, more positive ways. Guilt is invariably an emotion of the past, and whatever was done can never again be retrieved. It is one thing to learn from one's past mistakes and quite another to carry past, unfinished business into the present, particularly when one is feeling guilty about not measuring up.

Jane: That's MOTHER SUPERIOR. I get all kinds of lectures from her. (Bitterly.) She's just like Sister Angeline at St. Mary's, where I went to school. "Say your Hail Marys and Our Fathers, get your homework done, God doesn't like a shirker, watch how you dress, mind your manners, you're a young lady, ye reap what ye sow," ad nauseam. Jesus, I hated that!

CW: You hate it, but it sure sounds like you're living it. Small wonder you're feeling so lousy.

The crisis worker starts hooking up feelings with thoughts and actions. The response the crisis worker gets indicates that the burnout has spread out into the client's family life.

Jane: You know, I think that's why maybe Bobby and I are having problems right now. I really sound and act like a MOTHER SUPERIOR to him. Telling him what to do, always looking out for him. My Lord! He's 21 years old and I've started treating him like he was a 6-year-old. I haven't ever done that before. He's about like some of those clients I have to lead around by the nose.

CW: Did you hear what you just said? "He's about like some of those clients I lead around." First of all, I didn't know that was the business you were in. Sounds like Jane the handywoman. Fix 'em up the way you do your office. Second, I wonder how many people outside the office you've decided to fix up and look out for. I have to tell you that's one of the kinds of feelings I've had around you lately. Sure a lot different from how things have been in our relationship.

With this information, the client gives the crisis worker a chance to plunge into some core issues that have definable behavioral outcomes. By stating how she deals with Bobby, Jane is manifesting another of the typical signs of burnout: trying to treat significant others in her life as if they were in the therapeutic situation. Jane has fallen into a burnout trap of trying to be omnipotent by controlling other people in her environment (Van Auken, 1979). Paradoxically, she is hardly in control of herself. Her relationship with Bobby is problematic because one way of decreasing burnout is to have a satisfying family life, especially with one's children (Forney, Wallace-Schutzman, & Wiggers, 1982). Worse yet is that she has become autocratic in the therapeutic situation, so it is not surprising that a major component of her life that has been highly reinforcing to her is no longer so, and, in fact, has taken on some very negative connotations. The crisis worker lays that squarely on her. She is mixing up her characters and has replaced Dr. Jane with Jane the handywoman. This state of events is not so surprising since both characters are working in the same office. Jane needs a break in her day-to-day activities and needs to get away from the office to do it (Forney, Wallace-Schutzman, & Wiggers, 1982). Finally, the crisis worker relates and owns her own experience of having been treated the same way by Jane. She tries to make Jane aware that, like rings on a pond, the ripple effect from her burnout goes far beyond her immediate line of sight.

CW: Indeed, I wonder about your relationships other than those with Bobby, myself, and your clients. Anyone else you're trying to control right now?

Jane: (Frostily.) If you mean men, absolutely no, or anybody else, for that matter. When I get home at night, I'm so bushed all I want to do is fall asleep, but then all those clients go tumbling around in my head, and I start thinking about car payments, mortgage payments, how to straighten things out with Bobby, and I wind up getting about two or three hours of sleep a night.

CW: So right now you're so exhausted that you'd just rather be alone.

Jane: That's right, but I feel like I ought to be out mingling with people. I'm so damned isolated anyway.

CW: OK! I can understand that, and I'd agree with you, but let's look at right now. Seems as if you really need some time to just curl up in the fetal position, turn the electric blanket up to nine, and get your batteries recharged. Could you do that? I mean seriously, just go home and go to bed, take the phone off the hook, put the answering service on until Monday, and not get up for the whole weekend.

Jane: I suppose.

CW: No supposes. If you don't want to do that, we'll look at something else. But right now you look like the *Grapes of Wrath* and just seem to really need to rest before you think about doing anything else. Are you willing to call the contractor up and tell him you won't be there Saturday and Sunday without feeling guilty about it?

Jane: I could use the rest. All right! I'll give it this weekend.

CW: Fine. But there's one more thing. If you really get to feeling blue, plug the phone in and call me at home. I also want a report next week, so what time do you want to come in?

Jane: Sounds like I'm a client.

CW: Sounds like you're right. (Laughs.)

The crisis worker is basically assisting Jane to make a simple commitment to do one thing—get some rest. A critical component in treating burnout is revitalization (Tubesing & Tubesing, 1982, p. 160). Jane is physically fatigued, and the first order of business is to get her physical batteries recharged. A number of other options are available at this juncture, but the crisis worker follows Tubesing and Strosahl's (1976) advice to let the client make the choice of what treatment is appropriate. Keying on the client's own words about needing sleep, the crisis worker follows up and gains commitment to a specific behavior that the client will engage in over the short term. This is not a dramatic first step, but considering the least dramatic steps first is probably the way to go (Van Auken, 1979). The most important objective of this initial encounter is finding some short-term intervention techniques that the client is able and willing to utilize (Freudenberger & Robbins, 1979).

A particular behavior the crisis worker touches on is the use of the telephone. Private practitioners are notorious for taking phone calls from clients at all hours of the night and on weekends. Van Auken (1979) urges human service workers not to let clients run or, for that matter, ruin their personal lives. The crisis worker makes sure that Jane follows this dictum. Finally, the worker provides emotional support, but once Jane is able to ventilate her feelings, the worker is going to move into a problem-solving mode. Getting Jane out of the office and into bed is a first step in alleviating her burnout.

Next week.

Jane: I'll have to admit I do feel better. Couldn't sleep at all Friday night, but I got ten hours in Saturday. I can't believe it! I woke up and I was all curled up in the fetal position. The clients looked somewhat better this week. I can't say it was wonderful, but at least I wasn't an ogre to them. I guess what bothers me most about that is that I've lost all my creativity.

CW: OK! Let's talk about that a bit. You haven't been paying very much attention to the right side of your brain, so what do you expect? What could you do creatively that isn't client involved that'd get the right side of your head going again?

Jane: I've got a couple of articles I've been putting off—how about that?

CW: Got anything to do with clients?

Jane: Yes.

CW: Is that going to help you out?

Jane: I don't guess so, the same old stuff, only I'm writing about it.

CW: What else, then?

Forney, Wallace-Schutzman, and Wiggers (1982) propose that a variety of professional activities may be an excellent coping mechanism; nevertheless, the crisis worker confronts Jane about this suggested alternative. The crisis worker is fairly sure that the client's stress bucket is full to the brim professionally. Jane needs to become less, not more, involved in her professional life. Jane's response confirms the crisis worker's confrontation.

Jane: Well, there is something else. I bought this sailboat for Bobby and me. The Coast Guard Auxiliary is putting on a sailing class. It would sure surprise Bobby if the next time he came home I could handle that Y flyer.

CW: Is that something you want to do? Would like to do, not need to do it?

Jane: Yes!

CW: And not pile it on top of everything else. Really reserve some time for yourself to enjoy it.

Jane: You sure drive a hard bargain, but I can do it.

This is a wedge in the behavioral repertoire of the client that the crisis worker has been looking to find. Writer after writer in the burnout literature has promoted the use of leisure, particularly physical exercise, as a way of breaking up the dogmatic, work-brittle behavior of just going through the motions that often characterizes the burned out human service worker (Dowd, 1981; Freudenberger & Robbins, 1979; Savicki & Cooley, 1982). By proposing for the client a combination of leisure, physical exercise, and quality time with her son, the crisis worker has neatly integrated a number of positive interventions. The crisis worker now takes on the main issue of the client's private practice.

CW: Fine. Let's talk about your practice for a while.

Jane: You know as well as I do about that. Sure, I've got a great caseload now. But who knows, it might dry up next week, and then where would I be? The bills don't wait.

CW: Has it ever dried up? Even in the last recession?

Jane: No, it hasn't, but I keep expecting the worst.

CW: You've been in private practice eight years now, right? Has it ever been such that you didn't have enough clients to keep the wolves away from your door?

Jane: No. I guess there's something else. I feel a little foolish saying this, but it's almost like if I don't live up to my reputation and take on those really tough cases, I start feeling like I'm not the queen of the mountain. I mean in the past, I've been real proud of that, but now I don't seem to feel anything but that there's an albatross around my neck.

CW: Sounds like Superwoman again. I frankly admire you for dealing with those terminals' families, and you're right! Not many could do that. But if there's no intrinsic payoff, why are you fooling yourself into thinking you can heal the whole world? See the trap you've put yourself into?

Jane: Well, no! I guess I don't.

CW: OK! I want to try something. Maybe you've used it on some of your clients before. It's a game of "Who Told You?" I want you to move over to my chair and ask that empty chair, which will represent Jane, some questions. I'm going to stand aside and process as we go along, but it'll mostly be up to you. I want you to use all your insight as a therapist and really bore in and go to work on Jane's fictional goals, those crazy things she tells herself that have no counterpart in reality. All right, let's start.

Jane as CW: (Shifts chairs and gets a glitter in her eyes.) OK, toots! Who told you you had to be Superwoman?

CW: Now shift back.

Jane: Nobody really, I've just got a lot of responsibilities.

Jane as CW: Responsibilities, my foot! You've been going up that success ladder so fast you've scorched the rungs. Always got to show them. Be number one. My God! You little twirp. You're 43 years old and you still think you're back on the VA ward. Got to show them you're better than any man. Volunteer for the worst cases. Scared to death you won't succeed. And when you did, you were scared you wouldn't succeed the second time. Who told you that?

Jane: Nobody! It was reality. I had to be better than the men there.

Jane as CW: That was 20 years ago, nerd! The only men you deal with now are your clients. And that's another thing, is that why you're so damned afraid of going out with any other man? And don't give me that stuff about getting burned again, you know why that divorce happened, and it sure doesn't have anything to do with having good social relationships now.

Jane: It's just that with the financial obligations for Bobby, I really don't have the time.

Jane as CW: (Really angry and shouting.) I won't have that! How long will you be responsible for him? He's 21 years old. Who supported you when you were 21? I'll tell you who. You did! You just use that as an excuse. Just like you use all those clients as an excuse. You don't fool me, you little martyr. Oh, sure! You get those strokes. (Dripping sarcasm.) Just like Annette here said, "I really admire you, Jane." You go around fooling everybody, but worst of all you fool yourself. Look at you. Sitting here the pathetic little wretch. You don't fool me. You're not little Miss Goody Two-Shoes. Behind all that depression is a really angry, bitter bitch who's always going around being everybody's servant. So just who told you you had to be that?

Jane: (Breaks and sobs. The CW goes to Jane, gathers her into her arms, and hugs her for dear life. Five minutes elapse.) Good Lord! I didn't realize that was all in there. I really got on a roll.

CW: Neither did I, but I figured if anybody could get it out, you could. What have you got out of that?

Jane: Besides spilling my guts, which I haven't done in 25 years, I see now how I got into this. I really set myself up.

CW: What do you want to do?

Jane: Well, I'm not going to kill myself literally or figuratively. I've got some living to do, and while I'm not going to quit the practice, there sure are going to be some limits put on it.

The "Who Told You?" technique is a combination of Adlerian, rational-emotive, and Gestalt therapy that is extremely powerful. Given a person with the kind of insight Jane has, it often has dramatic results in pointing out the way clients delude themselves. By using Jane as her own therapist, the crisis worker provides no one for the client to rationalize to, attack, manipulate, or otherwise attempt to fool but herself. For a person with Jane's abilities and insight, that seldom happens for very long. Underneath most depression lies anger. If that anger can be mobilized, then the client has taken a major step toward getting back into control of the situation. By putting Jane in a position to view her behavior from outside herself and also giving her a stimulus to attack her irrational ideas by the "Who Told You?" technique, the crisis worker provides an arena in which Jane can combat the apathy she is experiencing.

Such a dramatic shift to being mobile is uncommon among the general populace and in Jane's case is a condensed version of what may generally happen. The crisis worker often has to provide the stimulus statements that are the core of clients' irrational ideas because of clients' poor cognition of their own negative self-talk. However, in dealing with highly trained professionals, it is not uncommon for such rapid shifts to occur. Given the initial stimulus, they may pick up on the technique and provide their own dialogue with little or no help from the crisis worker. When emotional catharsis occurs, the crisis worker then takes a nondirective stance and serves as little more than a sounding board as their fellow professionals put reasonable parameters back into their lives. At that point, human service workers who are clients tend to be able to make good decisions quickly about the behavioral, emotional, and cognitive aspects of their lives. Indeed, if burnout syndrome is successfully overcome, it is not unreasonable to expect that human service workers will come back to their profession with hardier personalities, stronger commitments to self and profession, better self-temperance, a greater sense of meaningfulness, and increased vigor toward their environment (Kobasa, 1979). Further, new coping styles that include greater self-awareness, increased self-insight, and a more direct approach to problem solving are likely to result for those who successfully navigate these treacherous waters (Cooley & Keesey, 1981). Finally, it is our own observation that human service professionals who have successfully conquered burnout respond not only to their work but also to their daily living with calmer and wiser choices, behaviors, and work style.

SUMMARY

"Burnout" is not simply a sympathy-eliciting term to use when one has had a hard day at the office. It is a very real malady that strikes people and may have extremely severe consequences. It is prevalent in the human service professions because of the kinds of clients, environments, working conditions, and resultant stresses that are operational there. No one particular individual is more prone to experience burnout than another. However, by their very nature, most human service workers tend to be highly committed to their profession, and such commitment is a necessary precursor to burnout. Private practitioners may experience burnout even more severely than their counterparts in organizations because of their professional isolation. All human service workers, public or private, tend to be unable to identify the problem when it is their own. No one is immune to its effects.

Burnout moves through stages of enthusiasm, stagnation, frustration, and apathy. In its end stage, burnout is a crisis situation. The crisis takes many forms. It can be manifested behaviorally, physically, interpersonally, and attitudinally. It pervades the professional's life and can have effects on clients, co-workers, family, friends, and the organization itself.

Recognition of the beginning symptoms of burnout can alleviate its personal and organizational ramifications. Raising consciousness levels in regard to the dynamics of burnout in training programs and conducting on-the-job workshops are important ways of halting and ameliorating its effects. Support groups within the organization that provide instrumental and emotional resources to victims are important. In the past, burnout has been regarded as a malady that resides only within the individual. That view is archaic. Burnout should also be viewed in a systems perspective and as an organizational problem.

Intervention may occur on both an organizational and an individual level. At its end stage, it is a crisis situation that calls for immediate, direct, and reality-oriented therapeutic intervention. Given corrective remediation, victims of burnout can return to the job and again become productive.

REFERENCES

Barad, C. B. (1979). Study of burnout syndrome among SSA field public contract employees. Washington, DC: Social Security Administration, Office of Management, Budget, and Personnel, Office of Human Resources.

Baron, A., Jr., & Cohen, R. B. (1982). Helping telephone counselors cope with burnout: A consciousness-raising workshop. *Personnel and Guidance Journal, 60*, 508–510.

Berkeley Planning Associates. (1977). *Evaluation of child abuse and neglect demonstration projects, 1974–1977: Volume IX. Project management and worker burnout.* Washington, DC: U.S. Department of Commerce.

Butts, S. (Speaker). (1986). *Therapeutic techniques, marriage and family therapy* (Cassette Recording No. 6611-12). Memphis: Department of Counseling and Personnel Services, Memphis State University.

Carroll, J. F. X., & White, W. L. (1982). Theory building: Integrating individual and environmental factors within an ecological framework. In W. S. Paine (Ed.), *Job stress and burnout* (pp. 41–60). Beverly Hills, CA: Sage Publications.

Cherniss, C., & Krantz, D. L. (1983). The ideological community as an antidote to burnout in the human services. In B. A. Farber (Ed.), *Stress and burnout in the human service professions* (pp. 198–212). New York: Pergamon Press.

Coffman, D. A., & Katz, C. (1979). Stress management: A structured group manual. Unpublished manuscript, University of Texas at Austin.

Cooley, E. J., & Keesey, J. C. (1981). Relationship between life change and illness in coping versus sensitive persons. *Psychological Reports, 48*, 711–714.

Daley, M. R. (1979). Burnout—smoldering problem in protective services. *Social Work, 58*, 375–379.

Dowd, E. T. (Ed.). (1981). Leisure counseling. *Counseling Psychologist, 9.*

Eastman, J. (1981, November). How you can beat job burnout. *Parade, 12*, pp. 16–17.

Edelwich, J., & Brodsky, A. (1982). Training guidelines: Linking the workshop experience to needs on and off the job. In W. S. Paine (Ed.), *Job stress and burnout* (pp. 133–154). Beverly Hills, CA: Sage Publications.

Farber, B. A. (Ed.). (1983). *Stress and burnout in the human service professions.* New York: Pergamon Press.

Forney, D. S., Wallace-Schutzman, F., & Wiggers, T. T. (1982). Burnout among career development professionals: Preliminary findings and implications. *Personnel and Guidance Journal, 60,* 435–439.

Freudenberger, H. J. (1974). Staff burn-out. *Journal of Social Issues, 30,* 159–165.

Freudenberger, H. J. (1975). The staff burnout syndrome in alternative institutions. *Psychotherapy: Theory, Research, & Practice, 12,* 73–82.

Freudenberger, H. J. (1977). Burn-out: Occupational hazard of child care workers. *Child Care Quarterly, 6,* 90–99.

Freudenberger, H. J. (1982). Counseling and dynamics: Treating the end-stage person. In W. S. Paine (Ed.), *Job stress and burnout* (pp. 173–188). Beverly Hills, CA: Sage Publications.

Freudenberger, H. J., & Robbins, A. (1979). The hazards of being a psychoanalyst. *Psychoanalytic Review, 66,* 275–296.

Hall, R. C. W., Gardner, E. R., Perl, M., Stickney, S. K., & Pfefferbaum, B. (1979). The professional burnout syndrome. *Psychiatric Opinion, 16,* 12–17.

Kell, B. L., & Mueller, W. J. (1966). *Impact and change: A study of counseling relationships.* New York: Appleton-Century-Crofts.

Kobasa, S. (1979). Stressful life events, personality, and health: An inquiry into hardiness. *Journal of Personality and Social Psychology, 37,* 1–11.

Maslach, C. (1976). Burned-out. *Human Behavior, 5,* 16–22.

Maslach, C. (1978). The client role in staff burn-out. *Journal of Social Issues, 34,* 111–124.

Maslach, C. (1982). Understanding burnout: Definitional issues in analyzing a complex phenomenon. In W. S. Paine (Ed.), *Job stress and burnout* (pp. 29–40). Beverly Hills, CA: Sage Publications.

Maslach, C., & Jackson, S. E. (1981a). *The Maslach burnout inventory.* Palo Alto, CA: Consulting Psychologists Press.

Maslach, C., & Jackson, S. E. (1981b). The measurement of experienced burnout. *Journal of Occupational Behavior, 2,* 99–113.

Maslach, C., & Pines, A. (1977). The burn-out syndrome in the day care setting. *Child Care Quarterly, 6,* 100–113.

Mitchell, M. D. (1977). Consultant burnout. In J. W. Pfeiffer & J. E. Jones (Eds.), *The 1977 annual handbook for group facilitators* (pp. 143–146). La Jolla, CA: University Associates.

Moos, R. H. (1981). *Work environment scale manual.* Palo Alto, CA: Consulting Psychologists Press.

Paine, W. S. (1982). Overview of burnout stress syndromes and the 1980's. In W. S. Paine (Ed.), *Job stress and burnout* (pp. 11–25). Beverly Hills, CA: Sage Publications.

Patrick, P. K. S. (1979, November). Burnout: Job hazard for health workers. *Hospitals, 16,* 87–90.

Patterson, C. H. (1980). *Theories of counseling and psychotherapy* (3rd ed.). New York: Harper & Row.

Pines, A. M. (1983). On burnout and the buffering effects of social support. In B. A. Farber (Ed.), *Stress and burnout in the human service professions* (pp. 155–173). New York: Pergamon Press.

Pines, A. M., & Kafry, D. (1978). Occupational tedium in the social services. *Social Work, 23,* 499–507.

Pines, A. M., & Maslach, C. (1978). Characteristics of staff burnout in mental health settings. *Hospital and Community Psychiatry, 29,* 223–237.

Riggar, T. F. (1985). *Stress burnout: An annotated bibliography.* Carbondale, IL: Southern Illinois University Press.

Savicki, V., & Cooley, E. J. (1982). Implications of burnout research and theory for counselor education. *Personnel & Guidance Journal, 60,* 415–419.

Savicki, V., & Cooley, E. J. (1987). The relationship of work environment and client contact to burnout in mental health professionals. *Journal of Counseling and Development, 65,* 249–252.

Sculley, R. (1983). The work-setting support group: A means of preventing burnout. In B. A. Farber (Ed.), *Stress and burnout in the human service professions* (pp. 198–212). New York: Pergamon Press.

Shinn, M., & Mørch, H. (1983). A tripartite model of coping with burnout. In B. A. Farber (Ed.), *Stress and burnout in the human service professions* (pp. 227–239). New York: Pergamon Press.

Spicuzza, F. J., & Devoe, M. W. (1982). Burnout in the helping professions: Mutual aid as self help. *Personnel & Guidance Journal, 61,* 95–98.

Tubesing, D. A., & Strosahl, S. G. (1976). *Wholistic health centers: Survey research report.* Hinsdale, IL: Society for Wholistic Medicine.

Tubesing, N. L., & Tubesing, D. A. (1982). The treatment of choice: Selecting stress skills to suit the individual and the situation. In W. S. Paine (Ed.), *Job stress and burnout* (pp. 155–172). Beverly Hills, CA: Sage Publications.

Van Auken, S. (1979). Youth counselor burnout. *Personnel & Guidance Journal, 58,* 143–144.

Warnath, C. F., & Shelton, J. L. (1976). The ultimate disappointment: The burned-out counselor. *Personnel & Guidance Journal, 55,* 172–175.

Watkins, C. E. (1983). Burnout in counseling practice: Some potential professional and personal hazards of becoming a counselor. *Personnel & Guidance Journal, 61,* 304–308.

■ Classroom Exercises: Case of Steve

Steve is an elementary school guidance counselor. He has worked eight years in an urban school system. In that time he has literally built a guidance program from the ground up. Career awareness/exploration, developmental guidance, individual personal counseling, and parent-training groups are but a few of the activities he has instituted with little budget and no help. When there was no money for materials, Steve cajoled civic organizations. When students needed dental work and could afford none, Steve got it done free. He has counseled such problems as child abuse, suicide attempts, drug addiction, and home break-ups and has done an excellent job. Teachers and parents have also sought him out for personal counseling; and he has done an excellent job with them too.

Steve is active in professional and civic organizations. When not working, Steve devotes a great portion of his time to his family: his wife, two daughters, and invalid mother. A keen sense of humor and a positive word for everybody typify Steve. His major recreational pursuits are working in his garden, carving duck decoys, and playing an occasional game of penny-ante gin rummy with some other teachers. Steve was just elected as outstanding educator of the year in the metropolitan area where he works. By any measure, Steve is doing an outstanding job, both professionally and personally.

Steve is just now at the National Elementary/Middle School Guidance Conference, which he has not missed in his tenure as a counselor. Actually, he is in a bar in the city in which the conference is being held. Steve is in the process of getting roaring drunk for the second day in a row. So far he has failed to put in an appearance at the conference, even to make a presentation he was scheduled to give. He cannot remember getting this inebriated since he got out of the service. To say that such behavior is highly unlike this conscientious young man is putting it rather mildly.

The only thing Steve is really sure of is that if he sees, hears, talks, or does anything that vaguely resembles counseling, he is afraid he will go stark raving mad. A not-so-subtle corollary to that neon sign that keeps flashing on and off in his head is that he no longer cares to be nice, friendly, brave, or obey any of the other Boy Scout laws to anyone for any reason. That includes his wife, with whom he had a fight before he left home. The fracas was over putting his mother into a nursing home. He immediately buries that horrid thought and broods over his shot of bourbon. At this particular moment, his good friend Mike, a buddy from Vietnam and graduate school days who is also a middle school counselor, walks into the bar, orders a beer, and sits down on a stool next to Steve. The following conversation takes place:

Mike: (Cheerful but concerned.) Hey, man! How you doin'? The chicks from Colorado told me you were in here getting hammered and said you told them to bug off. You must be getting choosy in your old age, those are some fine women. What's the deal?

Steve: If you want a drink, fine. If you wanta get inside my head, get the hell outta here and go back to the conference. I've had it with this stuff. I don't even know why I came, except this is a pretty nice bar. It's really quiet in here and people tend to their own business, catch my drift?

Mike: (Smiling but dead serious.) Uh huh! Well, watch my lips, screwball! This is the guy who sweated with you through the two worst pieces of your otherwise Prince Charming life. I am talkin' Nam and Stat II. I also remind you now that I am the godfather to your kids and haven't seen you this stewed up since we got back to Frisco from Nam. Besides which, I'm bigger than you and you can't throw me out. So what's eatin' on you, anyways? You're mad as hell about somethin'?

Steve: (Angry but depressed.) I don't know. I just know I don't want to be a counselor any more. So much misery. I feel like the little Dutch boy with not enough fingers to stick in the dike. If I counsel one more person I think I'll go nuts. Before I came here I put in my application at the post office to be a package sorter. At least I wouldn't have to listen or talk to packages, and the pay's better anyway.

Simulated Crisis Intervention before the Group

A volunteer takes the role of Steve. The group leader takes the role of Mike and starts active listening in the "fishbowl" with Steve. After two minutes at most, without doing anything more than exploring the problem, the leader gets up and leaves the chair. The leader then invites any group member to come and sit in the leader's place and continue the dialogue in a crisis intervention mode. Any time that a member becomes stymied, the member voluntarily gets up and leaves the chair. Another member is then invited to take the chair voluntarily. No questions are permitted by the rest of the group. Rather, any time a group member desires to offer input, that member gets up, taps the counselor on the shoulder, and sits down with Steve. This exercise should continue until Steve's situation is fully assessed and closure is reached regarding the crisis. At this point the leader may then process the counseling session. As openers, the following kinds of questions may be asked:

1. Did the crisis workers obtain an adequate assessment of the problem?

2. Referring to the list in the chapter, what behavioral, physical, interpersonal, and attitudinal indicators lead you to believe that Steve is in crisis?
3. What problems do you foresee when a friend also gets cast in the role of crisis interventionist?
4. What special ethical considerations must the crisis worker bear in mind?
5. What makes the crisis of burnout different from other kinds of crisis we have considered?

Simulated Intervention with Alter Egos

Four people from the group take roles, again using the case of Steve. One person portrays Steve and another person portrays Mike. Each of the other two people stands behind Steve or Mike, with their hands on Steve's or Mike's shoulders, respectively. These two people will become the *alter egos* of the client and the worker. As the dialogue between the client and the worker unfolds, the job of the alter egos is to reflect at a deep, affective level what they feel is occurring intrapersonally with the person behind whom each is standing. The idea is to bring out verbally the hidden feelings that are happening "here and now" as the exchange between Mike and Steve takes place.

Alter egos may feel free to vocalize their feelings at any time to their partner, to the other participant in the crisis, or to the other alter ego. Responses may be constructed in the form of a confrontation or a reflection, but they must target the feeling state of the person toward whom the statement is directed. Mike and Steve may respond to the comments of the alter egos, but they are allowed to direct their comments only to each other and *not* directly to the alter egos. If the alter egos have trouble breaking into the dialogue, the leader may stop the exercise and give some reflective responses to model the role of alter ego.

Alter egos tend to be somewhat timid about stating some of the feelings they detect in the dialogue. They should be encouraged to take strong guesses as to what their partners are feeling. The purpose of this exercise is not necessarily to reach resolution but rather to open wide the affective component of crisis intervention and to let participants fully experience feelings that might otherwise remain hidden. The process may go on until the leader feels that enough emotional content has been brought to the surface. At this point the role play is halted and the experience is processed. Process questions should concentrate on the affective dimensions of the exercise. These are typical questions:

1. What effect did the alter egos have on the session?
2. How did the client and worker react when the alter egos became involved?
3. What did the alter egos feel as they entered into the dialogue?
4. What difference do you see between this exercise and typical client-worker role plays?

5. What were your own feelings as Steve, Mike, and their alter egos became more deeply involved?

6. Often when dealing with affect, it seems the worker is not dealing directly with the problem or its resolution. Why, then, do you think that we believe that exploring affect is so important?

Simulated Intervention in Pairs

The group is divided into dyads: crisis worker and burned-out human service worker. Using the "Who Told You?" technique, the human service worker starts a monologue about his or her gripes, complaints, frustrations, perceived shortcomings with clients, bureaucratic problems, and so on. (If participants do not currently hold a human service job, they can role-play Steve or one of the examples from the beginning of this chapter.) As the burned-out worker unfolds verbally, the crisis worker will use a combination of active listening skills and "Who Told You?"

Such an approach is designed to confront the irrational ideas and beliefs the burned-out worker has built up about his or her job. The crisis worker should be on the lookout for any of the 11 irrational ideas that Albert Ellis maintains are endemic to a neurotic society (Patterson, 1980, pp. 68–70):

1. It is essential that a person be loved or approved of by virtually everyone in the community.
2. A person must be perfectly competent, adequate, and achieve in order to be considered worthwhile.
3. Some people are bad, wicked, or villainous and therefore should be blamed or punished.
4. It is a terrible catastrophe when things are not as a person wants them to be.
5. Unhappiness is caused by outside circumstances, and a person has no control over it.
6. Dangerous or fearsome things are cause for great concern, and their possibility must be continually dwelt upon.
7. It is easier to avoid certain difficulties and self-responsibilities than to face them.
8. A person should be dependent on others and have someone stronger on whom to rely.
9. Past experiences and events are the determinants of present behavior; the influence of the past cannot be eradicated.
10. A person should be quite upset over other people's problems and disturbances.
11. There is always a right or perfect solution to every problem, and it must be found or the results will be catastrophic.

As the crisis worker detects irrational statements like these, he or she should confront the client with "Who told you. . . ?" The idea is to confront the "shoulds," "oughts," and "musts" that propagandize clients into believing that they need to continue unproductive and debilitating ways of thinking and behaving. The exercise should be continued for 15 to 20 minutes and then the roles should be reversed. After the exercise is completed, all members rejoin the group and process the experience. Special emphasis should be given to comparing the irrational ideas brought out by each participant. The leader may want to list and tally each irrational idea so that all participants may start to experience the communality of ways in which they delude and fool themselves into making these irrational beliefs a dysfunctional part of their lives.

Index